Textbook of Management for Doctors

Dedication

This book is dedicated to my wife Anne
for her unfailing help and support
Omnia Vincit Amor.

For Churchill Livingstone

Publisher: Peter Richardson
Publishing Assistant: Prudence Daniels
Copy Editor: Holly Regan-Jones
Project Controller: Mark Sanderson
Design Direction: Sarah Cape
Indexer: Elisabeth Pickard

Textbook of Management for Doctors

Edited by

T. White PhD FRCS MB BS AKC MHSM

Consultant Otolaryngologist and Clinical Director,
Bath Royal United Hospital, Bath;
Visiting Fellow, The School of Management,
Bournemouth University, Bournemouth, UK

NEW YORK EDINBURGH LONDON MADRID MELBOURNE SAN FRANCISCO TOKYO 1996

CHURCHILL LIVINGSTONE
Medical Division of Pearson Professional Limited

Distributed in the United States of America by Churchill Livingstone Inc., 650 Avenue of the Americas, New York, N.Y. 10011, and by associated companies, branches and representatives throughout the world.

© Pearson Professional Limited 1996

All rights reserved. No part of this publication may be reproduced, stored in a retrieval system, or transmitted in any form or by any means, electronic, mechanical, photocopying recording or otherwise, without either the prior permission of the publishers (Churchill Livingstone, Robert Stevenson House, 1–3 Baxter's Place, Leith Walk, Edinburgh, EH1 3AF), or a licence permitting restricted copying in the United Kingdom issued by the Copyright Licensing Agency Ltd, 90 Tottenham Court Road, London, W1P 9HE.

First published 1996

ISBN 0-443-05158-5

British Library Cataloguing in Publication Data
A catalogue record for this book is available from the British Library.

Library of Congress Cataloging in Publication Data
A catalog record for this book is available from the Library of Congress.

Medical knowledge is constantly changing. As new information becomes available, changes in treatment, procedures, equipment and the use of drugs become necessary. The editors/authors/contributors and the publishers have, as far as possible, taken care to ensure that the information given in this text is accurate and up to date. However, readers are strongly advised to confirm that the information, especially with regard to drug usage, complies with latest legislation and standards of practice.

The publisher's policy is to use **paper manufactured from sustainable forests**

Printed in Hong Kong
CTPS/01

Contents

1. Medicine before the NHS   1
   Andrew Morrice, Tony White

2. The evolution of the NHS   9
   Tony White, David Allen

3. Doctors' involvement in management – the reality   21
   Jenny Simpson

4. The organizational structure of hospitals   33
   Tony White

5. Engaging doctors in management   47
   Helen Jones

6. Clinical directorates   57
   Tony White

7. Management development for doctors   67
   Adrian Turrell

8. The roles of medical directors   81
   David Grimes, Tony White

9. The roles of clinical directors   89
   Tony White

10. Practical aspects of clinical directors' and medical directors' appointments   99
    Tony White, Sally Watson

11. Giving talks and presentations   105
    Colin Coles

12. Effective writing   115
    Tim Albert

13. Managing people   127
    John Gatrell

14. Interviews and interviewing skills   135
    John Gatrell, Tony White

15. Being interviewed   149
    Tony White, John Gatrell

16. The management of meetings   157
    Tony White

17. Dealing with the media   165
    Nigel Duncan

18. Educational management   173
    Janet Grant

19. Managing for personal effectiveness   183
    John Gatrell

20. Team building and performance management   191
    Chris Grice

21. Change management   201
    Janet Grant, Rodney Gale

22. Managing a budget   211
    Rodney Gale

23. Business planning   221
    Martin Anderson

24. Marketing, marketing strategy and contracts   231
    Rodney Gale

25. Economics for clinicians   241
    Karin Lowson

26. Personnel, performance and staff appraisal   257
    Helen Witt

27. Quality in health care   273
    Richard Thomson

28. Managing some legal Issues   297
    Gill Strawford

29. Risk management   313
    David Bowden

30. Information and information technology in healthcare   331
    Tim Scott

31. Management of learning, professional development   341
    Giff Batstone, Mary Edwards

32. Further principles for clinical directors   359
    Tony White

33. Multiprofessional audit   367
    Giff Batstone, Mary Edwards

34. Doctors and management in the reformed NHS   379
    Alan Maynard

35. The Culture of a health commission   387
    Barbara Longley, Madeleine Gantley

36. Clinical and professional freedom   399
    Tony White

37. Ethics   413
    Roger Higgs

Index   423

Contributors

T. Albert BSc MIPD
Trainer and Consultant in Written
Communications,
Visiting Fellow in Medical Writing,
Wessex Institute of Public Health Medicine,
Southampton Medical School, UK

D. Allen PhD
Senior Lecturer,
School Of Epidemiology,
Manchester University,
Manchester, UK

M. Anderson
Management Accountant,
Raglan,
Gwent, UK

G. Batstone MB BS BSc FRCPath MSc
Director Medical Development Programme,
Kings Fund Development Centre,
London, UK

D. Bowden FHSM FRSA MA
Chief Executive,
Merret Health Risk Management Ltd,
Brighton, UK

C. Coles BSc MA PhD
Reader,
Institute of Health and Community Studies,
Bournemouth University,
Bournemouth, UK

N. Duncan
Head of Communications
British Medical Association,
London, UK

M. Edwards MSc BA RGN
Director of Nursing and Patient Services,
North Hampshire Hospitals NHS Trust,
Basingstoke, Hampshire, UK

R. Gale MSc Dphil MBA AMIMC
Senior Consultant Rodney Gale Associates
Hampton, UK
Fellow in Management
The Joint Centre for Education in Medicine
London, UK

M. Gantley MSc PhD
Lecturer,
Primary Medical Care,
University of Southampton,
Southampton, UK

J. Gatrell BA(Hons) PGCE FIPM MIMgt
Head of The Business School
Bournemouth University,
Bournemouth, UK

J. Grant BA MSc PhD CPsychol FBPsS
Joint Centre for Education in Medicine
London, UK

C. Grice MA MIPD BSc PGCE
Senior Management Advisor,
The Industrial Society,
Birmingham, UK

D. S. Grimes MD FRCP
Consultant Physician Gastroenterologist and
Medical Director,
Blackburn, Hyndburn and Ribble Valley Health
Care NHS Trust,
Royal Infirmary, Blackburn, UK

CONTRIBUTORS

R. Higgs
Professor of Primary Care,
King's College,
London, UK

H. Jones
Head of Leadership and Management Development Studies
North Yorkshire College of Health Studies
Innovation Centre
University of York
York, UK

B. Longley MB BS BSc MFPHM PtI
Public Health Doctor,
Wessex Institute of Public Health Medicine,
Winchester, UK

K. Lowson BA Econ(Hons) MSc IPFA
Director of Finance, Information,
Bradford Community Health NHS Trust,
Bradford, UK

A. Maynard BA BPhil
Secretary,
The Nuffield Provincial Hospitals Trust,
London;
Visiting Professor,
Centre for Health Economics,
University of York,
York, UK

A. G. Morrice BSc MB BS
Former Reader Fellow,
Wellcome Institute for the History of Medicine,
London, UK

T. Scott BSc
Senior Fellow,
British Association of Medical Managers,
Barnes Hospital,
Cheadle, Cheshire, UK

J. Simpson MB ChB DCH MBA
Chief Executive,
British Association of Medical Managers,
Barnes Hospital,
Cheadle, Cheshire, UK

G. R. Strawford MB BS MRCGP,
Medico-Legal Advisor,
The Medical Defence Union Ltd,
Sharston, Manchester, UK

R. Thomson MD MRCP MFPHM,
Senior Lecturer in Public Health Medicine,
Department of Epidemiology and Public Health,
Medical School,
Newcastle Upon Tyne, UK

A. R. Turrell BA(Hons) PhD,
Research and Development Coordinator,
Neurosciences Nursing Development Unit
Queens Medical Centre,
Nottingham, UK

S. Watson
British Medical Association
London, UK

T. White PhD FRCS MB BS AKC MHSM
Clinical Director and Consultant Otolaryngologist,
Bath Royal United Hospital, Bath;
Visiting Fellow,
The School of Management,
Bournemouth University, Bournemouth, UK

H. C. Witt MIPD,
Development and Training Department,
Royal South Hants Hospital,
Southampton, UK

Foreword

I am very pleased to have been invited to write the foreword to this book. In today's NHS, management is not an optional skill for clinicians but should be an important part of a doctor's training and education at all stages of his or her career. This is a wide-ranging work of reference which covers basic management skills such as information management and technology and quality in healthcare. It should prove useful to newly qualified doctors looking for an easily accessible introduction to some of the non-clinical skills they need to acquire and to more senior clinicians such as medical and clinical directors who have opted for significant or even full-time management responsibilities.

Doctors in management have a unique contribution to make in bridging what is often seen as a deep cultural division between managers and clinicians. More doctors should be encouraged to take up this challenge and, when they do, they need more effective support in their training and career development. The 'Textbook' is a welcome addition to the growing bibliography of texts for medical managers. Its authors are leaders in their field who have drawn upon solid research and extensive experience to produce lucid guidance to a complex subject. I commend this book to all doctors who wish to acquire or extend their skills in this essential area.

Alan Langlands
Chief Executive
NHS

Preface

Where there is no vision the people perish (Proverbs: Chap 29 v 18).

No one can precisely foretell the future of healthcare, but it will be determined by an interplay of factors and also, to some extent, by the legacy of the past. Local circumstances may influence precise outcomes in a given area, and technology, frequently predicated as a major factor, may be limited by economic factors and political and cultural resistance. The expectations of the public are rising. However, it is not always clear exactly what patients want – 'Care closer to home, but still in high-tech hospitals'?

For some time there has been a move from independence to interdependence, with the doctor increasingly functioning as a member of a healthcare team rather than as an isolated practitioner. The increasing managerial coordinating role of doctors has resulted in them becoming more isolated from the patient and having to place a greater emphasis on resource allocation. The increasing number and range of professionals has led to deprofessionalisation thus lowering the status of the professional. There is a 'bleeding away' of lower levels of work to less qualified staff. The possible introduction of more time-specific contracts, increasing expectations of changing jobs and new attitudes to work may all eventually affect professionals. And while all this is happening, a quiet revolution is occurring – changes in the delivery of healthcare, changes in treatments, changes in organisations – as changes in other services related to hospitals and changes in the way hospitals are managed are under way.

The influence exercised by healthcare professionals at the point of delivery is greater than that available to service deliverers in any other sector of employment (Loveridge 1992). As a result of economic contingencies, there have been increased attempts at greater administrative control of state employees, particularly in healthcare, where until recently there had been considerable autonomy. As a result medical control over the delivery process is changing and perhaps being eroded. It remains the case that the creation of a managerial hierarchy capable of designing and delivering healthcare services or, in terms used by institutional economists, of 'appropriating the idiosyncratic information assets' (Williamson 1985) of the medical professions, is to say the least problematical. All those who have to make the Health Service work require some common understanding of the issues facing the service, how to tackle them and the personal and managerial skills that are needed. All doctors, even junior doctors, end up in charge of the resources of others and are not simply providing their own time and resources. They need to have a basic understanding of the managerial culture appropriate for the Health Service.

The ideal would be to educate all healthcare professionals about the issues in a similar way, so that the day will come when a chief executive and consultant can sit together and have a common view of the world they are facing, a common understanding of the problems. To achieve long-term cultural change, where all the key players in the Health Service, including all the doctors, have some common base on which to approach the problems, will probably need a much more systematic and sympathetic approach, with management development being treated as a part of professional training.

At local level, there are very significant opportunities for change, although these depend heavily on the management ethos of the Trust. Some Trusts are very closed, secretive places, far from the open organisations they profess to be. Others give doctors the opportunity to be involved in changing the organisation. The true clinical directorate system is vital, where doctors do have significant responsibility and authority for the way the unit is organised and the way the work is performed. For the organisation to achieve the best results, doctors need freedom within the resource limits available to them. To obtain that degree of development requires encouragement, not only for the management to let go, but also for the doctors to become involved. In the Health Service there is no question that managerial power has increased greatly; however, doctors are still the single most powerful group in the Service, as they have many advantages that managers do not. Although the medical profession was perceived as having lost ground over the reforms, that will not be a lasting phenomenon. Public esteem gives the profession potential access to political power and the media are interested in what doctors have to say. The profession has networks which remain effective. There are very few Trust chairmen with the ability to stand up to a delegation and truly represent their consultant medical staff.

The doctors' problem generally, however, is that very few of them are interested in, or have taken the trouble to educate themselves in, management. They have not learned basic managerial skills, how to manage people, budgets and information. Perhaps they have not had the opportunity. All those areas of knowledge need to be broadened.

There will be a need for doctors in management, and perhaps it should be asked if it is reasonable to expect surgeons in their mid-fifties to do the same workload as those in their mid-thirties? In management there are very few managers who work in mainstream managerial positions beyond their mid-fifties; instead they act for consultancies, teach and enter research. If it is right for managers, why not for doctors, especially as managers do not have the physical and psychological pressures of practising in acute medicine? We may need to plan for doctors to enter management on a full-time basis. Clinical director or medical director may become the fourth stage of a career and could lead to chief executive. Many other healthcare systems in the world have at least a proportion of medically qualified chief executives. There are some very effective chief executives from non-medical backgrounds, but there should be a mix. Doctors' involvement in management applies not only to hospital medicine but also to general practice. A fundholding practice needs what any large practice needs, a full-time management partner who, in many cases, should be one of the doctors and should be paid as a management partner and not be regarded as a drain on the practice because they are performing a management role.

In the future, management education will be as important to doctors as their clinical and professional education will be introduced in the undergraduate programmes. A managerial content into the base programmes is already reflected in the GMC (1993) revision of syllabus guidelines. Ultimately every medical student will have some understanding of management, every qualified doctor will go through a systematic series of management programmes, and those doctors who go into full-time management, or virtually full-time management, will receive intensive management preparation training. In Project 2000, there is already some appreciation of managerial issues.

Maybe there will be the opportunity to enter management at the age of fifty and stay until retirement, but there would need to be flexibility about retraining clinical commitment. Some doctors would like to become managers, and this should be facilitated. In the main, however, it is likely that most will not want to move into management until they are older, as their clinical work is their main focus and provides them with most satisfaction. One of the tragedies of the early days of general management was the presumption that it was possible for consultants to be unit general managers on part-time contracts. This was a tragedy, and it has discredited the potential of doctors as managers. It was not a fair trial, and it was nonsense to pretend that somebody could be a unit general manager for only three days a week. If doctors want to enter serious management, the jobs have to be full time. If a hospital is divided into individual clinical directorates, they are often very significant businesses in their own right.

On the matter of overcoming the feelings of the doctors crossing the divide to become a manager, it might be easier to admit that that has already happened. The doctors no longer have to function in the role they have initially been trained for, but, because of their experience in practice, they are able to become much better managers. Quality is a major problem. As Drucker (1979) says repeatedly, 'all organisations need efficiency but above all they need effectiveness, an emphasis on the right results'. However, as Strong and Robinson (1990) state: 'although many new managers talk about quality, there must be grave doubts about how much they really know about the subject'. Since this is so, what happens to all the bold claims that are made about the new order? How can the vast new regulatory structures work, if there are few indicators of quality? How can managers direct the work of individual doctors in any rational fashion if they are ignorant of most medical outcomes?

The problem is compounded, as doctors often have not been willing to make the jump into management without suitable pay and conditions. Doctors have been obliged to straddle both worlds, but that cannot continue in a serious job demanding a full-time commitment. The situation will not improve until we see the two as a partnership. According to Loveridge (1992), survival at the local level of the strategic operational unit, whether a hospital or general practice, depends on the collaboration of general managers and senior professionals. He goes on to suggest a model closely resembling the US hospital, where the medical team works alongside the senior administrator. So, when we talk about doctors moving into management this then begs the question, how do we alter the culture so that managers and doctors are not at war with each other? To some extent they always will be, because the focus of their lines is so entirely different. The doctors, as long as they are in clinical work, focus their attention on the individual patient and are often indifferent to the budget, national resources or the difficulties of the hospital, whereas the manager thinks about the organization as a whole – society as a whole. What we can do is lessen the tension by educating people together and having more doctors on the other side of the fence, so that they do at least understand the issues that their colleagues are facing; however, the tension will never be completely removed.

Management, both administrative and clinical, will become more cooperative, with a greater sense of working together for a hospital rather than for a profession. Audit departments will become R&D departments and monitor the literature to advise professionals and management on current practice. Electronic journals and bulletin boards will be used to search for specialty-specific information. People may need to re-adjust their expectations. Today's junior doctors may find themselves training for positions that are very different from those they thought would be their goal – perhaps also reflecting the age in which we live. Although the service may be more efficient, it might feel less compassionate.

REFERENCES

Drucker P 1979 Management. Pan, London
GMC 1993, Tomorrow's doctors. Recommendations on undergraduate medical education. General Medical Council, London
Loveridge R 1992 The future of health care delivery – markets or hierarchies. In: Continuity and crisis in the NHS. Open University Press, Buckingham, ch 15
Strong P, Robinson J 1990 The NHS – under new management. Open University Press, Milton Keynes, ch 11
Willamson O E 1985 The economic institutions of capitalism. Free Press, New York

Acknowledgements

I would like to pay tribute to all those contributors who have worked so tirelessly to provide material for this book, and to all those unnamed colleagues, doctors, managers and academics who have listened, criticised, suggested and supported the many discussions about issues to be included. I would particularly mention Dr Hugh Platt, Regional Postgraduate Dean (Wessex) and John Gatrell, Head of The School of Management, Bournemouth University, for their unfailing help, support and advice.

David Rumsey and the staff of the Postgraduate Medical Centre Library in Bath deserve my thanks, for their unfailing cheerfulness and their willingness to search the literature for references. I apologise if I have failed to attribute or acknowledge any references used in this book.

My acknowledgements extend to the publishers, in particular Peter Richardson, director of healthcare publishing at Churchill Livingstone, and his colleagues, who ensured that the book proceeded smoothly into print.

Last but not least, my long-suffering family who have become accustomed to management issues as everyday family conversation.

1

Medicine before the National Health Service: an historical introduction

Andrew Morrice, Tony White

If the science of medicine is not to be lowered to the rank of a mere mechanical profession it must preoccupy itself with its history.

(Emile Littre 1801–1881)

This statement, made in the last century, still carries an essential message to all those involved in the care of patients today. British doctors are proud of the importance they place on taking an accurate history from their patients and the way in which this can ensure well-focused and effective care. Despite this fact, it would be safe to say that doctors have tended to give little energy to 'taking the history' of their own profession. Yet a clear history of medicine can do much to sharpen perceptions of the issues raised by the enormous changes occurring in our healthcare system. History created our present situation and the decisions and priorities we make today will soon become the historical legacy with which our successors will struggle. Whilst history may not strictly or precisely repeat itself, it is the case that many of the challenges of the present day find close parallels with the challenges of the past.

The aim of this introduction is to sketch out some themes from the history of healthcare and its organization in order to place the issues dealt with in this book in perspective. This brief historical survey does not aim to provide a complete account of the history of medicine. As the burgeoning literature and interest in the field indicate, we have in many ways only just started to explore many aspects of the medical past. This account is concerned with broad themes rather than fine detail. It is our particular aim to show that the organization of healthcare has often been to some extent an area of dispute and contention. Nothing is so detrimental to clear thinking about the challenges now facing healthcare than the idea that the conditions under which doctors worked in the past were stable, uncontentious or ideal.

An important first point must be that over the vast majority of the historical period healthcare has been a private matter, rarely carried out in any organized institution or structure. It was therefore not 'managed' as such. Although institutions called hospitals have existed for centuries it is only with the industrial age that we find institutions roughly resembling modern hospitals and which are their direct antecedents. It was only in the late 19th century that any structures for providing what we now term primary healthcare came into existence. (This account is therefore skewed, because it primarily considers these institutions, even in periods in which such organizations only represented a small aspect of the healthcare of the time.) The involvement of government in structuring or regulating medical life was a feature of the industrial age and only began in earnest with the Poor Law of 1837. Broadly speaking the structures organizing healthcare have been overseen by a number of powerful social institutions. In the mediaeval period the Church and the monastic system had this role. Following the Dissolution a little hospital care was organized under the auspices of the Crown. The Poor Law of 1601 allowed for the sick to be attended out of local rates. In the 18th century it was the corporate power of local groups of wealthy people who funded organized healthcare, then increasingly in the 19th and 20th centuries the state, through central and local government, has structured and endorsed medical care.

Hospitals have been, over the last 250 years, the prime site in which medical care has been developed to its current state of complexity. These institutions, with large concentrations of the sick (until this century most usually the sick poor), provided conditions under which doctors could meet, compete and collaborate and in which medicine could be practised and developed. However, very few were set up by and exclusively run by doctors. Although they have always been places in which doctors have worked, doctors' priorities and needs have not always been those at the top of the management agenda. The same has been true for the nurses and the other, newer professions working in the hospital setting. Indeed, for all these professions the use of hospitals as places of work has been an integral part of their development as professions. Their history and the history of hospitals are inextricably linked together in the wider history of changing society (Perkin 1989). The agendas of patients, professionals, institutions, governments and society at large have all had an influence in the organization and aims of hospitals and inevitably, at times, this history has been one of intense negotiation and even open conflict.

THE PREINDUSTRIAL ERA

Much of the history of the hospital in Western society up to the industrial era is closely linked with the organization and aims of the Christian Church, from the time of the adoption of Christianity by the Roman Empire. Of the hospitals founded in Britain between the introduction of Christianity and the Reformation the majority were 'places of resort' (the ancient meaning of the word 'hospital'). Most monastic institutions did not administer hospitals as such. They usually contained an apartment known as the infirmary, for the use of sick monks or nuns, although occasional travellers might be admitted. During the Middle Ages various religious orders founded places for the care of the sick. They were primarily places where poor people went when they could not be cared for at home by family or by the parish. The aim of these institutions was primarily to provide Christian charity. Hence such places would admit a variety of unfortunates whom we might not class as sick today and would emphasize comfort, support and alleviation of symptoms over attempts to cure disease. Some monasteries were, however, famed for their medicine and the larger foundations often had a particularly skilled brother among their number. Occasionally a physician or surgeon was appointed at a stipend.

The organization and administration of a lay hospital was similar to that of a monastic infirmary. The infirmarian became the warden, a kind of secretary or house governor. Physicians and surgeons were called in from outside when needed and some larger establishments had a paid but not full-time staff. In the later Middle Ages a number of institutions were set up by lay bodies to cater for special groups of sick people, under the patronage of the crown, the bishop of the diocese, a merchant guild or private benefactor. The boom in pilgrimage created a need to cater for those who became ill whilst travelling. Another special group of patients catered for were lepers, in institutions known as lazar houses. These places retained a strong ethos derived from Christian piety and had an important function in underpinning the social order. They demonstrated not only Christian doctrine in action, but also the concern of the powerful and wealthy for the well-being of the people (Granshaw & Porter 1989).

By the 16th century the mediaeval order was beginning to collapse. In terms of hospitals and their management, Church domination had degenerated to the extent that clerks licensed to practise medicine by a bishop could be, and often were, illiterate. Monastic and other houses were occupied less by the needy sick and more often by anyone who could exploit the rules of the foundation to their advantage.

Henry VIII, during a reign that brought with it profound upheaval, had a large impact on the organization of hospitals. As part of an overall pattern in which power moved out of the hands of the Church and into the hands of the monarch, vast numbers of hospitals were swept away in the Dissolution of monastic and ecclesiastical institutions between 1536 and 1547. The only institutions remaining were a few foundations belonging to corporate bodies, some houses in crown patronage and a few attached to a cathedral or episcopal see and nearly all of these were almshouses rather than hospitals in anything approaching the modern sense of the word.

The wholesale destruction wrought by Henry VIII's reforms in many ways created the conditions under which new arrangements were gradually built up before the industrial era. State interest in the management of the sick poor found its most lasting and important expression in the Elizabethan Poor Law of 1601. This law was the basis of much of the provision for the sick poor up until 1837. It gave the then non-elected local authorities the powers to raise rates to finance the support of the lame, impotent, old, blind and such others among them being poor or unable to work (Pater 1981). Thereafter a rudimentary system of medical relief arose under which those who were too poor to pay were supplied with physic by a parish doctor (Honigsbaum 1990).

FROM THE WESTMINSTER HOSPITAL TO THE WORKHOUSE INFIRMARY (1720–1837)

The 18th century marked the beginning of a number of important processes which resulted directly in the emergence of modern healthcare, producing both the impetus towards the development of a united medical profession and a ubiquitous lay hospital system in which that profession was educated and partly worked. The most obvious of these changes was the voluntary hospital movement. However, it must be borne in mind that at this time most sick people were not attended by doctors at all, but used a variety of lay healers or even family members and neighbours as their carers. Physicians were the medical attendants of the wealthy, but became increasingly involved in the care of the middle classes and poor, usually in a hospital setting, over the intervening period. Barber-surgeons and apothecaries provided some medical attention for the middle and artisan classes. The barber-surgeons as a group diverged, some successfully developing an increasingly recognizable form of hospital-based surgery. The work of others gradually merged over the next century with that of apothecaries and these doctors became known in many cases as general practitioners, a term that stems from the early 1800s. It refers first to general surgeons but came to apply to individuals from a number of backgrounds (Loudon 1979). However, these antecedents of today's orthodox profession competed on equal terms in an unregulated market crowded with all manner of itinerant and local healers and mountebanks (Bynum and Porter 1987).

From early in the 18th century, and increasingly as the century advanced, private individuals of the wealthy elite became concerned to demonstrate an interest in the well-being of the labouring and trading classes. Hospitals provided the perfect expression of this concern and were not primarily institutions designed for medical care (a theme familiar from the hospitals of earlier times). The main focus of these institutions was to provide care for the acutely unwell members of the 'worthy poor'. Admissions were controlled by the lay governors and were restricted in many cases to exclude children, the destitute, the chronically or terminally ill.

The first London voluntary hospital was the Westminster, set up in 1720 (Rivett 1986), and the first provincial voluntary institution was started in Winchester in 1736. A survey in 1719 revealed that while 23 English counties had no hospital accommodation at all, by 1799 nearly every county and many of the larger towns had its hospital, founded and maintained by private benefactors (Cartwright 1977).

The voluntary aspect of these institutions was reflected in the unpaid honorary nature of the posts taken up in these places by physicians and surgeons. These practitioners were not acting simply out of concern for the sick poor, but were keen to demonstrate their worth to the governors, benefactors and local elite on whose patronage their incomes as private practitioners depended. (The gaining of a public hospital post in order to access private practice, whilst never required in any written rule, statute or law in Britain, has been retained as a pattern of medical organization to this day.) It was in the setting of the voluntary hospitals that medical members of the comparatively small university educated class came into contact with the sick poor for the first time in any great numbers.

The availability of large numbers of poor patients to the 18th century physician and surgeon enabled them to develop new styles of medicine and medical education. In stark contrast to the situation in private practice, the patients in voluntary hospitals were passive recipients of charity rather than demanding customers in a buyer's market. In this context medical men were able to develop more objective and less individualized ideas about disease. Here also they were able to teach large numbers of students at the bedsides of people who could scarcely object to the presence of so many strangers. The lay governors of many hospitals discovered that ambitious young men would pay quite large fees to attend the sick as house pupils. This trend became increasingly important in centres such as Edinburgh (which in the early 18th century rapidly rose to a preeminent position as the leading centre of medical education in Europe) and London. In these places medical schools gradually developed, in which training centred around teaching at the bedside as well as lecture courses and, increasingly, dissection and anatomy classes (Lawrence 1994).

FROM NEW POOR LAW TO NATIONAL INSURANCE (1837–1911)

Between the early 19th century and 1948 a system and pattern of healthcare provision came into existence, which the National Health Service (NHS) inherited and endorsed with public funds. This period of change saw medical care make a number of important transitions, from largely domiciliary to frequently hospital-based medicine, from largely private to overwhelmingly state-organized and funded care, from an unregulated market to a virtual monopoly by orthodox practitioners, from older ideas about diseases and their causation to a modern pathological framework. For the purposes of this discussion we shall focus on organizational changes, but these interrelated strands of change cannot be seen in total isolation from each other.

Perhaps the earliest sign of increasing state involvement had been the Apothecaries Act of 1815, which legally enforced the Licentiate of the Society of Apothecaries (LSA) as a qualification. But the most influential changes came with a piece of legislation which was not at all medical in its original intention. The new Poor Law of 1837 was designed to tackle the problem of poverty in a society in which the old parish-based system of relief was no longer regarded as adequate. Its central feature was the principle of 'less eligibility' by which the care provided for the pauper had to be as unattractive as possible in order to prevent abuse of the system. The union workhouses set up under the act were designed to be not so much places of resort but places of last resort. Inevitably these places housed large numbers of the sick poor and many quickly set up infirmaries for them. The boards of governors of union workhouses employed medical men to provide a medical component to the system. The emphasis of the management of these institutions was firmly to get the poor back into the labour market as quickly and as cheaply as possible. It is not surprising, then, that such work was despised by medical men, although it was still preferable for many struggling to build up a practice from scratch, without the meagre salary such a post paid. Control of this institutionalized medical care remained in the hands of the local (lay) elite. In 1833 there were 10 000 (parish) workhouse inmates needing medical care and by 1861 the sick workhouse population had risen to over 50 000, compared to 11 000 patients in voluntary hospitals (Abel-Smith 1964). A census of sick poor taken in 1896 showed that of 58 550 sick, only 22 100 were in separate infirmaries, the large remainder being tended in general workhouses.

The running of hospitals and later public health services was not, however, left entirely in the hands of local bodies. In 1848 a short-lived body, the General Board of Health, was set up. Its intended role was to coordinate the efforts of the infirmaries and voluntary hospitals but it had little success. It was followed in 1871 by the Local Government Board which had a major role in structuring local services, including public health, until the creation of the Ministry of Health in 1920. In 1867 the Metropolitan Poor Act created a common fund for the fever and mental hospitals in London.

The 19th century also saw a proliferation of voluntary hospitals, many of which were created to cater for special groups of patients, such as foundlings, those with venereal diseases or women. Increasingly hospitals were set up to cater for emerging medical specializations, such as St Mark's Hospital (for diseases of the bowel) in London. In none of these institutions were medical men in control of the management. As the century wore on and medicine became increasingly well organized and confident of its claims to power and influence, this situation came to be resented. For many the idea that appointments to the staff could be under the control of a board of governors, whose only qualification was the ability to donate funds, rankled badly (Peterson 1978). Although the profession tended to perceive a need for more influence than it actually had at any given time, there was a steady acceptance of medical agenda setting. By 1888 all London infirmaries had been put in charge of a medical superintendent. This altered the balance of power in the running of the hospital and the boards were often forced to grant the requests of their medical superintendents.

With the emergence of powerful surgical and (to a lesser extent) medical techniques, the day-to-day running of hospitals became increasingly geared to the needs of the medical profession. The huge influence of the nurses trained by Florence Nightingale in the way hospitals were run in the second half of the 19th century was important for a number of reasons. It made a hospital stay much less hazardous for patients, well in advance of the 'germ theory' and bacteriological knowledge of the 1880s that subsequently explained its success. The Nightingale nurses also saw themselves as the natural servants of medicine, and doctors, in the hospital setting. This, along with the emergence of first antiseptic and then aseptic surgical techniques and the ability to chemically anaesthetize patients, enabled hospitals to provide interventive care on a large scale for the first time. The growing private market in surgery was catered for by the hospital consultants in many privately run nursing homes.

Hospitals at this time expanded not only in the scope of surgical and medical treatments offered but also in sheer size and local authority hospital provision became increasingly elaborate. Between 1891 and 1901, for example, the number of voluntary beds in England and Wales rose from 29 000 to 43 000. Infirmaries were now beginning to offer amenities approaching those of the voluntary hospitals. Rate payers failed to see why they should be required to support these 'palatial workhouse infirmaries' and also be pestered for money by the voluntary hospitals.

The latter fell increasingly into financial difficulty. Some of them, Guy's for instance, began to charge for outpatient attendance. Guy's also suffered particularly in this period since its wealth lay largely in land which lost both its absolute and rentable value in the agricultural depression of the 1880s. In the same period the governors of St Thomas's could afford to open only 13 of its 21 wards. In 1881 they opened some pay beds and Guy's followed suit in 1884. This system of payment spread rapidly to other hospitals and by 1890 15% of provincial hospital income came from this source.

In 1889 dissatisfaction prompted an enquiry into the

London hospitals by the House of Lords. They issued a report in 1892 recommending that all London hospitals should be placed under the control of an independent central board. The report ended with the warning that all hospitals would find it necessary to seek government or municipal support unless urgent action was taken. Argument, however, took the place of action, while the large voluntary hospitals fell rapidly and more deeply into debt. In 1896 the interest of the Prince of Wales had been enlisted. The Prince invited a number of leading doctors, financiers, industrialists and Church dignitaries to meet him and discuss the critical hospital finances. They agreed to collect and administer a fund, the Prince of Wales' Hospital Fund. Investigation showed that part of the hospitals' financial troubles resulted from amateur methods of costing and accountancy.

The middle classes were not really catered for in this system which had drawn its structure and ethos from the provision of relief to the sick poor, but it was beginning to offer types of treatment that would also be sought by the better off, and in settings which did not constitute a risk to health. These people were too wealthy to merit admission to voluntary hospitals, too proud to enter an infirmary and too poor to afford expensive home nursing, and their plight was not entirely solved until the inception of the NHS.

Many of the middle and artisan classes used the services of the general practitioner, who was seen as the 'family doctor' for the first time in the Victorian period. However, those poorest members of the working population found another way to gain access to medical care by forming medical clubs, friendly societies, provident dispensaries and so forth. These organizations contracted in the services of a general practitioner, often for astonishingly low capitation rates, and, through their lay boards, controlled many aspects of the doctors' work for their members. Capitation rates as low as 4 pence per head, per week were expected to cover the costs of medicines, appliances and premises as well as the doctor's personal equipment, transport and pay. The fictional club described by Cronin (1937), in which only 1 minute was allowed for a consultation, was probably not an exaggeration. Again this form of work was regarded as a clear second best to purely independent private practice and was the focus of intense unrest prior to 1911. However, the medical overcrowding which was to plague the profession until the early 20th century provided ample reason for doctors to seek and tolerate these posts.

The plight of the poorer GP, and the chronic financial embarrassment of the great voluntary hospitals coexisted with and was in stark contrast to the rising esteem for the medical profession and the medical sciences. Lord Lister, hailed as the discoverer of antisepsis (but who in many respects was no extraordinary innovator in surgery), represents this high public esteem. He was a celebrated figure rather like a great General or heroic explorer. Medicine, in a society which was turning away from the Church and towards the sciences for much of its understanding of life, became regarded as one of the major benefits of modern society. This was despite the paucity of treatments of any worth for the major causes of morbidity and mortality of the time, such as tuberculosis, cancers and syphilis. Doctors were seen as the best placed and most able people in society to tackle the problems of poverty, disease and physical inefficiency which after the turn of the century were widely perceived as pressing social problems. Beatrice and Sydney Webb, in their famous *The Doctor and the State* of 1910, clearly expressed the view that efficient provision of individual medical care was the key to promoting the health of the lower classes and society as a whole. This view would have astounded all but the most radical medical visionaries of the previous century and represented perhaps the most important victory for medicine prior to the chemotherapeutic revolution of the postwar period.

FROM NATIONAL INSURANCE TO NATIONAL HEALTH SERVICE (1911–1948)

This perception of the power of individual clinical care to solve social problems lay at the root of the reasons for the 1911 National Insurance Act's provision of medical care to the working population. This was the first time the state had intervened in any practical way in the provision of primary healthcare. However, as was often the case, this new provision retained many of the features of the preceding system. The friendly societies, provident dispensaries and medical clubs were given a 60% majority on the insurance committees created to administer medical benefit. As a result many doctors opposed it. But the reform was pushed through and 1912 saw the introduction of the panel system for general practitioner care as part of National Insurance, administered by civil servants. Doctors soon preferred the reforms and the income of general practitioners rose steadily in the interwar years. The system represented something of a triumph since doctors retained their independent contractor status, jealously guarded to this day.

Lloyd George's coalition was returned in 1918 and set up the Ministry of Health in 1919, to replace the Local Government Board, its role being a coordinating and advisory rather than an executive one. The first Minister was a qualified doctor, Christopher

Addison. As one historian has recently commented, the Ministry represented an endorsement of medical care over public health and was 'not a ministry of health at all, it was a ministry of clinical medicine' (Lawrence 1994).

Conditions were now conducive to a debate over the possible future structure of a state-controlled and funded health service. Addison set up a Council on Medical and Administrative Services under the chairmanship of Sir Bertrand, later Lord, Dawson which published a report on a proposed reorganization in 1920. The emphasis of this lay on bringing together preventative and curative medicine. Specialist advice would be available at a primary health centre, but the main working area of the specialists would be in the secondary health centres, located in a hospital capable of undertaking diagnosis, care and treatment of the more difficult case. The scheme considered that most cottage hospitals and some infirmaries could be adapted as secondary health centres although rebuilding would be necessary on some scale.

The Dawson Report was, with hindsight, more important as a sign of the interest in an overarching state organization and provision of medical services than as an influential milestone in structuring the national service. In many senses the interwar years represent a confused interregnum between the era of locally structured and funded medical care and the nationalized system of the NHS. Whilst the primary care system flourished the hospital sector was beset by difficulties. The profession was also deeply divided about how its future might be influenced by government. The essential dilemma for the profession was that it needed money from central government to fund its activities but it feared the impact of state interference in clinical settings and in private practice. There was, however, a growing body of opinion that government and professions should join in reforming medical care to be both more equitable and more efficient. It was equitability of funding, as opposed to efficiency of structure, which found expression in the form the NHS took in 1948. The interwar years were characterized more by crisis management than by visionary planning and in any case, structural change was often perceived as threatening the interests of the profession. The period 1911–1948, between National Insurance and the NHS, was not simply a period of planning and preparation for the latter service. It was rather a period in which the conflicting pressures exerted by doctors, doctors' organizations and state bodies were played out, with no clear direction or policy emerging from the process. The Second World War, and the special social, political and medical circumstances it generated, was more important in the making of the NHS than the peace that preceded it.

By the middle of 1920 the then Minister of Health found himself confronted by a crisis. The chairman of the London Hospital told the government that the voluntary hospitals would be unable to continue work unless the Exchequer provided one third of their income. The hospitals had tried to raise money by various means but had been beaten by rising prices. A number of hospitals found it necessary to close beds and two large London hospitals prepared to close down. Radical reform of medicine was now out of the financial reach of central government and the Minister had to devote all his energies to raising money to save the situation. The impetus for basic restructuring was not prominent again during the rest of the interwar years.

In 1929 the Local Government Act abolished the boards of guardians who administered the Poor Law and enabled local authorities to convert Poor Law institutions into municipal hospitals, therefore making hospital care more readily available (Wilson 1946). To placate doctors and voluntary hospitals who feared a loss of patients, a means test was applied and all those who could pay were expected to do so. Many doctors looked forward to a comprehensive service but those who might lose income attempted to frustrate it. Before 1930 many doctors had been concerned with the threat to their position under National Insurance, but now they perceived a more serious threat from the growth of the municipal services.

There still existed a division of the hospital service, one section depending upon voluntary subscriptions, the other upon the rates levied by borough and county councils. In the first the doctor was an 'honorary' giving his services freely, in the second he was a paid servant of the local authority. Proposals had already been made to end this separation and dual control, but the difficulties had proved too great and they had never been implemented. On the one hand both doctors and voluntary hospitals feared domination by local councils. On the other, powerful town halls saw no good reason to surrender an important part of their function. In the mid 1930s the majority of 'honoraries' attached to voluntary hospitals also held a paid 'consultant' post at a municipal institution. The teaching hospital 'honorary' often took his firm of students to the municipal hospital where the student benefited by seeing a type of patient not often found in the teaching wards. Cooperation became so close by the outbreak of war in 1939 that many doctors and administrators thought the future of the hard-pressed voluntary hospitals lay in the hands of local government.

Ideally BMA leaders wanted to free the profession

from both municipal rule and friendly society interference and the trades unions gave them the opportunity. The unions were alarmed at the way the insurance industry was influencing social policy. In 1936 the BMA had formed a joint committee with the Trades Union Congress. The combination was strong enough to influence government. Amongst other measures the government introduced in 1938 was a royal commission to study the whole question of workmen's compensation. It seemed, however, that the council of the BMA did not appreciate that national health insurance must imply some degree of national government control.

The outbreak of war in 1939 and the anticipation of huge civilian casualties from aerial bombardment led to the setting up of the Emergency Medical Service, which included under its auspices voluntary and local authority hospitals. For most of these hospitals this was a positive change, for although they were now managed within state plans they were adequately financed, in some cases for the first time in decades. This gave new impetus to the effort to formulate a state medical service for peacetime. In 1940 the Medical Planning Commission was formed to consider health services and in 1941 the government created a committee headed by William, later Sir William, Beveridge to consider the whole field of social policy. In 1942 the Commission produced an interim report calling for the creation of a comprehensive health service covering 90% of the population, which actually amounted to little more than an endorsement of proposals made in 1929 and 1938.

Five months later the Beveridge Report appeared calling for the removal of the insurance industry from state administration but also for the abolition of the approved society system. This seemed a proposal that doctors would find easily acceptable and in 1943, the Ministry plan presented to the profession was to organize all health services under local authority control with GPs employed on salary, and all under medical officer of health control. The BMA and colleges, however, made it clear that municipal control would not be acceptable. Civil servants failed to heed the warning and it was only on the intervention of Aneurin Bevan that local authority control was removed in 1945. (Only a limited array of community services ended up under local authority control and even those were taken away when the NHS was reorganized in 1974 when medical officers of health disappeared to be replaced by community physicians and public health officers whose role was to plan or evaluate rather than provide services.)

The plans for a health service included in the Beveridge Report of 1944 formed part of the promised 'new world' for the war-weary population of Britain. The postwar Atlee government immediately set about implementing Beveridge's recommendations in full to create the modern welfare state. In a White Paper published in March 1946 Aneurin Bevan suggested that instead of turning over all the hospitals to the local authorities, he proposed to adopt both voluntary and municipal hospitals and to administer them by regional boards consisting of members chosen and appointed by the Minister. These boards were in turn to appoint hospital management committees after consultation with local authorities, medical and dental staffs for each large hospital or group of smaller hospitals. Teaching hospitals did not form part of the regional structure and were to be administered by separate boards of governors.

Medical leaders still argued that the main problem in the proposals was the introduction of a salaried service, with the loss of clinical and contractual independence. It was also feared that the new system would effectively abolish private practice. Bevan made several concessions in this direction and famously commented that he would 'stuff [the doctors'] mouths with gold' in order to ensure that a state-funded service, free at point and time of use, was brought in. As had been the case in 1911, the government were confident enough that most doctors would join the new service therefore allowing them to ignore some of the demands of the BMA and Royal Colleges. The NHS came into being on 5 July 1948. Doctors' acceptance of the NHS, rather like their acceptance of the panel system, was largely due to their important role in budgetary control and the preservation of their clinical freedom. As Klein (1989) put it:

Implicit in the structure of the NHS was a bargain between the state and the medical profession. While central government controlled the budget, doctors controlled what happened within that budget. Financial power was concentrated at the centre; clinical power was concentrated at the periphery.

This was a remarkable gain for the medical profession and also, to some extent, for society as a whole, but it contained within it the seeds of much trouble to come. The NHS enshrined a relationship between the state and healthcare professions which had been the product of two centuries of change, but which was bound to come under strain as the social conditions and cultural assumptions underpinning it continued to change over the next half century.

In the next chapter we shall see how the NHS developed and examine the doctors' role within that process.

REFERENCES

Abel-Smith B 1964 The hospitals 1800–1948. Heinemann Educational, London

Bynum W F, Porter R (eds) 1987 Medical fringe, medical orthodoxy, 1750–1850. Croom Helm, London
Cartwright F F 1977 A social history of medicine. Longman, London
Cronin A J 1937 The citadel. Gollancz, London
Granshaw L, Porter R (eds) 1989 The hospital in history. Routledge, London
Honigsbaum F 1990 The evolution of the NHS. British Medical Journal 301: 694
Klein R 1989 The politics of the NHS, 2nd edn. Longman, Harlow
Lawrence C 1994 Medicine in the making of modern Britain 1700–1920. Blackwell Scientific, London
Littre E 1979 in The Oxford dictionary of quotations, 3rd edn. Oxford University Press, Oxford
Loudon I S L 1979 Trends in general practice. Royal College of General Practitioners, London
Pater J E 1981 The making of the National Health Service. King's Fund, London
Perkin H 1989 The rise of professional society, England since 1880. Routledge, London
Peterson M J 1978 The medical profession in mid Victorian London. California University Press, Berkeley
Rivett G 1986 The development of the London hospital system 1823–1982. King's Fund, London
Wilson N 1946 Municipal health services. Allen & Unwin, London

RECOMMENDED READING

Granshaw L, Porter R (eds) 1989 The hospital in history. Routledge, London
Klein R 1989 The politics of the NHS, 2nd edn. Longman, Harlow
Lawrence C 1994 Medicine in the making of modern Britain 1700–1920. Blackwell Scientific, London
Perkin H 1989 The rise of professional society, England since 1880. Routledge, London

2

The evolution of the NHS

Tony White, David Allen

Foolish the doctor who despises the knowledge acquired by the ancients.
(Hippocrates)

INTRODUCTION

When someone falls seriously ill in Britain more than nine times out of 10 they will be looked after by the NHS. In 1994–5 the NHS cost about £35 billion. Since that amount continuously increases with inflation it is useful to remember that about 5.6% of GNP is spent on the NHS. This compares with figures for 1989–90 for Germany 8.2%, France 8.9% and the United States 12.4%. Health economists believe that there is an economic relationship which is statistically significant between the wealth of a country and the amount of money that a country spends on healthcare. On that basis Britain spends slightly less than predicted. This, it is argued, is because the NHS is an efficient way of using resources. It is the government's second biggest item of expenditure after the social security budget (covering pensions and unemployment pay, etc.) and more than is spent on defence and education. Even after allowing for inflation the amount of money spent on the NHS (or resources used) has increased by about three times since 1949–50 when 3.9% of GNP was spent on the NHS. The question of whether the NHS is underfunded is not easy to answer in objective terms; need and demand are not absolute states but elastic concepts (Harrison et al 1990). These authors also point out that the ability to consume healthcare resources is apparently limitless. Allsop (1984) says that arguments about levels of funding are largely pointless since they say little about the efficiency of that spending.

Essentially the NHS is an insurance mechanism which allows the population to pay for healthcare when they are well and working so those who need care can receive it 'free at point of delivery' when they are sick and in need. As we have seen in the previous chapter, historically healthcare had been either bought by direct payment or those unable to pay could receive care in charitable institutions paid for by the donations of the rich or public charity. Until 1948 the voluntary hospitals generally concentrated on providing acute care, while the local authorities filled the gaps and provided long-stay care.

The wartime coalition government agreed that a comprehensive health service covering all aspects of healthcare, open to all, 'provided where needed, without contribution', was required and published a White Paper *A National Health Service* in February 1944. The Labour government of 1945 and its Minister of Health, Aneurin Bevan, were committed to the main proposals of the 1944 White Paper except for local authority control, preferring to develop new institutions: hospital management committees and regional hospital boards with members appointed by the Minister. The 1946 National Health Service Act set up new regional boards and management committees (which were really the only new institution in the NHS) to manage and co-ordinate the 2800 hospitals which were transferred to public control. The executive councils, set up originally by the 1911 Act, continued to control the work of the general practitioners, while the local health services (community services) remained with the local authorities. This tripartite structure, as it was called, and the NHS were born on 5 July 1948. Very little changed, the same people were doing very much the same things, although they were paid by a different source. What the NHS did change was the way people could obtain and pay for healthcare. No country's health service is unique; all countries have mixtures of organizations of health services (even Russia has long had a private sector). In Britain the private sector, although growing, is very small compared to the NHS.

The NHS is one of the largest organizations in the world. It employs about 1¼ million people. Allowing for the large numbers of part-timers, there are almost 1 million full-time equivalents including about half a million nurses. Countries such as Denmark and New Zealand have similar health services but there are six key aspects of the NHS which distinguish the NHS, although not uniquely, from other health service organizations. The first is the separation of primary from secondary healthcare. This of course dates back to the end of the 19th century when the BMA persuaded the general practitioners and hospital doctors to resolve their long-standing dispute over patients by accepting the convention that 'The general practitioners had the patients and the hospital doctors had the beds' and that with some exceptions, patients could only be seen in hospital after referral by a general practitioner. The 1911 National Health Insurance Act institutionalized this separation by paying only general practitioners and (at their own choice) not hospital doctors. This means that general practitioners act as gatekeepers to the NHS. This separation has had profound effects, particularly on the costs of the NHS, as Britain has an inpatient rate three quarters that of Germany and half that of the US.

Because the NHS is a national service, having to serve the whole of the United Kingdom and, like most British institutions, it was built on what went before, nothing about the NHS holds 100% true. The NHS ceased to be completely free at point of delivery when, in 1950, the Labour government introduced charges for some items and services. But even in 1992, after the government had repeatedly increased charges, revenue generated by charges still only covered about 5% of the total cost. The Labour government of 1945 decided the cost of the NHS should come out of general taxation, not out of a direct charge on income as in other European health insurance schemes nor out of local rates or taxes as in Sweden. General taxation was preferred for two reasons. First it was more efficient; the cost of collecting tax is about 2% of the total collected, while the administrative costs of European social insurance schemes are anything from 5% to 10% and for some private health insurance schemes can be more than 30%.

Secondly, payment for the health service out of taxes is more equitable; 'the biggest burden borne by the broadest backs'. Flat rate social insurance is a regressive tax, while the total tax take with PAYE is progressive and thus more equitable. Another distinctive feature is that the National Health Service is comprehensive, again with exceptions, covering all aspects of primary, secondary and also tertiary care in the community. Healthcare services in other countries may not cover primary care or some aspects of secondary care, like psychiatry or geriatrics, and many other health services do not have community services. The NHS is also open to all, although since 1985 foreigners who deliberately come to Britain for healthcare, as opposed to falling ill while visiting, and those not residents of the European Community or residents of countries that have reciprocal agreements (like Russia and Australia) have had to pay.

Finally, the NHS can be distinguished from most other health services because the government owns the hospital and either directly or indirectly employs all the staff, although trust status has subtly changed this relationship. This is significant because in Germany or France, once the government has passed legislation stating that specific medical conditions are covered, anyone presenting with those conditions is entitled to treatment, meaning that the cost of healthcare in those countries depends upon demand and is out of government control. Whereas in Britain, the amount of money given to the health service does not depend on the number of patients treated. It is the Cabinet who, as part of the annual PES (Public Expenditure Survey) review, decides how much funding the NHS and all other government departments receive and the NHS has to do what it can with that amount of money. As they say, 'The NHS is the envy of the world's finance ministers' for while other countries desperately try to contain health expenditure the British government has NHS expenditure under precise control.

So the six aspects which distinguish the NHS from healthcare systems in other countries are:

1. the separation between primary and secondary medicine
2. free at the point of consumption
3. paid for out of taxation
4. comprehensive service
5. open to all
6. the government owns the hospitals and employs the staff and precisely controls the cost of the NHS.

These features have not changed greatly since 1948 but while the underlying characteristics have not changed, to achieve the NHS's two underlying managerial and political aims of efficiency and equity, the organization and structure have undergone seemingly almost continuous change, at least in the last 10 years. Efficiency and equity were the two original political imperatives of the 1946 Act. The NHS was designed to make the provision of healthcare in Britain more efficient than the divided and competitive systems that went before and to provide an equity of healthcare in Britain that had not previously existed. These two factors have remained the guiding principles underlying all sorts of 'reforms' and reorganizations since 1948.

The DHSS (1972a) published a paper for reorganization implemented in 1974. Six years later the DHSS (1980a) published a further paper and in 1982 another reorganization took place. The following year the Griffiths Report (DHSS 1983) was published and implemented in 1984. In 1989 the government published its White Paper *Working for Patients* (DHSS 1989), introduced during 1991. According to Welborne (1990), all organizations are now experiencing very rapid and continuous change and he feels that it is important for all senior staff and managers to develop skills to manage such changes if they are to be effective in their jobs. But this is not a new experience; as long ago as 210 BC Petronius Arbiter said:

We trained hard – but it seemed that every time we were beginning to form up in teams we would be reorganized. I was beginning to learn, later in life that we tend to meet any new situation by reorganizing; and a wonderful method it can be for creating the illusion of progress while producing confusion, inefficiency and demoralization.

REASONS FOR CHANGE

These changes also beg the question as to their purpose. Is it to make the service better and if so, in what way? To treat more patients or to treat patients quicker or to treat patients for less money? Improvements in priority group services are frequently financed through cost improvement achievements or rationalization within the acute sector. The government appear to see change within the NHS mostly as a means of cost improvement and cost containment. In a sympathetic review of the NHS, Enthoven (1985) notes the tight limits under which the NHS operates and considers that it will find it increasingly difficult to meet the demands placed upon it.

Change has not only been concerned with finance but also with management and control. In spite of talk of decentralization, since 1982 central government has tightened its 'grip' on the NHS through such reforms as annual review systems, the application of performance indicators and trial management advisory schemes. Petchey (1986) describes an increasing disquiet, felt not only in government and the DHSS but also by staff within the NHS, particularly doctors, about the failure or shortcomings of consensus management which, he says, 'were experienced as cumbersome and time-consuming, leading to institutional stagnation and creating a lack of managerial accountability'. Although the assumption that consensus management may lead to institutional stagnation may be difficult to justify, he does not elaborate on this aspect.

The early reorganizations recognized that the NHS is a loosely coordinated system. During the Royal Commission on the NHS, Kogan et al (1978) echoed the DHSS statements from 1972: 'It is generally held that decision making cannot be undertaken by a chief executive of a single authority because of the integrative complexity of health care provision.' Schulz & Harrison (1983) claimed widespread support for the practice of consensus decision making as a means of managing the service.

RESOURCE ALLOCATION AND INCENTIVES

The 1976 Resource Allocation Working Party (RAWP) attempted to allocate money between the regions geographically, but more equally, based upon need as measured for acute care, by population adjusted by standardized mortality rates. In 1979–80 the poorest region was 9% below and the richest 13% above the mean but since then differences have been greatly lessened. The regions adopted the RAWP procedure to allocate targets to their areas and districts.

The 1977 Priorities Document said that the demographic characters of the population and disease were changing. There was an increasing elderly population, more degenerative diseases and fewer infectious diseases. In addition more needed to be done for long-stay patients and the health service needed change to reflect this. The Department of Health identified priority healthcare groups, like the elderly, mentally handicapped and mentally ill, and made care in the community a priority. It was an attempt to change the allocation of resources between patient groups. There has been some transfer of resources from acute to other groups but some argue that the transfer has not been sufficient, not even enough to keep up with the increased demand in those areas.

In 1980 the Black Report showed a comparison of healthcare between social classes and the probability of death of those under 65 of social classes 4 and 5 was twice that of those in social classes 1 and 2. Similarly for perinatal mortality of the two groups. The Report made many proposals, but the working party, having been set up by a Labour government, reported after the Conservative party was elected and the Conservative government were unenthusiastic. These findings remain a problem for the NHS.

The lack of adequate individual reward is an additional drawback. In private industry there are cost of living and merit-based pay increases for employees. During pay restraint, private organizations can manipulate the system to give non-cash benefits to reward their employees. Public service organizations have none of these advantages and are used as a tool of government economic policy. In a review of the incentives and economic efficiency of the NHS, Enthoven (1985) says:

> The system contains no serious incentives to guide the NHS in the direction of better quality care and service at reduced cost. There are few rewards for the manager who takes risks and makes the extra effort, and fewer rewards to hand out to staff.

Rewards are more than the ability to recruit the right calibre of employee or reward effective performance; they are also a measure of the value that an organization places on its employees and an expression of the value placed on them by society. To maintain, as governments do, that vocational reward is compensation enough for low pay compared to those in private industry may insult the employees. Estimates suggest that up to 10% of medical graduates never practise and a similar number drop out in the early years. And there is a growing tendency for medical consultants to take early retirement. Large numbers of nurses, once trained, never work or do not return to NHS hospitals. Increasing NHS defections highlight a growing gap between the philosophy of the NHS and that of the outside world. Companies appreciate that staff are an important and increasingly scarce resource, so they provide decent facilities to retain them.

For a health service to be effective it has to have some inbuilt slack capacity. This may be regarded as inefficient, but patients do not fall ill or have accidents at a steady daily rate. If there is a major disaster the local hospital(s) cannot say, 'We can only cope with 25% of the casualties today, the rest we will treat next week'. When someone has a heart attack you cannot say, 'Sorry we have had too many emergencies this week, we will admit you another time'. Although much of this slack is provided by staff goodwill, working extra hours without reward, their goodwill cannot make other resources available. Yet most hospitals make no provision for staff holidays, sickness or maternity leave, so that when these events take place there is no one to do the work. Routine work is not done or it is cancelled even though other members of the team are available. The result is a very efficient organization that becomes ineffective.

MANAGEMENT PROBLEMS

The NHS management finds itself, unlike private industry, without the authority to determine and direct all the activities of the organization. It does not have what is known as primacy. Management in the NHS is part of a coalition of managers and professionals which is entirely separate from the other coalition of the professionals, doctors, nurses and paramedical professions, of which the medical profession, for historical and logistical reasons of its relationship with the patient, is the most dominant. Klein (1989) considers that a striking feature of policy making in the NHS is the domination of the medical profession. He states that out of the NHS total British labour force of about 750 000, only some 45 000 are doctors, yet a review of the literature about policy making in the NHS is exclusively preoccupied with the medical profession. As Crossman (1972) said, the NHS is a 'consultant dominated service'.

THE FIRST REORGANIZATION (1972–74)

The participation of hospital doctors in management and their contribution to the efficiency of the hospital service was a major theme of the first reorganization and stemmed from doctors being able to direct the use of costly resources with varying but often considerable degrees of autonomy. After discussion between the Minister of Health and the profession in 1965, the Joint Working Party on the Organization of Medical Work in Hospitals was set up to discuss the progress of the NHS and particularly to review the hospital service. It produced three reports (MoH 1967, DHSS 1972b, DHSS 1974), known as the Cogwheel Reports because of the design printed on the covers. The first report recommended the creation of divisions of broadly linked specialities to include consultants and junior medical staff which would constantly appraise their services and methods of provision. Such divisions were likely to be set up on a faculty or speciality basis. Representatives of each division were to come together in each hospital as a medical executive committee which would coordinate the work and views of the division and provide a link with nursing and administration. The sort of problems they might consider included bed management and the organization of outpatient and inpatient resources. In fact, they became more a means of disseminating routine information, a discussion forum for problems, in addition to being an outlet for airing frustrations. Most hospital groups gradually implemented this scheme and by 1972 the second report was able to identify the essential elements of an effective Cogwheel system and to report that particularly in large acute hospitals, the system had been helpful in creating improved communications, reductions of inpatient waiting lists and the progressive control of medical expenditure.

The third report clarified the role of Cogwheel systems in the newly reorganized NHS, because an emphasis of the 1974 reorganization was the part played by multidisciplinary teams in integrated management, whereas Cogwheel had been set up as a doctor-dominated hospital-based arrangement. The third report suggested that Cogwheel should continue to deal with issues where the agreement and action of hospital doctors were the main needs, while problems requiring strong collaboration between all professional groups, both within the hospitals and in community services, should be the province of the district management teams and healthcare planning teams. It would still be appropriate for Cogwheel systems to concentrate on efficiency issues and it would be helpful for hospital doctors to see their clinical freedom in the context of teamwork and the necessity of sharing resources.

Cogwheel divisions did not flourish everywhere, however, but where they did (Levitt & Wall 1984), many required a considerable amount of administrative input. Support for the Cogwheel concept was nevertheless fairly general and an alternative was difficult to find given the clinical autonomy which consultants enjoyed. The Royal Commission noted an impatience amongst medical staff with the seemingly inevitable delays intrinsic within consensus management and they supported an executive team at hospital level which they thought would speed things up. The idea of unit management teams was endorsed in *Patients First* (DHSS 1979) and in a DHSS (1980b) circular on the new structure, but the involvement of doctors was somewhat ambiguously stated. Many doctors feared that the reorganization would be taken as the opportunity to deprive them of their clinical autonomy. Clinical freedom was, however, built into the reorganized service.

The 1974 reorganization had been intended to improve planning and the Priorities Document creating priority care groups lead to a planning system in which the Department of Health annually sent to the regions guidelines on how the NHS should develop. The regions interpreted these and sent regional guidelines to the districts who prepared short-term programmes as proposals for specific action, which were then submitted to the region for approval and, after negotiation, agreed. The regions then combined the district plans for submission to the DHSS where they were reviewed. But the intrusion of politics exacerbated discontent. A Green Paper and consultative Document in 1972 (DHSS 1972a) appeared to have had as its purpose a closer integration of preventative with curative medicine. As implemented in April 1974 the only overt effect was to make administrative machinery more cumbersome and to separate lay administration more widely from the working doctor. A hospital consultant now had to penetrate several strata of committees before arriving at the source of management. The nature of these new committees intensified the political aspect. The 1948 tripartite structure had come in for increasing criticism in the 1950s and 1960s because of the lack of continuity of care. The Cranbrook Report on Maternity Services in 1959 pointed out that expectant mothers could be treated first by their general practitioner, then referred to hospital for delivery and then discharged back into the community to be looked after by a midwife. Inevitably, as in other specialities with a high community content such as psychiatry and geriatrics, patients could 'fall through the cracks' and fail to receive the continuity of care they expected. During the 1950s and 1960s, as the health service was expanding and developing new services, planning became increasingly difficult because of the divided responsibilities of the several agencies.

In 1974 the health services were reorganized so that the family practitioner services joined with the hospital services to form health authorities. Hospital social workers joined the local authorities and the local authority nurses and doctors joined the health authorities. Local authorities became responsible for all social services, including meals-on-wheels and home helps, etc., while health authorities became responsible for all health services including community services. One of the purposes of the reorganization was to make planning easier, so if health authorities were to work with local authorities it was argued they should cover the same areas. The local authorities had, in 1973, just been reorganized, for the first time in about 100 years, into 80 local authorities in England so there had to be 80 health authorities to match. While some health authorities presented no problems others were far too large to manage and some of these 80 area health authorities were divided into districts to create 199 districts in England.

At each level (region, area and district) a management team of four officers was appointed. The four officers were the matron, now to be called the district nursing officer, who lost her 'hotel' responsibilities to an administrator (often the old hospital secretary), who lost his financial responsibilities to a treasurer/finance officer, and a medical officer or community physician, often the old medical officer of health transferred from a local authority. At the regional level, because of the RHA's responsibilities for planning and building new hospitals, there was also a works or estates officer. As part of the reorganization these teams were to make decisions based upon 'consensus', so in theory each member of the team could veto a decision. Figure 2.1

STRUCTURE OF THE NHS

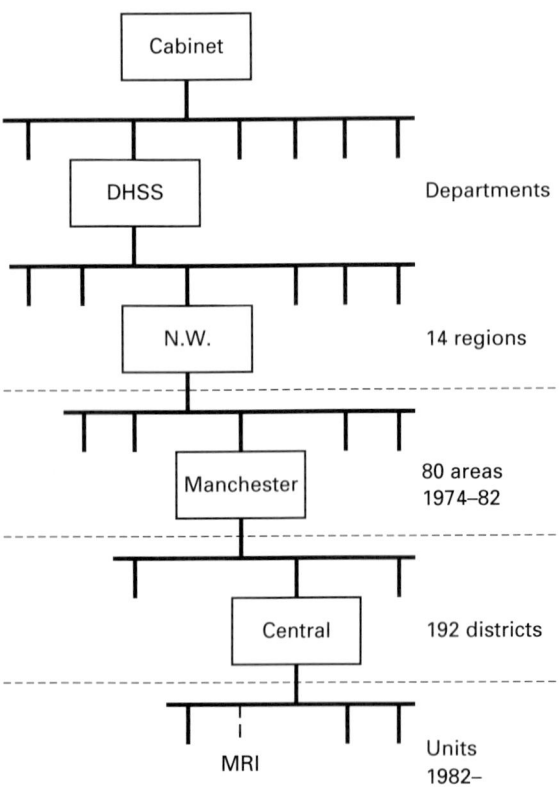

Fig. 2.1 Structure of the NHS

shows the structure in 1974 with the Secretary of State for Health a member of the Cabinet. He had a Minister for Health and several parliamentary private secretaries to help him. The Department of Health directly monitored the 14 regional health authorities in England (in Scotland, Wales and Northern Ireland the respective Secretary of State is responsible for the health services). The regional and area health authorities were legal entities in their own right (while districts were operational units and reported to the next level up – the area). The regions and areas had chairmen who were personally appointed by the Secretary of State and other members appointed from the local community. Each area or, where they were divided into districts, each district also had a new organization called a community health council (CHC) to represent the views of the population, which allowed the area and the district health authority to concentrate on the management of the service.

THE SECOND REORGANIZATION (1980–82)

The objective of the 1974 reorganization had been to achieve a more efficient way of providing the service. Having set up this structure with its emphasis on planning, the structure came under increasing attack for excessive bureaucracy and poor decision making. Senior staff tended to move away from the hospital to work on planning at the district level. There was criticism, particularly by the Royal Commission set up in 1976 by Harold Wilson, and when the Conservatives returned to power in 1979 they accepted the Royal Commission recommendations that there was too much bureaucracy and one of the tiers should be removed, though they did ignore most of the other recommendations. So in 1980 the new Secretary of State, Patrick Jenkins, published *Patients First*, which proposed that one tier of the management structure, the multidistrict area, should be removed and that the management of the hospital needed to be strengthened. Districts were therefore reorganized into units, intended to provide sensible managerial organization, like a client group or a geographical area or a hospital. These units were to be managed by an administrator, a nurse and a doctor elected by colleagues.

The emphasis had been on delegation; the message from the then Minister of Health, Dr Gerald Vaughan, was that the NHS, which had been complaining about too much departmental interference, should stand on its own feet. But the Public Accounts Committee of the House of Commons, the most senior committee of the House of Commons, cross examining ministers and civil servants about their multimillion pound budgets, took the view that it was all very well telling the health authorities to manage alone but that there needed to be proper accountability. The PAC said the health service should be more accountable to the Secretary of State and hence to Parliament. The next Secretary of State, Norman Fowler, in 1981 set up the Annual Review Process to, in his words, 'call the health authorities to account'. Annual reviews were at that time probably the most significant development in the management of the NHS since 1948. Each year the regional chairmen and officers met with ministers to discuss how the money was being used, the level of efficiency and plans for future development and which previous plans had so far been achieved.

Following the 1982 reorganization, unit management teams (UMT) were set up as a quartet of doctor, nurse, administrator and treasurer; in some cases they included a consultant and general practitioner. The planned role of these teams is not altogether easy to determine, nor is their corporate relationship to the district management team (DMT), although clear directions were given (DHSS 1982) on how doctors were to be appointed to the DMT following the 1982 reorganization. The consultant was to be elected by the consultant body and the general practitioner by all general practitioners in a district and serve for a limited period. This marked a change in some places where previously the District Medical Committee (DMC), itself a representative body, had elected the DMT medical representatives.

THE THIRD REORGANIZATION (1983–84)

The Griffiths Report (1983b) proposals recommended modification to this type of team decision making. Ironically, it was hospital doctors' criticisms of consensus management which probably did most to encourage the Secretary of State to ask for the Griffiths Report in the first place. The resulting proposals that there should be a general manager at district and unit level led the BMA to state that such a post should be held by a doctor, even though many doctors were doubtful that filling the role would be practicable given their comparative or total lack of management training and their prime commitment to patient treatment, allowing little time for a managerial role. That dilemma cannot be easily resolved. Doctors need to be involved closely with the decisions about healthcare, but do not wish to spend too much time away from their patients and other commitments such as teaching and research, etc. It was hoped that the Griffiths proposals would be an effective improvement on Cogwheel and on consensus management. However, things changed again with the reforms introduced in 1991.

To a certain extent the idea of a top doctor had been tried before with the medical superintendent in some hospitals and with the medical officer of health in local health authorities before the 1974 reorganization. Medical superintendents' posts atrophied well before 1974 but the medical officer of health was sometimes a highly influential officer in local authorities whose work was often widely appreciated, although not usually by hospital consultants. The holders of these posts did not find it easy to adapt to the different management principles following the reorganization and this has left community medicine in a somewhat ambiguous position.

Possibly this is one of the reasons why there were relatively few community physicians in the early 1980s. No one appeared to know whether community medicine was about the management of medical work or about the management of the health of the community. Unfortunately regional medical officers and district medical officers were not trained for management and their background was not the best qualification to give leadership to consultants.

Prestige in medicine has always been associated with possession of skills in the application of advanced technology. Consultants discount the views of regional medical officers, district medical officers and community doctors because they have no direct experience of the problems of being a consultant. This may of course be a phenomenon not unique to medicine but the consequence is that regional medical officers and district medical officers had little influence over consultants. Medical leadership might be strengthened by recruitment of leaders from the more powerful medical posts and those with formal training in management.

Despite the claims of the Hunter Report (1972) which had tried to amalgamate both the managerial and clinical responsibilities, the Royal Commission felt that the community physicians' role in planning, health education, epidemiology and environmental control should be encouraged. This implied that administrative tasks should be undertaken by administrators.

Doctors generally do not perceive the impact of their individual decisions on beds, facilities and costs (Weisbord 1976) and in general doctors have little interest in management problems. Some managers feel doctors are closed-minded and aloof and disinterested in the problems facing the administrator (Jacobs 1978). Jynton (1975) agrees that physicians have a tendency to establish themselves as role experts in health-related matters. Their 'domain' includes all parts of the hospital. According to Hanlon and Gladstein (1984) a common perception of departmental heads, many of whom were doctors, was that they were at best mediocre administrators with little sensitivity to the human side of management.

INTERPRETATION OF THE GRIFFITHS REPORT

It is now claimed by Griffiths (1991, 1992) that both doctors and managers misunderstood the implications of the Griffiths Report (1983b): 'Involve the clinicians more closely in the management process, consistent with clinical freedom for clinical practice. Clinicians must participate fully in decisions about priorities in the use of resources'. In the Audit Commission Annual Lecture in 1991 he said (Griffiths 1991): 'I personally believed and intended it to be liberating in the sense that doctors and nurses would have the opportunity of having a much greater say in the running of the health service'. And again in a speech to the British Association of Medical Managers in 1992 (Griffiths 1992), he reemphasizes this: 'From the very outset in 1983 I made it clear that I envisaged a strong role for doctors in the management of the NHS and my report subsequently confirmed that'. However, of greater interest is his statement on general management, in which he says: 'I did not intend that the result should be yet another profession in the National Health Service to work in parallel with other professions'. Not only were the Griffiths recommendations misunderstood or perhaps reinterpreted later, but also the medical profession, always fearing a loss of clinical freedom, felt unable to grasp the opportunity created and the reforms were effectively hijacked by the administrative management.

Fitzgerald & Sturt (1992), in discussing the Griffith Report, said: 'Despite the strong thrust provided by general management, limited progress was made on the inclusion of clinicians into management decision making'. Harrison (1988), offering an historical analysis up to the late 1980s, suggested that, 'Some change has taken place but that this has more to do with the *form* of relationships [between doctors and managers] than with the substance'. Enthoven (1985), while sympathetic to the thrust of the Griffiths Report, said that in different circumstances its recommendations might make a difference, but only if the structure and incentives in the NHS were changed more fundamentally.

The 1974 reorganization had created a management structure based upon professional hierarchies; all the administrators reported to the senior administrator, all the nurses reported to the senior nurse, etc. But with Griffiths all the managerial staff reported directly or indirectly to the general manager and that, combined with the annual performance reviews which gave the management specific tasks (such as moving a given percentage of the long-stay patients into the community), meant that the old professional structure was gradually moulded into a functional structure with directors of planning or personnel, etc. replacing district medical officers and district nurses, etc. Thus, there was a gradual evolution of the organizational structure. Griffiths was a more significant reorganization than any that went before, because whereas the previous reorganizations gave people new titles, the Griffiths reorganization meant people did different things. Where the structure in the 1974 reorganization had been prescribed in precise detail, the Griffiths recommendations related mainly to the concept of general management and the implications of the recommendations only evolved afterwards with time, thought and experience. While Griffiths gave general managers greater authority and power and lessened 'the shackles of professionalism' the general managers' freedom to act was overestimated and unrealistic expectations led to many problems particularly among the outsider general managers, slow to learn a new culture. The NHS with its caring tradition and particularly the power of the professional groups is a radically different culture from industry and commerce.

THE FOURTH REORGANIZATION (1989–91)

In the late 1980s there were a number of occasions when the Secretary of State for Health had to ask the Treasury for more money for the service. Despite these injections of extra cash there were frequent reports in the press of patients unable to receive appropriate care. Mrs Thatcher therefore set up a small ministerial committee to look at the NHS. As a result, the government published a White Paper in January 1989, *Working for Patients* (DHSS 1989). The government argued that they were spending a lot of money on the NHS and were not getting value for it; there were large variations in efficiency across the country. Their solution to increase efficiency was to separate purchasers from suppliers and create an 'internal market'. The stated aim of the White Paper was to give patients better healthcare and more choice of the services available to give greater satisfaction and greater rewards for those working in the NHS who successfully responded to local needs and preferences.

Five key measures were proposed. To stimulate a better service to the patient, hospitals would become self-governing NHS hospital trusts. Hospitals were to have the money to best meet the needs and wishes of patients and the money required would be able to cross administrative boundaries. A hundred new consultant posts would be created to reduce waiting times and improve the quality of service, to help give individual patients appointment times they could rely on and reduce the long hours worked by some junior doctors. To enable family doctors to improve service to patients, large general practitioner practices would be able to apply for their own budgets to obtain a range of services direct from hospitals. To improve the effectiveness of NHS management, region, district and family practitioner management bodies would be reduced in size and reformed on business lines, with executive and non-executive directors. The creation of trusts meant a substantial change in the role of DHAs, with neighbouring districts merging and DHAs merging with FPCs.

The system of funding by the RAWP formula was discontinued. Health authorities were now funded on a capitation basis, weighted to reflect the health and age distribution of the population and the relative cost of providing services. Each DHA's duty was to buy the best service it could from hospitals in its own area or indeed outside them, even from the private sector. There are 'core' services to which patients are guaranteed local access: accident and emergency including admissions, other immediate admissions, outpatient and other services to support these, public health, community-based services and other hospital services which need to be provided on a local basis. Every consultant was expected to participate in a form of clinical audit agreed between the management and the profession locally. Consultant contracts are with their trust and each trust agrees with consultants the scope and arrangement of their NHS duties. Clinical executives should take a direct part in the appointments procedure for consultants. Changes in the distinction awards scheme were proposed so as to reflect the wider responsibilities of consultants for the effective use of resources as well as the clinical merit of their work. The government's intention for the internal market was to reward the best and concentrate future development on the most efficient parts of the system.

Ministers protested that privatizing the NHS never crossed their minds, but it probably crossed Mrs Thatcher's mind. In the end she was obliged to settle for an ersatz market. The claim that the money would follow the patient aroused expectations of some kind of voucher system. But reality remained the same: purchasers could purchase no more than their budgets permitted and the voucher ensured no more than a place in the queue. Rationing continues under the new system as under the old. In time, the internal market should increase supply by promoting greater efficiency. The way the NHS works is a continuously changing and evolving kaleidoscope of a multitude of factors. It never stays still and so is never predictable or dull to study.

The National Health Service had now undergone the most radical of the many reorganizations in its history. There was intense discussion about ideas for reform which fell largely into two broad views: either replacing the tax-financed scheme with an insurance-based scheme or improving the use of existing resources by organizational change. The influence of American ideas on the first, being insurance-based, is very obvious but on the second theme less so, this being attributed to the influence of Enthoven (1985) who advocated an 'internal market' within the NHS. As Klein pointed out (1989):

There appeared to be a terminal irony in the fact that, after 40 years which had brought a regular procession of Americans to Britain to find out the secrets of the NHS's success, the process was being reversed: the anorexic were seeking a cure from experts on obesity.

Ministers failed to convince the majority of healthcare professionals that the reforms would have the desired effect. Nor indeed were doctors consulted, a point of interest as it was the first time that government had failed to consult the medical profession. The service continued to work because of inherited goodwill and almost any system can be made to function if all the members are willing to work within the organization.

There was also the danger that strategic planning would produce plans that did not actually happen. Implementation failure might occur because planning was separated from those that have to work the changes or because of hopeless optimism or because implementation problems are denied so that at best only compliance is achieved instead of commitment. At worst this could result in conflict. The consultants had accepted long-term contracts with the NHS and limits on total expenditure in exchange for job security and 'clinical freedom'. The NHS management has very little leverage to make their services responsive to patient needs. To change the speciality mix of its medical staff, a region, district or hospital has to wait for deaths and retirements. Improvements that do occur are often the result of accident rather than design or because of powerful individuals rather than effective management structure. This is because major organizational change in the health service is often based on assumption and belief rather than substantiated theory or observational evidence. One of those assumptions is that commercial organizational models are directly transferrable to public service enterprises.

So we came to the position that in 1989, in the face of a radical reorganization, the doctors were the ardent defenders of a nationalized structure. They had found refuge in the doctrine of central control, regional appointments for consultants and uniform terms and conditions of service to avoid interference from local authorities. Not only had the societies gone but now also the spectre of municipal control. Clinical freedom had been enlarged and the doctor no longer had to worry about the patient's ability to pay before deciding on treatment. The profession was enjoying greater freedom than at any time since club practice began in the 1820s.

Until 1948 every doctor had been trained in a medical school attached to a voluntary hospital. The student was reared in a spirit of the voluntary hospital. Voluntary hospitals ran on a shoestring. The hospital could only exist if everyone was prepared to help. Everything non-essential to the patient's welfare had to be cut to a minimum. Care without direct payment carries on a tradition from the voluntary hospitals that predated the NHS. Doctors gave their time free of charge in those hospitals, hence the name. This charitable background may still be affecting many consultants' attitudes, as an influential consultant aged 55, training young doctors today, would have been trained by consultants who entered medicine and had their attitudes shaped in the 1920s.

The voluntary hospital spirit was not forgotten quickly. One cannot identify a date at which goodwill started to run out, but the process was gradual. New doctors qualified had no experience of the voluntary hospitals and, more significant, they were trained by doctors who also did not have that background. Doctors became increasingly frustrated. The general practitioners were debarred from the hospital. The hospital consultants became swamped with a type of illness that could have been dealt with by a general practitioner. Specialized medicine and surgery became more complex and time consuming, but had to be fitted into the routine work. A highly trained and skilled specialist surgeon was to be found repairing hernias and removing ingrowing toenails. It was very useful and necessary but could have been done more economically by less skilled staff in primary health centres, had they existed, an idea first suggested in a report (Dawson 1920) on proposed reorganization of healthcare in Britain in 1920. This emphasized bringing together preventative and curative medicine. Specialist advice would be available at a primary health centre, but the main working area of the consultants would be in the secondary health centres, located in a hospital capable of undertaking diagnosis, care and treatment of the more difficult case. This idea was to surface again more than once, particularly with the birth of the NHS. Cartwright (1977) describes the Dawson Report thus: 'This revolutionary plan is one of the more important, although tragic, documents in the history of British medicine'.

What had gone wrong? Some would blame the senior doctors, suggesting that they are too conservative and unwilling to move with the times (Klein 1983). Yet it is the younger ones who are actively expressing disillusionment. Some point to increasing interference by party politicians. Perhaps we are passing through a transition phase from one form of medicine to another and such periods of transition are historically accompanied by convulsions. Curative medicine, although based upon science, is after all still primarily an individual art and creative artists do not take kindly to bureaucratic control.

SOME PRESENT DILEMMAS

The government believe a balance must now be struck between organization and freedom. There is a situation of mutual dependency. (Klein 1990) states:

The state became a monopoly employer: effectively members of the medical profession became dependent on it . . . the state became dependent on the medical profession to run the NHS and to cope with the problems of rationing scarce resources in patient care.

The healthcare industry is said to be under pressure to reduce costs and increase efficiency without sacrificing the quality of patient care. However, all those within the healthcare industry appear to feel that changes are strictly a cost reduction exercise with little consideration for the quality of patient care. No one has yet focused on the relationship between the two most powerful influences in hospital healthcare delivery, the manager and the doctor most involved in daily management, often called the clinical director. If the relationship between the most powerful actors in healthcare delivery becomes more cooperative and less adversarial, creative energy can assist both administrators and physicians (Simendinger & Pasmore 1984).

More than in any other institution, the hospital provides a unique arena for studying factors affecting cooperation among those in positions of power. Unlike industrial organizations the dual hierarchy of hospitals sets up barriers to, and at the same time necessitates, cooperation between doctors and their managerial colleagues. Over the decades there has been a gradual change from a doctor-managed healthcare system to a joint doctor/manager team. Some would argue that the pendulum has swung even further, to a primarily professionally managed hospital healthcare system. The challenge now is for the medical profession, in the words of Klein (1990), 'to run the NHS and to cope with the problems of rationing scarce resources in patient care'. Klein continues:

Given the certainty that conflict will continue and the possibility that the NHS may be living off an inherited but not necessarily renewable capital of commitment and loyalty is it possible to devise better strategies for managing the resentment generated by mutual dependency of the state and the profession?

LESSONS FROM INDUSTRY FOR THE HEALTH SERVICE

Griffiths (1983) emphasized the similarities as:

- the need to identify and satisfy real needs

- delivery of the highest quality of service
- securing a trained, motivated workforce
- setting short and long-term objectives.

More important, however, are the differences. Smith (1984) says differences do exist and highlights them as:

- Prime motive is service, not profit.
- Beneficiaries are the public rather than owners.
- Performance measures are more qualitative.

He brought together a group of NHS and commercial managers and asked them to identify those dimensions of organizational life which differentiate the NHS from private sector organizations. They found this relatively easy and identified nearly 50 such factors. They felt the following were the most important:

Commercial Organization	NHS
Coherent/single	Diffused/multiple
Power source – single profession	Power source – multi-professional
Few external pressures	Extensive external pressures including public image
Clear objectives	Diffuse objectives
Clear customer	'Confused patients'

They represent what Maslow (1972) called low synergy institutions. The reason why they are different is because hospitals are in fact professional bureaucracies and these differ in a number of ways, most notably because professionals have some control over task performance, task review and planning. Hospitals have few of the formal characteristics of industrial firms (Friedlander 1976); physicians and scientists are socialized to form a rational, autonomous, specialized, expert behaviour, which is antithetical to the organization of any but the most narrow individualized pursuits (Freidson 1970):

Health services are organized around professional authority, and their basic structure is constituted by the dominance of a single profession over a variety of other, subordinate occupations.

Early studies of hospitals by sociologists were made with studies of the factory in mind and in general their view was that improved communication within and across the organization would settle difficulties of operation. But one problem at least, that of reconciling expert with hierarchical authority, remained. And the degree of expertise is very important in this problem.

As Freidson (1970) puts it: 'Skill of such complexity and refinement that autonomy of judgement is necessary'.

Smith (1958) emphasized two lines of authority, administrative and medical, and drew attention to the difficulty of operating with such a system. Goss (1961) studied how autonomy of professional judgement could exist in a hierarchical and supervisory hospital setting and observed:

that the two lines of authority are both established and maintained by the segregation of administrative decisions from areas where professional judgement was considered necessary, the former freely made and enforced by the authority of office, the latter left to the 'authority' of the individual professional.

On this foundation Goss constructed an organization model called 'advisory bureaucracy'. Freidson (1970) refers to it as 'professional bureaucracy'. According to Engel (1969) and Scott (1965):

The essential characteristic is that professional work is free from the exercise of the authority of non-professionals even though the working professionals are technically subordinates in a bureaucratic system.

However, Bucher and Stelling (1969) feel that the concept of bureaucracy may be entirely inappropriate for professional settings. According to Weisbord (1976), hospitals require three different social systems and not one, as in industry. The links among the task system which administrators manage, the identity system which underpins professional status and the governance system which sets standards are extremely tenuous. Inglehart (1983, 1984) described the NHS not only as probably the nation's most popular institution but as also the largest and it is probably more complex than any other national enterprise. The average district health authority has (or had, before some split into trusts) many more employees than the average company. With unintegrated management, professional hierarchies and many external pressures, confusion of goals, internal competition for resources, differing disciplines all having differing internal goals, no organizational priorities, clinical freedom, contradictory perceptions of management, lack of a reward system and the need for organizational slack, it is not one of the easier organizations to manage.

REFERENCES

Allsop J 1984 Health policy and the National Health Service. Longman, London

Bucher R, Stelling J 1969 Characteristics of professional organizations. Journal of Health and Social Behaviour 10: 3–15

Cartwright F 1977 A social history of medicine. Longman, Harlow

Crossman R 1972 A politician's view of health service planning. University of Glasgow, p 22

Dawson B 1920 cited in Watkin B (ed) 1975 Documents on health and social services 1834 to the present day. Methuen, London

DHSS 1972a Management arrangements for a reorganised health service. HMSO, London

DHSS 1972b Second report of the joint working party on the organisation of medical work in hospitals. HMSO, London

DHSS 1974 Third report of the joint working party on the organisation of medical work in hospitals. HMSO, London

DHSS 1979 Patients First. HMSO, London

DHSS 1980a Circular HC(80)8 health service development. Structure and management, July 1980. HMSO, London

DHSS 1980b Patients first. A summary of comments received. HMSO, London

DHSS 1982 Circular HC(82)1 health service development. Professional advisory machinery, January 1982. HMSO, London

DHSS 1983 NHS management inquiry. Griffiths report. DA(83)38. HMSO, London

DHSS 1989 Working for patients. HMSO, London

Engel G V 1969 The effect of bureaucracy on the professional autonomy of the physician. Journal of Health and Social Behaviour 10: 30–41

Enthoven A C 1985 Reflections on the management of the National Health Service. Nuffield Provincial Hospitals Trust, London

Fitzgerald L, Sturt J 1992 Clinicians into management. On the change agenda or not? Health Services Management Research 5: 2

Freidson E 1970 Professional dominance: the social structure of medical care. Aldine, Chicago

Friedlander F 1976 OD reaches adolescence: an exploration of its underlying values. Journal of Applied Behavioural Science 12: 1

Goss M E W 1961 Influence and authority among physicians in an out-patient clinic. American Sociological Review 26: 39–50

Griffiths R 1983 NHS management inquiry. DHSS, London

Griffiths R 1991 Audit commission annual lecture by Sir Roy Griffiths, 12 June 1991

Griffiths R 1992 Speech to British Association of Medical Managers, 3 June 1992

Hanlon M D, Gladstein D L 1984 Improving the quality of work life in hospitals. Hospital and Health Services Administration September/October: 94–107

Harrison S 1988 Managing the National Health Service – shifting the frontier? Chapman & Hall, London

Harrison S, Hunter D J, Pollitt C 1990 The dynamics of British health policy. Unwin Hyman, London

Hunter R B 1972 Report of the working party on medical administrators. DHSS, London

Inglehart J K 1983 The British National Health Service under the Conservatives. New England Journal of Medicine 309: 1264–1268

Inglehart J K 1984 The British National Health Service under the Conservatives – Part II. New England Journal of Medicine 310: 63–67

Jacobs M O 1978 Administrators, boards, physicians must help change health system. Hospitals 52: 15.

Jynton R P 1975 Boundaries in health care systems (backfeed section). Journal of Applied Behavioural Science 11: 2

Klein R 1983 The politics of the NHS. Longman, Harlow

Klein R 1989 The politics of the NHS, 2nd edn. Longman, Harlow

Klein R 1990 The state and the profession: the politics of the double bed. British Medical Journal 301: 700

Kogan K et al 1978 The workings of the National Health Service. Research paper no.1 Royal Commission on the NHS. HMSO, London

Levitt R, Wall A 1984 The reorganised health service, 3rd edn. Chapman & Hall, London

Maslow A 1972 Synergy in the society and the individual. The Viking Press, New York, ch 14

MoH 1967 First report of the joint working party on the organisation of medical work in hospitals. HMSO, London

Petchey R 1986 The Griffiths reorganisation of the NHS. Fowlerism by stealth? Critical Social Policy: 87–101

Schulz R, Harrison S 1983 Teams and top managers in the NHS. A survey and strategy. Project paper no 41. King's Fund Centre, London

Scott W R 1965 Reactions to supervision in a heteronomous professional organization. Administrative Science Quarterly 10: 65–81

Simendinger E A, Pasmore W 1984 Developing partnerships between physicians and healthcare executives. Hospital and Health Services Administration 29: 21–35

Smith G W 1984 Towards an organisation theory for the NHS. Health Services Manpower Review: 3–7

Smith H L 1958 Two lines of authority: the hospital's dilemma. In: Jaco E G (ed) Patients, physicians and illness. Free Press, New York

Weisbord M R 1976 Why organization development hasn't worked (so far) in medical centers. Health Care Management Review Spring: 17–28

Welborne I W B 1990 The management of change. British Journal of Hospital Medicine 44: 53–55

3

Doctors' involvement in management – the reality

Jenny Simpson

The thinking behind bringing doctors into management has been well documented. Accountability, better control of resources and better clinical input to decision making are well-rehearsed and convincing arguments for the 'doctors in management' rhetoric. What, however, of the reality? What really happens when the highly skilled professionals in an organization take on significant management roles? How are the organizational arrangements affected? What happens to those who take up the challenge? To their jobs, their lifestyle and to their career prospects? This chapter firstly examines the specific issues brought to light by doctors taking a significant and influential role in management and then goes on to consider the theoretical underpinning factors that determine why organizations behave the way they do.

A survey was undertaken recently by the British Association of Medical Managers Simpson 1993) which aimed to establish information on clinical management. The factors critical to success in developed management structures have been identified and are described here.

Ten years ago or less, a doctor who expressed an interest in management was, at best, suspected of eccentricity, but more generally accused of a lack of clinical commitment. Now, however, a move into management, especially on a part-time basis, is widely regarded as a healthy and interesting development in a clinical career. This has been reinforced by a well-established trend in other countries, primarily the USA, Canada and Australia, in which doctors with specific talents in management progress in their careers by some form of management development, moving into senior positions in the management of their organizations.

THE IDEAL SCENARIO

The ideal of clinicians and non-clinical managers working in harmony demands a sharing of common values. Firstly, a belief shared by the entire organization that the hospital exists to care for sick and injured people. All other activities, whatever they may be, are secondary to this. To this end, each and every management process must have the patient at its heart.

Secondly, the driving force in the hospital must be its clinical teams, assisted and supported by management, financial and personnel expertise. The product of the organization is delivered by clinicians – nurses, doctors and other clinical professionals. It is they who have intimate knowledge of the needs of the patient and it is vital that this unique knowledge is harnessed in the effective management of the service. To do this clinicians must be helped and genuinely supported by management staff.

The third component of the ideal focuses on the design of clinical services, which must be geared to the needs of the patient rather than those of the staff. Clinical services, just as any other service, must be designed around the needs of the customer. In many instances the customers of the health service are ill, distressed and vulnerable and there is no justification for designing the service, in terms of appointment systems, facilities or access, merely to meet the needs of the hospital staff.

The fourth factor concerns the way decisions are made in the service. In an ideal scenario, decisions are taken on the basis of hard fact and expert knowledge rather than on the basis of politics or convenience. We are all familiar with the way in which apparently straightforward decisions sometimes result in a completely crazy outcome simply because of political interference – either within the organization or from external influences.

Finally in the ideal scenario, there is the concept of decisions at every level of the organization being taken in the light of a clinical perspective.

Elements of the ideal scenario

> - Hospitals exist to care for sick and injured people.
> - The driving force of the hospital is its clinical teams.
> - Services are designed around patients.
> - Decisions are taken on hard fact.
> - Decisions are taken with a clinical perspective.

THE COMPROMISES

In reality clinical management places considerable demands on both clinicians and managers. It is not by any means easy to lead an organization when much of the power and authority has been devolved to teams of professionals, particularly when those teams may not have significant management expertise and almost certainly have varying degrees of skill and interest in management. The general manager must strike a balance between retaining central control and a gradual letting go of the reins in parallel with development and education of clinical management teams. Many managers do not get this balance right and far fewer hit upon a formula that works for an entire hospital. Some do, however, and it is to these managers that we must look for guidance. It is a mistake to believe that decentralization of management is a structural issue involving merely the drawing up of a new set of organizational charts. In reality, it means a true devolution of management power. Some managers find it extremely difficult to relinquish central control. Equally, some clinicians are reluctant to take on the power and responsibility of a managerial role.

The effects of these changes spread far more widely than simply to the doctors and managers involved. The entire organization is affected. In particular the 'tribal hierarchies' which have formed a major part of our lives as clinicians for decades are no longer appropriate. The introduction of a directorate system of devolved management, in which all staff are accountable to the clinical director, leaves the director of nursing services without a direct managerial line to the nursing staff. In many organizations this type of change has led to some tension and indeed in some to outright war. It takes considerable skill and a thorough understanding of the principles of change management to bring about major organizational change effectively and with the minimum of pain.

THE NIGHTMARE SCENARIO

In a small number of hospitals the antithesis of the ideal scenario is developing. In such hospitals clinical managers may well be in place on paper – indeed, the organizational chart may well be extremely detailed and technically devolved. But, on analysis there is no devolution of management authority. This can be extremely confusing for the key players in the organization who, whilst they have a title and may have other evidence of the status of clinical director, such as an extra secretary or a management office, may be completely excluded from the decision-making process. The clinical director may have insight into his or her predicament or may be totally unaware of it.

There are hospitals in which clinical directors spend considerable amounts of time and energy attending meetings, preparing papers, making an active contribution. However, these contributions are never acted upon. Strategies greeted with enthusiasm are never implemented, even when a full agreement is reached at meetings. Another symptom of this particular and confusing organizational pathology is the existence of a parallel decision-making body in addition to that of the clinical management board. The general manager will meet with a group of non-medical managers on a regular basis who will, in fact, be making the decisions that run the hospital. Meanwhile, the clinical directors are meeting in the belief that it is their decision making that is the driving force. A common but less extreme variant of this syndrome is one in which clinicians are involved in the decision-making process, but only ever at an operational level. In this situation the clinicians are allowed to make decisions within their own directorate or affecting the whole hospital – such as whether the car park gates should lift up and down or swing out and in. However, they are excluded from the long-term decision making, from influencing the strategic direction of the hospital. This actually takes place in some inner cabal and is delivered as a fait accompli to the clinical directors.

Also to be found in the nightmare situation is hardcore resistance by the long-established tribal middle managers, those who may have been relieved of their traditional power base. These managers, if mishandled, feel extremely vulnerable and are capable of using complex damaging tactics to undermine every aspect of the directorate structure. For example, many middle managers are most reluctant to relinquish their role in holding meetings with directorate staff of their own discipline, even though this is clearly no longer appropriate in the new structure. They will make most strenuous efforts to maintain the old relationships and the status quo.

The nightmare organization may also be identified by an expectation on the part of management that clinical staff involved in the management process can do so without appropriate information, time or support. There is clearly a grudging attitude towards an involvement of clinical staff in management and little enthusiasm for providing administrative or clerical support or even investing in further clinical help to free up the clinical director for this role.

The nightmare organization is understandably characterized by a cynical and demoralized clinical staff who quickly reach the conclusion that an involvement in management leads rapidly to taking on the blame for the hospital's overspend without the slightest authority to do anything about it.

Elements of the nightmare scenario

- Clinical managers in place but on paper only; clinicians get the blame for overspend but no authority.
- Undermining of the devolved structure by tribal middle/senior managers.
- Expectation that clinical managers should be effective without information, time or managerial support.
- Demoralized and cynical clinical staff.

What does this mean for doctors entering the world of management?

For the doctor in management, whether it be as a clinical director with a 2–3 sessional commitment or as a medical director requiring a greater commitment in terms of time or even a move to a full-time managerial post, there is an enormous learning challenge and usually very little time to achieve it. Firstly, doctors in management must learn to direct their peers. Doctors are generally used to being single players, leading their clinical team. They are unused to being responsible for the actions of their colleagues and are unused to any form of hierarchy at consultant level other than seniority. Also doctors must learn to be directed as they learn to be managerially accountable for their actions – generally a new concept.

Secondly, doctors must learn to contribute to the management decision process. Traditionally doctors have influenced decision making in an advisory capacity, often using their professional power base to achieve whatever outcome they wished to see. This has frequently led to accusations of shroud waving and table thumping. In a decentralized management structure, medical professionals must learn to play a very different role, using their influencing skills to achieve outcomes that will benefit the hospital as a whole, working as a team, whether it be at directorate or at hospital board level. They must learn to allocate resources effectively to ensure the future well-being of the organization and its patients, not merely concentrating on their own particular speciality or service.

Finally, there is a full range of expertise that must be acquired. Finance, business planning, personnel management, marketing and strategy formulation are new areas of study for most clinicians, all of which are needed to some extent in the role of clinical or medical director. The busy clinician must also master perhaps the most difficult and trying challenge of them all, the management of time. For a clinician, all management activities inevitably represent a conflict with clinical or personal time.

Issues for doctors

- Learning to be both director and directed.
- Learning to contribute to management decisions.
- New areas of expertise and technical skills.

THE KEYS TO SUCCESS

Devolved management structures appear to work very much better in some organizations than others. Eight fundamental success factors were identified by the BAMM study and the following list gives some indication of the types of environment in which decentralized clinical management will thrive and therefore the conditions those contemplating a move into management should seek to identify in their own organizations.

1. Trust and respect on both sides between doctors and managers. In any organization there are tensions and this is even more so in complex organizations such as hospitals. There must be a fundamental trust and respect on both sides if clinical management is to survive. Essentially there needs to be a recognition of the differences between the managerial cultures of power and role and the professional cultures which are task- and person-oriented. Both clinicians and managers must then concentrate on shared values, shared goals and objectives and establish a shared view of what the organization exists to do. This requires flexibility, trust and time for all parties.

2. Debate and dialogue based on appropriate, accurate and timely information. The quest for achieving high quality, accurate information upon which doctors in management may base their decision making has dogged the health service for decades. Indeed, Florence Nightingale wrote in 1863:

In attempting to arrive at the truth, I have applied everywhere for information but in scarcely an instance have I been able to obtain hospital records fit for any purpose of comparison. If they could be obtained . . . . they would show what amount of good has really been done with it and whether the money was not doing mischief rather than good.

3. An appropriate level of consistent administrative support for clinical directors. Clinicians simply cannot take on additional, complex work without administrative help. The supportive organization will make strenuous efforts to relieve doctors of clinical duties by bringing in some form of additional clinical back-up; it will ensure that clinical directors are supported by business managers, finance and personnel expertise. It will tolerate the learning stages through which a clinician new to the world of management must pass and will make every effort to assist him or her.

4. Development of strong, powerful teams within directorates. Teams at directorate level must be allowed to flourish and thrive. They will meet many challenges and pressures; their survival will be dependent upon excellent communication and a determination to work together to deliver an excellent clinical service.

5. Development of a single management board comprising clinical and non-clinical managers. The entire hospital should be governed by a single decision-making body. The development of a second executive or 'administrative' body or, worse still, a plethora of such small committees with a bewildering array of three-letter titles, is a bad sign.

6. The definition and agreement on the role and job descriptions of the directorate members. There must be clarity as to what is expected of those who venture into management. Job descriptions should be made explicit and the objectives to which clinical directors and directorate team members are working should be made public and circulated throughout the directorate. Similarly clinical directors should be aware of the objectives to which the chief executive is working.

7. Open and explicit processes for election or appointment of clinical directors. Whatever the approach to appointment of clinical managers taken by a hospital, it must be open and explicit. The process must be fair with open access to all those interested in taking on a management role. Given that the clinical director must in the end be in a position to lead his or her colleagues, many chief executives involve the consultant staff in the process of appointment of clinical directors.

8. Formal contracts and an appropriate, agreed and explicit reward scheme for clinical directors. If the integrity of the new system is to be maintained, it is essential that clinical directors are rewarded in a consistent and open fashion. The mechanism of reward varies from hospital to hospital and ranges from financial incentive to clinical support to an increase in paid leave. Whatever the reward scheme chosen, it should be perceived as appropriate and should be explicit.

THE ABSOLUTE REQUIREMENT

A number of factors recur consistently throughout both the BAMM survey and subsequent studies, most notably the managerial services survey (Harwood & Boufford 1993). From this research, the following minimum requirements for successful implementation of developed management structures are drawn:

- **Chief executive**
  A strong, highly skilled general manager who is capable of, and totally committed to, relinquishing the existing power base and to leading a fully devolved organization. This commitment must be visible in every single decision taken within the hospital.
- **Doctors**
  A sufficient number of senior medical staff members with the enthusiasm, stamina and determination to take on a management role, to accept the burdens that this places on clinical work and to take on the challenge of learning how to do it effectively and efficiently.
- **Information**
  Recognizably accurate, timely and appropriately presented information detailing the clinical activity taking place within a directorate.
- **Investment**
  In support and education for clinical directors and their teams.

SO WHY BOTHER?

It is clear from the experience that medical management is by no means an easy task. Some doctors have become bitter and cynical as a result of tangling with management – usually those in organizations less than supportive of the idea of clinical management. On the other hand there are many doctors who, after their term of office has ended, have wished to stay on in their management roles, finding it difficult to step back from the more strategic perspective. Such doctors generally acknowledge the complexities of the task, but do in fact find the management role extremely stimulating, enjoyable and, above all, interesting.

Many are questioning now whether it is sensible to adhere to a time-limited term of office as clinical director or whether the system should be changed to allow those who have a particular interest or talent in management to train and take on a long-term position as clinical manager. Managers are also faced with the challenge of making effective use of talented, skilled and experienced former clinical directors and many are developing further management roles for such individuals.

Doctors are now presented with an opportunity to become involved in management. It is essential that that involvement is based on the right grounds: not to achieve status or to embellish the CV, not because a chief executive wishes to make his organization chart look neat and tidy but purely and simply to ensure that the finite resources in the NHS are invested as wisely as possible to ensure maximum accessibility to effective and high quality healthcare for all its patients.

THE BEGINNING

In his response to the Management Enquiry of 1983, Sir Roy Griffiths (DHSS 1983) stated: 'The nearer the management process gets to the patient, the more important it becomes for doctors to be looked upon as the natural managers'. Whilst much emphasis has been placed upon the latter part of this statement, it is the first part which exposes the structural situation which is the cause of much of the frustration, less than optimal efficiency and effectiveness and consequent disenchantment on the part of professionals that has characterized the NHS for many years.

The management process, certainly in 1983, was a long way from the clinical process and the patients. The gap is less pronounced now, but still evident in many organizations providing healthcare in the UK.

THE MANAGEMENT PROCESS

All organizations have processes which make things happen. They may be efficient or inefficient, geared tightly to the corporate aims or be completely off-beam. Nevertheless, processes are in place which provide the mechanisms of achieving whatever the organization sets out to do. The processes evolve or are put in place in response to a number of factors, of which three have the predominant influence:

1. Structure and systems
2. Power
3. Culture and values.

It is convenient, but entirely overly simplistic, to think of healthcare organizations as straightforward, relatively simple bodies to run. Certainly the degree of investment made in training and developing high calibre managers over the last 20 years would not indicate an overwhelming need for highly skilled individuals. Hospitals and other healthcare institutes are complex bureaucracies which pose considerable challenges to those at senior management level.

Many of the decisions to be made are not clean-cut and operational but are:

characterized by novelty, complexity and open-mindedness, by the fact that the organization usually begins with little understanding of the decision situation it faces or route to its solution, and only a vague idea of what that solution might be and how it will be evaluated when it is developed. Only by groping through a recursive, discontinuous process involving many different steps and a host of dynamic factors over a considerable period of time is a final choice often made.

(Mintzberg et al 1976)

For an organization to achieve what it sets out to do, it must have management processes that are uniquely tailored to its aims. This is not a one-off exercise to be conducted somewhere in a back room or on an away day; the management process must be constantly subjected to scrutiny and adjusted to fit development and change within the organization and constantly checked against the expectations of those it seeks to serve.

However, it is not possible to develop tightly geared management processes unless the aim of the organization is clear and shared amongst the totality of the workforce. So, why does a hospital exist? What is it for? It is obvious, of course – to make sick and injured people better. But is that always so? Or does it somewhat depend on the perspective of the observer? To the patient, the aims are clear; but are they always so clear to the finance director, to the chief executive or to the chairman, who has to fulfil obligations and political expectations from above (see Fig. 3.1)?

To understand the organization fully, it is necessary to examine the three major influencing factors on management process.

Structure and systems

Any observer of the NHS over the last few years will have noticed a preoccupation with structure. Organizational charts have been radically altered, pinned on the wall, altered again, sent out for consultation, been the subject of countless management board meetings and the cause of endless discussion amongst clinical staff. Should we have directorates? How many? Who should sit in which directorate? To whom are the directorates accountable?

Peters et al, in their article 'Structure is not organization' (1980) assert that the productive organization 'is not simply a matter of structure, although structure is important'. The authors go on to claim that effective organizations are dependent upon 'the relationship

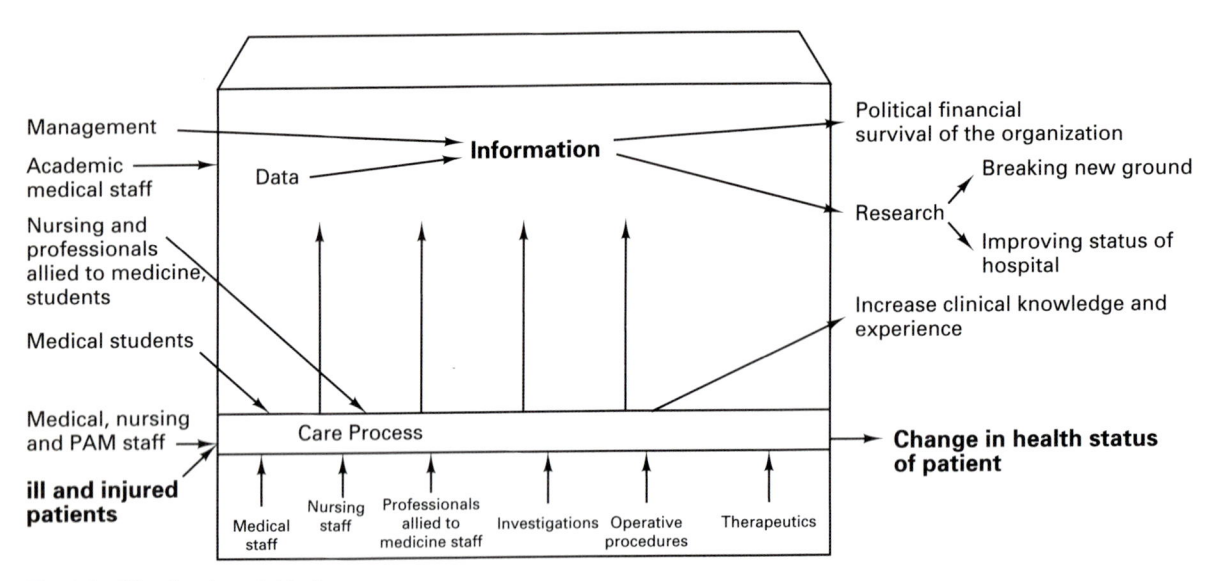

Fig. 3.1 What is a hospital for?

between structure, strategy, systems, style, skills, staff and something we call superordinate goals (shared values)' (Waterman et al 1988).

Insight into structures and the systems in operation within them, however, does provide an understanding of why things are as they are and thus suggests the basis for devising mechanisms for change. Whilst a knowledge of structure or the anatomy of the organization is fundamental to understanding, it is the impact of the structure on how things are done – how staff communicate with each other, what mechanisms are in place to ensure that the service is of consistent quality – that is of paramount importance.

Hospitals and healthcare organizations, like universities, are complex bodies. In Mintzberg's classification (1983), these organizations are professional bureaucracies, characterized by a reliance for their functioning on the skills and knowledge of their operating professionals. These organizations, which are unusual in that their skilled employees can act as if they were self-employed and yet receive a monthly salary, all hinge on a fine line between collegiality (working for common good) and politics (working for self-interest). Professional organizations carry out highly skilled, yet highly standardized tasks. Considerable energy must be expended in ensuring that the excesses are controlled, to ensure that patients or clients are not mistreated and that professional standards are upheld.

Mintzberg's theoretical view of the professional organization is that it relies heavily for coordination on standardization of skills, which is achieved primarily through formal training. Trained specialists form the operating core of the organization, working relatively independently alongside their colleagues but closely with the clients they serve. Most of the necessary coordination amongst the professionals is then handled automatically by their set of skills and knowledge – to a large extent by what they have learned to expect from each other. However, no matter how ingrained the knowledge and skills, the sheer complexity of the work ensures that considerable discretion remains in their application. No two professionals ever apply the skills in exactly the same way and professional judgements are required. Training of the professions is of paramount importance, as is the acquisition of universal standards.

In comparison with, for example, a manufacturing hierarchy in which the bureaucracy creates its own standards which are then enforced by line managers, the standards of the professional organization originate outside its own structure in the self-governing associations to which the professionals belong – the royal colleges and faculties. The external bodies set universal standards which they ensure are taught by universities and are used by all organizations practising the profession.

Other forms of standardization are difficult to rely on in the professional organization. Processes themselves are too complicated to be standardized directly by work analysts. Furthermore, the outputs of professional work are difficult to measure, although not impossible, as is demonstrated by the clinical audit process. Outcome measurement, however, still poses considerable challenges to the medical profession. The administrative structure of the professional bureaucracy, as described by Mintzberg, consists of a fully elaborated

The prereform hospital

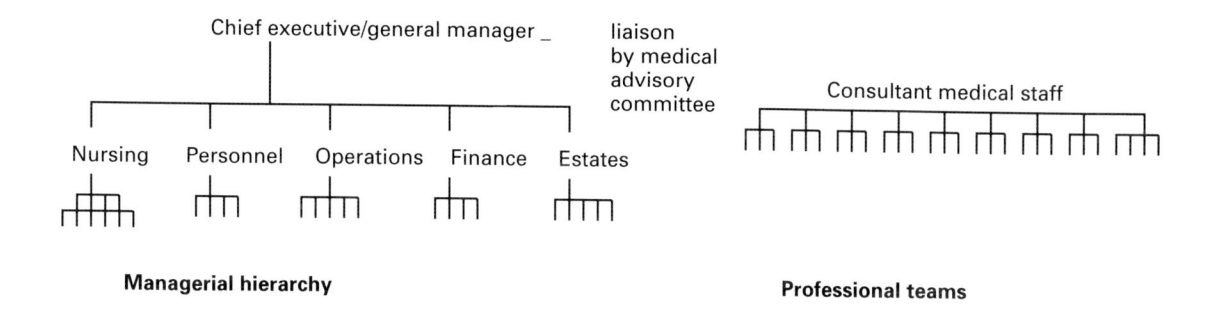

Managerial hierarchy: Chief executive/general manager — liaison by medical advisory committee — Nursing, Personnel, Operations, Finance, Estates

Professional teams: Consultant medical staff

The postreform hospital

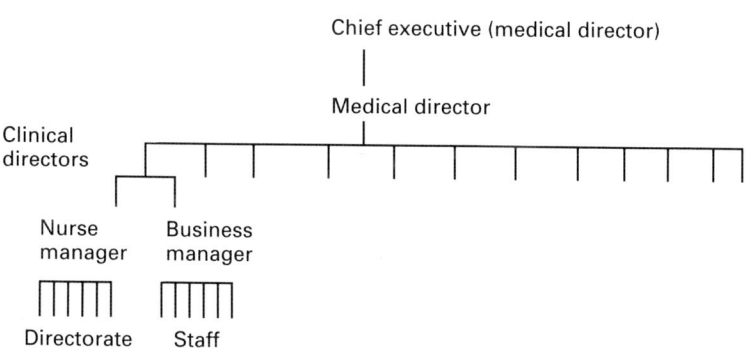

Chief executive (medical director) — Medical director — Clinical directors — Nurse manager, Business manager — Directorate, Staff

Fig. 3.2

support staff which is focused on serving the activities of the operating core of professionals. There is less of a need for middle line management or technical support in comparison with the manufacturing organization, but a considerable need for support staff throughout the organization – in laboratories, operating theatres, radiology departments, pharmacies, libraries, portering and clerical staff. For the support staff – often more numerous than the professional staff but generally less highly skilled – there is no democracy within the professional organization. Such support units as portering are likely to be managed centrally as hierarchical enclaves within the professional configuration. Thus what is commonly found in professional bureaucracies are parallel and separate administrative hierarchies, with very different management processes, decentralized and bottom-up for the professionals and centralized, top-down for the support staff.

In comparison with the support staff and professionals, the administrative structure is relatively thin and in comparison with their counterparts in entrepreneurial and manufacturing organizations, they would appear to lack the traditional power base. But that is far from the whole story. The administrator of professional work may not be able to control the professionals directly, but he or she does perform a series of roles that give considerable indirect power.

Firstly, the administrator spends much time handling disturbances in the structure. There are many jurisdictional disputes between the professionals – who should do what, when and where. Secondly the administrators, particular those at higher levels, serve in key roles at the boundaries of the organization, between the professionals inside and the influences of the outside, governments, purchasers, patient associations, benefactors and so on. On the one hand administrators are expected to protect professionals' autonomy, buffering them from external pressures. On the other they are expected to liaise effectively with those outsiders who support the organization, both politically and in terms of purchasing hospital services. This often leads outsiders to expect that these administrators are able to control the professionals. Thus external roles of the administrator – maintaining liaison contacts, acting as figurehead and spokesperson in a public relations capacity, negotiating the outside alliances – are of primary importance in the administrative structure of the professional bureaucracy.

This theoretical picture of the professional bureaucracy fits well with the way hospitals were organized prior to decentralization and the full involvement for doctors in the management process. There are many vestigial remnants of this structure present in hospitals and it is important to be able to recognize these in trying to make sense of today's organizational structures. The introduction of clinical directorates and multidisciplinary teams represents a partial move towards what Mintzberg terms 'the adhocracy' in which multidisciplinary teams are deployed to deal with the management of clinical services (see Fig. 3.2).

The structure is decentralized with the professionals having managerial responsibility for much, although generally not all, of the support staff. Thus the need for middle line management, one of the features of centralized hierarchies, is even less than had been the case previously. Prior to decentralization there was no management relationship between manager and professional staff. This resulted in decisions at the managerial level being taken without any real clinical input. Since the organization's business *is* the clinical process, this structure resulted in a considerable range of problems, not the least of which was the impossibility of non-professional managers attempting to control the activities of their professional colleagues.

In the decentralized structures all non-medical administrators are faced with the choice of accepting the doctors' role in management and arranging administrative and financial support around the professional team leaders or deciding to maintain a centralist perspective and ensure that no matter what the organizational arrangements look like on paper, in reality, devolution does not take place. This central control approach has taken the form of withholding information or of convening decision-making meetings of executive and managerial staff without involving clinical leaders.

Mintzberg concludes that in professional organizations, power does flow towards those who care to devote effort to doing administrative as well as professional work, so long as they do it well. But he stresses it is not a case of laissez-faire; 'The professional administrator maintains power only as long as professions perceive him or her to be serving their interests effectively' (Mintzberg 1988).

Power

In the early days of organizational psychology, it was accepted that the behaviour of organizations could be explained in terms of motivation theory, leadership theory, of organization structure and design. However, around 25 years ago, key writers and theorists began to suspect that other forces influence the way people think, feel and live in organizations. Organizations are complex entities, full of people working in a contradictory fashion, acting upon their own needs and changing their minds.

Power is a central concept in the study of human behaviour in organizations. It infiltrates all the other influencing factors on organizational behaviour and, whilst in many organizations it is regarded as not quite de rigeur to discuss power openly, an understanding of power bases and the responses of people to power plays is essential to the full understanding of how hospitals and other healthcare institutions work.

Power can be regarded as potential – the potential to do something, a base from which to work. The fact that an individual can bring together the appropriate resources to influence people to behave in desired ways is the essence of power. Resources are critical to an individual's power base and can either be organizationally determined, defined by the individual's role, status or title, or personally determined, a feature of the individual's personality, charisma, skill and even physical characteristics. Power is also defined as the degree of dependency of others on the resources held by individuals.

Power levers

The way in which an individual chooses to apply power is termed 'power lever'. Kakabadse et al (1987) identify seven such levers:

1. Reward power: the capacity to influence the rewards offered to others.
2. Coercive power: a punishment-centred approach to power. This can be organizationally or individually based.
3. Legitimate power: authority and control which stems from the individual's organizational position or role. The application of legitimate power is influenced by access to the relevant information, to relevant others and relevant networks.
4. Personal power: personal characteristics, which can be personality based (charm, charisma, flair) or physical attributes (strength, height, size and weight).
5. Expert power: specialist knowledge or skills.
6. Information power: ability to use information to support a particular point of view or alternatively downgrade other viewpoints.

7. Connection power: access to relevant others within and outside the organization.

Information provides a major power base. In itself, raw data has little influence. Information, when used either to support an argument or to downgrade other people's, provides an extremely powerful base from which to work. Kakabadse et al (1987) identify three categories of information:

1. Concrete information – the facts, figures, trends, projections, financial statements and reports which examine the effectiveness of the organization or parts of it. Access to the various levels of concrete information is related to position within the organization. Organizations generate substantial amounts of concrete information, but confidential reports concerning the long-term liability of the organization are likely only to be available to a selected few.
2. Process information – the processes by which people relate to and interact with each other.
3. Self-disclosure information – information which is normally of a private nature, freely offered by one individual to another on the basis of trust. This information would be embarrassing if it became public knowledge and it is important that the listener will not only be sympathetic and offer help but will also maintain confidentiality.

All three types of information are central to the operation of health service organizations. A particular feature of the NHS is the way in which information is used not only directly but throughout the entire organization, indirectly. Denial of access to accurate, timely and appropriate information has been used at all levels as a very effective power base. For many years information on patient admissions, clinical process and diagnosis has been collected mechanistically by low paid, low status staff and delivered automatically up the system to the central administrative bodies, but not to those providing the service.

Critical to the implementation of the Resource Management Initiative introduced in 1986 was the introduction of patient-based information systems, which delivered accurate, timely and relevant information immediately to those providing care for patients and, as a byproduct, delivered aggregate data for management purposes. It is the power of this information which has largely driven forward the principle of professional involvement in the managerial process. Without it the clinician in management reverts to making blind decisions; although because of the clinical perspectives this is still significantly more informed than is the case without clinical input, it is far from ideal.

As a result of the change in the information power base and changes in the other power levers at work, the health service has undergone a major change in its culture.

ORGANIZATION CULTURE

The culture of an organization is defined with difficulty. It can be described as a shared feeling between a number of people in response to situations within the organization. It is easy, however, to identify different cultural characteristics within different organizations when moving from one organization to another.

It is clear that becoming aware of the technical aspects of a new job is not sufficient to do it well. To be successful, it is essential to understand new colleagues, superiors and subordinates and their attitudes towards the work itself, to interact with colleagues, to mingle socially with superiors and other colleagues. After a time, the newcomer realizes there are certain ways of doing things, certain subjects that are taboo, certain people who are easily upset and others who are not. Attitudes develop within the organization which determine the behaviour of staff working in them. After a time these attitudes and behaviours become characteristics of a particular organization. Various organizational characteristics such as leadership, motivation of staff, organizational structure and style of communication all interact to produce the culture of an organization.

Handy (1976) suggests that cultures are deeper than just commonly agreed ways of perceiving the situation. He states:

In organizations, there are deep set beliefs about the way the work should be organized, the way authority should be exercised, people rewarded, people controlled. What are the degrees of formalization required? How much planning and how far ahead? What combination of obedience and initiative is looked for in subordinates? Do work hours matter or dress or personal eccentricities? Do committees control an individual? Are there rules and procedures or only results? These are parts of the culture of an organization.

Even within an organization, different cultures will prevail. Very different points of view and approaches will exist between those working, for example, in clinical operational activities and those working in research, those working in administration and those working in the clinical front line. These different power levers are used differently within various cultures. Harrison (1972) has identified four basic organizational cultures:

1. power
2. role
3. task
4. person.

Power culture

A power culture depends on strong leadership from a central power source such as one person or a small group, controlling and manipulating almost all activities within the organization. The organization functions mainly by staff anticipating issues, decisions and attitudes of those at the top. What happens in practice is that those at middle and lower levels quickly react to rumour and use the grapevine as the main source of information.

Role culture

The role culture is based on the concept of legitimacy, in that the procedures, rules and control, authority and information systems are considered right and proper and are not to be broken or transgressed. Great attention is given to job descriptions, definitions of authority relationships, procedures for communication and rules for settlement of disputes. The principal function of senior management is coordination and once direction is given, each of the functions, guided by rules and procedures, will work according to the overall plan.

Task culture

A task culture is one in which problem solving, application of expert knowledge, working in teams and both individual and group adaptability are highly valued. Influence is based on the application of technical expertise rather than positional or personal power. The predominant style is to work in team settings and the differences in individual objectives, status and style are quickly and happily sacrificed for the continued well-being of the team. Project and task force groupings are quickly formed to grapple with a particular problem and equally quickly abandoned on its solution. Formal roles have little meaning in such situations as judgement is based on expertise, control over one's work, easy working relationships and mutual respect for personal competence. As a result, the task culture and the role culture are anathema to each other; the former is based on sensitivity, on flexibility to the needs of the market and social environment. The latter needs to achieve somewhat inflexible long-term objectives and establish rules, procedures and control.

Person-oriented culture

The primary objective of the person-oriented culture is to serve the individuals in the group. This culture develops when the existing structures, rules and procedures are there to provide for the needs of each of the organization's or group's individual members. This is the least common of the four cultures and, Harrison (1972) suggests, offers a high order of moral values. A person–oriented culture is unlikely to predominate in an organization over approximately 100 people in size. In many organizations, however, individuals and small groups prefer a person-oriented approach but have to accommodate a stronger alternative culture. Some professional clinical staff, for example, may and often do hold strong person-oriented values but operate in a role or task culture. Many professional and academic staff tend to regard the organization as a base from which to pursue personal professional interests which often only indirectly add to the status of the organization.

In person-oriented cultures which are part of another but more dominant culture, control is always a problem. Managers within the organization are likely to discover that person-oriented specialists are difficult to manage. The normal range of sanctions brought to bear on erring individuals in organizations are often meaningless to the specialist and furthermore, the services of most specialists are in demand and therefore to move is no major problem.

The health service today exhibits all four of these cultures within individual organizations. Within the non-clinical management hierarchy, a power culture prevails with role cultures also existing within parts of the hierarchy. The current movement towards working in multidisciplinary teams, as in the task culture, is more characteristic of the way directorates work and within the medical fraternity, a person-oriented culture is prevalent. Identifying and understanding the types of culture in operation gives an insight into which power levers are most effective in achieving change and effective organizational function.

REFERENCES

DHSS 1983 NHS Management Inquiry. HMSO, London
Handy C 1976 Understanding organizations. Penguin, Harmondsworth, p 177
Harrison R 1972 How to describe your organization. Harvard Business Review
Harwood A, Boufford J I 1993 Managing clinical services. A consensus statement of principles for effective clinical management. BAMM/BMA/RCN/IHSM, London
Kakabadse A, Ludlow R, Vinnicombe S 1987 Working in organizations. Gower, London, pp 14–225
Mintzberg H 1983 Structure in fives: designing effective organizations. Prentice-Hall, New Jersey, ch 10
Mintzberg H 1988 The professional organization. Mintzberg on management. Free Press, New York, pp 180–181
Mintzberg H et al 1976 The structure of unstructured

decision process. Administrative Seminar Quarterly 250–251

Peters T J, Phillips J R, Waterman R H 1980 Structure is not organization. Business Horizons

Simpson J 1993 BAMM clinical directorate survey. Clinician in Management 2(4): 13–15

Waterman R H, Peters T J, Phillips J R 1988 The 7-S framework in the strategy process. In: Quinn, Mintzberg H, James (eds) Concepts, contexts and cases. Prentice-Hall International, New Jersey, pp 271–272

4

The organizational structure of hospitals

Tony White

It may seem a strange principle to enunciate as the very first requirement in a hospital that it should do the sick no harm.
(Florence Nightingale 1820–1910)

DOCTORS' INVOLVEMENT IN RUNNING HOSPITALS

There are many ways a complex organization can be run so it is therefore important to define the term 'running' a hospital. Chairmen of departments or clinical directors can have varying degrees of influence in planning and resource allocation and this influence depends very much on the degree of devolvement of central power and authority within that institution. Generally speaking the influence of clinicians in running hospitals had until recently been diminishing in a strategic sense, but had not changed in a daily operational sense. The relationship between doctor and manager has developed to a complex relationship regarding the doctor's involvement in the organizational problems of today.

We have seen in Chapter 1 that it was not until the late 19th century that the doctor began to play an important role in the hospital. Hospitals had been until fairly recently cottage industries and the craftsmen or the technicians were the doctors who ran their 'workshops' within them and maintained complete and total authority over their own areas. The doctor was not involved and indeed had no need to be involved in the management of the hospital (White 1991):

In early times the doctor was very much in control of the patient and that authority was unquestioned in the care of the hospital patient. Professional independence was reinforced as the centre of practice had been in the home. As hospitals gradually developed doctors continued to guard their position even when the patient was in hospital. In the second half of the twentieth century the hospital and medical treatment have become more complex. There are large numbers of people involved in treatment and the organization has grown in size with a move away from professional independence to interdependence.

Hospitals were of course neither generally founded by the medical profession or operated by them after founding and perhaps it would be interesting to speculate whether, had this been the case, they would have been very different institutions from the ones we know today. Doctors were not originally part of the organization, although they had a vital role to play in the organization and this explains why the doctor, with certain exceptions such as privately owned hospitals and nursing homes, was never in control of the institution. Many of today's difficulties facing the relationship between doctors and managers have arisen as the result of this historical development. Drucker (1977) states that, 'Hospitals everywhere present the same confusion of missions and objectives with resulting impairment of effectiveness and performance'. Should a hospital be, in effect, a doctor's work facility, as many older doctors believe? Should it focus on the major health needs of a community, should it try to keep abreast of every medical advance no matter how costly and how rarely that facility will be used or should it focus on preventative medicine and health education for the community?

These are only a few of the possible definitions and objectives of a hospital and every one can be defended, each one deserving a hearing. The effective hospital will be a multipurpose institution trying to strike a balance between various objectives. What many if not most hospitals do, however, is to pretend that there are no basic questions to be decided. According to Drucker (1977) the result, predictably, is confusion and impairment of the capacity of the hospital to serve any function and carry out any mission. One hospital stated its purpose as, 'To provide acute care that utilizes the most advanced diagnostic and therapeutic techniques available, to be a centre of medical excellence', but it then continues paradoxically by saying, 'and meet an agreed standard of quality within available resources'. Another mission statement began, 'We aim to be the finest district general hospital', but then went on to say, 'We also aim to be a specialist centre of excellence'.

When resources are scarce nothing worthwhile is accomplished unless those scarce resources are concentrated on a small number of priorities. Dependence on a budget allocation, placed at whatever level, seems to delay setting priorities. Being budget based appears to make it more difficult to abandon the bad things, the old and the obsolete practices. As a result Drucker (1977) feels that hospitals, like all service institutions, are more encrusted than businesses with the barnacles of inherently unproductive efforts.

MANAGEMENT OF HOSPITALS

Hospitals are often thought to have a unique administrative structure but in fact they have similarities to a number of human service organizations and inherent complexities: 'The large number of separate decision makers in the professions are what separate health care from most industrial and service industries' (West 1988). Nelson (1989), however, takes a different view: 'In many ways, health services are not different from any other service industry or, indeed, any manufacturing industry'. Drucker (1990) regards hospitals as one of a number of 'non-profit organizations' which do different things from business, which supplies goods or services, or government, which controls:

A business has discharged its task when the customer buys the product, pays for it, and is satisfied with it. Government has discharged its function when its policies are effective. The 'non profit' institution neither supplies goods or services nor controls. Its 'product' is neither a pair of shoes nor an effective regulation. Its product is a *changed human being*. The non-profit institutions are human-change agents.

They appear to agree that improved employee morale can improve organizational effectiveness. Davis & Cherns (1975) and Cummings & Molloy (1977) indicate that it has come to be accepted that an organization should be responsive to the social and psychological needs of its employees and that improvements in the quality of their working life are often linked to improvements in organizational effectiveness. Despite the government's expectations of hospitals to increase efficiency, consideration of employee morale has not appeared to be a feature of these demands. The complexity of the hospital, lack of goal clarity and the conflicting interests of different groups are formidable barriers to improving operating effectiveness and the nature of working within the organization (Hanlon & Gladstein 1984).

Nor is the hospital one organization, but a collection of empires which until recently were in competition with each other for beds, money, manpower and other resources. To many who worked in hospitals there was no higher authority than the consultant. Administrators were regarded as 'the mere servants of the kings'. They coordinated and tried to keep the building and the non-medical staff functioning. They would not, and it appeared could not, interfere in the way consultants ran their kingdoms. Neither could they, being without medical qualifications, make valid priority judgements between departments. The old district management teams often decided who should receive resources under pressure from the lobbying of a powerful consultant or group of consultants. But the consultant in his own department was autonomous. Only he decided how many patients to operate on, what type of operations to perform and how many patients were seen in his outpatient clinics. His power extended even over non-clinical matters.

Following the various reorganizations new kinds of administrators and managers took over, but they were still largely without power, respect or seniority. They were regarded only as housekeepers and they often had a hard time trying to control the hospital. Toynbee (1977) relates an anecdote showing how consultants operated in complete isolation from the rest of the hospital:

The administration had sent out directives to all consultants to admit only emergency cases. The laundry had ceased to function effectively and there was a severe linen shortage. The orthopaedic department suffered particularly since many of their admissions couldn't easily be categorized as emergencies. There was a lot of wheeling and dealing going between the consultants. I was with Dr Goodwin of the nephrology department one day during the dispute. He was pacing the wards, whispering to the sisters. In one of his wards he found that a prudent sister had stockpiled a vast amount of linen, plenty to keep his non-emergency admissions flowing. The sister was anxious that he shouldn't tell the administration that she had all this extra linen, as she wanted to keep it for her ward. 'Do you think we could? Could we just admit a few, do you think?' he asked her conspiratorially. He went down to the administrators in the end and, being careful not to disclose the ward in question, said, 'If I found the linen could I keep admitting my patients?' There was a fairly indignant 'no' from administration, who were hard put to find enough linen for their emergencies. Dr Goodwin huffed off in a bad temper and no doubt the administrators ordered a quick search of some of the ward linen stocks.

The consultants had almost complete autonomy, arguing amongst themselves in a series of complicated and unsatisfactory committees, each striving to increase the size of their empire. Few, it seemed, had any consideration for the general good of all patients, only caring for the rights of their own patients. There is a belief amongst consultants, unassailable and inviolable, that nothing, no authority in the world must come between them and their patients. They alone must have complete freedom to prescribe whatever treatment they feel is appropriate. It is on this basis that the consultants can build around them such powerful empires. There was no one above or below them to challenge that authority. Toynbee (1977) quotes one consultant's view:

I regard the health service as nothing more than a mechanism for paying for medical care of the patients, a sort of insurance, and nothing more. We consultants have no loyalties whatever to the health service, nor should we. All our loyalties are to our patients and the hospital.

Care without direct payment of course carries on a tradition from the voluntary hospitals that predate the National Health Service, doctors giving their time free of charge in those hospitals, hence the name. It is probable that this charitable background may still be affecting the attitudes of many consultants toward patients today. A consultant aged about 55, training young doctors today, will have been trained by consultants who entered medicine and had their attitudes shaped in the 1920s. According to Devlin (1985b):

There has been a sort of cosy consensus among the surgical oligarchy since the inception of the NHS or, more correctly, since the then oligarchies returned from the 1939–45 war and diecast the NHS in the most favourable view they took of the surgical practice they had known prior to September 1939.

Doctors also come mainly from higher income groups and were chosen for their aptitude in science examinations and it is not surprising that they are frequently lacking in the area of customer relations. This pattern may, however, be altering: 'That attitude is now changing, more schools acknowledging that people with only moderate academic achievement can cope well with the course and often have more to offer in terms of personal skills, attitudes and experience' (Lowry 1992). Patients effectively have no purchasing power and do not control the transaction in a market way. The consultant is paid a salary and the poor performer is paid the same as the best. Where the patient has a direct input into the choice of doctor and where an insurance fund rewards doctors for the treatments and service provided, as in the United States and many European countries, there is a greater incentive to keep the patient happy and informed about the treatment.

West (1988) drew a comparison between doctors and airline pilots:

It is widely accepted that planes need well-trained independent professionals to cope with whatever situation develops. But it is also accepted that the autonomy can be exercised within limits of financial and organizational efficiency set by the airlines.... Furthermore, customer safety requires detailed reviews every six months to check on the competence of the pilot in a range of situations.

CONSULTANTS' USE OF RESOURCES IN HOSPITAL

Doctors involved in the use of resources in hospitals demonstrate not only the extent to which they are major users but also that they manage those resources in a way directly denied to managers. It also demonstrates some of the lessons which clinical directors have to learn about the ways in which a hospital operates and the proportions of resources that go into various aspects of the running of a hospital. It also shows some of the areas in which change is occurring, for example in the culture of bed holding for status and empire building in general. Consultants use two main types of resources: those they control more or less directly and those where a task is referred to a service department. A clinical or bed holding firm is usually allocated a number of inpatient beds or wards with supporting facilities and outpatient clinic time at one or more hospitals. In addition, for surgical specialities there will be an allocation of theatre time with anaesthetic services and related equipment.

Directly controlled resources

Consultant beds have been equated with status and their use is often unwillingly surrendered to colleagues when for clinical or other reasons their occupancy falls. They may have been kept unnecessarily occupied to prevent emergency cases from other firms blocking next day's elective admissions, a problem especially common in winter. To be fair, we might consider how we would feel if on coming into work we found our desk taken over by others, leaving no room for us to do our own work. Without incentives, the choice of how beds are used might not be efficient for the hospital. A consultant has until recently usually taken no real interest in the management of hospital beds and faced few penalties for this lack of interest.

The use of operating theatres involves similar obstacles. Theatres, like beds, are not always used effectively and frustration results. One cause is lack of clear management and this could change in the new management structures outlined later. Since managers have no real control over the consultants they can only make sure that a theatre is ready to provide the service expected of it. They cannot make the service happen. Theatre user committees exist but for these to function effectively the consultant members may need to challenge each other about the use of facilities, something they rarely consider. Medical etiquette, loyalty to the profession and a 'medical mafia' serve to prevent change. The cost of underusage of theatres, or any other facility, is negligible to the consultant, but expensive for the hospital. Overuse causes overspends beyond budgetary allocations, provokes irritation in theatre staff who may have to work longer hours unpaid and can keep surgical colleagues waiting.

According to West (1988):

A more fundamental problem is the mismatch between the rate of detection of problems by GPs, confirmation by the consultant at outpatient clinics and final treatment. A patient may be diagnosed in minutes for a condition that will take hours of direct treatment and days of hospital stay. As a result, a waiting list starts to build up for either treatment or outpatient clinics . . . . There is no real incentive to improve performance.

For surgeons especially, there may be an imbalance between outpatient work and theatre time. It may not always be practical to change this, nor in the consultant's interest, nor may it be possible for the manager to change it because of resistance. In the past managers had no clear incentive to increase performance, where even if the number of patients treated increased, the income to the hospital did not. With a real internal market, the more efficient a hospital becomes, the more spare capacity may be revealed, although this may not be filled if purchasers have no money for extra work. A further issue is that a consultant and his firm using resources for one case do not allow this to affect the firm's decision about another case as it would have no immediate, direct or apparent effect on their total resources. The service is apparently free to them.

Investigations and resources

There are at least three ways in which overusage of resources by investigations may occur. The first, which might be called legal overusage and which tends to be more overt in the United States, is the overuse of resources as a result of defensive medicine. This is practised to avoid possible criticism especially if there is future litigation and usually means doing everything possible, even when the clinical gain may be small or non-existent. The second kind is professional overusage by inexperienced junior doctors in order to defend themselves against criticism by their seniors. Lastly there is a form of patient overusage, where there may be a need to demonstrate concern or to reassure the patient that a problem is receiving attention, is under control or is not a significant problem after all. There is also the significant problem of unreal expectations by patients of what can be done for them, sometimes reinforced by an abrogation of responsibilities regarding referral.

Whatever the extent of these forms of defensive medicine, particularly the last, because doctors are motivated to help people they may push this to the limit where they think it is at least worth trying. Nevertheless the lack of incentive facing doctors indicates that resources may not be used in ways that health economists and others might regard as efficient. The problem is that while everyone agrees waste is a bad thing, there is frequently no comprehensive agreement on the best course of action for a given patient with a given disorder and audit and protocols are at present in their infancy. They may also stifle innovation. With all this uncertainty it is probably wiser to think of improving hospital efficiency by eliminating obviously wasteful activities rather than trying to aim for medical consistency on patterns of resource use when there is no consensus on the right treatment.

Service controlled resources

So far we have only considered the so-called bed holding clinical departments; the service specialities have rather different problems with resources. They are the departments such as anaesthetics, pathology and radiology providing services to other specialities in the hospital. Faced with rising demand, they have either to increase their output from the resources available, which means everyone working harder (unlikely to be popular) or they can claim more resources to meet demand at the current level of efficiency (such extra resources rarely being available) or they have to restrict demand, which means disputes with clinical departments and difficult decisions about priority and rationing. It has been easier to pursue efficiency in the non-clinical support services such as cleaning, catering and the other hotel services, where there is no direct question of a threat to healthcare from reductions in staffing, although reducing or at least controlling demand is increasingly seen as an alternative way to cut expenditure within hospitals.

THE TRADITIONAL CONTROL OF RESOURCES

In some hospitals before the formation of trusts the district administrator already behaved as a chief executive and administrators and managers with strong personalities managed effectively. In other hospitals a different member of the team was the real manager and in some, doctors became involved in management. The doctor was not really regarded as an employee of that institution and until 1991, consultants, except those in teaching hospitals, were generally employees of the regional health authority. They advised managers of the hospital about what needed to be achieved medically and it was the task of the managers to do their best to satisfy those requirements. To some extent from 1948 until the late 1970s hospitals functioned in that way and each year more and more money was spent. Perhaps there were not as many increases as were happening elsewhere in Europe or as many as doctors would have liked, but nonetheless each year more money was spent. They were years of relative plenty.

Then came the years of famine, with cash limits in 1979 and cash planning in the early 1980s so that the old ways of running hospitals no longer applied. There is nothing unique about the National Health Service. Every country in the world is facing the problem of not having sufficient resources to achieve everything they would like to achieve and therefore having to make choices. So the question was raised, how to involve doctors in management. The Griffiths Report (DHSS 1983) emphasized the need for doctors to assume managerial responsibility by involving them in the management of resources. It was endeavouring to make them more cost conscious and suggested this may take place in two main ways:

1. by involving doctors in management within hospitals
2. by appointing doctors to general managerial posts.

DOCTORS' INVOLVEMENT IN THE MANAGEMENT OF RESOURCES

There have been a series of attempts to move away from functional budgeting and to involve doctors more, each attempt increasing the degree to which they have been given more involvement. These may be summarized as follows.

Clinical budgeting

There was a disparity between clinicians who make decisions about which patients to treat and managers who had responsibility for controlling a budget and keeping within cash limits. Managers did not see it as their role to negotiate with clinicians how resources should be used. Nor since the beginning of the NHS have doctors wished to fill that role. Clinical budgeting suggested that plans should be agreed by clinicians in conjunction with service providers and finance officers. Those plans should incorporate objectives for clinical activity, specifying the details of resources required into a financial statement. The essential change with clinical budgeting was the securing of an agreement with clinicians on a budget.

Experience from other countries showed that doctors had not regretted participating in clinical budgeting. One of the main advantages is strengthening the doctors' position when negotiating resources. It enables discussion on standards and quality of care and some consultants found this to be an incentive. Some managers paradoxically feel that giving doctors resource management type information could be manipulated by consultants and intensify their 'shroud waving' ability, not necessarily making them better team members. Consultants were also generally unhappy with management interference in medical workloads and frequently distrusted the accuracy of information.

Management budgeting

The Griffiths Report (DHSS 1983) emphasized the need to involve doctors more effectively in the management of resources. It pointed out what has been emphasized on many occasions, that it is the decisions of the doctors that largely determine how resources are used. Griffiths argued that clinicians should accept the managerial responsibility that went with the clinical freedom. He recommended that:

- Health authorities should involve the clinicians more closely in the management process, consistent with clinical freedom.
- Clinicians must participate fully in decisions about priorities in the use of resources.
- Clinicians need administrative support, together with strictly relevant management information and a fully developed management budget approach.

Although previously involved informally and implicitly, clinicians were in future to be involved formally and explicitly in financial management and decision making and to be responsible for those decisions. The proposals thus had profound effects on general managers, treasurers and other professional groups, especially nurses. The discipline of management budgeting also meant that doctors would be accountable for their actions to a manager who might not necessarily be a doctor, a move which would have little appeal to the profession. It was essentially, however, similar to clinical budgeting. A review of management budgeting (DHSS 1986) concluded that it had failed to achieve its objectives due in part to a failure to win support and commitment from key personnel, i.e. agreement with the absence of clear management structures, together with the rapid speed of introduction. Management budgeting was not just a matter of agreement between doctors and managers but required doctors to take responsibility for the budget, although accountability remained somewhat vague.

Resource management

A new initiative was therefore needed and in 1986 it came in the form of the Resource Management Initiative (DHSS 1986) which was co-sponsored by the Joint Consultants Committee and the NHS Management Board. Watson (1994, personal communication) takes the view that the initiative recognized two different directions from which to approach the involvement of clinicians in management. One was to establish information systems that would meet the clinicians' own specifications for supplying data on clinical activity and costs that would actually be useful to them in running the service. The other was to establish management structures (on the Guy's clinical directorate model) that gave them the responsibility and the authority to run their service. Indeed, the experimental sites were deliberately selected to include some of each type (e.g. Huddersfield for its information systems, Guy's for its management structure). The preliminary conclusion of the evaluation of the experimental sites carried out by the CCSC (1986) was that the two aspects were independent – those with clinical directorates found they would only work effectively if supplied with proper data through well-designed information systems, while those with information systems found they needed to revise their management structures in order to make proper use of the data.

The new approach was to aim for greater medical and nursing involvement, with a focus on measurable improvements in healthcare through better use of resources. There was a recognition that nurses and clinicians needed to be more involved than hitherto. The architect of the scheme, Mills (1987), stated:

> The resource management programme is principally about changing attitudes and encouraging closer team work in managing resources among patient care professionals and between such professionals and other managers.

Resource management was intended to provide accurate and useful information to clinicians about their practice and costs compared with colleagues in the same hospital, district or region. In a sense it was the forerunner of audit in that it sought to encourage doctors to review performance and improve standards of healthcare. While some consultants found this information interesting and even useful, some became anxious about comparisons.

Winning over clinicians to resource management would take time. Earlier initiatives had failed because they did not convince clinicians that they had anything to offer. Indeed, the DHSS used the words 'seriously antagonized' (DHSS 1986) and went on to say that 'there may be a case for suspending management budgeting development for the time being'; Devlin (1985a) said that it was:

> unrewarding for the clinician, a fact that management consultants agreed in private conversations. In a cutback situation the health authority is having to grab every penny it can and will only squeeze further consultants who improve their output. I think management budgets by incentive is fraudulent unless the clinician is prepared to go home and rest when he has reached his target output – doing more and more efficiently negates the savings the health authority is really out to achieve. Savings, not efficiency, is the real bottom line.

Resource management therefore emphasized human relations, whereas management budgeting was finance led. Resource management was concerned with making doctors more management conscious and accountable for the resources used. By now the doctor and manager had agreed the budget and the doctor had been given responsibility and made accountable.

CLINICAL DIRECTORATES

The term 'clinical directorate' has a number of interpretations and there is ample scope for confusion. Such is the complexity of organizations that a wide range of interpretations are now placed on clinical directorates, an additional problem being that organizational structure has not been created afresh but developed from a whole range of existing structures. Here clinical directors, clinical chairmen or heads of service (the terms vary between hospitals) are responsible and accountable for consultants and other medical staff within a directorate and have the authority to manage the directorate. The problem with such generalizations is that classic directorates can be more easily applied to acute hospitals. Community hospitals, however, with their traditionally more disparate and loose managerial structure, do not lend themselves so easily to the same basic structures. Community trusts may only have one medical director with no clinical directors; indeed, they may be called clinical director rather than medical director, even if they have a seat on the trust board.

In a classic case in an acute unit, the clinical director will be supported by a business manager and nurse manager and this is described more fully later. One of the problems in the health service is that we tend to use the same word for a number of things: many hospitals now have clinical directors and yet what they actually do regarding responsibility, authority and accountability varies from hospital to hospital. With true clinical directorates the doctor was finally given authority in addition to accountability and responsibility.

It is probably useful to summarize the changes in tabular form.

Date	Budgeting	Details	Control by
1948	Functional	Nursing Medical staff Estates, etc.	Managers
	Clinical	Agreeing finances	
1983	Management	More medical involvement	
1986	Resource management	Doctors supplied with information on costs, both absolute and comparative	
1989	Clinical directorates	Everything in directorate	Doctors

More important are the differences within the various stages of development, with regard to agreement, responsibility, accountability and authority which may be summarized as follows:

	Agreement	Responsibility	Accountability	Authority
Functional budgeting				
Clinical budgeting	Yes			
Management budgeting	Yes	Yes	?	
Resource management	Yes	Yes	Yes	
Clinical directorates	Yes	Yes	Yes	Yes

APPOINTMENT OF DOCTORS TO MANAGERIAL POSITIONS

Few doctors were willing to take general managerial posts. A small number were appointed in 1987 – less than 8% at regional and district level and less than 19% at unit level (Stewart & Dobson 1988). They were often on a part-time basis and the number has since fallen. Scrivens (1988) gives a number of reasons for this including limited interest in management roles, lack of training in management skills, lack of ability in management skills, lack of suitable financial rewards for doing so, meaning a cut in salary, a feeling from colleagues that one had crossed to the other side. There were also difficulties in maintaining a career when abandoning all or even part of clinical work.

SOME MODELS OF MANAGEMENT STRUCTURES

It is vital to recognize that structures on paper rarely reflect workings in practice, but it is useful to understand the more common structures in use today. Formal pictures of organizations often contain an element of wish or imagination and fail to capture the messiness or fudginess of most organizations as complex as the NHS (Gale 1993). It is also important to realize that parts of one structure can be superimposed on other areas and different parts of an organization may have different organizational structures. These structures began with the arrangement seen before the recent reforms applying to directly managed units, which was the traditional hierarchical model.

Consultant chairman of division model

The unit management team or board was chaired by the unit general manager and included a consultant, usually the chair of a consultant committee, often the medical executive committee. In addition there was normally the senior manager of nursing (the matron) and finance (the treasurer) and maybe also senior managers representing professions allied to medicine (PAMs) and unit general managers. There were four distinct levels of management:

1. top managers – DGMs
2. senior managers – UGMs and directors of functions
3. middle managers – assistant UGMs and heads of professions
4. 1st line managers – departmental heads.

As far as the doctors were concerned representation was via the consultant representative who chaired or sat on

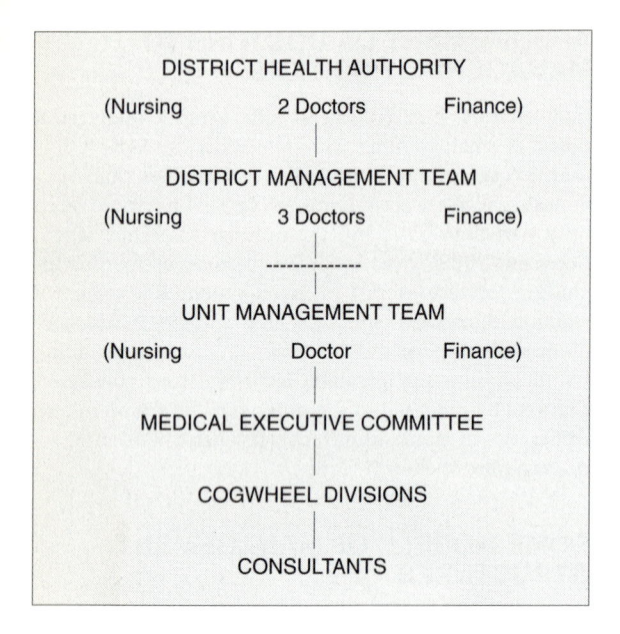

```
DISTRICT HEALTH AUTHORITY
(Nursing        2 Doctors        Finance)
              |
   DISTRICT MANAGEMENT TEAM
(Nursing        3 Doctors        Finance)
              |
     UNIT MANAGEMENT TEAM
(Nursing         Doctor          Finance)
              |
   MEDICAL EXECUTIVE COMMITTEE
              |
        COGWHEEL DIVISIONS
              |
           CONSULTANTS
```

the medical executive committee, composed of all the Cogwheel divisional chairs.

Above this was the district health authority composed of members selected from nominations received from several sources. Circular HC(80)9 (DHSS 1981) specified that the authority should include a hospital consultant, a general practitioner, a nurse, midwife or health visitor, a nominee from the region's medical school, a trade union member, four or more local authority nominees and seven or more general members. The consultant was usually a representative elected by the consultant body. The chairmanship was the gift of the Secretary of State although not apparently accountable to him. The selection of a candidate, according to Levitt & Wall (1989), was done via the 'old boy' network whereby those in influential positions in society suggest a suitable candidate. He usually acted as a bridge between the DHA and its officers, particularly the DMT.

The district management team consisted of the DGM, the district treasurer, the district nursing officer and three doctors, only one of whom, the community physician, usually the district medical officer or director of public health, was managerially accountable to the DGM. The others were the consultant and general practitioner mentioned previously. There were of course considerable variations in practice, particularly related to the size of the district and the roles and duties particularly of the public health doctor that changed in 1974, 1982 and again in 1990 with the respective reorganizations. Nevertheless the outline of the traditional model can be identified from this simplification of a very complex and diverse structure.

The clinical manager model

There are still two functional strands or columns to the organization, clinical and managerial, with little lateral relationship.

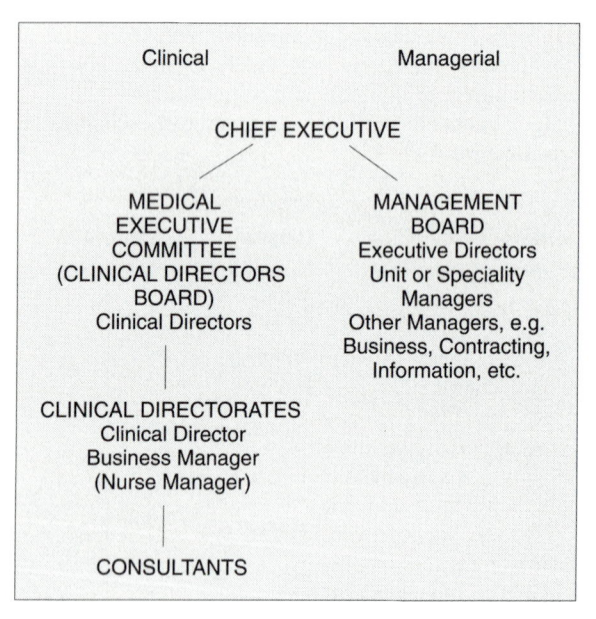

```
         Clinical                Managerial

                    CHIEF EXECUTIVE
                    /            \
          MEDICAL                MANAGEMENT
          EXECUTIVE                BOARD
          COMMITTEE             Executive Directors
       (CLINICAL DIRECTORS      Unit or Speciality
             BOARD)                Managers
         Clinical Directors     Other Managers, e.g.
                                Business, Contracting,
                                 Information, etc.
             |
    CLINICAL DIRECTORATES
         Clinical Director
         Business Manager
         (Nurse Manager)
             |
         CONSULTANTS
```

Here the services are delegated to a clinical manager and medical interests are regulated and advised through a separate column up to the chief executive. Operational management takes place through the managerial column, including the negotiation and agreeing of most activity, business and contracts. Although there may be clinical consultation, it is only advisory.

The clinical adviser or consultant coordinator model

In this variant the chief executive retains overall responsibility for the professional hierarchies and career development issues of managers with an arrangement for the consultant to act as clinical adviser, although being responsible for coordinating and monitoring the professionals within the directorate. Often the clinical coordinator or adviser does not hold full budgetary responsibility for the services provided by the team and also has no responsibility for the performance of other professional groups within the team.

```
TRUST BOARD
Chairman
Non-executive Directors
Chief Executive
Executive Directors (inc Medical Director)
        |
MANAGEMENT BOARD
Chief Executive
Executive Directors (inc Medical Director)
Unit or Speciality Managers
        |
CLINICAL DIRECTORATES
Doctor  Nurse Manager  Business Manager  Finance
                   Adviser
        |
CONSULTANTS
```

The true clinical director model

In a true clinical directorate model, on the trust board, with a chairman again appointed by the Secretary of State, are five non-executive directors together with the chief executive and five executive directors usually including a medical director, a director of nursing, a finance director and one other, often either a director of support services, business activity and contracts or human resources.

On the management board there sit the same five executive directors chaired by the chief executive (sometimes the medical director or maybe taking it in turn) and all the clinical directors. And below that the 'executive units' sit as a clinical directorate chaired by the clinical director with the business manager, nurse manager and all the consultants and heads of department within the directorate. Here the clinical director is a part-time consultant manager.

He assumes responsibility for the work of consultant colleagues and for nursing and support services within the directorate. The clinical director also holds all the budgets for staff and services relating to the directorate, has responsibility for all personnel issues and for day-to-day management of the directorate. Business and nurse managers support the directorate rather than belonging to professional hierarchies.

STAGES IN THE EVOLUTION OF CLINICAL DIRECTORATES

It usually takes a considerable period of time to progress or transform a public sector mentality to an entrepreneurial spirit. One might almost call it a revolution, but it is about empowerment and increased effectiveness, discarding functional budgetary systems that waste money and jettisoning bureaucracy and replacing them with decentralized, more responsive organizations that can take advantage of the information technology available today.

It is possible to track this evolutionary process in hospitals through a number of stages (Fig. 4.1). It is important to realize that not only may doctors and managers see themselves as being at different stages in the process, different doctors and managers may be at different stages, different departments at different stages. Frequently an independent outside observer may see things differently and the organization may drift between stages at different times in response to particular events.

1. Ignorance stage

Managers lack awareness of the need to involve professionals in management and the doctors lack interest.

2. Denial stage

Managers deny the need to involve doctors and the doctors feel that it is not part of their job to be involved.

```
TRUST BOARD
Chairman
Non-executive Directors
Chief Executive
Executive Directors (inc Medical Director)
        |
MANAGEMENT BOARD
Chief Executive
Executive Directors (inc Medical Director)
Clinical Directors
        |
CLINICAL DIRECTORATES
Nurse Manager    Doctor    Business Manager
        |
CONSULTANTS
```

3. Refusal stage

The managers now say they will not allow the doctors to be involved. This may be out of ignorance of the need to do so or fear of their becoming involved. At the same time the doctors are saying that they refuse to become involved. This is usually because of the feeling that doctors look after patients and someone else finds the money.

42 TEXTBOOK OF MANAGEMENT FOR DOCTORS

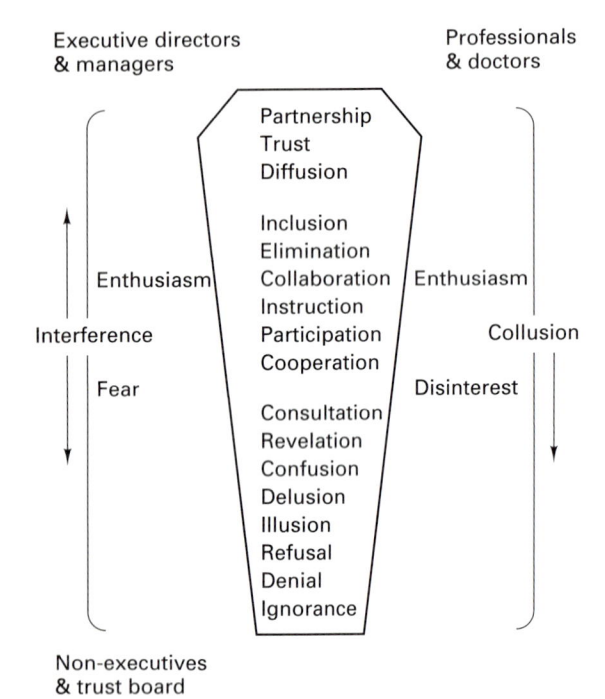

```
Executive directors          Professionals
& managers                   & doctors

                  Partnership
                  Trust
                  Diffusion

                  Inclusion
                  Elimination
    Enthusiasm    Collaboration    Enthusiasm
                  Instruction
    Interference  Participation    Collusion
                  Cooperation
    Fear                           Disinterest
                  Consultation
                  Revelation
                  Confusion
                  Delusion
                  Illusion
                  Refusal
                  Denial
                  Ignorance

Non-executives
& trust board
```

Read from bottom upwards. Note that each step becomes more difficult for both sides until the penultimate stage when trust is fully established.

Fig. 4.1 Stages in evolution of developed management (i.e. to clinical directors)

4. Illusion stage

The managers now pretend to involve the doctors and the doctors are under the illusion that they are being involved.

5. Delusion stage

The managers no longer admit to pretending to involve the doctors and really believe they are involving them. The doctors truly believe that they are genuinely involved.

6. Confusion stage

The managers are now questioning how they can really involve the doctors and the doctors are asking what they need to do to help.

7. Revelation stage

Suddenly the managers understand the need to really involve doctors and it comes as an equal revelation to the doctors that they really do need to become more involved.

8. Consultation stage

The managers feel that they need to talk with the doctors about how the process can progress. This tends to cause some initial suspicion with the doctors.

9. Cooperation stage

The doctors suddenly see the need, particularly as it might be in their own interest as well as that of the service and the patients to respond to this initiative. This stage represents the first real move towards the clinical advisory roles for doctors.

10. Participation stage

The doctors agree to respond to these advances and talks take place between the two sides to agree how the organization should progress towards devolvement.

11. Instruction stage

The organization receives help from experienced outside experts who not only act as honest broker but also have helpful suggestions as to how the organization may be structured, examples of successful structure, the advantages and pitfalls of these and are able to help with a process of arriving at a local solution. This stage should not be mistaken for efforts to bring in outside assistance to reinforce existing managerial prejudices. This can cause reversion to stage 4.

12. Collaboration stage

With the knowledge and experience gained from the previous stage, the parties consult, discuss and agree on the new local structure and establish a complete set of ground rules by which it will work. These are thoroughly tested with examples of 'what if', 'suppose we' and 'how would', etc. It is vital that all the rules are thought out and tested. Failure to do so causes reversion to stages 3–5.

13. Elimination stage

All functional management and most central management is eliminated. Because this often resulted in the loss of a number of central managerial jobs it was originally called the Dead Wood Stage but for obvious reasons required a different title! There is understandably sometimes delay at this stage as middle managers need to find alternative career opportunities. Failure to address this issue also results in reversion to earlier stages and disillusionment amongst enthusiastic professionals.

14. Inclusion stage

This refers to the inclusion of all clinical directors onto a single management board. Apart from the reasons discussed elsewhere this also ensures that they know what is happening and why. Failure to implement this stage really sets back the process, maybe as far back as stage 1, but often depending on the motives underlying the decision.

15. Diffusion stage

The managers by now should have devolved true authority rather than blame and the doctors should willingly have accepted responsibility in addition to the need to be accountable for this responsibility. By now real clinical directorates are being established.

16. Trust stage

There should now be a feeling of confidence and trust in and from both parties. Talking to professionals in the organization, you no longer hear the phrase 'the managers' or 'the management'.

17. Partnership stage

This final stage is the end result of a long and often difficult process for both parties but is the easiest part, for by the time managers and doctors have been through all the previous stages they will have achieved true decentralization of management.

It is important to understand a number of influences and reactions within this process. Firstly, there are outside influences which can speed up, delay or reverse the process. Some of these emanate from the two major parties concerned in the process but there are also influences for good or ill from outside. Apart from the obvious effect of central government who, by changing the rules, can profoundly affect the process, the trust board and its non-executive directors can interfere in the process by either encouragement or interference through enthusiasm or fear. For the managers, the chief executive and executive directors, the process is frightening. Managers have to learn to let go, but they are often fearful, sometimes rightly, of who will control the organization and how.

FUTURE ROLE OF CENTRAL MANAGEMENT

It should not be forgotten that some dilemmas fall to the managers. Some clinical directors have been given administrators or business managers to guide and brief them. This can cause resentment to those managers who feel that they could do the clinical director's job and are indeed doing much of it without the pay and responsibility to match. The radical change in the way a hospital is managed is not only a change facing consultants. The more senior managers and chief executive are affected in more ways than they think. Clinical directors agreed when their attention was drawn to this, in line with this comment from a leading healthcare academic: 'With the change to clinical directorates the managers are in new ground too, they too are not used to management either, having been administrators'. The Institute of Health Service Managers are also aware that this might be a problem (Charlwood 1992): 'For managers the future is a lot less distinct than it used to be'. There are also problems if there is a hierarchy of medical managers; what can the non-medical lay management do when they have reached a certain level and cannot go further? And what of their career structure if much of the management function is taken over by professionals? For the administrators it remains an unknown, unanswered question.

Decentralization of decision making and the use of the directorate structure may leave a few functions in the centre. Finance and personnel and other central support departments are not usually completely devolved and an arbitration function will need to be performed by the centre, so there remains a small enabling rather than a constraining role being performed by the centre and central support departments.

THE DOCTORS AND OTHER PROFESSIONALS

These people may affect the process for good or ill through disinterest, delaying or reversing the process or by enthusiasm in speeding the progress towards devolution. It is also possible for the professionals and the managers to collude, even unknowingly, to delay progress. This is partly professional tradition and training. Jaques (1978) defined a profession in this way:

At a certain stage of development the possibility of managerial control of professional members by non-members must be excluded. This happens when the latter can no longer judge the competence of such professionals nor assess the technical problems encountered. Only monitoring and coordinating role relationships are possible in this context.

Much of the work of the NHS is carried out by professionals largely working on their own or in very small teams. Indeed, the essence of professional work is that the individual has discretion to adjust the work to the situation and to have independence of action when required. But this independence may lead to a certain degree of isolation and it does not encourage a wider team approach within a profession. This is one of the issues being addressed by the changes that are occurring in hospitals to create a more team-oriented approach; as a medically qualified chief executive put it: 'We are trying to engender a team approach, delegating responsibilities and giving, for example, ward sisters control over everything that goes on on their wards'. Consultants are being given the opportunity to participate in management, the decision making and the changes which are occurring. Clinicians, rather than being alienated from decision making, are being brought to the fore. They are recognizing that they need certain skills for which they have not so far been trained. They very often need help, support and training to fulfil these roles, but many doctors are willing to do that if asked and the involvement is real.

Managers recognize the need for new skills, for consultants in general and clinical directors in particular, and the need for learning management as well as other general professional skills. Many managers support the view that the doctors should be involved, a typical comment being: 'Doctors with management flair and leadership skills should be encouraged to take their place in the management of the health service'. Some consultants do accept also that they have a responsibility in this direction. One said:

Clinicians are the people responsible for initiating the expenditure. It is therefore important for some clinicians to accept responsibility for management and to be prepared to play a leading role in managing the affairs of the hospital.

They must have responsible reasons for that involvement:

Furthermore doctors must be able to manage themselves and others and to assess and evaluate the proper use of available resources for the best, most effective and most efficient delivery of health care.

THE POWER SHIFT WITHIN HOSPITALS

There has been a profound power shift within hospitals which has resulted in destabilization of the organization with resulting fear and anxiety. The traditional view is that this is simply a shift in power from consultants to managers.

This view is based on the notion that consultants have lost power, status, influence, autonomy, job security and, to some extent as a result, their self-esteem. They fear becoming technicians. All this has led to a feeling of disillusionment, with a consequent increase in

```
CONSULTANTS  <———>  MANAGERS
     ↑                   ↓
GENERAL PRACTITIONERS <——— PURCHASERS
```

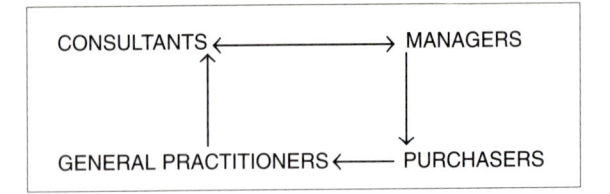

Fig. 4.2 The new paradigm

those seeking early retirement or a change of career and a desire by some, where possible, to abandon the NHS and pursue private or possibly independent practice.

For managers it has been assumed that they have acquired new power and authority, increased status, influence, greater responsibilities. But they too fear the increased accountability, they fear doctors (White 1993) and this leads to an inability to devolve. They too have lost security; if professionals take over much of the management of healthcare there may be less of a career structure for them.

But the shift in power is more complex. Research shows (White 1993) that the expert power held by consultants is more explicit and if it is ignored, the organization as a whole often suffers. The power shift for consultants is much more directed to the general practitioners and it is here that one needs to look for the partnership of the future to improve healthcare. For too long there has been a gulf separating primary and secondary care. Finally, for the managers there has been a loss of power to the purchasers, particularly where they have been general practitioners, and for the health authority and health commission purchasers there has also been a similar shift.

REFERENCES

Charlwood P 1992 Address given at conference on Managing clinical services. Centralisation in action. IHSM, BMA, RCN, BAMM, London
CCSC 1986 Resource management initiative: an evaluation of the six experimental sites. BMA/CCSC, London
Cummings T G, Molloy E S 1977 Improving productivity and the quality of work life. Praeger, New York
Davis L E, Cherns A B (eds) 1975 The quality of working life. Volume one: problems, prospects and the state of the art. Volume two: cases and commentary. Free Press, New York
Devlin B 1985a Second opinion. Health and Social Services Journal 95: 165
Devlin B 1985b Second opinion. Health and Social Services Journal 95: 490
DHSS 1981 Health services management membership of district health aauthorities. Circular HC(80)9. HMSO, London

DHSS 1983 NHS management inquiry. Griffiths Report. DA(83)38. HMSO, London
DHSS 1986 Health services management: resource management (management budgeting) in health authorities. Circular HN(86)34. HMSO, London
Druker P F 1977 Management. Tasks, responsibilities, practices. Pan Business Management, London, pp 137–147
Druker P F 1990 Managing the non-profit organization. Harper Collins, New York
Gale R 1993 Clinical directorship. A foundation course. Rodney Gale Associates, London
Hanlon M D, Gladstein D L 1984 Improving the quality of work life in hospitals. Hospital and Health Services Administration 12: 94–107
Jaques E 1978 Teams and leadership. Health services. Heinemann, London
Levitt R, Wall A 1984 The reorganized National Health Service, 3rd edn. Chapman & Hall, London, p 8
Lowry S 1992 Student selection. British Medical Journal 305: 1352–1354
Mills I 1987 Resource management feedback. DHSS, London
Nelson M J 1989 Managing health professionals. Chapman & Hall, London, p vii
Scrivens E 1988 Doctors and managers: never the twain shall meet? British Medical Journal 296: 1754–1755
Stewart R, Dobson S 1988 Griffiths in theory and practice: a research assessment. Journal of Health Administration Education 6(3): 503–514
Toynbee P 1977 Hospital. Hutchinson, London, Ch 6
West P A 1988 Understanding the NHS: a question of incentives. King Edward's Hospital Fund, London, p 99
White A 1991 Lecture given at Resource management for doctors course, King's Fund College, 10th December
White A 1993 The role of hospital consultants in management decision making and change. PhD thesis, University of Bath

5

Engaging doctors in management

Helen Jones

INTRODUCTION

Consultants who hope that their involvement in management will diminish the importance of full-time managers do not appreciate the complexity of running large organizations. Similarly, managers who assume they can achieve their objectives with disempowered consultants have lost sight of the main purpose of their work. What is needed, more than ever, is a comprehending partnership of the two that empowers both, for the benefit of the patient.

(White 1993)

The following pages describe an approach to engaging doctors, together with managers, in a management development initiative in Yorkshire which took place mainly between 1989 and 1993.

The dilemma described above was a recurring theme.

A group of consultants showed an interest in attending a series of management development programmes. Three or four weeks were spent at business school. The remainder of the programmes consisted of six or more monthly meetings of 24 hours in a mixed group of doctors and managers.

The purpose of the joint working was to address differences in the personal and professional values of the doctors and managers involved. The hypothesis was that such joint working would have creative and positive outcomes for patients and also for members of the group.

Evaluation was conducted by the author who also cofacilitated the programmes. There are many interesting outcomes, if no conclusive findings.

Everyone taking part in this initiative was 'engaged'. They willingly spent time learning new skills, exploring their own motivations and sharing experiences with each other over a period of about 18 months. They were personally involved in management roles and regularly reported back on progress in applying skills and ideas learned within the programme. They reviewed outcomes and revised plans as they worked together.

A culture now exists in Yorkshire resulting from these activities which has brought doctors and managers more closely into contact as friends and colleagues. The management development programmes have created a forum for debate, disagreement, conflict, constructive alternatives and collaboration.

Doctors need to feel that they are unique individuals who wish to take charge of their own transition from full-time medicine to part or full-time involvement in management. Managers need to be included in the transformation as they learn to work more closely with doctors. The transition is very significant for every doctor.

Gaps in understanding between managers and doctors are too great to be left to chance. Doctors and managers need to spend time together addressing real problems in a climate of mutual support and understanding; this chapter describes how such a climate was achieved.

Qualitative research methods were used 'based on the assumption that every situation is filled with multiple meanings and the social world is dynamic, shifting and constantly negotiated by the people within it' (Glaser & Strauss 1968).

BACKGROUND

Gareth Morgan, in *Images of Organization* (1986), says:

In talking about culture we are really talking about a process of reality construction that allows people to see and understand particular events, actions, objects, utterances, or situations in distinctive ways. These patterns of understanding also provide a basis for making one's own behavior sensible and meaningful.

Organizations are, according to Morgan, 'socially

constructed realities that rest as much in the heads and minds of their members as they do in concrete sets of rules and relations' (p 128). George Kelly, in *The Psychology of Personal Constructs* (1955), says, in his choice corollary: 'We choose for ourselves that alternative in a dichotomized construct through which we anticipate the greater possibility for the extension and definition of our system' (p 64).

The author has questioned the individual choices, particularly of doctors but also managers, within the socially constructed reality of the National Health Service. What is it which allows them as individuals to thrive, survive or lose morale?

In 1987 doctors were generally seen as reluctant to become involved in learning about what they perceived to be administration. Consultants were professionals, they said, experts in their fields, managing their specialties. Administrators looked after the rest. The shared activity was often extremely effective but sometimes fragmented. There was no generally agreed standard.

Roy Griffiths carried out the NHS Management Inquiry (DHSS 1983) and suggested that doctors could be appointed to general managerial posts or alternatively could be involved in management within hospitals. In 1986 the Resource Management Initiative began, attempting to make doctors more management-conscious and accountable for the resources used.

As a positive response to both sets of recommendations doctors in Yorkshire were offered protected study leave to attend management development programmes. The funding came from top sliced money at regional level. The author was asked to develop these early programmes for consultants and senior registrars.

Enthusiasts came along. Initially they came more from specialties like psychiatry, paediatrics, pathology, radiology and were only occasionally joined by physicians or surgeons. The organizers of the programmes decided that it would be more effective to work with enthusiasts first. Others would then become more engaged with the idea. This did happen.

The programmes lasted 6 months. Real learning takes place over time and any skills learned during a management programme only embed themselves through regular use in the workplace. Action learning sets were therefore formed. Reg Revans (1982) suggested that people are good at teaching others and learning from each other, particularly when they have an opportunity to put the learning into practice and to review progress month by month with supportive yet challenging colleagues.

Doctors seemed to take to this approach. Working with peers on stimulating exercises which displayed skills of negotiation, managing conflict, communication and assertion they could, often for the first time, talk about the things which really interested and concerned them. In those early days the themes were often about frustration and powerlessness and even fear, as the culture around them became one of general management, not administration. This newly developing culture was threatening to professionals.

Powerful learning networks were created and individual consultants began to recognize their joint strength. At this stage they began to want to work more directly with managers.

STIMULUS TO FURTHER ACTION

In 1989 a sum of money was allocated from the Department of Health to give hospital consultants the opportunity to attend business school. The intention was to engage doctors more actively in the management process.

The opportunity thus arose to pull together more formally the introduction of doctors to management. Managers at this stage were also included.

The timing was excellent. Large numbers of consultants in Yorkshire had taken part in the local management development programmes. They were stimulated by management theory and practice. 'Going over to the other side' and 'putting their heads above the parapet' were phrases used frequently in research preceding the early programmes (Jones & Watson 1989). What were seen as threats in 1989 were now perceived more as fascinating glimpses of another culture, another world, where doctors could gain stimulation and interest. One medical director, formerly a consultant psychiatrist, says:

Six years ago my intention, even before the NHS reforms were announced, was to learn how managers and management worked, so that I could get the better of them. In the intervening years I have continued my involvement with the management development programmes for very different reasons.

There are very personal, selfish reasons such as my own self-development, learning new skills and approaches to dealing with people in all sorts of settings, and finding out how to help managers do their jobs better . . . Attendance at the various courses and activities over the last few years hasn't made me into a manager but it has shown me that management skills are actually 'people based skills' rather than budgeting/financial based skills.

The author's approach to engaging doctors has been, from the beginning, based on the notion well illustrated by this medical director that 'People change things by changing themselves first' (Kelly 1955). Consultants wishing to change things in the National Health Service were no exception to this principle. What made individual consultants behave as they do? What were the values which motivated them? Were those values different from those which motivated managers and could there be any reconciliation of these perspectives through management development programmes based on personal learning?

George Kelly suggests that social relationships cannot be generated with any real value unless people engage with one another at a deeper level than that which usually exists between colleagues in the workplace. His sociality corollary reads: 'To the extent that one person construes the construction processes of another he/she may play a role in a social process involving the other person' (p 95).

RESEARCH AND EVALUATION

The author chose to develop this theme of sociality within a research protocol. When asked to evaluate the exercise, as part of the national management development initiative for doctors, she chose personal construct psychology as the framework.

'Engaging Doctors', the title of this chapter, implies the need to have an implicit understanding of what it is that makes doctors *want* to engage themselves. George Kelly (1955) suggested that a first principle of enquiry was that of 'credulous listening'. 'If you do not know what is wrong with a person, ask him; he may tell you' (Kelly 1955, pp 322–323).

The author was not interested to find out what was *wrong* with doctors but she *was* interested to know how they saw the world and what their core values were. Personal construct theory suggests that we all have core values, probably no more than seven or eight, by which we make our choices about the world and our future. The research undertaken was aimed at discovering those core values. Kelly describes this discovery in his organization corollary: 'Each person characteristically evolves, for his/her convenience in anticipating events, a construction system embracing ordinal relationships between constructs' (Kelly 1955, p 56).

PROCESS

A protocol was designed which involved every doctor and every manager in three separate interviews over a period of 12 months. The first one lasted about half a day, the second and third each about an hour and a half. The research aimed to find out what, for the participants, would be recognized as desirable outcomes from a management development programme and how they would rate themselves, now and in the future, on those desirable outcomes.

The outcomes were then used as elements in an elicitation exercise comparing similarities and differences between them. Following this exercise people's preferences on those similarities and differences were elicited. Finally a change grid was done. Each preferred position was compared with all the other preferred positions in order to identify the eight or nine key themes which controlled the behaviour of the person. These themes represented the core values held by that person.

MOTIVATION

Personal construct psychology suggests that motivation is not something which can be managed from the outside in. Motivation is what stimulates us into action and it is driven by inner forces. George Kelly proposes that it is our core constructs, our values, our anticipations, which motivate us:

When we laid down our Fundamental Postulate we committed ourselves to a particular view of human motivation. 'A person's processes are psychologically channelized by the ways in which s\he anticipates events.' The direction of his\her movement, hence his\her motivation, is toward better understanding of what will happen . . . our lives are wholly oriented toward the anticipation of events.

(Kelly 1955, p 157)

Research interviews aimed to identify the motivating factors for each individual. What were their anticipations?

METHODOLOGY

Over 200 people took part in the survey and were interviewed on two or three occasions. Each person spent three hours in an initial interview with the researcher (the author). There were four parts to the interview:

1. Rating desirable outcomes

People were asked to read and make sense of nine supplied desirable outcomes. These desirable outcomes were rated twice. The first rating was the position currently recognized. The second rating was the desirable position in 12 months' time following a combined business school and management development programme. A list of the supplied desirable outcomes is in Table 5.1.

Everyone was asked to add three further personally desirable outcomes for themselves after rating this grid. These personally desirable outcomes served as the main objectives for attendance on the programme. They were

Table 5.1
Many people have said that desirable outcomes from a management development programme would be as follows. Do these statements make sense to you? Where would you rate yourself, now (please circle) and in 12 months' time (please underline)? One is low and seven is high. E1 Developing your ability to lead, mobilize and channel human energy at all levels in the organization 1 2 3 4 5 6 7 E2 Appreciating the range of management resources necessary to you to manage well 1 2 3 4 5 6 7 E3 Learning to use your personal and managerial power to influence the quality of service provided 1 2 3 4 5 6 7 E4 Increasing your competence in budgetary control 1 2 3 4 5 6 7 E5 Accepting your need to work with and be supported by others 1 2 3 4 5 6 7 E6 Responding positively to challenge 1 2 3 4 5 6 7 E7 Demonstrating your commitment to high standards of management practice 1 2 3 4 5 6 7 E8 Getting things done and making things happen 1 2 3 4 5 6 7 E9 Sustaining your commitment and stamina in a continually changing world 1 2 3 4 5 6 7

Table 5.2
Doctor 1 Breaking down professional barriers Running with the ball (lower down the organization) Influencing colleagues **Manager 1** Appreciating the role others play in managing Building on individuals' strengths Developing commitment to the organization **Doctor 2** Teaching others positive optimism Using time to maximal effectiveness Not being intolerant **Manager 2** Taking off professional goggles Getting into policy not technical issues Improving person management abilities **Doctor 3** Balancing my life – clinical, management, home, etc. Learning about stress management (consultants need this) **Manager 3** Learning the language to communicate with doctors

Table 5.3 An example of elicitation
Interviewer: 'Is there some way in which two of these statements seem to you to be similar and different in some way from the third?' E1 (Leading, mobilizing, etc.) E2 (Awareness of management resources) E3 (Using personal and managerial power) **Person interviewed:** 'Well . . . E1 AND E3 are about personal development while E2 is about knowledge gathering.' The interviewer then writes on a card (see Table 5.4).

Table 5.4	
1a PERSONAL DEVELOPMENT	1b KNOWLEDGE GATHERING

the anticipations and predictions of people interviewed, their motivation to attend the programme. Some examples are given in Table 5.2.

2. The elicitation of personal constructs using the 12 desirable outcomes as elements

The process of elicitation is as follows. Each desirable outcome is written on a separate card – E1, E2 and so on. Triads of desirable outcomes are shown to the person being interviewed. Tables 5.3 and 5.4 illustrate the process.

3. Each of these personal constructs is laddered

'Laddering' is a technique used within personal construct psychology to help clarify the values underpinning statements made. It is based on the view (Kelly 1955) that all our unique ways of looking at the world are linked hierarchically to a set of core values. There are probably no more than eight or nine of these core values which control our behaviour. Hinkle developed this idea in his PhD thesis (unpublished) 'The change of personal constructs from the viewpoint of a theory of construct implications', Ohio State University, 1965. Laddering is illustrated in Table 5.5.

The interviewer asks which is the preferred position for the person, why that is important for him or her and what the opposite position would be. This is done systematically until a more abstract and philosophical statement emerges. This is likely to be a core value

Table 5.5 An example of laddering

Interviewer: 'If you look at the card on which is written: 1a Personal Development 1b Knowledge gathering, which, in general, is the preferred position for you?'
Person interviewed: 'In general I would prefer *personal development*.'
'Why is that generally important to you?'
'It allows *growth* and *creativity*.'
'What, for you, is the opposite of *growth* and *creativity*?'
'Stasis.'
'Are *growth* and *creativity* generally important to you?'
'They are absolutely vital, core values of mine!'

Table 5.6

1a	LEARNING FROM OTHERS	1b	closed to ideas
2a	HAVING DIRECTION/VISION	2b	reactive/no vision
3a	GETTING MOST OUT OF WORK	3b	budget controlling focus
4a	CHANGE THE UNDERDOG	4b	complacency
5a	WORKING WITH OTHERS	5b	doing it all yourself
6a	EXCITEMENT AND BUZZ	6b	dull and low level
7a	DOING THE BEST YOU CAN	7b	not using skills/talents
8a	STAMINA	8b	burnout
9a	GETTING REAL THINGS DONE	9b	just playing

Table 5.7 Extract from change grid

If you were to wake up tomorrow and find that you could keep your preferred position (IN CAPITALS) on one of these bipolar personal constructs but had to change to the other side on the other one, on which would you more easily move?

1a GROWTH AND CREATIVITY   1b Stasis
2a LOYALTY   2b Disloyalty

Table 5.8

If you were to wake up tomorrow to find that you could keep the preferred position on one of these bipolar personal constructs but had therefore to change to the opposite position on the second one, to which non-preferred position would you move?

1A 1B 2A 2B 3A 3B 4A 4B 5A 5B 6A 6B
2A 2B 3A 3B 4A 4B 5A 5B 6A 6B
1A 1B 2A 2B 3A 3B 4A 4B 5A 5B
3A 3B 4A 4B 5A 5B 4A 4B
1A 1B 2A 2B 3A 3B 5A 5B
4A 4B 5A 5B 6A 6B

and so on

---

underpinning the first statement. Unfortunately not all ladders come out as clearly as this one!

All the laddered personal constructs (personal values) are written on cards. The most important nine are selected by the person interviewed to be used in a change grid. Table 5.6 illustrates one person's choice.

In a change grid people are asked to prioritize between their personal constructs in a very specific way. They are asked, systematically, to make choices between their preferred positions so that on each occasion one preferred position is lost. Fortunately the loss is in the imagination only as the choices are extremely hard. Table 5.7 shows the form of questioning used by the interviewer.

If someone believes in *growth and creativity* and *loyalty* (two of the author's core constructs) it will not be easy to reject either of these positions. Is stasis preferable to disloyalty? In the last resort the author has to choose *loyalty* and is therefore forced to accept, temporarily, *stasis*.

After all nine cards have been considered in this way the result is genuinely felt by the person questioned. Individual core values are highlighted, scrutinized and put to the test in a way which is very powerful. The change grid identifies the comparative importance of each of the chosen personal constructs (values) and is self-evident to the person concerned. The principles by which the person lives his or her life are clearly prioritized and values held dearly are well articulated. Table 5.8 shows a section of a change grid.

Coping with the threat of change

The results of a change grid are useful, powerful pieces of information for a person about to embark on a development experience or change of career. Change is easy when the new experience is in accord with personal values but may be very threatening if unique personal constructs or attitudes about what is significant in the world are challenged. Doctors moving into management are very likely to be challenged in profound ways.

4. A core process interview follows

Eight incidents in the person's life from birth to the present day are reviewed with a particular focus on the happy times when they felt good about themselves and their surroundings. A description of this approach from *Biography in Management and Organization Development* (Jones 1992) follows:

In brief, each person is asked to divide their lives into four or five sections, from birth to the present day. In each section, from the youngest age until now, I ask them to recall moments, feelings, sensations, and experiences which were, for them, fulfilling and motivating. These are times of feeling at one with the world and with themselves. My questioning of these memories is quite discreet. The focus is to identify what were the special qualities, the important patterns and themes which were around at the time of those moments. The incidents are written down by the interviewer.

In the script the interviewer highlights what for them is the important statement which links the events and gives purpose to their lives. Nearly always, people look and feel very good at such identification. Often they say they have not thought in this way before. Always they feel there is a 'personal truth' being expressed. It feels good. The blocks to development are now considered. Most of these have already emerged in the change grid.

The important focus of the core process exercise is to identify what is positive and fulfilling. Kelly's theory suggests that we will always choose for ourselves that option for the future which gives us maximum room for development. The core process exercise reflects how we have reacted to such choices in the past when we have felt successful and good about ourselves. It allows the option of choosing to recall a 'good' self, a validated self (Rowan 1989).

The statements which emerge from these stories are usually quite simple but they are always acknowledged by the storytellers as an accurate reflection of their own motivating experience. Table 5.9 gives examples of some of the core process statements.

At the end of the interview the findings from the two kinds of process – change grid and core process interview – are compared. They are often very similar in outcome though different in form. The one validates the other.

People being interviewed are very 'engaged' in the process. The interview itself is a developmental experience and is usually remembered vividly and with some emotion. Core process interviewing follows change grid interviewing so that the final feeling experienced is a positive and validating one.

Table 5.9 Some care process statements

'It is important to be confident in my technical and professional self. I am not God's gift and do have limitations. However others do too and will support me. We are all in the same boat, together we can go forward.'

'I enjoy being a competitive person who is anxious to achieve and contribute and be recognized. Meeting the right person in the right place at the right time, to have some luck and make the right decisions are important to me.'

'I have an appreciation of coming from a solid family . . . so many of my youthful dreams have come true allowing me to live a life of contentment, enjoyment of interests, family and environment. I have to take responsibility for knowledge and influence.'

'I have to have a challenge to go for and to be interested in doing because I think I can make a personal contribution. What motivates me and involves me is dealing with people.'

'The burning things that keep me to the centre part of the pack are having fun with company, having long-term responsibility and feeling free to do my own thing. I can and will change once someone criticizes me but I will not let things interfere with my own time, me. As well, I still need to be wanted!'

TWO INTERVIEWS – ONE THEME
Developing self-awareness

The reason for this approach stems from the principle referred to above – that people change things by changing themselves first. Identification of core values through the process described above is important. Unless people are consciously aware of the hidden drives which motivate them as individuals they will be able neither to choose to accept nor to resist change which is perceived as an imposition.

Change

Doctors and managers are currently being asked to change at a very rapid pace. Many people describe themselves as upset, confused, irritated or frustrated by the changes. If people know their own core values they are better able both to understand the frustration and to appreciate the excitement they may be feeling in the face of such rapid change.

All the doctors and managers involved in this work expressed an engagement with the process and the philosophy. They treated the experience as one of being mentored.

DESIGN OF MANAGEMENT DEVELOPMENT PROGRAMMES

The findings from this research project informed programmes designed to bring doctors and managers together in a working and developmental context. Enough information was available to ensure that doctors and managers taking part could work together although their values were often very different. Debate was sharp and challenging. Work in action learning sets complemented large group work. Support was available as well as challenge. Gradually differences became less evident and mutual support grew. Disagreements were constructive and no longer 'doctor' or 'manager' bashing.

THE COMMON GROUND

The common ground shared between everyone was the willingness to be involved in this experiment:

- being involved personally in the indepth interviews
- taking part in the business school programme
- taking part in ongoing action learning sets
- taking part in a larger group meeting of 20 people.

A negotiation opportunity

Negotiators try to find common ground from which to explore different territories and these programmes were the negotiating area for the doctors and managers involved. Space and time and a confidential context were available for them to explore their differences and people looked forward to these monthly opportunities. Facilitators helped the process.

CATEGORIZATION OF PERSONAL CONSTRUCTS

A key feature of personal construct psychology is the notion of uniqueness; each individual has a unique and individual view of the world. The findings of the interviews described above were therefore difficult to compare with one another. Measurement of change in values and attitudes of the individuals concerned was simple. The four processes were repeated at each successive interview and any changes noted and discussed. It was not necessary to share this material with anyone else unless the person involved wanted to do so.

However, there is another feature of the theory – that of commonality. People do share things in common. They develop language together from shared experience of family, school, education, culture, religion and other activities.

Table 5.10

	Doctors	Managers	Totals
Male	30	25	55
Female	4	9	13
Totals	34	34	68

Did the personal constructs of the doctors differ in any major way from those of the managers? A categorization exercise, combined with a celebratory conference, was carried out with the sample shown in Table 5.10 (Jones & Gibbs 1993).

NOVEMBER 1992

Over 100 people attended a conference for chairmen, chief executives, medical directors and participants held to celebrate the management development work with doctors and managers together.

One test of the effectiveness of this process was the high level of noise at the meeting as people met and began to resume contact with each other.

CATEGORIES FROM ROUND TABLES

In the afternoon they sat at round tables on each of which was a pile of cards. On the cards were the personal constructs they had each produced during their interviews before and after their management programmes. No names were attached and there was nothing to indicate whether the cards came from doctors or managers.

Look, reflect, wonder

The task was for them to look, reflect and wonder about the meanings underlying the statements on the cards. It was interesting to observe the way the task was tackled. It can be disconcerting to be faced with a pile of apparently meaningless cards and to make sense of them. People faced with this type of situation vary in their responses and this group was no exception.

Sorting

Graham Gibbs of Huddersfield University, who helped in the design and analysis of the exercise, commented:

> My impression is that some groups of doctors and managers did 'better' jobs than others... Doctors especially were concerned to 'get the job done' rather than agonize about

what category a construct should go into and preferred not to leave constructs in a 'rag bag' category. Groups had to be warned not to focus solely on one end of the bipolar constructs . . . when bundles were combined at the second stage, there was a tendency to look only at the 'key construct' at the top of the bundle hence missing some of the range and variation of constructs included in that bundle.

Graham Gibbs' comments reflect the very crucial consideration that since individuals are unique in the ways in which they construe the world, the minute they begin to connect their ideas together there is a moving away from the real personal meaning of the constructs. Any group or organization attempting to represent individual views is inevitably going to suffer from such loss of pure individuality.

Graham Gibbs continues:

However, the group of seventy doctors and managers did manage to come up with a small number of categorizations of the constructs which a substantial number were happy with. In one sense, the fact that any subgroup could do this, let alone the whole group, suggests the existence of an underlying set of construct categories which were to some degree exemplified in individual personal construct sets. Several of the categorizations contained a large number of relatively homogeneous and coherent constructs. In other words, to the doctors and the managers and to us, it seems as if the categorizations are MEANINGFUL.

The author's own observation of the exercise was that it seemed to manifest a shared understanding between the groups which had certainly not existed before. A language had developed to help these groups of people make better sense of each other's points of view. There were, however, differences still in evidence. Table 5.11 indicates some of the differences revealed.

Graham Gibbs commented that although the results were not in fact statistically significant they do draw attention to a clear difference between doctors and managers in terms of the kinds of constructs they tend to place in their top three. Overall this categorization exercise acted as a learning and developmental experience for doctors and managers, showing evidence of alternative values and also allowing each to recognize others' points of view.

The significant feature of the exercise is to emphasize that the best people to analyse their personal constructs are the people themselves.

An example of a category of constructs is shown in Table 5.12.

CATEGORIES OF PERSONAL CONSTRUCTS AND PERSONAL VALUES

On the whole doctors were looking for personal development whereas, initially, the managers were looking for organizational improvement through the partnership. Later these objectives began to merge.

There are too many different personal constructs to give a fair sample but Table 5.13 illustrates the sort of things one particular group of doctors and managers expressed as important to them jointly. This list is a

Table 5.11

	Doctors	Managers
Most important construct	High standards, fulfilment	Effectiveness, teamwork
Second most important construct	Integrity, teamwork	Effectiveness, vision
Third most important construct	Vision, fulfilment	High standards, achievement
Top three constructs combined	Fulfilment	Effectiveness, high standards

Table 5.12

Teamwork	People on their own
includes	includes
Learning from others/cooperation	Singlehanded
Work through others	Isolation
Empowering	Alone

Table 5.13

ACHIEVEMENT as opposed to FAFFING ABOUT
TEAM LEADERSHIP as opposed to DICTATORSHIP
MAKING THINGS HAPPEN as opposed to MISSED OPPORTUNITIES
COPING WITH CHANGE as opposed to NOT COPING
RESPONDING POSITIVELY as opposed to NEGATIVELY
TO CHALLENGE as opposed to ACCEPT STATUS QUO
AWARENESS OF FOIBLES as opposed to NOT ACKNOWLEDGING FOIBLES
STRETCHING AND DEVELOPING as opposed to DRIFTING
MANAGING STRESS WELL as opposed to CONFUSION AND UNHAPPINESS
POWER AND CONTROL as opposed to BEING POWERLESS
MAINTAINING PERSONAL INTEGRITY as opposed to BEING DEMORALIZED
ORDER as opposed to MESSINESS

mixture of personal constructs taken from different people but all recognized as important by the group of doctors and managers who considered them.

CONCLUSIONS

'Engaging Doctors' has been the subject of this chapter. It has described how doctors in Yorkshire were helped to take an interest in management. Later managers joined the experiment. This early work preceded the recent NHS reforms.

From 1989 to 1993 research involving over 200 doctors and managers was undertaken. The focus of the research was the values and attitudes held by doctors and managers undergoing change during the NHS reforms. Doctors and managers were asked to talk about the desirable outcomes they would want from a management development programme. They were asked to identify personal values and to look at the implications of challenge to those personal values. They were also asked to reflect on their personal motivations.

Later they were involved in development programmes alongside one another where it was appropriate to address their differences and similarities in action learning sets.

They jointly addressed service issues with an interest in moving them forward in constructive fashion. The assumption was that better partnerships between doctors and managers produce better conditions for patients and colleagues.

What are the implications of the study? The results indicate that:

1. Management development programmes are powerful ways of influencing individuals during times of change.

2. It is important to identify objectives both for the organization and for the individual.

3. Individual values will be challenged by development and change in the environment.

4. It is important to identify the values which are at stake for each individual. Such knowledge adds strength and choice to the experience which follows.

5. Doctors become engaged by the exploration of their personal motivation. They, and managers, appreciate the time taken to explore their personal realities in advance of development work. Their stories are not often told and rarely heard.

6. The telling of the personal story, the articulation of values sometimes not at the forefront of the mind, is very powerful.

7. Core process interviews reflect the values expressed in change grids.

8. What people would most like to retain stems from these happy experiences. The threat of losing what matters to us as individuals is often unrecognized unless these values are described and acknowledged.

9. The whole process is in itself developmental (individual interviews, small and large group work, conferences, review and evaluation).

10. The numbers involved indicate a groundswell of 'engaged' doctors in the Yorkshire region which is likely to represent the view of doctors elsewhere.

11. Full analysis of the work undertaken is yet to be completed.

FINAL THOUGHT

The quotation which began this chapter, taken from Tony White's book *Management for Clinicians*, describes a crucial partnership in the National Health Service. The work in Yorkshire has been successful in addressing the issues at a fundamental level through the use of personal construct psychology and a participative approach to management development.

REFERENCES

DHSS 1983 NHS management inquiry. HMSO, London

Glaser B G, Strauss A M 1968 The discovery of grounded theory – strategies for qualitative research. Weidenfeld & Nicolson, London, p 67

Jones H 1992 Biography in organization and management development. Management Education and Development 23(3): 199–206

Jones H, Gibbs G 1993 Doctors and managers working together in Yorkshire during times of change. Paper delivered at the Kellyan Research Conference at Huddersfield University

Jones H, Watson J 1989 The paradox of training. Paper delivered at the International Congress of Personal Construct Psychology, Assisi, Italy

Kelly G A 1955 The psychology of personal constructs. Norton, New York

Morgan G 1986 Images of organization. Sage, Beverly Hills, p 128

Revans R W 1982 The origins and growth of action learning. Chartwell-Bratt, Bromley, p 538

Rowan J 1989 Sub personalities – the people inside us. Routledge, London

White A 1993 Management for clinicians. Arnold, London, p v

6

Clinical directorates

Tony White

Tempora mutantur, et nos mutamur in illis.
Attributed to Emperor Lothar I (795–855)

ORIGINS OF CLINICAL DIRECTORATES

A culture exists within the medical profession which does not recognize or acknowledge the value of management skills (Gatrell & White 1995). Managers are accorded low status by professionals and this deters clinicians from assuming management roles. Career and professional disincentives and lack of reward for management activity also inhibit doctors from becoming involved. They often consider a prime interest in patient care does not, indeed should not, allow them time. The medical profession frequently have few relevant management skills and often feel disadvantaged faced with experienced professional managers.

Consultants who see their involvement in management as diminishing the value of full-time managers do not appreciate the complexity of running large organizations. Similarly managers who think they can achieve their objectives with disempowered consultants have lost sight of the main purpose of their work. What is needed more than ever is a comprehending partnership of the two that empowers both for the benefit of the patient (Kennedy 1990). Other authors and authorities (Stewart 1986, Maxwell 1992a, 1992b, personal communication) have talked of bridging this divide, as no one really wants a division (NHSTA 1989).

For a long time there was increasing discontent and frustration among doctors involved in trying to run clinical services in acute hospitals. They worked long hours and felt that there was little support from management. They were not really sure what management could or would do for them; indeed, management's purpose was to them obscure, so much so that further involvement of doctors in management seemed only likely to increase the consultants' burden and deprive them of clinical freedom. For many doctors, management was regarded as a lowly function (White 1993), a housekeeping role, a household chore and a manager was accorded the low status of an administrator amongst stars. This view was supported by Handy (1985) in his symbolism of the different styles of management and cultures found in organizations with Dionysus, the preferred god of artists and professionals, as the model of people who owe little or no allegiance to a boss:

Dionysians recognize no 'boss', although they may accept coordination for their own long-term convenience. Management in their organisation is a chore, something that has to happen like housekeeping. And like a housekeeper, a manager has small renown: an administrator amongst the prima donnas is bottom of the status lists.

The dilemma, however, was that existing arrangements were unsatisfactory and failing. Medical executive committees and other so-called executive groups were in fact working at best as advisory groups and at worst as talking forums and safety valves for discontent. Neither could the problems of each consultant or faculty be represented to management through a chairman or the minutes of these meetings.

It took the increasing crisis of lack of funding and cost containment in the late 1980s to bring matters to a head. There was a growing realization that a large proportion of the expenditure of an acute hospital was undertaken on the direct orders of doctors (White 1993). By involving them in the decision-making process these costs might be contained.

Many have argued over the years, especially since

Griffiths (1983), that the health service needs more clinicians to take a greater part in management. The White Paper *Working for Patients* (DHSS 1989) included proposals for ensuring consultants were involved in management in hospitals and given responsibility for the use of resources. Consultants now had the opportunity to become involved in hospital management provided managers were prepared to let go (see Chapter 4) and should be encouraged to take this opportunity to re-establish their role in the management of hospitals.

HISTORICAL BACKGROUND

Cost containment was not a phenomenon peculiar to the UK. For more than a decade American hospitals had been struggling with this problem and their response was to consider cost controls and more efficient management to reduce expenses while others tried to concentrate on the more profitable services. Unfortunately the less profitable services were typically provided by teaching hospitals and to survive they needed to look to innovative approaches in both medical care and management practices.

Medical practices were aimed to reduce the length of inpatient stay by greater emphasis on outpatient investigation and more day surgery. Management practices were changed to encourage more doctor involvement, since as previously stated most of the cost came from doctors' decisions. A new management structure had therefore to be devised, decentralizing control and placing responsibility for costs in the hands of the consultants. This new approach is 'usually traced back to North America, in particular to the so-called clinical director model developed at the Johns Hopkins Hospital in Baltimore' (Disken et al 1990). Johns Hopkins had operated with a management structure 'designed to control expenditures by placing responsibility for costs in the hands of physicians' (Heyssell et al 1984). They adopted a decentralized management system frequently used in industry (Drucker 1973) which for the first time involved doctors in management decisions and shifted operating responsibilities and financial accountability to the clinical departments. Two consequences of this change were described by Heyssell et al (1984). The first measured financial performance where cost increases were held below state and national averages and the second described management factors which were:

1. the necessary willingness of corporate officers to delegate the decision-making authority to functional unit management;

2. the willing assumption of this responsibility by the functional unit directors (doctors), a role they have tended to shy away from.

A third issue considered in some detail by the authors was that the change needed the acceptance and support of professional nursing staff. Finally it required the development of management and financial information systems to support this decentralization. Heyssell et al also highlighted the transfer of responsibility to accompany the authority in making decisions. (This important triad is discussed more fully in the Chapter 9.) This necessitated some strengthening of the doctors' management skills but more importantly it required central administration to redefine its own role, an issue sadly not fully addressed by many hospitals in the UK.

The involvement of doctors clarified and expedited the decision-making process, but did require an extra commitment of time and management support. In addition, nursing directors assumed similar increased departmental responsibilities so a management organization was created that was more accessible than a central bureaucracy.

A fourth issue considered important is the provision of intelligible management information to help with operational decisions at unit level. A final issue is communication. All of these are discussed later in more detail.

Some hospitals have attempted to encourage their medical professionals to participate more in managing the hospital by becoming responsible for their colleagues as part of the management structure. Other hospitals have felt that the extent to which they are truly involved depends on the degree to which those professionals, as managers, have been given some financial independence in the operational management of a department or directorate, an issue discussed in Chapter 4. One chief executive's comment was typical: 'You need to give them [the doctors] hands-on control of the money'. This view is supported by West (1988) who says: 'A great deal will depend on the extent to which managers (professionals involved in management) at each level have some financial independence'. Equally important is the extent to which clinical directors take a corporate view and see themselves as part of the hospital management, West again: 'Equally important is the extent to which such managers (professionals involved in management) see themselves as part of the hospital management or first and foremost as part of their own department'. This is sometimes described as breaking out of tribal groups as opposed to being first and foremost part of, and representing, their own department. This departmental or representative attitude is typified by the following comment of a clinical director: 'I represent the department, put my department's point of view and generally fight to get what my department feels it needs. And also to make sure we do not lose out to other departments'.

It is helpful to recall that there have in the past been specialized managers of certain so-called service departments of the hospital, for example an X-ray department represented by its superintendent or consultant radiologist, the pathology laboratory probably by a consultant pathologist, the audiology department by an audiological scientist, consultant otolaryngologist or audiological physician and beyond that the ward sister, the firm consultant, etc., but they were usually competitors for resources, not allies within the organization and the resources they were given were set by those in local control of the whole service.

There is no one clinical directorate structure; there are many variations and no one example seems to be clearly better than another, but whatever arrangement is chosen, for it to work well it has to be that which is best suited to that hospital, given all the local factors of size, history, personalities and whether the hospital is on one site or several. What has gone before to a very great extent influences what is developed so it is also important to realize that what now might be termed traditional directorate structures are more suited to acute units, whereas community units which have different traditions of control and a looser, more diffuse management structure often do things differently. There are, however, certain principles associated with success or failure. In any study of this, one of the problems encountered is that what hospitals assert they have chosen as a clinical directorate structure does not always bear resemblance to what an outside researcher observes. A vital factor is the true degree of decentralization of management. Again structures and charts are meaningless unless there is true devolvement. Indeed, for success it is probably necessary to decentralize further than the clinical directorates, down even to clinical teams within the service. This may present a new and difficult experience for clinical directors who may then come to understand the reluctance of some senior managers to devolve.

There appear to be no hard and fast rules for splitting the hospital into specific types or numbers of clinical directorates. Factors to take into account are the size of the hospital, the total number of consultants in the hospital and the numbers of consultants within each speciality. And what works in acute units is not necessarily transferrable to community units. The directorate structure should not be applied mechanistically but in accord with the culture of the unit.

In an acute DGH the ideal seems to be groupings of similar specialities with roughly some equality of size. A major centre with a large specialist unit would probably have separate directorates for those units, but directorates of more than about 40 consultants are probably too large, whereas those with a dozen or less are too small. Fifteen to 20 consultants is a comfortable figure to work with but again there are no hard and fast rules. Another useful rule of thumb is that medical and support service directorates can be larger than these figures as they usually contain less disparate groupings. The activity and control of the surgical specialities where services and activities are somewhat different has a far greater effect on hospital income and these specialities often require slightly smaller directorates. Ultimately it depends on the enthusiasm and ability of the clinical director but also on the time and resource given them by the organization. The more support and time given, the larger the directorate can be, although the effort required is not necessarily proportional to the size of the directorate alone. Other factors such as the amount and complexity of work and contracts need to be taken into account so that surgical directorates with many purchasers and contracts can be more demanding than medical directorates.

The greatest danger is that of appointing too many clinical directors who then regard themselves as representatives of their department and fail to take a corporate view. Their number then prevents effective contribution to the management board which becomes overly large and in some instances there are so many that the operational management board is separated from the meeting of the clinical directors. On the other hand a balance needs to be struck, for the other side of the coin is the situation where too few clinical directors are represented on the management board, there are too many consultants in each directorate and the professionals feel undervalued, underconsulted and totally managed rather than involved in management.

Differences and anomalies often appear to exist for reasons of personality, history and lack of management control. There are many hospitals which for local reasons have managed their directorate structures in differing ways, for instance where hospitals are split between two or more sites. In such circumstances certain specialities, even though relatively small in their own specialist hospital or site, may have their own directorate as a result.

Large hospitals with perhaps 200 consultants may have more than 30 (sub)directorates although these are grouped into about six or eight clinical directorates with the remainder as associate clinical directorates. The clinical directors of the associate or subdirectorates are responsible for running them in exactly the same way, except that associate clinical directors do not sit on the management board but meet regularly with their particular clinical director, their spokesman who negotiates for them on the board although he is not their representative (see Chapter 9).

COMMUNITY, MENTAL HEALTH AND PRIMARY CARE MODELS

Most of the foregoing comments apply typically to an acute unit and some community and non-acute units have tried to use or adapt acute clinical directorate models. However, most non-acute units have found it necessary to alter the typical acute model in some way to suit their particular needs. Nevertheless, the principle of decentralizing clinical management is the key to success.

Such units tend to be characterized by being more widespread and having smaller working teams. This usually means that a typical clinical management team of doctor, business manager and nurse manager, that Harwood & Boufford (1993) call 'the traditional triad', is unusual. They describe either a functional or speciality head, usually but not always a consultant, who coordinates all the services within a locality or all the services across a whole unit. Professionals from nursing, social work, psychology or occupational therapy often undertake these roles. Alternatively speciality heads coordinate professional groups or clinical services and report to a general manager in charge of one or more localities.

PITFALLS OF SETTING UP CLINICAL DIRECTORATES

Failure to decentralize

The biggest pitfall is where the old Cogwheel division remains unchanged but the titles of the various leaders and heads are altered. For instance, the head of department becomes the clinical director and the general manager becomes the chief executive. In such an event there is the illusion of change, but disappointment when hoped for improvements do not occur. Stamping clinical director on somebody's back and then forgetting about them does not work. Clinical directorates having minimal or no representation on the management board and no structure for direct communication with that board carry a representative rather than a corporate role.

Neither the management structure nor the hospital environment necessarily determines the attitudes of the consultant to his management role. Unfortunately the enlightened attitude of one or two clinicians will be no match for the majority view of the failure to decentralize. Unfortunately some of the doctors involved in management have been those who want to build their own empires.

Confusion over roles

In hospitals where failure to decentralize occurs there is often confusion over which committee has a management role and can make decisions and which are talking shops, to air problems.

It is important that once the management board is established, clinical directors' decisions are honoured. According to Watson (1994 personal communication):

It can be tempting for a chief executive who fails to get the desired decision from the management board then to circumvent the agreed structure in order to implement his/her preferred policy. For example, funding for a project in a particular department is turned down by the management board when weighed against other priorities. The chief executive then goes privately to the clinical director concerned and does a deal in which the project is funded after all, perhaps with certain conditions. That this is happening will soon become evident to other members of the management board and the credibility of the structures will be completely undermined.

Items at executive committees requiring a decision which is difficult or painful may be referred to other non-executive committees such as the medical staff committee, a body of all consultants in the hospital, to avoid the painful decision and its personal consequences. Too often medical committees avoid taking difficult decisions. A new structure should never be set up without knowing exactly who makes decisions and on what. No new management structure should be published unless it is for true consultation and discussion and unless all the details have been thought through. One or two examples of problems should be run through the system as a trial to check that the mechanisms are fully understood. The means of approaching problems should be clear even if the solution is not. Chantler (1992) sets out four points that he considers important to the introduction of clinical directorates:

1. Professional and management accountability are discrete and should not be confused.

2. Decentralization should be encouraged to produce a broad and flat management structure for operational purposes with clear definition of responsibilities and

authority (which must be commensurate) and accountability.

3. Management commitment of the professionals involved in general management at clinical directorate level should be part-time so that they can continue to fulfil their professional responsibilities. To be successful teamwork must be encouraged and the leadership of the team does not need to be defined in advance but does need to be determined.

4. Adequate information systems should be introduced and these should be determined by the clinical needs which should have primacy as well as the management requirements.

DIFFERENT MODELS OF CLINICAL DIRECTORATES

The range of models found is almost infinite between two extremes of a spectrum. Mumford (1989) describes a typology of roles along a continuum:

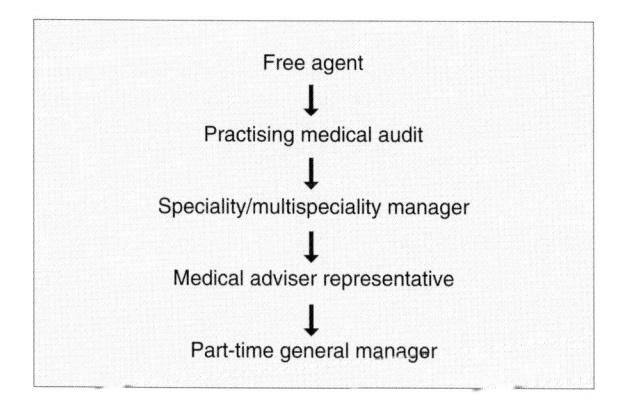

```
Free agent
    ↓
Practising medical audit
    ↓
Speciality/multispeciality manager
    ↓
Medical adviser representative
    ↓
Part-time general manager
```

Although Fitzgerald & Sturt (1992) feel this is useful in showing the different perspectives on patients, financial responsibilities and the sphere of interest, they point out that it does not explicate the issues of accountability. However, as discussed in Chapter 9, the 'vital quartet' (White 1993) of agreement, responsibility, accountability and authority are more important factors in the continuum. There are other flaws in Mumford's model, not least that medical audit (now clinical audit) is educational rather than managerial (DHSS 1989, SCOPME 1990, Batstone 1992).

THE TRADITIONAL TWO MODELS VIEW

True manager

At the one extreme is the true manager, the clinical director, chief, chairman, director of faculty, head of service (the terms vary), the clinician leader of a care group or speciality and half manager, half clinician. They are the manager of a unit or department allocated or negotiating a budget with senior management and responsible for spending that budget, who has two contracts, one as a clinical consultant, the other as a manager. Therefore, properly placed in general line management, they are bound by the ethos of being a manager. They manage staff other than their own immediate junior staff, nurses, administrative, clerical and secretarial staff, for example, although professionally nurses remain accountable to a senior nursing officer.

It is a part-time activity as they are generally practising clinicians so the quality of support staff is vital. These directors are responsible and accountable for the planning of the service, allocation of the resources and all operational work including the specification of internal contracts, taking responsibility for service planning and service development and working alongside a speciality manager, responsible for daily operational management. This clinical director is at the heart of the process and is the key decision maker. This draws the clinician into corporate responsibility, accountability and influence.

The difficulty lies in combining the time-consuming management responsibility with a clinical practice. There are problems of time and motivation to say nothing of the cost to the service of the loss of 'hands-on clinical work'. At present there are few clinicians in this type of role. There appear to be two main reasons given for this: firstly that there are few clinicians with the necessary management expertise for the role and secondly there are few who wish to undertake such a role.

The chairman

At the other extreme is the position previously known as the chairman of division, a representative who has been labelled a clinical director but for whom nothing else has changed. Here a speciality manager agrees activity targets between the chief executive and purchaser(s). The directorate is then provided with management support by the speciality manager who either holds the budget or devolves it to the business manager. Management responsibility then lies with the full-time managers and clinicians concentrate on clinical work, where they remain on the periphery in purely advisory capacities and consequently are less directly or truly involved in management. Managers in this situation are really managing professionals directly and the clinical director is actually a clinical adviser.

There is support for this view of two distinct models

from the Institute of Health Services Management (Disken et al 1990); they describe the differing clinical management structures at six Resource Management Initiative (RMI) sites as also clustering around two distinct models.

The first is the traditional model where a consultant is elected as chairman of a clinical division; a medical advisory structure produces medical representatives for the management board and nurses, therapists, technicians, etc. are managed in their own hierarchies. The second is the true directorate model where the clinical director is accountable to the chief executive and sits on a management board; medical representatives are no longer involved in the management board and nurses and other core staff in each clinical service are managed by the clinical director who holds the budget. Disken et al also see these models as being at opposite ends of a spectrum. These authors did not find a unit showing a pure version of either although as the work was published in January 1990, the latest reforms had only just begun.

THREE MODELS VIEW

Moore-Smith & Darby (1993) describe three organizational models of clinical management based on the work of Disken et al (1990).

The consultant coordinator

This is the old style hospital management with no devolvement of responsibility or authority.

- The chief executive retains control and accountability for professional and managerial hierarchies.
- The consultant coordinates and monitors colleagues.
- The consultant does not hold the budget.
- The consultant is not responsible for the management or performance of other team members.
- Teams are not corporate and not accountable for budget or performance of group.

The clinical general manager

The operational management of clinical services is delegated to clinical managers who may be from any professional background.

- Medical/management relationships are conducted through medical representatives but there is no explicit contract between consultants and managers.

The consultant manager

Operational management of the clinical service team is highly decentralized.

- The chief executive is in contract with the consultant manager who coordinates colleagues and other medical staff.
- The consultant holds the budget for staff and services within the unit.
- The consultant is responsible for day-to-day management, recruitment and selection, staff appraisal and staff development.
- The chief executive is no longer a manager but a negotiator and coordinator of clinical contracts.

Moore-Smith & Darby (1993) regard each of these models as a stage in the development of the role of clinicians in management. The consultant coordinator is the old style of hospital management with no devolvement of ownership or responsibility. The clinical general manager he regards as an 'idealist' solution and presumes a massive shift in cultural attitudes within the hospital and within individual professions. The consultant manager is the classic clinical director model where the directorate is managed by the clinical service team of clinical director (consultant), nurse manager and business manager.

CHAIRMAN OR CLINICAL DIRECTOR

Before considering various models it might be helpful to look at the characteristic organizational features of the traditional model, where the consultant is coordinating head or chairman of a team or department.

- Individual consultants prescribe treatment and care for their patients.
- The chairman is elected from the consultants within the faculty or division.
- All the chairmen sit on a medical executive committee.
- The chairman of that committee is elected by the committee.
- That elected chairman sits on the management board.
- Nurses and other professional groups are managed within their own separate hierarchies and each has a separate functional budget.

Sometimes the chairman of the MEC might be a senior consultant who is not a chairman of a division or faculty but who has been appointed by a caucus of senior consultants within the hospital.

The clinical director model differs in a number of important ways.

- The clinical director is accountable to either the chief executive or via the medical director.
- The clinical director holds total authority for the budget and is responsible and accountable for the service.
- Medical representatives of each and every faculty or division may no longer be represented on the management board.
- The nurses and other staff in each clinical directorate are managed by the clinical director, although professional accountability remains distinct.

It might be appropriate to state that the clinical director does not necessarily have to be a consultant, but could be another senior professional within a department. Ross (1992) stated: 'The most suitable person should be the clinical director, not necessarily a doctor' and Goodrich (1990) argued a similar case in midwifery.

SPECIFIC EXAMPLES

The Johns Hopkins model

Each functional unit is headed by a functional unit director (clinician). Reporting directly to each is a nursing director and an administrator, the three functioning as a management team, accountable for all direct costs associated with the operation of the unit, including services from other departments, such as laboratory, medicine and radiology. Costs that pertain to the operation of the institution as a whole, e.g. central personnel administration, security, accounting, billing and insurance, are allocated to the functional unit. Each unit may use services such as housekeeping, dietary and maintenance from central hospital departments, but the unit may also switch to other providers. Each functional unit has of course to operate within the general policies of the hospital. It was felt that management strategies directed by physician managers were more likely to be successful as they could influence the behaviour of their colleagues.

The original Guy's model

As originally set up, clinical directorates were established, each headed by a clinician assisted by a nurse manager and a business manager. The business managers were mostly chosen from professional hospital administrators but could be a nurse or other professional such as a scientific officer. Some directorates shared a business manager. Management accountability was seen as very distinct from professional accountability. Clinical directors were not elected but appointed with regard to their management capabilities as seen by the chairman of the board and the district general manager.

Responsibility was then decentralized to the directorates so that over 60% of total staff reported within the directorates. These comprised doctors, nurses, clerical staff, scientific staff, etc. Centralized outpatient appointment and management arrangements, admissions, management of waiting lists, etc. were dismantled, the responsibility being assumed by the individual directorates. Rules for bed borrowing were defined and the authority of the ward sister over the ward re-established, including management of the ward budget.

The British Medical Association model

The BMA CCHC Guidance Notes state:

Although the ultimate managerial responsibility for a unit lies with the accountable officer, the executive responsibility for the management, finances and other resources of the unit should be carried by a single management body which contains a significant number of senior medical staff as full members.

BMA model hospitals have a single management body on which all clinical directors sit as full members, this body having full executive authority for the unit's management, finances and resources. Clinical directors elected by consultants in that speciality are responsible for certain personnel and peer review matters such as medical audit, but cannot override the clinical judgement of colleagues.

BASIC PRINCIPLES OF CLINICAL DIRECTORATES

Certain principles seem necessary if clinicians are to be properly and genuinely involved in management. These include decentralization of authority and responsibility and the development of teamwork between different professional groups. It is important that the management skills of the other groups, the business managers and nurse managers, are also developed. It is vital that the clinical director does not remain as a chairman with a new title and no authority, ending up as a glorified middle manager taking the responsibility for reductions in services together with all the budget restrictions. This may well curb clinicians if they have a management contract for the general management component of their work since they can be instructed to do certain things as a manager which they would never contemplate as a clinician. This would be a middle management role that does not affect the allocation of resources. This was initially a common phenomenon and is really little more than the old style Cogwheel chairman, representative of his colleagues but not part of the management chain who has alongside him a business manager who is part of the management chain and between them they manage the unit. The clinical director here does not carry budget responsibility, is not part of line management, but is the doctor representative of colleagues, negotiating with the manager. The only new feature in this organization is that the management structure is allied to the clinical structure.

SOME CONCERNS ABOUT CLINICAL DIRECTORATES

Kennedy (1990) raises concern that there may be serious flaws in the clinical directorate model, ultimately making it unworkable for consultants and bad for nurses and others. He challenges the clinical directorate concept by asking a number of questions about the management responsibilities of the consultants, whether clinical directors can successfully direct consultant colleagues and whether there is true representation. But most authorities would not regard a clinical director as a representative in the way that the chairman of division was a representative because, for example, he should be selected rather than elected and take a corporate rather than a departmental view.

Neither is a clinical director a director in the sense of ordering people, particularly his colleagues, how to treat patients, etc.; hence the dislike of the term by some hospitals and consultants. Some still label the role 'chairman', 'consultant in administrative charge', 'head of the department' or 'head of service'. The actual title is less important than the functions. This reflects the work of Boyatzis (1982) who in discussing the functions of management jobs states that:

> The title of the job they hold is not related to this distinction. Titles are often granted on the basis of prestige value to the job occupant, others in the organization or the environment external to the organization. Having the word 'manager' in one's job title does not necessarily mean that person is a manager.

What is important is that a review and evaluation of a departmental organization should focus on the roles of the clinical director, business manager and nurse manager as a clinical management team. Such a review should include consideration of the following, a summary of some of the views of many clinical directors with some inevitable overlap:

- Is there proper delegation of authority from the chief executive?
- Is there proper responsibility, accountability and authority?
- Is the clinical director fully supported to make best use of skills and time?
- Are colleagues in the department aware of the implications for the hospital of the decisions they make?
- Is there collaboration, cooperation and teamwork?
- Are decisions being made at the level of impact?
- Is initiative, innovation and risk taking encouraged?
- Is appropriate management training given?
- Is there adequate recognition given for the work in the way of remuneration and a career structure?

THE CRITICAL SUCCESS FACTORS

There needs to be clear and explicit coordination at all levels of the organization about its purpose, goals and involvement in clinical management and what the roles of all the members of clinical management teams and managers are. This means that the trust board must ensure effective involvement of clinical management teams (clinical director, business manager and nurse manager) in strategic planning. There has to be role clarity for both the medical and nursing directors. They need to lead and clarify responsibilities for quality standards at both organizational and directorate level. Where appropriate they may need to take a lead in clinical audit including encouraging audit across directorates. There needs to be a focus on outcomes, quality, efficiency and effectiveness, all discussed in detail in later chapters.

There has to be a single decision-making operational management board responsible for integrating strategy and operations, consisting of trust board executive directors and clinical directors. This ensures that there is an effective link between the trust board and the clinical management teams, ensuring that use of resources is consistent with the defined goals. It also ensures that quality patient care does not suffer from financial considerations.

Decentralization has to be supported by the genuine devolution of authority as well as responsibility and support systems have to be put in place. This means truly involving clinical management teams in specifying their requirements for finance and information systems and taking account of these requirements. Managers' roles need to change from direct management to facilitatory roles and support and training may be required to assist this process of change. Similarly clinical management teams may require assistance; for example, financial advice to help with their decision making.

There needs therefore to be an investment in training and professional development with appraisal sensitive to the needs of the clinical management team members. Appraisal skills training is therefore urgent and vital (see Chapter 26). Attention to team building (see Chapter 20) will encourage clarification of roles as well as team development. In addition succession planning needs to be addressed early and as a continuous and ongoing process.

The clinical management team should regularly define and review strategic goals and objectives as well as resource needs and ensure that they fit into the organization's strategy, revising them as necessary. For this, team building and mutual support are essential. Interpersonal skills must not be subordinated to the pressure of financial and informational skills and knowledge. This means that the organization has to make time available to the clinical director and the priorities within the clinical management team must be decided. Here too there needs to be a focus on outcomes, quality, efficiency and effectiveness by regular monitoring and review, as well as a regular appraisal of individual skills and behaviour, training and development needs. There needs to be willingness to risk and innovate and this requires delegation of responsibility and authority to all members of the directorate.

THE 10 FUNDAMENTAL PRINCIPLES

The findings of research (White 1993) suggest that there are probably 10 basic principles for effective clinical management.

1. The roles and the relationships of the trust board and management board need to be explicit and clearly defined.
2. There must be a single operational management board on which all the clinical directors sit.
3. The role of the medical director has to be explicit and clearly defined.
4. The roles of the clinical directors need to be explicit and clearly defined.
5. Decentralization is vital in finance, information and contracting.
6. Authority needs to be truly devolved.
7. There needs to be internal charging thought through with explicit rules.
8. Lines of communication need to be explicit and clear, upwards, across and down.
9. Relationships between directorates and all medical staff of the hospital need to be maintained, encouraged perhaps through an independant medical staff committee.
10. The structure and number of directorates need to be thought through, balancing the factors for and against too many or too few.

The consensus statement from the BAMM/BMA/IHMS/RCN (Harwood & Boufford 1993) summarizes and reinforces these critical success factors and shows that the organization must have an explicit commitment to the following.

1. To progressively improve and explicitly develop approaches to quality in healthcare, efficiency and effectiveness of patient care.
2. To create an environment in which all staff in a clinical group can innovate, take risks and feel empowered to act to improve patient care.
3. To make decisions on the use of resources explicit and consistent with defined goals.
4. To contribute to the development, understanding and implementation of shared corporate goals, both within the individual clinical group and in the unit as a whole.
5. To fully exploit the skills and experience of the clinical management team members.
6. To promote a culture of investment in the education, training and development of the members of the clinical group and of the clinical management team.
7. To ensure the availability of accurate, timely, patient-based information to support the process and create a culture of decision making based on this information.

CONCLUSIONS

The clinical director needs to lead the directorate, take a role in hospital planning, be an ambassador at corporate level and involve the body of consultants in the management process. There also needs to be a changing of mind sets and boundaries by some of the people involved, both clinicians and managers.

The change in culture and the time scale necessary need to be considered; it is easy to change the structure but it takes longer to change the culture. You may not expect to see any change in, say, 2 years.

Once the decision has been made in principle to implement an organizational management structure based on clinical directorates it is essential to dismantle all existing representative and advisory machinery. A bureaucracy is very difficult to dismantle as the bureaucrats within it will resist. Regions, districts, administrators, managers, executive directors and bureaucrats hang on to power. There is a need to dismantle old structures before new ones are added. Without this, old parallel structures with management roles tend to subvert the new structure.

There continues to be a need for a forum for all consultants to discuss matters of interest and importance to them, reflect views, etc., such as a medical staff committee which is independent of the management structure of the organization. Indeed, it may need to meet more often but it must not be and must be seen not to be, part of the managerial structure and have no explicit or implicit managerial role. It is not possible to run an old Cogwheel divisional system alongside or mixed with a clinical directorate system.

It is important that the clinical directors meet with their directorate at least monthly. It is also important that the clinical directors as the management board meet regularly under the chair of the medical director or chief executive. Hospitals tend either to alternate the chair or have one as chair and the other as deputy. It is vital that this management board is not subverted by a parallel board of managers who take the decisions which are then rubber stamped by the management board of clinical directors. The staff committees, often known as medical staff committees, are important in an open organization, but they have no role in the management structure.

One other change is important when considering the switch from a divisional system to a clinical directorate system. The former was doctor-dominated and had no involvement with the nurses and other professionals except as observers. The clinical directorate system works with nurse managers, business managers and heads of departments, all discussing business matters relating to the directorate.

REFERENCES

Batstone G 1992 Making medical audit effective. Joint Centre for Medical Education, London, Module 6, p 1

Boyatzis R E 1982 The competent manager. A model for effective performance. Wiley, New York

Chantler C 1992 Address given at the conference Managing clinical services. Centralization in action. IHSM, BMA, RCN, BAMM, London

DHSS 1989 Working for patients. HMSO, London

Disken S, Dixon M, Halpern S, Shocket G 1990 Models of clinical management. Institute of Health Services Management, London

Druker F W 1973 Management tasks, responsibilities and practices. Harper & Row, New York

Fitzgerald L, Sturt J 1992 Clinicians into management. On the change agenda or not? Health Services Management Research 5(2): 137–146

Gatrell J, White A 1995 Wessex management development for doctors project. NHSTD, Bristol

Goodrich H 1990 Are clinical directorates the death knell for midwifery? Nursing Standard 4(37): 43

Griffiths R 1983 NHS management inquiry. DHSS, London

Handy C 1985 Gods of management. Souvenir Press, London

Harwood A, Boufford J I 1993 Managing clinical services. A consensus statement of principles for effective clinical management. BAMM/BMA/RCN/Institute of Health Services Management, London

Heyssell R M, Gaintner J R, Kues I W, Jones A A, Lipstein S H 1984 Decentralized management in a teaching hospital. New England Journal of Medicine 310(22): 1477–1480

Kennedy P 1990 A better way than clinical directorates. Health Services Management October: 211–215

Maxwell R 1992a Speech at Managing clinical services: decentralization in action conference. London, September

Maxwell R 1992b Speech at Royal College of Physicians workshop. London, November

Moore-Smith B, Darby W 1993 Models of organizational support for clinical directors. In: Hopkins A (ed) The role of hospital consultants in clinical directorates. The synchromesh report. Royal College of Physicians/King's Fund, London, pp 33–42

Mumford P 1989 Doctors in the driving seat. Health Service Journal 99: 612–613

National Health Service Training Authority 1989 Doctors and management development: policy proposals from the National Health Service Training Authority. NHSTA, Bristol

Ross P 1992 Address given at conference on Managing clinical services. Centralization in action. IHSM, BMA, RCN, BAMM, London, September

SCOPME 1990 Medical audit – educational implications. SCOPME, London

Stewart R 1986 Involving doctors in GM. Templeton series, paper no 5. NHSTA, Bristol

West P A 1988 Understanding the NHS: a question of incentives. King Edward's Hospital Fund, London

White A 1993 The role of hospital consultants in management decision making and change. PhD thesis, University of Bath

7

Management development for doctors: theory and practice

Adrian Turrell

OVERVIEW

This chapter, in four sections, begins by describing some concepts and models to explore the nature of management development. These ideas are followed by a discussion surrounding the management development needs of doctors. The third section considers how these needs could be met (i.e. issues about workshop design) followed by some speculations and conclusions about what all this means for the future of management development for doctors.

MANAGEMENT DEVELOPMENT: MODELS AND CONCEPTS

It is important to clarify the terminology, concepts and models used here. One of the enduring themes of management development programmes for doctors which I help to run is the need to debunk management theory; interpreting management jargon is an essential first step in this direction.

The first of these models to introduce is the *inner* and *outer* worlds (adapted from Pedler 1987). This model at its simplest illustrates the nature of our individual inner world – the self – and the outer world which we must engage with. The inner world comprises the various aspects of ourselves which make each one of us unique: our physical abilities, skills, behaviour and personality traits, our emotions, knowledge and intellect, values, attitudes and beliefs. Each of us brings a range of inner strengths and vulnerabilities to whatever external situation we face. The outer world describes the nature of the external realities which confront us. The outer world is more fully represented by a series of interrelated circles which cover the breadth of our external contacts whether socially, professionally or in the family. For these purposes, however, the focus is on the outer world of work, which comprises three broad elements:

1. First, the work role – the scope of our work responsibilities and functions.
2. Second, the organization in which we work (the organizational relationships, cultures, tasks or structures we must participate in).
3. Third, the wider environment in which our organization exists and to which it must respond (patients, pressure groups, GPs, other health/social care organizations, the government, the treasury, professional bodies, other associations, etc.).

The extent to which any of us – in terms of our inner world – engage in this outer world is largely defined by the nature and extent of the role we have and how thoroughly we undertake it. For example, given a strategic role the role holder would expect to spend longer understanding and managing the wider NHS environment than if the role was purely operational.

In this context I am interested in the extent to which the managerial role of doctors requires them to understand and deal with *both* the inner and outer world realities arising from being a clinician in management and in particular, exploring the impact each world has on the other. The premise is that if doctors are to be effective managers (or in modern parlance, if they are to demonstrate the necessary management competencies, i.e managing self, the role, organization or environment using Fig. 7.1) they must master these inner:outer world dynamics. Management development for doctors therefore should offer pathways to achieve such mastery.

At this point it is important to address one element of training nomenclature which recurs below: the word 'development'. This chapter is deliberately titled management *development* for doctors rather than management training for doctors. The difference between the two requires clarification at this point since I use the term in a way which determines the role and expectations of facilitator and participant alike, in relation to

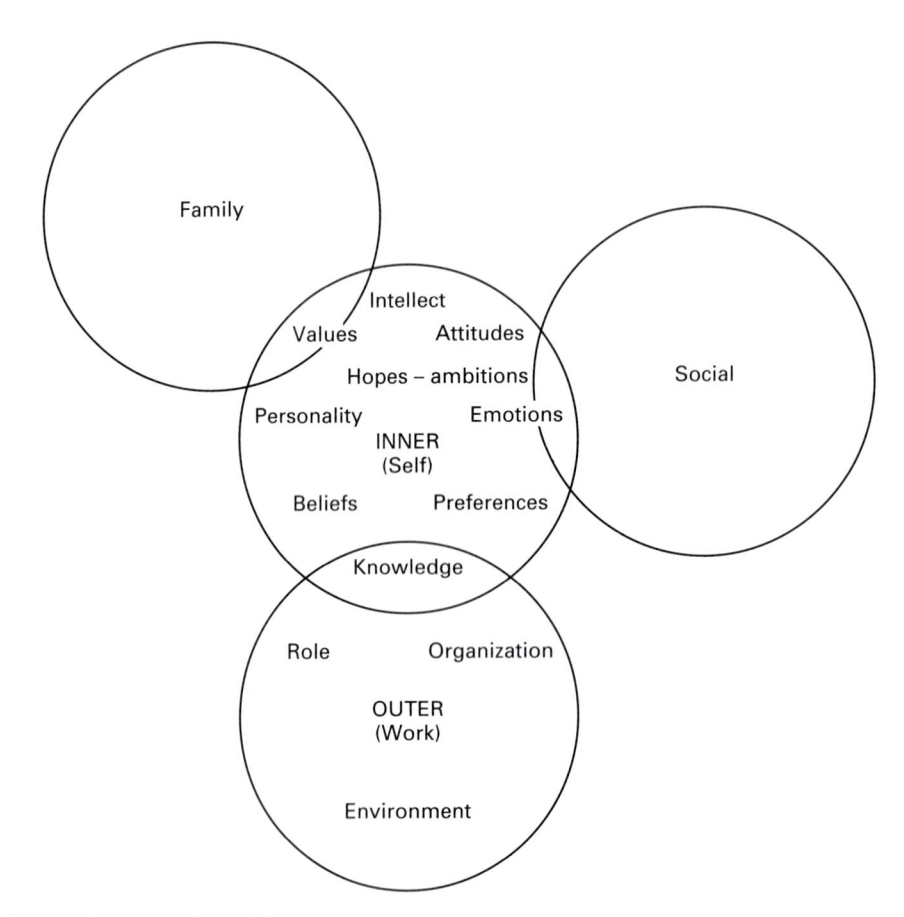

Fig. 7.1 The inner and outer worlds model

both the content and design of a learning experience (see Boydell et al 1992). A summary of some of the differences between training and development is contained in Table 7.1.

Development addresses *both* the inner and outer worlds of Fig. 7.1. Training is predominantly about the outer world only: it is driven by the needs and demands of the organization; it is about grasping the technicalities of role effectiveness. The depth of learning in a developmental experience is greater than that which might be expected in a training experience:

An individual may be said to have learned when his behaviour after the learning occasion remains significantly different from his behaviour before . . . Learning is not an acquisition of new knowledge so much as a rearrangement of the old.
(Revans 1971, pp 100 & 106)

Training may impact on self-awareness and contribute to behaviour change, but it will do so as a by-product, by accident. Development is designed to challenge and change the inner; it will do so explicitly and directly, not by chance. Moreover, a positive development outcome will affect long-term behaviour in a wide range of situations; it is like learning to walk, it cannot be unlearned. Such changes in behaviour become useful to life as a whole rather than just work. Development outcomes therefore tend to be holistic. Training outcomes tend to be specific to a situation, job or organization; their relevance is bounded. Training might be seen as superficial given that it does not deal with individual self characteristics which inevitably affect motivation, aptitude, attitude and hence the effectiveness with which skills or knowledge learnt are deployed and expressed by the individual.

Development activity can be focused in a number of ways. It can be related to:

- the person as a whole (personal development);
- their managerial role(s) in part or as a whole (management development) or
- the organization as a whole (organization development).

Table 7.1 Features of development and training as learning experiences

Development characteristic	Training characteristic
Emphasis on inner *and* outer world	Strong emphasis on outer world
Learning is about self and work	Learning focuses on work demands
A holistic approach	A job-led approach
Designed to link to personal and work goals	Designed to meet work goals
Tends to be non-directive/inner-directed	Tends to be other-directed/job-directed
Control rests with learner	Control rests with expert/teacher
Learner experience/ideas are important	Expert ideas/experience are important
Mistakes provide valuable data in learning	Mistakes are to be corrected/forgotten
Long-term change in behaviour producing more effective action is a good outcome	Increased technical knowledge/skill is a good outcome
Because self is changed, retention of what is learned is high	If not reinforced, knowledge/skill atrophy over time may be high

In each case outcomes are about securing long-term improvements in performance. Thus organization development is often described as a process of changing organizational culture (Burke 1987, p 9) – the values, loyalties, reward systems, informal and formal structures and processes which determine the behaviour of the employee are altered to facilitate easier achievement of organizational goals. As Boydell et al comment in defining development, 'Development involves working with individuals, groups, organizations ... to enable them to cross a threshold into a new state of being that is of qualitative significance to them and their life' (1992, p 13).

The process of personal or management development is complex. In my view the individual manager *develops* (positively or negatively) through their experiences, reflections and responses to the interaction between their *inner* and *outer* worlds. A manager is almost certainly bound to develop in some way through time because of exposure to external pressures and experiences. But it is empowering the individual to recognize and control the scale, pace and direction of that development which often fails to take place. If this fails to happen, though the individual develops they may feel a victim – they perceive their behaviour as driven by external forces, not mediated through a process of self-checking and personal choice. For example, individual time management problems are not resolved merely by considering the manager's volume of work, scheme of delegation or through a technical review of job design. It is also about addressing personal attitudes to work, definitions of success, fear of failure, need to control, personal scales of values and priorities in life. Tools and techniques are only part of the picture of improving the individual's time management strategy. The disappointment of going to a workshop to address issues like time management is often due to the half-truth that technical solutions or new structured approaches to managing workload are the whole answer. The failure to address the relevant characteristics of the individual self in this situation is to treat us as robots, without choice or values, or clones of the perfect rational person.

The concept of management *development* espoused here fits well with some other commonly used management learning approaches. For example, the pioneering work on action learning championed for 30 years by Professor Reg Revans legitimizes and validates the need to deal with inner and outer world issues. So, in his work Revans defines action learning as:

a means of development, intellectual, emotional or physical ... to achieve intended change sufficient to improve his observable behaviour ... the learning achieved is not so much an acquaintance with new factual knowledge ... conveyed by some ... expert or teacher ,

but rather, action learning is described as 'development of the self, not merely development by the self of what is known in the external world' (Revans 1982). More broadly, experiential learning – which forms a significant element of many developmental approaches in healthcare organizations – is described by Woolfe as follows:

Experiential learning is seen as actively challenging people at an emotional level. Without such challenge no change is possible ... learning places the self under the microscope ... for the student who is sufficiently open to look at self, learning offers a big opportunity for re-evaluation, to put the self into new relationships with the world.

(in Hobbs 1992, p 5)

Similarly, self-managed learning (another learning method) recognizes that learning is unlikely to have a very powerful and enduring impact if the individual is not committed to the learning process by investing some of their self (ideas, energies, values, etc.) into the learning experience.

Development is about learning about the relationship between ourselves and the outer world in a way that promotes greater personal effectiveness – qualities which we carry with us not only in the job, but beyond it. Taking these ideas into account, their implications in terms of the design features of a management development experience for doctors are discussed in more detail in the third section of this chapter. Before doing so, I shall describe some aspects of these inner and outer worlds in which NHS clinicians as managers operate, which in turn helps to define the scope and focus of their need for management development.

MANAGEMENT DEVELOPMENT NEEDS: INNER AND OUTER WORLDS

I have suggested that the outer world as illustrated in Fig. 7.1 (as it focuses on work) consists of three aspects:

1. the role;
2. the organisation; and
3. the wider environment in which the organization functions.

Beginning with the last of these, few could have predicted 5 years ago the nature and scale of changes which have been visited upon the NHS with the advent of the NHS and Community Care Act. Professionals and managers have coped remarkably well amidst sea changes in almost every aspect of their internal and external business which have flowed from this legislation and its predecessor White Papers.

It is as well to remember that the environment in which doctors have practised has never represented a simple managerial set-up. The NHS has long been recognized as one of the most complex organizations in the Western world. This inherent complexity has been compounded by the establishment of NHS trusts, GP fundholding and a healthcare market. Formerly the complexities of the NHS were made less taxing by the relatively easy to grasp planning, funding and management structures and processes operating uniformly from local to national level. These arrangements have been exchanged for circumstances in which providers have to manage multiple and uncertain income flows, where the planning intentions of purchasers may or may not coalesce with those of providers and where the investment decisions of purchasers may no longer only marginally affect existing services. This creates a climate of insecurity for providers and a world of wide-ranging change possibilities for clinicians.

Health service manpower tables for Britain (IHSM 1994) suggest there are 1.2 million healthcare workers in the NHS, which is therefore one of the largest employers in Europe. But even prereforms, the NHS did not have a particularly strong reputation for investment in management development. The logistical difficulty of helping so many employees through such radical and ongoing changes is considerable. Doctors may have benefited more than most in the last years in terms of access to management development since the adoption of resource management strategies. The growing literature, characterized by Peters and Kanter (Peters & Waterman 1982, Peters & Austin 1985, Peters 1989, Kanter 1992a, 1992b) suggests that a failure to see employees as *the* critical resource for enlivening and revolutionizing healthcare production is a huge error of judgement. The ideas, motivations and energies of the medical workforce could be harnessed to create vibrant, responsive and flexible solutions in this rapidly changing NHS environment.

Such has been the scale of change that it is perhaps best illustrated by the advent of a new NHS paradigm. Paradigms have been defined by Handy as 'a way of viewing the world' (Handy 1993). Table 7.2 contrasts some of the characteristics of the pre and post-reform paradigms which affect the tasks, structures, processes and relationships in the NHS.

The significance of this shift in paradigm is that it provides the backcloth against which doctors, managers and NHS staff as a whole view their roles and the functions and performance of their organizations. Most doctors have lagged behind mainstream managers in appreciating, and certainly accepting, the nature of the paradigm shift illustrated in Table 7.2. Amidst profound changes such as these – taking place in such a short time – there are also significant if conflicting pressures on doctors reflecting the demands enshrined in separate but related national initiatives such as the Patient's Charter, the New Deal for junior doctors, the Calman Report, etc. These specific initiatives, together with the overall thrust of the reforms, represent by far the biggest challenge to the power base and wit of the medical profession since the inception of the NHS in 1948. If this scale and pace of change were not enough, a tight, if not stringent, medium-term financial climate in the public sector seems assured. Continuing efficiency gains will therefore be sought from the NHS which will demand more and more changes of clinicians.

The NHS managerial environment has also changed almost beyond recognition in the past 3 years. The separate accountabilities of purchasers and providers, the bureaucratically complex relationships between the two resulting from contractual arrangements (particularly in

Table 7.2 NHS Pre and post-reform paradigm characteristics

Prereform paradigm	Post-reform paradigm
Tendency to permanent incremental change	Real prospect of progressive/radical change
Relative employment security	Relative employment insecurity
Professional-led development	Purchaser-led development
Principle of equitable access	Principle of effective services dominant
Dependent/interdependence	Interdependence/independence
Integrated, unitary, uniform structures	Separate, plural, complex structures
Cooperative behaviour	Coalition/competitive behaviour
Input focused/sensitive	Output/outcome focused/sensitive
Individualism and professionalism	Team-ism/corporatism/cross-professionalism
Expectations of real growth	Expectations of nil growth
Preservation of provider status quo	Rationalization of providers

inner-city and urban areas), together with the imperative to meet a growing number of national priorities or objectives (far more than any private sector business of equivalent size would think sensible to address) all add up to a formidable challenge; perhaps even overload.

The two other elements of the outer world – the organization and the role – are, or should be, driven by the dynamic of change in the NHS environment. As such, the nature of healthcare organizations in the next 10 years may change considerably; the impact of the public sector funding situation and local market forces will lead to a rationalization of providers especially where competition exists in populated areas. The advent of community care policy and the developing role of primary healthcare will change the focus and territory of some healthcare organizations, as will the changing demographic profile of the country. The disappearance of the district general hospital model is now being widely predicted as a consequence of some of these changes. Organizational infrastructure – information technology systems, financial management systems, general management structures – will all have to adapt further to the demands and opportunities created by the new postreform NHS paradigm. This all suggests that the nature of the organizations in which doctors train and gain employment will undergo significant change and that as a result doctors' working practices will be directly and significantly affected.

In respect of the inner world, until an individual can manage themselves they can hardly be expected to manage anything else. The ability to adapt positively to a changing role, organization or environment is crucial to the maintenance of effective personal performance. Personal management (for example, stress management, time management, assertiveness) depends on having the right mix and strength of inner qualities such that personal flexibility to adapt and resilience to maintain integrity amidst external pressures are assured.

In expressing some of their inner world doctors, perhaps more than any other NHS group, have the ability to fundamentally alter patient activity and decision chains in healthcare settings. Doctors bring to their work a set of values and although these may not be shared by other colleagues or managers, they inevitably influence clinical behaviour particularly as they become fully fledged consultants. Clinical choices are not just resolved on nuances around technical judgements. This should be recognized and the tensions and pressures it creates dealt with openly and honestly. It would also seem important to be sensitized to the consequences of one's own particular personality traits, aptitudes or preferred work content. Too often professionals get locked into work behaviours and roles due to their technical or academic ability, rather than because of their work preferences and enthusiasms, which can result in morale and motivation difficulties which again spill over into the external world, sometimes in damaging ways but at the very least creating work ineffectiveness. Apart from anything else, self-awareness in areas such as these might further increase the numbers of students failing to complete their training or making poor career choices which undermine NHS performance for years to come and thus quality of health outcomes.

MANAGEMENT DEVELOPMENT FOR DOCTORS: ISSUES AND ARGUMENTS

Having briefly illustrated the inner and outer world issues which are relevant to or likely to impact on doctors, a *developmental* approach to doctors which seeks to improve their managerial effectiveness is preferable to a more superficial training approach. Certainly at this time of great change and challenge to the medical profession it is shortsighted to ignore the inner sensitivities of doctors which can be productively examined within a management development learning framework. Having stated this, it is crucial to recognize that there are aspects of the doctors' inner and outer worlds which combine uniquely to create a particular kind of momentum (or resistance) to engage in management development. Indeed, broadly speaking, individual doctors' inner and outer world dynamics could mirror their intrinsic and extrinsic motivations to engage in management. For example, the developing practice of requiring doctors to answer questions on management at interview provides an extrinsic motivation to raise their awareness of managerial matters. If this link to intrinsic and extrinsic motivation holds, the strongest learning outcomes would accrue from an approach which tapped into both sets of motivations. Certainly ignoring intrinsic factors would be naive and ill-judged.

Inner:outer world tensions are not just about management knowledge and skills but about understanding how management will impact on the clinician – for example, their attitudes, values and relationships – and hence draw on self-knowledge and self-perceptions and encourage self-development. The kinds of problems which medical managers face, such as redefining the boundaries of clinical autonomy and freedom, cannot be adequately resolved without dealing with fundamental issues such as ethics, power and status, which in turn require inner awareness and personal re-evaluation.

Another potential difficulty in engaging doctors in management development is that management cannot be learnt in the same way as doctors learnt and practised medicine. As Carl Rogers remarked:

> It seems to me that anything that can be taught to another is relatively inconsequential, and has little or no significant influence on behaviour . . . the only learning which significantly influences behaviour is self-discovered, self-appropriated learning.
>
> (1967, p 276)

Empirical, scientific or academic approaches to learning do not help to discover much about or define management. Experiential learning is much more relevant. The implication of this for doctors is that they may not be comfortable with, or accept the legitimacy of, management learning methods if they stray far from traditional didactic approaches. There are no scientific laws to govern management behaviour. Doctors, on balance, are expected to make objective judgements; managers, on balance, cannot even if they wanted to.

Adair illustrates the power of experiential learning in some evidence he produced (1985, p 168):

Table 7.3 The extent to which 120 chief executives felt their chosen 'top 20' management attributes were developed mainly by on-the-job experience

Management attribute	Ranking amongst top 20 attributes[1]	Extent to which attribute developed by academic study[2]	Extent to which attribute developed by on-the-job experience[2]
Ability to take decisions	1	1	9
Leadership	2	0	9
Integrity	3	1	6
Enthusiasm	4	1	6
Analytical ability	7	0	9
Understanding of others	8	1	8
Ability to spot opportunities	9	0	9
Ability to meet unpleasant situations	10	0	9
Ability to adapt quickly to change	11	1	9
Willingness to take risks	12	0	8
Enterprise	13	1	4

Table 7.3 (contd)			
Management attribute	Ranking amongst top 20 attributes[1]	Extent to which attribute developed by academic study[2]	Extent to which attribute developed by on-the-job experience[2]
Capacity to speak lucidly	14	4	5
Astuteness	15	1	9
Ability to administer efficiently	16	1	9
Openmindedness	17	2	6
Ability to 'stick it'	18	3	4
Ambition	20	2	5

Adapted from: Adair 1985, p 168

[1] Respondents in this survey of 200 chief executives (of which 120 replied) were aked to allocate a maximum combined total of 10 points to indicate the extent to which they felt the management attribute in question was developed by academic study or on-the-job experience. For example, the chief executives felt that leadership attributes were overwhelmingly developed by on-the-job experience, whereas capacity to speak lucidly was only marginally so.

[2] The 'top 20' attributes *not* felt to be mainly developed by on-the-job experience were: willingness to work hard (ranked 6) and willingness to work long hours (ranked 19) with an equal (3:3) likelihood of being developed by academic study and on-the-job experience; analytical ability (ranked 7) was felt to be mainly developed by academic study (7:2).

The table and footnotes show the top 20 attributes ranked as most important in management by 120 industrial and commercial chief executives and the extent to which, out of a maximum combined score of 10, these 20 attributes were mainly developed by academic or professional work. The right-hand column demonstrates the heavy reliance on real work experience in acquiring essential management behaviours, skills or knowledge. Good managers are not best described as those able to expound theory and deal with abstract concepts or apply rigorous scientific research methodology by gathering all the data, testing all assumptions against hypotheses before making generalizations or taking decisions. The ability to deal with theory, engender innovation and harness the creative power within an organization is of course important, but day-to-day managerial action cannot proceed on the basis of a scientific model. Aside from anything else the day-to-day business of management often centres on being able to utilize the gifts and capacities of employees in demanding circumstances and their behaviour is not predetermined by some fixed laws of nature and thus predictable.

Given these arguments, effective management performance for doctors is best achieved by engaging doctors in management development experiences which deal with the realities of inner:outer world interactions. In this context the model below suggests a process to help doctors to identify their individual management development needs, which in turn would feed into the design of a management development experience. Fig. 7.2 below suggests management development needs are identified by comparing our current stock of management qualities with those required to be effective in a future management capacity. The future situation we compare with might be that where we are working more effectively in the same role and organization or being effective in a different role, organization or environment. Identifying what those critical qualities are in a future role can be achieved by, at one extreme, creating some kind of competency framework or, alternatively, using critical incident analysis to reflect on the behaviours demonstrated in a successful or unsuccessful manager operating in such a role. The areas in which these two snapshots of the current and future role performance do not match become the focus for management development.

MANAGEMENT DEVELOPMENT DESIGN: CONSIDERATIONS AND IMPLICATIONS

From the arguments and assumptions above, management development experiences for doctors should be designed to address two interrelated sets of issues:

1. those relating to the medical managers' inner and outer worlds;

IDENTIFY MANAGEMENT DEVELOPMENT NEEDS

Current state of management
- knowledge
- attitudes
- behaviour

utilized in current management role

Future stock of management
- knowledge
- skills
- attitudes
- behaviour

required to be effective in a future management role

MISMATCH?

DEVELOPMENT NEEDS

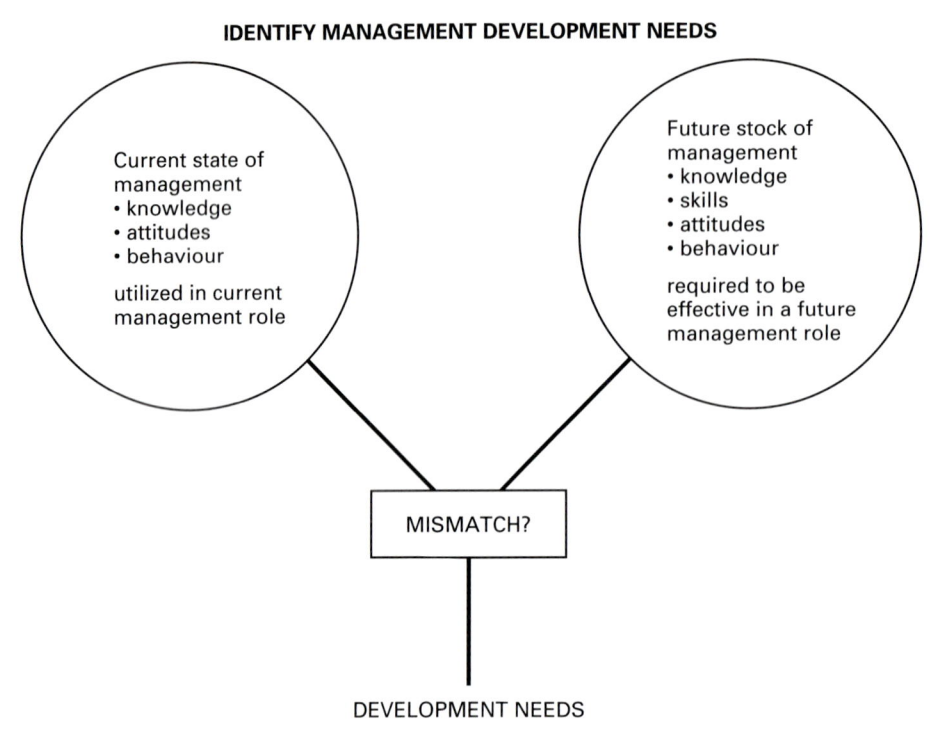

Fig. 7.2 The mismatch model

2. those which help to clarify the management performance currently achieved and that expected in the future.

The link between these two sets of issues is straightforward: role performance, whether now or as required in the future, is a product of how the individual deals with the inner:outer world management demands. Grasping this point justifies the need to move beyond mere knowledge or skill/technique acquisition in a management learning experience. Accordingly a variety of learning methods should therefore be deployed as well.

Creating a setting in which the comparisons between inner and outer world and current and future job performance can be made is perhaps best done by providing learning opportunities which raise awareness about these sets of issues and bring home their implications to the individual through self-perception inventories, simulations, questioning experts or high performers. Opportunity for reflection is crucial in such a process, as is the space to check out self-perceptions with peers or facilitators. Taking stock of a learning opportunity at regular intervals by making links back to simple reference points – such as Fig. 7.1 and Fig. 7.2 above – so that connections can be made is also helpful.

Awareness raising of both inner and outer worlds is something which needs to take place on an on-going basis, although clearly in ways which relate directly to the managerial responsibilities or issues facing the participant. Some commonality of needs amongst participants helps to simplify the learning process within a group. It is best to research beforehand the extent to which the individuals in a group have common needs and the areas in which they diverge so that learning content can be perceived to be relevant to most people most of the time. Evaluation of learning experiences can prove very useful in this respect: openly asking participants how helpful or unhelpful particular inputs or exercises were to their needs.

On this premise, the nature of the common needs of participants will vary between groups targeted. For example, awareness of the manager's *outer* world as a medical student is rightly restricted to a focus on role and the organization as a vehicle for discharging the responsibilities of their role. At the other extreme, clinical directors and medical directors need to have a fairly sophisticated understanding of their organization and the environment in which it works to make informed and sophisticated managerial judgements.

I would argue, however, that inner world awareness should be a strong theme whichever group is targeted. As management responsibilities grow, so do the demands on the person and so does the propensity to hide personal vulnerabilities from others. At more senior levels recognizing personal weaknesses may not be politic. On this basis continuing to develop self-awareness is legitimate at all levels of management responsibility. Yet the focus on self is often problematic for doctors to grasp, given that doctors in training are not encouraged to consider the role of self-awareness in becoming an excellent medical manager. Anecdotes illustrating the paucity of practical support to deal with personal management problems such as stress are commonplace amongst junior doctors. As Woolfe observes, 'Stress occurs when there is a misfit between the characteristics of the person and the environment... stress resides neither in the environment nor in the person, but in the interaction between the two' (in Hobbs 1992, p 15). Dealing with issues such as stress by recognizing them as a mismatch between outer world demands and inner world resources may make these kinds of topics more acceptable.

Individual inner and outer world dynamics are not static. People change, so do their roles, organizations and the gamut of influences and pressures which make up the environment. It has already been argued that inner world issues should legitimately be revisited throughout management careers. The same holds for aspects of the outer world. Knowledge of the range and impact of changing political or professional policies, priorities or expectations should be continually re-appraised, not treated on a once-for-all basis.

The need to confront inner and outer world issues at regular career intervals suggests that management development activity should be a continuing experience for doctors. The reality, however, is far from this. In many areas of the country, doctors are not targeted for any such experiences until reaching senior registrar grades. Even if they benefit from some management training at this point, having access to further management development opportunities as a consultant to build on earlier material is not by any means a universal experience. Forgetting for the moment the important distinction I have made in this chapter between management training and management development, the two charts in Figs 7.3 and 7.4 illustrate and compare typical current management learning experiences of doctors (Fig. 7.3) with what might be viewed as an ideal pathway of continuing (not continuous) management learning (Fig. 7.4).

The 'ideal' management learning pathway shown in Fig. 7.4 indicates that a positive correlation should exist between the breadth and sophistication of management development input to doctors and their time/career path as a doctor. In part there seemed some irresistible logic to this: at the earliest stages of training, awareness

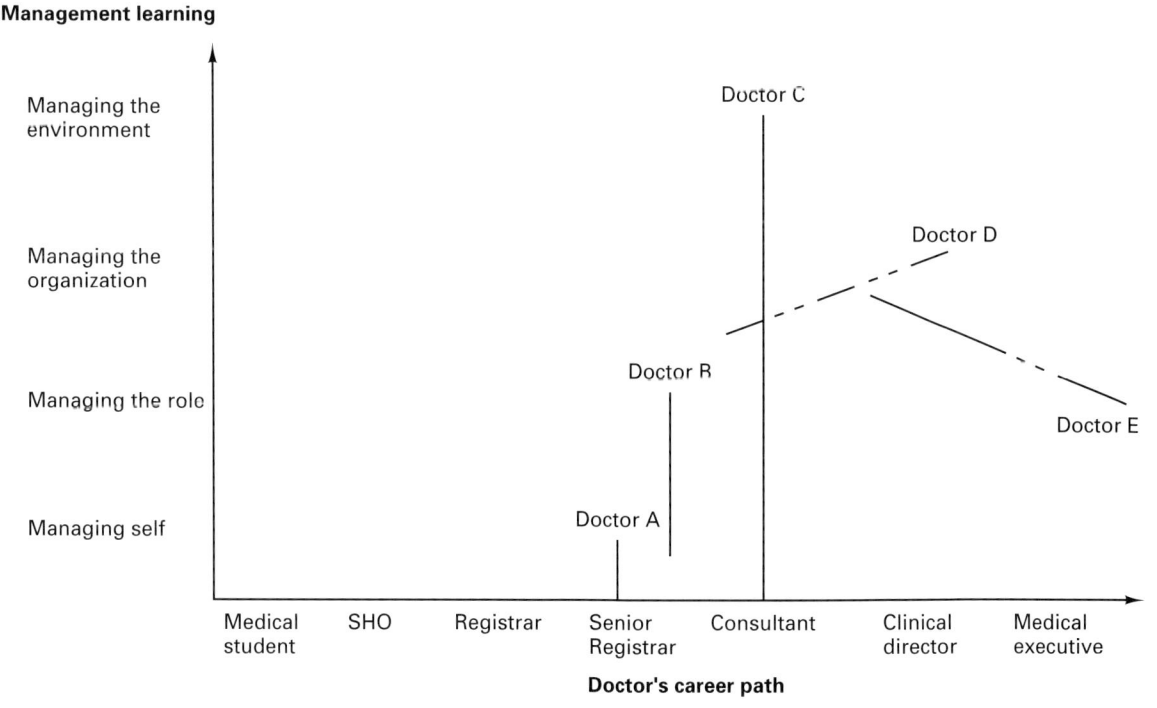

Fig. 7.3 Some realities of a doctor's management learning paths

Management learning

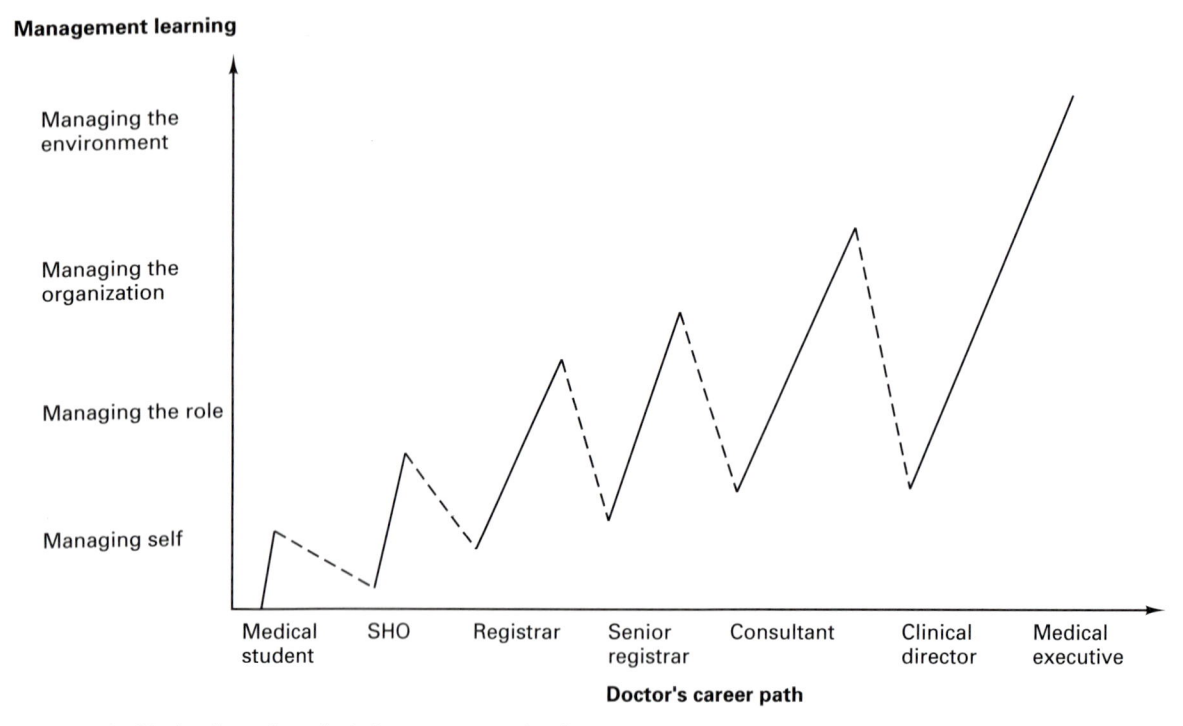

[Chart Y-axis from bottom to top: Managing self, Managing the role, Managing the organization, Managing the environment]
[Chart X-axis (Doctor's career path): Medical student, SHO, Registrar, Senior registrar, Consultant, Clinical director, Medical executive]

Fig. 7.4 An ideal pathway for a doctor's management development

raising at the most general level about the key organizational features of the NHS seemed essential. This should be built on as doctors begin to deploy NHS resources and work with colleagues within and without the medical profession, certainly at senior registrar level when there are responsibilities for managing junior colleagues, the need for more formal input in terms of communication and interpersonal skills, time management, etc. Thus although the relationship between management development input and time in the medical profession may be inexact, I would argue that the trend is not; management learning should be progressive and continually supplemented or built upon.

It is this feature, the early and progressive build-up of management development for doctors, which in my view constitutes good practice and the best foundation on which to establish an effective medically managed NHS.

One implication of Fig. 7.4 which has yet to be seriously addressed in the majority of the areas of the UK is the need to build up management development for doctors prior to becoming senior registrars. Clearly a major obstacle to management learning prior to higher specialist training is sponsorship: who would invest in management development for junior doctors on rotation and when they had to frequently move around the country to gain experience and employment? There are perhaps two motivations which could be tapped here. The first is the fact that junior doctors on a day-to-day basis make decisions which, intuitively, commit a considerable quantity of healthcare resources (investigative tests, follow-up clinic bookings, admissions to beds, etc.). Would it not represent a good investment for them to be helped to make good managerial as well as clinical decisions? A second payback to the NHS from the early input of management development could be a reduction in drop-out rates of medical students and doctors in training prior to accreditation. A focus on personal management issues here could pay dividends. Thus recent evidence from the BMA on stress amongst the medical profession suggests that tackling personal management issues in the early stages of training may be highly cost-effective (BMA 1992), as would be a greater emphasis on counselling skills of senior doctors.

The caveats to the simple graph above – and the relationship it depicts – are numerous. The graph inevitably oversimplifies the position of individual doctors' need for management development which will vary according to their personal needs and responsibilities within their speciality, within their organization and through time according to the national/local management agenda. In practice, management development input should be focused and built up on a modular basis, giving opportunity for applying knowledge and skill acquired outside work back in the workplace to address today's issues.

The other false assumption which might be inferred from Fig. 7.4 is that managing self, role, organization or environment are separate and self-contained issues. Patently they are not. Indeed, they are closely interwoven although circumscribed to a greater or lesser extent by the boundaries of a medical manager's role at any point in time.

Comparing Fig. 7.4 with Fig. 7.3, the latter identifies the instances where management learning is provided on a 'too little .. too late' basis or where doctors are exposed to the 'quick fix': the 2, 3 or 4-day course on management. Of course, the reality may be that the quick fixes or the 'just in time . . . just too late' input is better than no management input at all. Tangible benefits *do* of course accrue from the one-off management training courses: they may stimulate interest or convince of the need for more management development.

In terms of preferred direction, however, the rolling forward of management learning experiences seems to have overwhelming merits: the difference between the Fig. 7.4 approach and the Fig. 7.3 approach is perhaps illustrated by contrasting the effectiveness of trying to help someone cope when continually out of their depth in management waters by throwing them a life jacket rather than teaching them to swim!

Good practice is not just about instituting regular management development experiences for individual doctors; it must be about establishing positive learning environments in which doctors can be facilitated in their learning in the workplace. Attention should be paid to influencing organizational culture and to building up the infrastructure within organizations to support management learning for doctors – through, for example, mentoring schemes, shadowing, journal clubs, self-development or action learning groups, secondment, job enrichment and so on. The advantage of building up organizational infrastructure such as this is that the short-term gains from management learning opportunities (typically witnessed in end-of-workshop evaluations) can be built on and sustained. Since management learning is about doing and not just thinking or testing behaviour in a non-work situation, the need to create opportunities for learning to be expressed is very important.

Notwithstanding all the comments made here about the desirable features of a management learning experience for doctors, predicting the shape and scale of these opportunities in the future is difficult, not least because there are many factors which could influence the impetus behind local management learning for doctors. For example:

- the nature of the link between doctors' learning and organizational objectives;
- investment priorities of postgraduate deans;
- training and development capacity within healthcare organizations;
- pressure to accredit management learning experiences;
- the merits or otherwise of multi-professional training;
- the impact of national policy changes (e.g the Calman Report);
- the difficulty of demonstrating clear outcomes from management learning;
- trade-offs between the volume and quality of management learning;
- development of undergraduate curricula to reflect management issues;
- royal college examination requirements in relation to management;
- recruitment practices for consultants;
- the differences in speciality career paths (compare GPs, public health physicians, surgeons, physicians, community-based and service specialities).

Management development for doctors can be used as a means to numerous ends. The political, economic and managerial will to engage doctors in management is not clear and the central drive to management development is not strong nor uniform. Who will 'own' management development under the new NHS management structure is unclear. Planning blight is a real threat to local investment in management learning for doctors. Whether management continues to be treated as marginal to doctors' training will be signalled by the perpetual reluctance to give space to management on undergraduate and postgraduate training/education programmes, in exit exams for senior trainees and in job interviews. The latter have certainly changed in recent years; the former have frequently not.

In relation to the final point in the above list, the diversity of doctors becomes an issue. Once at senior registrar level, for example, the need to recognize different career progression pathways becomes crucial. Management development experiences must scratch doctors where they itch and here there is an issue about structuring programmes around common agendas: public health, acute, primary and community care doctors share a common training as medical students but soon their clinical interests diversify, as do their organizational needs. Yet doctors in primary and secondary healthcare must work together if they are to be most effective, so finding opportunities for doctors to train together after they have specialized is very important. Similar links should be made with other professions other than in the immediate context of work.

CONCLUSIONS: WHITHER MANAGEMENT DEVELOPMENT FOR DOCTORS?

Notwithstanding the number of possible influences on management learning opportunities for doctors, if it is accepted that management responsibility is rightfully devolved to those closest to where care is delivered then it seems inconceivable that doctors *en masse* (rather than exceptionally) can do other than make an informed contribution to most of the critical issues confronting healthcare policy and practice into the next millennium. It seems self-evident that, perhaps more than any other professional group in the NHS, doctors have the ability to thwart changes or frustrate progress towards economical or political goals deemed essential at national level. Thus, for example, discriminating between patterns of health investment, different types of healthcare intervention and service configuration – the difficult issues of the future – should engage the minds and hearts of clinicians *per se* if satisfactory decisions are to be made in the dilemmas concerning the targeting of limited resources to unlimited health needs. A failure to achieve this – at least for the new generations of doctors who have been or are being trained in the reformed NHS – could easily translate into a failure to effectively or imaginatively deal with the changing realities in the NHS for the next 20 years.

Given that consultants more than any other professional group are likely to remain a part of a healthcare organization for a very considerable part of their professional career and given that for many years they will strongly influence (for good or ill) the utilization of resources of all kinds, the methods by which patients are treated and the healthcare outcomes in a particular locality, it seems remarkable that so little emphasis is placed on bringing consultants systematically into the world of management rather than leaving then standing on the sidelines. Learning by experience – so often a good description of management learning – is taken very literally in the case of these doctors. However, doctors' opportunities to make the most of this, given most doctors' part-time commitment to work in formal management roles, suggest that unrealistic expectations are being foisted on them.

Certainly enormous progress has been made over the last 10 years in attracting doctors to take up management responsibilities and to engage in some management learning. As a result, some clinicians have risen to the management challenge and become fully fledged medical managers, most commonly through their leadership of directorates. The roles available to clinicians willing to take management responsibilities in healthcare organizations may change as supporting managers above or below clinical directors are stripped out. In this scenario, the tables may be turned: as doctors apply themselves in increasing numbers to management roles and as management becomes an accepted part of medical training, the current momentum to cull the much-maligned grey-suited non-medical manager may accelerate.

An alternative, more pessimistic scenario is one of withdrawal: that doctors become unable to engage in management because of growing and conflicting pressures on their time. The paramount need to maintain contract performance and spend more time training juniors will push doctors into a narrow healthcare interventionist role. If this were to happen it would represent a failure to build on the interrelationship between the managerial and clinical cultures within the NHS. It would mirror the inefficiencies of the current separation of clinical and management training for doctors which fails to recognize that decisions taken in primary diagnosis, investigation, referral, secondary diagnosis, treatment or intervention and rehabilitation are unmistakably a combination of managerial and clinical judgements. Managing patients, technology, colleagues and time are the day-to-day dilemmas which clinicians of all colours try to grapple with. Doctors have to engage the healthcare organization in which they work and manage that environment to achieve the clinical results they believe are desirable. Exposing these managerial processes, tasks and values, making them explicit in clinical practice, is essential if day-to-day 'management' is not to be automatically seen as yet another additional demand on the time of clinicians. Doctors at all levels are already managers to some extent: managers of themselves, their time, the staff around them, the facilities they call upon and use, the patients they treat. The question is whether investment is targeted towards making them more effective managers and whether they can extend their repertoire of management behaviours to suit the developing role they may have and the organization or environment in which they work.

Like many areas of the health service, management learning faces both opportunities and threats in the marketplace competing as it does for scarce resources, most of which are utilized in order to yield direct patient care benefits, rather than indirect benefits associated with management development. But survive and prosper it must if the benefits of the reformed NHS are to be fully realized.

REFERENCES

Adair J 1985 Management decision-making. Gower, Aldershot

BMA Board of Science and Education 1992 Stress and the medical profession. BMA, London

Boydell T, Leary M, Pedler M J 1992 From training-and-development to training and development. TRANSFORM, Sheffield

Burke W W 1987 Organization development: a normative view. Addison-Wesley, Reading, Mass.

Handy C 1993 Understanding organizations, 4th edn. Penguin, Harmondsworth

Hobbs T (ed) 1992 Experiential training. Practical guidelines. Tavistock/Routledge, London

IHSM 1994 The health services yearbook. IHSM, London

Kanter R M 1992a The change masters: corporate entrepreneurs at work. Routledge, London

Kanter R M 1992b When giants learn to dance: mastering the challenge of strategy, management and careers in the 1990s. Routledge, London

Pedler M J 1987 Applying self-development in organisations. Department of Employment, Sheffield

Peters T J 1989 Thriving on chaos: handbook for a management revolution. Pan, London

Peters T J, Austin N 1985 A passion for excellence: the leadership difference. Collins, London

Peters T J, Waterman R H 1982 In search of excellence. Harper & Row, New York

Revans R W 1971 Developing effective managers. A new approach to business education. Longman, London

Revans R W 1982 The origins and growth of action learning. Chartwell-Bratt, Bromley

Rogers C 1967 On becoming a person: a therapist's view of psychotherapy. Constable, London

8

The roles of a medical director

David Grimes and Tony White

A la guerre, les trois quarts sont des affaires morales, la balance des forces réeles n'est que pour un autre quart.
(Napoleon I 1769–1821)

INTRODUCTION

Earlier chapters have shown how hospitals have always had an arrangement in which the consultant body has elected a representative to act at the interface with management. The medical director sits in a culture that has changed dramatically from the days of the chairman of the medical executive committee. Not all doctors understand this. The position and responsibility of the medical directors of hospital and community trusts must be seen in the light of major cultural changes. It is a statutory requirement of the reforms of April 1991 that an NHS trust has a medical director as one of its executive directors (DHSS 1989):

> The government proposes that the board of directors of an NHS hospital trust should be constituted as follows. . . . . The executive directors will include the general manager of the hospital, a medical director, the senior nurse manager and a finance director.

In theory this person can be appointed from outside and in some cases advertisements have been placed in the medical press for such positions. Generally, however, they are appointed from within the consultant body of the trust.

The medical director still fulfils the role of the former chairman of the MEC in the sense of acting as a bridge between senior management and the consultant body and in this respect must have the confidence of both. This is much more than, and different from, representing the medical staff views although some trusts see their medical director as also having a representative role (Harwood & Boufford 1993). The trust board must develop a corporate identity with corporate objectives and the medical director must form an important and perhaps leading part of this corporate function. It is therefore clear that the trust board needs to appoint its own medical director and not have a consultant effectively appointed by the medical staff for reasons which might not support this corporate view. On the other hand, the trust board can only develop a good working relationship with the consultants if the medical director has strong support from the clinicians. It is important that the chief executive and chairman of the trust board consult closely with the chairman of the medical staff committee in making the appointment of the medical director.

RESPONSIBILITIES

This creates for the holder the most challenging balancing act of remaining a clinician while being very much a part of the management of the hospital and is a role which is still evolving. According to Harvey (1993), 'Some medical directors provide management expertise, some provide medical support and others do administrative work'. Gough (1993) feels that there appears to be no universally accepted view of what a medical director's role is: 'Few are clear about what their job should entail', while according to the consensus statement of principles for effective clinical management (Harwood & Boufford 1993), 'The role of the Trust medical director is relatively new, and is developing differently across the service'. However, Sims (1993) feels that while trusts may vary enormously in size and scope of services, 'The medical director's role remains the same. The job is basically to communicate between the board and medical staff and to advise on the future development of the Trust'.

The roles of a medical director are many and varied but essentially it involves selling the quality medical services of the trust, guaranteeing their delivery and furthering their development and ensuring that this is the prime focus of the board. In considering the issues it is also important not to confuse the trust boards, which are generally for strategic management and where medical input is from a medical director and the management boards which are for the operational management of the hospital or trust, although they may from time to time need to take a strategic view and where medical input comes from the clinical directors. This is discussed in detail in Chapter 4. The roles of the medical director and clinical director are also different, although in some hospitals this is confused.

TRUST BOARD

The medical director must attend meetings of the trust board, held usually once a month and taking up half a day and would be expected to make reasoned and useful contributions to discussion highlighting the medical view and also the technical and professional limitations of any changes that might be proposed for the service. He or she is the only one member of that board still working in the clinical arena.

In addition there will be attendance required at the weekly meeting of the senior management team of the executive directors. This requires the three key managers, chief executive, director of nursing and medical director, to be able to work closely together mutually respecting each other's area of work. Initially a board may spend much of its time developing the rules and regulations for the new trust but of increasing importance in the future will be the development of strategic roles, seeing beyond operational matters, looking for market opportunities for and threats to the services provided by the trust.

The medical director has a number of direct responsibilities to the trust board and these can be considered under the following headings.

Consultant appointments

When a retirement is about to take place it should not automatically be assumed that the person concerned will be replaced. The medical director needs to have an impartial view as well as a vision as to how the service might be developed in the future with any new appointment. The general pattern for the future is likely to be of an increase in consultant numbers but perhaps a slight change in consultant activity and the balance of activities. The replacement of a consultant may well form part of a business plan and clearly the clinical director and the Director of Business Services will need to work with the medical director in deciding how the service might need to be changed. The medical director needs to work closely with the clinical director and the director of human resources in drawing up a job description and job plan for any new appointment as well as for ensuring that the advertisement is placed. The appointment committee for consultant appointments will involve the medical director and clinical director as the minimum consultant attendance from within the trust. The royal college assessor will continue to be present but it is possible that the consultant from a neighbouring trust and, unless there is a major teaching component, the university representatives may cease to be members of the appointments committee (see Chapter 14).

Junior doctor issues

Major changes are taking place in the hours worked by junior doctors and also in their training, resulting from the Calman Report. The medical director, as well as being aware of these changes, would be expected to bring them to the attention of the trust board together with the implications these changes have for the future of the service, particularly in the organization. The medical director and the director of human resources would be expected to give an overview of junior doctors' issues but the clinical directors would need to be involved in the detail. The medical director might need to act as a catalyst to some clinical directors if they do not appreciate the inevitability and speed of implementation of these changes. A common failing of doctors is that they tend to spend management time rather fruitlessly arguing against changes that have been agreed nationally rather than responding to these changes. Frequently this sort of discussion tends to make committee meetings unnecessarily long.

Continuing professional development

A major part of any present-day human resources strategy is personal development plans for all staff. In respect of medical staff the medical director is expected to become actively involved. Junior staff training is generally well covered by regional speciality training committees, the postgraduate clinical tutor and royal college tutors within individual departments. The medical director would be expected to make certain that these are in place and functioning well. In respect of consultant staff, the medical director would be expected to work with the director of human resources to make certain that appropriate training and study leave are taking place and also to encourage and enable management training for consultants to occur so that succession of clinical directors in the future is assured.

Continuing medical education

The medical director represents educational issues to the trust board but the responsibility for these will be shared with the postgraduate medical tutor. Proposals in the Calman Report put a great emphasis on the quality of training of junior doctors and this will become an increasing responsibility of clinical directors. The medical director is likely therefore to have a major coordinating role working closely with the postgraduate medical tutor. Continuing medical education (CME) for consultants is likely to be a responsibility shared with the director of human resources.

Clinical audit

Each trust will have inherited its clinical audit organization from the previous health authority and this may present a problem in that clinical audit has tended to cross trust boundaries and involve general practitioners and some aspects of public health. The former district or perhaps the trust itself will have a chairman of an audit committee whose appointment historically has been relatively informal. Clinical audit is an important function of a trust in either looking at problems in the provision of service or alternatively in identifying areas of success. There will need to be a dialogue between the trust and the purchasers of healthcare as they will wish to know details of quality and value for money which should be forthcoming from clinical audit. It is the responsibility of the medical director on behalf of the trust board to make certain that clinical audit processes are in place and furthermore that there is a useful dialogue between the health commission and the trust in respect of the clinical audit budget. It is also important that the audit committee and its subgroups at directorate level are auditing aspects of care that are of interest to the purchasers and the medical director will be expected to be part of such negotiations. The medical director will not be the chairman of the audit committee but is likely to be involved in his or her appointment.

Contracting

The details of contracts set between clinical directorates and purchasers will be the responsibility of the clinical director and the business manager. There is, however, an overview required in initiating the contracting process and in general making a trust an attractive business proposition for potential purchasers. The medical director has a role here and might work in cooperation with the Director of Business Services. It is suggested that trusts maintain close links with general practitioners, whether they be fundholders or not. It is sensible for the medical director to hold regular meetings, perhaps only twice per year, between general practitioners, coming forward usually from the local medical committee, and the clinical directors. This can be a useful forum for keeping general practitioners informed of hospital developments and also determining areas of common interest where the service to patients might be improved.

In general the medical director has an important task in informing local purchasers about developments within the hospital, new facilities that have been made available, new ways of doing things, developments in research and the appointment of new staff. The Director of Business Services usually issues the purchasers with details of waiting times and can work closely with the medical director in developing a newsletter which could include waiting times, details of new developments, details of newly appointed staff, educational issues written by other consultants, important messages obtained from scientific meetings attended and perhaps some of the results of clinical audit. The medical director should have a high profile in public events, especially at the interface with real or potential purchasers and needs a suitable attitude and approach, especially with general practitioners, as well as superb communication skills.

Research

Each trust may have inherited from the former health authority research funds of varying size depending upon the type of trust, etc. These funds need to be spent sensibly and clearly medical advice is necessary. The medical director will probably take a role in this, perhaps forming a small committee which might include the postgraduate medical tutor and another consultant with significant research experience.

Quality

Quality is a major issue in the process of NHS reforms and contracts should be established on the basis of quality rather than cheapness. The trust board and the senior management team have a major responsibility for developing a quality initiative within the organization and this needs to be led mainly by those directors with clinical contacts. It is usual for the director of nursing to be given the main responsibility for quality assurance and development but in achieving this will need to work closely with the medical director. One of the advantages of medical directors being primarily and remaining practising clinicians is that they will have a much better feel for quality initiatives and may indeed be able to pilot them in their own clinical practice. They have the task of spreading a quality ethic throughout the medical staff. This may not be an easy task as historically the NHS has been much more concerned with quantity than quality. Indeed to many clinicians today, the quality issue is relatively trivial when the waiting list is so significant and so many people are waiting so long for treatment. Dealing with waiting lists has been a major clinical responsibility but now the purchasing authority has to decide the number of patients to be treated at a given quality and a given price. For all those concerned with healthcare, a major aspect of quality is accessibility to treatment and the length of time a patient needs to wait. It is in respect of waiting times and waiting lists that the medical director and the director of corporate development will need to work in close cooperation with the purchasers of care. If there are organizational efficiencies which will allow a greater volume of new patient activity at the same level of expenditure then this needs to be encouraged. Examples of this are moves from inpatient admissions to day-case activity and abandonment of the previously accepted norm of routine outpatient follow-up of discharged patients. A major quality issue is outpatient organization and reduction of waiting times and waiting lists so consultants should take a radical look at outpatient follow-up activity and reduce it to the absolute minimum, effectively thereby sharing care with general practitioners. This requires a major cultural change led by the medical director.

Complaints

Here there is a certain overlap with quality and the medical director should be involved not only with clinical complaints but also the management of untoward incidents and medicolegal matters. There is a key role to play in advising the board on risk management where this involves clinical issues and this ties in with issues of clinical audit, quality control and research.

Again this is an area of activity that the trust has to manage and the responsibility is usually devolved to the director of nursing and quality as the complaints are usually of a clinical nature. Complaints about the organization need to be dealt with by the director of corporate affairs and complaints against medical staff and medical treatment will need to be dealt with by the medical director. It is an area of activity that should not take up too much time, however. Complaints against an individual consultant will normally be referred directly to that consultant but if there is a pattern of multiple complaints about one doctor or one department then the medical director would need to become involved.

OTHER HOSPITAL COMMITTEES

Any trust is likely to find itself facing major organizational problems with decentralization in such areas as medical records, coding, resource management. The organization may therefore call upon the medical director to take part in ad hoc committees on such subjects. Becoming involved is largely a matter of choice, particularly if there is already a consultant in the organization with a major interest in one of these issues, when the medical director might delegate authority and involve them. The advantage of this is that it spreads the committee workload and gives other consultants opportunities for involvement in management.

DEPUTIES

It is not usually recommended that the medical director has a deputy as it would be difficult to know how a formal deputy would keep in touch. When the medical director is absent on holiday, etc., then the chief executive or trust board might require information or advice as a matter of urgency. The chief executive will need to use judgement as to where to get that advice from; one of the clinical directors or perhaps from the chairman of the medical staff committee.

RELATIONSHIPS

Clinical directors

In the traditional model the chair of Cogwheel divisions met with the chair of the MEC who was the single point of formal contact between the consultant staff and senior managers. Things have changed for the better. As has been described in Chapters 6 and 9, the clinical directors now have a direct relationship with their chief executive. In some trusts, the medical director has taken on overall responsibility for clinical services and therefore the clinical directors report to him or her, an issue discussed in Chapter 9. This is, however, an unusual situation and would give the medical director the most important role on the trust board and therefore by far the most time-consuming. The clinical directors may report directly to the chief executive who maintains responsibility for clinical services and the medical director remains in an advisory role to the trust board rather than in a line management arrangement. This arrangement seems to work very well in many trusts and allows the medical director to remain at a certain distance from the mainstream of decision making and take a much less threatening role in respect to the clinical directors. This position may change over the years once the corporate image of trusts develops.

When chairing the management board of clinical directors, the proposals from directorates can be prioritized and coordinated. Whether chairing that meeting or not, there is a responsibility for communicating the policies from the trust board to the clinical directors and helping to implement them and also providing a link for the clinical directors to the trust board.

The relationship of the clinical directors to the chief executive is entirely vertical and one of the problems is horizontal communication. The directorate structure still represents the traditional way in which hospitals are organized, into departments determined by a certain part of the body (for example, ophthalmology) or simply a medical way of doing things (surgical as opposed to medical gastroenterology). Boundaries are already being altered by, for example, the development of neurosciences centres and oncology departments but perhaps for the future we need to see the trust managerial functions reorganized. These might be, for example, an acute admissions unit, a trauma unit, a day unit, a five day ward, rehabilitation service, etc. Private hospitals tend to work very much in this way with multiple specialities sharing a given ward whereas the NHS tends to be much more territorial. The medical director will have a future role in bridging the gaps between the directorates and encouraging them to work together in, for example, multiuser day units and five day wards.

It is important that clinical directors are a catalyst for change as the pressures for improving hospital efficiency are going to become greater in the future. The medical director should bring in ideas of this sort from outside the trust to see if they might work within it. The medical director must therefore be readily available, able and willing to give advice at any time to any clinical director to help them out of any difficulty within their part of the organization. The clinical directors are the most important part of the trust: the strength of the trust can be seen as the sum of its parts and each of the clinical directors is responsible for one of those parts. If they are all working well then the trust will work well. The clinical directors therefore require a lot of support and the medical director should be at the heart of this process.

Consultant staff

An important task is effectively to communicate the board's views and decisions to the medical staff. As the consensus statement (Harwood & Boufford 1993) puts it: 'In either case, the medical director is the clinical link between clinical directors and the trust board, and is usually a senior practising clinician'. The medical director should be a practising clinician and it is essential to retain clinical credibility. According to Collins (1993) the attributes necessary to retain that credibility relate to the six Ps – patient, practitioner, public, politicians, press and peers. It is only at present in exceptional circumstances and in exceptional trusts that the medical director has become a full-time appointment with no clinical duties so there is usually a normal day-to-day working relationship with other consultants, sharing in their frustrations and problems and being fully aware of current clinical issues.

It will be necessary to keep the consultant staff up to date with changes taking place within the trust, to bring to their attention on a regular basis the appointment of new consultants and to try and develop within consultant staff a constructive approach to change rather than endless discussion about whether the change should have been made in the first place. For example, the Calman Report indicates very radical changes to higher specialist training within this country. The medical director must make certain that the consultant staff as a whole, in addition to the directorates, are well prepared for such changes, to be proactive rather than reactive.

The support for the clinical directors can also be at this level in that the medical director tries to bring about the concept of teamwork within the trust. Traditionally, consultants have been very much individuals working within the health service rather than for it. Things are changing with the new contracting process as contracts are made between purchasers and directorates rather than with individual consultants. This means that in meeting a contract, a group of consultants must work as a team. This is a new philosophy and some consultants have difficulty in coming to terms with it. What it means in practice is that an individual consultant, in failing to understand the corporate responsibilities of the directorate, may seriously interfere with the ability of a directorate to meet a contract, to the detriment of the group of consultants rather than the individual. The medical director has an important role in the immediate future in supporting the clinical director in this respect and in general, helping the consultants as a whole to understand the realities of the NHS in its present form.

Discipline

The other responsibility of the medical director towards the consultant staff as a whole concerns discipline. According to the CCSC working party on medical directors (BMA 1993):

> In certain forms of disciplinary action, such as the intermediate procedure and professional review machinery, the medical director should act as the equivalent of the regional director of public health (see HC(90)9 and CCSC guidance for full details of the procedures). Serious disciplinary matters will require referral to the trust board, with the right of appeal to an independent body outside the trust.

Managing difficult doctors is an issue that every medical director faces. Burnett (1994) identified it as the single largest problem mentioned by medical directors in a questionnaire. Historically the difficult consultant has been tolerated because disciplinary issues have been tortuous and the organization could survive with them or in spite of them.

In respect of the teamwork responsibilities on corporate views identified above, the difficult consultant may be a great embarrassment to immediate colleagues within the same speciality or directorate. Such a difficulty will usually require an informal word and this is best dealt with by the medical director, not as close to the individual concerned as the clinical director, for whom the difficult consultant may be a much greater threat. If the informal approach does not work and the difficult consultant continues to create problems then disciplinary hearings will need to take place. At a formal level these will involve both the medical director and the chief executive. If, on the other hand, there are problems with the health of an individual consultant which is interfering with his ability to undertake clinical functions then the 'three wise men' system should be invoked. The medical director should not be one of the three but should make certain that the trust does have three consultants identified from the body as a whole who have respect and who agree to form a committee of 'three wise men'. They should usually be brought into action by the medical director and report to him. No matter what disciplinary procedures are brought against doctors, they would need to be coordinated by the medical director.

The medical staff committee

The consultants within trusts should maintain a medical staff committee (MSC) as a forum in which all consultants can meet together for a number of purposes. These may be merely social, for example the organization of an annual dinner or a dinner to mark the retirement of a colleague, but the MSC is a forum for discussing major changes taking place within the NHS, changes that are often ill understood initially and require quite a lot of debate before they can be put into action locally. The MSC has a role in bringing consultants forward to sit on representative committees or to undertake roles such as postgraduate medical tutor, chairman of audit, 'three wise men' and membership of the ethical committee, etc.

Finally the MSC might have a reactionary role in demonstrating consultant solidarity against threats upon the profession. It is unfortunate that so much MSC time is traditionally devoted to grumbling about car parking arrangements, a widespread problem with no easy solution and on which much time can be wasted.

It is helpful if the medical director remains a member of the MSC and indeed this is only natural if he is a practising consultant. But he should never be the chairman of the medical staff committee nor a member of any negotiating committees set up by the MSC.

Junior doctors

It used to be common practice for a junior staff representative to attend the meetings of the medical executive committee. With the directorate model, this is no longer considered appropriate as the junior doctors do not have a management function, which is not an ideal situation as particularly the more senior juniors do have management training needs. Their needs and concerns do need to be expressed at the senior management level and this should be provided by the medical director, usually working together with the director of human resources. The concerns expressed by the junior doctors would probably be standards of accommodation, conditions of service including entitlement to study leave and finally training requirements. Especially with the latter two categories, there is an overlap of responsibility with the postgraduate medical tutor and indeed it might be better if the latter were to oversee the training needs of junior doctors. In many trusts, the budget for study leave is managed by the postgraduate medical tutor and when this is a satisfactory local solution it should continue.

Management board

The usual arrangement is for the management board to meet once a month. Such a meeting may be chaired by the chief executive, the medical director or both in turn and involves the executive directors, including the medical director and all the clinical directors. Some suggest that the medical director should meet with clinical directors separately, such a meeting being exclusively for doctors. This proposal is probably merely a hangover from the times of mistrust between doctors and managers, when objectives were entirely different. Where such an arrangement does exist it is likely to prove to be unnecessary time spent in committee and is likely to disappear.

The trust board

There will be little or no day-to-day contact between the non-executive members of the trust board and indeed the chairman, except at times of particular crisis. They are likely to come into contact only at the formal meetings of the trust board, but the medical director must always be available for advice over clinical issues.

Contacts with the chief executive, on the other hand, need to be very frequent and usually daily as there is so much overlap of responsibilities. Chantler (1994) suggests that the medical director should act as deputy to the chief executive. This close working relationship is important if the medical director is to avoid taking managerial responsibility for all clinical activity, which as mentioned above would make the role full time. The medical director and the chief executive must work together as a team with mutual respect and trust. If this is lacking and if there is no sense of common purpose then the trust cannot function as a successful organization.

External relationships

The medical director needs to act as spokesperson for the trust on clinical matters and be prepared to communicate freely with public and press. There is also a requirement for professional external relationships, with all general practitioners, visiting them periodically either with the chief executive, director of nursing or business development to discuss their clinical requirements and assist in securing contracts. It is also necessary to maintain with the chief executive or director of finance a similar continuing dialogue with the purchasers and GP fundholders.

THE MEDICAL DIRECTOR'S CONTRACT

The role of medical director is probably one that will grow in the future. At present most consultants who become medical directors will take on between two and four sessions of work per week. While the National Health Service has what many would consider an unrealistically small number of consultants relative to the amount of work undertaken, it means that consultant clinical time is vital to the organization and to have a full-time medical director might be seen as an extravagance. With the passage of time it might become a necessity but it is clearly a job which will evolve in the future.

The medical director should have a formal contract and the practical details of this are discussed in Chapter 10. The appointment is made as a result of a formal interview conducted by the chief executive and the chairman of the trust. This committee would normally obtain the view of the medical staff committee or its chairman.

CONCLUSION

The post of medical director carries a tremendous potential for work. If the work is to be minimized then it is important individuals trust each other. Keep committees as small as possible; learn and practise chairmanship skills; organize and control meetings to produce decisions within a reasonable time by preventing unnecessary and futile discussion on issues already decided elsewhere. The important thing is that consultant staff, clinical directors, medical director, chief executive and trust board should have a common purpose. This does not mean that life will be easy and there will always be financial constraints and problems previously unforeseen. We hope, though, that these circumstances will in the future be met by a spirit of cooperation which has been conspicuously absent from the NHS in the past.

REFERENCES

BMA 1993 CCSC guidance for clinical directors. British Medical Association, London

Burnett C 1994 Questionnaire survey on dilemmas of the medical director. BAMM conference, Brighton, October

Chantler C 1994 Dilemmas of the medical director. BAMM conference, Brighton, October

Collins C D 1993 Medical director in practice. Hospital Update Plus 19(4a): 42–43

DHSS 1989 Working for patients. HMSO, London, p 23

Gough T 1993 Tackling the concerns of trust bosses. BMA News Review. February. Vol 19.2: 30

Harvey L 1993 Reported in tackling the concerns of trust bosses. BMA News Review. February. Vol 19.2: 30

Harwood A, Boufford J I 1993 Managing clinical services. A consensus statement of principles for effective clinical management. BAMM/BMA/RCN/IHSM, London, p 15

Sims J 1993 What is a seat on the board worth? Healthcare Management 1(3): 46–49

9

The roles of a clinical director

Tony White

Hos successus alit: possunt, quia posse videntur.
(*Virgil, 70–19 BC*)

INTRODUCTION

There has been considerable research on the managerial activity of chief executives and general managers but although some research has been undertaken in healthcare management, it is sketchy and inconclusive and almost entirely restricted to senior management such as executive directors. It has ignored the equivalent of the corporate middle manager and the role of consultants in hospital management activity.

In many ways it is unfortunate that there is no universally agreed definition of a manager's role but it is accepted as often fragmented, diverse and usually reactive, constantly responding to the actions of others. Indeed, Zaleznik (1977) described it as organizing resources, motivating, rewarding, providing goals and objectives, while Mintzberg (1973) identified 10 managerial roles: figurehead, leader, liaison, monitor, disseminator, spokesman, entrepreneur, disturbance handler, resource allocator and negotiator. This will be discussed in detail later.

Clinicians in management need to be clear about the differences between professional and management accountability, although some do not see this as important or a problem, ensure that responsibility and authority are decentralized in equal measure and accept that the role of the clinician in management is as a part-time member of a team providing the necessary range of management skills. The leadership role of the clinician is very important and cannot be fulfilled satisfactorily unless clinicians are still practising.

Clinicians have unique contributions to make to healthcare management and it is around these factors that the role of the clinical director should be established. They should be service strategist, resource allocator and quality assurance manager.

- Defining the service which the directorate is able to provide including inputs from personal expertise, interest and research.
- Proposing service developments and modifications.
- Defining and monitoring quality standards.
- Advising on resource allocation priorities.

Management can be broadly divided into two parts: guidance or strategic management and delivery or operational management. The trust board of a hospital has primarily a strategic management role with the medical input from a medical director and this is discussed in Chapter 8 on the role of the medical director. The management board has primarily an operational management role although it may from time to time need to take a strategic view; its medical input comes from the clinical directors. The roles of the medical director and clinical director are therefore distinct and different.

The broad task of a clinical director is primarily operational management. Secondly, although not a representative of the directorate, in reflecting a 'clinical voice' the clinical director should have a voice in strategy. Thirdly, it is vital that they must have an adequate voice in the corporate decision-making process. This chapter is limited primarily to doctors' involvement in the management structure at directorate level.

As discussed in Chapter 6, many hospitals have increasingly been experimenting with variations of the so-called clinical directorate management structure. This is the latest in a series of efforts, discussed in earlier chapters, to secure the active participation of clinical staff in the management of a hospital. A previous chief executive of the NHS made this plea at a seminar on clinical directorates (Nichol 1991): 'Doctors and managers must build up a relationship of mutual dependence if the NHS reforms are to work'. He went on to say that there was a need to sustain the unique doctor–patient relationship and then build a new and mutually supportive doctor–manager relationship, an issue addressed in other chapters.

CLINICAL DIRECTOR: ELECTED OR SELECTED?

There is confusion over whether a clinical director is or is not the representative of clinical colleagues. There are important differences between election and selection and it is an issue underlying a number of problems that have surfaced. As Jaques says (1978): 'Elected representatives must be distinguished from individuals who are appointed by some external agency to advisory or executive bodies because they are typical of the group from which they come'. The representative can have more problems with and complaints from colleagues, particularly in difficult decisions, because he is a representative rather than an appointee, as the basis of the roles are different. It is important therefore for this difference to be understood.

How many clinical directors are the most effective number for effective corporate management and decision making? It might be considered possible to have every faculty, speciality, department and cost centre represented on the management board and this would produce a very flat management structure. The BMA (1990) emphasize, 'the requirement that the management body is not too large to be unworkable'. But in their latest guidance (BMA 1994) they state that:

Some units have combined some specialities to form superdirectorates. Although this has often been for reasons connected with ease of decision making and to avoid too large a board, it has also lead to problems of accountability and conflicting areas of interest for specialities.

One problem, however, is that if every faculty and speciality is represented, this often causes confusion in the minds of the clinical directors who then are more likely to view their role as representatives of their department, continuing to exhibit tribalistic, departmental attitudes, whereas they should be exhibiting corporate and visionary attitudes.

There is the strongest identification with groupings of patients rather than a profession. In other words doctors identify with their department and speciality and feel only secondary loyalty to the hospital. If you ask a consultant what they do for a living they invariably say, 'I'm a surgeon', 'I'm a doctor', 'I'm an ophthalmologist'. They never say 'I work for St Elsewhere's'.

Similarly staff feel more responsible for standards of care throughout the directorate rather than exclusively those of their own profession. Tribalism has to be confronted with more explicit shared responsibility. This entails a consciously managed process which must be seen to erode traditional tribalism. These attitudes can be summed up by the following typical comments from clinical directors: 'I put my department's point of view'; 'I make sure my department doesn't lose out'; 'I gain a sympathetic hearing from my colleagues for the problems of my department'; 'I represent my department and enable it to get the support of others for things we need'. These comments usually reflect a centralized management attitude in the organization. There has to be more relevant participation in the running and development of the service and a commitment to corporate management. It is the difficult shift from fighting one's corner to fighting for someone else's.

Clinical directors in truly devolved hospitals do recognize that their role is not as representative when they begin to move towards not just representing themselves or their own speciality but speaking on behalf of other people, absorbing the interests of other groups and taking on board the five-year plans of others and trying to mesh them into a larger organization, accepting that for the greater good, their directorate or department may need to yield to another.

GENERAL PRINCIPLES

The appointment of a clinical director needs the support of the majority of medical staff within the directorate. The clinical director is the organizational head of the directorate, responsible for the organizational and strategic management, although the day-to-day management minutiae usually need to be delegated to the business and nurse managers. The clinical director is line manager of the nurse and business managers and therefore responsible for such management duties as objective setting and performance appraisal for these staff.

He is accountable for the management performance of clinicians who have accepted budgetary responsibility within the directorate but not clinical responsibility for the diagnosis and treatment of individual patients of those other clinicians. Actual job descriptions vary greatly even within provider organizations (Harwood & Boufford 1993) but there are certain broad features and commonalities as well as some underlying basic requirements and themes.

RESPONSIBILITY, ACCOUNTABILITY AND AUTHORITY

These are the three vital criteria for a successful clinical director and each requires defining. Their importance is also discussed in Chapter 13. The division of responsibilities must be clear and the degree of authority vested in the clinical directors unambiguous, for without this clarity, accountability will be indistinct.

The definition of responsibility is relatively easy to agree but responsibility for what has also to be agreed. A common view is that budgetary authority should be for all staff – medical, nursing, secretarial, administrative and other professionals – and non-staff, including medical and surgical equipment and drugs, ward supplies, etc. But the reality depends on the model chosen and local decisions and agreements. And responsibility to whom? This should be to the management board but responsibilities to the unit need to be considered, as well as the directorate itself, the faculty, the department and the speciality.

There is also the question of loyalty and responsibility. Are they different? Responsibility involves being accountable. Does loyalty mean adopting hospital policy and accepting the constraints of management or should it mean doing what one thinks is best for the organization in the long term? Kanter (1989) offers a prospect in post-entrepreneurial organizations of a different definition of loyalty:

There is often no such thing as a 'chain' of command, and people work under different leadership for different purposes... There is encouragement for people to test limits, challenge traditions and move in new directions... Decentralization of decision making responsibility puts more power in the hands of people at lower levels to make decisions and exercise judgement... Professionalism... transcends the organization... Post-entrepreneurial organizations produce so much change that they cannot offer the same incentive for unquestioning obedience.

Accountability

As part of the triad with responsibility and authority comes accountability. This invariably increases the focus of budgetary awareness, better financial information is then sought and budgetary performance more closely monitored. The responsibilities require accountability, not only for the level and quality of service but also for the production of data which demonstrate and confirm this. Clinical audit and quality management then become more relevant and continuous multidisciplinary activities. Because standards are largely determined by doctors themselves, they can then be understood, owned, relevant and achievable.

And to whom are clinical directors accountable? They have not always seemed comfortable being accountable to the chief executive although chief executives invariably felt that the clinical directors are or should be accountable to them. Doctors have tended to feel more comfortable when reporting to another doctor and some enlightened chief executives recognize this, so that their clinical directors report to the medical director rather than the chief executive. A survey by Davies (1995) showed that nine clinical directors were responsible to the medical director and eight to the chief executive. More clinical directors appear now to accept that they are directly accountable to the chief executive than would have been the case previously. Harwood & Boufford (1993) showed in their questionnaire analysis that of 52 clinical directors, 65% were managerially accountable to the chief executive/UGM. Of these clinical directors, 75% were doctors. The BMA (1994) recommend that in order to ensure corporate responsibility, accountability should be to the management board but a meeting of medical directors (BAMM 1994) reflected that:

Whilst in most cases clinical directors are directly accountable to the chief executive, medical directors are increasingly assuming direct control and responsibilities for clinical directors and for all medical manpower type issues.

Authority

Talk to doctors about authority and they mostly think of authority to get their colleagues to do what is required of them. But authority for a clinical director is different. Talk to managers and chief executives and they hesitate at the thought of giving doctors more authority. This is because authority is power (its definitions, descriptions and classification are set out in more detail in Chapter 32).

How do clinical directors exercise authority over and gain the acceptance of clinical colleagues? How do clinical directors influence the behaviour and clinical work of colleagues? They do not usually need to be *given* authority over colleagues as their colleagues already put themselves into a quasisubmissive role by accepting them as director and agreeing to their acting in that role.

The British Medical Association (1990) argues that individual consultants still have continuing responsibility for their patients, although that clinical freedom is subject to the limits of law, ethics, contracts, professional standards and resources but that Clinical Directors cannot commit colleagues to workload or resource agreements, discipline or sanction colleagues or override colleagues' clinical judgement. They can of course negotiate on behalf of consultants agreed workloads and monitor that agreement. They can coordinate medical personnel matters, peer review and clinical audit. And none of this precludes any consultant still talking directly to management about their own practice.

Both managers and doctors exhibit considerable confusion over the authority required by a clinical director to undertake the role. The *Oxford English Dictionary* gives three definitions of authority:

1. The power or right to enforce obedience (not relevant to the role of a clinical director).
2. Delegated power (coming from the chief executive and management board and which is often reluctantly given as decentralization and devolution of authority is a generic problem).
3. Personal influence especially over opinion, which is earned and comes from respect. (Despite the lack of line authority some clinicians do have considerable success in managing colleagues. The processes used by the successful ones are based on representing, involving, consulting, trading, using personal power, the skilful use of information and often the ability to fit their work into a broader picture, all discussed in previous chapters on management skills. White (1993) describes three approaches a clinical director needs and the importance of knowing when each should be used.)

However, not all the tasks required of a clinical director fall into this third category and it is here that problems arise when management and even trust boards expect results which clinical directors cannot hope to deliver, in spite of the board's pleading that they have made the clinical director fully responsible and accountable. In such circumstances, and White (1993, 1994) gives examples, only true delegated authority or power will deliver. There are often tensions around this problem of the centralist/decentralist approach and not solely confined to hospitals (Osborne & Gaebler 1992) and it is a theme referred to in several other chapters.

A clinical director having responsibility for a job, no matter how accountable, does need authority to 'get the job done'. This vital ingredient is often missing and it is here that many problems lie because it comes back to the way in which the system works, i.e. process rather than structure.

Hospitals are no longer expected to provide a limitless service; they 'earn' money from contracts for treating patients. Part of their responsibility is to provide an emergency service, but a significant part of their contracts is to undertake non-emergency work in line with agreements. The new system has not always filtered down to directorate level where they often work with fixed annual budgets allocated by management which the clinical directors have no real control over.

CLINICAL DIRECTORS' ROLES

Mintzberg (1973) carried out some classic research on the 10 roles of managers, suggesting that they are under constant pressure to acquire and disseminate information, to develop strategies without time for analysis, to influence the behaviour of others without being dictatorial, to react sensibly to external initiatives without creating an impression of weakness, all of which require a manager to develop a network of relationships which depend critically on the art of communication. He refers to management roles as:

- Interpersonal roles – leader, figurehead or liaison.
- Informational roles – as monitor, disseminator or spokesman.
- Decisional roles – the planner, disturbance handler, resource allocator and entrepreneur.

Handy (1985) describes the three roles in more everyday terms as:

- leading
- administrating
- fixing.

The Audit Commission (1995) defines the elements of the clinical director's role as:

- Implementation of service and training contracts.
- Medical staff planning (e.g. skill mix of doctors and deployment).
- Consultant job plans – specification and review.
- Continuing medical education and other training for consultants and staff grade doctors.
- Directorate policies on junior doctors' hours of work, supervision, tasks and responsibilities.
- Implementation of medical and clinical audit.
- Development of management guidelines and protocols for clinical procedures.
- Speciality level induction and information packs for new doctors.

THE RELATIONSHIPS

Roles and responsibilities of other key staff within the directorate need to be defined and this will depend on the model chosen locally. Thought needs to be given to the relationship of the clinical director to the medical director, general manager or chief executive. One of the key factors to success or failure is often the relationship between the clinical director and the business manager and nurse manager, or speciality manager where these are combined, and White (1993) has set this out in a classification of clinical directorates. Fig. 9.1 shows

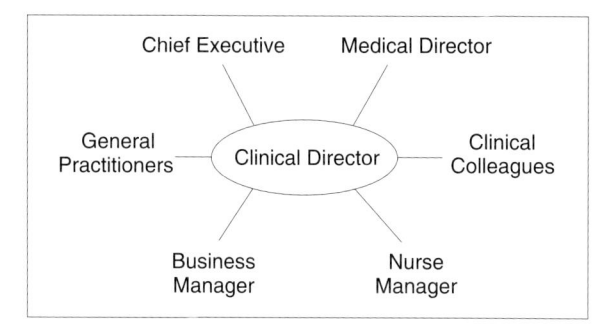

Fig. 9.1 Clinical director's relationships

some of the important relationships required of the clinical director.

SOME SPECIFIC CLINICAL DIRECTOR RESPONSIBILITIES

The budget

A budget is a control device to restrict expenditure and balance the finances of the organization. The actual setting of the budget should reflect the strategic goals of the organization but often reflects the present situation or historical budget setting. The key is to ensure that those responsible for activity which reflect the budget own and are responsible for achieving that goal so it is mandatory that the budget cover the costs of that activity. These issues are discussed more fully in Chapter 22.

Budgets are not fixed but need to be constantly reviewed as at the outset they only represent a best guess at future activity and also have to allocate resources within the financial constraints of the organization. Things do not always work out as expected and views, expectations and demands can change. If budgets can be revised up as well as down it is not a problem; unfortunately there is a tendency for funds to be removed rather than awarded so that games are played such as spending money early in the year before it can be taken away, deliberate errors of coding to hide money, erroneously using someone else's budget, clogging up the accounts system, disputing the figures and proving them wrong, delay or omission in entering large items of expenditure and delay in or failing to reveal income.

The more those responsible for the budget are involved in the setting process and the more accurately they are informed of their financial position, the fewer games are played and the better the organizations financial control. The clinical director must therefore direct and support negotiation and management of such soundly based budgets. Significantly, Harwood & Boufford (1993) found that 66% of clinical directors had little or no influence on the size of the budget, although a similar number had a major or moderate influence on the allocation within the directorate.

Clinical directors will require an understanding of budgets, financial planning, managing contracts, costing and pricing of services and the interpretation of financial information, possibly even encouraging colleagues to identify income-generating opportunities. It is generally regarded as good practice for directorates to have named accountants within the finance department supporting the directorate.

As far as the actual budget is concerned, there are four basic types and the subject is discussed in greater detail in Chapter 22.

1. **Lump sum**: involves allocating a fixed sum to produce a given service with no details of how the money will be applied. Block contracts are possible examples. In some senses such a budget may be motivational for the budget holder, giving considerable freedom of action and leaving little control with the allocator of the funds. It rarely, however, leaves much scope for freedom of action.

2. **Steady state**: where there is very little change from the previous year. It assumes that there will be no change in strategy or the external business although there may be an inflation adjustment. It is very common and makes changes in an organization extremely difficult.

3. **Activity based**: work is broken down into component activities. A value is then placed on these activities and a decision made about how much to allocate to each. Some contracts for fixed numbers of procedures at fixed prices fall into this type. It does allow for some adjustment to be made in the activity of an organization.

4. **Zero based**: the ultimate method for adjusting the activity. The budget is allocated on the basis of what the organization needs for the future rather than on what it does. It requires much effort, involves much trauma and is used sparingly, but can be employed to rationalize services in some organizations.

Depending on the model chosen and local decisions, the clinical director may decide to accept financial responsibility for provision of defined services and should certainly encourage financial awareness among colleagues and participate in financial review of the directorate. He or she should advise on clinical priorities to ensure the directorate stays within budget, ensure mechanisms are in place to monitor financial performance and that corrective action is taken as appropriate operating within the statutes, rules and conventions of the trust or self-governing unit.

Capital expenditure

The clinical director has to be and usually is the most influential member of the clinical management team over capital expenditure within and on the directorate. The problem is usually, however, that persuading the organization to find and spend the capital is really dependent on the presentation of a sound business case for such investment of capital. For further details see Chapter 23.

Activity and business planning

A clinical director has to have a major influence on the activity of the directorate and analyse and identify opportunities. He or she needs to be able to lead a discussion to analyse issues and make decisions, for example agreeing realistic achievable activity levels through contracts. This ensures that a business plan and the monitoring activity that follows is acceptable to colleagues. An increasingly important role for clinical directors is the analysis and identification of opportunities and the encouragement and development of awareness of business planning in colleagues.

Meetings and discussions with medical and other staff may be necessary before agreeing work patterns and targets within the directorate and monitoring progress through the year. For example, surgeons may need to meet and discuss operation targets with anaesthetists, theatre and ward staff. There is also a responsibility for analysing progress against the plan, as well as expenditure against budget, at least at monthly intervals and taking appropriate action if the results are not matching targets.

A work agreement within the available budget needs preparing and arguing as a business plan and this should include an opportunity to bid for a budget increase for the directorate each year. This requires good information in support of the case and it is the role of the business and nurse managers to ensure that such information is timely, reliable and available to the clinical director. Indeed, the business manager should also have a major influence in the business planning process with the clinical director.

As clinical director, you do need to 'get your hands on the money' if you are to play any significant role in management. You also need to ask who really makes the decisions and how. As an example, take a recent piece of equipment and find out who really made the decision to buy. If you are to be part of the management structure you have to be part of that process. You also need to be informed of the total budget position of the hospital as your budget in isolation is meaningless. You need to be honest with yourself as well as the other members of the management team about your financial position. It is no good saying that everything is fine when you are really overspent. It is no good saying, 'Well it is only a little overspend'. It is no good retreating into the defence of, 'It is not really an overspend but an underfund'. Those days are gone. You are the manager now. It is important that clinical directors, business managers and nurse managers meet with the financial director regularly and state their financial position. It is also important, if the clinical director is to work effectively, to have access to regular, timely and accurate financial information. This really means on-line access, perhaps read-only enquiries to the general ledger. This speeds up the process and also increases the trust between directorates and the finance department.

Your budget is likely to be made up of about 80% pay, i.e. salaries, and 20% non-pay, i.e. other outgoings. If you have an overspend you should agree a figure for this with the finance officer and get that in writing over his signature. Computer printouts have a nasty habit of being changed. By this stage you may well find that the finance department have already discovered some errors and the overspend is not as bad as was originally stated. If not, then identify every single item. Miss out nothing. You may need to go and spend some time to find these things out. Accept nothing on trust. Have all requisitions go through you and be signed only by you. Look at maintenance contracts for items of equipment which might have long since been abandoned. Look at estate items closely. Watch out for double invoices. And never forget that sometimes items get charged to the wrong directorate.

On the income side, make sure that you have at least one line set aside for income. A key error is the organization not billing the source of this income. Although a balance has to be struck between corporatism and individualism, directorates do need to retain about 50% of savings made and a large proportion of the income generated. The remainder has to go as a form of 'corporate tax'. If all the money or an unreasonable amount goes to the organization then people do not play the game for very long. The rules need to be set out beforehand. Remember that management retains power by not setting out the rules beforehand.

Contracts management

This involves directing and supporting the service or contracts manager in negotiating and agreeing achievable and realistic contracts, then managing and controlling clinical activity to ensure that the contract requirements are met. Between you, you should ensure that mechanisms exist to manage and control activity levels to contract requirements and coordinate medical input into establishment and maintenance of accurate information on activity and costs. Negotiation of contracts without clinical director involvement is at best regrettable, at worst a disaster. Watson (1994, personal communication) explains that:

> In some of the sites I visited during the 'Managing Clinical Services' exercise it was clear that the urgency of the contracting process had significantly undermined the devolution of real decision-making to directorate level, particularly where structures were already in place that had been working well before the introduction of purchaser/provider.

Support for this view came from McClean et al (1994) who found that the 'majority of clinical directors are not involved in setting contracts'. They went on to state that most are 'excluded from negotiations with health authorities and GP fundholders'.

Marketing

The clinical director clearly needs to be involved in marketing but initially it is primarily a business manager's function. This is discussed in more detail in Chapter 24.

Regrettably many hospitals manage the negotiation of contracts at a 'higher' level without clinical director involvement and at the very least, efficiency of the organization suffers as a result. Some hospitals negotiate contracts at business manager level or through a business or contracts department with little or no medical input, which leads to all sorts of problems and often alienation between general practitioners and hospital clinicians who never have the opportunity to talk together.

Monitoring of contracts

This is too often carried out above the level of clinical directorate and regarded as a central function. This is undesirable as there is invariably delay in the publication of data, so much so that it can be common for a directorate to see itself as overperforming and slowing down as a consequence when in fact the real situation is that they are underperforming and should be speeding up! Some have likened this phenomenon to trying to steer a supertanker.

INTERPERSONAL ROLES

These are leadership roles and many doctors have difficulty with these, which may at first sight seem odd but consultants especially see themselves as autonomous. As clinical director you are the leader of the directorate and have to take full responsibility for devolved operational management. You need to be creative, innovative and ambitious, an enabler and facilitator, always pursuing excellence. A high degree of motivation and enthusiasm is required to set the style and pace of the directorate.

The management style of the directorate is determined by your manner, behaviour and actions as clinical director. You lead and are accountable for the decision-making process, but always ensure that you are empowering others to make decisions. If you take on all the roles of the team not only does your clinical work and leisure time suffer but you are not providing satisfactory leadership and a sound role model, nor allowing others to make their contribution. A major responsibility is to provide an effective and successful role model for other staff.

You have a responsibility to determine directorate organizational behaviour and standards. You largely determine what the directorate does and how. You are responsible for audit, review and evaluation, staff development and appraisal. You determine whether the directorate has a high or low profile.

Leadership may be defined as the ability to inspire and influence others to work towards the attainment of objectives and goals. This is vital to the task of getting work done by and through others (Appley 1969) which is often used as a definition of management. It is essential to choose a method of leadership most appropriate to the situation (see Chapter 10). People need to be motivated and a challenge which allows a feeling of achievement followed by recognition often works. Clinical directors need strong leadership qualities, setting up and running, with the help of business and nurse managers, the management process within the directorate. You need to be able to recognize good ideas, analyse problems, make decisions, accept responsibility and be accountable for those decisions. The scope for leadership and flair is boundless.

Remember delegation of leadership means people are more in touch with leadership. Taking responsibility and accountability and provided with the appropriate authority, the doctor is able to be part of the corporate hospital management. So it is necessary to invest people with a sense of identity in the directorate. You need to create a team spirit not only amongst the clinical management team, but amongst all the members of the directorate.

You need to establish clear complementary and effective roles and responsibilities with others in the directorate, reviewing and updating them as skills develop. Clear, informative, relevant and comprehensive communication, review and evaluation are important. Your responsibilities include representing directorate business at corporate level, developing corporate responsibility and skills in oneself and within the directorate, and demonstrating motivation, commitment and enthusiasm for the management process.

The clinical director acts as spokesperson, coordinating medical input into management information. You are the main link with other directorates and the hospital management system. The opinion and content of messages going out of the directorate must be realistic and accurate and the incoming messages must be loud and clear. Information and communication skills and networks are important and the director must use considerable influence to ensure that these are good.

Consulting with others and taking advice is about building strengths, not admitting weakness. Many clinical directors feel particular vulnerability in expressing a need for guidance and learning for themselves (Wraith & Casey 1992). This can hinder personal, professional and directorate growth and is not a good example for colleagues. Directorate culture must be to support all staff development within the group. External resources provided by other sites, academic institutions and organizations should be fully utilized to ensure the fullest professional development of staff.

QUALITY MANAGEMENT

The clinical director must organize effective clinical audit mechanisms, with reporting of audit as required by the organization, and ensure that mechanisms are in place to ensure that improvements and changes are monitored. Managers as providers desperately need clinicians to explain changes in practice, to evaluate new practices, to indicate dangers in existing practices and to prioritize demands on limited resources. New techniques require investment in expertise and equipment which may have long-term benefits, such as more favourable outcomes, less inpatient time, less recurrence surgery and more acceptance from patients.

Purchasing authorities equally need doctors to explain quality matters and advise on value issues and priorities relating to demand. Coordinated and integrated hospital and general practice audits must become incorporated into quality aspects of contracts. Increasingly measurements of health gain may be specified in business plans and contracts which will then be monitored and it is here that purchasers will look to doctors to provide information and it is from clinical audit that doctors will seek to learn this. This requires information systems to enable collaborative audit between hospital, general practice and community health services to take place.

Part of the current role of clinical directors is to ensure that effective audit mechanisms are in place and that reporting of audit is occurring: this role is dealt with more fully in Chapter 33. The managing of a balance between quality, quantity and cost, particularly quality in contracts, will probably be part of the clinical director's future role.

There has to be a major professional input into standard setting, overseeing development of protocols and service specifications as required for purchasers. There is probably less need for the clinical director to be involved in the monitoring of quality standards, other than ensuring that they *are* monitored. Many of these issues demonstrate the vital necessity of clinical directors being involved in all contract discussions and negotiations.

Harwood & Boufford (1993) identify the function of customer orientation, which is normally lead by the nurse manager with the business manager being influential. The clinical director supports the team members in this. Responsibility for the quality management of the organization is brought closer to the patient with an impact on the quality of service delivered. Quality is understood and embraced as an integral part of everything everyone does. The patient should be the primary focus of everyone's effort. Success is defined in quality terms. Achievement should be recognized, broadcast through the organization and rewarded. People then begin to see the wider impact of their own particular and unique contribution to the success of the whole.

CORPORATE MANAGEMENT

This is a two-way process of communication between the directorate and organization, providing a clinical perspective to corporate management, giving clinical colleagues the opportunity to debate and influence management policy decisions and enabling clinical colleagues' views to be represented to management. In the other direction it ensures clinical colleagues are informed of management decisions and the clinical director has a clear role in ensuring that all members of the directorate understand management policies, to which he will properly have been a party.

The clinical director will therefore be participating in hospital strategy and policy formulation, contributing to effective decision making within the hospital for which he has to recognize corporate responsibility, while at the same time setting and monitoring directorate objectives and policies and ensuring that they are consistent with the overall objectives of the hospital.

The need for the clinical director to keep the directorate informed of management policy and pass on views from the directorate to management requires effective communication to all members of the directorate. This involves three factors:

1. talking
2. debating
3. listening.

You need to express what has to be done, with confident and clear instructions, how it is to be done, by whom and when. In a highly complex organization like a hospital this is a multidirectional process which needs to reach superiors, peers and subordinates.

Ensuring good communication within the directorate and between other directorates is a process of people relating to one another. Listening is demonstrating empathy, checking understanding and providing feedback. An ability to prevent and diffuse potential areas of difficulty with staff and colleagues is also vital. A clinical director needs to be able to relate in groups or one-to-one situations, lead discussions and meetings competently, prepare and present arguments based on facts and resolve competing claims for limited resources. All these issues have been discussed in detail in earlier chapters.

Everyone acknowledges the benefits of comprehensive, open and effective channels of communication. The most favoured method of communication is the cascade principle. Lateral communication below board level is important, but does your hospital listen as readily as it talks? Do you as clinical director have an adequate voice in the corporate decision-making process? If not, that needs to be changed. And maybe your hospital is still running with the old organizational structure while paying lip service to the new? Is the management structure of your hospital the most effective forum for corporate decision making?

INFORMATION MANAGEMENT

It is important to convince colleagues and management of the necessity for accurate and timely information. It may be necessary to review and refine available information. Information, often the source of centralized management power, has to be freely available and shared and it needs to be accurate, up-to-date, timely, clinical and patient-based to support the directorate in appropriate decision making. Information management has three main roles:

1. monitoring and using the information for problem analysis and solving;
2. disseminating information, for instance to effectively inform management decisions;
3. coordinating and acting as spokesperson or coordinating medical input into management information.

As far as information systems are concerned, most clinical directors are likely to have only a modest influence on the systems installed in hospitals, which are regrettably often more geared to demographic record keeping and financial management rather than useful clinical, audit or directorate-orientated functions. The subject is fully covered in Chapter 30.

CHANGE MANAGEMENT

The process of change is described by some authorities as a step-by-step process. (This is discussed in Chapter 21.) First there is recognition of the need for change, then identification of the problem and alternative strategies for dealing with it. The selected strategy then needs to be chosen, the change implemented and finally an evaluation of the success or otherwise of the change. This is important as you have a responsibility to make the best use of resources. It can also prove whether the change was wise or whether further change is necessary.

Change is never easy (Machiavelli 1514); people resist it for many reasons. Kaluzny & Hernandez (1988) identify three types of change as a function of whether ends or means or both are involved. Technical change involves modification of the means by which activities of the organization are carried out; there is no change of goal. Transition change involves organizational goals but not the means of achieving those goals. And transformation, the most extreme form of change, involves change in the goals and the means to achieve them.

HUMAN RESOURCES

This covers two main areas, the motivation of teams and individuals and the coordination of the administration of medical staffing within the directorate. The latter covers the medical input into the selection and appointment of junior and senior medical staff. This latter could reasonably be devolved to another consultant within the directorate. There is clearly a major influence on the recruitment of extra clinical staff.

The clinical director will not have a major influence on the staff workload or recruitment of other disciplines, as nursing staff will be influenced by the nurse manager and administrative staff generally by the business manager. Skill mix is generally organized on a similar basis. The need for the recruitment of non-clinical staff should be a major consideration for the clinical director in collaboration with the business manager, although

Harwood & Boufford (1993) found that only 20% of clinical directors, as opposed to 70% of business managers, had a major influence in this area.

One final matter needs careful thought and preplanning; how matters will be handled and the financial implications supported in the event of long-term sickness of a directorate member. This may have significant financial implications for a small directorate.

STAFF APPRAISAL

As far as clinical staff are concerned this is a major role for the clinical director although it would not be unreasonable for this to be devolved to another consultant in the directorate. Nursing staff should be appraised by the nurse manager or members of the nursing team. As far as the non-clinical staff are concerned, this should be lead by the business manager but appraisal of the nurse and business managers should be by the clinical director. This subject is dealt with in detail in Chapter 26.

DECISION-MAKING ROLES

These are the fixing roles. Vision and a capacity for growth and learning are required, as is an evolutionary and optimistic outlook rather than doubt and anxiety about change. Implementation of change should be a flexible and continuing process towards a considered objective. Feeling positive about change enables people to live comfortably with uncertainty and apparent contradictions. You are responsible for the responses to change. Uncertainty can even become the expected way of life rather than a threat. You need to focus on solutions and opportunities rather than the problems.

The greater flexibility demanded of staff should encourage learning. Any innovatory practice needs to be considered, evaluated and rewarded if successful. The organization must expect and accept mistakes, learning from them and modifying practice accordingly. Risk taking and its consequences need to be supported.

Dealing with conflicts is often a problem, as doctors have difficulty with negotiation and believing in teams. They see committees as looking after territories rather than the whole organization and may have difficulty in thinking strategically. You may need to make a stand on critical issues but problems must be faced openly and honestly. This relates very much to working with people, being aware of others and seeing things from another person's perspective, reading or interpreting other people's thoughts and feelings even when they are not obvious, developing others and working as a team.

REFERENCES

Appley L A 1969 A management concept. American Management Associations, New York

Audit Commission 1995 The doctors' tale. The work of hospital doctors in England and Wales. HMSO, London

BAMM 1994 Medical directors meeting. London, November 24/25

BMA 1990 CCSC guidance on clinical directorates. British Medical Association, London

BMA 1994 Clinical directorates. British Medical Association, London

Davies A H 1995 A profile of surgical clinical directors. Annals of the Royal College of Surgeons of England (supplement) 77: 13

Handy C B 1985 Understanding organizations, 3rd edn. Penguin, London

Harwood A, Boufford J I 1993 Managing clinical services. A consensus statement of principles for effective clinical management. BAMM/BMA/RCN/IHSM, London

Jaques E 1978 Health services. Appendix B Definitions of concepts. Heinemann, London

Kaluzny A D, Hernandez S R 1988 Organizational change and innovation. In: Shortell S M, Kaluzney A D (eds) Health care management: a text in organization theory and behaviour, 2nd edn. Wiley, New York, pp 380–381

Kanter R M 1989 When giants learn to dance. Unwin Hyman, London, p 338

Machiavelli N 1514 The prince VI (trans. G Bull). Penguin, Harmondsworth

McClean Jones McCarthy 1994 Connecting clinical directors. Reported in health services management. Clinical Directors Survey Vol 90 No 4: 6

Mintzberg H 1973 The nature of mangerial work. Harper & Row, New York

Nichol D 1991 BMA News Review 17(1): 10

Osborne D E, Gaebler T 1992 Reinventing government: how the entrepreneurial spirit is transforming the public sector. Addison-Wesley, Reading, Mass.

White A 1993 Management for clinicians. Edward Arnold, London

White A 1994 The role of hospital consultants in management decision making and change. PhD thesis, University of Bath

Wraith M, Casey A 1992 Implementing clinically based management. Getting organizational change underway. The Resource Management Unit of the NHS Management Executive, London

Zaleznik A 1977 Managers and leaders: are they different? Harvard Business Review 59: 64–78

10

Practical aspects of clinical and medical director appointments

Tony White, Sally Watson

When two men in a business always agree, one of them is unnecessary.

(William Wrigley Jr)

PRACTICAL ASPECTS

Taking on the role of a clinical director does not bring great rewards for a doctor, either financially or in terms of career progression. Indeed, it must be recognized that it often does not bring job satisfaction either and may create disillusionment, alienation from colleagues, stress and financial disadvantage. The reasons why doctors are prepared, sometimes enthusiastic, to take on the role are complex but usually relate to a sense of responsibility, a wish to protect and develop clinical services and pressure or support from colleagues.

Although the practical aspects of taking on the role are certainly not in themselves a motivation to doctors, it is clearly desirable to organize the job in such a way as to ensure that they do not present a barrier. The following aspects in particular need to be considered.

APPOINTMENT PROCEDURE

Clinical director

It is not usually necessary or appropriate to advertise clinical director posts or to set up a competitive selection process. The important principle is that the individual appointed must command the confidence of the staff in the directorate. As stressed elsewhere, this does not mean that he is elected as their representative. There are important differences between the two and these have been discussed (see Chapter 9). The representative can have more problems with, and complaints from, his colleagues in difficult decisions because he is a representative rather than an appointee, as the basis of the roles are different. To some extent the choice may be limited by those willing to undertake the role.

The appointment will ultimately be made by the chief executive on behalf of the trust but it is vital to devise a process which explicitly includes the directorate staff, particularly other consultants. This might involve the chief executive or the medical director on his or her behalf talking to individual members to ascertain their views. Alternatively the directorate might be asked to deliberate and put forward an agreed name. If this name is not acceptable an alternative nomination should be sought until agreement is reached. Because the relationship between the clinical director and other consultants is not that of direct line management but a more subtle one based upon leadership, it is unlikely to work if the choice of clinical director is simply imposed upon staff without their agreement.

The need for accountability is probably another essential reason why the clinical director is appointed, but with the support and the confidence of the consultants within the directorate. It is also important for a directorate not to put a 'wrecker' in place with the hope of fighting change or avoiding it or until 'hopefully' it goes away.

In some hospitals the competencies of clinical director applicants have been assessed before being appointed to directorates while in others training or agreement to training is an essential part of the appointment procedure.

In an small audit of surgical clinical directors, Davies (1995) found the mean age of clinical directors to be 51 (range 45–61) years and the mean time since appointment as consultant to be 16 (8–26) years.

Medical director

The medical director is appointed by the chairman of

the trust board, the non-executive directors and the chief executive. Again, it is important that those responsible for making the appointment ensure that the medical director has the confidence of the consultant body as a whole. This confidence and associated credibility normally require that the appointee is a member of the clinical staff of the trust, certainly at the time of appointment, as a number of such appointments have been made to consultants prior to retiring fully from clinical practice. In order to maintain the confidence of clinicians, the medical director should normally maintain some clinical workload, albeit reduced. When appointments have been advertised outside, it has also been usual to offer clinical sessions to the appointee.

TENURE OF APPOINTMENT
Clinical director

A fixed tenure is desirable to obtain the benefit of fresh ideas from changing directors, but they should be sufficiently long in post for the holder to learn all facets of the job and to have time to put the acquired knowledge and skills into practice. Few clinical directors expect to take on the job permanently and consultant colleagues would be unlikely to be comfortable with their doing so. It is usual for the tenure of appointment to be set at 3–5 years. A shorter period would be insufficient to allow the clinical director to acquire the necessary skills and put them into practice. There is evidence which suggests that some jobs are not fully learned for over 3 years, so it would be a mistake to move before that time or potential may never be fulfilled. A longer period would be possible, providing that the clinical director continues to command the confidence of colleagues; this can be achieved by providing for the appointment to be renewable annually after the first 5 years. A degree of challenge must exist in the job otherwise it becomes tedious and dull; a reasonable view is that about 7 years could be about right with the option to go earlier. One of the problems about being too long in post is that it leads to a separation from colleagues and credibility can be affected by being away too long. And it should not be forgotten that jobs do change. There should also be a rolling programme of appointments and retirements within the hospital to ensure that not all the clinical directors change at once.

Medical director

Much the same applies to medical directors as clinical directors. The tenure of the appointment should be specified in the contract (saying whether it is without term, rolling or for a fixed period). If it is renewable then the procedure and criteria for renewal should be specified.

CONTRACT AND JOB DESCRIPTION

The duties and responsibilities should be clearly set out in an agreed job description which will form the basis of a formal contract between the director and the trust. This ensures that both parties understand the formal position and are appropriately protected. The managerial and clinical contracts should be kept separate, but taken together may be regarded as equivalent to a whole-time contract. The BMA offers an example of a job description for a clinical director (BMA 1994). The clinical director's accountability for managerial duties will be specified; this may be to the chief executive or to the management board. This contract will be in addition to the existing basic consultant contract which it is vital to retain because clinical duties will continue throughout the clinical directorship and may be fully resumed at the end. The arrangement of duties, agreed periodically in the consultant's job plan, will clearly need to be amended to reflect the increased proportion of time spent on managerial duties, probably with a commensurate reduction in fixed clinical commitments. In a survey of surgical clinical directors, Davies (1995) found the mean time spent on directorate business was 10 (3–20) hours per week.

A range of different solutions may be negotiated to deal with the issues of reward for medical and clinical directors and for time and clinical cover to enable the work to be carried out. These will vary according to the size of the unit, workload and resources available and the preferences of the trust and director concerned. They would need to take account of the amount of time involved, the level of commitment and responsibilities, management skills brought to the role, compensation for loss of private practice and perhaps an 'inconvenience factor'. These issues will clearly affect the medical director more than the clinical director.

For clinical directors ratification is a means of formalizing the appointment. There should be a formal agreement with budgetary responsibility identified. Participation in budget-setting exercises should be mandatory. Responsibility for different groups of staff within the directorate should be identified.

The terms and conditions of service for hospital medical and dental staff (para 14) provide for up to two temporary additional notional half-days to be payable to clinical directors or to those who provide clinical cover for colleagues to enable them to take on the role. Some clinical directors may opt for this extra remuneration;

others may feel it is more important to negotiate reduced clinical commitments in order to take on the extra work.

For medical directors there are three main types of contractual arrangement to cover the extra work and responsibilities: payment of extra notional half-days or sessions, an enhanced consultant salary or an extra salary under a separate contract.

It should be noted that temporary additional notional half-days taken in excess of a whole-time or maximum part-time contract are not superannuable. In future, as more trusts move away from national terms and conditions of service, clinical directors may find it attractive to negotiate packages involving a salary increase (as opposed to additional notional half-days), which would then be superannuable if the post were held in the last 3 years before retirement. Termination of an appointment should be by 3 months' notice by either side.

The BMA (1993) stresses the importance of incorporating in the contract of medical directors a right to take up any temporarily dropped clinical commitments once the contract comes to an end, whatever the reason. And it also stresses that a similar commitment should be written into the contract of clinical directors (BMA 1994). Under HC(85)9, consultants who temporarily drop permanent contracted hospital sessions to become part-time general managers have the right to resume their previous clinical sessions on ceasing to be a general manager and have a right of appeal against changes in the content of sessions they have temporarily dropped. These rights should apply to consultants who take on the role of medical director.

SUPPORT

Probably the most important factor in allowing medical and clinical directors to carry out their role effectively while maintaining a clinical workload, is the provision of high calibre and appropriately trained support staff. For clinical directors, this applies particularly to the business manager, but it is also vital that key staff in the finance and information departments are dedicated to the affairs of the directorate and are adequately trained. The level of secretarial support available to the clinical director may also need to be upgraded if the directorate is to function effectively.

Sufficient support staff are essentially a business manager and/or nurse manager together with secretarial support. Meetings of the directorate should be attended by all consultants in the directorate, nurse manager and business manager and by all heads of department within the directorate. Meetings between clinical director and business manager should range from daily to weekly and the directorate should meet as a whole monthly. Where appropriate, members or representatives of other staff in the directorate should also meet. There should be sufficient, accurate and timely information available to the clinical director to enable him to carry out the work readily and easily and support will be needed to allow him to meet remaining clinical commitments.

APPRAISAL

There have been suggestions that clinical directors should be appraised or subject to individual performance review (IPR) for their management role. Most chief executives appear to consider this valueless and indeed it is far from likely that consultants would participate.

SUCCESSION PLANNING AND OVERLAP

The issue of succession planning for clinical directors is an extremely difficult one. The succession should be planned and phased and should not be merely by seniority. One of the problems for the first wave of clinical directors was the lack of management skills and training at or prior to appointment. This should not be allowed to be an issue for the successors. They need to be fully trained prior to taking up their appointment, particularly in smaller units. The choice of the first clinical director may be obvious; a suitable candidate may also be identified as a second. However, where the directorate consists of only a handful of consultants, those who have not come forward during the first 8-10 years may prove to be either reluctant or unsuitable to take over and a newly appointed arrival might find it difficult to command the confidence of colleagues. Nevertheless, the issue must be dealt with and an important principle is to identify a successor at an early stage.

In larger directorates it may be possible to appoint an assistant or deputy clinical director, who would have the opportunity to learn the ropes, including attending management board meetings in the absence of the clinical director, before ultimately taking over. Where this is not possible the appointment of a successor before a predecessor's retirement with a 3–6 month overlap is highly desirable to allow the new incumbent to gradually and smoothly take over. It might be worth considering the possibility of input from the retiring clinical director and other clinical directors in the reselection or succession procedure.

RE-ENTRY PROBLEMS

This is an issue which has received little attention. What

will you do with your time, how will you cope with relationships with your colleagues and reintegrate personally? You may have fallen behind in your practice, your skills may have been difficult to keep up to date, your clinical sessions may well have been taken over by someone else, your perceptions and attitudes will have changed and you will no longer be sharing problems with those having a common interest. You will experience a sense of loss, loss of information, not knowing what is going on. You can help your successor by being supportive but it is important not to interfere or be critical of your successor unless asked for your opinion or advice. This relationship between successor and succeeded can be difficult to handle for both parties.

You may feel that your interest in teaching and research, which inevitably suffered when you undertook a management role, will again fill your time and interest. You need to be honest with yourself as you may in reality have been fed up before and wanting something else. Whatever your reasons for taking on the job, management experience will have given you a new perspective and you can never return to that prior state of knowledge. It is best to look forward and see how you can best use your new experience.

TRAINING

Management training should be provided as necessary. At present in many hospitals it falls between study leave and management expenses and in the end nobody pays. For many years the health service has turned a blind eye to continuing education and neglected the responsibility and welfare of the staff. Yet the benefits of training for managerial positions are well documented (Handy 1993, Blanchard & Johnson 1983). A hierachy of development needs for doctors at all levels and grades has now been fully researched (Gatrell & White 1995). This has enabled a checklist of training needs to be produced in a form which enables the identification of individual personal development plans.

At present management development provision for doctors is provided unevenly around the country. There is evidence from the aforementioned research that those regions which have been most successful in initiating and sustaining management development for doctors have been those with central specialist support functions, usually staffed by professionals with a background in the design and provision of management training.

There appears to be little evidence of junior doctors attending clinical directorate meetings and whereas senior registrars and registrars were encouraged to attend, this no longer seems to be the case. Davies (1995) rightly raises the question 'as to how the consultants and directors of the future should gain the skills required to cope in the ever changing management infrastructure within the NHS'. It should be part of training for junior doctors.

CONCLUSIONS

Discussion in this chapter and elsewhere has already demonstrated the importance of clinical directorates and indeed the constitution of any new management structure being approved and supported by the consultant body. Consultant involvement in management has until recently been a controversial issue. Some still take the view that doctors should only practise medicine for which they have been highly trained and not 'dabble' in management for which they have certainly until recently had no training. 'My job is to treat patients' is a familiar expression. The alternative view is that management needs strong clinical input and advice, without which inappropriate decisions and actions may be taken. Given a hospital's acceptance of the value of clinical input into management, there needs to be some explicit obligations on the part of the organization.

Emphasis needs to be placed firmly on the need to avoid contracts or arrangements where priority for investigations and treatment is based on anything other than clinical need, irrespective of whether the patient is from a budget-holding general practice, health commission purchaser, extracontractual purchaser or the private sector. The monitoring of this must be the responsibility of the clinicians.

All information has to be freely available except in so far as it may relate to individual and identifiable patients or members of staff. The obligation in a publicly funded service is to public accountability, rather than commercial secrecy. Full explanations of decisions should be given to relevant staff ahead of implementation and whenever possible, in time for amendments in the light of consultation. Weaknesses as well as strengths in the provision of clinical services should be identified and honestly acknowledged.

There needs to be a continuing emphasis on reducing bureaucracy and simplifying the administrative processes. One of the greatest problems in changing the existing management structure is that a bureaucracy is very difficult to dismantle as the bureaucrats within resist and cling on to power.

REFERENCES

Blanchard K, Johnson S 1983 The one minute manager. Fontana, London

BMA 1993 CCSC guidance for medical directors. British Medical Association, London
BMA 1994 CCSC guidance for clinical directors. British Medical Association, London
Davies A H 1995 A profile of surgical clinical directors. Annals of the Royal College of Surgeons of England (supplement) 77: 13

Gatrell J, White A 1995 Medical student to medical director: a development strategy for doctors. NHSTD, Bristol
Handy C 1993 Understanding organizations. BPCC Hazell Books, Aylesbury

11

Giving talks and presentations

Colin Coles

AIMS

The aims of this chapter are:

- to review common problems people have with talks and presentations, both from the presenter's and the listener's points of view;
- to explain why the prevailing educational model causes these problems to occur;
- to examine a more appropriate educational model for giving talks and presentations;
- to explain the theoretical bases for this model;
- to provide a checklist for people to apply this model when giving talks and presentations.

COMMON PROBLEMS

Talks and presentations do not always have to cause problems. They can be extremely valuable and even satisfying for both presenters and listeners. People often enjoy speaking on their favourite topic and can feel a sense of achievement having got their point across. Equally, people who attend talks and presentations can get a great deal from them and frequently find them enlightening and even entertaining.

However, talks and presentations can also be a great problem for presenters and listeners. From a presenter's point of view, the kinds of problems include:

- I know so much that I don't know how to cut it down to what is important;
- I don't know enough about this subject to make it worthwhile speaking on it;
- I don't know anything about the audience and what they already know or what they want me to talk about;
- I don't know anything about the location and where facilities are available;
- I don't know how long I have to speak for and if there will be time for discussion;
- I don't know who else is speaking and how what I have to say fits with their talks.

Some of these problems must be addressed by the people who organize talks and presentations. They reflect on how well they brief speakers about the time and place of the talk and its purposes. Other kinds of problems involve ensuring that one's presentation is appropriate to the needs of the people listening and how it relates to the rest of the presentations being made. Other problems reflect the speaker's inability to get across what they want to say in a way that is interesting to the people there.

Listeners have rather different problems:

- I can't cope with all this information being presented in such a short time;
- I can't understand the relevance of what is being said;
- I am sure I'll forget most of this;
- I doubt very much that I'll be able to apply this information when I want it;
- I am feeling very demotivated by this presentation because it is reminding me of everything I don't know.

When talks and presentations are a problem, whether from the presenter's or the listener's viewpoint, it is usually because an inappropriate educational model is being employed – one that can best be described as 'pot-filling' (Coles 1989). This occurs when large amounts of information are presented out of context without any opportunities for people to consider its application to their own circumstances. Speakers 'pour out' their information to the recipients, who act rather like pots waiting to be filled. The presenter is active, the receiver is passive. Knowledge is a quantitative phenomenon which flows from the one to the other. For the receiver, becoming knowledgeable is a matter of taking on board what the presenter has to offer, who after all knows more than you do.

Educationally, there are considerable difficulties with this 'pot-filling' model. On the face of it the information being presented may be entirely appropriate. Presenters can convince themselves that the listeners 'need' this information. However, doing this fails to address two very important questions – important in an educational sense. First, is the listener in a position *to receive* all this information? And second, does the listener know *what to do* with this information once it has been received? When presentations go wrong, the answer to both of these questions is a resounding 'No'! Or, more probably, the questions haven't even been asked. So what is the alternative?

AN ALTERNATIVE MODEL AND ITS THEORETICAL BACKGROUND

A much more appropriate model is shown in Fig. 11.1. Paradoxically, the information being presented closely resembles the information being transmitted during 'pot-filling'. The major difference is that consideration has been given not just to the context in which the information is presented but also to what the receivers of that information could be doing with it to make it useful to their own circumstance. This will be explained further in due course. Before that we should perhaps examine the model's theoretical background.

For much of the first part of this century theories of learning were dominated by the work of Pavlov in Russia with classical conditioning and Skinner in North America with operational learning. Indeed, this led to the development of an entire school of learning psychology called behaviourism. By the 1960s, a number of educational theorists were arguing against this and two broad themes emerged, one a cognitive view of learning and the second humanistic.

Recent views of cognitive learning theory go back to Bartlett (1932) in the 1930s who emphasized that *what* we learn is influenced by *how* we learn. Learning was seen as 'information processing'. Incoming information from our senses passes to short-term memory where it is processed before being stored in long-term memory, and information already stored in long-term memory has a crucial role in assisting the processing of new incoming information.

A library is a good analogy (Broadbent 1975). The librarian processes newly acquired books using the library's classification and storage system and then shelves them appropriately. Anyone wishing to retrieve a particular book goes to the index and finds where the book is located. In human learning, we store new information in accordance with our own cataloguing system and when we want to remember something – retrieve that information – we do so using the same system.

An information processing view of learning helps explain why the pot-filling model makes talks and presentations so grossly inefficient. Listening to lists of facts out of context, without a clear purpose, means listeners are unlikely to process the information effectively. The information remains abstract – it lacks personal meaning for the listener – so is arbitrarily attached to some other stored information or remains unattached. In either case, the information will be difficult to retrieve.

When we forget something, this is not due to 'fading' of the memory through some process of decay. Rather, forgetting is an 'active' process of 'interference' where new information has made inappropriate links with stored information. This is rather like replacing a library book on the wrong shelf: the book retains its quality but is useless because it cannot be retrieved.

An important contribution to this information processing view of learning was made by Ausubel (Ausubel et al 1978) who emphasized the value of what he called an 'advanced organizer' – some prior knowledge that helps us process new information. When giving talks and presentations this means ensuring that the listeners are 'prepared' in some appropriate way. We will see later how this can work in practice.

In the 1970s, work in Gothenberg (Marton & Saljo 1976a,b) introduced the terms 'deep and surface processing'. Deep processing happens when people attempt to understand the meaning of what they are learning. Surface processing occurs when people rote learn or memorize. Deep rather than surface processing leads to better recall and application of what is being learnt.

The work of Kolb (1984) extends this view. Learning occurs best when it starts with actual experience on which learners reflect, derive abstract principles for themselves and apply those principles to new situations.

In a similar way, Schon (1983, 1987) argues that professional development requires a process called 'reflection in action' – a kind of dialogue professionals have with themselves in order to define the problems

| Context for learning | Appropriate information | Opportunities for education |

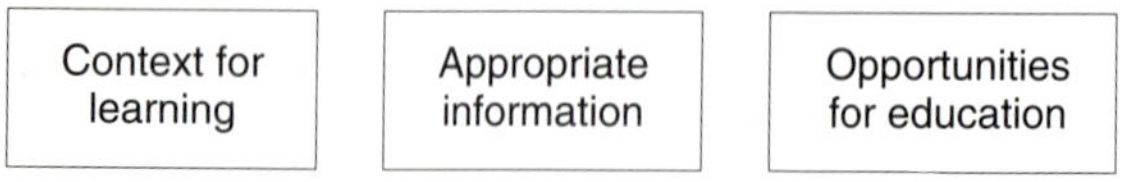

Fig. 11.1 Contextual learning model

they face and to carry out 'on the spot experimentation' by subtly modifying what they are doing to meet the unique demands of each situation they must deal with.

Polyani (1966), too, suggests that much professional knowledge is implicit and personal. Professionals might appear to practise in similar ways yet their knowledge base can be quite different. It would be wrong to assume that there is some core knowledge that underpins professional practice that can be transmitted through professional education. Rather, professionals must be allowed to create an understanding of their own personal knowledge through the opportunities afforded by professional education (Eraut 1994).

Professional learning, then, is much more than merely being given information. It is concerned with the processing of information and is highly dependent upon what we already know or have previously experienced. Knowledge-getting is a process which is unique to each individual. When, as a speaker, you give a talk you might believe you are presenting the same information to each of the listeners, yet everyone there will process it uniquely. Speakers must recognize a difference between the information they think they have presented and the information that the listener has actually received and stored.

A further implication of cognitive learning theory is that the traditional 'basic firsts' approach, where theory is presented before practice, is inefficient. People must first have some relevant experience or be given some concrete example to enable them to process effectively the abstract information, facts and principles a speaker presents to them.

Above all, effective learning is concerned with learners attempting to establish more and more complex networks of knowledge rather than storing information as discrete and separate entities. High quality learning results from learners 'pulling things together', that is, by constantly structuring and restructuring what they know into a more and more elaborated knowledge. Such a knowledge is the basis for problem solving and high quality professional practice (Norman 1988).

Humanistic learning theory is the second thread of learning psychology to run through the 20th century and arose at a time when occupational psychology was becoming established. The introduction of automated work practices and repetitive business routines lead to studies of employees in the workplace itself. Perhaps for the first time employment began to be looked at systematically from the point of view of the employee, not just to improve worker efficiency but to aid training through the analysis of job performance.

These studies showed that the quality of the working environment was an important consideration. Excessive noise, heat, fumes, fatigue, etc. gave poor performance. Improvements to the working environment lead to increased efficiency. Moreover, workforce morale affected efficiency. People who felt valued and had self-esteem performed better than those without. Giving employees constructive feedback on their work increased their efficiency. Perhaps even more significantly, performance improved when people had the opportunity to observe the results of their own efforts and discover where they could make improvements.

In the 1960s and 1970s similar concepts were applied to the world of education. Rogers (1961, 1983) developed the notion of learner-centred education – the learner should be the focus of education with the teacher providing support. For Rogers, learning was a 'self-actualizing tendency' (1961). Learning should be related to the problems people face. If so, it occurs automatically because learners will want to know how to solve their own problems. The teacher's responsibility was to provide a supportive environment, to facilitate learning.

This approach was developed further by Knowles (1988, 1990) in relation to adult learners. He introduced the term 'self-directed learning' where learners are encouraged to set their own learning objectives and seek their own solutions to their problems. Crucially, learning needed to relate to people's own experience and be perceived as relevant.

Piaget (1972) had shown that children's thinking passed through a series of developmental stages. Perry (1970), working with college students, demonstrated that young adults continue their intellectual development. Students begin their studies by seeing knowledge as right or wrong and then as dependent on the context in which the knowledge is located. Ultimately, they commit themselves to a particular view of knowledge. The teacher's role, according to Perry, is to help students through these developments, though the transitions are sometimes difficult and painful and teachers need special skills to help students grapple with their uncertainties.

This shift to learner-centred education, as well as pointing out new roles for teachers and learners, also emphasized the relationship between our intellectual and emotional states of mind. Maslow (1970) suggested that people have 'hierarchies of needs'. We must address our physiological needs – food, drink, shelter, etc. – before our social and emotional needs – belonging, contentment. Only then can we address our intellectual needs.

Two strands of educational enquiry, then, have developed this century. One considers learning as the processing of information, the other considers the learner's state of mind. In short, people will learn best when they are helped to reflect on what they already know, on some experiences they have had or on their routine practice. Through this they should identify their strengths and weaknesses, set educational objectives for themselves, deal with these objectives satisfactorily, evaluate their progress in meeting them and as a result apply what they have learnt to their own circumstances. The teacher's role is to provide a conducive environment in which this can occur, monitor the learner's progress, provide constructive feedback as appropriate and intervene appropriately as necessary in order to facilitate the learning that is occurring.

THEORY INTO PRACTICE: APPLYING THE MODEL TO GIVING TALKS AND PRESENTATIONS

How can we turn all this theory of learning into the practice of giving talks and presentations? Let us look more closely at the contextual learning model, which was briefly described earlier. What do the stages of the model involve and what do they mean for speakers and presenters?

The context for learning

The learning you want the listener to engage in takes place in a context. The speaker's task is to ensure that the context is an appropriate one. The listener's context is not just the cognitive state but also the physiological, emotional and social one. To pay attention to this means, as Ausubel puts it, finding out what the other person already knows and proceeding from there. This applies not just to what the listener knows but also the experiences the listener has already had, as well as the analytical frameworks the listener has developed. Often, though, listeners do not know what they already know or even that they have an analytical framework. In fact, they may need help to reflect on and recognize their own starting point.

Within the listener, the physiological and emotional context should be a satisfactory one. Most are aware that hunger, tiredness, physical discomfort, etc. can make learning difficult. Paradoxically, perhaps, strong emotions (such as being humiliated) can either facilitate or inhibit learning, switching you off or engaging you more fully.

The learning context also concerns what is going on around the listener. Speakers must ensure the environment has minimal distractions and relative comfort. The learning 'environment' can also be deliberately manipulated in subtle ways to facilitate learning, for example, by presenting some relevant experience prior to or early on in the learning sequence. This can also mean providing the listener with some appropriate example or illustration to form a basis for the person to learn.

Finding out where the listener is at the start of a talk can be done more easily in some settings than others, such as small group and one-to-one teaching, by asking people questions like: What do you know already? What misunderstandings do you currently have? What do you do in your work? What problems do you face? What do you want to know about or know how to do? This is not quite so easy, of course, in a lecture. You have to make some assumptions about where the listeners are, but these can be informed assumptions. You could, for example, carry out some enquiries with them prior to the educational event or ask the organizer, who ought to know. Another possibility is to pose your audience a problem. Ask them to reflect on their own experience, perhaps review recent cases or examine the way they routinely deal with certain conditions. Present an example of someone's practice, perhaps in the form of a video recording.

Speakers' checklist for establishing the learning context

1. *Administration* Check the exact time of your talk, the date and the venue. Telephone the organizer a few days beforehand for the arrangements. This also reassures the organizer you will be there.

2. *Facilities* Make sure you know how to get to there. Check the parking. If you are travelling by public transport, ensure that you can get there in time. Where is the talk to be given? How big is the room? What facilities does it have? If you are planning to use audiovisual aids, ensure they are available. Will somebody set them up for you? If you really do need a projectionist, ask for one in good time.

3. *The programme* When do you give your talk in relation to the rest of the programme? Is there an opportunity, such as a break for refreshments, for you to set up audiovisual materials, place handouts for people to collect a copy, etc.?

4. *The topic* Make sure you know precisely the topic you have been asked to speak about. If there are any ambiguities, check with the organizer well in advance.

5. *The audience* Who will be in the audience? How many people will be attending? What does the audience already know about the topic? What problems do they face? How does your talk help? Should you carry out a pretalk survey of their problems or what they know already? Ask the organizer to help you with this. Do you want the members of the audience to have carried out

some task before they come along? Do you want them to bring along examples of typical problems that they have or questions that they might like to pose?

6. *Arrive in good time* Get the feel of the place and of the audience. Listen to other speakers. You might refer to what they said. Watch and listen to how others present their talk, you can pick up some good ideas this way. Arriving early has other benefits. Get your audio-visual materials and equipment sorted out. If there is a projectionist, make contact. If you are using slides, get them loaded into the projector in good time. If you have the opportunity, check your slides on the screen before the audience comes in (or during a break). It is surprising how often, in haste, slides get reversed or inverted. If you are using the overhead projector, check this too. Does it have a spare bulb? Are the surfaces and lenses clean and free of dust? Again, it is surprising how often equipment needs a wipe over – keep a clean tissue handy. Do you need to use overhead projector pens? Don't rely on them being there – take your own. Check other facilities such as the lighting arrangements. Do you have to dim the auditorium lights yourself? Do you know how this works? Do you have to change the slides yourself? Is there a pointer? Is there an amplification system? Do you need to wear a roving microphone?

Another very good reason for being early is to put the organizer's mind at rest. Contact the organizer to say you are there.

7. *At the start of the lecture* Make a few general (but relevant) comments right at the start. This way you get used to speaking in that particular auditorium and the audience can get used to you too – your voice and style, etc. Humour at this point is a possibility, but be careful; it is amazing how often people try to be funny but fail. Perhaps be neutral; thank the organizers for the invitation and for the kind words of introduction, but don't spend too long on all of this. You probably have a limited time slot so don't waste too much of it on your introductions.

8. *Set the scene for your talk* Say what you are going to say and prepare people for any activity you will be announcing during your lecture. Establish any ground rules for your session. Will you be unconventional in any way? Will you be expecting the audience to do something? Do you expect them to take notes? Is there a handout?

9. *Handouts* These can be useful for conveying the overall structure of the talk. Use them, too, for additional information you do not want to cover in your talk. Handouts are useful for references and follow-up reading. Leave blank spaces in handouts for people to fill in notes themselves. If you are concerned that people will be busily reading the handout rather than listening to you, you could give the handout at the end, making sure that you have told your audience in advance that is what you are going to do.

10. *State what you see to be the aims and objectives of your talk* Not just what you hope to cover, but what you hope the audience will get out of it. What do you expect they will be able to do afterwards? How does your talk help with their problems?

11. *Use some kind of 'advanced organizer'* If they did some work before they came, refer to it now. Ask if they have any questions at this point. Say a little about what you have found out (either from your own researches or from talking with the organizer) about where you think they are coming from regarding your topic. Say what assumptions you are making. Use an example (as concrete as possible) relevant to the audience's work or pose some problem that they might typically face. Very importantly, use case studies or clinical examples at this point. The more concrete your organizer at this stage, the more likely the audience will be tuned into listening to what you have to say.

Information

The second aspect of contextualizing learning is to make available appropriate information. Educational content is usually abstract. On its own, it might carry very little meaning for the listener. It is likely to be novel. Take care to ensure that the information you present has a clear relationship to the learning context you have just established. For example, if the listeners have been asked to undertake some experience prior to the talk or if you have presented examples and case studies at the start of a talk, ask yourself if the information you now present clearly relates to those examples? Put another way, relevance is important. The information presented must be relevant to the listener's context, not yours.

In practice, when planning a talk or presentation you need to consider simultaneously the learning context you will establish and the information you want to present. Clearly there are dangers that the context and the information may not match, or perhaps more worrying, that the listener does not recognize the mismatch and wrongly connects theory and some other practice they have in mind.

Paradoxically, this establishing of the context through giving examples and then presenting information is the complete opposite of how most talks or presentations are structured: facts are often presented *before* their application. Theory tends to come before practice. The reverse, practice before theory, works better. Try it yourself.

Information can of course be presented in different forms, the most common being words – either printed or spoken – pictures and sound. As for words, printed information is different from spoken information. Reading out loud a text prepared for publication sounds dull and lifeless. The reverse, writing down spoken information, is equally unpalatable; it appears trivial and inexact. Written presentation must rigorously follow the rules of grammar and syntax. When speaking we can allow ourselves greater freedom because we rely more on the tone and inflection, as well as gesture and other non-verbal communication.

The level of complexity of the language we use, whether written or spoken, is also a consideration and can be analysed in terms of 'word density' using a device known as a Fog index (Table 11.1; see Chapter 7). This indicates the level of complexity of the language you are using and its likely impact on different groups of people depending on, for example, their level of education. On this index an article appearing in a learned journal will score higher than one in a tabloid newspaper, which in turn will be more dense than a child's fiction book.

The situation is the same with spoken presentation. Bernstein (1971) has distinguished between elaborated and restricted use of language. An elaborated code is used in an intellectual discussion while a restricted code is more likely to be used in everyday conversation. Just as with a Fog index, elaborated language is more involved, has longer sentences, more clauses, more adjectives, more polysyllabic words, etc. A restricted code uses shorter sentences, fewer adjectives, shorter words and conversational terms and phrases.

Information can be presented in other ways such as audiovisual presentation. Pictures can be shown either as still photographs or as moving images, such as film and video recordings. Presentations can use symbols, tables, diagrams, cartoons, etc. A very important consideration is the amount of information presented. People often present too much information on slides and overhead projector transparencies. Sound (without pictures) can be very evocative if used sensitively.

A final consideration is whether information should be given at all. Many presenters see their responsibility as giving people information and are much less concerned with encouraging people to seek out information for themselves. Yet educational events should encourage others to direct their own learning and this might mean finding things out. Speakers should perhaps ask themselves what they *shouldn't* be saying, as much as what they should. What can be left for the listener – perhaps as a follow-up to the talk?

Checklist for presenting information

1. *Content*   A spoken lecture should not rely on the speaker reading out something that has been written in advance. Speaking and writing are quite different. Supporting notes are useful. If you find it helpful, write out notes for your opening and closing statements and even read them out (making sure that you have written them as you want to say them). If there are some important sections in your talk, write these out too, but keep them to the minimum.

In your notes, summarize the main points you want to make. Keep your notes on sheets of paper or possibly on cards (5" × 3" file cards are very useful). Keep your notes (or cards) held together in case they get out of sequence. Staple together sheets of paper or punch holes in the file cards and fasten them with tags.

Check your language style. From time to time tape record a talk you have given and have part of it typed up for you to analyse. What is the Fog index of your talk? Is your language structure too complex or perhaps too simplistic?

2. *Structuring your talk*   Your talk will have at least an implicit structure. Give thought to the way you structure your talk. How will you make this structure explicit to your audience? The structure will depend on your objectives – what you want to achieve and how you intend to achieve this.

Set out the structure of your lecture as you prepare it. Can you represent your talk as a diagram showing how the points interrelate? State your structure quite explicitly to your audience near the beginning of your talk. This could be in your handout. Then, as your talk proceeds, refer to the structure from time to time to show your audience where you have got to in your talk. Emphasize the key features of your structure. Say, for example, 'I want to cover three things . . . . .'.

3. *Audiovisual aids*   Your audiovisual aids can help display your structure, perhaps on an overhead projector transparency. As you proceed you could uncover

---

Table 11.1   The Fog index (after Albert 1992)

Select a passage of 100 words ending with a full stop.

- Calculate average sentence length of the passage (100 divided by the number of sentences).
- Count the difficult words (three syllables or more, but excluding two-syllable words that have become three syllables with plurals or with endings like -ed or -ing. Also ignore technical words but not jargon and proper nouns).
- Add together the average sentence length and the number of difficult words and multiply by 0.4.
- The result will be the reading score.
- Language with a reading score of 14 or more requires a university degree!

areas of it to reveal different aspects of the topic and to show where you have got to. Similarly, an overhead projector transparency can be built up using successive overlays. Alternatively, keep the overhead projector transparency with the structure of your talk on all the time and show the different points you want to make using slides.

There are a number of key points to remember whatever audiovisual presentation you use.

- Restrict the amount of information on the screen to what you could read from the back of the hall. This is perhaps the biggest error of most presenters. If you find yourself saying 'You won't be able to read all of this', ask yourself why you are showing it!
- Do not use your slides as prompts for what you are going to say next. Have these on your notes or cards.
- Always project on the screen exactly what you are saying. If the wording is even slightly different, the audience will be reading the slide and not listening to you. Better to keep quiet and let people read your slide than to start saying something else while the slide is on the screen.
- Have blank slides or alternatively switch off the projector from time to time.

Opportunities for elaboration

The third element of contextualizing learning concerns opportunities for elaborating (Coles 1990). Even if you have set an appropriate context for learning and made available appropriate information, there remains the need to make the connections between the information and the context. This is a task which only the listeners can perform; the speaker cannot do it for them. So the speaker's tasks are twofold. First, get listeners to make their own connections and second, ensure these are the correct ones.

Elaboration occurs through a 'conversation' – ideally between the speaker and the listener, provided the speaker adopts a role that encourages elaboration by the listener. Educationally, this is best seen in group discussion, private study, through computer-assisted learning and even while people are revising for examinations. It is more difficult when giving talks and presentations – one-to-one conversations are impractical – but it can be done and should be encouraged. Essentially it requires your listeners to hold their conversation with themselves, because of the way you have structured your talk, through the emphasis you have placed on them making the connections for themselves.

As we saw earlier, gaining knowledge is much more than merely acquiring information. It is an active process where the listener takes in information and makes it personal. Knowledge is not the quantitative accumulation of facts but the qualitative transformation of information into an elaborate structure. Knowledge is greater than the sum of the bits of information that form its parts. People of course need to understand what they are learning but must internalize it too – make it their own.

The good presenter encourages this process of elaboration, whatever kind of presentation is made (Gibbs et al 1992). Some listeners do it quite naturally, others have to learn how to elaborate their knowledge. Elaboration is evident when people make intuitive leaps in their understanding, when they gain sudden insights and when 'things fit together'. Frequently these experiences are highly motivating and they provide the all-important intrinsic rewards associated with 'learning for its own sake'.

So effective learning is concerned with people constructing their own personal meaning of what they are learning. They elaborate their knowledge when they make connections between what they already know and what they are now learning and by reconstructing their existing knowledge to give it new and enhanced meaning. The bottom line of learning is knowing something differently.

In many ways, this third phase of contextual learning is the most difficult to conceptualize, particularly when giving talks. It is concerned with what is going on inside the listener. It is not enough to establish an effective context for learning nor to make available appropriate information. If the listener does not also 'handle' the information in such a way that elaboration occurs, then the talk or presentation will have been less productive than it might be. Speakers need to ask themselves how they can help this process happen by what they do and say.

What is important here is the listener's personal perception of their role in the educational event. What do they see themselves as having to do in order to learn from it effectively? If people have been brought up to believe that their role is a passive one – just sit there and wait to be told things – then learning is not going to be as effective as if they had taken a more active role in the educational process. The problem is that years of experiencing formal lectures has led many people to adopt a passive learning role. Not only are they unaware of how to go about active learning, but speakers are not skilled in providing them with appropriate opportunities for doing so.

Encouraging active learning is easier to achieve in one-to-one or small group teaching through some form of dialogue than when giving talks and presentations, where speakers must work harder and be more deliberate in assisting listeners to see what they might do to elaborate their knowledge.

Checklist for establishing elaboration

1. *Active learning* A typical audience can pay close attention for up to 20 minutes or so. After this they begin to lose interest. So it is important that you 'engage' your audience in what you are trying to convey. Change the 'focus' every so often. Reengage your listeners from time to time.

2. *Establishing the context* at the outset is important for active learning. If listeners *want* to know what you think they *need* to know, they will be attentive. If they see there is a problem (and it is *their* problem too) they will listen. The presenter, through the context, can help listeners become 'engaged'.

3. *Promote active learning through:*

- describing relevant clinical cases, events, practical examples, etc. at the start of the talk and referring back to them during the talk;
- posing questions at the outset and during the lecture itself. Keep referring back to these too;
- using 'buzz' groups. Ask people to pair off to discuss a particular topic. (The term 'buzz' refers to the sound this will create in the room. Some lecturers find this quite intimidating, wondering if they will ever gain control of the audience again.) Try it, especially for:
  — reviewing or applying what has just been said;
  — allowing the audience to think about questions they want to ask.

Buzz groups work best when you are well prepared. Ensure the audience knows what they should do. For example, you might say 'At this point I'd like you to turn to your neighbour and discuss . . . . You have two minutes for this. Then I'd like you to raise any questions that you have.' But be prepared for:

— people not being used to this way of working;
— people not discussing the proposed topic;
— the audience coming to the wrong conclusions;
— the audience feeling it is wasting its time or becoming bored.

An extension of the buzz group is for pairs to amalgamate into fours to share their ideas before proceeding. This can be quite helpful because individuals and even pairs can be reluctant to report on the outcome of their discussions and might welcome the opportunity to confirm their views with another pair. Groups of four also have more chance of elaborating their knowledge through hearing other people's views.

Articulation – This is a way of elaborating. It simply means getting listeners to put into their own words what you have been saying. Articulating helps you see things more clearly.

4. *Summarizing* Whether or not you use buzz groups it is useful at times throughout your lecture to summarize what you have said already and where you wish to go from here. This is also a good opportunity to refer to the structure of the lecture to indicate how you are progressing through it.

5. *Application* This means encouraging listeners to take the information you have presented and to use it in their own situation.

6. *Problem solving* This means getting people to use information gained in one situation to solve a problem in a quite novel setting.

7. *Concluding remarks* This is another good opportunity to encourage elaboration. Summarize the main points of the talk. Better still, get the audience to do this for themselves. You could announce this by saying 'We've got five minutes left, so before I ask for questions you might like a minute or two just to reflect on what I have been saying. Jot down some notes of the main points of my talk as they have applied to your own circumstance, and note any questions you want to ask me. I'll tell you when time is up.' It is very important to give this last instruction – the time scale – because almost inevitably somebody will start straight out with a burning question they have in mind without allowing other people the opportunity to reflect.

In your own summary of your talk, keep the number of points to the bare minimum. In a half-hour talk you can probably communicate three main messages, no more. Simply say to your audience 'Three important points I'd like you to take away from this are . . . . .'.

8. *Invite questions relevant to your talk* Some people might want to broaden the discussion and there is a fine dividing line between questions relevant to everyone and topics that only some of the audience might find appropriate. Be prepared to say 'Perhaps we could talk about this afterwards as it seems rather a specialist area'. Try to judge whether a question from one person is likely to be representative of what many of the audience would like to hear about. Keep your answers relatively short. If you can't answer the question in a couple of sentences, suggest you talk about it afterwards.

9. *Before you close,* say what the audience could be do-

ing in their own circumstances with the information you have been communicating. This is a failing of many speakers. The preparation work you put in prior to the lecture will pay off handsomely at this point. If you cannot suggest how they might apply the information you have presented, perhaps you shouldn't have been giving the lecture in the first place!

10. *Talking with people after the lecture* Some people may want to discuss with you afterwards. Remember that your talk is probably one of several on the programme so you should not take up too much time by this. Be prepared to talk to people at some other time. Have available some name cards with your address and telephone number so that people can contact you. Interesting though it is to continue talking about your topic, there are other things you need to be dealing with after your talk.

AND FINALLY.... SOME GENERAL POINTS ON GIVING TALKS AND PRESENTATIONS

Timing

The cardinal rule is: 'Keep to time'. If you are unfamiliar with your material, practise it beforehand. It often takes longer than you think. Time yourself and add a few minutes as a margin of error. If you arrive early, see if there is a clock in the lecture room or check this out in advance. Alternatively, take your own. A small travel clock is easier to read quickly than a wrist watch provided you have somewhere to place it, for example next to your notes. If you find yourself running out of time, be prepared to cut part of the main body of your lecture and move straight to your concluding remarks. However, you might want to tell your audience that you are doing this, particularly if you have given them the overall structure in advance – they may wonder why part of the talk is missing. Whatever you cut out, don't omit your concluding remarks.

Take away all your audiovisual materials, notes and unused handouts

Projection rooms are full of the slides people have left behind!

Feedback

Does the organizer use a feedback sheet which audience members complete? If you have any say in its design, ensure it is as brief as possible. Ask three or four closed questions about the relevance and interest level of your talk, which the audience members might rate on a four-point scale (from very good to very poor). Importantly, leave a space for people's open comments. These are often much more useful than a rating scale. Then ask a few open questions: What would you suggest I include from my lecture in any future talk I give? What would you suggest I omit? What do you suggest I include that I omitted today? What are your general comments on this presentation?

Contacting the audience again

Some days after the talk you might consider contacting some of the audience to discuss it further with them, particularly regarding its relevance to their day-to-day work. The people attending might have been impressed at the time but on returning to work may find difficulty in applying much of it. Alternatively, they might have left your talk somewhat perplexed and worried because you challenged them but on reflection found a great deal more in what you said than perhaps they thought immediately afterwards. Either way it is very useful to know.

REFERENCES

Albert T 1992 Medical journalism: the writer's guide. Radcliffe Medical Press, Oxford

Ausubel D P, Novak J S, Hanesian H 1978 Educational psychology: a cognitive view, 2nd edn. Holt, Rinehart & Winston, New York

Bartlett R C 1932 Remembering. Cambridge University Press, Cambridge

Bernstein B 1971 On the classification and framing of educational knowledge. In: Young M F D (ed) Knowledge and control. Collier Macmillan, London

Broadbent D E 1975 Cognitive psychology and education. British Journal of Educational Psychology 45(2): 162–176

Coles C R 1989 Diabetes education: theories of practice. Practical Diabetes 6: 199–202

Coles C R 1990 Elaborated learning in undergraduate medical education. Medical Education 24: 14–22

Eraut M 1994 Outcomes and professional knowledge. In: Burke J (ed) Outcomes, learning and the curriculum. Tomorrow's doctors: recommendation on undergraduate medical education. General Medical Council, London

Gibbs G, Habeshaw S, Habeshaw T 1992 53 interesting things to do in your lectures. Technical and Educational Services, Bristol

Knowles M S 1988 Self directed learning: a guide for learners and teachers. Jossey-Bass, London

Knowles M S 1990 The adult learner: a neglected species. Gulf, Houston

Kolb D A 1984 Experiential learning: experience as a source of learning and development. Prentice-Hall, New Jersey

Marton F, Saljo R 1976a On qualitative differences in

learning. I Outcome and process. British Journal of Educational Psychology 46: 4–11

Marton F, Saljo R 1976b On qualitative differences in learning. II Outcome as a function of the learner's conception of the task. British Journal of Educational Psychology 46: 115–127

Maslow A H 1970 Motivation and personality. Harper & Row, New York

Norman G R 1988 Problem-solving skills, solving problems and problem-based learning. Medical Education 22: 279–286

Perry W G 1970 Forms of intellectual and ethical development in the college years: a scheme. Holt, Rinehart & Winston, New York

Piaget J 1972 Intellectual development from adolescence. Human Development 15: 1–12

Polyani M 1966 The tacit dimension. Doubleday, New York

Rogers C 1961 On becoming a person. Constable, London

Rogers C 1983 Freedom to learn for the eighties. Charles E Merrill, Columbus, Ohio

Schon D A 1983 The reflective practitioner: how practitioners think in action. Jossey-Bass, San Francisco

Schon D A 1987 Educating the reflective practitioner: towards a new design for teaching and learning in the professions. Jossey-Bass, San Francisco

12

Effective writing

Tim Albert

THE PURPOSE OF WRITING

One of the most misleading – and pretentious – phrases used by scientists is 'in the literature'. The kind of writing dealt with in this chapter has nothing to do with literature, which is generally written by enthusiasts for themselves and only rarely is considered good enough to be published and shared with others. The kind of writing discussed here is more functional and concerned mainly with putting messages across and not just out. Good managers will find this skill invaluable.

Communication seems easy enough when we talk to people face-to-face. Yet, mysteriously, those who can hold an audience spellbound at a party can, when armed with a word-processor, use convoluted constructions and obscure words that will baffle a reader before the second full stop.

The rest of this section will elaborate on this theme and will reveal the all-important but often neglected principle behind all effective writing. It will also show how 'medical writing' often goes wrong. The next section will look at the process of writing, on the assumption that a good technique aids efficiency as well as understanding. Style will be the subject of the third section, which will give seven guidelines for effective writing. But good writers have to use many different styles and the final section will list a number of different 'writing products' and give specific tips for each.

By the end of this chapter, you will probably not be able to turn out perfect prose for all audiences. This is a skill that needs constant refining; as Alex Paton (1985) says: 'Don't believe people who tell you that writing is easy'. Nevertheless, you will know the main features of the craft; the rest will be up to you.

I will follow the model from all good textbooks and propose a definition. Effective writing is the use of words in a permanent and readable form which sends a message from one person to another, accurately and completely. As stated above, it is different from literature; as argued below, it is different from scientific writing, which has evolved a form and function of its own. The nearest kind of communication is speech, which has the advantage of providing us with instant feedback.

Unfortunately, many writers allow themselves to be distracted. When they approach a piece of writing they somehow adopt a new personality. Behind each of these people seems to stand a half-remembered English teacher, who berated them for breaking rigid rules and rewarded them for long new words. They now feel that impenetrability means intelligence and that anything written simply is 'childish' and of little value.

Medical schools have reinforced this position, encouraging young men and women to reject 'real English' in favour of the particular language of medicine. When communicating with other doctors, this is acceptable. When communicating with other people, it becomes meaningless gibberish.

Further traps await. Medicine, like all other professions, is highly competitive. Writing is in black and white. Those who have to commit themselves take great care not to offend their peers and, if possible, try to impress upon them their own grasp of the subject. This is an effective way of ensuring that the message fails to get through.

There is a key to effective writing and it involves an important shift in attitude. Imagine the path that should exist between writer and reader. There are difficult barriers along the way, such as the reader's lack of time, lack of interest and lack of knowledge. The task of the writer is to break through these barriers and, unless they do this, the whole process is a waste of time. Thus the all-important rule is: write with your reader's interests in mind at all times.

This is easier said than done. We may have one

all-important principle, but this principle allows for all other rules to be broken. For instance, if the reader will understand better when you split an infinitive, then you should split one. If the reader has limited knowledge, you should simplify. If the reader needs to come away with a vague or softened message, then you should wheel out your euphemisms. Apart from our single principle, there are no hard-and-fast rules. That is the fascination.

THE PROCESS OF WRITING

On many of the courses I run, doctors cite lack of time as their most pressing writing problem. Others talk about writer's block, that state of suspension in which they sit for hours at a time in front of a blank sheet of paper or an empty screen. There are some simple tricks that can ease you through this problem and this section will reveal them.

One trick is to accept that it takes time – usually more than you think – to write well. Therefore some activity – such as golf, sleeping, watching television – will have to go. You will also find it helpful to approach the writing process logically: understanding the different phases, and how you approach each of them, will help you to be more efficient.

Forward planning is also helpful. Work out what you want to achieve in writing, how you can achieve that goal and what immediate steps you need to take. Avoid huge undertakings, like 'writing a paper for the BMJ' or 'doing the annual report'. Break these down into small units, such as 'five possible topics for a BMJ article' or (1) the mission statement and (2) the chapter headings for the annual report. Put a time limit on these tasks. This will help you to ease the burden of guilt that many of us carry because we feel that we are not 'writing enough'.

Setting the brief

Unless the writer is clear in purpose, the reader stands no chance. Clear writing is rooted in clear thought and you will only get your message across if you are absolutely clear in your own mind what that message should be.

Tackle this problem at an early stage by what I call 'setting the brief'. This stage unites four elements:

1. the purpose or theme of the writing
2. the audience or market
3. the length
4. the deadline.

Formulate the purpose with great care. It is not the same as a title, which is a marketing device whose main goal is to attract the reader; this is best added later, once the product is finished. 'We conducted an experiment which found that most mice died after ingesting product x' will give a writer more direction than 'A study of mice and the ingestion of product x'.

The purpose should consist of one clear idea only. Thus '. . . a few mice did well, most showed no effects one way or the other and some of them died' is too complicated. All these features are important and all will be included in the writing but at this stage, for the sake of clarity, you must make your own priority by choosing the single most important feature.

The exact wording is important. Substitute 'people' for mice or 'got better' for 'died' and the whole shape of the writing will change.

You do not need to be seated at a desk to do this task. Sitting in the bath or walking along country lanes provides ample opportunities. As Henriette Anne Klauser points out in her excellent book on the process of writing (1987), 'ruminating time' is an essential part of the writing process. Do not feel that this is not real work, because the thought you invest at the beginning will pay a rich dividend by the end.

However, as any good freelance journalist will tell you, having a theme is worthless unless it is matched with a market. This market may be a postcard, memo, business report, newsletter, newspaper article or original journal paper. The tighter the audience, the more effective the piece will be. A common error is to try to write for too many publics: if you need to reach different types of readers, then write a separate piece for each. For instance, both the structure and style of a report on quality in fracture clinics will differ depending on whether it is written for the public, GPs or purchasers.

Third, you should decide how long your piece of writing should be. Many people believe that this length is determined by the importance of the subject (which really means how much they happen to know about it). However, our overriding principle that the audience's interests are paramount demands that the true determinant must be what the chosen audience will bear. Writing too much is not a sign that the writer is well informed but rather a sign that he or she has failed to make basic decisions on what, for the audience, is really important.

The final element is a deadline. This will also help to shake off any burden of guilt. It should be realistic and allow ample time for revisions and changes.

Doing the research

Once you have a clear brief, you should write it down, as

in: 'I am going to write a 1200 word report for the management board by January 1 on the need to improve fracture clinics'. All you now have to do is to expand these 20-odd words into the 1200 required. In other words, gather the facts or do the research.

Scientists now have a problem. The word 'research' seems to trigger off a knee-jerk reaction that ends with a literature survey from the nearest medical library. The ensuing pile of paper will confuse the writing process rather than advance it.

The best start, as Klauser suggests, is 'mind-mapping'. This involves writing down on a clean sheet of paper the elements of the theme. Then start jotting down questions and thoughts that you will need to deal with, taking them out like the branches of a tree (Fig. 12.1). This should take between 10 and 20 minutes and by the end of it you will have thought the matter through clearly. As Klauser points out, it is important to let this 'right brain activity' flow. Resist the temptation to be critical (introduce 'left brain activity') at this stage.

This right-side brainstorming will give you the main research questions. You will be surprised how many of the answers you already know or can easily find. The others you should now specifically seek out. In this way you are writing to the brief, not to the subject.

Fig. 12.1 Flow chart (mind mapping)

A few other principles are important at the research stage. Make sure that you keep good notes, in case there is any dispute. If you speak to others, make sure that you tell them why you are talking to them. Do not steal other people's ideas without attribution and, if you use more than a few lines, make sure that you have the appropriate permission.

Planning the writing

You will now have three things: a clear brief, a mind-map flowing all over the page and a pile of notes, charts and figures. Your task is to use these elements to produce a piece of writing that will take the reader through from beginning to end. Reading – and therefore writing – is a linear process and you should now start to convert your material into a linear plan.

The basic structure of any piece of writing has three elements: the beginning, the development and the end. The beginning has a clear function, which is not (as some people have been led by their teachers to suppose) to summarize what they are going to say but, crudely, to attract the reader's interest. You should plan it first, as a separate unit, by asking: what in my material is likely to interest the reader most? You should then add a way of linking this to the rest of the text, preferably by setting up some dynamic which will only be resolved at the end of the writing.

Writing the ending should be straightforward. If you have a good brief then your last paragraph should answer or summarize the question it poses.

The difficult part is constructing the argument that will take the reader from beginning to end. To do this successfully you have to understand that all writing is made up of two different types of matter, 'flesh' and 'bones'. The bones, similar to what grammarians call 'topic sentences', usually appear at the start of each paragraph and take the argument forward. The flesh is the supporting or illustrative material, such as facts and figures or quotations. These explain or elaborate but do not argue.

Any piece of writing should have an even-paced structure; in other words the bones of the argument should appear at regular intervals throughout. A good test is to take a highlighter and mark all the key sentences so that you are left with a mini-version of what you have written. If you find, for instance, that there is a large gap between highlighted sentences, the writing has become flabby. If there are too many highlighted sentences, the writing is overcomplicated.

Writing

Once you are satisfied with your plan, put your research away. You should know enough about the main implications, even if some of the details escape you. Remind yourself of your brief and check that it is still valid. Block off at least an hour, find a quiet room with no telephone, arm yourself with your plan and start writing.

Most writers suggest that you write the whole piece (or, if it is a long one, a large part of it) in one go. Don't worry about the details: they can be added later.

Once you have finished your first draft, put it away for a few days (or at least overnight). When you return to it, relatively fresh, you can start the real work.

Rewriting

Leave the piece for as long as possible, then start revising. This, according to Klauser, is where you should encourage the left-hand side of your brain. You will now have a chance of seeing your work objectively. You should also be able to see some of the simple errors that you made, such as 'wee' when you meant 'week' or '1984' when you meant '1994'. Now is the time to put in – or check – those details that were missing from your first draft.

This stage is vital. As Michael O'Donnell (1987) says: 'To forge simple, direct prose you need to rewrite and rewrite and rewrite and rewrite'. Do not be afraid to rewrite several times (this chapter took about 10 drafts).

Once you are satisfied with it, you should start showing it to others. This is a vital part of the process but, unless you handle it carefully, it can be fraught with problems. The two important rules are, first, to show your writing only to those who can improve it and, second, to understand that some of the changes they suggest will be meeting their agenda, not yours.

Most people advocate showing writing to three different types of people. The first is an obsessive, who will spot those silly mistakes that have so far eluded you. This can be threatening: it is, after all, a piece of your soul that they are criticizing. But grin and change it.

Also show your work to someone who knows something about the subject you are writing about. Do not choose the world's greatest living expert because he or she will usually produce a level of detail that you will rarely need.

Third, show your piece to a member of the audience. This may seem obvious but how often do we do it? A useful technique, devised in America, is 'protocol analysis'. This involves giving a typical reader a tape recorder and asking them to talk aloud giving their reactions. This can reveal many ways in which writing can be improved.

You may wish to add to this list a fourth person, who will represent the views of the organization in which you work. This can be useful in revealing infelicities, often unintentional, which are better discovered before publication. It can also be a good way of spreading the political risk.

With all these people, beware. They will usually exceed their brief. Thus the expert on pollution will pontificate on punctuation and the grammarian on medical ethics. All these people have agendas of their own and, if you ask them to comment, they will feel that they are failing if they do not. One solution is to tell them exactly what you want them to comment on.

GOOD STYLE

Many people confuse style with personality. For the kind of writing we are talking about, good style means the ability to attract predefined readers, maintain their interest and put across information clearly and completely. Good style is not a mandate to show off or a mark of learning. It should not intrude.

However, doctors, scientists and managers often think that it should, judging by the extraordinary styles of some of the most eminent. Some students have said that, if they write along the lines I recommend, their professors will fail them in their examinations. The value of emphasizing that the readers' needs are paramount becomes clear: if the reader wants obscurities, put them in. But the general goal should be simplicity and the following guidelines will help.

Sentences

Sentences are the basic building block of thought – and writing. They should each be clear and self-contained and flow on one from another. Unless the thinking is clear, the sentences will not work.

Avoid long sentences, which usually indicate unclear thought. Good writers can make long sentences work though probably not as often as they would like. A good rule of thumb is four to five sentences for every 100 words, which is not the same as saying each should be 20–25 words long; variation is important.

Do not overuse 'cough starts' with subordinate phrases, such as: 'At 14% of the practice, the number of patients with asthma is higher than the national average'. These are often difficult to follow and even downright ambiguous: 'As the first subject for the experiment, the professor chose amputation'. Perpetrator or victim?

Be careful of inserting long subordinate clauses in the middle, like a sandwich too thick for the modern mouth. Consider the following sentence: 'Specific regulatory genes, some of which may be switched on for only a few days during fetal development, carry all the information needed for the normal development of the embryo'. Dividing this sentence into two makes it far more digestible.

Use the active

Each unit of thought focuses on a person, group or thing; in other words it has a subject. This usually

---

Questions of style

Acronyms Most common style is to use capitals if each letter is pronounced, otherwise upper and lower case: BBC, WHO but Unesco and Aids.

Amongst Archaic waste of two letters. Prefer 'among'. Similarly, 'while' not 'whilst'.

Capitals Slow the reader down and should also be kept to a minimum. Avoid pompous initial capitals, as in 'the Doctors', 'the Nurses' but 'the patients'. Words like 'Department', 'Authority' and 'Mission Statement' do not need initial capitals.

Christian names This term is not appropriate for multiracial societies. Prefer 'first name'.

Comprise Does not take 'of'. But 'consist of'.

Exclamation marks Overdone. Should be used (sparingly) for exclamations and not to signal weak jokes.

His Applies only to a man's possessions. Use 'his or her' or put into plural, as in 'their'. Avoid stereotyping doctors as male and nurses and patients as female.

Hopefully Wrong when used for 'I hope', as in 'Hopefully, the meeting will be good'. Meetings have no feelings.

Hyphens Use sparingly, when they point the reader to the right meaning, as in 'answered carefully-prepared questions' or 'answered carefully prepared questions'.

Include Splendid word for writers, because it allows for any complaint that the list is incomplete.

Lists Be consistent: (1), (2), (3); (a), (b), (c) or bullets. See style book of target publication for guidance.

Monologophobia The fear of using the same word more than once in the same passage. This fear is overrated and can lead to confusion when authors use 'study', 'research' and 'investigation' in one paragraph.

Quotation marks and full stops If the quotation is only part of the sentence, finish it with the quotation mark before putting the full stop: He said it was an 'appalling waste of money'. 'It is an appalling waste of money.'

Try Takes 'to' not 'and'.

Very Use very occasionally.

should be made the early focus of the sentence. Thus: 'The *doctor* saw the patient' or 'Take the *child* to hospital'.

Yet over the past century scientists have adopted a curious grammatical construction which contradicts this principle. This is the passive voice, as in 'The patient was seen by the *doctor*' or 'Urgent admission to hospital is indicated'. Apparently introduced on the grounds that it was more objective, the passive has flooded through the writing of doctors and scientists, spilling over into such pomposities as: 'It was decided that we should take our holidays in Scandinavia this year'.

The passive has three disadvantages. The first is that it requires more words. The second is that it becomes less vigorous. And the third is that the writer often fails to state who actually performed the action, as in: 'Any problems that the patient may be experiencing are discussed and an individual action plan for their asthma is worked out'. By whom?

The passive does have a place. It is useful when the object of an action is more important than the subject, as in: 'The Prime Minister was attacked by a bystander'. It is also useful when causality has yet to be established: 'The Prime Minister was attacked'. And it is useful when a writer, quite deliberately and for political reasons, wishes to make things unclear. Thus, 'Redundancy has been chosen as the preferred option' rather than, 'We have made you redundant'.

A complicating factor, often used to justify the passive, is the common argument that professional people should not use the first person ('I' and 'we'). Why not? If a scientist has done something, it becomes part of the science and manipulating language will not make it more or less objective. In fact, 'The test tube was shaken' gives less information than, 'I shook the test tube'.

The real reason for discouraging the first person is usually more political than scientific. It helps to ensure that individuals cannot be singled out for praise (and promotion?). It also distances the author from subsequent blame. Be brave: instead of, 'It has been noted in the literature by the present authors', substitute 'They have written' or 'We have read'. Instead of 'It is believed', substitute 'I believe' (or 'I disagree with the commonly held belief').

Writing in the active is one of the most effective ways of improving dense prose. As Gowers (1986), one of the leading authorities on effective style, remarks drily: 'Overuse of the passive may render a sentence impenetrable'.

Be positive

The timidity which appears to have encouraged the passive also appears in another form, which involves using a negative whenever possible, apparently to avoid the slightest chance of giving offence. Thus 'not quite right' rather than 'wrong', 'unpleasant' rather than 'nasty', 'not on time' rather than 'late'. Even more confusing are double negatives, as (in an earlier draft of this chapter): 'This is not to say that the passive should never be used'. 'The passive has its place' is neater and simpler to understand.

Make every word count

Do not use a long word if a short one will do. There are many examples: 'performed' rather than 'did'; 'elevated' rather than 'raised' or 'higher'; 'unpleasant' rather than 'nasty'; 'principal intention' rather than

Table 12.1 Overweight words: those in the right-hand column should be used whenever possible

additional	more
anticipate	expect
assistance	help
attempt	try
approximately	about
calculate	work out
commence	start
consensus	agreement
currently	now
determine	decide
donate	give
elevated	raised, higher
endeavour	try
enquire	ask
exceedingly	very
facilitate	ease, help
following	after
implement	use, carry out
indicate	show
individuals	people
initially	at first
maintain	keep
participate	take part
prior to	before
purchase	buy
rapidly	quickly, fast
remuneration	pay
resources	cash, funds, money
requested	asked
required	needed
retain	keep
subject	person
sufficient	enough
subsequently	later, after
uncommon	rare
utilize	use
whether	if
vigilance	care

'main aim'; 'termination of life' rather than 'death' (for a fuller list see Table 12.1). I recently came across 'apices of triangulation' rather than 'three points of the triangle'. Using such phrases is not a sign of cleverness.

Distinguish carefully between technical words and jargon. A technical word or phrase is one used in a particular profession to have a precise meaning and for which there is no other alternative. 'Skill mix', 'health gain' and 'empowerment' may trigger the right reactions among certain groups of insiders but when such phrases are used for the uninitiated they become jargon and should be avoided. Equally pernicious are the fashionable but meaningless clichés, such as 'in the final analysis', 'bottom line' or 'gold standard'. This is imprecise and lazy writing.

Do not use words unnecessarily. Some can simply be struck out, thus: 'learning' and 'experiments' rather than 'learning situation' and 'experimental setting'. 'Absolute perfection' and 'two-way dialogue' can easily be replaced by 'perfection' and 'dialogue'. 'An increasing number of registered medical practitioners' can become simply 'more doctors' (see Table 12.2).

Most of us lapse into pomposities at the first opportunity and one of the best ways of guarding against this is the occasional use of a Fog test. The one I favour, be-

Table 12.2 Pompous phrases

an increasing number of	more and more
arrive at a consensus	agree
at a district level	district
at the end of the day	finally
at this point in time	now
collective agreement	agreement
comprehensive range	range
experimental situation	experiment(al)
for the moment	now
in accordance with	agrees with
in addition	also
in general terms	generally
in order to	to
in the present case	here, now
it is clear that	clearly
it is essential that	... must
it is possible that	... could
it is our opinion	we believe
last but not least	finally
learning situation	learning
two-way dialogue	dialogue
medical profession	doctor
small child	child
weight of evidence	evidence
were not predictive for	did not predict
medical profession	doctors
within a short period of time	soon

Gunning Fog Test

Step one Count out a passage of 100 words. Make sure it ends with a full stop, even if it comes out at slightly more or less than 100 words.

Step two Calculate the average sentence length by dividing 100 by the number of sentences in the passage chosen.

Step three Count the number of words with three or more syllables. This figure gives you the percentage of difficult words. Don't count:
- proper nouns
- combinations of easy words, like 'photocopy'
- verbs that become three syllables when you add 'es', 'ing', 'ed' (e.g. 'committed').

Step four Add the average sentence length (step two) to the number of difficult words (step three).

Step five Multiply the total in step four by 0.4 to get the reading score.

Version one
Within two weeks of your receipt of this notice, the pressure at which water is supplied to your property will be reduced. The benefits of the pressure reduction are a decrease in the volumes of water lost through leakage and a reduction in the frequency of burst mains resulting in fewer interruptions to your water supply to facilitate repairs. Often, customers notice no effect to their water supply as a result of this work, however, if you consider your water supply is inadequate after the pressure is reduced, please check, that your secondary stop tap (often located under the kitchen sink) is fully open.

Version two
I am writing to tell you that we will be reducing the water pressure to your property within the next two weeks. We are doing this in order to cut the number of repairs to leaking and burst pipes. This should mean fewer interruptions to your supply. You will probably not notice any difference. But if you do not think your water supply is adequate, please check that your secondary stop tap is fully open. This tap is usually under the kitchen sink. If it is fully open, please contact our customer service section on ....

	Version one	Version two
Sentences	3	7
Avge s length	33	14
Long words	11	7
Total	44	21
Fog score (x0.4)	17.6	8.4

Typical reading scores

6–8	Airport novels
8–12	Tabloid press
12–16	Serious papers
14–18	Medical journals
18–22	Lawyers' letters

Table 12.3 Clichés

acid test	at the end of the day
back burner	ballpark figure
coal face	empowerment
focus on the grassroots	future requirements
health gain	key initiative
last but not least	learning curve
ring fencing	run with the ball
remedy the situation	role to play
more research is indicated	up in the air

Table 12.4 Common spelling mistakes

accommodation	achievement	argument
attendance	believe	benefited
committee	consensus	definitely
fulfil	guarantee	hygienic
independent	indispensable	liaison
miscellaneous	occurrence	omitted
perseverance	privilege	referral
successful	unnecessary	until

cause it is simple to use and to understand, is that invented by Gunning (1971). For some time it fell into disrepute, mainly because the inventor expected to produce an index that would correlate with US high school grades.

Nevertheless, the Fog test has its uses, as long as we realize that it simply measures long sentences and long words and provides a useful way of comparing different pieces of writing. A study of patient leaflets (Albert & Chadwick 1992), for instance, showed that about 17% were written in the same kind of style as a medical journal. Do not use this test whenever you write, but do use it occasionally to see if your style is running away with you.

Be specific

Effective writing is also specific. Use nouns and verbs ('things' and 'action words') rather than adjectives and adverbs (descriptions). Thus, 'She has a small practice in a pretty village' becomes more vivid once a few facts are inserted: 'She serves her 1000 patients from an ivy-clad cottage from where the village herbalist once dispensed comfrey and lemon balm'.

Do not fall into the trap of simply stringing nouns together, as in 'second generation ethnic household' or 'potential married woman returner'. They have a dangerous habit of acquiring unintended meanings.

Also avoid making good verbs into ponderous nouns.

'This helps in the understanding of the spleen' is better as 'This helps us to understand the spleen'.

Watch for parallels

Putting across a message in words is a difficult process and it is easy to confuse the receiving brain. Make sure that your constructions are parallel; in other words keep to the same structure throughout. 'The consensus is that he is a good clinician, but his administrative skills are bad' is better as 'He is a good clinician but a bad administrator'. Similarly, 'Smith's experiment succeeded but all Jones's mice died' is obviously easier to understand as 'Smith's experiment succeeded but Jones's experiment failed'.

Check grammar and spelling

Much has been written about the poor standards of doctors' (and other professionals') grammar and spelling and many of these comments are true. I take the view that it is probably too late to correct what should have been inculcated at an early age and the most important thing is to know your weaknesses and to ensure that someone is available to correct them (see section on revision, above).

Nevertheless, grammar is important because it can destroy the meaning of a sentence. 'The administrators, who arrived early, held a meeting' is different from, 'The administrators who arrived early held a meeting'. 'The administrators, who arrived early held a meeting' is neither one nor the other. (For a list of common errors, see Table 12.5.)

These examples also illustrate the fact that the point of grammar is to set up a system of rules that enable us to understand each other. These rules should not be rigid and they change over time. Many of us were taught that we should never split infinitives, use 'and' or 'but' at the beginning of a sentence or end with a preposition. The latest edition of Gowers says that, under certain circumstances, we can.

Correct spelling is also essential for understanding. 'Elevated' is different from 'alleviated', 'casual' from 'causal'. Spellcheckers can help up to a point but even they are fallible. Shakespeare, for example, would not have been alerted to: 'Two bee oar knot two bee . . .'

Do not be obsessed by political correctness

All languages change. In recent years a chair has become not only something that you sit upon but also a person who leads a meeting or committee. Other

Table 12.5 Eight common grammatical mistakes

1. *The incomplete sentence* Can be used occasionally, but often creeps in through faulty punctuation, as in: 'The management board decided to close down the hospital. Having considered all the evidence'.
2. *The floating comma* Do not 'leave' a phrase without signalling your return: 'The doctors, however disagreed' is wrong. 'The administrators, who arrived early held a meeting' is wrong and ambiguous.
3. *The misplaced possessive* In general, the apostrophe comes before the s for singular (one doctor's) and after the s for the plural (several doctors'). Most people now agree that s can go after s (St James's). 'It's' is a contraction of 'it is' and not a possessive.
4. *The dangling modifier* The habit of qualifying something which is not mentioned until later in the sentence or not at all. As in 'Unable to speak, the doctor gave me an enema' or 'The chairman having spoken eloquently, the meeting ended on time'.
5. *The movable tense* Choose one time-frame and keep to it. Not: 'The speaker added... He also says...'
6. *The misplaced phrase* Connected phrases should stay together and not wander off to the other end of the sentence, as in 'We talked about several diseases in the restaurant'.
7. *Inconsistent numbers* The subject of a sentence must agree with the verb. 'Managers and politicians is in agreement' is obviously wrong, but it gets complicated when collective nouns are introduced: 'A group of doctors was...' or 'The company are...'. 'None' is a contraction of 'not one' and is always singular.
8. *Faulty pronouns* Use 'I', 'he', 'she' and 'we' only if they are the subject of the sentence; otherwise 'me', 'him', 'her' and 'us'. Thus, 'She and I were talking with him' and 'He was arguing with her and me'.

phrases are even more cumbersome. Some phrases we learnt as children are no longer acceptable.

For the writer the trick is to bear in mind the needs of the real audience and not let political correctness undermine your overall goal. When you do your first draft, do not examine each word to see if it might be offensive. That is a sure way of producing unintelligible documents. Write with your own vocabulary, then show the copy to an activist. He or she will be delighted to point out when your words are unacceptable. Of course, it is up to you to judge whether to change them or not.

DIFFERENT TYPES OF WRITING

One of the main themes of this chapter is that writing is a flexible tool. Provided that you work to the rule that the reader's interests are paramount, you should be able in principle to write anything from a learned paper in a scientific journal to a snappy guidance note for patients. Nevertheless, there are some differences, mainly in style, and this last section will give various tips on how to tailor your writing for specific markets.

Management reports

Doctors in management spend much of their time writing. Define the brief carefully (see above) and pay particular attention to the real audience. Is it the management board in general (or a single powerful figure on that board), the general public or a particular interest group? It is unlikely to be for other doctors, so avoid technical words and jargon unless, of course, your main aim is not to get a message across but to show that you are clever and they were wise to hire you.

Study other reports from your organization. These should show you the house style. Classify the reports into those that have succeeded and those that have failed and look for differences in the way they were written.

Pay particular attention to the structure. You will usually have to impose a further level of 'bones', i.e. headings and subheadings, but within each of these sections the usual guidelines will apply. Use the introduction to attract the reader and show the pay-off for *them*. Use the development for a structured argument and not just a compilation of random data. Use the conclusion to put across the message you wish to stay in the reader's mind. In addition, give a summary, so that busy readers can at least have a quick overview.

Writing for publication

Although many journal editors say that they encourage good style (as in short words and active constructions) the reality is often different. When working on a scientific paper, make sure that you choose your target journal at an early stage so that you can meet the editor's expectations. Look at the language it uses, try a Fog test on some of the articles and keep to that style. One journal recently rejected two articles on the grounds that they were a 'bit thin'; they had a Fog score of about 12. When I rewrote one with righteous – and pompous – anger, it had a score of 22 and was rapturously accepted.

Look at markets within markets. Each publication has its own structure (editorials, original papers, short reports, books reviews, letters) so work out in advance where your contribution will best fit. Write to the right length. There is no point submitting a case report to a journal that does not publish them or sending a 3000-word editorial when the usual length is 850 words.

For original scientific papers, use the IMRAD structure: Introduction, Methods, Research and Discussion. In communication terms, this structure is a curiosity: the important part always appears at the end (which is one reason why abstracts are more and more important). Nevertheless, this is the convention and you flout it at your peril.

When submitting to the 'lay' press, the same general principles apply. Do not write anything until you have worked out its ultimate destination. Study the style of the publication and also its structure. Then look at the shape and style of the articles in each section. As stressed already, do not write anything for publication until you have chosen its target market. Make sure that your target publication carries the kind of articles that you wish to write.

Press releases

In some organizations, the function of press releases is to show the management board that people in the press office are doing their job. The real purpose of press releases, however, is to alert publications to potential stories.

First, make sure that there is a story; in other words it is something that is likely to be published, as opposed to something that you want to see published. Construct your brief carefully: a common mistake is to put out a press release on one subject while giving a keen reporter a clue for an even better story, not necessarily in your interests to see published. To say that Professor Smith has been appointed is one thing (though not very interesting); to say in the fourth paragraph that he is conducting 'simian studies' is asking for trouble.

The structure of the press release follows the style for news stories. This is known as the 'inverted triangle', in which the first paragraph defines the whole story. The rest follows in decreasing order of importance.

Layout is important: make sure that the package is appropriate. Use double spacing and clear margins. Keep to two pages maximum; if you have extra information that you think is essential, put it in an appendix or 'Notes to Editors'.

Use a title to attract the editor's interest, but do not expect this to appear as a headline in print. Writing headlines is a particular skill and anyway, it is unlikely that your version will fit the publication's style – or the space set aside for the headline.

Finally, make sure that you have a contact number at the end of the press release. And that someone will be there when a reporter calls.

Memos and letters

The most appropriate structure is the inverted triangle. Put the important part (i.e. the pay-off for the reader) in the first sentence. Under no circumstances should you use the IMRAD structure, which reverses this principle. Busy colleagues may well lose heart and stop reading and your buried message will not get through.

Pay attention to the start of the memo. This should be reader-oriented. 'You' should appear before 'we' or 'I'. The first few words should not be boring, as in 'I am in receipt of your letter' or 'The car-parking working party of the senior management group. . .'. With some letters, however, you may wish to ignore this rule in the interests of politeness. Some people expect a welcoming cough: 'Thank you for your letter' or 'It was good to meet you the other day'. This reinforces our main rule: the interests of the reader are paramount.

Keep a cynical eye out for people who read between the lines. A letterhead where the top half consists only of patrons' names will make the receiver seem small. A request for a stamped addressed envelope may sound mean. 'It's' instead of 'its' will suggest that you are uneducated.

If you are using an envelope, check that the contents are the right ones and that all extraneous slips of paper have been detached. A health authority once received an estimate from a firm of solicitors, with a note attached: 'This is a sprat to catch a mackerel'. Such carelessness can undo hours of careful writing.

Newsletters

Articles for newsletters should follow the rule for news stories and press releases; the first paragraph should do all the work by defining the story and interesting the reader.

Write to your audience and remember that you are competing with many other documents, many of them professionally produced. Keep words and sentences short and simple. Be wary of the *Pravda* factor: you should not combine news with propaganda. Do not impose value judgements, such as 'We are very fortunate to have someone of the calibre of Professor Smith', unless you attribute the opinion and put it in inverted commas.

Make sure that each newsletter has an editor, someone who can impose his or her personality and style by taking decisions on what can or cannot be published. The editor, or someone nominated by the editor, should subedit each contribution to ensure that the style is consistent and the language reader-friendly. Do not underestimate the time needed to do this.

Do not hide the words by putting them in small print. Make sure that each page has constant elements, such as headlines and some illustrative material, that will help to involve the reader. Keep to a simple style. The most important thing, as ever, is to try to see things from the point of view of the reader, not the organization.

CONCLUSION

Throughout this chapter some common themes recur. Work out carefully what you want to say and how you want to say it. Adopt the appropriate structure and style. Above all, think of the real audience – and treat comments from others with the appropriate pinch of salt.

Do not expect to enjoy the experience of writing. Few professional writers, if any, say that it is easy. Do not expect the skills to come easily, particularly at first. But if you persevere and learn from your many mistakes, you will find that you have at your disposal an extremely useful tool.

REFERENCES

Albert T, Chadwick S 1992 How readable are practice leaflets? British Medical Journal 305: 1266–1268

Gowers E 1986 The complete plain words, 3rd edn. HMSO, London

Gunning R 1971 The technique of clear writing. McGraw-Hill, New York

Klauser H A 1987 Writing on both sides of the brain. HarperCollins, San Francisco, pp 25–55

O'Donnell M 1987 Write for money. How to do it 2. BMJ Books, London, p 198

Paton A 1985 Write a paper. How to do it 1, 2nd edn. BMJ Books, London, p 207

FURTHER READING

Albert T 1992 Medical journalism: the writer's guide. Radcliffe Medical Press, Oxford

Goodman N W, Edwards M B 1991 Medical writing: a prescription for clarity. Cambridge University Press, Cambridge

Hughes V 1990 English language skills. Macmillan, London

O'Connor M 1991 Writing successfully in science. HarperCollins, London

Shortland M, Gregory J 1991 Communicating science. Longman, Harlow

Strunk W, White E B 1979 The elements of style, 3rd edn. Macmillan, New York

13

Managing people

John Gatrell

There are many aspects to management. If one single characteristic of a successful manager can be isolated as of critical importance, it is the ability to get the best from people. Managerial work has been studied and defined in a wide variety of ways since the process of management became an observed part of organizational life during the 19th century. An early definition, by Fayol (1949), divides management into five elements:

1. planning (deciding what needs to be achieved and developing a plan of action);
2. organizing (bringing together the resources to meet the objectives of the organization);
3. commanding (directing and maximizing the effectiveness of personnel);
4. coordinating (unifying and harmonizing the activities of the organization);
5. controlling (verifying that everything occurs in accordance with expressed command).

This definition has been useful in providing a basis for the study of management in organizations. A more recent explanation of how managers carry out their functions is provided by Mintzberg (1973). He has defined three sets of managerial roles. The *interpersonal* role arises from the status and authority of the manager. The roles of figurehead, leader and liaison are encompassed in this set. The second set is *informational* and includes monitoring performance, disseminating information and acting as spokesperson. Finally, the *decisional* roles are entrepreneurial, disturbance handler, resource allocator and negotiator.

Some tasks performed by doctors in the performance of their everyday professional activity include elements which could be described as managerial. These would include time management, resolving conflict and engendering team spirit. In addition to these elements, there are some activities which arise because some doctors assume responsibilities outside their medical role. These latter activities vary, in most cases, with level of seniority of appointment. They also vary with speciality, size of unit, between general practitioners and hospital doctors and by individual choice. They are likely to include budget management, negotiating, interviewing and contributing to the strategic development of the unit.

Burgoyne & Stuart (1976) developed a model which identifies the qualities of an effective manager. These are divided into three clusters which form a hierarchy. The first cluster is concerned with awareness of surrounding data and facts, which is based on contextual knowledge and past learning, including professional studies. Second in the hierarchy is a cluster of qualities and skills which enable the manager to interpret situations and to handle the uncertainty of unfolding events. This is achieved by analytical problem solving, using social skills to communicate with and influence others and by maintaining emotional stability and responding purposefully to events. Finally, there is a group of 'metaqualities' which support the development of managers and their ability to acquire the qualities and skills to meet the sometimes unforeseeable demands of specific situations. These are creativity, mental agility, balanced learning habits and skills and, finally, self-knowledge.

One detailed study of senior managers in a mix of public and private sector organizations in the USA provides a useful summary of managerial competences (Klemp & McClelland 1986).

Among the intellectual or cognitive competences are:

- planning/causal thinking – seeing implications, analysing causal relationships;
- diagnostic information seeking – seeking information from multiple sources to clarify a situation;
- conceptualizing/synthetic thinking – identifying

patterns, interpreting events, identifying important issues in complex situations.

Influence competences are described as:

- concern/need for power;
- personal/directive influence (personalized power);
- collaborative influence – operates effectively with groups, involves others;
- symbolic influence – creates impact by setting personal example.

An additional competence is:

- self-confidence – sees self as a leader, the most capable person to get things done.

It may be easily seen that these definitions, particularly the more recent, emphasize the relationship between the role of the manager and their effectiveness in working with others. This chapter sets out the key issues surrounding the role of a manager in relation to people. These are dealt with here under headings which are most relevant to the work of doctors – leadership, delegation and motivation. Firstly, a brief review of managerial approaches to the relationships is presented.

MANAGERIAL BEHAVIOUR AND RELATIONSHIPS

McGregor (1987) proposes two opposite sets of assumptions made by managers about human nature and behaviour. He refers to them as Theory 'X' and Theory 'Y'. Although they oversimplify and are expressed as extremes, they do represent recognized philosophies under which managers' inclinations to act are frequently shaped. They relate to the hierarchy of needs model which is described below.

Theory 'X' managers make the following assumptions:

- the average person is lazy and has an inherent dislike of work;
- most people must be coerced, controlled, directed and threatened with punishment if the organization is to achieve its objectives;
- the average person avoids responsibility, prefers to be directed, lacks ambition and values security most of all.

McGregor argues that the style of management suggested by these assumptions is no longer relevant in today's organizations, where people's views and expectations are shaped by changed social structures, education and non-work activities.

Theory 'Y' managers make a quite different, opposing set of assumptions about people:

- work is as natural as rest or play;
- people will exercise self-direction and self-control in the service of objectives to which they are committed;
- commitment to objectives is a function of rewards associated with their achievement;
- given the right conditions, the average worker can learn to accept and to seek responsibility;
- the capacity for creativity and problem solving in organizations is distributed widely throughout the population;
- the intellectual potential of the average person is only partially utilized.

The Theory 'Y' approach is regarded by McGregor as a more effective basis on which to develop managerial systems and approaches. If the organization is to get the best from its members, the administration of employment through performance appraisal, promotions and reward systems, team and individual development and training should be founded in Theory 'Y', rather than in Theory 'X'. As with other models for understanding managerial work, this approach offers guidance rather than certainty. It is recognized that individual differences between people, and variations in types of organization, can mean that adopting a style of management based on Theory 'X' can be more effective, at least in the short term.

LEADERSHIP

The relationship between leadership and management could be explored in depth. For the purpose of this chapter it is sufficient to confirm that, while all managers should be capable of leading, not all leaders are managers. There are roles within the medical profession, such as consultant, which call on the postholder to act as leader in relation to junior posts.

It is difficult to generalize about leadership. Essentially, it is 'a relationship through which one person influences the behaviour of other people' (Mullins 1989). Models and theories of leadership are many and various. They range from the traditional 'leaders are born, not made' perspective to the more modern view that leadership is a complex process which involves a range of skills which can be acquired through learning and practice.

Leadership traits

The traditional assumption has been that effective leaders possess distinguishing characteristics, such as enthusiasm, self-assurance, initiative, intelligence and so on. Considerable research has failed to arrive at a consensus on such traits, particularly because there are many notably successful leaders who are deficient in a significant proportion of the defined traits. There is still some interest in identifying personality traits of successful leaders. Interest has shifted, however, to other approaches to leadership.

Leadership styles

Styles of leadership are usually defined as occurring on a continuum between 'authoritarian' and 'democratic'.

Five separate styles are commonly defined:

1. Tells – the leader chooses the course of action to be followed, communicates it to subordinates and expects acceptance without debate.
2. Sells – the leader anticipates the possibility of resistance from subordinates and attempts to persuade them of the merits of the decision.
3. Consults – the leader presents a problem to the team and invites suggestions and advice before making the decision.
4. Participates – the leader joins the group in arriving at a decision, inviting the group to assist in defining the problem.
5. Delegates – sometimes referred to as 'empowerment'. The leader develops staff and creates an environment of trust in which subordinates accept responsibility for problem solving and decision making. This is not always described as a style of leadership. For a detailed explanation of delegation, see below.

The difference between one style and another reflects the locus of power between the leader and the led. Authoritarian leaders hold on to their power and use it to direct the work behaviour of their subordinates. They retain the right to make decisions, reward and punish. More democratic styles lead to the delegation of decision making or at least the sharing of authority and control. Some writers have argued that people will be more productive when working in a democratic environment (Blake & Mouton 1964, Likert 1961, McGregor 1987). They provide evidence that supportive styles of leadership help to create job satisfaction, reduce grievance rates and result in less intergroup conflict. There is some doubt, however, that participative styles are always effective in enhancing work group performance. Style alone is insufficient as a determining factor, although its importance is now recognized.

Situational leadership

This approach starts from the proposition that the effectiveness of the characteristics and style of the leader is contingent upon the variables involved in the leadership situation. Prominent among these variables are the type and size of organization, the nature of the immediate challenge facing the group and its preparedness to deal with it, and the pressure of time constraints. Other variables include the favourability of the leadership situation (Fiedler 1967), the quality and acceptance of the leader's decisions (Vroom & Yetton 1973) and the maturity of the led group (Hersey & Blanchard 1988). The last of these provides a useful insight into leadership models in general. Appropriate leadership style is defined as the balance between task-oriented and relationship-oriented leadership behaviour:

- task-oriented behaviour focuses on directing the actions of followers, defining their roles and setting goals for them;
- relationship-oriented behaviour concerns the extent to which the leader engages in listening, encouraging and supporting followers.

These two dimensions are used to produce four leadership styles – telling, selling, participating and delegating. Choice of leadership style is dependent on the state of readiness, or maturity, of the follower group. Thus, the telling style is suited to an immature group which needs high levels of guidance and structure and is less in need of relationship concern. Next, selling style emphasizes both relationship and task behaviours and is suited to groups which have growing maturity and are in need of support through the team-building process. Participating style emphasizes two-way communication and support but allows freedom to the group to determine task decisions. At the other end of the continuum, delegating can be used only with a mature, well-trained group which is capable of managing its own tasks and relationships.

There are many forms of leadership, with no one best way. Likert (1961) found that authoritative, task-focused style could result in high productivity in the short term because of compliance based on fear. Long-term improvements in performance are more likely to result from participative styles which accommodate group and individual needs.

DELEGATION

The concept of delegation is simple. The practice is rather different. It involves high levels of skill and understanding. Delegation is usually interpreted to mean passing down authority and responsibility to others at a more junior level. It is also possible to delegate laterally to colleagues and even upwards when, for example, a staff member is called away and a more senior person takes over the work. Authority and responsibility go together. Authority is the power and the right to take appropriate action in a given situation. Responsibility, in a corporate sense, is an individual's answerability to a senior for the successful accomplishment of a task. It would be unreasonable to delegate responsibility for an activity without giving the person authority to act. Equally, if that person is given authority, they should be held responsible for outcomes. This does not mean that the senior can delegate *ultimate* responsibility. Their role will be to delegate effectively and give support, encouragement and reasonable protection to their staff. The senior remains accountable to higher authority for all the activities, whether medical or managerial, within their control.

There are many benefits which can arise from delegation. Good time management involves making the most effective use of all staff resources, including your own. Tasks which can be carried out satisfactorily by subordinates should not be routinely undertaken by senior staff. Delegation leaves senior staff free to make profitable use of time by concentrating on important tasks and planning to avoid problems. Staff training opportunities arise out of delegation. It also allows assessment of suitability for future development and promotion. Specialist knowledge and skills are demanded of staff by the complex nature of healthcare. Rapid changes brought on by technological development and government influence increase the complexity of the work. It is impossible for one individual to carry all the knowledge and skills necessary to ensure effective performance of the unit. Delegation provides a mechanism for controlled sharing of the workload.

Mullins (1989) identifies six stages in a planned and systematic approach to delegation:

1. Clarification of objectives and design of structure – clear command, communication and coordination between the various levels of authority. Policies and procedures must be defined in order to provide a framework for the exercise of authority and the acceptance of responsibility.

2. Agreement of terms of reference – define the task. Areas of responsibility should be identified clearly. End results, rather than detailed instruction, should be emphasized. The division of activities and responsibilities should be established and agreed.

3. Acceptance of authority and responsibility – select the person. Subordinates must be helped to understand and accept the extent of, and restrictions on, the authority and responsibility delegated to them.

4. Briefing, guidance and training – subordinates should be told where, and to whom, they can go for further help and advice. They need to be confident in their own ability to cope with the new responsibility. This will come from effective instruction and adequate resources being made available. Colleagues and other individuals within the organization who will be affected by reallocation of responsibilities must be informed of the change.

5. Time limits, check points and performance standards – adequate standards of performance and realistic time limits must be agreed. Wherever possible, achievement should be measurable against clearly defined criteria.

6. Freedom of action – the subordinate should be left alone to get on with the job. It is a fundamental requirement of successful delegation that the senior is prepared to trust the subordinate and demonstrate that trust by standing back once the task has been delegated. 'The true nature of successful delegation means that the subordinate is given freedom of action within the boundaries established and agreed in the previous stages' (Mullins 1989).

An additional stage is evaluation of performance and recognition of achievement. Effective control should mean that the senior will be aware of the satisfactory completion of the delegated task. This should be noted and feedback given to the successful subordinate.

Difficulties with delegation

Difficulties arise largely as a result of the emotional link we have with our own job. We worry that another person might not do it as well as we would, or worse, they might show us up by being much better at it! It is often easier to do it than explain it to someone else. Sometimes we feel uncomfortable about asking others because they are too busy or the task is unpleasant. We might fear one of the consequences of delegation, which is a feeling of becoming underemployed. Handy (1985) suggests this is 'the most insidious, but most ignored, perverter of organizational efficiency'.

Above all, there is the need to show trust in our subordinates, so that they can develop as we have done. A tension arises because of the relationship which inevitably exists in the 'trust/control relationship'. The amount of control we retain reduces with any increase in trust we demonstrate in the person to whom we delegate.

MOTIVATION

The performance of any individual in the conduct of their work is likely to be dependent on three variables.

Firstly, the *ability* to complete the task to a satisfactory standard, which is a combination of aptitude and development. Secondly, the tools and facilities for the job must be available; they must have the *opportunity*. Thirdly, they must be *motivated* to complete the task. Thus, it has been stated that performance is the product of ability and motivation.

Good managers, it must be assumed, are able to understand what motivates their workforce and act in order to get the best from them. They must also be capable of harnessing those energies towards the successful achievement of corporate goals.

The study of work motivation has produced many texts since the beginning of the 20th century. For each text, there seems to be yet another theory to show managers how to get the best from a workforce. Motivation, in this context, is concerned with why people choose a particular course of action and persist in that action in preference to others. The underlying concept of motivation is the existence of *needs* which give rise to *drive* to take *action* in order to achieve desired *goals* which meet the needs and create *satisfaction*.

Human needs are said by Maslow (1987) to be arranged in a hierarchy, with basic needs dominating higher order needs until the former are reduced. His model is often presented as in Fig. 13.1.

Physiological needs include food, water and warmth – the basic requirements of survival. Safety and security are provided by freedom from threat of physical attack, protection from deprivation and by predictability and orderliness. Social and love needs are met by a sense of belonging, friendships and the giving and receiving of love. Esteem is focused on the self and involves the desire for confidence, status and the respect of others. Self-fulfilment (described by Maslow as self-actualization) is the realization of one's full potential. This may vary widely from one individual to another. Some authors have suggested that a sixth need, which follows self-fulfilment, is self-awareness.

Maslow argues that these needs are hierarchical and that a need which is satisfied is no longer a motivator. Hence, as lower level needs are met, so the driving force of behaviour becomes the higher need. Needs do not have to be fully met. There is a gradual emergence of a higher level need as lower level needs become more satisfied. He also makes it clear that the hierarchy applies to most, not all, people. It is not necessarily a fixed order. Exceptions will be evident. Some people, driven by a creative and self-actualizing urge, will ignore more basic needs. Others, with high ideals or values, may become martyrs and give up everything for the sake of their beliefs. It follows that, in order to provide motivation for changes in behaviour, a manager must direct attention to the next higher level of need.

Maslow's theory is difficult to test empirically. Those attempts which have been made give only tentative support. The theory has been influential, nonetheless, perhaps because of its simplicity and universality. It spawned a string of suggested approaches, sometimes referred to as 'content' theories, which focus on the things which motivate. Among the best known of these is the work of Herzberg (1974). The latter produced an influential model, known as the dual factor theory of motivation and job satisfaction.

The first set of factors, if absent, lead to dissatisfaction. These are generally extrinsic to the job and include salary, working conditions, security and organizational policy and administration. They are called 'hygiene' factors by reference to the medical context in which they may be regarded as preventive and environmental. If 'right', they do not create satisfaction. If 'wrong', however, they can cause dissatisfaction and subvert the motivational efforts of managers. It is important for managers to make sure that these factors are acceptable to the workforce. If they are, the second set of factors can serve to motivate by encouraging greater effort and performance. These are generally intrinsic and can create satisfaction. They are referred to as 'motivators' and include achievement, recognition, responsibility and the nature of the work itself.

Hygiene factors can be related to the lower levels of Maslow's hierarchy of needs and the motivators to the higher levels. If the work situation is acceptable regarding hygiene factors, it does not follow that workers will be satisfied. They will merely not be dissatisfied. If dissatisfied, it will not be possible to improve their performance by use of the motivators. If sources of dissatisfaction have been removed, then it should be possible to create opportunities for job satisfaction to be obtained. This will be mainly achieved through job

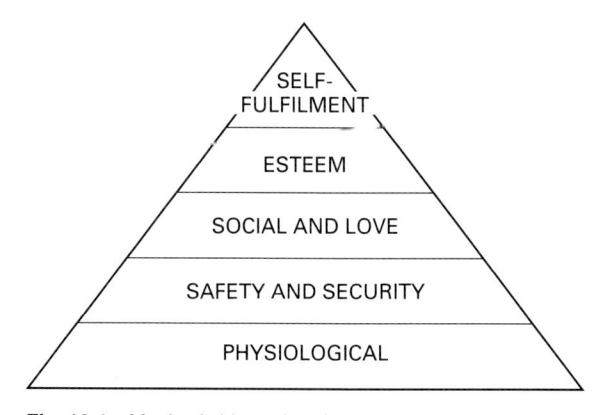

Fig. 13.1 Maslow's hierarchy of needs model

restructuring or 'job enrichment'. This means building the job into one which can generate in the holder a sense of achievement, responsibility or other motivating factor.

Various studies replicating that of Herzberg have supported his results. There is also a view that the data could have been used to demonstrate different outcomes (Vroom 1982). Others have argued that the theory does not account for individual differences. A given factor might be a source of satisfaction for one person but cause stress or dissatisfaction in another. This is particularly relevant in relation to manual workers, who did not feature in Herzberg's research, which focused on accountants and engineers.

The work of McClelland (1976) led to a further content theory of motivation. He and his colleagues identified three main arousal based, socially developed motive forces. These were:

1. affiliation (n-Aff)
2. power (n-Pow)
3. achievement (n-Ach).

These correspond broadly to Maslow's highest order needs for love and society, esteem and self-actualization. Their relative impact on behaviour varies with each individual. It was also possible to identify differences according to occupation.

Follow-up research focused on individuals with a high need for achievement (McClelland & Burnham 1976), in whom they identified three common characteristics: a preference for personal responsibility, the setting of moderate goals and the desire for concrete feedback on performance. They like to be personally responsible for solving problems and getting results. They also like to attain success through their own efforts, rather than as a member of a team. The recognition of others is not as important as their own sense of accomplishment. A second characteristic is the tendency to set moderate achievement goals and to take calculated risks. If the task is too difficult or too risky, the chances of success would be reduced. If the task is too easy or too safe there would be little sense of achievement from success. Thirdly, feedback on performance should be prompt, clear and unambiguous. It helps to confirm success and give the sense of satisfaction which comes with achievement.

A second 'family' of motivational theories emphasizes the study of process, rather than content. These seek to provide a better understanding of the relationship between variables which influence work behaviour. Process models are generally more able to accommodate individual differences. Among the best known is 'expectancy theory'. It emphasizes an individual's perception of the probability that particular outcomes will result from specific courses of action. The model which is best known is that developed by Vroom (1982). It is based on three variables: valence, instrumentality and expectancy.

Valence is defined as the attractiveness of, or preference for, a particular outcome to an individual. If a person has a preference for a particular outcome, valence is positive. Where avoidance of a particular outcome is preferred, valence is negative. If the person is indifferent to the outcome, valence is zero. Valence is the *expected* satisfaction and is distinguished from the value attached to the actual outcome, once achieved.

Instrumentality is best understood if we distinguish between first-level outcomes and second-level outcomes. First-level outcomes refer to actual performance in the work. For some, this will be an end to be valued for its own sake, as 'a job well done'. For others, the valence of the performance outcomes is determined by the second-level outcomes which may, for example, be derived from the financial gains resulting from satisfactory completion of the task. Second-level outcomes are need related. Instrumentality is the extent to which first-level outcomes lead to second-level outcomes.

Expectancy is a perception of the probability that the choice of a particular action will lead to the desired outcome. It relates effort expended to the achievement of first-level outcomes.

Fig. 13.2 shows that expectancy (the perceived probability that effort will lead to first-level outcomes) and instrumentality (the association between first and second-level outcomes) are linked in Vroom's model. The strength of the valence of an outcome is determined by the extent to which that outcome leads to other outcomes. Expectancy (E) is measured on a value range of 0 to +1.0. A zero probability that an action will be followed by an outcome is rated 0, and certainty that a particular action will result in the outcome is rated +1.0.

The strength of the valence of an outcome is based on the instrumentality, which is measured from −1.0 to +1.0. If, for example as shown in Fig. 13.2, it is believed that good work performance always results in a wage bonus, instrumentality will be +1.0. On the other hand, if good work performance is not expected to lead to a bonus, or the bonus will be paid regardless of performance, then instrumentality will be −1.0.

Motivation (M) may be expressed as the equation $M = \Sigma(E.V)$. There are likely to be a number of second-level outcomes to any action (for example, see Fig. 13.2). Each possible outcome (E.V) is computed and they are summed to give a single indicator of the attractiveness to the individual of the contemplated behaviour.

This model, as with others derived from it, is useful in explaining the process by which people weigh and

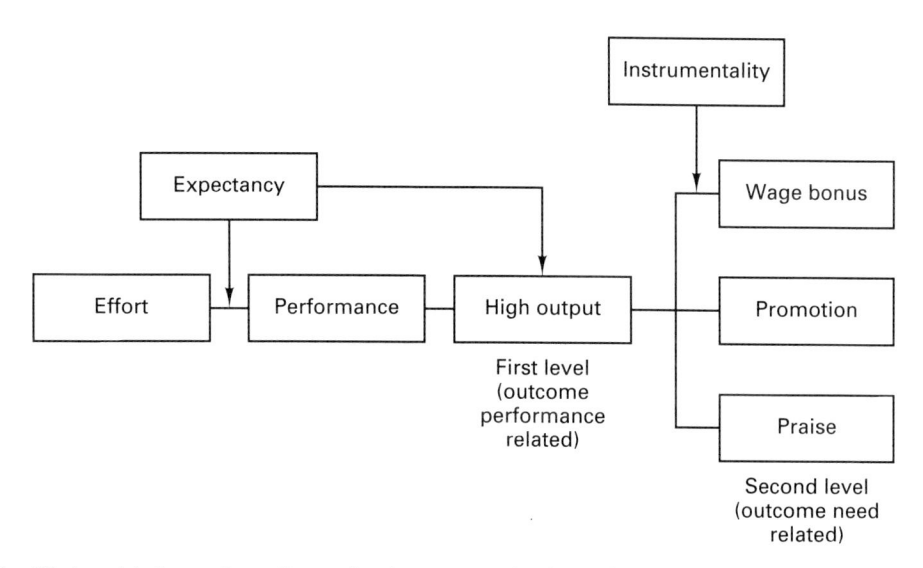

Fig. 13.2 Simplified model of expectancy theory showing an example of a performance-related first-level outcome

evaluate the attractiveness of different alternatives before committing themselves to specific courses of action. The models do not, however, reflect the actual decision-making steps taken by an individual.

Goal-oriented behaviour has been explored by Locke (1968). This provides a further insight into motivation. Goal setting may be viewed as a motivational technique rather than a theory. A number of management systems emphasize the importance of agreeing work goals with employees, whose behaviour is thought to be determined by their goals. Locke suggests that people's values give rise to emotions and desires which they strive to satisfy through their responses and actions. Goals direct work behaviour and performance and lead to certain consequences or feedback. People with specific, measurable goals will perform better than those without. Also, those with difficult, though achievable, goals will perform better than those whose goals may be easily achieved.

In general, theories and models of motivation are unable to provide universal solutions to the challenge of motivating people at work. They do, however, help us to understand the complexity of the process and take us away from management approaches linked to fear and punishment once common among traditional managers earlier in the 20th century.

SUMMARY

The work of a manager has been described in various ways. It encompasses planning and organizing work activities, coordinating and controlling the use of resources, communicating information and using personal attributes and competences to influence and lead others. Leadership styles range from the authoritarian, who makes decisions and tells subordinates, to the democratic, who involves subordinates in the decision-making process. There seems to be a relationship between style and effectiveness, but this is affected by the leadership situation.

Effective managers of people are able to delegate effectively. They define clearly what is expected and guide and train those to whom authority and responsibility are given. The relationship between control and trust means that we must relinquish control as we expect subordinates to accept more and this involves developing trust in their ability to cope.

Motivation to work involves a complex set of needs which create drive for action. Needs have been seen as hierarchical, forming the basis for more detailed models of motivation.

REFERENCES

Blake R, Mouton J 1964 The managerial grid. Gulf, Houston
Burgoyne J G, Stuart R 1976 The nature, use and acquisition of managerial skills and other attributes. Personnel Review 5(4): 19–29
Fayol H 1949 General and industrial management. Pitman, London
Fiedler F E 1967 A theory of leadership effectiveness. McGraw-Hill, New York
Handy C B 1985 Understanding organizations. Penguin, Harmondsworth

Hersey P, Blanchard K 1988 Management of organizational behavior. Prentice-Hall, New Jersey
Herzberg F 1973 Work and the nature of man. Staple Press, London
Klemp G O, McClelland D 1986 What characterizes intelligent functioning among senior managers? In: Sternberg R J, Wagner R K (eds) Practical intelligence: nature and origins of competence in the everyday world. Cambridge University Press, Cambridge
Likert R 1961 New patterns of management. McGraw-Hill, New York
Locke E A 1968 Towards a theory of task motivation and incentives. Organizational Behaviour and Human Performance 3: 157–189
Maslow A H 1987 Motivation and personality, 3rd edn. Harper & Row, New York
McClelland D C 1976 The achieving society. Irvington, New York
McClelland D C, Burnham D H 1976 Power is the great motivator. Harvard Business Review 54: 100–110
McGregor D V 1987 The human side of enterprise. Penguin, Harmondsworth
Mintzberg H 1980 The nature of managerial work. Prentice-Hall, New Jersey
Mullins L J (1989) Management and organisational behaviour. Pitman, London
Vroom V H 1982 Work and motivation. Krieger
Vroom V H, Yetton P 1973 Leadership and decision-making. University of Pittsburgh Press, Pittsburgh

14

Interviews and interviewing skills

John Gatrell, Tony White

Let me have men about me that are fat; sleek-headed men and such as sleep o'nights. Yon Cassius has a lean and hungry look; he thinks too much: such men are dangerous.

(Shakespeare, *Julius Caesar*, Act 1 Scene II)

INTRODUCTION

The purpose of interviewing and selection procedures is to appoint the best person for the job. Judgement is made about the match between each applicant and the requirements of the job. Shakespeare's Julius Caesar reminds us that many individual characteristics are used as a means of judging people. Not all of them are necessarily reliable. The procedures explained in this chapter are intended to reduce the risk of error and to ensure that the employment decision is a good one. Best practices in the recruitment and selection of doctors are considered. The chapter also identifies the principles underlying good practice and suggests how these principles should be applied. This is fair to individuals, the needs of the service and ultimately the patients. Elements to be considered include job descriptions, person specifications, advertising, applications, shortlisting, references, pre-interview visits, interview panels, interviews, decision making, after the interview, legal issues and monitoring.

There appears to be a growing trend on the part of organizations to take a more systematic and visible approach to the selection process. The principles of good practice in recruitment arise from codes of practice, legislation and the use of properly trained staff. Selection, by definition, involves a process of discrimination. The opportunity arises for selectors to emphasize candidate 'acceptability', or the 'good chap syndrome', rather than suitability based on task-based criteria (Townley 1991). Equal opportunities guidelines aim to ensure that discrimination does not occur on the basis of characteristics which are irrelevant to the requirements of the job, which restrict selectors' choice and are unfair to applicants. The BMA (1994) states those key principles as:

- the establishment of a systematic approach to recruitment and selection;
- the specification of the requirements of the post;
- the selection of individuals against those requirements.

Selection practice among British organizations is often at odds with that found in other, more successful, economies such as Japan and the USA. Japanese companies frequently employ several screening devices such as aptitude tests, occupational personality tests and group exercises as well as interviews (White & Trevor 1983). Department of Health (1982a,b, 1990a) circulars have attempted to standardize current procedures for consultants, senior registrars and registrars. Such guidance is also issued by many health authorities and trusts. Implementation of equal opportunities policies requires an emphasis on good advertising practice and achieving a balance between limiting personal information required of candidates and monitoring of gender and ethnic origin of candidates and employees.

STAGES IN THE SELECTION PROCESS

Job description and person specification

It is self-evident that, if a decision is to be made regarding the suitability of an individual for a given post, then that post must first be properly defined. All recruitment begins with the preparation of a job description and a

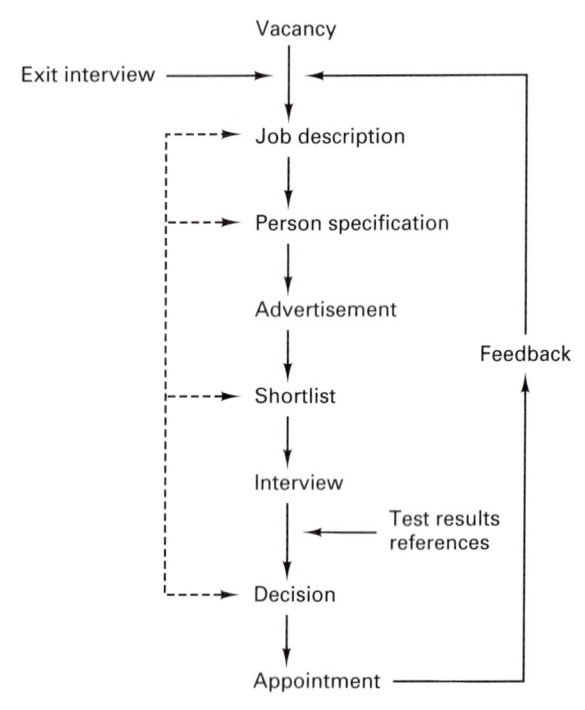

Fig. 14.1 Stages in the selection process

person specification and these should form the basis of the selection process in advertising the post, shortlisting and assessing applicants at interview.

Job description

The job description should identify the location(s) of the post, its title, grade and speciality, the duties of the post including clinical, administrative, managerial and research components. There should be some description of the accountability of the postholder within the organization and the main conditions of service, hours of work and duty rotas, as well as education and training facilities and a salary scale. This amount of detail is often neglected in the case of house officer and SHO posts, where the job description is only seen after appointment.

Prior to advertising, job descriptions should be drawn up by the appropriate doctor(s) with the assistance of personnel staff to ensure that they are in line with good personnel practice and not discriminatory. The job description forms part of the contract and nothing in it should contradict anything in the contract. The job description should be sent out with every application form, so it is important that it is kept up to date.

Person specification

The person specification is derived from the job description and outlines the qualifications, skills and experience required to perform the job. The person specification should list what is essential and what is desirable. Drawing up a person specification concentrates the minds of those involved in the selection process on the criteria they will use to judge candidates. The person specification should be used by the appointments panel for the shortlisting process and at the interview. It is good practice for applicants to be given copies of the person specification together with the job description when they apply so that they know by what criteria they are to be assessed

For single-handed general practitioners, the FHSA or health board has responsibility for sending potential applicants a fact sheet containing details of the practice and practice area (DHSS 1990b). Such information is also useful for applicants for partnerships. In general practice partners should agree on a written job description and person specification. Advice and guidance on equal opportunity issues and how to draw up a job description and person specification are available from the LMC or DHSS (1990b) or Ellis & Stanton (1994) and Gilley (1994). General practitioners who need information about practice job descriptions and person specifications can obtain guidance from the BMA (1993c) which produces a booklet on the subject.

Advertising

NHS guidelines (NHSME 1994) recommend that all posts are advertised. Preregistration house officer posts are an exception, usually only being advertised if the matching schemes with medical schools are unsuccessful. Such systems are fragmented and can be unfair to medical students (BMA 1994). They are also open to abuse by consultants who may prefer to 'fix' their vacancies in advance. This system can also make it difficult for students who wish to work outside their region to be considered for a post.

Advertising procedures for hospital doctors apply equally to vocational training schemes and to GP assistants. The procedure for advertising general practice principal posts differs between single-handed practices and partnerships. The FHSA or health board advertise single-handed vacancies, but with partnership vacancies the individual practice decides whether to advertise. There appear to be no central guidelines relating to the advertisement of research posts by universities. These appointments are, of course, subject to the provisions of the Sex Discrimination and Race Relations Acts and the codes of practice, all of which recommend open advertisement and formal selection procedures. Other methods of inviting applications for posts (e.g.

Post   Registrar in Accident and Emergency

Trust/health authority   St Elsewhere's Hospital

Location   Anytown

REQUIREMENTS	ESSENTIAL	DESIRABLE
Qualifications/training a. Professional qualification b. General professional training	MBBS, FRCS General surgery & medicine at SHO level	ATLS course DA or MRCP or MRCEP. SHO in paediatrics/anaesthetics
Knowledge/previous Experience Clinical expertise in speciality/subspeciality	SHO A+E 6/12 Broad base of related SHO skills	SHO A+E 12/12 SHO in orthopaedics SHO neurosurgery/plastic Experience O/D, burn, resuc
Previous training Management/audit	Understanding of audit Understanding of management of A+E departments	Personal experience of audit project(s)
Academic achievements Research/publications	None essential	Has made some presentations Has one or two publications, at least, submitted
Skills a. Leadership skills b. Organization skills c. Communication skills	Good team leadership skills A team player/planning toras Good interpersonal skills	Departmental general Managerial ability Equitable personality Consistency, reliable
Other requirements	Not overconfident. Aware of limitations. Can cope with changeable situations	Ability to involve and consult others. Not a 'loner'. Thoughtful

Completed by (name & title)   A Smith - Consultant

Signed _____   Dated   25.12.94

Fig. 14.2 Example of a person specification for a registrar in A&E (Source: BMA 1994: Guidelines for good practice in recruitment and selection of doctors)

headhunting and targeting) are occasionally used but these methods must be fair to all potential applicants and not effectively screen out minorities or members of one sex (IPM 1991). Failure to advertise is one of the greatest causes of racial and sexual discrimination. The advertising of all posts should attract applications from a wide range of candidates, ensuring that sources of good candidates are not neglected or overlooked. Advertising posts should be the norm. Full-time consultant, associate specialist and staff grade posts may be advertised in such a way that candidates unable for personal reasons to work full-time are able to apply.

Shortlisting

Objective shortlisting requires the use of agreed criteria which are developed from the job description and defined in the person specification. These criteria are carried through to the interview. All those participating in the shortlisting process should receive copies of all applications together with the agreed job description and person specification. It is good practice for all members of appointment panels to be involved in shortlisting applicants, although this is not always practical. A member of the human resource department or, for general practice, a personnel specialist, may be available to advise on relevant equal opportunities legislation. Notes made by those shortlisting should be retained on central personnel files and reasons for not shortlisting should be clearly documented. The interviewing panel should receive a formal report of the shortlisting procedure and any member of the panel should have the right to see the applications of anyone not shortlisted.

In general practice shortlisting is usually undertaken by existing partners, sometimes with a practice manager. Shortlisted candidates may wish to view in confidence the practice accounts so that they can ask questions about the financial arrangements at the interview, as well as gaining access to the existing partnership agreement. In trusts, shortlisted applicants for consultant appointments may also wish to have confidential access to detailed financial accounts of the trust.

References

It is important that the value and use of references is fully appreciated by those who rely on them within the selection process. Their use for selection has been the subject of considerable debate. Some argue that they are of little value other than for confirming simple factual information, such as that the applicant worked in a particular post for a given period. There are risks for referees in passing judgement on the standards of performance of candidates. Unless assessments can be substantiated, a referee could become the subject of a successful action in libel. It is generally agreed that references should only be read after all the candidates have been interviewed. It is not infrequent for unsolicited references to be provided in support of candidates (NHSME 1991). The chair has a duty to remind panel members that such unsolicited references should be disregarded. The main purpose of references should be to verify factual information regarding characteristics of an applicant's experience and qualifications as indicators of that person's suitability to the post. References are frequently unstructured and vary in content. Structured references are often used and these help to ensure that the same questions are answered by all referees. This gives a more accurate and reliable picture of applicants, although it may be useful to have a final open question for further comments. Unsolicited references should form no part of the selection process (BMA 1993b). Phone calls by panel members to referees are regarded as acceptable only if they are carried out for all applicants or are confined to clarifying specific facts arising from the application. Such references should be confined to the candidate's ability to do the job and not be indirectly or directly discriminatory. Personnel departments should bring references to the selection panel's attention only when the decision about a candidate is being made. Any use of references should be overt. Reference to unsolicited and informal references should be avoided, as these can lead to unfair, and potentially unlawful, discrimination.

Pre-interview visits

Doctors deciding whether to make an application may wish to visit a hospital or unit before applying for a post. Pre-application visits are a two-way process and important for potential applicants to assess whether they wish to proceed with their application, particularly in more senior posts. They will wish to obtain as much information as possible from the hospital, local consultants and local junior doctors. Potential consultants may wish to meet the clinical director, the medical director and other consultants in the department to discuss the job and the hospital. The advertisement, job description or other literature sent out to prospective applicants should contain details of how these visits are to be arranged. Normal practice is for the contact appointments to be made through the departmental secretary, but it is important that time is set aside for this and all candidates are given equal opportunity and treatment.

Informal pre-interview visits are widespread in the health service, particularly in medical appointments

(King Edward's Hospital Fund 1990). They are for the benefit of candidates to get to know about the job and potential colleagues. However, all candidates must be given the same opportunity to make such visits and be accorded equal treatment. The Department of Health (1982a) circular advises that such visits should not form part of the selection process. This opportunity could be used in some cases to circumvent procedures aimed at making formal selection fairer. Candidates may be asked discriminatory or inappropriate questions which would not be asked openly at appointment panels. If such information is used in the selection process, this could be shown to contravene the equal opportunities legislation and result in legal proceedings against the employer or practice.

Interview panels

Panel interviews for selection represent the norm in most large public sector organizations. Private sector selection procedures generally depend more on one-to-one interviews combined with other selection methods such as psychometric tests. It is also more usual for those with responsibility for selection to have received skills training. Where health authorities have provided training for staff involved in selection, medical staff are less likely than other groups to have received it (King Edward's Hospital Fund 1990). Senior medical practitioners are therefore less likely than other staff to be aware of the provisions of the codes of practice and of their legal liability. Where employing authorities have been found guilty of discrimination, it has commonly been attributed to lack of training. Panel chairpersons and members should take the responsibility to acquire skills in interview techniques and equal opportunities legislation (NHSME 1993c, BMA 1993c).

Panel membership is defined by statute for the appointment of consultants (DHSS 1982b). For senior registrars and registrars membership is advisory. There are no guidelines for the composition of interview panels for SHOs and house officers. For consultants the membership of advisory appointments committees (ACCs) was reduced with the reforms 'with flexibility for additional members where necessary' but must contain:

- lay person, usually trust chairman or non-executive director;
- chief executive of trust or representative;
- medical director or consultant representative;
- local consultant of same speciality;
- royal college assessor (who has no right of veto);
- university representative (when the post has a substantial teaching or research commitment).

There is no statutory maximum number for the selection panel but the above minimum with a local and medical majority is recommended on appointment committees. The Joint Working Party on the Review of the Appointment of Consultants reaffirmed that 'Appointment of consultants will continue to be centrally-determined and controlled by statute' although trusts can set terms and conditions of service, introduce short-term contracts and performance-related pay for non-medical staff, but not set its own criteria for determining what constitutes a specialist.

For senior registrars, the panel membership is advisory (DHSS 1982a) and normally consists of a lay chair, a representative of the university, a representative of the appropriate royal college, a representative of the postgraduate dean and one consultant from each hospital on the senior registrars' rotation. The minimum number for a committee is five. There is no maximum. There is sometimes considerable cost in time and expenses paid. When the numbers are large, no panel member has time to ask more than one question. The quality of data collected on candidates is likely to be considerably less reliable than in smaller, more manageable panels.

For registrars, the panel make-up is also advisory (DHSS 1989). It should consist of at least five members, a lay chair, a representative of the university, royal college, dean of postgraduate medicine and one consultant from each limb of rotation. If the rotation is within one hospital then two consultants from that hospital should be present on the panel.

Senior house officer selection panels follow no set procedures. Recruitment of SHOs is often informal and undocumented so that fairness and efficacy are difficult to assess and sometimes a single consultant interviews and decides. The short term nature of HO and some SHO contracts (6 months) tends to lessen concern. These posts, so early in doctors' training, can have great influence on their later careers so the decision can be important.

Most house officer posts are filled through medical school matching systems. Nearly all schools have schemes where a computer programme can be used to match the students to consultants. Posts and students remaining unallocated find places either by word of mouth or through the clearing house scheme, now abolished (NHSME 1993b). Attention has been drawn earlier to the potential abuse of such systems. Equal opportunities in house officer appointments are improved if made by a properly constituted appointment panel, perhaps within a closed matching system.

Associate specialists are personal appointments which are not advertised, but made on an individual basis for established doctors who are unable to complete higher professional training or to accept the full responsibility of a consultant appointment. Staff grade doctor is a non-training career grade which is intended to provide a career in hospital medicine for doctors who also do not wish to or are unable to train for consultant status. Appointments for both follow a probationary year and may be held until retirement. In some circumstances, employers may offer fixed term appointments up to a period of 5 years renewable each year. The advisory appointment committee for staff grade doctors must comprise at least a lay chair, a professional member from outside the district appointed on the advice of the appropriate college or faculty and a professional member employed in the district in the relevant speciality (DHSS 1988). Senior clinical medical officers (SCMOs) and clinical medical officers (CMOs) working in community health services are broadly equivalent to associate specialist and staff grade doctors respectively. No appointment procedures are laid down, but they normally follow the procedures for staff grade doctors. For hospital posts generally the optimum number of panel members should be between three and eight. A larger number of members on a selection panel can be intimidating and is often counterproductive.

In single-handed general practices the FHSA or health board decides whether to shortlist and interview candidates themselves or whether to appoint a selection committee to act on their behalf (DHSS 1990b), which usually involves a representative of the LMC.

Panel members should declare any personal interest in applicants which may be regarded as significant to the selection process. It is important that this is done at the beginning of the selection process and that new information is not introduced during the final discussion of the appointment.

Timing

Perhaps the most common criticism made of interviewers is that they fail to manage the timing of the interviews. Running late has a number of undesirable side-effects. Unfortunately, this is such a common occurrence that it is taken for granted by panels and interviewees alike. The problem usually stems from an unwillingness to accept the fact that interviewing is a complex process and takes a lot of time if it is to be done well. Making an employment decision, which has critical influence on the lives and careers of the candidates as well as patients and colleagues in the organization, should be a slow and deliberate process. Sufficient time is needed, seldom less than an hour for each candidate for senior appointments. Time should be allowed for reflection, discussion and writing up of notes between interviews, coupled with adequate time for discussion at the end of the interviews. Failure to do this leads to long delays for candidates who are scheduled for later in the day. This causes stress and prevents them from performing as well as they might. It also puts pressure on the panel and can lead to hurried, ill-considered decisions.

Interview process

Communication is the transfer of ideas, facts and feelings between two or more people in order to achieve an understanding between them. Conversation is a natural form of informal communication between people. A meeting is a more formal example and is often managed with an agenda and followed up with minutes, including action points. The interview is a conversation which has a purpose and is directed towards its object by the interviewer. It falls somewhere between a formal meeting and a conversation. Practice in the management of the selection interview varies widely. Many commercial organizations avoid large panels because they are seen as cumbersome and ineffective as a means of collecting data of sufficient quantity and quality to make such a critical decision.

Interview structure

Interviews normally follow a pattern which permits the acquisition of essential data by the interviewers and gives candidates a chance to get to know a little more about the culture and other aspects of the organization. There are four stages. The first is concerned with making the candidate feel at ease and prepared for the process. This is often achieved by a brief, informal question and answer session between the chair and the candidate, usually on an inconsequential topic such as the weather, the candidate's journey or even car parking problems at the interview venue. Introductions are also made at this stage. The second stage commences within a few minutes and is the dominant part of the interview, taking up perhaps four fifths of the total time available. This stage focuses on acquiring information about the candidate's life, educational and work experience, checking panel members' perceptions based on the application form and curriculum vitae and exploring leads which arise in the course of the candidate's responses to questions. The success of the interview depends heavily on the skills of the panel members as questioners and, above all, as listeners. Relevant techniques are described in more detail below. The third stage of the interview gives the candidate the opportunity to question the panel. This may take up relatively little time, especially if preinterview procedures have given candidates adequate detail regarding the job and organization. It is unhelpful to take up the panel's time in giving detailed answers to questions about terms and conditions of employment. These are best deferred by the chair until after the interview, when a one-to-one meeting with a relevant person can save time and deal properly with issues of importance to the individual.

Preparing to interview

The Institute of Personnel and Development recommends that interviewers should plan the structure and content of the interview in advance. Preparing questions in advance will ensure that all the necessary issues are covered in the interview to enable the panel to assess individuals against the selection criteria in a consistent manner and make informed selection decisions. It is good practice to set aside time before the interview during which the chair will normally ask members to indicate priorities and concerns regarding the candidates. Discussion of the process is also critical. If the sense of a 'conversation with a purpose' is to be maintained throughout the interview, then the flow of information must be managed with care. All members need to understand the chair's approach and agree their own contribution.

It is also important to agree on how the panel members will be introduced to the candidate. Decisions on levels of detail (candidates usually forget names and titles as soon as they hear them, if there are too many), whether or not to shake hands and who will collect and bring in the candidate can have a significant impact on the time it takes to put the candidate at ease.

Candidates are often unskilled in presenting themselves and doctors untrained at interviewing for selection. Some research has shown that inexperienced interviewers make up their minds very early, even within a few minutes of the start of the interview (Eggert 1992). This leads to an interview in which questions are framed which serve only to confirm the interviewers' prejudices. It is important for the chair to discourage this approach by allowing time to discuss such issues before starting the first interview. On the other hand a more recent experiment (Tomorrow's World 1995) has suggested that last impressions are important.

Other issues for the panel to consider before the start include arrangements for the comfort of the interviewee. Physical barriers may exist if the room is too small, causing candidates and interviewers to feel uncomfortable and cramped, or too large so that both parties can feel daunted. It may be too hot or too cold so that

either party may feel uncomfortable. Untidiness can be a distraction and the layout of the furniture with large desk or chairs for interviewers and small chair for interviewee is a power game to avoid. A large table can form a barrier but is common enough in medical interviews to be generally acceptable. Other barriers can include poor positioning of the interviewee, such as facing a window, interruptions, distractions in glass offices or distracting actions of panel members such as shuffling papers.

Problems can also arise which inhibit the flow of information between parties to the interview. Mental and emotional barriers can arise from lack of understanding, bias, status, failure to establish rapport, which can result in the candidate feeling uncomfortable and tense. Lack of confidence can also be distracting in the case of an inexperienced interviewer or candidate. Language problems may arise from the use of jargon by the interviewer.

Questions – types and uses

The two core skills of interviewing are asking questions and listening effectively. The interviewer needs to understand when and how to use questions to guide and control the interview. Some types of question are likely to be unhelpful and could even damage prospects of success. Others may be useful only if used at the right time. Interviewing requires a high degree of skill, the acquisition of which should be based on knowing how to choose a question to suit a need. Some types of questions, with examples, are shown below.

Introductory questions

These help to put candidates at ease, enabling them to adapt to the interview environment, gauge the sound of their voice in the room and generally begin to relax. They are innocuous and might include such questions as: 'Did you have any difficulty travelling here today?', 'What were your first impressions of the town?' or 'How did you find our car parking facilities?' (assuming they are satisfactory!).

Open questions

Open-ended questions generate discussion and allow interviewers to probe for facts and clarification of details. They are used for exploring, gathering information and encouraging the candidate to talk freely. They might include: 'Why do you want this job?', 'What would you bring to this hospital/practice?', 'Tell us about your early experiences as a junior doctor', 'Why did you choose to undertake research in that area?' They usually start with 'Why . . .', 'How . . .' or 'Tell me about . . .'. They cannot be answered with 'Yes' or 'No'.

Probing questions

Use these to explore in greater detail experiences and associated feelings, actions or events which have been mentioned by the candidate in an earlier answer: 'What happened then?', 'What did they say during feedback?', 'How did you feel at that point?', 'What did you do to achieve that?'.

Reflective questions

These enable the interviewer to check understanding and to elicit further information about a particular aspect of a candidate's most recent response, perhaps about sensitive aspects of their experience. They involve selecting a few words from the candidate's most recent response and feeding them back as a question. They encourage the candidate to continue talking, without asking directly: 'So, you felt unsure about your ability to undertake work at that level?'. This type of question is often used in counselling.

Closed questions

These are useful when checking facts, but may lead to the interviewer doing most of the talking, with the candidate answering 'Yes' or 'No'. Inexperienced interviewers sometimes get trapped into a series of these questions, as they are not allowed sufficient time to frame their next question properly. 'Did you find any difficulty in analysing the results?', 'Does your journey to work take long?'

Leading questions

A question which gives the candidate the answer by implication is known as a leading question. They are commonly used by inexperienced interviewers, but are generally unhelpful because they merely encourage the answer which the interviewer wants to hear. 'We consider teamworking to be an important aspect of our approach to achieving excellent results. Are you good in a team?' or 'Starting your PhD is a really good idea and once complete should be useful. Will you finish it?'

Multiple questions

Another trap into which inexperienced interviewers frequently fall is triggered by their desire to be helpful to the candidate. In elaborating their first attempt to ask a question, they end up asking another question, which can cause confusion. 'When you were in a situation with a colleague who had a problem, did you confront her directly or was it on an informal basis after the meeting and what did she say?' The candidate is uncertain which question to answer first. Ask one question at a time and only try to clarify a question if the candidate asks for more help.

Behavioural questions

Many writers on selection argue that the only reliable indicator of a candidate's future performance and behaviour is what they have already done and how they have carried out tasks and reacted to given situations in the past. Getting them to talk through their use of their skills and judgement in previous events tells us much more than asking them to speculate about possible future events. The approach usually requires the use of an open question followed by a chain of probing questions, each of which is prompted by leads in the candidate's responses.

'Think of an example where you successfully influenced a group of people and changed practice?' . . . 'What happened then?' . . . 'How did you react?' . . . 'What did he/she say?' . . . 'Why do you think that approach worked?'

or

'Think of an example where you had to communicate unpleasant news to someone' . . . ' How did you approach the problem?' . . . 'What was the end result?' . . . 'How did you achieve it?' . . . 'How did you feel?' . . . 'What did you do then?'

The candidate should be given time to think of the example, even though this usually results in a quiet moment in the interview.

Using silence

We are usually uncomfortable if a long silence occurs during a conversation. This leads us to fill it, sometimes with a thoughtless contribution which does not add, and may detract, from an interview. Silence can be used to put gentle pressure on an interviewee and can be an effective way of getting at details which they may not otherwise have released. It requires a discipline and common understanding not always found in inexperienced panel members, who must stop themselves from talking while the time passes. At the end of a response to an open question it can be effective to wait for a few seconds to allow the interviewee to continue to give more detail or to expand on the last point made.

Interview behaviours to avoid

Questions are sometimes asked by untrained interviewers which reflect stereotyping around assumptions made about particular groups of people. For example, assumptions that women of a particular age may be intending to start a family or, if they have a family, that women with young children may be unreliable in attendance or that women may be unable to carry out physically demanding work. Apart from being false assumptions, they may result in a successful legal action against the potential employer. Other assumptions arise around working relationships – that a woman working with men or a man working with women will cause problems or that a black person working with white colleagues may have problems getting on with the team.

Halo and horns effects

The halo effect can occur when an interviewer is impressed by the fact that a candidate's experience or interest matches their own, such as studying at the same university, playing cricket or golf. The interviewer may consequently spend time seeking positive feedback from the candidate to support this initial impression and ignore negative evidence. The horns effect, on the other hand, occurs when a candidate shows interests or experience which is not of interest to, or contradicts the values of, the interviewer. In this case, the interviewer subconsciously seeks negative evidence to support the prejudice.

Effective listening

Candidates respond more effectively to interviewers who not only listen but can be seen to listen. Regular eye contact should be maintained throughout the interview and occasional nods or sounds of approval are used to encourage the candidate to continue developing full answers to the questions. Brief notes may be made of important facts, but it is important to ensure that note-taking does not become distracting. The notes record information to be used in the selection decision, so interviewers should check that they have all the information needed to make an assessment.

Assessment and decision making

The most difficult challenge facing members of the panel is that of reserving judgement until after all of the candidates have been interviewed. Sufficient time must be set aside at the end of the interviews to consider each applicant fully. In deciding on the merits of each candidate, rating scales for a range of attributes are sometimes helpful. The attributes might include personality, appearance, presentation, qualifications, experience, research, management ability and so on depending on the nature and level of seniority of the post. These will have been considered at an earlier stage in the process and should be recorded in the person specification. Selection criteria must be objective, job-related, non-discriminatory and applied consistently to candidates. The panel should concentrate on facts, past performance and current circumstances, using all available data including references and any test results. The chair should ensure that all members of the interview panel are allowed to express their views about candidates in an attempt to reach a consensus. The decision should be formally recorded. Reasons for rejecting unsuccessful candidates and for appointing a second candidate if the preferred candidate fails to take up the appointment should also be recorded. Records should be retained for at least 6 months (at least 3 years in Northern Ireland (DoED 1989)) as they may be required if a complaint is made to an industrial tribunal. The panel must be prepared to reject all candidates if none is found to match the agreed requirements of the post.

The proceedings of the committee are strictly confidential, as are notes, references and other documents and the references must be collected at the end.

Appointment

The successful candidate should be informed of the panel's decision by an authorized person. This constitutes an offer and an acceptance by the candidate at this stage can create a legally binding agreement in the form of an employment contract. Care should be taken to ensure that all necessary pre-contract procedures have been followed. Failure to do so could lead to financial loss in a lawsuit. It is good practice that offers of employment should be made subject to an occupational health assessment of the successful candidate. The purpose of a pre-employment assessment is to ensure that the individual is fit for the job (Lunn & Waldron 1991); for example, to ensure satisfactory hepatitis B status and to advise on the capabilities and limitations of those with disabilities.

Giving feedback to unsuccessful candidates is often regarded as an essential part of the interview process. This is not generally the case in private sector organizations, other than for internal candidates. An appropriate member of the interview panel should be made responsible for providing feedback.

Evaluation

A post-appointment review, perhaps a few weeks or months

into the appointment, is good practice. Problems and failures at interview may be due to poor interview technique, lack of appropriate experience, unsuitably constituted panel, poor chairmanship, unreliable references or many other possible causes. These should be considered in relation to the appointee's performance by those responsible for managing the process.

EQUAL OPPORTUNITIES LEGISLATION

An optimum selection decision is more likely to be achieved if irrelevant criteria such as race and gender are excluded from the selection process. Allen (1988), Esmail & Everington (1993) and McKeigue et al (1990) have shown that some categories of candidates, such as women, certain ethnic groups and overseas doctors, often fail to gain posts for which they are qualified. There are many possible reasons which they highlight which are discussed elsewhere (BMA 1993a,b). The NHS Management Executive (EOC 1994) states that fair recruitment and selection procedures are essential to ensure equal opportunities in employment and that equal opportunities practices have two purposes, justice for the applicants and enabling the selection of the best available candidate.

A survey by the Equal Opportunities Commission in 1990 (EOC 1990) into women's employment in the NHS revealed a lack of equal opportunities practices in the recruitment and selection of all NHS staff in many health authorities. Out of the 87% of regional and district health authorities which responded to the survey, 22% did no staff training in recruitment and selection, 39% had no written management guidelines on sex or marital discrimination and 23% included potentially unlawful discriminatory questions on their application form. This patchy record is confirmed by considerable anecdotal evidence that the NHSME's equal opportunities guidelines are often ignored (NHSME 1991).

It is wise to rely on the up-to-date knowledge of an experienced personnel professional regarding employment legislation. The following is a guide to the range of legislation affecting the employment decision. The main acts are:

- Sex Discrimination Act 1975, Sex Discrimination Act 1986 and Sex Discrimination (Northern Ireland) Order 1976 which make both direct and indirect discrimination on grounds of sex and marriage unlawful.
- Race Relations Act 1976 renders direct and indirect discrimination unlawful if it is made on grounds of race, colour or ethnic origin.
- Fair Employment (Northern Ireland) Acts 1976 and 1989 and Fair Employment Monitoring Regulations (Northern Ireland) 1989 make direct and indirect discrimination on grounds of religious beliefs or political opinion unlawful.

These acts make it unlawful to discriminate, either directly or indirectly, on the grounds of sex, race or marital status. Discrimination can take two forms, direct and indirect.

Direct discrimination occurs when someone is treated less favourably than others because of their sex, because they are married or on racial grounds.

Indirect discrimination occurs where, although everyone is treated the same, there are requirements which are such that members of a particular sex or race are at a disadvantage compared with others and married people are disadvantaged in comparison with single people and these requirements cannot be justified. Although conditions are applied equally to men and women, their effect is to preclude one sex. For example, the normal career and life pattern of women are different from those of men as a consequence of family responsibility and childbearing. Women may be less mobile than men. Insistence on a conventional career path can be indirectly discriminatory.

Exceptions to racial or sexual discrimination can be made where there are genuine occupational qualifications. It is lawful to discriminate where it can be shown that the job has a genuine occupational qualification, for example, a physiological requirement such as in the interests of authenticity for an actor or model or because it is more effective for welfare services to be provided by one particular racial minority. It is for the employer to prove the case for discrimination.

Equal opportunities in recruitment and selection procedures (NHSME 1991) state that there is a statutory duty (under SI 1982/276) to advertise consultant posts unless the Secretary of State's prior permission to dispense with advertising has been given. There are several important exemptions to this rule; among these, consultants facing redundancy can be relocated to other posts without the post being advertised. Such practices are likely to continue with future redundancies (Mawhinney 1993).

Goal One of the programme (NHSME 1993c) is aimed at equal opportunities policies for recruitment and selection. It recommends that NHS trusts and health authorities include in their business plans a local objective to increase the proportion of minority ethnic staff in areas and grades where they are underrepresented, within a specified time scale, until fair representation is achieved. The objectives of the programme include training for all staff involved in selecting candidates and monitoring of applications, shortlisted candidates and successful candidates at medical interviews.

The General Whitley Council has developed a comprehensive series of agreements to support equal opportunities policies (NHSME 1994). They have recommended good practice in recruitment and selection procedures stating that these are an essential contribution to ensuring equal opportunities in employment. Staff involved in the recruitment process should receive training in equal opportunities. Employers are urged to ensure that job descriptions and person specifications are drawn up and made available to all applicants and employing authorities should keep data on applicants for jobs and shortlisted applicants. The General Whitley Council recommends that the policy should be included in staff handbooks to be disseminated widely to all employees in order to obtain the commitment of all staff and management to equal opportunities.

Positive action

Covers a range of measures which employers may lawfully use to help women or people from ethnic minorities compete for a job on an equal footing with everyone else. It means encouraging applications from members of one sex or from ethnic minorities to take advantage of employment opportunities where they have been underrepresented in the previous 12 months. It does not involve discriminating in favour of one particular sex or a certain racial group at the point of selection. Unless there is a genuine occupational qualification, that would be unlawful.

Disability legislation

UK legislation on the employment of disabled people is significantly different from other employment legislation. The term 'disabled' is generally applied to a variety of people with many different characteristics. For employment purposes, current UK legislation uses the following definition: 'people with a disability which substantially handicaps them in obtaining or keeping employment which, apart from that disability, would normally be suited to their age, experience and qualifications'. This definition covers a far wider range of disabilities than is popularly supposed. As well as the more obvious and visible disabilities (blindness, deafness, loss of use of limbs, etc.) many disabilities which can sometimes affect employment are not immediately obvious (e.g. heart trouble, mental illness, epilepsy, colour blindness, etc.).

Rather than making it illegal to discriminate against disabled people, the Disabled Person's (Employment) Act 1944 (amended 1958) sets out a requirement for employers of more than 20 people to employ at least 3% of their workforce from the register of disabled people which was set up when the law came into force. The law is difficult to enforce because the situation in the UK at present is that there are insufficient registered disabled people for all employers with a workforce of 20 or more to meet the quota. There may be many reasons for this, but one of these is likely to be a reluctance by disabled people to register. Disabled people are not required to register and many choose not to do so because they perceive that there are more disadvantages than advantages in being so labelled. There are therefore likely to be many more disabled people in employment than the registered number would imply.

Codes of practice

The Commission for Racial Equality and Equal Opportunities Commission have produced codes of practice which give recommendations and guidance on how to avoid racial and sex discrimination. The codes do not have the force of law and are not legally binding but are approved by Parliament. The extent to which their provisions have been observed is normally taken into account by industrial tribunals when considering cases of alleged discrimination.

LEGAL RESPONSIBILITY OF THE APPOINTMENTS COMMITTEE

Consultant appointments are governed by a statutory instrument (NHSME 1994) while senior registrar and registrar appointments are covered by guidelines for NHS employing bodies set out in DoH circulars (DHSS 1989). Guidance includes reference to equal opportunities and states, for instance, that a candidate who feels unfairly treated in the appointment is entitled to seek redress through an industrial tribunal or a court of law. There are no central guidelines for senior house officer and house officer appointments, but general recommendations are made for the recruitment of all doctors in the hospital or community health service by the NHSME (1991). All members of selection panels share responsibility for ensuring equal opportunities in the selection process. The chairperson of the panel carries particular responsibility for the conduct of the committee. All members may be required to account for their decisions and actions so they must be provided with adequate guidance and training to ensure that they can carry out their responsibilities effectively.

General practitioners, when employing both medical

and non-medical staff, must abide by relevant employment legislation. General practitioners as independent contractors are not obliged to follow any standard procedure. When general practitioners appoint a new partner they appoint a doctor to join them in a legal and business partnership. There is a different procedure for the appointment of single-handed general practitioners. When a single-handed practice becomes vacant the Medical Practices Committee (MPC) decides whether to allow the vacancy to be advertised. Responsibility for advertising the vacancy is then passed to the Family Health Services Authority (FHSA) or health board (DHSS 1990b). These are encouraged to involve the Local Medical Committee (LMC) in the shortlisting and selection process. They are also responsible for drawing up criteria for the shortlisting of potential candidates and informing the MPC, which will advise the successful candidate. Existing partnerships can apply to take over a single-handed partnership. Unsuccessful applicants have a right of appeal to the Secretary of State.

MONITORING

The NHS Management Executive (NHSME) has recommended that applicants and successful candidates at medical interviews are monitored on the basis of race, gender and speciality. An effective way to carry out equal opportunities monitoring is to include a standard sheet for each applicant to complete, which is separated from the main application before shortlisting. This form can include questions about sex, age, ethnic origin, nationality, marital status, number of children and disability not available to those shortlisting and conducting the interview, which can then be organized by the personnel department. In 1992 the Equal Opportunities Commission (EOC 1990) revealed the piecemeal record of monitoring throughout the country. Of the 87% of health authorities who responded to the questionnaires sent out, 43% said they monitored their workforce and/or their job applications by sex, but only 2% of districts stated that they monitored both applicants and employees.

NHS employers have responsibility for equal opportunities monitoring of their workforce and selection procedures and should take appropriate remedial action where necessary. From September 1993 the NHSME began the central collection of ethnic monitoring data (NHSME 1993c). In September 1994 the NHSME introduced an improved information system to enable progress in achieving equal opportunities for ethnic minority doctors, from all groups including general practice, to be measured more effectively including monitoring applicants and appointees.

OTHER TYPES OF INTERVIEW

The selection interview is one of many different types of interview which are frequently conducted in employing organizations. Many principles and techniques apply to all types, particularly those relating to questioning and listening.

Performance appraisal

It is widely felt that postgraduate medical education leaves a lot to be desired. It has been suggested that an educational supervisor should be able to discuss training problems and that juniors should have mutually agreed objectives for knowledge and skills acquired at the end of a post so that performance might be evaluated by a review, an approach extensively used among management and nursing in the NHS. This concept is discussed fully in Chapter 22 on personnel, performance and staff appraisal, but for the moment all we need to accept is that it is a two-way process where both parties agree future activity plans and appropriate help and guidance can then be given to enable these objectives to be met. The consultant with direct responsibility for the work of the junior will therefore need to carry out interviews and supervise the individual performance review. The discussion during which objectives are drawn up must be a two-way exchange of ideas. There should also be regular informal discussions to monitor and review progress. While this process is very much a combined responsibility with each playing equal roles, for the purposes of this chapter it is convenient to consider each player's role and call them interviewer and interviewee. Dialogue should be open and relaxed so it is important to choose a time when neither party is under pressure. It also requires the prior collection of all relevant facts.

For both, however, it is important to prepare for the interview by considering and setting out the objectives of the exercise, allocating sufficient time and considering the structure of the interview. All too often the interview is carried out without a clear understanding of what it is trying to achieve. Relevant headings have been listed as follows (Mosley 1993):

- management of patients;
- note taking and legibility;
- communication between members of the clinical team and between nursing and medical colleagues;
- development of technical skills;
- presentations at hospital meetings;
- examination achievements;
- research.

Interviewer

Needs to be familiar with all previously agreed targets. If there are deficiencies then examples need to be available to substantiate points of concern. The interview needs to be structured so that the best use is made of the available time. A framework needs to be established and agreed to this end and might include:

- outline of purpose of meeting;
- a report from trainee on their latest period of work;
- assessment of performance with reference to previously agreed targets;
- discussion of shortcomings;
- agreement on programme to rectify any shortcomings;
- agreement on targets and any necessary training.

The interviewee needs to be put at ease, particularly as this is a new process to medical training and consultants are not yet skilled in carrying out such interviews. Suspicion and anxiety have to be recognized and addressed. Ample warning needs to be given to allow the trainee to prepare for the interview. The interview is for joint assessment and joint decisions, not someone in authority passing judgement.

Allow the trainee the first opportunity to comment on how they feel about their progress. Do not interrupt but make notes for reference if necessary. If targets have been met there is no problem unless the targets were too simple. If they have not been met then the cause needs to be identified and corrective action agreed. The cause of failure may not be within the sphere of influence of the trainee but only of the consultant. But if it is through the failure of the junior, then it should be established whether this is through negligence or lack of knowledge and skills. Where targets are met or even exceeded then praise is called for. How rare that is! Any commitments made to juniors at the interview should be fulfilled at the earliest opportunity. Consultants also need to pay attention to their own shortcomings as teachers.

Interviewee

The junior will probably have a good idea about what they want to achieve during their time in the job and also usually a very clear idea of their deficiencies. They need adequate time to prepare for the interview.

Counselling interviews

The counselling is of a special nature and the three stage model, developed by Carkhuff and amplified by Egan (Fryer 1985), is helpful for understanding the process.

Stage 1 explores and focuses and requires good active listening skills, open questions and the ability to move the interview forward. The second stage pieces together the picture from stage 1, seeing themes and broader issues, deepening self-understanding and increasing awareness of the need for action, helping to set specific goals. The third stage designs and implements an action plan. It is also important to know when to direct an individual to a specialist agency.

Factfinding interviews

These may be used for gathering information for management control or the handling of a crisis, corrective action to change performance to agreed standards and finally dealing with complaints, grievances and disciplinary matters and these are dealt with elsewhere.

SUMMARY

Selection procedures in hospital and community health services are costly in terms of consultant time, money, effort and stress. Solutions may be reducing the number of people required to sit on a selection panel and reducing the number of selection panels by increasing the number of rotational training posts which permit longer contracts to be offered. But if selection procedures are fair and seen to be fair, there will be less likelihood of complaints. These can be expensive in terms of time, staff morale, resources, reputation, legal fees and the cost of damages awarded to those discriminated against.

REFERENCES

Allen I 1988 Doctors and their careers. Policy Studies Institute, London
BMA 1993a Childcare for doctors in the NHS. British Medical Association, London
BMA 1993b Patronage in the medical profession. British Medical Association, London
BMA 1993c Assistant in general practice. Framework for a written contract of employment. British Medical Association, London
BMA 1994 Guidelines for good practice in the recruitment & selection of doctors. British Medical Association, London
DHSS 1982a Health services management. The appointment of consultants and senior registrars. HC(82)10. HMSO, London
DHSS 1982b The National Health Service (appointment of consultants) regulations 1982 (SI 1982/276), as amended in 1990 (SI 1990/1407). HMSO, London
DHSS 1988 The new hospital staff grade. HC(88)58. HMSO, London
DHSS 1989 Health services management. Appointment procedure for registrars. EL(89)MB/68. HMSO, London

DHSS 1990a Health services management. The appointment of consultants and directors of public health. HC(90)19. HMSO, London

DHSS 1990b GP practice vacancies: revised selection procedures. HN(90)26. HMSO, London

DoED 1989 Fair employment in Northern Ireland, code of practice. Department of Economic Development, London

Ellis N, Stanton T (eds) 1994 Making sense of partnerships. Radcliffe Medical Press, Oxford

EOC 1990 Equality management: women's employment in the NHS, a survey report by the equal opportunities commission. Equal Opportunities Commission, London

EOC 1994 Recruitment and selection procedures, NHS management executive. Equal Opportunities Commission, London

Eggert M 1992 The perfect interview. All you need to get it right first time. Century, London

Esmail A, Everington S 1993 Racial discrimination against doctors from ethnic minorities. British Medical Journal 306: 691–692

Fryer M 1985 Counselling skills. National Marriage Guidance Council, Rugby

Gilley J (ed) 1994 Women in general practice. British Medical Association, London

IPM 1991 The IPM equal opportunities code. Institute of Personnel Management, London

King Edward's Hospital Fund for London 1990 Equal opportunities task force. Racial equality: hospital doctors selection procedures. King Edward's Hospital Fund, London

Lunn J A, Waldron H A 1991 Concerning the carers: occupational health for health care workers. Reported in BMA 1994, above

Mawhinney B 1993 Letter dated 15 March to John Chawner, Chair Central Consultants and Specialists Committee. Reported in BMA 1994, above

McKeigue P M, Richards J D M, Richards P 1990 Effects of discrimination by sex and race on the early careers of British medical graduates during 1981–7. British Medical Journal 301: 961–964

Mosley J G 1993 An explanation of the role of individual performance review in surgical training. Annals of the Royal College of Surgeons of England 75 (supplement)

NHSME 1991 Equal opportunities in recruitment and selection procedures: doctors and dentists in the hospital and community health service. HMSO, London

NHSME 1993a NHS management executive. Flexible training report of the joint working party. HMSO, London

NHSME 1993b NHS management executive circular EL(93)15. HMSO, London

NHSME 1993c Ethnic minority staff in the NHS: a programme of action. HMSO, London

NHSME 1994 Report of the joint working party on the review of appointment of consultants. EL(93)94. HMSO, London

Tomorrow's World 1995 MegaLab experiment. 23rd March, BBC TV

Townley B 1991 Selection and appraisal: reconstituting 'social relations'. In: Storey J (ed) New perspectives on human resource management. Routledge, London

White M, Trevor M 1983 Under Japanese management. Heinemann, London

15

Being interviewed

Tony White, John Gatrell

O wad some Pow'r the giftie gie us
To see oursels as others see us!
      (Robert Burns, *To a Mouse*)

This chapter is intended to provide guidance for doctors applying for a job. While this mainly affects those in the junior or training grades, research indicates that just under 30% of consultants considered that presenting themselves well in job interviews was of high or very high priority. A little under 20% of partners in general practice responded similarly (Gatrell & White 1995). Applying for new posts should generally be part of a well-organized and programmed career plan, with each move having specific objectives. This may be for additional training in a special field, a lighter job to enable you to read for an examination or write up a thesis or a jumping-off post where you acquire specific referees for a later post. Time spent discussing your planned programme with college tutor and regional advisor or postgraduate dean is usually well repaid. And when planning speciality moves, never forget the reviews of the specialities published regularly in *Health Trends* which show numbers of doctors in all grades of all specialities and therefore career prospects.

FINDING AND ASSESSING JOBS

It is important to know and understand the market, which varies with specialities. You can do this by attending meetings, talking to people and doing some investigative research. You may also find that keeping a record is useful as your data accumulate. Using a library, the *Medical Directory* and journals helps to identify hospitals, staff, names, etc. The *Medical Directory* is also useful for calculating approximate ages and estimates of retirement dates. Also do not forget that your referees may retire, so plan ahead. Assemble facts for your curriculum vitae.

While in the library look for advertisements and ring up for details and application forms. Do this even for jobs in your speciality that you may not plan to apply for as you will rapidly get a feel for the market. When ringing also request general details of the hospital and ask for a specimen contract. You can then arrange to visit, try to talk to several people and look around. Always make appointments and never turn up without doing so. Whom you should see will depend on the level of seniority of the job you are interested in but for a consultant appointment, we suggest you try to see consultants within the department, clinical director, medical director, junior doctors, chief executive and chair of trust.

You have to ask yourself the question, 'Is it the right job for me?'. In order to answer this, you need the details and job description as a minimum. Following this, you might find it useful to talk to others who may know more about you, the situation generally, the job and the hospital. This might include your chief, consultants, clinical tutor, regional adviser, referees, the regional postgraduate dean and of course colleagues and contemporaries. Provide yourself with as much information as possible from region, hospital, local consultants and local junior doctors.

CURRICULUM VITAE

In general any panel has difficult time constraints, so help them by being clear and concise, ensuring your curriculum vitae is typewritten, well prepared and presented, accurate and up to date. O'Brien (1985) feels that the standards of curricula vitae submitted for posts at all levels are often abysmally low. The CV needs to be fully complete with personal details, qualifications, speciality experience, general experience, prizes, research and publications. There should be no disguised or hidden gaps and it should present you in the best light but without being misleading. If you are in any doubt about whether something should or should not be excluded then seek advice, perhaps from your referees. Always add achievements outside your career. It is not a process to be hurried. Allow yourself plenty of time as it is an important feature of your application which can involve a number of decisions on what to include or exclude, layout, etc. A neat curriculum vitae may give an impression which tips the balance in your favour at shortlisting.

There are several acceptable ways of planning the curriculum vitae. It is important that it should be orderly, methodical, neat and comply with the instructions for applicants sent out by the hospital. The correct number of copies must always be supplied, however unreasonable this may seem. Some hospitals require an application form to be completed. This may be a standard form for all members of staff and therefore seem inadequate for more senior medical posts, if only due to lack of space. Unless a curriculum vitae is specifically excluded it is usually best to fill in the form, referring to the appropriate page of your curriculum vitae.

A word processor makes keeping a curriculum vitae up to date very much easier. Regular updating is also useful even for an established consultant, as research grant applications, trials and applications to societies and professional organizations often require a curriculum vitae. Unless you keep your CV up to date it is easy to forget publications. The safest way of updating this is to add items as they become appropriate. Beware the danger with word processors of overdoing the use of multiple elaborate fonts and changes in size of lettering. It is best to keep it simple and elegant.

Content and headings

It is usual to start with personal details but certain things are not required such as marital status, number of children, nationality and general education including schools attended. Examination results and honours or distinctions may be briefly listed. Items such as GMC registration number and whether the applicant has right of abode in the UK could be requested and therefore included. It is usual to give a full list of your degrees and other qualifications with dates awarded under this heading.

It is acceptable to include undergraduate education and you should include date of entry and graduation from university, college or medical school together with any honours and distinctions. Any genuine reason for postponing or even failing an examination should be briefly indicated if this has resulted in delay, as someone invariably notices. If there are no mitigating circumstances for such an occurrence then you will merely have to state the dates and hope no one notices. Scholarships, prizes and other awards should be listed.

There is considerable debate over whether previous appointments should be put in chronological or reverse chronological order. Whatever you decide, put the nature or designation of the post on the left, the dates of tenure on the right and underneath a brief summary of your experience including your service commitment, clinical experience, teaching, research administrative experience, etc. as appropriate. You will also probably want to classify these under general and speciality experience.

For your present appointment some people feel that this is better placed before the previous appointments and this would fit naturally if you place them in reverse order. The layout should be similar to the above. Do not forget to list any separate components of your job, for example a clinical side, an academic side and the research component. Remember, too, that you may need to emphasize certain parts in the light of the requirements of the job you are applying for.

With publications, accuracy is particularly important. Interviewers sometimes check one or more publications, more for the quality than their existence, and will understandably be unimpressed if they cannot find them. So give the fullest details including title, authors, journal or book, year, volume and page numbers. As your publications become more plentiful you may wish to classify them as original papers, abstracts, editorials, chapters in books, books, reviews, letters, etc. and perhaps also according to those in which you made a major contribution where there is more than one author. Add posters and presentations at scientific meetings, but only if you delivered the address. Again you will need to give the full title as well as the name, date and venue of the meeting. Poster displays are often published in abstract form and would normally then appear under the list of publications, but it is not unreasonable to indicate both under the one heading. Do not be tempted to fatten the curriculum vitae by making one piece of work appear as a number of separate contributions. It is acceptable, however, to show a piece of work progressing from a local presentation to an international meeting and finally full publication.

Learned societies and committee membership may include other non-clinical or medical societies if you feel you can justify their inclusion and committee chairmanship or a period as secretary would indicate managerial experience. Other interests, whether cultural, sporting or recreational, should be mentioned especially if they feature distinguishing excellence. Team sports give the impression of team membership and a captaincy may suggest team leadership. Similarly, committee membership of a university or hospital club suggests organizational and administrative ability.

Lastly, a short covering letter should accompany the curriculum vitae, submitting your application, mentioning the post for which you are applying, stating that you are enclosing copies (state number) of the curriculum vitae and the names (state number) of referees.

PRE-INTERVIEW VISITS

Usually known as pre-interview visits, these should be more correctly known as pre-application visits, as your decision to apply will probably be based on this visit unless you already know the hospital and job very well. Arranging the visit is usually explained in the advertisement, job description or literature supplied by the hospital. It is usually a question of telephoning the departmental secretary, who will organize things according to arrangements for candidates to visit. If all else fails you can ring the human resource department and ask for local advice and assistance.

Assemble a list of questions you would like to ask, some being more appropriate to ask the medical staff and others the managers. They will also depend on what grade of appointment you are considering. Those relating to the job itself might include whether the job provides what you need for your career plan and whether it is accredited with relevant authorities. You will be able to identify the rotations and where you will slot in to these and that there are no restrictions due to existing trainees' present contracts. Find out who controls the rotation and whether you have influence in your placement. You might want to define the exact nature of the work and check the on-call arrangements. How flexible is the on-call rota and what happens when people are on annual leave, sick leave and study leave? What facilities are available for research and is research encouraged? Will you be given time, how will you get papers typed, can you get equipment, is there space, is anyone interested, what research has been done in the department recently and is there a good library? If this is your last move to a consultant appointment you will also need to know how secure the post is, what changes are envisaged for the unit and hospital, what plans there are for changes of the staff mix and how the Calman Report will affect you.

What are the local rules and policies on study leave and what funds are there for expenses? Do you have to live in on-call, do you have to pay for the accommodation and what is it like? How secure is it? And where can you park? How secure is that? Then you may want to consider incremental points, moving expenses, etc., transferring distinction awards, private practice. And do not forget house prices, travelling costs to work, car parking costs, local schools and school fees. Check not only on entitlements but willingness to pay. Although there are no questions you should not ask, remember not to dwell unduly on your rights and entitlements with medical staff. There are also some things you will need to know just in case you are asked any questions other than about yourself and your career to date. Basically these are the same sorts of questions you might be asked in the interview and are discussed later. People you meet will talk about you and the job while you are trying to find out about the job and the department and hospital. Allow the consultant(s) to tell you what is required of the applicant as you will then be in a better position to fit yourself to the role. This may also require a revision of your curriculum vitae.

Although this is not the selection interview, it is a time for mutual assessment and you need to present well and create the correct impression. Give your best suit a trial run for the interview. The more informal the setting the greater will be the impression you may create. Try to appear competent without being overconfident, deferential without being obsequious and pleasant without being overfriendly. Take some copies of your curriculum vitae and reprints of papers in case you are asked and your list of reminders for questions. Take some food or chocolate with you. You will almost certainly be offered coffee, but you will not perform at your best with hypoglycaemia.

Allow plenty of time for the journey whether by public transport or car. Hospital parking is almost always very difficult, finding a department in a large hospital is not easy and receptions seem invariably to be staffed by people who have only the vaguest notion of the whereabouts of different departments. And try and tidy up before you arrive in the department. It has usually been raining or is very windy the day you choose to visit. Arrive a few minutes early, introduce yourself to the secretary or receptionist and when introduced to your hosts, make sure they have your correct name. Candidates with similar names have been mistaken for one another. Try to make a sensible impression; remember that this is not the selection interview but also that your host is not being interviewed. By all means refer to your notes, but it is polite to ask if you want to write notes and do not forget to thank your host. When talking to other members of staff try to find out if they are happy with their work, the unit and the hospital. Beware anyone who is very discouraging; they might be correct in their advice but they might also be applying for the job! You might also do well to check the accuracy of the job description with other staff.

If you are applying for a consultant job there are a number of issues which need to be brought out with both doctors and senior managers. These may include problems facing department/unit/hospital, the roles of doctors in managing these problems, the role of clinical directors and medical director within the trust, the management of hospital or unit generally, clinical audit, etc. and also how you feel about some of these issues. You should use the opportunity to find out about the hospital, get the chief executive's and chair's view of the world so that you can reflect this when answering their questions at interview. You need to gauge their interests and mirror their world. Avoid any strong philosophical or political views. And ask for a copy of the finances and annual plan.

Before leaving the area you might consider buying a local newspaper to survey the local property market and identify some of the local estate agents. And if you feel really confident you might want to buy a local map. Certainly tidy up and complete any notes about the job, department, etc. as there may be some weeks until the interview and you will forget the details.

APPLYING FOR THE JOB

Applications for jobs should be clear and concise, typewritten, well prepared and presented, accurate and up to date. They may be submitted either on an application form or by curriculum vitae. The choice of which is used seems to vary. Some posts require one or the other, some require both. An application form has the advantage of excluding information not relevant to the application, thereby standardizing the process and making it fairer. CVs leave more scope for the individual to show creativity and initiative. The applicant has more control over the selection process by including or excluding information from a curriculum vitae. Long application forms can be time consuming to complete and with the popularity of word processors and relative lack of typewriters, forms are more difficult to complete unless done by hand when they do not look so neat. Most doctors therefore prefer to use curriculum vitae.

A practical solution would be for employing authorities to send out guidance notes with the job description and person specification, listing the information which does not need to be included in the curriculum vitae. Guidance notes would generally be similar for specific grades or specialities and would obviate the need to rewrite the curriculum vitae for each job application.

Names can lead to selection bias (Esmail & Everington 1993) and a pilot scheme for medical appointments in which the name of the applicant is shown on a detachable front sheet and not on the curriculum vitae is in progress. Consideration may need to be given to further research in this area to reduce the chances of surnames causing racial discrimination in the selection process (BMA 1994).

You might want to leave your application with the department of human resources at the end of your preinterview visit; at least you will know that it has arrived safely. If you post it, send it recorded delivery or put in a stamped addressed envelope for an acknowledgement, or even both. The authors know of one consultant application that was lost after being received! Also allow plenty of time not only for the mail to arrive at the hospital but also for it to go through the internal postal system there.

REFERENCES

Referees are not only vital to the application but their choice is important. It will be you who chooses them and this requires considerable thought. They obviously need to think highly enough of you to support you and understand their role. The referee needs to be a consultant you have worked for, preferably recently and, certainly for more senior posts, the speciality is relevant. If they will be serving on the advisory appointments committee, its a matter of debate whether you should use them.

Without fail, seek their permission, if necessary in writing, before submitting your application. Always supply them with details of when you worked for them, plus a copy of your curriculum vitae. They may have forgotten a lot about you and may not know what you have done since leaving them. Also let them have details of the post for which you are applying so that the reference is appropriate to the post. You may wish to discuss your preinterview visit with your referees to enable them to do this. Also supply the likely date of the interview so that if the referee is away, at least the secretary will be able to notify the appointing hospital. It reflects badly on a candidate if the named referee has not sent a reference as it may be assumed that the fault lies with the candidate not having allowed sufficient time for the preparation, typing, signing and posting of the reference. It is useful to find out what address the referee wishes to use for the correspondence. And it shows courtesy and attention to detail to get their qualifications correct.

The process of how shortlisting is carried out has been discussed in the previous chapter. There remains, however, the possibility of 'trial by sherry'. The rules with regard to questions about race, family plans, sexual orientation and marital status are as for the selection interview, but you may find yourself faced with people who feel they should have been on the selection panel but are not and who need to flex their egos. You need to be diplomatic in avoiding these questions.

DAY OF INTERVIEW

Prepare everything the day before and allow more time than necessary for your journey. If it is any distance away it may be worth the expense of staying nearby so that you have a relaxed start to the day with plenty of time to arrive. Do not miss out on eating, arrive early and calm and with possible questions and your answers totally revised and memorized. Your general principle should be to convince the panel that you will successfully complete your training and achieve your goals or, in the case of a consultant appointment, make a delightful colleague.

Being interviewed

This used to be a taboo subject in the profession although there have been a few articles (see Further Reading) on the subject in the medical press from as early as 1947; these need to be read with care now as the law, codes of practice and fashion have changed. You can always discuss the subject with colleagues and contemporaries but the resulting discussion can often be highly charged with anecdotal experiences from people not necessarily able to give objective, relevant and up-to-date advice. As Drife (1985) points out, if you are on the shortlist, assume the job is there for the taking and do not be overawed if you find yourself competing with a 'home' candidate.

As you will have seen from the previous chapter, the size of the appointments committee tends to grow as the seniority of the post rises. The members of the selection committee may or may not know one another but almost certainly the chair will not know everyone on the panel. So you can be reassured that even some of the panel members may feel in strange surroundings.

As a general rule you should dress to reassure and fit the stereotype of the post for which you apply. You are hardly likely to impress the panel selecting a consultant surgeon or physician appointment dressed in jeans. In most people's minds doctors dress in a quiet, sober, conservative manner and the flamboyance of excessively loud ties, bow ties, etc. may not endear you (although you may get away with similar excesses in shoes and socks as these are generally hidden below the table). For women the same general rules apply. On the other hand you do need to stand out a little so try to be very smart and not frayed at the edges.

Go into the room positively, smiling and determined to enjoy it. It will not be as bad as a viva examination. Be relaxed but businesslike. Sit upright, be friendly, smile with perhaps a degree of authority and look initially at the chair who should put you at your ease. Be courteous. Know your curriculum vitae by heart. Be enthusiastic for the job.

Interview questions

Answer the questions, which are invariably not difficult but only attempting to get you to talk about yourself, with the right mixture of confidence, intelligence, charm, humour, enthusiasm, honesty and maturity. Address your answer initially to the questioner but look around and try to engage all the panel. Do not be monosyllabic nor loquacious. If asked closed questions avoid the temptation to give simple yes or no answers. Try to expand the answer to allow the interviewer time to recover; making him or her feel uncomfortable will gain you no friends. Again, balance is important. If there is silence after your answer you are being invited to continue. Do not be embarrassed by silence if you need time to think about your answer and do clarify a question if you are not clear what you are being asked. With multiple questions try to remember the individual questions or clarify before answering.

Routine questions about your journey or finding the place help break the ice and enable you to settle yourself and these are usually followed by some questions to clarify any queries with your curriculum vitae. The questions then tend to move to asking your reasons for wanting this job or what attracted you to the job? This is your opportunity to show that you have researched the hospital. Have you identified any challenge that the institution faces? This leads naturally to how you see your career developing or perhaps where you see yourself in 10 years. You might be asked, if you had money to spend when you arrived in your new job at the hospital, what would you spend it on? And slightly trickier, what you think of the hospital or what you have to offer the hospital. Typical questions ask about research you have done or intend to do, your experience and knowledge of clinical audit, government reports which affect you and the service generally, as well as possible future plans and changes in the NHS. Sometimes this leads to general questions about doctors' involvement in management, the responsibilities in your present post and any achievements and changes you have dealt with, which may reveal something of your management qualities.

Then there may be questions which reveal 'what makes candidate tick'. These are usually about hobbies and outside interests. Avoid suggesting these might interfere with your work! Aptitudes and outside interests are a measure of whether you are a well-rounded personality. They may try to reveal your virtues and weaknesses, maybe asking about your mistakes directly or your aptitudes and ambitions. Answers tend to reveal your personal values. Such questions gauge your self-awareness, intellectual honesty, maturity and dependability and may relate indirectly to your team membership characteristics. Or they might ask how you would change your present job or what would be your priorities with unlimited funds for research. There are no right answers to these questions. They are not really the same as tricky questions intended to impress the committee with the questioner's skill. If you are asked that sort of question, stay calm and if you are struggling remember that only better candidates get asked difficult questions in order to separate them and also committee members usually have sympathy for candidates being given a difficult time by colleagues. A good chair will intervene in this situation.

Questions about your greatest achievements, challenges or responsibilities, etc. are an attempt to obtain a record of your standards, your qualities of management and relationships as well as your leadership style and ability and whether you are a process or people-orientated person. Questions about relationships are trying to assess your personality – social or self-contained, conforming or independent, extravert or sensitive, phlegmatic or excitable – as well as whether you would rather be a 'big fish in a small pool' or vice versa.

Try to identify the real question and if in doubt ask for clarification but do not waste time looking for hidden catches. Remember, they are usually seeking reassurance. Do make sure you are answering the question asked. Be enthusiastic and do not give evasive answers. Be prepared to explain gaps in your curriculum vitae and why there are lots of locum appointments. And do not show undue interest in holidays, study leave, time for research projects, etc.

Try to appear friendly, cheerful and smiling. Body language helps, with a businesslike, authoritative attitude, professional appearance and energetic approach. Remember to keep your voice calm. Allow yourself time to think before answering so that your replies are considered and logical; do not be tempted by silence to leap in and say something ill considered. And remember synchronization. When asked questions in visual terms such as 'How do you see your career developing', answer with the use of such words as 'picture', 'clear' and 'focus'. If asked in kinaesthetic terms, 'How will you handle the reforms affecting your department', answer with words like 'move', 'impact' and 'impress'. And similarly with questions in auditory terms. Finally keep your animation and gestures limited and try not to wave your hands and arms about in an excited nervous fashion.

At the end of the interview you are generally invited by the chair to ask the panel any questions you might have. While it will not count against you to ask a question, it is acceptable and indeed desirable not to do so. Certainly it is not the appropriate moment to ask about pay, time off for research or other reasons, holidays, etc.

Presentations

This is a developing method of helping to assess candidates for consultant appointments and is thought to be a reasonable way of assessing the vision of candidates in relation to the future of a unit, whether they have grasped the problems of the unit in preinterview visits and have a realistic expectation of what they are coming to. Some candidates like it as a way of being in control of the first half of the interview; others feel uncomfortable making presentations, particularly as they feel that it will not usually be a part of their everyday work. It does illustrate the importance of making sure you collect useful information from clinical director, medical director, chief executive and chair when paying your preapplication visit.

AFTER THE INTERVIEW

One of two things should occur. Either you will be called back to the panel when the chair will offer you the job or one of the panel members will come and offer you words of advice and counselling about the reasons for your failure this time, whether you need to change anything and how to go about that. It might also be suggested that you discuss your career plans with others such as your postgraduate dean or regional advisor.

If you were not shortlisted the problems to consider are careless curriculum vitae writing, poor references or maybe insufficient or inappropriate experience. If in doubt you should seek advice from referees, chiefs, clinical tutors, college tutors, regional advisors and postgraduate deans. If failure occurred at interview and you feel it went badly, it probably did. Consider poor interview technique, unfavourable references and again seek advice from all sources. If you feel things went well at interview, then you were not the most appropriate candidate but there will be other opportunities. Finally, if you are accepted, it is probably safest to await written confirmation and agree the start date before resigning your present post.

REFERENCES

BMA 1994 Guidelines for good practice in the recruitment & selection of doctors. British Medical Association, London

Drife J O 1985 Be interviewed. In: How to do it, vol 1, 2nd edn. British Medical Journal, London

Esmail A, Everington S 1993 Racial discrimination against doctors from ethnic minorities. British Medical Journal 306: 691–692

Gatrell J, White A 1995 Medical student to medical director. A development strategy for doctors. NHS Training Authority, Bristol

O'Brien E 1985 Prepare a curriculum vitae. In: How to do it, vol 1, 2nd edn. British Medical Journal, London

FURTHER READING

Articles

Dick G 1979 Conduct an interview. British Medical Journal 1: 42–43

Bourns H K 1991 References for medical posts – how best to utilize them. West of England Medical Journal 106 (i): 11–12

Bertram, R 1988 Anatomy of an interview. The Times, 1st September

Evans N 1991 There must be a better way. British Medical Journal 303: 1483

Foot S, Horton J 1992 More luck than judgement. Health Service Journal 102: 22–24

Books

Ailes R 1988 You are the message. Dow Jones-Irwin, Wokingham

Laborde G Z 1983 Influencing with integrity. Syntony, Palo Alto

Pease A 1981 Body language (overcoming common problems). Sheldon Press, London

Wainwright G R 1985 Body language. Hodder & Stoughton, Sevenoaks

White T 1993 Management for clinicians. Edward Arnold, London

16

The management of meetings

Tony White

Too many open minds should be closed for repairs.
(Toledo Blade 1989)

INTRODUCTION

Meetings are universal in any organization and are a common event in the NHS. They are also an important management tool but many are a waste of time and most hospital meetings take longer than necessary. The main reasons for this are:

- lack of clear objective(s);
- lack of preparation;
- no agenda or late presentation;
- too many participants;
- the wrong participants;
- lack of leadership and control;
- poor presentations;
- digressions and repetitions;
- time wasting on why, rather than how;
- lack of outcome or equivocal decisions.

REASONS FOR MEETINGS

Every meeting should have an objective and you as manager should have a personal objective. It may be the same as the stated objective of the meeting or it may be different, in which case you may have a problem. Your interest may be only marginally different or totally different from the others. Weigh the objectives and make choices. You may feel the need to move the meeting to a conclusion that will only benefit yourself and which may not be in the hospital's best interest. Personal agendas can destroy meetings and members may be heavily defensive in order to protect their personal agenda.

Every well-run meeting, whether formal or informal, is based on three essentials:

1. careful planning
2. clear aims
3. teamwork.

TYPES OF MEETINGS

There are many different kinds of meeting but hospital meetings commonly fall into three categories:

1. routine regular meetings, e.g. committee meetings;
2. small group meetings arranged for a specific purpose;
3. workshops, impromptu and brainstorming meetings for a specific purpose.

PLANNING FOR MEETINGS

All meetings need careful planning yet many only have papers and even agendas circulated on arrival at the meeting and people turn up for these events equally unprepared. It is sloppy management practice to run meetings without circulating a properly prepared agenda and all the papers in advance to allow members time to read and consider these matters. Only in very exceptional circumstances should papers be circulated at the meeting. In such circumstances the members should be allowed time to read and consider the papers. Any other course of action means consultation is a sham.

Always go to the meeting knowing what you want to achieve and never go unprepared. Consider the decisions that might be made, what problems will be solved, what actions will be taken, what information can be learned. Do not assume that what you wish to achieve will be understood by others. Many meetings are run on the assumption that everyone knows what the task is. Members may be required to provide facts but think they are there to provide advice or reach a decision.

There should be concise accurate summaries about the problems being addressed, with options already identified. If more information is required it should be made available with the documentation but not as part of the summary. A meeting may be the opportunity to put across a message so if you have an objective, always have a prepared statement available when the opportunity presents itself. A seed sown today may be important for later. To make sure you do not miss a point, use notes.

- Never read a prepared statement aloud.
- Never use a memorized statement.
- Speak naturally using notes.

If you are organizing the meeting you will need to consider where to meet. There are a number of advantages to holding a meeting in your own office if it is of a suitable size. This obviously allows some degree of control which would be impossible elsewhere. You have the opportunity to play the gracious host, of course, and it may save you time if the alternative is a meeting in another building. Finally it gives the opportunity to terminate the meeting when you choose. But never insist on meeting in your own office if this creates tension, as there can be advantages to meeting on neutral ground. By deferring to the other person, you may gain an advantage.

Remember that seating arrangements can have a profound effect on behaviour in a meeting. Sitting yourself behind a desk creates a barrier. A peer should be met in a more comfortable area or around a table. You are more likely to get candid advice or new ideas when the person you are meeting is not feeling vulnerable. If you are dealing with a peer in their office who remains behind a desk you can diminish their control by remaining standing or moving about the room. You have a height advantage and their eyes have to follow you.

In meetings face to face, the mood will be intensified especially in large groups where the energy is focused. A full circle is most intense. This is not necessarily good or bad as such but depends on what you are trying to achieve. It does make control more difficult since all the parties are of equal status but discussions can be creative and stimulating. Semicircles are good for problem-solving meetings and provide a good balance of control and sensitivity. Everyone can see everyone else but they can also focus on you as discussion leader. Do not fill a room with more people than it can comfortably hold.

Long tables are wonderful control mechanisms but do possess limitations. They are useless for brainstorming sessions. It is impossible to see others down the same side and as a result discussion between people is limited. This can be an advantage with two allied troublemakers who, if placed a few seats apart on the same side of the table, can have their effectiveness minimized. Obviously you will need to establish assigned seating to accomplish this goal. In informal meetings, however, you might plan where to place the most critical participants, perhaps a valuable team player and a troublemaker. Sometimes a group that meets regularly may establish tacitly assigned seating.

Always be aware of other sources of influence at a meeting and position yourself where you can easily make eye contact. To some extent where you sit will depend on your purpose. If you want to be uninvolved pick a position that permits that. If you are seeking to win a point, pick a controlling position. At a long table this will be at either end; in a three-sided arrangement this will be either side of the chair or at either end. At a long table an ally at the other end of the table will give you maximum support in handling a difficult meeting.

Next time you are at a meeting observe where people sit and see how it influences their roles. Observe the quiet, apparently unassuming member who has developed a technique to suit their own agenda. An ideal position is opposite the chair so that you can talk directly to them and include others as well. If you are going to be a competitor to the chair, sit as far away as possible. Where the participants sit may shorten the meeting when clear lines of authority are established and the meeting is kept under control.

AGENDAS

Whoever controls the agenda controls the meeting because a skilled chair does not allow anything on it that does not serve their own interests. Each meeting should have a correctly constructed agenda, not a shopping list. Agendas are sadly often too brief and too vague, which only encourages people to pile on additional items. You must also tell the members of the meeting enough about the item for their contribution to be useful, so summarize the task on the agenda and attach all relevant papers. Each item should provide enough information to allow the participant to do any necessary preparation and to understand what you hope to achieve.

There are also different kinds of tasks. You must indicate whether an item is for information, discussion, action or all three. Meetings often fail because participants are not clear about what is on the table and what is expected of them. Circulate the agenda well in advance to allow members to do their homework. For regular routine meetings this is vital, to allow them the opportunity to seek advice from their own staff or colleagues.

It is revealing to see people at meetings thumbing through sheaves of papers, trying to understand their purpose. There should be concise, accurate summaries about the problem being addressed, with options already identified. Papers distributed at a meeting are valueless. Passing out a report at a meeting is a total waste of time as it cannot be considered seriously and nor will it be read afterwards. It is only valuable as a technique for bluffing an item through and is a distraction, shifting the focus away from the matter in hand. There is a strong relationship between the length of time people are given to consider items before the meeting and the positive decision-making process at the actual meeting. It also reduces the length of the meeting as members are adequately prepared for what is to be discussed and this results in a more valuable contribution. Not least, the chair is also fully briefed on all the topics for discussion and will have better control of the meeting, as it may be necessary to resolve any potential problems in advance.

The agenda should be the plan of action for the meeting. It is helpful to schedule items in order of relative importance. It may be necessary to request action plans from key players before the meeting, which can be discussed ahead of the meeting to produce an appropriate agenda. This will help everyone focus on the objectives of the meeting, the issues to be discussed and what is expected of them by way of preparation before the meeting.

Group all the agenda items into routine items first, items for information only next and those for discussion/decision last. This enables half the agenda to be achieved quickly, giving a good sense of pace and achievement to the meetings. Any Other Business should not be an item for a weekly or monthly meeting. It might be acceptable for, say, regional meetings which perhaps only convene every 6 months or so. It is very difficult for the chair to control the timing of meetings which have such an open-ended item.

Do your homework, as there is no excuse for laxity which slows down a meeting and sends a clear message to others that the meeting is of little value. It is always very clear who has and who has not done their homework. As chair, never talk the group through material page by page as this gives the message that preparation is unnecessary. Guess expectations and then exceed them. A few minutes of extra preparation will give you credibility with others.

Talk to people before the meeting and do not limit your discussion to the meeting. Not only are people flattered to be approached, it will enable you to hear things you will not necessarily hear at the meeting. Sophisticated participants will be talking to each other before the meeting.

If, after the meeting, someone asks how the meeting went and your best reply is, 'We had a good discussion', there is a problem. Every meeting is a winner or a loser but you do need some yardstick by which to measure success or failure. These might be considered as follows:

- meetings to inform have to present and receive a predetermined amount of information;
- brainstorming meetings are not successful unless a certain number of new ideas are generated;
- meetings to delegate are not successful unless each participant has a clear idea of their respective assignment.

Therefore for each meeting set a measurable, attainable objective by which success or failure can be measured.

AIMS

Everyone needs to work together and agree on aims, if not detail. A small group, whether a patient support group or a departmental meeting, may be for talking, listening or sharing problems. A committee normally aims to make and agree decisions, plan how those decisions should be carried out and share out the tasks amongst its members. Meetings may have more than one purpose and concentrate on different aspects during relevant parts of the meeting, so the membership has to be very clear about its purpose and when the style changes. The aims need to be agreed and the most successful meetings are usually those which have been planned.

TEAMWORK

Only those people who can influence the fulfilment of the objective of the meeting should attend. Unnecessary participants, like unnecessary meetings, are a waste of time. That does not mean that anyone who may oppose the objectives should be excluded. That may do more harm. A successful meeting is dependent on those present, but that depends on who is invited. You should normally invite those:

- whom it is essential to invite;
- who can provide what is required;
- who are in favour of the objective;
- who will oppose the objective;
- who will sit on the fence;
- who can cause trouble if not invited.

Of course hospital policy often determines who should attend. The more specific the objectives, the fewer participants there should be. The question then arises as to how many people should attend. It has been said that the length of a meeting is proportional to the number of people attending. The more participants, the more difficult it is to achieve objectives. No one should feel the need to be at a meeting if the objective is of no particular concern to them so if you are invited to a meeting, attend only if it will be useful to do so.

The psychology of group dynamics is important. A meeting of two people should provide excellent communication and a useful outcome. Unfortunately the process may have to be repeated with several individuals and if the outcomes are different this could create problems. Small groups from three to nine individuals invite candour, intimacy and real results. According to Nelson (1989), people 'are often reluctant to speak up in meetings of any sort involving more than four or five people, especially when they are juniors amongst a number of more senior' people. When the group reaches 10 or more people, acting and a sense of theatre come into play as opposing parties try to impress colleagues by aiming for effect rather than results. When the group reaches 12 or more then two leaders or groups are likely to emerge.

Kieffer (1988) says that 'there is a tendency for meetings to drift towards collective incompetence'. As Macaulay (1991) puts it, groups of individuals are far more likely to err than individuals. Regular staff meetings with a long agenda produce few results and often the same issues appear time and again for discussion. At the heart of collective incompetence is the so-called 'group mind', where people meeting together have an enlarged mind with tremendous capacity which can achieve effective results but also has severe limitations. The group mind has a number of flaws. People dislike inconsistency and attempt to eliminate it. This mental conflict or cognitive dissonance occurs when information challenges group beliefs. The group reacts to preserve its preconceptions. This is common amongst medical committees.

Dissociation from the task may occur. A member may believe they are less well informed than the rest of the group and although disagreeing, may vote in favour to remain accepted within the group. The group may then reach a decision based on the lowest common denominator. Ultimately this may not solve the problem but it saves feelings and egos. The factors affecting group thinking may be miscommunication, outside pressures, personal agendas and a pattern of meeting that becomes traditional and ingrained. Professor Parkinson is reputed to have stated that the time spent on any item on the agenda will be in inverse proportion to the sum involved.

Then there is the problem of strains between the various members representing different groups, between their representational role and their corporate role, between their personalities and backgrounds. They may all have different visions of the future. They all require emotional maturity to face these tensions, but how rarely those tensions are allowed to surface. Everyone remains polite and reserved. It is unnatural for people not to talk about these discomforts openly. Quality does not emerge by talking about it. Teamwork does not result from talking about it. The group needs to do these things. The best teams are not necessarily the brightest but those of the right mix.

It is also useful to distinguish the social leaders who deal with people rather than issues or process. They converse before and after the meeting and are sensitive to the feelings and emotions of other people, enjoying the contact of meetings. The process leaders look for order, distinguishing process from structure. They are very quick to focus, to notice when the discussion goes off track although they may not have the personal skills to retrieve it. Meetings usually require both social and process leadership.

DURATION OF MEETINGS

Time wasting is the commonest problem with most meetings. The following list will be readily identifiable to anyone who has attended meetings in hospitals or medical management meetings.

- Fighting losing or lost battles.
- Discussing items when a decision has already been made (maybe elsewhere), especially when you know this.
- Discussing items not within the group's power to decide or even influence.
- Socializing. The problem here is usually that the members of the group are unaware of the purpose of the meeting.
- Disseminating information. Use other methods where possible. Instead of taking time to prepare a written report short enough to read, someone may call a meeting. This is not only wasteful but it can be dangerous as oral communication can be subject to more misunderstanding. If you are looking for ways of reducing meetings or the length of meetings, cut out those items which are for information only.
- Persuading people to do or become involved in things. This should be done outside the meeting. Make sure that everything that can be done before the meeting is done, as the meeting can then concentrate on the primary objectives.
- Decision making but not understanding what part of

the decision-making process the group is responsible for, whether agreement to a decision, consultation before a decision, decision requiring the agreement of more than one group, enhanced commitment to a decision, gathering information for a decision to be made elsewhere or actually to make the decision. It is also important to know whether all the preliminary steps to making a decision have been completed.
- Presentation of new ideas when members comment and nearly everyone has suggestions for improvements as they have not been given the opportunity to study the proposals in advance and are seeing them for the first time. Discussions are lengthy and suggestions are numerous so revision takes a long time. If the committee members had been consulted beforehand, better results might have been achieved in a shorter period of time. Aim to get alliances and support in advance of meetings.

PRODUCTIVE MEETINGS

There are ways of distinguishing whether a meeting is useful and productive. At the end of every meeting the objective should be restated and the results of the meeting summarized. Assignments and follow-up actions should be clarified and these can appear alongside the minutes. For a meeting that you are attending, you could ask yourself: What is the purpose of this meeting, what do I expect to accomplish and how will I distinguish success from failure? After the meeting ask yourself, was I correct about the task, were the other participants clear about the task and objectives, did the meeting achieve the objective(s) as stated in the agenda? Thus, was the meeting a success or failure? And if a failure, why and what could be done to improve the next meeting?

CHAIRING MEETINGS

Skill is required to manage meetings effectively and few doctors have had any training in this. You can usually predict the outcome of any meeting by who will be chairing it. Control and authority come from the chair's perceived commitment to the meeting and its objectives and the chair's skill in supporting the group to achieve those objectives. If you as chair are thought to have your own agenda or support some members over others, your authority will be restricted. Your comments as well as your objectives should be limited. The less you say, the greater your strength but very often the chair spends most of the time talking. Your primary concerns are the interest of the group, the integrity of the meeting, the achievement of the group objectives and the aims and objectives of the organization as a whole. Managing the chair covers a number of key characteristics:

- *Communication.* An important function is to help with communication, being the voice of the group mind. This does not mean speaking most. Look out for possible misunderstandings, words or phrases whose meanings are unclear or ambiguous, generalizations that lose meaning. Watch for wrong assumptions being made or statements removed from context. And remind the committee that the last statement may not be its final position.
- *Anticipation.* Organize the meeting with the tasks of the committee in mind. Ask yourself what objectives you are aiming to achieve from the meeting and what strategy and steps you will need to achieve them.
- *Personnel management.* Managing a meeting is about managing people and having a congenial personality is not enough. You need to be able to sense disagreement or harmony, agreement and opposition, confusion and certainty and bring it all together. You need to unite the group and be united with the group, friendly and complimentary. Although distance confers authority it can also produce both conscious and unconscious resentment.
- *Adaptability.* Although you should stay strictly with the agenda, be prepared to adapt should something unexpectedly turn out to be important. This does not mean allowing digressions, repetitions and pontifications and all the other wanderings one sees so often in medical meetings, but knowing when the discussion should be allowed to flow unhindered to achieve the objectives of the meeting.
- *Neutrality.* The chair represents the group to the group. Over 90% of what you say should be a reflection of the group or the process, rather than of you as an individual. Decide your position before the meeting on all the major issues, although be prepared to change your mind. Make an effort to form preliminary opinions on all issues. Your opinion may be decisive, although during the meeting you must remain neutral. If you as chair argue your position with peers you will have difficulty paying attention to the process, thereby placing your own identity over that of the group. Your attention should be directed entirely to the process and not the structure. You must also try to predict issues which require further discussion, or limited discussion and debate, to structure the meeting effectively. You should rarely influence the substance or structure but you do determine what appears on the agenda and this is generally more important than what is said. If you want to influence structure it must be done subtly and sparingly. Only

when all other efforts fail should you attempt to influence the outcome, by expressing substantive opinions. If you wish a particular point to be advocated it is far better to arrange for another member to do it for you. In the end your continuing effectiveness as chair, as strong neutral and fair, embodying the group as a whole, is more important than your effectiveness on any one issue.

The chairperson should sit in the most visible spot. From there they can be seen and heard and by seeing and hearing they are in control of the meeting. At the end of a rectangular table and farthest from the entrance is best. Or sit at the centre of the longer side of a rectangular table although this does not command as much attention. Do not sit next to the head of the table as this gives authority to the person at the head, thereby weakening your own authority. If the table is round or oval visualize it as rectangular and sit at the end farthest from the entrance.

Remember that starting on time and ending on time is for the mutual benefit of the group. To make a dull meeting less dull shorten it by setting a time limit on it. And stick to it. Always state the time the meeting will end. If it does overrun it is invariably the fault of the chairman. Time management experts have shown that people are more likely to turn up on time for a meeting scheduled at 9.10am than one at 9.00am because the former is more specific and many people allow themselves to be 10 minutes late for a start on the hour. And if you want to shorten a decision-making process, vote. Make the decision even if you do not have every single known fact. People do not like decisions and often feel that not making a decision will keep them out of trouble. When discussion is endless you must vote.

Don't neglect consultation. Members assume that you alone possess the input from all other members and will shift to a quasisubordinate role if they think that you possess the whole picture. If it becomes clear that you have not consulted, then your control and credibility are justifiably threatened.

Your consultation also gives you the opportunity to detect any hidden agenda. You will then have more information than your meeting partners and this will assist you in achieving your aim from the group. Nothing breeds authority like success and a pattern of successful meetings will have everyone wanting to work with the winner. Give credit where it is deserved, otherwise you risk jealousies and loss of authority. It is always more difficult to move from informality to formality than vice versa so always begin on a formal note. In meetings with peers, subordinates and superiors, if you want honest input make sure you ask lowest ranking members first, but if you want conformity ask the highest ranking person first.

Maintain courtesy. If you really want valuable contributions, treat all your participants with respect. Some may be smarter than others, some will be more creative, others better workers and yet others more influential, but they all have some contribution to make. Do value the introverts who do not contribute often; they may have a useful offering.

The more rigorous and demanding the requirement for membership in a meeting, the more the participants will enjoy and contribute to the meeting. However, there is a difference between setting high expectations for success and effort and setting unrealistic goals. Participants need to feel like winners by achievement. Speak of 'we' not 'I', especially when success is achieved. Make the task appear important, value participation, communicate confidence. Even when you have to be critical, put your positive comments first. Always look for the positive in any statement and if you must disagree, disagree with the statement, not with who says it. Congratulate the group as you move on; last statements are often remembered. Summarize actions and create expectations for future meetings. Bring a positive attitude and don't bring any of your other problems to the meeting.

Begin the meeting by getting announcements out of the way first and then move to simple issues to gain momentum. The energy of the meeting diminishes as it progresses. Consider more demanding issues early on if you are looking to get your own way rather than accepting serious contributions, as time dwindles endeavour to push your items through. If possible, the meeting should begin and end on positive notes. Being positive at the beginning can set up a feeling of success for the remainder of the meeting. That momentum can be helpful later so try to finish with an item that makes people feel they have achieved something. Failing that, try to summarize the positive things that came out of the meeting. Set a goal. Focus everyone on that goal beforehand so that after the meeting you will be able to say clearly what has been achieved.

Keep the meeting moving. When the issue is clearly ripe for conclusion, offer your summary, clarify and summarize points of agreement and opposing points of view. People often hear things differently, so your primary task is to make sure each person hears things in the same way. Take it step by step. When a particular task is completed, state the conclusion and make sure everyone is together before moving on. Make it clear what has been completed and what left open.

Do not draw attention to latecomers by restating what has gone before as this devalues those who were on time. Do not remark on lateness as this only adds further distraction. If you know in advance that someone is coming late, note it for the group so that it does not appear as a criticism of the meeting.

Most discussions involve many tasks to reach a conclusion and different tasks require different processes. You cannot have an effective discussion by approaching the tasks, the problems and the people all at the same time. Separate process from structure. If part of the group is discussing structure and part process you will need to get the group back on the same track. Distinguishing process and structure and separating and ordering tasks are among the most critical techniques for ensuring success.

Before addressing the structure the group will need to know the process for making a decision. Who has decided or will decide the criteria by which the decision will be made? Will all solutions be presented before discussion? Will one or three be recommended? Will decision be by consensus, by majority or by the chair?

Separate problems from people. What is the basic problem and the goal to be achieved? Separate the problems when there is more than one. Divide problems into subproblems which can be addressed, whenever possible as separate issues.

Gather the facts. Remember facts seldom speak for themselves. When dealing with people the perception of facts is more important than the facts themselves. Facts are just arguments heard in different ways and usually dependent on who presented them.

Always ask for multiple solutions if possible and pick the best solution. Decide who should implement the solution and make sure it gets done. There are three common problems:

1. defining the problem;
2. creating the basis for genuine consultation;
3. confusing the consultation with making the decision.

There are similarities with medicine itself. What seems to be the problem? Something seems to be wrong so let's discuss it. How long has it been a problem (gathering the facts)? Then detailed examination of the facts or distinguishing the problems. Looking for more than one cause (the differential diagnosis). Then a treatment or solution to solve the problem, although the group should offer more than one before a decision. Be careful not to allow consideration of the solution to go over old ground and begin the discussion again.

REDUCING MEETINGS

Always consider alternatives to meetings. Perhaps your objectives could be achieved with a phone call or letter or maybe the purpose is only the dissemination of information. Satisficing is all too common (Allison 1971). In choosing, human beings do not consider all alternatives and pick the action with the best consequences. Instead, they find a course of action that is good enough, one that satisfies. Organizations are often happy to find a needle in a haystack rather than searching for the sharpest needle in the haystack.

Meetings without results are a waste of time and usually only lead to more meetings. Meetings may take place for the wrong reasons. There may be hidden reasons for meetings, some related to specific personal agendas. They may be a substitute for work. They may indicate a need to share responsibility for a difficult problem, to avoid making a tough decision or even any decision. Meetings can be networking channels which all too easily become 'talking shops', a means of spending time with peers or those higher in the organization, to find reassurance or attention or to reflect power. And some committees meet regularly, publish a lengthy agenda and extensive minutes even though they may not have any real purpose. It is important to recognize that there is a subtle but nonetheless important difference between a stimulating discussion and a productive meeting.

Committee meetings are only effective as long as they have objectives which can be fulfilled. Many hospital committees have long since forgotten their original objectives and rarely consider their function and usefulness, often forming new ones in preference to disbanding old ones. Committees should regularly audit their value and purpose. Often situations are created to provide topics for the agenda.

Small group and brainstorming meetings usually consist of four to six people, picked and assigned to achieve a specific task. It is useful to define how it is to be achieved and set tasks for individuals. The group can then meet to pool the information obtained. The process may need to be repeated until the objective has been achieved but when this happens the group should be dissolved.

There are times when it is not appropriate to hold a meeting and maybe you are unsure whether to do so or not. Ask yourself the following questions:

- What do I hope to achieve by the meeting?
- Will the correct people be at the meeting to achieve that goal?
- Does the group have the authority to achieve that goal?
- Can the desired outcome be achieved by other means?
- Will I be properly prepared in time?

If the answers to these questions are not satisfactory then you should not be holding the meeting.

CONCLUSIONS

- Spend more time in preparation and less in the meeting because meetings fail in inverse proportion to preparation and in direct proportion to meeting time.
- Avoid a meeting likely to go nowhere. More mediocre meetings mean less capable management. Fewer, better managed meetings mean more effective management.
- To get the most out of a meeting limit the risks and focus the group to achieve your purpose.
- Keep the meeting on course by discussing only one issue at a time.
- Limit the number and types of tasks to be undertaken.
- Wider participation in meetings may be healthy but can simply lead to the need for the creation of smaller subgroups to serve the function of the original group.
- Limit the number of participants as meetings can fail in direct proportion to the number of people present.
- Once all the vital participants are there start the meeting; do not wait for latecomers.
- Remember the key functions of an agenda:
  - assisting in preparation for the meeting;
  - telling the participants in advance what items are to be considered;
  - mechanism for order and control;
  - standard by which success or failure can be measured.
- The agenda must be circulated about 2 weeks ahead of the meeting to allow time for the attached papers to be read by the committee members, discussed with colleagues and pondered over.
- When writing an agenda specify what is required of the meeting under each item.
- Do not have Any Other Business in frequent and regular meetings.
- Never distribute documents at a meeting and expect valuable comments.
- When preparing for a meeting, decide what you want to accomplish. You may need to ask yourself the following key questions:
  - What has to be achieved?
  - Do I have the authority?
  - Does the group have a mandate?
  - Who is attending the meeting?
  - Is there anyone I should speak with before the meeting?
  - Who will support and who will oppose the items on the agenda?
  - What are the priority issues to be discussed and/or decided? And in what order?
- If you are organizing a meeting for a specific purpose which is not a routine meeting you will need to consider:
  - Where should the meeting take place?
  - When is the appropriate time?
  - How or what will be the process of the meeting?
  - How will decisions be reached (consensus, implied understanding, custom and etiquette, etc.)?
- At the end of the meeting, summarize what has been achieved and relate conclusions to original intentions in a positive upbeat fashion. Make the members feel their effort and time were worth it.
- Always end on time.
- And never forget that there are times when it is not appropriate to hold a meeting as the outcome can be achieved in other ways.

REFERENCES

Allison G T 1971 Essence of decision. Explaining the Cuban missile crisis. Little, Brown, Boston

Blade T 1989 Too many open minds should be closed for repairs. Cited in: Daintith J, Isaacs A (eds) Medical quotes. A thematic dictionary. Facts on File, Oxford

Kieffer G D 1988 The strategy of meetings. Piatkus, London

Macaulay T B 1991 Meetings are central to your own career success and effective management. In: Blanchard K, Johnson S (eds) The one minute manager. Collins, London

Nelson M J 1989 Managing health professionals. Chapman & Hall, London

Parkinson C Northcote (1958) Parkinson's law or the pursuit of progress. John Murray, London

17

Dealing with the media

Nigel Duncan

WHY IT IS IMPORTANT TO DEAL WITH THE MEDIA

Why should the media form any part of a textbook of management for doctors? After all, it was not so long ago that doctors were advised to avoid any contact with the media for fear of being accused of advertising. So what has happened to alter this old advice?

What began with the first daily newspaper in England in 1702 has now become a massive media communications industry. The media – radio, television, newspapers, news agencies and magazines – see its function as being to inform, to educate and to entertain. It has become the essential source of information for the public. But its role has also become a central one in the democratic process as well. The media shapes the daily debate on current affairs, often determining the agenda and bringing influence to bear on Parliament and government. It reports on all aspects of life and health is a major ingredient in the news menu. The issues of health which interest the media embrace both the clinical and the political – the latest breakthrough on cancer as much as a change in the structure of NHS management. In recent years radio, television and newspapers have devoted much more time and space to the subject of health. All the main national newspapers now publish weekly health pages or supplements containing the latest health news and the fact that fictional and documentary television serials about life in a hospital or a general practice are among TV's most popular programmes today is recognition of the ever-increasing public interest in health and the practice of medicine. On the political front, the National Health Service has been a major political issue since the service was established in 1948. The NHS now costs some £40 billion of taxpayers' money and it is hardly surprising that the NHS should figure so largely in the minds of politicians and the media. At the same time the growing moral and ethical dilemmas facing doctors as a result of the advances in science have become issues of great fascination to the media and to the public.

For all those working in the health service, including doctors, this attention provides an opportunity for better communication between the medical profession and the public and for raising public awareness about health matters. Doctors cannot afford to ignore the media. Because of the sensational or simplistic way in which the media often reports difficult and sensitive medical issues, many doctors naturally feel suspicious about publicity and there is a frequent sense of friction between doctors and journalists. But responsible journalists should be regarded as essential allies in the quest for communicating the health message to the public at large. No longer should doctors blithely retreat behind the 'no comment' barrier when contacted by a journalist. Quite apart from the fact that 'no comment' replies encourage suspicion and scepticism, the days of reticence and medical mystique have long disappeared.

Today doctors can safely be named and identified on radio and television or in the press, providing they are not saying anything which is intended to attract patients. Anything which can be described as advertising a doctor's services would still be regarded as unethical behaviour. Doctors should still avoid being named where a particular surgery is being publicized or where a particular patient is being discussed.

For many years senior hospital doctors have had written into their national terms and conditions of service a fundamental safeguard of the right, indeed the duty, to speak out as independent professionals where the interests of their patients are concerned. Paragraph 330 of their terms of service (NHS 1994) reads:

A practitioner shall be free, without the prior consent of the employing authority, to publish books, articles, etc. and to deliver any lecture or speech, whether on matters arising out of his hospital service or not.

But since the establishment in 1991 of independent NHS trusts, with the power to alter these national agreements, this freedom of speech has been under threat. For newly appointed doctors, the protection of paragraph 330 may no longer apply. Instead, the government has issued new draft guidance for NHS staff on relations with the public and the media. This states that the individual interests of patients must be paramount but it also raises the possibility of disciplinary action against employees if disclosures are made 'unjustifiably'.

If the medical profession does not represent its corner in the media, others will fill the vacuum – especially those who wish to encroach on the role of doctors. The media has become an essential vehicle in particular for those seeking change, whether in the way healthcare is provided or in the level of resources devoted to health. Such doctors may be seeking changes to improve the health service for their patients or to improve their own working conditions. In either event, the media is the vehicle which carries that message most effectively to the public and to Parliament.

Doctors occupy an enviable position in this country. The image of the medical profession is still extremely high. This means that doctors' views are given considerable weight by both public and politicians. Public opinion polls consistently put doctors at the top of those occupations most respected by the public. As one commentator remarked, drawing a comparison between politicians and doctors: 'The public believes people in white coats rather than men in grey suits'. Doctors therefore start with a considerable advantage in their dealings with the media.

But many doctors not surprisingly have very little understanding of the media or the way it works. Either they have had no contact with journalists or they have had an unfortunate experience of being misquoted or misunderstood. This chapter is designed for them.

WHO ARE THE MEDIA?

'The media' is a collective noun covering both the printed and the broadcast word. Basically it is the dissemination of information. In the context of this chapter, the media covers newspapers, news agencies, radio, television and magazines. Competition is fierce, not only among rivals in the same media sections, such as *The Independent* and *The Times*, but also between the different sections, such as television and the national daily press. At the same time, newspapers, magazines and the broadcast media also feed off each other, following up and copying each other's stories in a thoroughly incestuous way. What is published in the morning newspapers may influence early morning radio and television news broadcasts, while interviews on radio and television later in the day will be picked up and used by the following morning's newspapers. Similarly, stories that appear in the weekly medical press will be picked up and used by the national press.

The press

Newspapers are in business to make a profit. These days it is a much more profitable business than it used to be because of new printing technology. Newspapers' income is derived from advertisements and sales. There are more national newspapers in the United Kingdom than in any other country in the world – 10 national dailies and nine national Sundays. In addition there are more than 90 regional dailies, 12 regional Sundays and 700 regional weeklies. The national daily press can be divided into 'quality' broadsheets and the popular tabloids. There are the five quality dailies – *The Financial Times, The Times, The Daily Telegraph, The Guardian* and *The Independent* – and five main popular tabloids – *The Mail, Express, Mirror, Sun* and *Star*.

The circulation war, particularly among the tabloids, is extremely fierce and leads to measures such as price cutting, 'exclusive' stories and serialization of popular books in order to attract readers. All the national newspapers have journalists who specialize in health. Many of them have been covering health issues for a considerable number of years and have amassed great expertise and knowledge and a wide range of contacts and experts in many different fields of health. The quality newspapers tend to have a team of two or three specialist health correspondents covering both political and clinical issues, while the popular papers have just one health correspondent each. On any one day there could be four or five different health stories in each national newspaper.

There are nine national Sunday newspapers, many of them stablemates of the daily newspapers. The four quality newspapers are *The Sunday Times, The Observer, The Sunday Telegraph* and *The Independent on Sunday* and the popular Sunday papers are *The Mail on Sunday, The Sunday Express, The News of the World, The People* and *The Sunday Mirror*. Health correspondents on the Sunday newspapers often have more space in which to write about health stories. These journalists will usually spend several days and possibly several weeks preparing their stories.

While all the national newspapers have their head

offices in London, outside the capital there are many important regional newspapers, both morning and evening papers. These include papers such as *The Birmingham Post*, *The Liverpool Post*, *The Yorkshire Post* and *The Northern Echo*, many of them with a long history and high circulations in their areas. Most of these larger regional newspapers have their own health correspondents, who would concentrate their efforts on writing about health news in their own geographical area or finding local angles to national health news.

There are also hundreds of local newspapers, most of them small weekly publications based in towns up and down the country. The quality of these newspapers varies considerably, from those with more advertisements than news and others which are excellent publications covering all aspects of interest to the local community. Health news in these newspapers tends to be covered by young general reporters or by stories supplied from news agencies.

Seven thousand magazines make up the rest of the press. These include some 2400 consumer magazines, women's magazines and special interest publications devoted to specific subjects, such as cars, computers or a particular sport. Finally there is the specialist press, which includes the medical press, such as *Hospital Doctor*, *Healthcare Management* and *The Health Service Journal*. These magazines are circulated almost exclusively among health professionals and many are distributed free to doctors, their revenue coming almost entirely from pharmaceutical advertising.

Most newspapers, national and local, are owned by one of the few large newspaper groups, such as News International, Mirror Group Newspapers, Northcliffe and United Newspapers. Many of these groups also have an interest in radio and television stations

Radio and television

Radio and television are run by the BBC and by a number of independent commercial organizations. Radio comprises the five national BBC channels, a large number of local BBC radio stations and an equally large number of commercial stations covering the major cities and towns throughout the country. Many of the stations are devoted entirely to pop music.

Television is confined to the four major channels, plus the satellite and cable channels. These channels are served with programmes made by a plethora of independent producer companies. Even the BBC, which once retained responsibility for producing its own programmes, now contracts much of this task out to a number of independent programme makers.

News agencies

There are a number of independent press agencies whose role is to provide newspapers with stories and feature articles. Chief of these agencies is the Press Association, which is owned by a number of national and regional newspapers. The PA, as it is known, has a large staff and covers major national and regional stories, sending them out 'on the wire' to most of the national newspapers and to many regional newspapers. The PA ensures that in each area of the country it has a local journalist, known as a 'stringer', who will keep them informed about local news and provide them with stories when they occur. That is often how local stories suddenly appear in the national newspapers.

A number of cities and towns will also have smaller press agencies serving just that area.

WHAT IS NEWS?

What sort of issues are the media interested in and how do doctors know whether their story will interest journalists?

There is no strict definition of news and no clear rules about what is a newsworthy story. Even journalists are never certain which of their stories will or will not be published in newspapers or broadcast on radio and TV. News judgement and news values are entirely subjective. In general, however, news refers to something new or original that has happened – the opening of a new hospital or the closure of an old one, for instance, an announcement about the withdrawal of a drug, the findings of a new research project or the latest treatment for curing a particular disease. Any controversy, particularly between doctors, is also likely to be regarded as news.

The media is basically interested in news which will interest or matter to their readers, listeners or viewers. Therefore, what interests the readers of *The Sun* may not be regarded as news by BBC Television's Nine O'Clock News. The more people who are likely to be affected by a story, the more likely it is to be published. Most news stories can be divided into two categories – events that occur without warning such as disasters or leaks from some committee or report and stories that emanate from 'diary' events. These include events such as court cases, the publication of annual reports, major conferences and speeches, all of which have been planned for some time. The weekly and monthly medical journals are also a continual source of stories for the national health correspondents, who are quite prepared to 'lift' such stories and rewrite them for their own newspapers with an attribution.

Some events, such as the opening of a hospital with a speech from a visiting dignitary, will have been planned for many months. Such 'diary' events are likely to be attended by local journalists and reported by the local media, who will have planned their coverage for some time. If the visiting dignitary says something of national interest, a few paragraphs might appear in the national press as well. Other events, such as the sudden announcement of job losses at a hospital, may be made known to the media without any forewarning or at a hastily organized press conference.

Most news comes under the heading of 'diary' events or planned news. Some will be the result of press statements or press conferences. National health correspondents are inundated by organizations and people trying to interest them in publishing or broadcasting a particular issue. Most of these items will be of no interest to national health correspondents. They may include advertising 'puffs' from public relations companies, 'soft' news from charities or glossy packs from drug companies.

The government and the Department of Health are constant sources of news. The DoH issues more than 650 press statements each year. Although many of them contain major news announcements and will be covered in the national press and on radio and television, some are simply government propaganda. These will be quickly ignored by journalists.

In short, doctors wanting to know whether their stories are of interest to the media should try contacting journalists to find out. There is no better way than trial and error.

HOW TO TALK TO THE PRESS

Newspapers are run by many different types of journalists. There are the editors at the top, who take sole responsibility for what appears in their publications, and there are the reporters who talk to people and write the stories. In between is a wide assortment of individuals who influence the way in which a story eventually appears in the newspaper. There are news editors, who often decide what stories should be covered and whether or not what the reporter eventually writes is strong enough to be published; there are subeditors, who cut and shape a story to fill a particular space and who, most importantly, write the headlines above stories; and there are leader writers who write the anonymous editorials representing the views of that particular newspaper.

For most doctors, the only journalists they will come across are the reporters – usually specialist health correspondents, general news reporters or freelance journalists. Freelance journalists who are not employed by any particular newspaper or broadcasting organization, supply stories that are either specially commissioned or offered for sale. Freelances can be extremely important and, indeed, something like a quarter of all feature articles in the quality newspapers are written by non-staff journalists.

Any conversation with a journalist, whether by telephone or in a face-to-face interview, should be seen by a doctor as an opportunity and not a threat. It is an opportunity for doctors to put a positive message across to whatever audience the journalist is addressing. Doctors should not resent enquiries from journalists. At the same time they must always remain cautious in their dealings with the media. There are many pitfalls awaiting the unwary and even the experienced. For this reason some preparation should always take place before any interview or conversation with a journalist.

When contacted by a journalist, doctors should first of all be absolutely clear:

- who the journalist is working for;
- what issue the journalist wants to know about;
- in what form the reported interview is likely to appear;
- what the journalist's deadline is.

During this preliminary conversation, the doctor should try to discover how knowledgeable the journalist is about the issue in question. An experienced health correspondent will need far less of a background briefing on a subject than a general news reporter or a younger journalist. If the request is to take part in a radio or a television interview further details should be sought, such as:

- whether the interview will be live or recorded;
- where the interview will take place;
- whether other people will be interviewed at the same time.

Some doctors will feel confident enough to answer the journalist's questions immediately but for those not used to handling the media, the best advice is to ask the journalist to telephone again in a few minutes or later in the day, depending on the urgency. The doctor should then spend a few minutes, or possibly longer, thinking out what it is they want to tell the journalist. They should write down a few positive points they would like to get across to the public.

It is best for doctors to regard all conversations with journalists as 'on the record' – that is, that anything they say can be quoted and will be published in the press or be broadcast. Those more experienced in handling the media sometimes like to talk to journalists 'off the record', enabling them to discuss the background to a particular issue without actually being quoted by name. This is also what is meant by giving 'unattributable' comments. Doctors wanting to adopt this approach should establish right at the outset of a conversation what the basis of the discussion should be. But talking to journalists off the record or unattributably is not generally advisable as it can lead to misunderstandings. Even leading politicians, who are well used to dealing with the media, often get into extreme difficulties because their 'off the record' comments sometimes appear in the newspapers.

Some journalists are more knowledgeable about health issues than others. In general, national newspaper health correspondents will have a good understanding about a health issue and may have written about the subject many times before. On the other hand, a general news reporter from a national newspaper will have very little grasp about health issues. Local journalists or journalists from the medical press may have some knowledge but may still require a quick 'teach in' about the details of the subject before a doctor can safely assume that they understand the subject sufficiently.

Doctors should obviously keep in mind that if they are talking to the medical press their comments will be read by their medical colleagues; if they are talking to a national newspaper they will be read by the wider lay public; and if they are talking to a local journalist they will be read by local people, including their patients. Doctors should remember to talk in simple terms, avoiding medical jargon where possible and mentioning patients and patient care where possible.

If doctors want to approach the media themselves in order to give them some information, whether national or local, the quickest way is to pick up the telephone and talk directly to the journalist. This is much easier when the doctor knows the journalist personally. It is also much easier when there is a 'peg' available on which to hang their story. This is journalese for a story which is currently in the news and which might be added to by what the doctor has to say. For example, a government announcement may have been made about the latest national waiting list figures. If a doctor has local evidence which throws some light on the reasons for the national increase, the government announcement is the 'peg' on which they can approach a journalist with their piece of news.

If a doctor is going to contact a journalist direct, it is best to avoid the busier times of the day or the week. For national newspaper journalists the best time is the morning, before they start writing their stories, and for weekly journalists it is best to avoid press day – the day when the newspaper or magazine is being published. A few enquiries beforehand should clarify this situation.

A doctor who has been interviewed by a newspaper reporter cannot expect to be shown the story before it is published. Only in exceptional circumstances will journalists offer or agree to show their 'copy' to the doctor before it is published. Usually this will be because the journalist will want to ensure the story is absolutely accurate.

Another easy method by which to bring an issue to the attention of the public is to write a letter for publication in a newspaper. This may be in response to a particular article that the newspaper has published or it may be raising a new issue which might be of interest to the readers of the newspaper. Doctors should remember to keep their letter short, to avoid medical jargon and to make sure they have informed their colleagues beforehand if they think this is relevant. Letters to the tabloid newspapers should be much shorter than those to the quality newspapers. It is then advisable to ring the letters page editor of the newspaper to say that a letter is being sent. Copies of the letter should be retained, in case the letters editor rings the doctor back to try to discuss some proposed amendments or cuts. It is best to write to one newspaper only, but if that newspaper does not publish the letter the same letter can be sent to another newspaper.

The most effective way of ensuring that a news item reaches all the media is to issue a press statement or press release. A good press statement should be simple and brief – no more than one, or at the very most two, sides of A4 paper. It should set out to answer the five 'Ws' – who, what, when, where and why. These are the questions journalists will want answers to if readers are to understand what the story is about.

The first paragraph should summarize the whole story, the second and third paragraphs should set out the details and the final paragraph should give a quote from the relevant doctor or report if there is one. It helps to include a number of quotable phrases or 'soundbites' to encourage journalists to report the item. Finally, the press statement should be dated and a contact name and telephone number should be included at the end so that the journalist can ring for further information. Home and work telephone numbers should be given.

Some press releases will need to be embargoed. This is the procedure by which journalists are prevented from publishing the information in the press statement until a specific time. This time should be clearly set out in bold at the top of the statement, such as 'Not to be published before 00.01 hours Monday February 2'. Finally, doctors sending out a press statement should warn their colleagues in case they are contacted by the media.

A statement for the national newspapers should be addressed to the health correspondent and either posted or faxed. A follow-up telephone call is also advisable. A statement for the local media should probably be addressed to the news editor unless there is a known health correspondent.

When a news item is too complex to explain in a press statement or when it is important enough, a press conference can be organized. This could be on an issue such as the publication of a major new report or of important new research findings. Often the basis of a story might be old but may be given a new twist by some recent development, such as the failure to reduce junior doctors' hours of work. A good local story, such as doctors' strong reactions to the closure of a local hospital ward, will attract the local media. Attracting the national media may be more difficult because there will always be competing events.

Press conferences should be held ideally in mid-morning and invitations should be sent out at least a week in advance. A convenient venue should be chosen and it is usually more effective to have two or three people to give the press conference, one of whom should act as chair. A rehearsal immediately beforehand is advisable. The event itself should last no longer than an hour or so, with brief opening statements from each of the panel and then sufficient time for journalists to ask questions. It is not necessary to provide alcohol or lunch to attract journalists; coffee and tea will be sufficient. If the story is strong enough, journalists will attend. Special arrangements may have to be made for radio and television interviews to be conducted immediately before the press conference or just afterwards. Usually these will be recorded and not live.

Media doctors

Some doctors work partly or exclusively in the media and are employed to provide general medical advice. Those in practice must be careful not to appear to advertise their own services while providing their advice. Only general advice should be given and patients corresponding with the doctor should be advised to see their general practitioner. Doctors who take part in radio phone-in programmes or who provide telephone 'helpline' advice to patients other than their own are advised to keep their advice general rather than specific.

RADIO AND TELEVISION INTERVIEW TECHNIQUES

Radio and television regard health as an issue of increasing interest, both for news programmes and for documentaries. As a result, not a day goes by without some health story featuring on radio or television. Doctors are in great demand from journalists wanting comments on a whole variety of stories. What are doctors' views about the latest hospital prescribing figures? What is the medical profession's view about the growth in day surgery? Do doctors believe that more money should be spent on the health service? The questions are endless.

When doctors are contacted by journalists from the broadcast media, the same principles apply as when they are approached by newspaper journalists. Any approach should be regarded as an opportunity and not a threat. It should be an opportunity for the doctor to put across a positive message on behalf of the medical profession. The opportunity to appear on television, for instance, is an opportunity to speak to millions of people. Viewing figures for news programmes increase during the day. Just over 1 million people tune in to breakfast news programmes; nearer 5 million listen to lunchtime television news; between 7 and 10 million listen to the evening news programmes. No other medium allows a doctor to reach so many people at once.

Any nervousness doctors might have at taking part in such interviews should be more than outweighed by the knowledge that they are being asked because they are the experts. They will always know more than the journalist and most of their audience. That at least should give doctors a sense of self-confidence.

But however much of an expert a doctor is, taking part in radio and television interviews requires careful preparation. Doctors should also be prepared for the fact that such interviews often take some time, particularly if they have to travel to a studio. When approached by a broadcasting journalist for an interview, doctors should first of all find out as much as possible:

- What does the journalist want to know and why?
- How much does the journalist know already?
- Are other people being interviewed?
- What is the programme – is it for the news or for a documentary?
- Will the interview be live or recorded, on the telephone or face-to-face?
- Who will conduct the interview? How long will the interview last?

It is perfectly acceptable for a doctor to ask such questions. In fact, it is essential if misunderstandings are to be avoided at a later stage. It will enable a doctor to know more about how much detailed information will be required, who the audience will be and how much time will be required for the interview. In this way the doctor is helping to establish the agenda and to shape the ground rules.

Having found out this information, a doctor should then spend some time preparing for the interview by listing a few positive points that need to be put across. Between three and six points should be identified – not less than three because the interviewee may run out of things to say and not more than six because an interviewee is likely to have difficulty remembering them all. By rehearsing these points beforehand a doctor will manage to retain some control over the interview and not simply be led by an interviewer's questions. The art of a radio or television interview is to answer the questions in a way that puts across those positive points identified beforehand. It is important to listen closely to the questions and if they are a long way from what the doctor wishes to say, to select one of the predetermined positive points by saying: 'I think the most important thing to say is . . . .' or 'Much more important, I think, is the fact that . . .'. The more positive and informative the doctor is, the more acceptable such a response will sound.

Doctors who sound more confident and reassuring in interviews are more likely to be listened to by their audience. People listening to the radio or watching television have very short attention spans. Many of them are only half listening to the person being interviewed. It is important, therefore, for interviewees to sound convincing. Doctors should be positive and not defensive. Answers should be kept clear and simple and the use of medical jargon and complicated initials should be avoided. Colloquial language should be used wherever possible. Statistics should be used only where necessary and then should be explained simply. Percentages, for instance, should be reduced to 'one in three' or 'four out of every 10 patients'.

When taking part in recorded interviews, it is important for doctors' replies to questions to be self-contained, stand-alone statements. This is because the questions are often edited out before being used and only the answers will be heard. Therefore, in answer to the question 'Do you think the NHS is underfunded?', the reply should not be 'Yes, it is and that's why we have got long waiting lists'. Rather it should be 'I certainly believe the NHS is underfunded and that is why we have got long waiting lists'.

Doctors who live some way from a major studio may often be asked to go to a small local studio to do a 'down the line' interview. These are conducted by journalists who are many miles away in the main studio. If it is a radio interview, the doctor will have to wear headphones and talk to a disembodied voice at the end of a microphone. If the interview is for television, the doctor will simply talk direct to a camera. It is easy in these situations to end up by talking too much. The best way to avoid this is to think of such interviews as telephone conversations and to talk slowly and clearly.

Radio

It is particularly important in radio interviews to sound convincing and enthusiastic. Interviewees should speak slowly and clearly, avoiding 'ums' and 'ahs'. It is sometimes a good idea to keep a list of the positive points on hand during the interview.

Television

Television interviews are accompanied by many distractions, particularly if they are taking place in a studio. The interviewee will be surrounded by sound and lighting people, make-up people and producers. During the interview it is important to pay no attention to the camera. The doctor should look at the interviewer and not at the camera. Even if the interviewer is looking elsewhere or studying papers, the interviewee's gaze should remain firmly fixed. An upright seated position should be maintained during the interview to avoid fidgeting, slouching or swivelling on the chair. Those who normally use their hands to emphasize a point while speaking should not be afraid to do this during a television interview. Sometimes this can be very effective, provided it is not overdone. It is important during television interviews to act larger than life. Television has a tendency to deaden the image and so it is important to use facial expressions, to smile or nod when being introduced and even to shake the head if disagreeing with a point being made.

Doctors should always try to retain control of any interview and not to be led down a path of questions determined entirely by the interviewer. Interviewees should not fall for the interviewer's pregnant pause, encouraging them to go rambling on and eventually to say something unwise or unprepared.

Pitfalls

Among the many pitfalls to avoid when being interviewed by any journalist are questions which start 'So what you are really saying, doctor, is . . .'. Interviewees should always answer in their own words. Caution should also be exercised in answering multiple questions. Interviewees should always attempt to answer on their own positive points.

Doctors are often disappointed when a 10 to 15 minute interview is reduced to a few seconds when actually broadcast. Unfortunately this is a fact of radio or television life and applies as much to Prime Ministers as it does to others. The only consolation for doctors in these circumstances is the knowledge that their few seconds of interview may well be heard or seen by millions of people.

HOW TO COMPLAIN

If doctors have a complaint to make about a television programme, either about its factual content or taste, they should write to the Broadcasting Complaints Commission. Complaints against a newspaper can be taken up in a number of ways. If the newspaper has misrepresented the doctor or misunderstood a particular story, a letter to the editor explaining the position is the easiest recourse. If a factual error has been made by the newspaper, a short correction can be requested by telephoning the editor, the news editor or the journalist who wrote the story.

If a national newspaper refuses to publish a correction or a letter seeking to set the record straight, other action can be taken, such as writing to the readers' representative. In 1989 all national newspapers agreed to establish their own system of readers' representatives or ombudsmen, whose job it is to consider complaints from readers. These could range from the failure to publish a letter to a lapse in taste or a breach of confidentiality.

Where cases of more serious complaint occur, a doctor can approach the Press Complaints Commission*, which was set up in 1991 as a successor to the Press Council. Its role is to enforce a code of practice framed by the newspaper and periodical industry. The Commission consists of editors and members of the public and its code of practice embraces issues such as accuracy, misrepresentation and harassment.

Its section on hospitals, for instance, states:

i) Journalists or photographers making enquiries at hospitals or similar institutions should identify themselves to a responsible official and obtain permission before entering non-public areas. ii) The restrictions on intruding into privacy are particularly relevant to enquiries about individuals in hospital or similar institutions.

CONCLUSION

Dealing with the media is a task which today's doctors must embrace but it requires patience, practice and time. Not everything will run smoothly; mistakes and misinterpretations will occur. But doctors and the medical profession as a whole have more to gain than lose from approaching this task openly and confidently.

---

*1 Salisbury Square, London EC4Y 8AE. Tel: 0171 353 1248

REFERENCES

National Health Service 1994 Hospital, medical and dental staff: terms and conditions of service (England and Wales). DoH (Welsh Office), Cardiff.

18

Educational management

Janet Grant

INTRODUCTION: TEACHER-MANAGER AND EDUCATIONAL PRUCHASER

Not so many years ago, a chapter about educational management would have confined itself to the management of learning: to the actions of the teacher and the learner. Managing education was largely seen as a matter of defining educational objectives, planning the teaching and learning methods that would enable the student to achieve those objectives and designing the assessment system that would show whether or not mastery of the objectives had been achieved (Davies 1976, Mager 1962). The teacher-manager was seen as a person whose task was to plan, organize, lead and control the learning process (Davies 1971).

> When a teacher or instructor deliberately creates a learning environment in his classroom with a view to realizing predefined objectives, he is acting as a teacher-manager
> (Davies 1971)

The teacher-manager as the direct provider of training is still a useful concept but it is no longer sufficient in describing all the management functions which are necessary for the effective implementation of postgraduate medical education in the new NHS. It needs to be supplemented by the concept of the educational purchaser whose job is not as a teacher at all but as a person who ensures by negotiation, communication, planning, setting contracts, monitoring and facilitation that effective training is occurring throughout the organization.

In postgraduate medical education in hospitals today, the teacher-managers are the consultants supported by their teams and clinical tutors who have a contractual responsibility to provide training. Speciality tutors have a provider-regulator role, reflecting the national standard-setting role of the royal colleges themselves. The college regional educational advisers are best seen as local regulators of national standards. The educational purchasers are the postgraduate deans. Clinical directors may also take on a managerial interest in education and training. The boundaries are often blurred and these roles are not always clearly specified or understood. And yet they have to be discharged, so it is as well to have a framework according to which education and training tasks can be analysed, planned, allocated, modified and evaluated.

This chapter will set out the complex context of postgraduate medical education and will consider the managerial tasks to be performed, including auditing educational provision. It will also describe and discuss a managed system of training for senior house officers which impinges on the roles of teacher-manager and educational purchaser.

THE CONTEXT OF POSTGRADUATE MEDICAL EDUCATION

Postgraduate medical education is a complex phenomenon, involving the deployment of people, time and resources. All doctors, regardless of status, are involved in education and training in some way, whether as a teacher, a learner or an organizer. Yet all have the primary task of patient care and have other calls on their time. At the level of opportunity costs, training has resource implications. At the level of the postgraduate centre, study leave budgets and trainees' salaries, the resource implications are even greater. Postgraduate medical education has not fully escaped the marketplace and the purchaser-provider framework.

Multiple agencies

Postgraduate medical education is singular in having at least four powerful agencies impinging on it, sometimes in an uncoordinated manner. These are the royal colleges, the General Medical Council, the postgraduate deans and the local management. Each body has its own interests and cooperates with the others in what is almost a voluntary manner. Levels and methods of joint working vary considerably at national, regional and local levels. Within the hospital, it is as well to discover whether the trust managers are aware of college requirements for training, whether the clinical tutor and speciality tutors meet and coordinate and what each sees as their role. There is often enormous duplication of effort (for example, in reviewing progress with trainees) which could be streamlined.

Service pressures

The most powerful contextual factor in the delivery of postgraduate medical education is, however, service pressures. Trainees in hospital medicine, despite currently having half their salaries paid for from the postgraduate dean's budget, are still employed as doctors. They provide patient care. They are not supernumerary, as are vocational trainees in general practice settings. The 'ever present and perennial problem of over-burdening service pressures which exclude almost all other activities for SHOs' (Grant & Marsden 1992) have been documented (Grant & Marsden 1988, 1992). These pressures are now increasingly being matched by those experienced by senior staff as patient throughput and clinical contracts combine with the New Deal, decreasing junior doctors' hours and imposing new shift arrangements. Hopes of fitting training into such a background are not enough: it has to be managed into place and supported managerially very carefully.

Time for learning, time for teaching

The service pressures and accompanying factors mean that time for learning or for teaching is at a premium. A common response to this problem until recently has been, strangely, to ask for more of what cannot be had rather than to seek a solution which is feasible. So calls have gone out for dedicated time for formal learning of one sort or another. This has been stimulated by the half-day release scheme for trainees in general practice. The time called for is usually a half-day per week.

But protecting time from the ravening beast of the service is more easily said than done. This is even true of the general practice vocational training scheme trainees. A recent study (Bouchier Hayes et al 1992) revealed that only 37% of VTS trainees working on hospital attachments attended more than 75% of the available study half-days, while 14% attended less than a quarter of the half-days on offer and 10% attended none. The two main reasons for non-attendance were pressure of work (67%) and inability to find cover (45%).

Another form of dedicated time is in the series of short meetings which many departments put on for their house officers and senior house officers (SHOs). Although some specialities, such as accident and emergency, are developing methods of ensuring that all SHOs attend all meetings, this is rare in most specialities where meetings are characterized by the insistent interruption of the trainees' bleeps and far less than 100% attendance. Many trainees also complain that the meetings are usually in a lecture format which does not allow them an active part in determining the content or the orientation of the meeting (Grant & Marsden 1992). This is a problem for the local teacher-manager.

Integration of service and training

Postgraduate training in medicine, as in any profession, is largely a process of ordered induction into the profession over a number of years. It therefore occurs in the context of practice. It can occur in no other place if it is to be effective. The strength of postgraduate medical education derives from the same source as its weakness: integrated service and training. The challenge to the teacher-manager or to the educational purchaser is to make that integration work without detriment to either component. To try to separate them through protected time is detrimental to both sides.

Educationalists recognize the importance of this integrated training as preparation for professional practice. They call it 'situated learning' (Lave & Wenger 1991) and define it as 'legitimate peripheral participation in the practice of a discipline' whereby the trainee acquires skill and knowledge to perform by engaging in the process, to begin with, to a limited degree and with limited responsibility for the ultimate outcome. This is the position of a preregistration house officer.

Over a period of years, the participation gradually becomes less peripheral until the trainee ceases training and has central participation with full responsibility as a consultant. Situated learning describes perfectly the progress of a trainee who gradually takes more and more personal responsibility for decisions about patient care. For the teacher-manager, educational manager or other standard setter (such as the royal colleges) the task then is to decide what experiences provide the proper context for learning to take place.

New imperatives

In addition to the context of postgraduate training,

there are new imperatives which impinge. Training is now controlled by contracts, in the same way as all other services offered by the hospital. Contracts are subject to monitoring and there is therefore the need to provide documented evidence of training.

The Calman proposals (Department of Health 1993) for higher specialist training also add to the push towards better managed postgraduate training. These proposals alter the structure of the higher training grades whereby registrar and senior registrar become one combined grade, having in-training assessments of progress in lieu of the check which moving from grade to grade formerly offered. The advent of the Certificate of Completion of Specialist Training means that training has to be clearly specified so that conditions for award of the Certificate are known and can be demonstrated. Failure to award the Certificate may give rise to appeals against the decision. In such cases, documentary proof of training will be necessary.

The Calman proposals edge postgraduate training further towards becoming a manageable or managerially based system by stating clearly that the assessment of doctors in training will be based on differentiated levels of competence, be structured and interactive and have opportunities for discussion between assessor and trainee. Such assessments require development against an expected set of competences and training experiences. This in turn necessitates specification of curriculum and specific training standards. The royal colleges have been assiduous in responding to this task and have laid down a framework of content for situated learning at successive levels of increasingly central participation in the practice of the discipline, against which the teacher-manager can plan the training provided and the educational purchaser (the postgraduate dean) can develop contracts and monitor provision.

This new era of organized and structured training against a background of increasing service pressures brings with it an equally increasing need for tight management of the training programme. The training period is to be shorter than hitherto and will have a defined beginning and end, in between which will be intensive and planned training activities. To achieve a consistent standard and deliver to the regulators' (royal colleges') specifications will require more than either simple training skills or the old definitions of educational management as just the management of the curriculum. It will require systems.

So, the new imperatives are those of curriculum definition, stimulated by Calman, and learning systems to deliver training to deadlines, budgets and defined standards. The concept and necessity of learning systems has been recognized by the General Medical Council in its recommendations on undergraduate medical education (GMC 1993) and this will undoubtedly extend rapidly to the postgraduate sphere.

The task of educational management in postgraduate training is therefore a fast-developing one, which is becoming a necessity. It might be useful, therefore, to draw together the components of educational management as it affects this field.

EDUCATIONAL MANAGEMENT: A DEFINITION

Educational management refers to all those mechanisms, systems and processes whereby educational provision is planned, implemented, monitored, evaluated and improved. Proper educational management along with proper financial accounting and control should enable judgements of cost–benefit, efficiency and effectiveness to be made.

We have seen that the educational management task is shared in any region by a number of players: dean, regional advisers, speciality and clinical tutors, consultants, senior registrars and registrars. Responsibility for the provision of training is also shared by the trust chief executives who are party to the deans' educational contracts.

We can divide these responsibilities between:

- the region (postgraduate dean and regional advisers). These responsibilities might also be discharged at national level through the postgraduate deans collectively, the royal colleges and the Department of Health. However, for our purposes we shall limit the discussion to regional level;
- the trust (chief executive's office) and clinical directors;
- the consultant's team.

Educational management will include, at least, the following for each of these.

Postgraduate deans and regional advisers

- Negotiation of educational policy and contracts, with internal and external agencies, e.g. royal colleges, speciality tutors, consultants.
- Development of educational strategy in conjunction with interested parties.
- Establishing a clear process of decision making and clarifying overlapping and dual responsibilities between different agencies (college representatives and dean's networks).
- Developing stable organizational structures, e.g. in the dean's office and in the postgraduate centres, to support effective educational provision and control.

- Ensuring and supporting appropriate curriculum development and innovation, e.g. by ensuring a budget for innovation, dissemination of new educational ideas, by professional development of the dean and clinical tutors as trained educationalists.
- Development of systems of data gathering about educational provision and its quality. This includes ensuring systematic evaluation of educational provision.
- Allocation of roles and responsibilities, i.e. negotiation and agreement of contracts with providers at trust level.
- Identification of lines and means of communication, reporting and accountability between deans, regional advisers, clinical tutors and speciality tutors.
- Setting the educational climate and styles of educational leadership through regional educational policy and practice.
- Ensuring training and support for key persons in the educational system, e.g. deans, clinical tutors, postgraduate centre staff, consultants, registrars/senior registrars.
- Negotiating and/or ensuring implementation of the 'curriculum' as set by the royal colleges or other relevant bodies.
- Delegating (to associate deans and others) responsibility for specific aspects and processes of educational planning and provision. Delegation requires specification and feedback.

The trust

- Negotiation of educational policy and contracts, with the postgraduate dean.
- Development of educational strategy for the trust in conjunction with interested parties.
- Ensuring and supporting appropriate curriculum development and innovation, e.g. by ensuring a budget for innovation, by supporting the professional development of consultants, registrars and senior registrars as teachers or teacher-managers.
- Development of systems of data gathering about the educational provision and its quality. This includes ensuring systematic evaluation of educational provision.
- Allocation of roles and responsibilities to discharge the conditions of the educational contract.
- Identification of lines and means of reporting and accountability between clinical tutors, speciality tutors, educational supervisors, clinical directors, consultants and registrars/senior registrars.
- Setting up lines of communication with and between key persons, e.g. by boards and meetings as well as by centralized and circulated reporting.

- Setting the educational climate and styles of educational leadership through local educational policy and practice. This might include raising the profile of education by ensuring that it is an agenda item at trust meetings.
- Ensuring training and support for key persons in the educational system, e.g. clinical directors, consultants, registrars/senior registrars.
- Setting standards for selection and promotion of staff at all levels which include performance as a trainer or teacher-manager.
- Delegating or accepting responsibility for specific aspects and processes of educational planning and provision. Delegation requires specification and feedback.

The consultant's team

- Deciding the style and methods of education and training in the department.
- Ensuring that everyone understands and discharges their education and training roles.
- Ensuring that teaching staff have appropriate skills.
- Inducting trainees into the educational programme of the department.
- Keeping records of education and training in the department.
- Monitoring and/or evaluating education and training in the department and giving feedback to all concerned.
- Raising the profile of education and training, e.g. by ensuring that it is a regular agenda item at directorate meetings.

Clearly, educational management requires the skills of running systems, managing people, planning education, delegating, communicating and supporting against a thorough background knowledge of educational practice and educational possibilities and a realistic view of what is possible, given the complex context of postgraduate training in medicine.

Educational management requires an overall strategic perspective with simultaneous attention to local detail and tactics. Many aspects of educational management are synonymous with or can be seen in the same light as business management – but educational management is always informed by educational theory and good practice.

AUDITING EDUCATION

One of the managerial tasks of the educational purchaser or teacher-manager is to ensure that the quality of educational provision is as it should be and to offer support and means of improvement if it is not. This can be done by means of both monitoring and evaluation.

Monitoring is the process of making prespecified observations about the characteristics of training and the training environment. This can be done objectively through checklists, questionnaires and other forms of data collection and reporting. Monitoring should be undertaken against known standards.

Evaluation is the process of gathering information about part or all of an educational programme for the purpose of making judgements about its merit or acceptability, on the basis of which development can occur.

Auditing education involves elements of both monitoring and evaluation.

Although it is possible to develop local systems for auditing postgraduate medical education, many postgraduate deans are implementing the PEAKit (Postgraduate Education Audit Kit) (Joint Centre 1993) for data collection. The PEAKit can be used equally well by trusts, directorates or individual consultants.

The PEAKit is a collection of forms and measuring instruments that have been specially developed to audit every aspect of postgraduate medical education in hospital locations. The PEAKit contains measuring instruments and checklists that relate to:

- the fabric and facilities of postgraduate training;
- the administration of education and training;
- the training activities that take place;
- the outcomes of the education process.

The postgraduate education system includes the following elements:

- *Inputs* The resources, buildings and equipment.
- *Capacity* The services on offer such as courses, meetings, ward teaching, counselling services, teaching skills.
- *Activity* The activity carried on or the use made of the services offered. These are sometimes called 'outputs'.
- *Outcomes* The impact of the educational activities on the quality of the doctor produced and the service delivered to patients.

The various PEAK forms relate to one or more of these elements.

The education audit cycle

The audit process in education reflects that of clinical or medical audit. It is characterized by a cycle of activity, as depicted in Fig. 18.1. The PEAKit is predominantly concerned with measuring performance but offers help

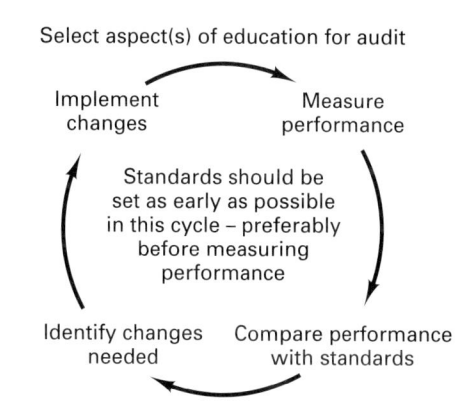

Fig. 18.1 Cycle of activity

and guidance on agreeing or setting standards and on managing the change process that is needed to complete the audit cycle or loop.

The audit cycle should be based on agreed standards. The results of data gathering can only be interpreted as acceptable or not if a standard is set against which to compare results. There are no national standards for postgraduate medical education, although clear curricula specified by the royal colleges and postgraduate deans' contracts based on them may start to resemble such standards.

In the absence of imposed standards, the local teacher-manager might want to set local standards. The PEAKit is designed so that this can be achieved in collaboration with interested parties such as college tutors, clinical directors, trainees or other teachers. Standards should be realistic and locally shared and relevant if the educational audit is to be welcomed.

As a managerial tool, educational audit can be used to:

- improve local educational provision;
- educate or inform others;
- justify the place of postgraduate training;
- identify and remedy local problems;
- provide information to help plan future strategy;
- assure the quality of education and training;
- enrich funding debates;
- satisfy contractual obligations;
- monitor trends in performance;
- make comparisons.

The PEAKit indicates that:

the main purposes and the uses to which the data from audit will be put should be known to all who agree to participate. It is also prudent to plan how the results of the audit will be presented and fed back to the participants. The main aim of audit is always to measure against standards and provide the

Table 18.1 Selection and use of PEAK forms

PEAK form number and title	Used to measure	Should be used for routine data gathering	Audits administn of education	Audits education provision	Best administrd directly	Best distributed
1 Population data	I		✔			
2 Audit diary of centre activities	I A	✔	✔			
3 Log of work	I C	✔	✔		✔	
4 Centre fabric checklist	C		✔			
5 Centre activities and services	C A		✔			
6 Presenter's evaluation of administration	A	✔	✔		✔	
7 Administration of meetings	A		✔			
8 Discussions, interviews and counselling	A		✔			
9 General administration	A		✔			
10 Library services	I C A		✔	✔		
11 Meetings evaluation	A	✔	✔	✔	✔	
12 Provision of in-service teaching and learning	C A			✔		✔
13 Comparative perceptions of education	A O			✔	✔	
14 Clinical climate questionnaire	I C A			✔	✔	
15 Educational climate questionnaire	I C A O			✔	✔	
16a Exam performance (by grade)	O	✔		✔		
16b Exam performance (by exam)	O	✔		✔		
17 Exit questionnaire	O	✔		✔		✔
18 Career development	A O	✔		✔	✔	
19 Training objectives	O	✔		✔		✔

direction for change to improve provision. Audit should never be used to judge individuals, to apportion responsibility, or otherwise blame individuals or groups.

As a properly managed part of the education development process, educational audit can be a powerful tool for improvement.

Table 18.1 shows the PEAK forms and their use (Joint Centre 1993). The PEAKit is clear that the effective use of these forms is predicated on careful planning, thorough negotiation and practical management of the data collection process.

SERVICE-BASED LEARNING: A MANAGED SYSTEM OF TRAINING

Having discussed the context of postgraduate medical

education, the new imperatives pressing on it, the nature of educational management in relation to postgraduate medical education and the idea of auditing educational provision for the purposes of improving it, we should now consider an example of a managed system of training: service-based learning for senior house officers (Joint Centre 1994).

Service-based learning was designed and developed through large-scale research, consultation and field testing. It was designed to fit in with the conditions of postgraduate training and the new imperatives which were discussed above. It is also a system which takes into account the basic tenets of educational management. It is an entirely manageable system.

The derivation of the system is described elsewhere (Grant & Marsden 1988, 1992). The structure of the system is represented in Fig. 18.2.

The documentation which accompanies service-based learning consists of:

- The service-based learning record: a small booklet in which the SHO can record learning plans (including incidental learning), study of brief learning materials (BLMs), completion of self-assessments, attendance at meetings and study leave taken. In addition, the SHO's accumulation of learning credits is noted in the record book. The service-based learning record is used to:

  — guide and structure learning;
  — provide evidence that a proper training programme has been provided and followed for which credits can be awarded.

The service-based learning record documents systematically the learning experiences which trainees currently use to great effect. It also extends these and moulds them into coherent sense around an identified 'syllabus'. The system as a whole provides support for these educational experiences and enhances them.

- Brief learning materials: a set of specially written learning materials in 15-minute 'bites' which cover the whole of the potential curriculum for the SHO. BLMs are arranged in groups of five or six, each group being accompanied by a self-assessment exercise. The BLM sets are kept in the department or on the ward where the SHO is working for reference whenever required. This supports the SHO's usual approach of reading up about patients seen and of referring to texts in the course of service work. But SHOs complained that frequently this was not possible because texts were too bulky for the time available or were located in the library which was too far away to visit when needed. BLMs solve these problems.
- Self-assessment booklet and model answers: each SHO keeps a book of self-assessments to accompany the BLMs. A senior in the department keeps the book of model answers to which the SHO refers on demand.
- Central credit record: a record of the SHO's credit accumulation is kept to ensure that the post is offering the appropriate educational opportunities. The

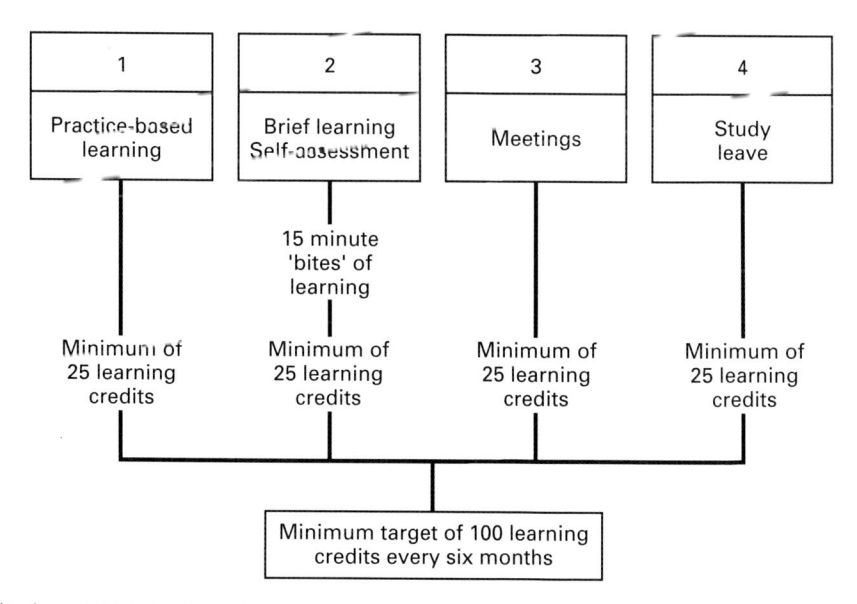

Fig. 18.2 Service-based learning: the system

central record is kept either by a senior or by the postgraduate centre.
- Guidelines for departments and postgraduate centres: a set of guidelines explaining how to implement service-based learning is provided with the materials.
- Overhead transparencies for induction: a set of overhead transparencies for the consultant's use during SHO induction to the post is provided with the materials.

Strands of service-based learning

The four strands of service-based learning mirror and support the types of situated and other learning that currently occur in postgraduate medical education. Together they make a coherent, managed system that fits in with training and service patterns and is amenable to monitoring. The strands are as follows:

1. Practice-based learning involves spending a few minutes at the end of each 'business' session (ward rounds, outpatients) or at other appropriate times, such as during scheduled meetings, discussing with the SHO what problems, issues or interesting topics arose about which the SHO would like to learn more. A learning plan is then noted down in the SHO's record book. This may consist of further reading, practice, observation, discussion with a particular senior, visiting another ward or clinic, studying departmental protocols or any other appropriate activity. The SHO then undertakes the new learning and reports back to the senior.

2. Brief learning and self-assessment involves the provision for SHOs of brief learning materials for individual study when and as needed. Study of brief learning materials would often arise from the learning needs identified in the practice-based learning strand or from service experiences. When a complete set of BLMs is read, the SHO tackles the self-assessment and checks with the model answers.

3. Meetings covers organized departmental and postgraduate centre meetings. To attract learning credits, meetings should have an element of SHO participation (group work, case discussions, exercises or other learning activities) or be generally agreed to be of good educational value.

4. Study leave makes a contractual provision for SHOs to take up to one week of study leave in preparation for Part One or Part Two examinations. Study leave could be used as attendance at a course or as private study. It must be planned at the beginning of the post.

The four strands of service-based learning function in parallel. Each is designed to respond to the individual learner's needs or to build upon the educational opportunities of service provision or to help the trainee to construct a personal path through the 'core curriculum' of the speciality.

Learning credits

Learning credits are accumulated for learning activities in all four strands. One learning credit is equivalent to one hour of study and the trainee is expected to achieve a target of 100 learning credits in a 6-month period, made up of a personally appropriate programme of learning reaching the minimum credit targets shown for each strand.

At 2-monthly intervals, the trainee updates a central credit record held in the hospital postgraduate centre or by the senior. If clear difficulties are being experienced in finding time for study (and therefore in accumulating learning credits), this is followed up by the hospital clinical tutor or by the consultant. This provides a means of identifying problems and solving them, whether they derive from the trainee or from the circumstances of the department in which the trainee is working.

When the target number of learning credits is accumulated, the trainee receives a Certificate of Service-Based Learning signed by the postgraduate dean, the clinical tutor and the trainee's consultant.

Individual learning needs and individual training circumstances

Service-based learning enables the trainee to construct a personally relevant 'curriculum', to choose to study those topics which are best suited to personal interests and career intentions and to the opportunities of the post. The brief learning materials can also be used to construct a broader 'curriculum' than the post itself offers.

Service-based learning also offers the teacher-manager or educational purchaser a means of assessing the training achievements of a department and of intervening and offering assistance if those achievements are less than expected.

Service-based learning has the strengths of building on current training methods, ensuring that the training opportunities of each department are fully exploited and demonstrating in a public, recorded manner that training does occur as part of the service experience of the trainee.

Service-based learning: a managed system

Service-based learning has the elements of a managed educational system.

It is a clear system with known inputs, capacity, activities and outcomes. The system involves clear processes, roles and responsibilities. Importantly, these are distributed across the team so that no unrealistic burdens fall on any particular individuals. Service-based learning provides support for hard-pressed clinicians who are discharging their educational responsibilities under difficult conditions. It has built-in systems for monitoring the activities of both trainee and training department. It sets the educational climate in a department and sets standards for training at appropriate levels. The processes of induction, guidance and recording ensure that there is a shared understanding of the system and a shared, coherent implementation.

CONCLUSIONS

Educational management is an indispensable part of the senior doctor's current repertoire. It involves skills of negotiation, planning, support, control, communication and documentation. Monitoring and improvement are part of the current imperatives. There is support available in the PEAKit and in the system of service-based learning (currently available in a limited number of specialities). Some other skills might necessitate new training, others are simply a matter of applying to education and training the principles of management which are applied to other aspects of the clinician's work. All are eminently achievable and can be incorporated into the processes of everyday working with only moderate effort.

REFERENCES

Bouchier Hayes T A I, Golombok S, Grant J, Rust J, Styles W McN 1992 The hospital component of training for general practice. Report to the Nuffield Provincial Hospitals Trust. NPHT, London

Davies I K 1971 The management of learning. McGraw-Hill, London

Davies I K 1976 Objectives in curriculum design. McGraw-Hill, London

Department of Health 1993 Hospital doctors: training for the future. HMSO, London

General Medical Council 1993 Recommendations on undergraduate medical education. GMC, London

Grant J, Marsden P 1988 Senior house officer training in South East Thames, vols 1 & 2. Joint Centre for Medical Education, London

Grant J, Marsden P 1992 Training senior house officers by service-based learning. Joint Centre for Education in Medicine, BPMF, London

Joint Centre for Education in Medicine 1993 PEAKit: postgraduate education audit kit. Joint Centre for Education in Medicine, London

Joint Centre for Education in Medicine 1994 Service-based learning. Training materials for senior house officers in paediatrics and accident and emergency. Joint Centre, London

Lave J, Wenger E 1991 Situated learning: legitimate peripheral participation. Cambridge University Press, Cambridge

Mager R F 1962 Preparing instructional objectives. Fearon, Palo Alto

19

Managing for personal effectiveness

John Gatrell

A wise man learns when he can. A fool learns when he must.
(Duke of Wellington)

Continuous personal development is a well-established aspect of employment in many organizations. Many professions have embodied it in formal requirements for maintenance of professional status. An individual doctor may arrive at a personal development plan by a number of routes. Some organizations have introduced systems for identifying development needs and monitoring performance in order to ensure that the needs are being met. These are sometimes called performance appraisal schemes and are explained elsewhere in this text. Systems such as these are important in updating technical knowledge and skills. They seldom address the less obvious personal effectiveness needs of doctors, such as self-management skills. The latter usually encompass time management, communication and influencing skills, handling stress and self-awareness. These are normally assumed to have been learned through life experience or to be in place by the end of initial training. In reality, they are seldom addressed as part of the usual education and training received by professionals in their early career stages. Once a career is embarked upon there is little time to step back and reappraise personal effectiveness. In any case, most doctors are unwilling to admit to inadequacies in relation to their personal effectiveness. Indeed, many senior doctors seem to be unaware of weaknesses in their interpersonal performance (Gatrell & White 1995).

TIME MANAGEMENT

Time is a remarkable commodity. Every day we are each given an equal portion. No person can steal it. No matter how much time we waste today, tomorrow's entitlement remains untouched. Such forgiveness and generosity can be both a curse and a blessing. A curse because it lulls us into illusory self-confidence and a blessing because it is never too late to start again.

How well do you use your time? Ask yourself the following questions. Try to answer them as honestly as you can. Do you:

- consciously set time aside each day for planning?
- prioritize tasks and deal with them in order of importance?
- work at an uncluttered desk?
- tell others if they are disturbing you?
- say 'No' if asked to do something trivial?
- avoid taking work home?
- spend enough time with your family and on leisure pursuits?
- feel in control of your career and life in general?

If you have answered 'Yes' to all of these questions, you should be passing on your skills and awareness to others. For those who are less in control of their time, there is still hope. The following guidelines are intended to get you started. They may enable you to make considerable changes to the way you organize your life.

There are four steps in the process of developing effective control of time. These are defining goals; developing awareness of time; planning; and implementing plans using relevant skills and techniques.

GOAL SETTING

The first thing to recognize is that, when thinking about organizing our lives, it is unhelpful to separate work and 'non-work'. The balance we achieve between these two elements should be the product of a total perspective on our lives. It is difficult to achieve a balance if we define each element as distinct and different. Each contributes to our total experience of life. Contemplating the whole, rather than its parts, is essential at the planning stage.

Take a sheet of paper and write down your 'foreseeable life goals'. These are likely to be attainable within the next year or two. Think of them as starting from now. They might be personal, family, social, career, financial, community and spiritual. Work quickly, without limiting your ambitions.

Next, review and refine these goals into statements that imply action. Some may be immediate, such as: 'Spend more time with my family'. Others may require considerable balancing of resources: 'Continue to invest to secure my retirement'. You can omit those which are too farfetched. Perhaps taking a one-year sabbatical is a goal which should be postponed at this stage in your career.

Prioritize these goals. This involves taking decisions about yourself. Take into account your own values and circumstances. At this stage it is preferable to work alone, although some of the decisions will affect the lives of others and you may feel that you are unable to proceed without consulting them. Do so, but reflect independently on their advice and opinions before sharing your conclusions. This is part of the process of accepting personal responsibility for the management of your life. It can be difficult to address some of the uncertainties you will uncover, but not as difficult as living without purpose. All of your goals may be important, but some will be more important than others. Use the prioritized list to begin to develop your approach to time management at work.

The next stage in the process is to develop a sense of time. This does not mean becoming a 'clock watcher'. It is more concerned with raising your consciousness of how effectively you organize yourself to achieve your goals. How do you really spend your day? It is helpful to draw up an analysis of a typical working day by keeping a time log for a few days. You can use an ordinary desk diary. Draw up a simple code for the most common activities in which you are engaged. This will enable you to record easily the activity in which you are currently engaged at frequent (15 minute) intervals throughout the day. List the activities and record the time spent on each in a typical week. Ask yourself if this reflects your priorities. Are there activities that take up time but contribute little or nothing? What would happen if you stopped doing them completely? How much of your time do you keep to use at your discretion? Are you spending time on work that could be delegated to others? It also helps to consider the relative proportions of your day or week which are devoted to non-work priorities, such as sport, family, personal development or simply relaxing or reflecting.

LONGER TERM PLANNING

It can be challenging to move away from habits of mind which cause us to focus on the present, especially if our normal working day keeps us very aware of the next urgent problem or task. It is vital to set aside time to lift thoughts to the longer term. Define goals for your personal development and professional accomplishment for the coming year. Write them in a way which will permit you to measure your success in achieving them. Acquiring the resources to achieve these objectives is, of course, an integral part of the process. There is no point in defining desirable but unrealistic objectives, or too many.

Effective planning is impossible without a diary system. There are many options, including pocket diaries, electronic personal organizers, wallcharts and desk diaries. Choose the one which most closely matches your working situation. If you have a secretary who maintains an appointments diary, build in time to make sure your own diary is updated on a frequent and regular basis. Your secretary should also protect short periods of time for regular review of plans.

Set aside time (between 10 and 30 minutes) at the beginning of each day to list your tasks and prioritize them. Some doctors prefer to do this at the end of each day in preparation for the following day. You may find it helpful to use a simple system of letters or stars to indicate priority, for example:

*** Must be done today
** Should be done today
* Might be done today

It is crucial to understand the difference between tasks which are urgent and those which are important. Urgent but unimportant tasks should be done quickly, but given a small amount of your time. Important, non-urgent tasks can be scheduled for later in the day, week or month and given sufficient space in your diary to complete them properly at the first sitting. Some tasks will be a mixture of both.

Work through your list, completing each task before moving on to the next. Set a time limit for each task based on its priority. Some of your time may be largely outside your control. Use your daily planning session to make best possible use of the rest. Do not worry if, at the end of the day, you have not completed them all. Simply transfer them to your list for the following day. Each week, review your list and schedule the coming week's key tasks.

CONTINUOUS IMPROVEMENT IN THE USE OF TIME

There are many small ways in which you can improve your effectiveness. Together they can have a considerable impact. Many of the following suggestions require practice. Do not give up if they do not work first time.

Avoid procrastination. Set starting times for tasks you might be tempted to put off. Forget about finishing the task – concentrate on starting it. Make your deadlines public. Reward yourself for completing unpleasant tasks. Learn to say 'No' to unreasonable or low priority requests from others. It takes practice to do this assertively and without offending.

For those who have one, working effectively with a secretary is a crucial first step. Doctors could improve their own performance by being more aware of how to use their secretarial support. Many (although not all) grossly underutilize their medical secretaries who often possess an array of skills about which the doctor knows little or nothing. One of these skills is likely to be diary management. This involves avoiding the scheduling of unnecessary meetings, protecting 'prime time' and balancing different demands on the doctor's time while they are left to deal with important core tasks. This is just one example of how your secretary can help. Others may include dealing, at first instance, with virtually all of your incoming and outgoing communication. Your secretary will need careful training by you. A clear understanding between you both of your expectations needs to be complemented by mutual trust. This is not easy to achieve. The benefits will soon pay for the time spent in generating it.

Incoming paperwork should be handled only once. Most mail can probably be dealt with by your staff, if they are adequately trained. Do not put a letter down until you have written or dictated a reply. If you really cannot act immediately, do something, even if it is just to set a time and date for when you will take action. Established routines for working at your desk are essential. Treacy (1991) suggests that one of four decisions can be made about each piece of paper that lands on your desk:

1. Should I act on it?
2. Should I pass it on to someone else's desk?
3. Does it belong in my filing system?
4. Should I throw it away?

Reading is an important method of personal development for all doctors. Scan lengthy documents before deciding that you need to read them all. Highlight key points so that you can refer back to them easily. 'Speed-reading' can be useful for those with many large documents to absorb, but is no substitute for good judgement when deciding what to read (Buzan 1988).

Writing clearly, simply and concisely is essential for effective, first-time communication. Consider the purpose, jot down key points, then arrange them in a logical order. Use short sentences, avoiding jargon and formal language.

Telephones save time when used appropriately. They are sometimes used inappropriately and end up creating more problems than they solve. Try keeping a time log of your telephone use during one week. A stopwatch will help. You may be surprised at the total time taken up. Before using the telephone, make a quick note of what you wish to say. Keep the conversation on track and bring it to a polite end when you have completed your business. Better still, delegate others to make, answer or return telephone calls for you. Mobile phones can be a mixed blessing. Ask yourself 'Would (or does) having one give me more, or less, control over my life?'

Meetings can waste a lot of time. First, ask yourself if the meeting is necessary or if you need to attend. If you have called the meeting, prepare an agenda, set a time limit and communicate these to others before it starts. Encourage them to prepare for the meeting. During the meeting, if you are responsible for its conduct, discourage irrelevant discussion. If you call meetings regularly it is worth considering attending a training course on managing them. Alternatively, for a useful guide to meetings, see White (1993).

Delegation can be painful. Giving away tasks you enjoy, or feel you cannot trust others to do, may be the only way to release time for what you need to do to achieve results. Effective delegation requires you to set and communicate realistic performance standards. Staff may need to be trained to accept new responsibility and be authorized to act on your behalf. Support and appreciation of good performance should be readily given. There is more on delegation elsewhere in this text.

The reward for successful time management is being able to answer 'Yes' to the questions at the beginning of this section. The enjoyment of career and life are worth the effort.

ASSERTIVE BEHAVIOUR

An innate characteristic of the work of many doctors is fragmentation and unevenness of work rate. One essential skill needed by doctors in the protection of their work routines is the ability to prevent others from unnecessary, disruptive interference. This can be a common cause of frustration and poor performance, particularly for those doctors who hold management or supervisory responsibilities, no matter how small. Those who work in teams need to be able to manage their working arrangements with others. Maintaining good working relationships while avoiding exploitation of goodwill can be difficult. Achieving and maintaining a satisfactory level of independent control while still contributing fully to cooperative tasks requires a high level of social and group working skills. Among these is the ability to act assertively when required, to decline taking on further demands when already fully loaded.

There are many reasons why people find it hard to say 'No' to even unreasonable demands which are made of them. The more obvious reasons cluster around the difficulty of deciding what tasks should, or should not, be a part of their role. Equally, they may be unable to determine what is a reasonable workload. Job descriptions can help, but they are seldom sufficiently detailed to remove all uncertainty and, in any case, constant changes in detail mean they are seldom kept up to date.

It is difficult to deal with colleagues such that good relationships are always maintained without constantly succumbing to their demands. Unhealthy conflict can arise if we appear to be negative in our responses. Smith (1975) suggests that, in addition to 'fight or flight' responses to conflict, we have been conditioned to respond passively by parents who teach us to 'turn the other cheek'. He argues that verbal communication is one of the distinguishing characteristics of humans and that we can learn to deal with differences and solve problems jointly by assertive use of our reasoning power. Harris (1970) describes the impact of early life experiences on our later behaviours. In developing the concept of transactional analysis, he outlines the nature of 'life scripts'. These are responses which we learn early in life and which help to shape our view of ourselves and hence our behaviour when responding to others. Building on the work of Eric Berne (1964), Harris suggests that our behaviour is shaped by our use of life data which are derived from early experience of key relationships. Hence, interactions with others are shaped by our tendency to respond from the 'parent', 'adult' or 'child' within us. Since the interaction is two-sided, the response we give is frequently drawn out by the type of initial message we receive. Parental instructions, which are likely to be judgemental and directive, tend to call out the child in us and vice versa. Overriding the tendency to behave in this predetermined manner is difficult. It requires the learning of new ways of reacting to requests and demands on our time.

The first and most basic requirement we have in developing the ability to act assertively is to recognize the 'assertive rights' of human beings. Smith (1975) describes a few of these as:

- the right to judge your own behaviour, thoughts and emotions and to take responsibility for their initiation and consequences upon yourself;
- the right to offer no reasons or excuses to justify your behaviour;
- the right to make mistakes – and be responsible for them.

Dickson (1982) adds, among others, the rights to: 'be treated with respect as an intelligent, capable and equal human being' and 'to express my feelings'.

The latter text recognizes and deals with the special problems that affect women in their careers and lives. Extensive research into women in employment confirms the difficulties faced by women who are attempting to build a career (Fincham & Rhodes 1992, Crompton & Sanderson 1990). Problems facing women training for a career as a doctor seem to be especially acute, particularly in certain specialities (Maddock & Parkin 1994). Learning assertive behaviours can help women to overcome the prejudice and career management problems which are likely to face them in their lives.

Assertive behaviour is not aggressive, nor is it passive. It does not infringe the assertive rights of others. It allows each party to an interaction to depart with their own self-respect intact. Ideally, it should leave each party feeling 'OK'. It is usually concerned with helping individuals to acquire what is rightfully theirs, to say 'No' to what they do not want or to enable them to handle criticism.

Most people recognize their own need to behave assertively when they reflect on their inability to refuse requests for assistance from colleagues, friends or family members which they realize place unreasonable demands on their time or other resources. The early life conditioning referred to above is the most common reason for this weakness. Having convinced ourselves that we have a right to say 'No', the next task is to learn how to say it assertively.

There are two sides to saying 'No'. The first is to recognize how simple it is to find the word. It helps to practise saying it without apologizing excessively or making complicated excuses. The dominant reason for experiencing difficulty in refusing an invitation or request is the feeling of guilt which results. The rights referred to above will, if remembered, help to assuage the guilt. So, also, will be the continued use of the skill, so that it feels normal. A refusal to a request is not a rejection of the person making the request. Once this fact has been learned the process will become much easier to use. The other side is to develop the skill of saying it using a tone which is at once friendly but firm. The way in which we look and express ourselves has a greater impact on the communication than the words we use.

Sometimes, the person with whom we are dealing is persistent in their demands. This increases the challenge, but need not create a problem. The key to success is calm repetition. Smith (1975) refers to this technique as the 'broken record'. It enables you to feel comfortable in avoiding manipulative verbal side-traps, argumentative baiting and irrelevant logic. Simply keep repeating your requirement or refusal in a calm and assertive manner until the other person accepts it.

Handling manipulative criticism can cause difficulty. Assertive responses encompass a range of options. The first is to calmly acknowledge to the critic that there may be some truth in the criticism, yet leave yourself with the right to determine what you will do about it. A stage beyond this is to strongly agree with hostile or constructive criticism as it is given, accepting your faults without resorting to denial. This has the effect of reducing your critic's anger or hostility without making you feel anxious or defensive. There is still no need to apologize if you do not wish to do so.

If it does not weaken your position or threaten your self-respect, it is acceptable to seek a workable compromise with the other person. This involves recognizing that a 'win-win' situation can be achieved by agreeing to concede something of your own position, while retaining your right to protect your own needs.

The objective of assertive behaviour is not to win all your conflicts at the expense of someone else. It is, rather, to maintain your own position and protect your own rights as a person while dealing effectively with the demands of others around you. It should always be your aim to respect the equivalent rights of others. It is this which differentiates assertive from aggressive behaviour.

HANDLING STRESS

Most professionals become familiar with the concept of work overload at some stage in their careers. For many, the effects can be recognized in the deterioration of their capacity for taking on new challenges and maintenance of normal lifestyle and family relationships. A less obvious side-effect is the impact uneven work patterns can have on health. Stress is often blamed as the instrument which directs the ill effects. It has been described as the modern affliction, the trigger for a multitude of physical and mental disorders, including heart disease and cancer. Before we become too taken up with the evil nature of stress, it may be helpful to attempt to define it. Most authors of management texts prefer to see it as describing a spectrum of states of mind, which includes stress as a positive, as well as a negative, concept. Thus, it may be described as 'a demand made on the adaptive capacities of the mind and body' (Fontana 1989). It is only when demand becomes more than the mind and body can handle that its effects become undesirable. Before this stage, it can act as a spur to greater achievement and satisfaction at work.

In order to understand the stress in our lives, we need to assess the external demands which are made on us (and which we make on ourselves) and our own capacity for handling that stress. People vary widely in their personal capacity for dealing with work overload. What appears as a major problem to one person may be an exciting challenge to another. Personalities and their approach to work-related stress have been assessed according to type. Complete the following questionnaire. Answer each question 'yes' or 'no'.

1. Do you characteristically do several things at once (e.g. telephoning, holding a conversation and jotting notes on a pad)?
2. Do you feel guilty when relaxing, as if there is always something else you should be doing?
3. Are you quickly bored when other people are talking? Do you find yourself wanting to interrupt or get them to hurry up?
4. Do you try to steer conversation towards your own interests, instead of wanting to hear of those of others?
5. Are you usually anxious to finish each of your tasks so that you can get on to the next?
6. Are you unobservant when it comes to anything that is not immediately connected with what you are actually doing?
7. Do you prefer to have rather than to be (to experience your possessions rather than to experience yourself)?
8. Do you do most things (eating, talking, walking) at high speed?
9. Do you find people like yourself challenging and people who dawdle infuriating?
10. Are you physically tense and assertive?
11. Are you more interested in winning than in simply taking part and enjoying yourself?
12. Do you find it hard to laugh at yourself?
13. Do you find it hard to delegate?
14. Do you find it almost impossible to attend meetings without speaking up?
15. Do you prefer activity holidays to dreamy, relaxing ones?
16. Do you push those for whom you are responsible (children, subordinates, partner) to try to achieve your

own standards without showing much interest in what they really want out of life?

It has been suggested that personalities can be divided into those who are driven by ambition and the need to achieve (type A) and those more laid-back people for whom life is a series of experiences which may be outside their control, but can be nonetheless enjoyable (type B). People with extreme type A personalities will have answered 'Yes' to all 16 questions above. If you have responded positively to 12 or more of the questions, then you are likely to have significant type A tendencies. Type A persons like deadlines and pressures, are impatient to move on to new challenges and can be intolerant of the failure of others to measure up to their own standards of commitment. Unfortunately, this approach to life can lead to type As drawing more upon themselves than they can reasonably cope with and finding they have fewer coping mechanisms as the pressure rises to breaking point.

Maintenance of a balanced lifestyle, in which sport, leisure and family pursuits are given equal place with work, is seen as an essential prerequisite for achieving healthy stress levels. This will help to ensure that the volume and nature of the workload does not outpace the individual's capacity for managing the work. This is usually easier said than done in modern working environments, where pressure to absorb increasing demand is often linked to organizational survival. Techniques of time management, as described above, can be used to begin redressing the balance between work and leisure activities.

Another, complementary, approach is to increase the capacity of individuals for coping with high levels of stress. Changing lifestyle is not easy but can be managed, especially if the consequences of failure to do so are taken into account. People with type A personality will be able to recognize the kinds of things which can be done to reduce the risk of stress. Paradoxically, they can be most effective in implementing change programmes to improve themselves. Finding and developing non-work interests which provide an antidote to overwork can make a good start to the process. Competitive sports, such as golf or sailing, help to improve physical fitness and to separate people from work pressure for significant periods of time. Learning to delegate, which is discussed elsewhere in this text, is also vitally important for people with type A personalities.

Some writers on stress management advocate the use of relaxation and meditation techniques. These range from undertaking simple physical exercises to the acquisition of understanding of Eastern philosophies and habits of mind. They do not work for everyone. It has been argued that regular meditation, even for only a few minutes each day, builds ability to concentrate and handle emotions and aids physical relaxation. Some people find it difficult to acquire the mental discipline associated with such an approach, although simple physical relaxation techniques are within the scope of most. A wide range of books on stress management and relaxation techniques is available. Many replicate the basic approach. An example of advice on meditative technique is shown below. Try it, in case this is what is right for you. It requires practice to become competent, so you should persevere before deciding it does not work for you, perhaps only for 5 minutes the first few times, rising to 10 or more after a week or so.

- Choose a suitable room or place where you are guaranteed peace and quiet, free from interruption. Sit in a comfortable upright chair. Keep your body upright throughout. It may help to imagine that your head is held up by a connection with the ceiling above you. Allow your muscles to relax as much as possible while still keeping an upright posture. Close your eyes.
- Remaining as calm as possible, start to focus on your breathing. You will find it helps to concentrate on either your nostrils or your abdomen, but not on both. Count 1 for each breath as you finish breathing out. Count up to 10, then down again until you reach 1. Keep repeating this process.
- As thoughts arise, allow them to drift without paying attention to them. Do not try to drive them away. Concentrate on your breathing. Allow other thoughts to come and go without hindrance.
- After the meditation session is over, rise slowly from your chair. Try to maintain the poised awareness which you experienced while meditating. Apply the same approach to thinking about the sights and sounds around you as you go about your everyday activities.

This approach will not remove the sources of stress. In serious situations radical life change may be necessary, such as a change of career direction. Meditation and other techniques are, arguably, a way of managing stress, rather than allowing it to manage us.

Changing the way we think about our lives is more difficult. It has been suggested that the following characteristics are found in those who handle stress most effectively (Woodcock & Francis 1982).

- They shelve problems until they are capable of dealing with them. They do not dwell on issues with which they cannot cope.
- They deliberately relax after coping with highly demanding and stressful tasks, usually by undertaking contrasting activities.

- They take a wider view of situations and do not become bogged down in detail.
- They control the build-up and pace of stressful situations by planning and intervening to prevent themselves from becoming swamped.
- They are prepared to confront difficulties or unpleasant issues.
- They know their own capacity and do not permit themselves to become overwhelmed by events.
- They can cope with being unpopular.
- They do not commit themselves to very tight deadlines which are unlikely to be met.
- They actively limit their involvement in work in order to maintain a balanced lifestyle.

The above section on stress management is intended to provide an insight into the issues. It does not deal with the responsibility which those supervising the work of others have ensuring safe and realistic work programmes for them.

CONCLUSION

The concept of a 'career' as a lifelong progression through predetermined hierarchical stages is no longer viable in developed economies. Discontinuous change is the norm and this does not allow for jobs for life. People who wish to sustain employment opportunities in satisfying work environments must be aware of their learning needs at all times throughout their lives. Continuous self-development is achievable by those who understand that learning is not a process which occurs automatically. It must be managed. The learning process requires that each individual discovers their personal learning goals and organizes events so that they can be met. We each have a preferred learning style. This may emphasize 'bookish' learning or active testing of ideas. It may focus on interaction with other people in group situations or 'back-room' theory and abstract concepts.

Learning also occurs when time is set aside for reflection on experience, as well as setting up opportunities for practice.

REFERENCES

Berne E 1964 Games people play. Grove Press, New York
Buzan T 1988 Speed (and range) reading. David and Charles, Newton Abbot
Crompton R, Sanderson K 1990 Gendered jobs and social change. Unwin, London
Dickson A 1982 A woman in your own right. Quartet Books, London
Fincham R, Rhodes P S 1992 The individual, work and organization. Weidenfeld & Nicolson, London
Fontana D 1989 Managing stress. British Psychological Society/Routledge, London
Gatrell J, White A 1995 Medical student to medical director, NHSTA, Bristol
Harris T A 1970 I'm OK – you're OK. Pan, London
Maddock S, Parkin D (1993) Barriers to women doctors in the north western region. NWRHA, Manchester
Smith M J 1975 When I say no, I feel guilty. Bantam, London
Treacy D 1991 Clear your desk. Business Books, London
White T 1993 Management for clinicians. Edward Arnold, London
Woodcock M, Francis D 1982 The unblocked manager Gower, Aldershot

20

Team building and performance managers

Chris Grice

The subject of team building is one which often elicits the response 'Why?'. It takes time to build a team – time we rarely have to spare – and team members are changing all the time. As for 'managers', this is almost synonymous with the 'men in grey suits' image of the 1990s and vies with the image of a 'professional carer'. Worst of all, 'performance' raises the spectre of interminable debate about budgets, throughput, measurement and evaluation.

It is hoped that the following chapter will allow doctors, as professionals, to consider these emotive topics with objectivity and come to their own decision as to whether team building is worth the effort (or even possible) in their particular circumstances.

BASIC PRINCIPLES

Peter Stemp (1988) has written: 'Small teams generate high commitment . . . The advantages are clear'. He goes on to encourage all those with the power to organize the work of others to create these small teams, implying that this is the universal panacea for all organizational troubles. What remains unclear is whether it is the small team or the high commitment which is advantageous. And how small (or large) is 'small'?

Alex Smith (1983) states: 'Experience shows that the best size of team is somewhere between four and fifteen'. He adds that: '. . . in highly complex, varied, high level work, . . . the number would be nearer four . . .'.

Let us now consider the size of a group of healthcare professionals delivering care to patients. In a single-handed GP practice, the number may well be close to four, but few wards or departments in the hospital setting have so few staff, especially if the care group includes those who are not permanently based in that location.

We have all experienced the situation when an extra pair of hands would be extremely valuable, so why should there be an upper limit on the number in a team? Or a lower limit for that matter? To answer these questions it is necessary to take a look at some of the ways in which a 'team' is different from a group of people working towards the same objective.

First of all, let it be quite clear that 'work groups' can and do achieve a great deal in organizations. It's just as well they do, because waiting for a team to be built before anything is achieved would paralyse every organization in the world! An important aspect of effective team building is that the team achieves as it develops, providing reinforcement of 'teamlike' behaviour and encouraging members to continue with their collective and individual development towards being a team.

A critical aspect of the argument in favour of 'teams' at work is that they are in some way 'better' than other work groups; they achieve more, perform better, are more effective. At least they are when they are 'mature'. As the team members are essentially the same before and after team building, the answer lies not in what they know but in how they apply that knowledge to the tasks confronting them.

A simple model for the evolution of a work group into a team has four stages labelled 'forming', 'storming', 'norming' and 'performing'. The key features of each stage are as follows.

Forming

At this stage the individuals are governed by a series of rules and regulations which have been worked out for them by the organization, often by the team's most senior person in terms of hierarchy. These are seen as the given boundaries of activity – what can or cannot be done. Each person may be aware of their own tasks and may even be aware of the expected collective outcome.

In some cases, the tasks of others in the group may be known, especially if they impinge on those of the individual. But who does what and how is usually imposed.

Discussion in these groups may be about work but will rarely address personal feelings about work or individuals' value systems. 'Work is for working' is the common attitude. This stage is often labelled 'king and court' as the outcomes tend to be directed by the most senior person without recourse to consultation.

Storming

The most important aspect of this stage is that the individuals in the group start to debate in depth issues related to their work. In particular, the underlying purpose of their work becomes collectively important. Those in authority often find themselves confronted with the question 'why?' and requests for a 'mission' statement may arise. Individuals also challenge each other and the environment may become turbulent for some time.

It is often the case that collective performance is impaired, especially when the leader is unaware of what is going on or is unable to facilitate the process. The success, or otherwise, of team building attempts often hinges on the ability of the team to survive this predictable dip in performance. In addition to the internal turmoil, pressure from other organizational groups for a return to the previous standards of performance is sure to mount. It is important, therefore, that performance outcomes are carefully considered prior to launching a team building exercise and that other groups likely to be affected by the changes are given due consideration.

Team building is not an exercise that takes place in laboratory conditions, but occurs as part of the ongoing work of the organization as a whole. It is an interactive process, both internally and across the boundaries with other work groups, departments and individuals. To ignore the effects of 'storming' internally on others is to doom the effort to probable failure in organizational terms.

It is incumbent on the nominal team leader to negotiate the conditions which will allow the 'storming' stage to occur successfully. This is often about short-term variations within longer term guarantees and the importance of fulfilling these at every stage is fundamental if the 'licence to team build' is not to be withdrawn. The situation facing most wards provides a good illustration. While senior staff of all disciplines remain in the team for periods of years, there is a planned periodic turnover of, for example, junior medical staff. Each time this happens, the team must spend time and effort sharing ideas and beliefs with the newcomer(s). Ethical and professional beliefs may raise particularly heated debate and working relationships may become strained whilst these issues are worked through. As individual team members have both social and professional relationships outside the team boundaries, the internal upheaval becomes common knowledge and the value of such tension to the quality of patient care challenged by those in authority. Equally, the impact of internal upheaval on lateral relationships with other groups and departments may not be acceptable to these others, especially if the debate leads to widespread polarization of views between individuals, teams or professions, as the whole organization can be disrupted.

Norming

Once the objectives of the team and the value systems are clearer, the process of developing protocols can begin. Even where a formal system of regulations is applied to the whole organization from a central 'command post', teams at this stage will work out their own ways of doing things within the imposed framework. Importantly, these 'house rules' are agreed to by the whole team – they represent 'normal' behaviour.

Performing

This stage of team development is characterized by high performance, because no effort is wasted. The team has worked out for itself the best way of doing things and acts accordingly. When a new challenge has to be faced, the team will collectively agree the way to proceed.

There are several other characteristics of the performing team which identify it from the less mature groups. The leadership of the team is vested in the member best qualified to lead at the time, by reason of specialist knowledge, closeness to the problem or experience of the situation, rather than by hierarchical status (see p 191). Criticism from outside the team is accepted and considered objectively, with subsequent action avoiding 'kneejerk' reactions.

Above all, there is an intense pride in collective achievement and frequent review of progress made. It is when a team has reached this stage that the performance becomes much better than that of the original work group and the dip in the 'storming' stage can be recovered. Of course, sustained performance at this higher level means that the organization benefits in the long run and, as the mature team is characterized by self-monitoring and evaluation, adaptation to all but the most extreme challenges should be achieved with little disruption and no radical dips in performance.

The four stages are not mutually exclusive. Indeed, it is common for the process of team evolution to be spiral, with frequent returns to the storming stage. This is, in fact, absolutely necessary, if only for a short time, every time a new face joins the team as every member needs to share the underpinning value system which the team has built up. If this does not happen, either the team will modify its values or, more likely, the newcomer will be rejected, with disruptive effect.

In healthcare, the knowledge, skill and experience of individual team members are essential to achieving a successful outcome. But whose knowledge, skill and experience are required? Perhaps a better question would be 'Whose can be left out?'!

The multidisciplinary team is a widely accepted concept in healthcare today and it gives us a major clue to one aspect of a successful team. Simply stated, 'Nobody's perfect, but a team can be'. The individual members of a team all have gaps in knowledge, have different levels of expertise, specialize in different fields. The four-stage model of team building suggests that, in mature teams, each team member is recognized for, and recognizes, their own potential and is equally aware of all the others in the team. It further suggests that each team member is encouraged in their personal development, as this will enhance the collective resources available to the team.

A team, therefore, is an integrated social unit, as well as a group of individuals working towards the achievement of the same task. As team size grows, this integration becomes looser and large work groups tend to break down into smaller units with which the members can cope socially. Theories about team size reflect this natural process.

The assertion that commitment is a clear advantage appears unchallengeable, but there is a significant risk in creating a highly committed team. In the absence of clear purpose and objectives, even well-established teams can become dysfunctional. The social bonding which is the key to effective teamwork can become an end in itself and if this continues for any length of time, refocusing the team on organizational objectives may meet with resistance. This is particularly true in times of radical change and was frequently apparent when much of the residential care for those with learning difficulties was moved from large institutions to smaller community-based units. The advantages to the residents were largely unchallenged but many of the care team members experienced strong feelings of loss and isolation and retained positive feelings towards the 'old hospital' which had nothing to do with the care of residents.

In practical terms, therefore, every team needs a clear awareness of organizational direction, as well as being comfortable with its internal processes.

LEADING THE TEAM

Many tomes have been written in pursuit of 'effective' leadership. John Harvey-Jones (1988) provides valuable insight into an important principle: '. . . it is only when you work with rather than against people that achievement and lasting success is possible'. The question remains as to what leaders and their teams should work at.

Attention has to be paid to the tasks facing the team. The achievement of these tasks gives the team its purpose and justifies its existence. In work groups, these tasks are the sole focus and where a team is brought together for the duration of a shortlived project, the vast majority of collective and individual effort will be applied to 'task' activity. The same is true when rapid change is imposed at time of crisis.

Consideration of the natural reaction to a crisis gives insight to other valid areas of attention for the team leader. The first concern is to tackle the crisis and avoid immediate disaster. This being achieved, the individual will normally heave a sigh of relief and relax the effort in the 'doing' arena. In many cases there will be reflection on how the crisis came about and perhaps some ideas generated as to how to avoid repetition in the future.

For a group of people to go through this process together is less common, but it is an essential element of working together as a team. The leader should not, therefore, merely drive the team towards task achievement but should also foster the collective approach and encourage team members to discover the best ways of working together for themselves.

From time to time, individuals will require personal support. At the lowest level, this requires the team leader to give feedback on how the person is doing. This should cover the social aspects of team membership as well as task achievement and needs to be constructive and regular. In this way, any specific problems can be addressed early enough for remedial action to be easy. The situation to be avoided is that which can occur when a team member behaves in a slightly unacceptable way, but does so with increasing frequency. Eventually, this behaviour has to be confronted and a major disruption results, disturbing the rest of the team as well as the individual concerned. This in turn upsets the smooth functioning of the 'teamwork' and has a detrimental effect on task achievement. In dealing with individual team members, the leader should aim to operate a 'no surprises' philosophy, which means providing feedback as soon after the event as is possible.

In addition to feedback about behaviour, support for

the individual may include help in identifying development opportunities and training needs, facilitating solutions to problems, providing emotional support and a whole range of other things at different times. To achieve this, and undertake all the other roles of the team leader, requires a considerable time investment and this in turn limits the number of people that can be 'led' effectively. Hence the restriction on maximum size of team and the reason why, in complex environments, smaller teams are suggested as being more appropriate – more time has to be spent on individual support and developing effective collective activity.

The team has, therefore, three broad areas of activity which require attention:

1. achieving the tasks;
2. building team working;
3. supporting individual team members.

This, of course, is true of all team members, not just the nominal leader, and in mature teams all three areas are effectively addressed. This is not to say that every team member will be equally involved in each area of activity but it is likely that a mature team will demonstrate not just the technical skills required to achieve the task, but also the social skills to cater for the other two areas. This will be considered further below.

In large organizations, nominal team leaders have additional tasks, which in broad terms can be viewed as 'representing the team'. This involves a whole range of 'communications' activities, including:

- taking the views of the team outside its boundaries and sharing these with other groups in the organization;
- fighting on behalf of the team from time to time;
- acting as the team 'post-box' for incoming communications;
- being involved in strategic planning, where this affects the team.

Above all, as the team representative, it is the nominal leader who will be held accountable for collective team performance by the rest of the organization. The role of clinical director makes these 'representative' functions of the leader very clear.

A successful team leader must be aware of five separate directions in which they are required to take effective action. The first of these is central, as it involves awareness of self – the leader's own tasks, abilities, feelings, etc. With so many different aspects involved, successful team leadership demands both breadth and clarity of vision. It is hard enough to juggle a large number of irregular objects with eyes open – blind spots are an unnecessary complication.

The second direction for action is towards the team itself, involving the broad areas outlined above.

The third direction is vertically upwards, towards those in the organization with line management responsibility for the team leader and the team. Such upward activity very often includes members of top management outside the direct line of reporting (e.g. chairpersons and non-executive directors), especially when development situations are involved. It is through this line of communication that the majority of information about the rest of the organization is made available, certainly where issues of policy and overall direction are concerned. Taking effective action in this direction is thus essential if the team is to remain in step with the organization as a whole.

The fourth direction is laterally towards other groups with which the team interacts directly on a regular basis. The ability of the team to be effective in its task achievement is often determined by these interactions and the quality of these activities often leaves much to be desired. Where such relationships exist, it is important that, on a day-to-day basis, all team members develop effective 'boundary management' skills to use when they interact with members of other groups. The leader needs to be able to use these skills in both one-to-one and group-to-group situations.

In healthcare, professional bodies, both regulatory and advisory (e.g. royal colleges, GMC, UKCC, BMA, CSP, IHSM), form an important group which has to be considered carefully. Opinion about best practice may differ between professions (e.g. on the patient's right to die with dignity) and this can make the development of an agreed protocol difficult in a multidisciplinary team. On other occasions, the disciplinary function of a professional body may place a team member in a situation where failure to conform to management demands could result in dismissal, but conforming would mean a breach of the professional code of conduct, possibly resulting in striking from the Register and thus disqualification from practice.

An example of this was experienced by a newly appointed night duty sister in charge of the multidisciplinary team. The senior officer on call was the director for the multispecialist 20-ward hospital, which was 'on take' 24 hours a day. The sister's role was to coordinate services, provide advice, floating cover and temporary relief for each area, ensure nursing standards were met and support junior staff. The agreed procedure for drug checking required two qualified nurses due to the complexity of the regimes and the sister acted as the second nurse across the hospital at night.

At handover, the director advised her that a patient required 'specialling' on an open ward and that as no staff were available, she would have to be ward-based herself to do this. The sister discussed the unsafe practice and levels of care, but was overruled and told to 'get on with it.'

The sister then contacted the liaison officer at another hospital in the unit, but was refused extra staff on the grounds that the budget was exhausted. She was also threatened with disciplinary action if she did not 'get on with her job', as her colleagues had in other weeks (when the hospital had benefited from more staff). Fortunately for the sister, her appeal to the chief nurse was treated professionally. He arrived, assessed the situation and organized the additional staffing. From the professional (i.e. patient safety) point of view, the sister had no choice but to obtain help, even if this overspent the budget. Not to have done so would have left her in breach of her professional code of conduct (even if no harm came to anyone) and liable to professional disciplinary action. To break the budget limits would have been flagrant disregard of the direct instructions of her line manager and the liaison officer and disciplinary action had been promised for non-compliance.

Successful leadership of multidisciplinary teams requires sensitive handling of professional dignity, starting with an appreciation of each team member's professional affiliation and values associated with this. It is important that these relationships are undertaken with insight and breadth of perception and, above all, even-handedness, irrespective of the profession of the leader.

The final direction to which attention must be paid is outside the formal organization completely. Various sections of the community at large interact in various ways with healthcare teams, both directly and indirectly. Important groups include:

- patients, their relatives and friends;
- suppliers;
- politicians, both local and national;
- the media, both local and national.

In this direction, the team leader represents not just the team but the whole organization. Furthermore, it is often action which is recorded and reported, not words. Consistency of words and action from all members of the team including the team leader is essential if activity in this direction is to be effective. It is not just 'Big Brother' who watches, although he watches everybody all the time!

This direction of activity is probably most sensitive to the influence of effective, self-generated team protocols, not only regarding direct activity but also regarding every phase of working in the team. If the protocols are agreed, they are likely to be consistently applied, the outside world will know what to expect and any challenges to the team from this direction will be on philosophical grounds rather than on quality of enaction of plans.

THE PERFORMANCE MANAGER

Nominal team leaders have special representative tasks to undertake on behalf of the team. They are also held accountable for the performance of the whole team over a period of time. This accountability is not just to their line managers but to the team, other groups in the organization and to the community at large. But most of all, this accountability is to themselves.

In this respect, each team member shares accountability for performance with the nominal leader – nobody can escape asking themselves the question 'Did I measure up?'. Unfortunately, data regarding personal performance are usually scarce and are seldom in a readily usable form. A lot of 'interpretation' has to be applied and it is easy for this to become distorted, seen as it is from one side only. It is no easy task for even the most dedicated and determined individual to retain the objectivity necessary to undertake effective self-monitoring, and hence self-management, of performance over any length of time. It is, of course, possible for individual aspects of personal performance to be monitored accurately, especially where linear measurement can be applied. In the more qualitative areas of assessment, however, things become much more difficult to do alone.

In the mature team, all individuals share a responsibility for observing the actions of both themselves and their colleagues and for providing feedback on these observations. There is also a joint understanding that this feedback will be constructive and meant to enhance future team performance by helping members develop greater individual or collective effectiveness. The key to achieving this desirable state is that all team members respect their colleagues' observations and value their opinions. Mutual trust is required and this takes time, because shared experiences and collective openness are indispensable.

In most working situations, the nominal team leader has an important role to play in 'managing' both the performance of all the individual team members and the collective performance.

Collective performance management is more than identifying the sum of the individual contributions. It involves consideration of the most favourable approaches to the challenges faced by the team, organization of team members to the best collective effect and retaining a flexible view towards 'ideal' allocation of resources. It is essentially an overview of all current and future activity undertaken by the team and requires the ability to rise above the pressures of daily task/team/individual activity and apply a wider perspective. This is sometimes referred to in texts as the 'helicopter quality'.

Individual performance management is usually associated with the process of getting each reluctant worker to achieve progressively more, given the same resources. Blood out of a stone. One of the biggest advantages of developing a team is that the collective commitment to achieving the team's objectives overrides individual reluctance to contribute and self-motivation becomes strong.

There are, however, five questions which have to be answered before a team member can even attempt to make an effective contribution. These same five questions also need to be answered when considering collective performance and provide a basis for individual self-monitoring, so having the answers is critical to anyone who embarks on managing the performance of others.

The first question – 'Who is my boss?'

Superficially, this may seem an elementary question, simply answered by reference to an organization chart. However, as discussed above, in healthcare there is often the possibility that an individual will owe allegiance to both a line manager and to a professional hierarchy. In project situations, each member of the project team may have a different line manager, in addition to the nominal leader of the project team, who is accountable for the outcome of the project to the organization through yet another line! What is clear is that each team member is entitled to know about each and every line of accountability to which they are subject.

'Who is my boss?' is not about accountability alone. Indeed, as far as achieving effective performance is concerned, accountability is less important than support. The 'boss' is the person to whom the individual can turn for help and guidance when necessary. This is the opposite side of the accountability coin – bosses have obligations to those who report to them as well as the right to hold people to account.

In practical terms the boss is normally a senior colleague, manager or team leader and, if the support function is working well, there is seldom need for draconian measures to be applied as far as accountability is concerned. Problems are sorted out as they occur, any shortfall on expected outcome can normally be predicted and appropriate remedial action can be undertaken in time to have maximum effect.

The second question – 'What is my job?'

The normal job description is rarely of use when it comes to identifying the role of an individual and when the actual tasks to be done need identification, no documentation can cover the full range of duties undertaken over a period of time.

It is the nature of work that the required tasks change through time and the effective team varies the tasks it undertakes in response to these requirements. Flexibility is crucial.

Fine. But where does that leave the team member? Badly applied, the principle leaves everyone with the dilemma of 'Should I do that?'. Guessing can be effective, if the guesser has a large database of related information, but guessing in ignorance is sure to lead to one of two equally unacceptable outcomes as often as not. These outcomes are duplication of effort (which may also be seen by colleagues as invasion of their 'territory') or tasks not being tackled by anyone. In extreme cases, both may occur simultaneously, as a person takes the decision to do one thing at the expense of another which is part of their function, only to find that this priority task has been undertaken by another as part of their allocated duties.

What is required to avoid such inefficiencies as far as possible is frequent review of each person's job in light of the collective needs of the team. Changes should be agreed between the individual and the team leader and these should be shared with other team members so they are fully aware of individual responsibilities within the collective need. Where 'special' tasks are to be undertaken, and these do not interact with the work of other team members, the collective task does not demand that such disclosure of change take place. However, the team building aspects of leadership suggest that it might be advisable to keep everyone informed of all such changes, in the interest of openness between team members.

The third question – 'What is expected of me?'

The answer to this question is essentially about standards. Some standards are imposed by the organization, some by the law, some by professional bodies. In broad terms, it is very difficult for an individual team member to influence this group of standards and the process certainly takes a long time.

A second set of standards are those agreed by the team as their internal rules. These often vary considerably from those laid down by the organization and, while the variance is often such that the internal standard is higher than that laid down, this is not always the case. Even where variance is towards a higher standard, the merit of this has to be viewed in the light of the resources available and the effect on collective outcomes of the redirection of some of the allocated resources to enable the higher standard to be achieved. Each case should be assessed individually and the team as a whole have to agree to any changes in internal standards – attempts to impose changes normally result in even greater waste and may even lead to the collapse of the team.

In addition to these standards, there are standards which are agreed between individuals and their senior colleagues or line managers on an ongoing basis. These standards are those applied to the tasks in hand and are often specific to a given time period – for example, undertake 10% more procedures this year than last.

Standards may be quantitative, as in the example above, or qualitative but they must always be clearly understood by all concerned if they are to be useful. As well as being clear, useful standards are always feasible, if challenging. Nothing makes a standard more useless than its impossibility. What happens in these circumstances is that the team create their own standard, which they unilaterally decide to work to. In most cases, this is readily achievable and the potential for improving performance is greatly reduced.

The fourth question – 'How am I doing?'

If tasks and standards are clearly understood by everybody, team members can, with some confidence, undertake self-assessment of their performance. In the mature team, sharing is completely open and honest and peer assessment by team members can be a powerful aid to performance enhancement on both an individual and collective level.

In reality, the need for supportive feedback on performance from the team leader is strong within each team member and, as outlined above, regularity of feedback is beneficial. This does not preclude interim feedback sessions when the need arises – indeed, it is essential that any deviation from agreed standards is addressed at the time, if major remedial effort is to be avoided. Equally, opportunities to reinforce outstanding performance should be taken as early as possible, to maximize the chance of these behaviours recurring.

The fifth question – 'Where is it all leading?'

There are at least two different levels at which this question must be answered if the team are to be able to identify a common purpose for their activity. As this is the central point of developing team values, the answers to this question are fundamental to the ability of any work group to progress towards being a mature team.

At the most immediate level, team members need to be clear as to the goals of the team in the immediate future. They also need to be clear about how their personal contribution fits into this collective endeavour and how the others in the team fit in.

At the broadest level, the long-term objectives of the whole organization need to be clear, as does the way in which the achievement of team goals contributes to this. In essence, this means that each member of a team will be aware of both the operational plan and the strategic plan of the organization and will be able to identify the worth of individual and collective achievement to these.

Individual needs for this sort of information will vary considerably. For some the need (usually labelled 'interest') will be very high and they will seek out the information without prompting or assistance. In other cases, the need will be very low and the team leader (or other members) may find it difficult to demonstrate the significance of these relationships to the individual. In general terms, the need for such information is likely to be higher in teams than in work groups, as the latter tend to be focused on the immediate task at hand rather than the purpose of achieving that task.

WHO'S IN THE TEAM?

Meredith Belbin (1981) identified eight principal 'roles' which members of successful teams commonly demonstrate. These roles do not relate to the actual tasks which the members undertake but reflect contribution to the process of team working. The conclusions drawn about process roles and achievement were in no way prescriptive, but rather indicated broad relationships. The most widely applicable observation was that successful teams either demonstrated all the process roles or were aware of their deficiencies and made appropriate allowances.

Another general point was that each of us tends to adopt one of these roles naturally, but 'secondary' roles may be played if the circumstances require this. Furthermore, about 30% of team members take little or no part in these process activities – the reason for this is obscure – and are labelled as 'makeweights' by Belbin.

Each of the eight types identified demonstrates typical characteristics – both strengths and weaknesses – and undertakes specific functions within the team. A brief summary is given below.

The coordinator

Mature, confident and trusting of others, coordinators make good chairpersons. They are good at clarifying goals and promoting decision taking. They are not normally the most creative nor the most clever members of the team.

The shaper

Shapers are dynamic, outgoing and challenging. They are very good at finding a way around obstacles but tend to suffer from 'short fuses' and are easily provoked.

The plant

When an imaginative solution to a problem is required, the creativity of the plant is indispensable. Solving difficult problems is their strength, although the solution may often be very unorthodox and communicating the merits of this to less 'brilliant' team members may be beyond them. Without help in this direction, the sensitive plant may well take offence and withdraw.

The resource investigator

Usually extrovert in the extreme, resource investigators are the true enthusiasts of the team. They are the source of numerous contacts outside the team and are keen to identify and introduce every 'latest development' to the way in which the team works. Their biggest failing tends to be a lack of 'follow-through', as their initial enthusiasm can be replaced very quickly by the next 'latest' idea.

The implementer

The opposite to the resource investigator is the implementer, who is conservative, reliable and specializes in turning ideas into practical applications. The need to be sure of the utility of proposed changes can make them slow to respond to new suggestions and they may be seen as inflexible by more dynamic colleagues.

The monitor evaluator

Strategic judgement and lateral thinking are the qualities provided by the monitor evaluator. Cool and discerning, with accurate judgement, few options escape the consideration of these people. They are often seen as being cold and uninspiring – the 'wet blanket' of the team – and they can be the cause of much frustration. Nevertheless, they provide an essential ingredient in the successful team mix.

The completer

Doing the job is the focus for completers. They are conscientious and have an eye for detail which allows them to spot oversights at the planning stage and put them right as the task progresses. Above all, they get the job done on time. But they do worry! And they tend to trust nobody but themselves to get the job done at all, so they rarely delegate effectively without support.

The team worker

Team workers are the 'lubricators' of the team processes. They are good at listening to all the others and frequently reduce the friction between different points of view. They are very perceptive of interactions between team members and try to achieve progress through accommodation and compromise. In crunch situations, however, they tend to lack the decisiveness required to take the team forward.

Later work on the subject recognized that specialists may be required to provide technical knowledge otherwise absent from the team and without which progress cannot be made. Because of this critical input, specialists are usually 'leading' the team when they are contributing in this role.

As has already been noted, mature teams will assign the practical (as opposed to nominal) leadership of the team to the person best qualified to lead at that time. Caring for a patient through a long illness and convalescence will usually require the skills of many disciplines and care will often take place in a number of different places, including GP surgery, hospital and the patient's home.

Where the care team is well established and functions in a mature way, the leadership function will pass smoothly from GP to surgeon; from surgeon to nurse; from hospital to community; from professionals to relatives/friends, etc. Each phase of care is led by the relevant individual. The ongoing communication required in this protracted process is often very difficult, requiring, amongst other things, compatible records and few care teams have achieved this to date. Nevertheless, the value of this system is being recognized and progress is being made.

Critically, the one member of the large team who is a member of all the subteams (and may be the most important person of all) is the patient. The success of clinical management is dependent upon their cooperation and involvement. Why then can they never be seen as the leader? Perhaps a review of this question is overdue. The patient can provide continuity in feedback, praise and direct information about the effect of individual and team activity on themselves and others in the 'team' who are not part of the immediate subteam, including relatives, friends and even the local Post Office from which the pension is drawn. In short, 'supportive' leadership. Arguably, the patient is favourably placed to communicate with and thus influence and direct all the team to achieve common goals, whether these be mobilization or death with dignity. Earlier, the question 'Who is my boss?' was mooted. 'The person(s) to whom I am accountable' was one reply. Philosophically, this may be the strongest reason of all for considering 'patient led' care teams.

IN CONCLUSION

Performance managers in healthcare have an awesome responsibility for achieving the best possible outcome for patients within the resources available. Whilst material resources remain finite, the most obvious way of achieving more seems to be creating more effective use of what is available. Even when allocation of resources to care activity is perfect (and debate on this subject is far from exhausted), developing team working will provide individual and collective commitment to collective performance which will harness the goodwill of those who choose a career in healthcare and focus the effort on patient benefit.

Key features to develop are:

- consideration of the feelings of everyone;
- awareness of the full membership of the team;
- mutually agreed objectives and procedures;
- respect for the contributions of all;
- objectivity in considering external comments;
- a balance of both technical and process skills;
- a problem-solving attitude to change;
- appropriate leadership at each stage of care.

Team building will not occur without the effective delegation of both responsibility and authority to act to each member of the team. The boundaries of this responsibility and authority need to be clear to all, as does accountability. In short, excellent communication between team members is a prerequisite.

The role of the leader at the start of the process cannot be overestimated. Belief in the process and the courage to disseminate personal power amongst the rest of the team are essential.

The challenge is great, but the potential benefits are limited only by the almost infinite collective creativity and synergy of the mature team.

REFERENCES

Belbin M 1981 Management teams – why they succeed or fail. Heinemann, London

Harvey-Jones J 1988 Making it happen – reflections on leadership. Collins, Glasgow

Smith A 1983 Structure of work groups. In: Notes for managers. The Industrial Society Press, London

Stemp P 1988 Are you managing? The Industrial Society Press, London

21

Change management

Janet Grant, Rodney Gale

Change – the planned or unplanned response of an organization to pressure arising from individuals, groups or coalitions inside and outside the organization.

Change does not always lead to a better organization, nor does it always lead to an organization in equilibrium. For these reasons, change should not be initiated unless the potential benefits outweigh the potential risks.

A major change is a process whereby a little of the external environment becomes incorporated into the organization. Both are altered by the process. The outcome of the change cannot be predicted from the determinants or the process of change.

Passive organizations do not seek to innovate and are only open to stimuli within a narrow range. Active organizations strive to innovate and have wide definitions of the environment to which they respond and from which they draw ideas.

Change is not something that should be entered into lightly or because you cannot think what else to do with your time. There will be more than enough essential changes to keep you occupied. Over the years, there have been interesting changes in management thinking on change and the best ways to assist or accelerate it. These have reflected the prevailing management culture. Today's culture centres on involvement and empowerment of employees in lean and flat organizations.

We assert that change is better if managed. Change will happen without management, but it is unlikely to be satisfactory or lastingly effective.

ORDERS OF CHANGE

Change comes in different orders.

First-order changes are the small, slow, incremental changes that are the stuff of normal life. They usually involve very few people or very few systems. They occasionally stress us, but rarely. We are usually unaware of how much has changed by this slow, gradual, stepwise process. We could think of introducing a new piece of surgical equipment or a new pharmaceutical product or a minor change to a ward procedure. Dealing with these changes involves a little learning and a little familiarization. They are challenging but not threatening.

Second-order changes imply some change in the status quo, a stress on relationships within the organization and they affect many people and systems. Second-order changes imply a number of people having to alter their behaviour. They need careful management. Most of our contribution is to the better management of second-order changes, although the techniques can be used to tackle first-order ones better too. Harmonizing individual firms into teams, greatly increasing the throughput of a theatre suite or the introduction of management systems that reduce the staffing levels are possible examples of second-order changes. They involve large numbers of people and interests and potentially involve some people being perceived as net beneficiaries at the expense of net losers.

Third-order changes are those that seek to alter the culture or belief systems of organizations. The concept of culture change is currently fashionable in the NHS, but culture changes are extremely complex and need a very long time. They should not really be attempted by the unskilled. It is also arguable that they cannot be tackled directly at all. Culture is a bit like an iceberg in that most of it is hidden until the circumstances demand its appearance. Culture can only be slowly shifted through a series of behavioural changes. It is debatable whether the change to minimally invasive surgery and day-case treatment is second or third order. It is not just a behavioural or organizational change that is needed as there are huge training and retraining implications. After the initial euphoria, there are some aspects of doubt and resistance starting to surface as the longer term implications become clearer.

CHANGE IN MEDICINE

There is an extensive and rapidly growing literature on the management of change. There is, growing in parallel, a realization that the context of change is important to its process and its outcome (Pettigrew 1985). All change management writings rest on a theoretical view of the nature of organizations and the way they function. Spurgeon & Barwell (1991) have reviewed many of these in the context of the National Health Service.

Context is important in relation to change and particularly in the context of the advent of gurus who offer quasi-religious, globally relevant, easy solutions to very complex problems. It has gradually become clear that, whilst there may be universal theories of change, they are only given meaning when adapted to the precise context in which they need to be used. Pettigrew et al (1988) illuminated the role of context and indeed of local history in determining the change process. Pettigrew et al (1992) have tackled the question of why different health authorities respond to the same stimulus in different ways and at different speeds. Local context and local history are paramount.

Pettigrew et al (1992) introduce the concept of receptive and non-receptive contexts for change. The receptive contexts are the promoters or enablers of change. They cover the environment, goals and leadership, the intraorganizational relationships, the history of change locally and the nature of the current change. A harmony among the set of variables enables change.

This description has the virtue of highlighting the complexity of the change process and the number of variables that need to be considered, but it still remains more descriptive rather than prescriptive. The concern of this chapter is for those who wish to promote, encourage, stimulate or lead change in their own institutions or organizations.

Turrill (1986) produced a booklet on change in the NHS that was firmly based on previous experiences in ICI. Much of the thinking on change in the industrial context of ICI was conditioned by that company's success in innovation and expansion. It was constrained only by its imagination and strategic capability. Change is seen as a process of:

- taking stock of the current situation;
- imagining or deciding where you want to be;
- planning how to get there.

Resource constraints are not a major issue because new investment can be justified if there is a reasonable prospect of a return and private sector companies have access to capital markets. Turrill is low on the messy interpersonal details that tend to dominate most change processes, in our experience. A recent book (O'Connor 1993) is better on these issues and also deals with conflict resolution. Spiegal et al (1992) have produced a model of change in general practice that emphasizes teamwork and collaborative approaches.

CHANGE IN THE NHS

One of the major problems facing anyone trying to manage change in the NHS is the resource constraint. The capital resource is bad enough and there are no meaningful mechanisms for injecting venture funding into the system. The human resource constraint is even greater. There is an unwillingness to acknowledge that well-managed changes demand human time and effort. The system does not stop while the changes take place and so the change management task becomes an additional burden on top of normal clinical duties. There should be a recognition that anyone managing a complex change optimally would not also be able to meet a full clinical workload.

To anchor our thoughts in medicine, we have to differentiate between the stimulus and response, between the sources of pressure for change and the organizational response. All change can be viewed as a process whereby influences from the environment become internalized and become part of the new organization (Plant 1987). The environment impinges through the agency of individuals or groups or representational structures. The environment itself encompasses legislation, government policy, resource distributions, attitudes, opinions, technologies and knowledge. Ideas come from research or experience, from people inside or outside the organization and from groups affected or excited by the stimulus.

One of the current issues in the NHS is the number of changes that appear from the NHS Executive. These are mostly perceived as imposed changes rather than being proper organizational responses to an environmental stimulus. The changes are also perceived by many to be only part of some form of 'master plan' that is being pushed through in stages. It is more likely that the genie of market forces, having been let out of the bottle, is out there causing hallowed practices to be questioned.

CHANGE AS AN ORGANIZATIONAL RESPONSE

Change can be perceived as an organizational response

to an environmental stimulus that seeks to improve along a particular critical dimension or it can be a response to remove something bad from the organization. Many parts of the NHS have felt the recent round of changes to be in the latter category. This distinction between excising the bad and nurturing the good or new is important in the change management process we describe later.

It is easy for the organization and its members to recognize the presence of something bad. They may not all agree on the causes and cures of such problems as underutilized theatres, closed wards, low bed occupancy, high readmission rates, but they can agree on their existence.

The end result variable of the change process is also relatively uncomplicated and readily identifiable in the opposites of the above. There is a neatness and simplicity arising from a bounded problem with a clearly obvious and detectable endpoint, albeit a complex problem whose solution may well touch many facets of the total organization.

It is, however, much more difficult to promote change that will improve the organization at some future point when there are no apparent problems to be overcome. This challenge is faced by those aiming to introduce novel service delivery methods or to reorganize a management system to improve the future market position of a trust. They have to be driven by a vision of the future and a vision of the benefits of changing and a faith in their appropriateness.

Aspiring change leaders need to communicate a vision of where the changes could lead and the potential advantages of pursuing such a route; this has to be of greater perceived benefit than the cost of disrupting a system that is already working tolerably well. It is difficult to convince those members of the organization who are averse to risk that it is worthwhile to set out on an uncharted course just on the strength of a vision.

Change for future benefit needs to be promoted and led very carefully. By its very nature, it will be led by visionaries who have the ability to foresee a new order of things and a strong motivation to take their organizations with them. Acts of faith are inherently dangerous to individuals and are equally so to organizations. Visionaries can be wrong and can often be narrowly focused. The actions of the leaders shape the change process and determine the ultimate success criteria by which the impact of the change will be judged.

On the other hand, it is difficult to generate the momentum needed for changes with future benefits from an artificially assembled group who, perhaps, lack the personal drive to see changes through and cannot formulate a clear vision at which to aim. Charismatic leadership has a central role in the type of change that is future orientated.

Gradualism, or a series of small second-order and first-order changes, is the mode of change management most likely to succeed. This approach has the merit of allowing the organization to learn to change, to learn from its own success in tackling a small change. Tackling change more gradually diminishes the centrality of visionary leadership and increases the emphasis on managed processes. The vision needs to be part of the process and needs to be the guiding light in which more pragmatic management processes are able to move the organization towards its visionary goal. The same pragmatic approach helps to manage the changes needed to overcome a short-term difficulty in an organization.

A model of change in medical education

The model we describe below was derived from the practice of medicine and medical education through properly designed experimental methods and has been returned to medical education in the form of several demonstration projects which have served to refine the model (Gale & Grant 1990a,b,c, Nicholls et al 1992). It is thus distinctive in its anchorage.

Authors on change management rely on the systematization of their own experiences to derive theories or frameworks. This approach produces theories that may lack broad applicability. The underlying experience may also be private sector dominated. The public sector and medicine especially are different and merit their own theories and models.

Our primary research was conducted in 1989 at a time of rapid change in government policy. We dealt with a broad section of medical practitioners, from general practitioners and medical school teachers to consultants, postgraduate deans, statutory and regulatory bodies and government representatives. We interviewed a total sample of 55. Their thoughts and views were content-analysed to reveal 54 categories of response, which were further refined to produce the model described below.

There were three strands to the model: professional characteristics or culture; strategic stages or core steps; and tactical choices or styles.

Professional characteristics are as follows:

- Consultation
- Demonstration
- Evolution
- Ownership
- Power to hinder
- Commitment
- Energy and enthusiasm
- Motives.

These have to be noted and dealt with in any change initiative that is not merely to be forced into place, but is to be negotiated. These cultural fundamentals reflect the views doctors have about themselves and about their roles, their relationship to patients and to other members of the healthcare team. They also reflect the distributed power structures that apply. Individual consultants take individual responsibility for their actions and this leads to a culture of independence that matches the resource and clinical decision-making independence that exists. It is vital that the consultants have a sense of ownership of any proposed changes, otherwise there is a chance that their undoubted power to hinder may be invoked. If consultants do not cooperate or remain neutral, it is difficult to promote any meaningful or lasting change.

Doctors, along with most other people, like to be asked or consulted and not told and coerced. Their scientific training makes them respect demonstrations or proofs. The conservatism associated with the practice of medicine leads doctors to prefer gradual development rather than radical leaps into the unknown.

Doctors are also quite suspicious of each other and are generally not keen to see any particular speciality, other than possibly their own, achieve a disproportionately advantageous share of the available resources. So the actions and motives of those wishing to lead a change are up for very close scrutiny. Change leaders must communicate energy and enthusiasm for what they do. They must demonstrate commitment to the cause without wavering but, above all, they must have unblemished credentials and untarnished motives for being involved. Change leaders who have too much to gain personally may find it hard to arouse sufficient following.

The core activities and tactical choices in the model for change management that arose from the research project are described in Table 21.1.

Each of the core activities and the associated tactical choices is discussed in more detail after this change management health warning.

It is extremely dangerous to assume that because a representational model of the process can be constructed and presented, the model is a prescription or detailed blueprint for change management. We have already been at some pains to show that context and complexity of change are confounding variables that are all-important when it comes to local details. The model is at best a guide or map which lists the major stages without telling you how far apart they are or how long you need to spend at each or how best to get to the next one. Change management is not like cookery or painting by numbers. It is a far more fluid process that requires considerable judgement and subtlety.

Table 21.1 A model of change in medicine

Core activity	Tactical choices
1. Establish the need or benefit	Do not sell solutions, lobbying consultation, conjunction of local or national circumstances
2. Power to act	Ownership, key people, using committees, borrowed power, positional power, political or external power, expertise, charisma, information, resource control, indebtedness, prior agreement to act
3. Design the innovation	Feasibility, resources needed, starting time and duration, scale and degree, avoid losers, predict barriers and pathways
4. Consult	Leadership, teamwork, talking and explaining, listening
5. Publicize widely	Vision, presentation, amending proposals, communication
6. Agree detailed plans	Produce plans
7. Implement	Demonstration projects, have an implementation strategy, avoid scheming and bypassing, key people, opportunism, pathways and barriers are activated
8. Provide support	Overcome difficulties, encourage new behaviour, expect resistance, deal with objections
9. Modify plans	Accommodate small alterations, compensate losers
10. Evaluate outcomes	Needs met, benefits realized, modifications needed, evaluation strategy

Establish the need or benefit

Managing change to meet perceived needs is probably more common than changing to reap benefits, but it is necessary to represent opportunity as an equally powerful starting point to need.

In terms of the tactical choices open to the change leader, the major lesson derived from our research and demonstration projects has been the realization that many change initiatives fail because the change leader is attempting to impose already worked out solutions. This contradicts the fundamental principle of achieving a wide ownership for the change initiative. The change leader has to chart a narrow course between explaining the change idea and prescribing it precisely. For people to join in with a change idea, they have to feel that they can influence it and become part of it, rather than merely sign up to it.

We experienced a graphic example of trying to sell solutions among a group of keen and active medical students at the Free University of Berlin. They had been enthused with the idea of problem-based learning and had organized their faculty to help them. They worked hard, fostered other groups to start and eventually convinced the vice chancellor of the merits of the idea. They worked out a scheme and presented it to the authorities who controlled the examination process and the awarding of degrees. This body rejected the solution and even failed to recognize an opportunity or need.

The change would have been better managed if effort had been put into winning the support of the regulators and securing their agreement to run a pilot project, rather than in preparing a well worked out solution without their knowledge or involvement.

Our model is about the process of change and we think it is possible to decouple the change itself and the process of managing it. We do not try to tell you what to change but how to maximize your chances of success. This of course is not completely tenable since the type of change attempted will have a bearing on the change strategy adopted. A WHO (1991) publication attempted to identify different strategies for initiating change locally, but even this document assumed that the desire for change already existed somewhere in the system.

Power

One view of change is that it is a political process (Carnall 1985). As such, power plays an essential role. The power need not be the naked, forceful, coercive type we are familiar with, nor the sweet-talking persuasive type so beloved of politicians on the extremes of their parties. There are many forms of power, some of which we list as tactical choices. Not all change leaders will have the full range, but it is surprising how many most can muster.

It is worth repeating that the change leader needs to assemble sufficient power or influence at the outset to see the changes through to their conclusion. It is very little use being on the brink of introducing the new ward management system only to discover that you have not actually involved the director of nursing. There should be no difficulty in finding the required amount of power to see through the desired changes. One potent source of power which is available because of the persistent hierarchical tendency among medical practitioners is borrowed power. Put simply, you reach up the hierarchy to where a being of sufficient gravitas sits and you enlist their support. Thereafter, you act in their name. An influential specialist could use, 'I am sure the president of the college would wish to see this phase of the work completed a little more expeditiously'. An ambitious senior registrar might be heard to proclaim, 'The chair of the consultants' committee is backing my project and supports my approach'. A clinical tutor might say, 'I am afraid the postgraduate dean would not sanction such a move'.

The earlier example of the Berlin medical students is a good negative one. They failed to appreciate that the regulatory body had the power to approve or block any proposed initiative. The regulatory body therefore needed to be involved at the outset.

We have detected a wide range of personal influencing styles that have been used to encourage fellow consultants to participate in the induction and counselling initiatives at both places where we have conducted demonstration projects, such as:

- Expertise
- Position and authority
- Information
- Charisma
- Resource control
- Indebtedness.

The power of expertise in one's own field often carries over into all other fields of endeavour that are entered. An expert is given greater credibility in all matters, even outside their range of expertise.

The power of position depends upon the importance or influence of the role. The role of clinical tutor has grown considerably in recent times. The reforms of postgraduate education have caused a better definition of the job of clinical tutor and increased contact with unit management and financial functions. There is often a specific contract covering the duties and responsibilities of the role and, above all else, the role has much higher visibility within the hospital. These factors all combine to increase the positional power and authority of the clinical tutor.

Likewise, the role of clinical director has the potential for positional power. Well-run hospitals acknowledge the importance of clinical judgement in resource allocation decisions and have devolved such powers to a practising clinician acting in a part-time management capacity.

Information power is the product of the rise of accountants in our society and the rise of computer-based storage and retrieval systems. The power is not so much knowing the information but knowing how to operate the computer system in order to get at it.

Charismatic power is somewhat more difficult to define but may be thought of as the ability to influence people because of the way you are, because of your personal qualities or personal characteristics. This power is either obvious or inaccessible. It is difficult to train someone to be more charismatic and it is a power that works to differing degrees with different colleagues. One person's charisma is another's nausea.

The power to control resources or access to resources is another potent source of influence. It is the material analogue of information power. It can be used destructively to block initiatives or constructively to encourage new developments.

Indebtedness is the principle whereby an act of consideration to a colleague initiates a future reciprocal favour. Vast positive spirals of cooperation and helpfulness can be built on such a simple device. Equally, vast negative spirals result if it breaks down. There is a more populist manifestation of the principle in organizations which states: 'Be nice to people on your way up the organization lest you meet them again on your way down'.

We are only advocates of elective change, where the participant has the freedom not to go along with it. With sufficient power, coercive change is possible. Coercive methods can work quickly and once. If you are seeking an organization with intrinsic health and inner harmony, please do not try to introduce change coercively.

Design the innovation

At the design stage, it is necessary to sacrifice the purity of an idea in order to make progress. Wide consultation, keeping an open mind and involving all the key players in the process lead to a dilution and broadening of the original concept in order to foster wide ownership. Wide consultation often improves an original idea, too.

In some circumstances, particularly when the change is moderately small and concerns a small number of people, the design task may be left to a small and trusted group. This is not the ideal recipe, however, for major reforms. Task groups may prove helpful but they need to be controlled by a more representative body.

Doctors are very busy people and do not always have the spare capacity to invest in active participation in change. The concept of seeking general agreement of all involved and then licensing a small group to execute the design may actually have wide validity. This is especially the case when moderately small changes are being attempted. The important issue is then one of communication between the design team and the wider group of stakeholders. This is discussed below.

Refine

The refinement stage can vary in length and complexity depending on the number of people or processes involved. The major need is to access a wide body of opinion and to keep in touch with all those holding a stake in the outcome. It is generally fatal to a change initiative to design the solution behind closed doors only to spring it upon an unsuspecting world when they least expect it. There is a strong tendency to do this if the change idea is contentious or controversial. There is a feeling that all may be lost if news of the change gets out before the group has worked out what to do. It may be harder to work in the open, but the final product is better and so are the attitudes and relationships that survive the experience.

The refinement process is a way of further spreading ownership of a change idea, canvassing the opinions and views of others and of communicating to let people know what is going on. If communication with committees or important people that may be involved does not take place, their support and goodwill could be lost or could be transferred elsewhere.

Communication is best when it is personal and verbal. Clearly there are time and resource implications in striving for this ideal. Other forms are used: the brief note, the committee paper or an interim report. The form of communication must be adjusted to the local context.

Publicize

Publicity is a way of communicating with a wider audience beyond the immediate stakeholders and of keeping everyone informed of the whole picture as it develops. We encountered a negative example of the use of publicity in our change management demonstration projects. We had divided the task of producing induction programmes for new SHOs into a number of smaller, speciality-based projects which together formed the project. The leaders of smaller projects were not always in possession of the overall picture of where the project was going or who else was working on it. The smaller groups were not communicating with each other to report progress and share views and there was not enough project team effort available to provide the role centrally.

There is a presentational aspect of publicity which needs to be accommodated. It is better to tell the truth and be open, but to err on the side of understating the magnitude and impact of proposed changes. This is difficult for those with a strong belief in insurance where it is fear of the worst that prompts action. You do not wish to invoke fear of the worst.

Detailed planning

Moderately complex changes cannot be managed without detailed implementation plans which tell everyone concerned where to go and what to do. This includes staff and users of an organization. Too many changes go wrong because of an impatience to see something actually in place before it has been properly designed and publicized. Others fail because of a 'travelling hopefully' philosophy that denies the need for anticipation and detailed planning of who does what, where, when and to whom. Much of what has been attempted to reduce junior doctor's hours under the New Deal has suffered from an urgency to implement before proper planning had taken place and the implications of all the moves had been thought through. Medical education has apparently suffered in some places as a result of such a lack of planning and anticipation of difficulties.

Implement

Implementation strategy depends on circumstances. Our demonstration projects have revealed a rapid implementation mode for change that has been undertaken with a mandate from a committee or other powerful body and is in a relatively accepted area of developmental need. In these circumstances the solution is so highly valued by all that they will tolerate a slightly less refined product. The change must be sufficiently developed to be taken seriously and can then be refined by the process of evaluation and modification.

The scientific basis of medicine leads to a high premium being placed on the demonstration project. If it is possible to operate such a demonstration, this is a powerful route to implementation. Running the demonstration project allows everyone to gain valuable experience and to improve upon the original design. It also allows people to 'view the finished product' and to anticipate what might happen if the pilot project were scaled up.

Provide support

Unless the changes are supported and reinforced, people will gradually drift back to the familiar ways of doing things. There has to be a concerted period of reinforcement and encouragement to allow people to settle down into the new ways so that they become the new status quo. Providing support has aspects of continuing to smooth the pathway of change by removing obstacles that have arisen and aspects of communication and feedback to the key players on the progress of the reforms or changes.

In our demonstration projects, we introduced an evaluation step soon after a major implementation. This was designed to detect any actual or perceptual problems and to provide positive feedback to those who had been involved. We included the providers and recipients, consultants, PRHOs and SHOs in the feedback, because creating a positive climate for the new ways of working was a high priority and the junior medical staff were important in this process. We used both formal questionnaires and interviews and informal channels of information to guide us. In the course of supporting a change, minor alterations or improvements to the system can be incorporated.

Modify plans

For changes that relate to periodic events, such as a 6-monthly induction meeting, it is possible to adopt a rolling programme of change management and development. Rather than spending a long time in designing and refining the innovation, it is possible to produce the first detailed plan and try it out in practice, as a continuing series of demonstration projects.

The lessons from this experimental development approach can then be absorbed and built into the next event, using the concept of modifying plans each time.

Given that the starting plan is moderately robust and the original idea is close to what is needed, the developmental strategy can give rise to an acceptance of continuous change and improvement. The first implementation is very important. It must be good enough to generate more successful features than features needing modification. This method is not a charter for badly worked out change, but a method to accelerate development upon a firm foundation.

If the initial plan is way off the mark, the developmental strategy harbours the danger of the whole initiative becoming discredited. It is also not recommended for changes to more continuous or frequently repeated processes, where there is no breathing space between events.

Evaluate

We have already discussed the part played by evaluation in the progress from implementation onwards. We need to differentiate this interim evaluation from the more open and enquiring evaluation which needs to take place near the end of the change initiative and which is designed to check whether the new system actually works for all involved and whether the change solved the problem or delivered the planned benefit.

Interim evaluation is also important. A change leader needs a constant supply of information on how well each stage is progressing. A good change leader tunes in to a variety of information sources and uses a variety of evaluation methods to gather information and make minor adjustments on the basis of what is discovered. Change management is much more a process of action learning than a static scientific experiment that has to run its course before we can know its result. Change management involves constant adjustments and shifts of direction based on the frequent evaluation of parts or stages of the process.

We summarize below our experiences of working in change management in medicine, over a number of years, in the form of distilled tips. They loosely relate to the critical stages of the model but the fit is not that precise.

Eleven steps for efficient change

1. Attempt to change only what needs changing. If it works, leave it alone.

2. Talk, talk and talk again. Explain your ideas to friends and colleagues, seek allies, convince others, listen and amend your ideas.

3. Always promote the opportunities of change or the benefits. *Do not try to sell your solution or your blueprint.* Ownership of the change initiative and its outcome is a vital issue.

4. Have available a broad vision of how things might be after the change so that you can have outline discussions with people and offer them some anchorage in the future world.

5. Make sure you have the organizational power to see the change through. Get key people on your side or involved early on. Independent practitioners have a very powerful veto if they are not consulted and not involved.

6. It is far, far better to try a small change that succeeds than a huge one that fails or goes astray. The organization learns to accept change through its own success. Bite-sized chunks!

7. Never plot change in secret and then spring it upon an unsuspecting public. It is far better to work in the open and to keep everyone who will be affected by the changes informed.

8. Be prepared to alter proposals, to accommodate other viewpoints. A compromise that spreads ownership may lead to 80% of the original concept being implemented, whereas failure to accommodate others' views may lead to 100% of the original concept failing.

9. Try to think the changes through to implementation and try to anticipate future difficulties or obstacles in your chosen path. The art of good change management is to design your way around the obstacles.

10. Spend your time discussing, designing, refining and publicizing and do not be tempted to rush headlong into implementation with an ill-conceived plan that will fall apart at the first hurdle.

11. There is a place for the written word but only as a confirmation of direct communication. Do not manage change by memo.

CHANGE MANAGEMENT TOOLS

This section introduces two techniques or tools that can be used to assist in the planning of major change or even minor change. They are as follows.

The People Chart (Fig. 21.1) is used to list those affected by the change and those with power or influence to alter its course. This is very useful at the early stage of a change initiative when you wish to make sure you have thought of everyone affected by the change and have gauged their power in relation to it and their degree of support. Good change needs this sort of detail.

PEOPLE CHART

PERSON	POWER	INFORM/ INVOLVE	PRO/ ANTI	ACTION & TIME SCALE

Fig. 21.1 Planning change with a people chart

The force field analysis (Fig. 21.2) is used to weigh up the attitudes and factors which tend to favour a particular change or tend to oppose it. Force field analysis rests on the work of Lewin (1951) who reasoned that organizations are in a state of dynamic equilibrium. They are as they are because the forces trying to push in new directions are balanced by the forces against and so equilibrium or status quo prevails.

Change is a process that seeks to move the equilibrium to a different point. There are those who propound change theories based on Lewin's work that talk of unfreezing the organization or thawing it out of its equilibrium before making changes.

The NHS reforms in the Thatcher era were quite successfully initiated by Kenneth Clark who challenged the status quo quite rapidly and drew the professions into belated debate and dialogue. Unfortunately, the subsequent changes were coercive which hardened many against them.

The force field is used at any stage of change management to take stock of the current situation. It is especially useful right at the outset. The force field analysis method requires a listing of the forces helping or assisting the desired change and those opposing it. Forces can be people, groups, representative bodies, ideas, attitudes or local conditions.

The forces need to be listed in some rough order of importance and matched, as far as possible, so the most potent force for is matched by the strongest opposing force. When the list is complete the size and weight of the opposing forces need to be assessed. If the opposition is huge and powerful and you do not have to make a change, go off and use your time for some other pursuit. If the change is really necessary, then try to redesign the change to remove some of the opposition or to convert them to your side. Change management needs artful pragmatism and not heroic onslaughts against overwhelming odds.

Below we give a listing of factors, derived from our research interviews, that helped or hindered the change process. The list of barriers illustrates the point that it is easier to oppose something than it is to promote a new idea.

The following lists were derived during the research we undertook. They are included without editing or further comment.

Pathways to change

- Shock from adverse case studies
- Evidence of learner difficulties or problems
- Pressure from a disadvantaged group
- Panic induced by poor financial circumstances
- Acceptance of inadequacy
- Manipulation of budgets or organization
- Mergers or acquisitions
- National ratings
- Tradition of change
- Avoidance of something worse
- Litigation climate
- Prizes or achievable targets
- Government support or pressure
- Incentives to accepters
- Student pressure
- Avoidance of embarrassment
- Professional pride
- A new dean or department head
- Luck
- Change of key staff
- Teamwork
- Supportive peer or discussion group

Barriers to change

- Service workload
- Lack of time or loss of free time
- Refusal to accept responsibility

FORCE FIELD ANALYSIS

FORCES FOR THE CHANGE	FORCES AGAINST THE CHANGE

Fig. 21.2 The use of force field analysis

- Sticking to contract terms
- Lack of educational skills
- No financial rewards for change
- Total clinical independence
- Costs
- Mistrust of management
- Non-enthusiasts perverting projects
- Current performance assessment methods
- Lack of political or organizational will
- Strong prevailing opinions
- Unwillingness to make a stand
- Small capacity to accept change
- The need to learn new skills
- Someone else's idea, not mine
- Threat to status
- The nature of medical training itself
- Perceived roles
- Perceived threats to the nature of clinical freedom
- Feelings of being watched or observed
- Love of the status quo
- Limited channels of competence
- Having limitations exposed, a cover-up
- Consultants' attitudes
- Constantly disputing facts or information
- Diverse and diffuse power structures
- Preservation of useful myths
- Protection of perceived territory
- Prejudice
- Lack of understanding
- No agreement with the aims of the change
- Suspicion of change leaders' motives
- Confusion
- Key opponents 'not yet dead'

CONCLUSION

We have shown that managing large changes can be both difficult and potentially damaging to the organization. Change should only be attempted when needed. The process of change can, however, be managed to optimize its chances of success.

REFERENCES

Carnall C A 1985 The evaluation of organizational change. Gower, Aldershot

Gale R, Grant J R 1990a Leading educational change. Journal of Course Organisers Spring 2: 63–71

Gale R, Grant J R 1990b Guidelines for change in postgraduate and continuing medical education. The Joint Centre, London

Gale R, Grant J R 1990c Managing change in a medical context: guidelines for action. The Joint Centre, London

Lewin K 1951 Field theory in social science. Harper & Row, New York

Nicholls M et al 1992 How to run an induction meeting for house officers. British Medical Journal 304: 1619–1620

O'Connor C 1993 The handbook for organizational change. McGraw-Hill, Maidenhead

Pettigrew A 1985 Contextualist research: a natural way to link theory and practice. In: Lawler E (ed) Doing research that is useful in theory and practice. Jossey-Bass, San Francisco

Pettigrew A et al 1988 Understanding change in the NHS. Public Administration 66: 297–317

Pettigrew A et al 1992 Shaping strategic change. Sage, London

Plant R 1987 Managing change and making it stick. Fontana/Collins, London

Spiegal et al 1992 Managing change in general practice: a step by step guide. BMJ 304: 231–234

Spurgeon P, Barwell F 1991 Implementing change in the NHS. A practical guide for general managers. Chapman & Hall, London

Turrill E A 1986 Change and innovation. A challenge for the NHS. Institute of Health Services Management, London

WHO 1991 Changing medical education: an agenda for action, CUHO general

22

Managing a budget

Rodney Gale

We are all more familiar with budgets than we probably know or accept. They seem to embody some of the unsettling aspects of managerial culture and to be imbued with mysticism and implied difficulty. Nothing could be further from the truth. Budgets are, however, an intimate manifestation of the managerial style and culture prevalent in your unit or practice. As such, the budget setting and control process is contaminated with all the good and bad aspects of the overall management process and management style. Autocratic managements set budgets in an autocratic manner, much to the ultimate detriment of the unit. The whole thrust of modern management thinking is towards employee empowerment and distributed responsibility.

Budget setting is one issue we will explore later; budget control and budget monitoring will also be dealt with. Communication channels and interdepartmental links are at their most vulnerable and their most exposed when budget information is discussed and produced. The production of budget information is almost certainly in the hands of accountants who apply the highest professional standards to the process. The use of budget information is a managerial task that is not invalidated if the information is approximate or is estimated, but is invalidated when the information is late. There are distinct tensions in this area which we will return to later.

We will discuss what to do when your budget is going off course and offer you some informal advice for surviving budget battles.

The first task is to put the budget in the context of the unit's operational plan and to demystify the underlying concepts.

BUDGETS AND PLANS

A budget is best thought of as a £ sign in front of a plan. The plan is the primary document; it describes what the unit or practice is trying to do over the budget cycle. The budget cycle is just the period between setting budgets. An annual cycle is normal, but in some fast-moving industries the cycle can be as short as 3 months. It is also normal to link the budget cycle to other planning cycles. You can start to appreciate the complexity that is developing.

The annual planning and budget cycles are geared to the financial reporting dates which usually follow soon after the end of the financial year. There is extraordinary scope in the private sector to choose any convenient financial year and convenient year end and to change it if it suits, although this can be disruptive. In the NHS, the government financial year prevails and the year ends on the March/April borders. Then comes month 13. This is a wonderfully elastic mythical month that stretches lazily into the summer months and allows time for all the accounting surprises to come to light and all the outstanding creditors to submit their invoices for payment. Month 13 allows the accountants to neaten the figures, to vire money from underspent to overspent areas (by agreement) and to balance the books.

Budgets are part of management accounting; they are forward looking, they are produced according to the company's own formulae and are not for public consumption. However, the sum total of all the individual budget performances makes up a large part of the statutory accounts that hospitals are required to produce for ministerial, if not public consumption.

Planning processes

In order to understand better the delights and pitfalls of managing a budget it is useful to examine how the overall budget is built up.

In a well-managed organization, the planning process

would call for costed plans from each unit over the coming year. These represent the desires and aspirations of the unit; what they would do if only the general manager would allocate them a suitable slice of the corporate cake. These imaginative plans would be refined and scrutinized and after several iterations, much negotiation and not too much disappointment, would become the strategic plan for the organization.

If money were no object, all the unit plans could be accepted and all aspirations could be funded. Some of the computer companies in Silicon Valley worked roughly like this during their heyday in the late 1980s. Creative ideas were needed and new products were important. Money was flowing in so fast that it was better just to spend it than to worry about accounting for it. Times changed as competition and market saturation bit into the gold mine and prudent control of resources became the imperative.

In reality, the strategic aims and the financial position of a company or organization dictate the overall amount of money it has to invest in particular aspects of its operations, in marketing, in R&D, in manufacture, in department X or department Y. The budget-setting exercise is one which, in theory, is designed to allocate the resources in the optimum way for the company to achieve its overall objectives. This may not be the same as each individual department or unit achieving its own selfish objectives; the aggregate view is important.

In today's healthcare, much the same applies. Hospitals hold contracts to supply services to residents of a number of health districts. The mix of services provided has to match the income that can be derived from meeting the contracts. This is the baseline. Individual clinicians may well harbour different personal aspirations. They may have a particular specialization, a personal research agenda, a career development agenda, an acquired view of the way their profession should be conducted, a college role, a private practice. Any or all of these could provide a conflict with the base organizational and operational needs of their unit.

In this environment, it is not possible nor desirable to fund every individual unit's individual requests. There has to be some form of collective corporate view arrived at or ultimately imposed upon them and they have to be modified by negotiation. In this situation, a budget is fundamentally a control device to restrict, or sometimes to encourage, expenditure on a particular area or in a particular unit and to determine the balance between the competing parts of an overall organization. The budget-setting process should thus reflect the strategic ambitions of the whole organization and not the selfish interests of a few parts of it. Unfortunately, it all too often reflects the status quo and the present power bases or the power of the various lobby groups who have the ear of the directors or managers or who represent the more 'fashionable' specialities.

The way the budget is set and managed has a strong influence on organizational behaviour and 'game playing'. The ideal is to have everyone feeling they received a reasonable deal and that no one had exceptionally favourable treatment. From a manager's point of view, the key skill is to make sure that those who are responsible for the activities that constitute the budget feel a sense of ownership and responsibility for it and work to achieve good financial performance as part of a corporate body, the hospital or the general practice. As careers progress, doctors find themselves with budget-setting responsibilities within their own departments and have to act managerially.

USING BUDGETS

We are all using budgets in our daily lives. We set aside sums of money to pay the mortgage, to buy food, to buy clothes, to have holidays, etc. We set aside other sums for the future and against contingencies. Our income determines the amounts we can afford on each item and the standards we can afford to aspire to. We manage our money to get the best out of it, whatever our needs or our circumstances are. We make difficult choices about what we can and cannot have, what we can and cannot do.

I was brought up with a budget called pocket money which arrived every Saturday. I learned many lessons from it. I could spend it all on big items on Saturday morning or make it last all day. I graduated to smaller items and made it last all week; distributed pleasure. Then, having accepted the absolute finality of my allocated sum for many years, I started to sue for an increase to reflect my maturing needs. Next, I took to bargaining for exceptional items outside the pocket money system, a sort of extra pocket money or capital allocation which preserved my pocket money revenue. Then I learned to work with my sister and we pooled our funds to open up new vistas of purchasing power. Then I began to compare my budget with school friends' and felt acute injustice which was only satisfied by comparability arguments with my parents and a further increase. These were early 'shroud waving' experiences as I expertly conjured up images of the family's humiliation before my school chums if more funds were not allocated to me. Never a thought went to where the money would come from or what benefit the family would have to do without in order to satisfy me. I never really understood that it was a 'zero sum game' so that anything that I gained was lost by someone else.

Productivity deals followed as more money could only be extracted in return for the provision of domestic services. Item of service payments were calculated and soon became the vehicle for further increases in funds by arguing up the unit price as I considered my time to be increasingly valuable. This went well until the dreadful day of competition when my sister started providing domestic services at half my rate!

BUDGET TYPES

There are four basic types of budget or budget-setting process:

1. steady state;
2. lump sum;
3. activity based;
4. zero based.

All budgets are some hybrid of these four pure types.

Steady state implies very little change from last year. It assumes that there is no change in the strategic intent of the unit concerned and no change in external circumstances and merely uses last year's categories with suitable inflation adjustments. It is difficult to rebalance an organization using this type of budget setting, but it is used in postgraduate education and in many service planning situations. In recent years, the steady state approach has meant a steady erosion of funding, particularly in inner city areas of the NHS which are seeing funds transferred to outlying suburbs and rural areas as funding is gradually moving to a per capita basis. There are many difficulties in adjusting the crude allocations of healthcare spending to take account of different population needs, different degrees of deprivation with consequentially higher costs of treatment and local disease prevalence. These give rise to a sense of felt injustice.

Lump sum methods involve allocating a fixed sum of money to produce a given volume of output and leaving aside all the detail of how the money will be applied to produce the outputs. It can be motivational for the budget holders, but leaves the allocating manager with little control. The block service contracts that currently exist between health authorities and hospitals are similar to lump sum budgets with a slightly enhanced specificity. They require the hospital to provide all the services demanded by the local population for a fixed sum.

Activity-based budgeting, along with activity-based costing, is a rediscovered method that allows for some adjustments to the balance of an organization. The work of a unit is broken down into its component activities. It has then to be decided how much the organization values these activities and how much to allocate to them. This contrasts with the steady state method that does not challenge any of the current activities. The American system of item of service payments is an activity-based one. The value for each unit of activity is only calculated once it is known how many units have been performed in total.

Zero-based budgeting is the ultimate method for adjusting an organization. It involves forgetting current activities and cherished modes of working and looking very hard at the structure the organization needs to achieve its purposes. Budgets are then allocated on the basis of what the organization needs for the next and future years rather than on what it is or what it does. You can appreciate the effort and trauma involved and easily understand that this mode should be used sparingly. The functions analysis groups that were part of the early 1994 NHS reforms were given what amounted to zero-based briefs. The 1993 Tomlinson Report did not respect the role and function of the prestigious hospitals that had accumulated in the capital.

OTHER SOURCES

The primary budget-setting process can be distorted or even undermined by other sources of finance outside the budget mechanism. There are considerable debates over other sources of funding that are available to hospitals or particular units within them. These funds come from a number of sources, some of which are more properly accounted for than others. When these funds are outside the normal budget allocation process and are used to modify the intentions of the budget, they can potentially lead to a loosening of managerial control and accountability.

Such sources as charitable bequests and donations provide steady income streams and pools of investment capital for development projects. Monies that come from charitable sources to support research staff get partially included with service funding because it is very difficult to make a clean separation between service activities that support research but which incidentally treat patients and patient treatments that have value to research projects. Pharmaceutical companies make payments to clinicians for the conduct of drug trials or the recruitment of patients to such trials. Recruiting a patient to a trial takes longer than treating them normally and so some of this payment should compensate the unit for the extra time needed to treat its quota of patients. Consultants sometimes receive advisory contracts from equipment companies or pharmaceutical companies in return for their guidance. Some choose to put some of such income into their departments. There are other income-generating activities such as courses or conferences.

The picture is gradually blurring. There may be several sources of money outside the main contract incomes that could potentially distort the strategic intentions of the hospital or practice, particularly since such monies are controlled by individuals. Some would say that successful public appeals, whilst being helpful in supporting the NHS, add a potential distortion to the use of budgets as control devices. The Great Ormond Street Appeal effectively blocked the movement of the hospital to a new peripheral site. Many NHS auditors are concerned to ensure that such additional monies are properly accounted for.

There are thus difficulties in maintaining the strategic intent from the top of the organization whilst allowing a bottom-up approach to developing budgets and allowing local income generation to distort the patterns of service in favour of those who have more time or potential to secure additional funding.

BUDGET BASICS

It is axiomatic that a budget should both reasonably cover the costs of the expected activities and be achievable within the powers of the budget holder. A budget that is clearly ridiculous in either of these respects will detract from a sense of local ownership and will not be a source of motivation and challenge. A budget that is patently impossible to achieve can lead to loss of morale and disruptive behaviour. I have known hospitals facing cash squeezes who allocated budgets to operational departments that did not meet the costs of the staff salaries. If staff reductions are being hinted at, they should be negotiated with more candour and honesty and their consequences should be discussed with all those currently depending on the service being trimmed.

One problem with the cash-limited NHS is that there is a tendency to spread the available resources as thinly as possible. 'Bread and scrape.' This preserves as much as possible but cuts out the possibility of investing resources to save money through improved working methods or techniques. It takes money to save money.

A recent management invention in healthcare has been topslicing. This is a wonderful device that allows top management project and budget needs to be funded in full, without recourse to unseemly debate, justification or accountability to those who have given up resources. The remainder is then divided among the worthy causes such as patient treatment. The tide is turning against topslicing just when the middle layers of organizations are deciding that if it is all right for the top, it is all right for us. Accountability is the current thrust.

MARKET SYSTEMS

Within market systems, the competing organizations have to plan their actions against uncertain incomes. If their goods or services do not attract buyers, their sales income falls and they have to trim their operations to stay within the limits of their financing arrangements. Organizations can go on losing money for years providing their lenders are happy or have no way out. In commerce a company that is trading, albeit not too efficiently, is better for the lenders than a company that has to be broken up and disposed of.

With the advent of some of the aspects of the market system to the NHS, similar considerations are starting to apply. The market system, the balancing of supply and demand through the mechanism of price, is currently distorted by regional health authority funding mechanisms and their willingness to support particular institutions. The likelihood is that the market mechanism will develop and will play an increasing part in rationalizing service patterns. Once unleashed, market forces take on a life of their own and do not allow for the adjustments and fudges needed to ensure we get the NHS we all want.

The budget process will force organizations to look at income and match planned expenditure to that income. The consequences of avoiding this discipline will be decline and more or less rapid closure. There are tendencies in the commercial world for people to be unduly optimistic about the income they will attract and unduly conservative in estimating how much it will cost them to operate the organization to capture those incomes. The estimates of both income and expenditure must be as accurate as possible.

Historically, hospitals have only been concerned with distributing money to spend on services, but now the discipline of matching planned costs to expected contract income is becoming the necessary discipline. It is also becoming a more uncertain process as a greater purchasing power is vested in fundholding general practitioners.

ORGANIZATIONAL FORMS

Let us assume that all is well managed and the budgets are set in a way that retains realism and allows the components of the organization to feel able to achieve their part in the overall plan.

Within most organizations, there are parts which 'trade' in that they handle customers and generate payments and others which provide services to these departments. In hospitals the medical and surgical specialities are predominantly trading whilst the support departments, such as radiology, pathology, anaesthetics, for example, are effectively part of the cost of the trading departments, although they also sell some services directly outside the hospital. The trading departments are termed profit centres because they have to manage both income and costs and the support departments are cost centres because their task is to minimize the cost of their services within an acceptable quality. So radiology, for example, would pass on all its costs to users through its charges for services.

The NHS reforms have added a large degree of complexity to the process of securing an income for a hospital. Depending upon location and specialization, hospitals could receive income from one main district health authority or commission, several others in the surrounding districts, remote health authorities and health commissions and fundholding general practitioners. Each budget has to be negotiated on an annual basis and delays in settling them can lead to a 'planning blight' for the hospital, unable to commit itself to a particular level of service. There are fudge factors called ECRs or extracontractual referrals to deal with rare cases that need specific treatments.

However the money arrives, the components of the budget are likely to be:

Income

- Expected income by contracts, sales, grants, topslicing, etc.

Expenditure

- Expected staff costs, possibly by grade.
- Expected expenditure on materials such as dressings and pharmaceuticals.
- Expected expenditure on catering, laundry and cleaning, etc.
- Expected expenditure on fixed items such as buildings, heating, estates, etc.
- Planned investments, capital needs.

Each of these categories is likely to be broken down further and to contain explicit details. There has to be a balance between the precision required and the uncertainty involved. This is particularly the case with staff in times of high turnover. It is quite normal to put in the salary applicable to the midpoint in a grade rather than use actual salaries. Salary bills are aggregated and considered on a total hospital basis.

The budget may also have information on the phasing of all these items, that is, the precise timing of the expenditure. The importance of this is for the management of cash. The income comes monthly or upon sending an invoice and yet the salaries have to be paid regularly. It is not possible for all departments to spend large parts of their budgets at the same time because the hospital would run out of cash and would have to incur overdraft or other emergency financing costs.

Some of the costs of an organization are met by spreading them across the income-generating activities or as a levy on staff. These costs are called overheads. They are the costs of the hospital being there and being supported ready for the trading departments to be available for treating patients. The heating, lighting and estate costs, the management and personnel costs, the canteen and other hotel services costs are examples of overheads. These things must be paid for out of the income generated by trading activity or by treating patients under contracts. The pricing mechanism deals with this. It is more fully discussed in Chapter 24.

BUDGET MYTHOLOGY

There are many myths and beliefs that surround budgets which need to be aired and dispelled.

Budgets are not fixed and rigid. They can, and should, be reviewed. They are more like continuous assessment than final examinations. When a budget is set, it represents the best guess of future events and allocates resources within organizational strategies and constraints. Things do not always turn out as we expect and the prevailing views within organizations change. Budgets are frequently reviewed midyear to reflect altered circumstances.

We have already described the multiple contract nightmare that many hospitals have to live with. Loss of a contract, alteration of a contract, the late acquisition of a contract, extra funding for waiting list initiatives can all distort the initial picture. Under these circumstances, adjustment is necessary and budget holders have to expect a degree of flexibility.

Provided budgets are adjusted up as well as down, there are no lasting consequences and no implied criticism, there may well be an outbreak of understanding. If, however, there is a general tendency for the removal of funds from budgets, there may be game playing induced to hide money and protect interests. Such games include spending the money early in the year so that it cannot be taken away, making deliberate errors of coding so as to use someone else's budget or to clog up the accounts department, disputing the budget figures and being able to prove them wrong, forgetting to enter large expenditure items or failing to reveal income items.

The more it is possible to involve those responsible for working to a budget in the process of setting the budget and the more they can be kept informed of their financial performance and the overall financial performance of the trust or hospital, the fewer the games played and the better the financial control.

In my view, there should be a formal acceptance process for a budget, whereby the budget holder signs to agree that the budget is reasonable and achievable within known assumptions. This process helps to push the ownership of the budget and the responsibility for its proper management to the right level. It should also be possible not to sign a budget that is thought unreasonable. There are other issues with devolving budgets to small operating units and these concern potential losses of economies of scale and potential duplication of effort.

BUDGET MONITORING

Having anchored budgets in the planning camp and demonstrated some of the complexity in setting budgets, our next need is to monitor what is actually happening. The year has started, money is flowing in and out as patients come and go. Resources are being consumed. The accountant's job is to take all the purchase requisitions or orders and log them against the correct budget heading. The hours worked by each member of staff within a department or budget grouping are also added in. You will start to think of the old maxim in computing: 'Garbage in – garbage out'.

We could also add that information that is late or inaccurate contributes to the lateness and inaccuracy of the management accounts and reduces the effectiveness of monitoring: 'Late in – mortal sin'.

The accountants need to log each patient and to determine from whom their cost of treatment is recoverable, if anyone. Costs and patients treated will be attributed to individual departments by the coding system.

There are some genuine difficulties and some cultural difficulties to overcome. The genuine ones arise because of pricing policies. Suppose you order some dressings. You will probably fill in a purchase request, maybe an electronic one, which will be processed somewhere within the hospital, hopefully as close to your point of work as possible, or even outside. Your order may be put together with others and may be sent to a central supplies office or direct to a supplier. It is not until the invoice from the supplier is actually settled that you know precisely how much the goods cost. A notional sum of money may have been taken out of your budget, which may or may not bear any relation to what the final charge was. This may or may not be adjusted when the precise sums are known. You may have forgotten the dressings by the time the reconciliation takes place. This makes it difficult to keep precise control.

Most budget systems are now computer based. Every category of income and expenditure will have an identifying code number. One university I work with has a 16-digit code, explicit enough not only to identify the person placing the order and the purpose it met but the state of the weather at the time of ordering! The code directs the income or expenditure to the correct store within the accounting system. All expenditures of a related nature are grouped together. When information is printed for control purposes, each code's totals and transactions will appear on a separate line of the printout. These are called budget lines. The last line contains the summary of all the lines and is called the bottom line, the one that really matters. There may be a line for full-time staff, a line for part-time staff and another for agency staff. The difficulty is the trade-off between the number of lines required for management information and control and the problems of inaccurate coding which increase with the complexity of the system. Within coding circles, an error rate of 5–7% is considered normal. Adopting fewer codes will tend to smooth out the errors and the useful information, too! Opting for a greater number of codes will produce more detailed information but will produce an increase in the uncertainty and instability within each line of the printout.

The cultural differences are those between accountants and budget holders. Accountants are bound by strong professional standards. They have to operate consistently which means operating to the rules at all times. They adopt the maxim of prudence. This means that expenditure is considered to have taken place as soon as you place an order whereas income is only credited when the cheque is in the bank.

Accountants also seek order whereas clinicians live with variability. Accountants take the annual budget allocation and divide it into 12 equal monthly portions. They sometimes allow for the variability in months, but not always. The problem is that activity levels are not constant. Some specialities have a winter peak of activity or other variations as disease patterns alter with the seasons. This is important in the application of control systems, as we shall see later.

We are all familiar with basic budget monitoring systems in the form of bank statements and credit card accounts. These record the transactions and the costs of each. They have money flowing in and money flowing out. Computer printouts of hospital budgets are achieving the same purpose with slightly more complexity and detail, but with the fundamental simplicity of a bank statement.

The ideal monitoring system is one that is easy to operate and causes very little extra work to be done. We live in a far from ideal world. In looking at the financial performance of a department, the clinical director, the lead clinician, manager or project leader has to decide when the financial information is indicating the start of something nasty or when it is 'a mere blip', as Nigel Lawson discovered to his personal political costs. There are, however, time, material and human costs involved in finding out. It is much better to save the detailed investigations for the things that really matter rather than struggling for precision in an area of inherent uncertainty.

Monitoring techniques

The most widely applied monitoring technique is variance analysis. Variance in accounting speak means difference; the difference between what actually happened and what was planned to happen. Variance has a sign and a sign convention. Since income and expenditure have signs too, opposite signs, you can predict the gross lack of standardization. You have no choice but to work out your local convention or, better still, to ask your accountant. A positive variance is usually taken as a good thing. Positive variance arises if the actual contract income is more than planned or if the expenditure on staff, materials or any other outgoing was less than planned. An annual budget allocation under any heading is divided into 12 equal parts and the actual expenditure is compared with the planned on a monthly basis and sometimes cumulatively.

We all know from experience how easy it is for things to slip off plan. We often underestimate the labour needed for our activities, we often get the timing of purchases wrong, we underestimate the materials needed. We can be knocked off course by the unexpected or the need to treat rare conditions with moderately costly drugs. The division into 12 parts and the failure to build in seasonality or other variability means that we will always be off plan until the end of the year.

Some use a percentage variance above or below planned expenditure to trigger an investigation, others use monetary values only. The latter method avoids spending time tracking large percentages of small totals. On some critical expenditure categories, very tight variance bands may need to be specified. There is usually a good explanation for the variance, such as a delay in recruitment or earlier than planned purchasing or delay in contract negotiations which means it will go away in future months. There are, however, those trends such as increased overtime or agency staff expenditures which imply structural problems and may need managerial intervention.

ILLUSTRATION

We can best illustrate some of the other principles of budget management by using the monthly printout from the urinary dynamics department of St Kidding's NHS trust (Fig. 22.1). In the modern world, informa-

St Kidding's NHS Trust

Department: Urinary Dynamics   Period: 6   Date: 1996

£'000		plan	This month actual	variance	Month-1 variance	Month-2 variance	Cumulative plan	actual	variance	
1	INCOME									
2	Bulk contract	100	100	–	–	–	600	600	–	
3	Secondary contracts	10	20 (E)	10	(10)	(10)	60	20 (F)	(40) (D)
4	GP fundholders	20	10	(10) (H)	– (I)	– (J)	120	110	(10) (G)
5	Subtotal	130	130	–	(10)	(10)	780	730	(50) (C)
6	EXPENDITURE									
7	Medical staff	50	70	(20)	(20)	(20)	300	370	(70) (K)
8	Nursing staff	30	35	(5) (M)	(10)	(10)	180	220	(40) (L)
9	Auxilliaries	10	10	–	(1)	1	60	60	–
10	Consumables	10	10	–	(5)	(5)	60	80	(20) (N)
11	Therapeutic agents	15	15	–	(6)	(4)	90	110	(20) (O)
12	Subtotal	115	140	(25)			690	840	(150)
13	OVERHEADS									
14	Department	5	6	(1)	(2)	(4)	30	40	(10) (P)
15	Central	10	9	1	2	(4)	60	60	–
16	Total	130	155	(25)	(52)	(56)	780	940	(160) (B)
17	Profit & Loss.		(25)						(210) (A)

Fig. 22.1

tion is power and so some small adjustments have been made to the figures to preserve the trust's competitive edge. Please do not try to compare the figures with any real examples.

The key skill in budget management terms is to sort out minor and expected variations from structural and problematic changes. You only have limited time and energy to spend so you have to learn to home in on the important numbers first. It is not possible nor worthwhile to investigate every little variation from plan. Peaceful is the budget holder who has found an explanation for the biggest variances.

The first crucial test is face validity – do the numbers look about right, were they what I was expecting? If not, are there errors in the figures or just things I was unaware of? If satisfied, we move on to look in more detail.

Headings

The budgetary information is normally presented in the form of a matrix or grid. The rows or horizontal lines represent different categories of income or expenditure and the columns or vertical lines represent times or cumulative time periods. There will usually be some form of heading and other department identifiers to ensure the budget is really yours.

In our example, the heading tells us the department and the period. In this case 6/12 of the year, half way. Line 1 is just a heading. Taking line 2, block contract income, as an example, we can illustrate how to read across the grid. Under the heading 'this month', we find the planned income for month 6, the actual income and the difference or variance. The next two columns show the variance in the previous month and the one before that. These are useful in determining the magnitude and direction of any trend in the figures. Under the general heading 'cumulative' are shown the planned and actual incomes for the year to date. That is the sum of the first 6 months. The variance is also shown. Each line in the budget statement produces an exactly similar set of data for its relevant category of expenditure or income. The bottom line is a summation of the data.

The bottom line

The trained eye goes first to the bottom right-hand corner, the right-hand side of line 17, and looks at the profit and loss figure, in this case, item A (210). This means we are apparently £210 000 worse off than the plan suggested. Accountants have the habit of putting negative numbers in brackets, although some use a minus sign. In order to understand the large variance, we need to work with the cumulative variance column.

We notice our expenditure variance of (160), item B, and an income variance of (50), item C. These indicate that our overall shortfall of £210 000 was made up of a £50 000 lower than expected income, item C, and a £160 000 greater than expected expenditure, item B. We have adopted the convention of showing positive variances as beneficial and negative ones as harmful to the good of the unit, so that a surplus of actual income over planned income would be a positive variance, whereas a surplus of actual expenditure over planned expenditure would be a negative variance. Conventions vary, however, and it pays to ask your management accountant about those in use locally.

Income

We need now to delve more deeply into the variances in income and expenditure in order to understand and explain them. Being an optimist I like to look at income first and try to think of ways to increase it. Because of a shortage of time and effort to review figures, the rule in budget monitoring is big numbers first; big variances. This means both positive and negative variances because they both need to be understood.

Income is shown on lines 2, 3 and 4 of the budget statement. Our eyes go first to item D on line 3, which tells us that our secondary contracts are £40 000 below budget for the first 6 months. Working back along line 3, we further notice that all the income from this source arrived this month, items E and F. An explanation might be a delay in securing the firm agreement on these contracts. This would mean that the problem would soon correct itself and needs no urgent action.

Line 4, item G, shows a total variance of £10 000 in GP fundholder income and item H shows an identical variance this month. Could we have alienated the local fundholders and driven them elsewhere? Up till now the income has been steady, items I and J, so this needs investigation.

Expenditure

Expenditure information appears on lines 7–16 of the statement. We are seeking to understand the cumulative variance of (160), item B. Using the rule of biggest numbers first and working first on cumulative variances, our eyes alight on line 7, item K, and we note overspending on medical staff of £70 000. Looking along line 7 we see this has been a steady pattern for the past 3 months. Is it a problem?

If we are running at higher than average activity levels with distorted case mix, this may be a temporary imbalance between planned and actual expenditure. If, on the other hand, we have just filled a consultant vacancy with a dynamic person who escaped from a London teaching hospital, the salary problem may be permanent, at least until merit awards are done away with.

Line 8, item L, shows the nursing expenditure to be up by £40 000. Evidence of higher activity? This month's figure of £5000, item M, was lower than last month and the one before which both registered £10 000 overspends. So, if it is increased activity causing the variance, then the activity is slowing down.

Line 10, item N, and line 11, item O, both show more than planned expenditure on consumables and therapeutic agents which seem to confirm increased activity. Looking along each line, we note that the variance for this month is zero in each case whereas it was between £4000 and £6000 for the past 2 months. It is possible to speculate that the increased activity levels in past months may now have subsided. The budget holder needs to exercise judgement to determine whether the activity levels will fall below average and thus correct the cumulative expenditures or whether this is a sign to take more drastic action, such as restricting access to patients from certain health districts or cancelling clinics.

We may have convinced ourselves that overspending is due to increased activity, but this does not fully explain the medical staff costs. We may have a merit award problem too, or high locum costs. We need more detail to resolve the matter so we look at the components that were aggregated to form the totals on each budget line. We need the help of our accountants to do this effectively.

The last of the numbers that should trouble us is line 14, item P, and the overspend of £10 000 on departmental overheads. These should be under our control and we should find an explanation. It could be due to increased activity levels and unplanned overtime and temporary staff costs, but you should be able to find out and rectify the cause.

BUDGET CONTROL

Having spotted the anomaly or trend, what do you do next? There are several levels of budget control available to the budget holder. In demand-driven healthcare situations some of these may not be available or may be more difficult to operate.

Organizational level

Self-control

It is our contention that if budgets are devolved to the lowest possible level and owned at that level, then the staff will act responsibly and do their best to keep within their budgets. If the budget is 'theirs' and 'they got it wrong', the motivation of individuals to prove the point may be stronger than that to stay within their budget.

Other organizational methods are to designate departments as cost or profit centres. The former only worry about reducing expenditure, the latter have to balance income and expenditure. In industry, particularly in risky markets, parts of a company are designated as separate legal entities. So if the R&D department goes bust, the rest of the company is not affected. We have not reached the stage of St Elsewhere's Surgery plc, but the concept has merit in instilling into staff that exceeding your expenditure targets and/or falling short of your income target has real consequences and is not just a futile management game, leaving aside the argument as to whether it is appropriate to divide treatment of patients into separate little boxes in the first place.

General level

One control technique that is widely practised is management by exception. This means that you concentrate on the major problem areas to the exclusion of all others. This is a reasonable means of allocating scarce time. It may, however, have behavioural consequences. The budget holder's time is spent with those who have overspent most so there may be a danger of rewarding the less competent and failing to praise those who were within budget.

There are a number of control options which operate immediately to cut costs. Boosting income is altogether a much trickier art. The first option is gradually to restrict expenditure in certain categories, such as travel or consumable items or training courses. In other words you put up hurdles so that only the motivated can be bothered to jump them.

The next level of severity involves banning expenditure in certain categories. More drastic action may be needed, such as curtailing particular activities. An example might be a ban on recruitment. Another approach to overspending may be to shift resources from underspending areas. The challenge here is to avoid rewarding incompetence or there will be tough times ahead. Mergers between projects or departments may achieve economies of scale, a euphemism for getting rid of staff, or there may be other structural solutions needed. Cash-hungry universities and some hospitals are very fond of restricting telephone calls to local only.

The third level is known as 'slam shut', a term familiar to engineers and North Americans. This means drastic action.

The healthcare equivalent is the closure of a ward or the suspension of cold surgery. These moves do not avoid the fixed costs of equipping and staffing the hospital, but they do save on consumables, therapeutic agents and agency staff. Since most budgets are between 70% and 80% staffing costs, the only meaningful way to cut into costs is to find ways to reduce staff levels or to reduce core staff levels and to use others flexibly to meet demands. This so often requires extra resources to invest in new equipment or to train staff for new procedures and, all too often, such resources are not available.

FURTHER READING

Almost any textbook on management accounting will provide comprehensive coverage of this topic. My personal choices are:

Ellwood S 1993 Cost methods of NHS health care contracts. Chartered Institute of Management Accountants, London

Flynn R 1992 Structures of control in health management. Routledge, London

Hadley R, Forster D 1993 Doctors as managers. Longman Scientific, Harlow

Horngren C T Introduction to management accounting 7th edn. Prentice-Hall International, New Jersey

Scott J, Rochester A 1990 Effective management skills: managing money. Sphere/British Institute of Management, London

Secret M 1994 Mastering spreadsheets, budgets and forecasts. Pitman, London

Sizer J 1989 An insight into management accounting. Penguin, London

Tomlinson Report 1993 Hospital Doctors: Training for the Future. Department of Health, London

23

Business planning

Martin Anderson

INTRODUCTION

It is now a mandatory requirement for all NHS trusts to provide what is called a 'strategic direction' document at least every 3 years and a business plan every year. As a result, clinical directors and managers are increasingly being asked to provide business plans for their own directorate or department and there is a need for greater understanding of business planning.

Business planning is a relatively new concept within the health service and even experienced managers are still feeling their way, so that the quality of guidance given to clinicians and the way the process is managed is not always all it might be. To make matters more difficult, there is no standard list of subjects that must be dealt with in business planning and the contents of plans will vary from one organization to another. You therefore need to understand the purpose of business planning so that you can decide for yourself what is or is not included.

However, to try and make the chapter as specific as possible, where examples have been quoted these tend to be based on planning within a directorate of an acute hospital unit and, as the majority of secondary healthcare providers are now trusts, the chapter focuses on trust requirements, although it makes little difference whether a unit is managed by a directly managed unit (DMU) or has independent trust status; the disciplines of business planning are the same.

The first section sets out what the planning requirements are for trusts so that clinicians can identify where individual directorate plans fit in the overall scheme. The second section looks at what a business plan is and what the benefits of producing one are. The third section sets out the process of preparing a plan and the final section suggests typical contents of a business plan for a directorate of an acute hospital.

PLANNING REQUIREMENTS FOR TRUSTS

The strategic direction

The strategic direction is a document that all trusts must produce at the time the trust is formed and at least once in every 3 years thereafter. It is intended to look forward 5 years and identify the likely strategic shifts and developments in service delivery and establish broad objectives. Typically, formulating a strategic direction for any healthcare organization will involve an evaluation of:

- advances in medical and surgical practice;
- public awareness and expectations;
- demographic changes;
- the economic outlook;
- the local healthcare market and other related markets;
- national priorities including *Health of the Nation*, *Caring for People*, Patient's Charter and value for money;
- local regional DHA and GP fundholder priorities and future purchasing power;
- community health councils;
- other pressure groups.

In the light of this evaluation and taking into consideration existing strengths and weaknesses, trusts are expected to identify their broad objectives of scope, size and style of service. To aid the achievement of these objectives, supporting strategies need to be set out for:

- quality improvement;
- human resources;
- research and development;
- information;

- continued financial viability and improvements in value for money;
- estate usage and capital investment.

The resulting document is expected to be predominantly descriptive and concise. Circumstances change, of course, and any trust can review and change its strategic direction if it becomes necessary. It may, for example, submit amended proposals after a review of strategy resulting from the appointment of a new chairman or chief executive.

The trust business plan

The overall trust business plan is intended to be a natural extension of the strategic direction and to convert the broad objectives into specific terms. In contrast to the descriptive nature of the strategic direction, the business plan is intended to be a detailed document covering the forthcoming 3 years. In practice, nearly all trusts have found it extremely difficult to plan in the required detail for anything more than 1 year, reflecting the lack of experience and a degree of misunderstanding as to the purpose of the process. Trusts are expected to submit a draft skeleton business plan to the NHSME by 31 October each year, setting out the likely proposals contained in the full plan. The skeleton is intended to be no more than three or four pages long with drafts of the full plan being submitted by the end of January. All trusts are expected to publish a summary of the final plan and make it available to the district health authority, health commission, community health councils, GPs and members of the public.

The directorate plan

A centralized plan that does not involve and obtain ownership from the individual directorates responsible for fulfilling contracts has only limited merit and increasingly individual directorates and departments are contributing to the planning process. Typically instructions are being issued to clinical directors in September, obtaining directorate plans by mid-October to form the basis of the trust's skeleton plan.

THE BUSINESS PLAN
What is a business plan?

A business plan is a report that sets out in detail what an organization is trying to achieve and how it proposes to do it. That organization might be a company, a hospital, a charity, a department or even an individual. It normally covers a period of between 3 and 5 years. As is pointed out by West (1988):

. . . It is not a form of clairvoyance which will predict what will happen to the (organization) in the future. In fact it is quite the opposite: it is an instrument of the present developed through trial and error and using the (organization's) experience and achievement in the past to plot the way forward realistically. The plan will aim to achieve the most advantageous and workable compromise between what an (organization) wants to do and what it can do. It will show how its proposed policies are integrated and how one issue affects another.

The size of a plan can vary enormously and there is no predefined norm. Anything less than 10 pages would suggest that insufficient care has gone into the preparation whereas a plan in excess of 50 pages tends to lose its impact.

What is the purpose of a business plan?

The purpose of a business plan is to make an organization identify its key objectives and show how these will be delivered in the next and, in the case of the NHS, the following 2 years.

In particular, the plan is likely to indicate:

- anticipated levels of contracted and ECR activity;
- the financial consequences of service development;
- any service changes or developments and how these relate to national and local priorities;
- quality standards to be achieved;
- estate development and maintenance proposals;
- information systems development;
- research and development activity;
- income and expenditure patterns, identifying cost pressures and cost improvements;
- risk analysis and contingency plans.

In support of their plans, organizations should submit a set of financial returns in proformas containing:

- actual income and cost figures for the previous year;
- forecast figures for the expected outcome of the current year;
- budget figures for the first year of the plan;
- planning figures for the following 2 years.

Taken together, the text and proformas should:

- demonstrate that the trust has planned to meet its financial obligations of breaking even, earning the target return on assets and remaining within its EFL as well as providing value for money;
- demonstrate that the trust's plans are based on realistic planning assumptions about, for example, purchasers' intentions, inflation and efficiency gains;
- provide a detailed forecast of the trust's activity.

Why is it called a business plan?

It is called a business plan purely because its origins have tended to be in business where there is even greater emphasis on the financial aspects and where plans were originally used mainly for bank lending and recruiting investors. NHS plans are also frequently used as part of the process of competing for funding and in this respect hospitals, community care providers and even GP practices are really no different. One of the main differences that does, however, exist between the private sector and the NHS is that the latter uses business planning as an essential part of accountability in the use of public money, which in turn leads to a much greater openness.

Who should prepare the plan?

It is neither desirable nor practical that a clinical director should sit down in isolation and prepare a business plan. It is up to each individual to determine how they organize themselves and their staff to do it and some of the benefit will be lost if the problem is not approached as a team effort. Equally, an opportunity will be wasted if the preparation is merely delegated to management and neither medical or nursing staff are involved. In the final analysis, however, the plan must belong to the directorate as a whole although the clinical director takes ultimate responsibility.

What are the benefits of business planning?

Effective management always requires some degree of planning. The larger the organization the greater the need to delegate and to plan and make the best of limited resources. The annual planning process should be taken as the opportunity to stand back from everyday activities and concentrate on exactly what the organization is trying to achieve and how best to do it. It also provides the ideal chance to consider the longer term and what effect changes in purchasers' priorities, clinical practices and GP fundholders will have on the directorate. Similarly, one can also agree how the unit might react to variations in the assumed prognosis, how weaknesses will be rectified and strengths made the most of. Whilst few would argue with this philosophy and most claim that they already do plan or that the information is already available in some shape or form, the need to produce a plan as a written document does not always meet with such universal agreement or enthusiasm! The preparation of a written document does, however, fulfil a number of very important purposes:

- It forces a degree of focus, objectivity and attention to detail that would otherwise not exist.
- It provides the opportunity to involve clinical, nursing and management staff in the development of their directorate.
- It provides an effective means of communication to other departments endeavouring to provide effective support.
- It provides an effective and clear means of communication to the board. Equally, it provides the board with the confidence to delegate authority knowing that the directorate's plan is at one with the overall strategy.
- It provides the groundwork for business cases, development bids and capital applications and gives credence to a clearly thought out and consistent strategy.

MANAGING THE PROCESS

Business plans are rarely about individuals. They are normally about organizations with a lot more than one person involved and the merit of a single individual preparing and writing a plan in isolation is doubtful. It is therefore important to establish a team from the outset. There is no need to be too prescriptive as to who should or should not fulfil what role but the important thing to remember is that when a clinician is responsible for a hospital directorate or GP practice, the plan must be theirs and not that of a delegated planner. Many clinical directors do not have sufficient time allocated to management to spend it painstakingly going through the discipline themselves and may well need a general or business manager's support. Many clinicians find the financial aspects of planning particularly difficult and often coopt an accountant on to the team. However, to get as much ownership as possible, we recommend that the planning team tries to do its own calculations on the 'back of an envelope' initially itself and get the accountant to check the figures afterwards. This means that if and when the first year of the plan evolves into a budget, the authors will understand and identify with the figures.

Setting objectives

No business plan can sensibly be prepared without having a clearly defined set of objectives and these need to be agreed and understood from the outset. Objectives can, however, mean different things to different people and it is important to stress that this is not a discussion about mission statements or general aims. Objectives in this context should include explicit targets or goals that management and staff can say have or have not been achieved when performance is reviewed. Objectives can equally be problems that management already has to cope with or is likely to experience in due course.

Argenti (1968, 1993), for example, argues that an organization can have only one objective and that this will be a fundamental *raison d'être*. As often as not, it will be the same reason that the organization was formed in the first place. If the organization fails to meet that single objective, it fails to exist. He also argues that what we often think of as objectives are frequently in effect constraints. In healthcare, the objective is provide treatment for the sick, not to make income match expenditure or to produce a 6% return on assets – these are constraints! In the case of a department or directorate, the objectives should be agreed between the chief executive and the department head and in the case of an entire organization, typically by the board of directors or trustees, etc. However, they are frequently vague and descriptive and need to be put into a quantified form. If no objectives explicitly exist or you are planning for an organization for the first time, now is the time to get the objectives agreed.

To provide the necessary focus and limit the options, it is helpful to remember the acronym that objectives should be SMART, i.e. they should be Specific, Measurable, Attainable, Relevant and be given an appropriate Time scale over which to achieve them.

Specific

Always try and be specific in setting objectives. Don't forget, other people have to understand what you mean and an objective that merely states 'We want to improve the quality of service provided to patients' implies rather more hope than intention. If, for example, the department has a particular problem with cancelled outpatient clinics, a specific objective would state 'We aim to reduce the number of outpatient clinics cancelled from the current average of 10% to 5%'.

Measurable

It is not always easy to choose objectives that can be measured, but every effort should be made to do so or find proxies that could be used as relative indicators. If, for example, you set an athlete the objective of training for a 4-minute mile but had no stopwatch, measuring progress could be difficult!

Attainable

Objectives must be realistically attainable within the time scale of the plan. However, as part of the purpose of business planning is to evaluate alternatives within the restraints of such things as limited finance, it is possible that objectives set at the outset may have to be reassessed. In the example above, it might have been agreed that achieving 5% cancellations in the short term would be too expensive but that 7% could be achieved.

Relevant

Objectives must be relevant and seen to be relevant. This is perhaps a statement of the obvious but don't forget, you will be expected to explain and justify why the objectives have been set and why one objective is more important than another.

Time scale

Objectives should always have time scales attached to them. Does the outpatient clinic cancellation target of 7% have to be achieved in 12 months or 3 years? As implied, this could have a significant impact on finances if it had to be achieved in 12 months as opposed to 2 years.

There are two further points that should be stressed in setting objectives. Firstly, objectives frequently conflict with each other and should ideally be prioritized as this helps other members of the planning team to understand the problem. Secondly, don't set more objectives than can sensibly be managed. It is not possible to prescribe the precise number as some will be easier to achieve than others, but trying to do too many things at once merely makes the plan more difficult to implement.

Agree the period and timetable

The time period that the plan covers may have already been agreed but for those preparing a plan for their organization for the first time this may not be the case. You therefore need to decide whether the period will be typically 3 years, 5 years or 10 years. Whilst 10 years may seem a little extreme, if the plan involves a major investment in new buildings, a 10-year approach may be essential. The acid test is knowing what you are trying to achieve; is it to produce a detailed budget for the forthcoming year or a genuine longer term plan of campaign? It is one of the purposes of a business plan that it influences the budget-setting process which, given the relatively slow way that the NHS adapts to change, is unlikely to be so effective if only 1 year is looked at. Business plans must try and look beyond the short-term horizon and predict what will happen in the future and clearly demonstrate that managers know how they will react to it. It is worthwhile establishing responsibilities and a timetable from the start and don't forget, preparing a plan should be the main opportunity each year to 'see the woods for the trees'. It really is a good idea to get away from the normal work environment for a day to think the situation through before setting the wheels in motion.

Agree assumptions

One of the greatest frustrations of planning is always the lack of information and planners have to learn to come to terms with this. Indeed, if everything was known and certain, you would not need business plans. As examples, planning would be so much easier if one could predict with accuracy:

- how many patients will want treatment in the future;
- what each patient was going to be suffering from;
- how many would require surgery;
- how many could be treated as day cases and how many inpatients;
- how long each would require treatment for.

Added to this are all the uncertainties over resources. For example:

- How much capital will be made available for new equipment?
- Will there be enough skilled staff available?
- Will I be let down by other service providers?

It is possible to make reasonable informed guesses in many instances and there is usually a lot more information available than at first might be expected. It is necessary to gather as much information as you can within the time and resource available and accept that it will be necessary to make certain assumptions regarding the future. Some will inevitably be wrong but, rather like undertaking controlled research experiments, if you have put forward a hypothesis, it is much easier to quickly appreciate the implication of an incorrect assumption than if a hypothesis had never been made at all. All assumptions should be clearly set out in any final documentation. This will help not only to remind you what you had assumed when you come to review progress but also let other people know the basis of your thinking. Typical assumptions that doctors would normally have to make might include:

- the ratio of emergency to elective cases;
- the anticipated case mix;
- ratios of day case to inpatients;
- numbers of GP fundholders;
- purchasers' priorities;
- price tariffs.

Distinction should be drawn between assumptions over which you have some form of control as opposed to those over which you do not. A typical weakness of plans from inexperienced planners is the assumption that activity levels, for example, are almost completely outside their control. Whilst this may be so for emergency work in acute units, it is not the case in elective work, particularly in the longer term, and part of the purpose of planning is to actually control and influence activity.

Evaluating the alternatives

Having determined the assumptions it is essential to identify the different alternative courses of action, each of which will have its own associated problems relating to buildings, people, finance, etc. The question is, how far do you take it? It is often difficult to draw the line between what is a business plan and what is a strategic plan. In general, departmental business plans in the health service have, in the author's opinion, wrongly placed too great an emphasis on short-term plans prepared within a timetable that does not permit clinicians to influence their destiny. Plans are being formulated long after major purchasers have decided on their purchasing intentions and the so-called business plan is little more than a budget supported by narrative. Having said that, it would not be practical for a department or small organization to undertake a major strategic review each year and planners must form their own opinion as to how broadly to evaluate. A lot will depend on the degree of change going on around them. The written plan itself need not necessarily document all the alternatives that have been considered. However, it should reflect that thought has been given to the possible alternatives.

Preparing to write

Evaluating the alternatives should have provided over half of the benefit to be got from writing a business plan, i.e. the thinking through, the team building and finding the best course of action. It is now necessary to prepare the written document and share the findings with others. Before deciding exactly what the business plan should contain, it is important to consider for whose benefit the document is being prepared. This will dictate not only how much has to be written but also to some extent the style and explanation required. For example, a plan prepared purely for one's own staff would not need to spend much time describing the current facilities and recent history, the use of jargon might be acceptable and a short sharp document would suffice. A plan prepared for a board of directors or trustees, which

Number pages and provide an index

In the majority of cases, business plans are not prepared exclusively for use by the author and are reviewed by other people. Frequently the reviewers have a number of plans to get through and it is infuriating when pages, if not paragraphs, are not numbered.

Use a word processor

Plans frequently have to be rewritten several times over and this is extremely frustrating on a typewriter, not to mention time wasting. Similarly, plans frequently do not change dramatically from one year to the next and with a word processor there should be no need to start completely from scratch each year.

Use comparative data

Objectives should be expressed in specific or relative terms and it is often helpful to compare performance against other providers or departments. For example, 'Waiting times for a first outpatient appointment in orthopaedics is 6 weeks compared to an average of 5 weeks within the hospital as a whole. However, the nearest alternative provider has a waiting time of 8 weeks'.

Quantify statements

Quantify statements wherever possible. Only too often there is a tendency to use statements such as 'Waiting time for a first outpatient appointment has improved'. A more useful piece of information would have been 'Waiting time for a first outpatient appointment improved from an average of 8 weeks in December 1993 to 6 weeks in December 1994 but still falls short of the objective of 4 weeks'.

Use of best estimates

Use of best estimates in business planning is often both necessary and essential in the absence of better information. In fact, it is often much better to provide an estimate rather than provide no data at all or spend a disproportionate amount of time and effort obtaining the necessary information. The only important thing to remember is that if an estimate is used, then the narrative should clearly say so. A good example of where clinicians can use their best estimates is in case mix and workload analysis. Often the information on past case mix is poor and clinicians have to estimate future needs without the benefit of accurate historic data. The same is also true when it comes to estimating the amount of resources needed for each case type.

Use time scales

It is important to be clear in plans as to when action needs to be taken or when objectives are expected to be met. For example, 'We aim to reduce the waiting list for non-urgent waiting list operations from the current position of 24 months to 18 months by 31 March 1996 and 12 months by 31 March 1997. To achieve this objective, a new staff grade surgeon must be in post by 1 September 1994'.

Use tables, graphs and charts

Wherever possible, use tables, graphs and charts if information can be shown more effectively as a result. This is particularly relevant where data are shown over a number of years or where the relative movement of figures is more important than the absolute numbers themselves. Examples of this are shown later on.

Use appendices

Business plans should be concise and effective. Clogging up the main body of text with a lot of data is not recommended and good use should be made of appendices.

THE PLAN CONTENT

There is no one layout that can be recommended when writing a business plan and a lot will depend on the nature of the objectives that have been set. Not surprisingly, those matters that are important should be discussed at greater length. Typically, where individual directorates are required to produce plans as part of an overall process, a specific format will normally be requested because it makes plans easier to review. The NHSME guidance on business plans also specifies that data such as activity and finance should be shown for 5 years, i.e. the actual data for the preceding year, the expected outcome of the current year and the 3 years of the plan period. Set out below is a suggested content which includes 10 separate sections and is based on producing a plan for a directorate within a trust hospital. It totals no more than 16 pages excluding tables and appendices, the typical content of which is described below.

1. Executive summary

The executive summary should stipulate for whom the plan has been written, for what purpose and what time period is covered. It should set out the objectives and main problem areas that the plan addresses. For each objective or problem, it should state clearly what the position is now and what the organization intends to do at key milestones during the plan period, together with the expected outcomes. The summary should describe the main impact that the plans have with regard to such matters as human resources, quality, information, capital and revenue. Draft plans that are conditional on agreement to capital expenditure should indicate what matters need approval. The executive summary should also list the main assumptions that have been made, changes to which could substantially alter the proposed actions and plans.

2. Introduction

An introductory section may not always be necessary, particularly if the plan is being prepared for internal use and where readers are already quite familiar with the activities of the department or directorate. However, if it is for external use, it is important to use the introduction to set the scene. Typically it would include a summary of existing services provided, the staffing and management and the facilities available, etc. Planners should beware spending too much time and effort describing existing facilities. For beginners this is sometimes known as the 'comfort zone' because it is so much easier and certain to describe what is going on now rather than in the future. The introduction should at most be two sides of A4 and possibly only one.

3. Historical review

An historical review is useful where business plans are being prepared regularly each year. This section should set out briefly how an organization has performed against its previous plan over the previous 12 months, highlighting its successes and failures. Good planning tends to evolve rather than be an instant success and it is important that planners can demonstrate that they appreciate where incorrect assumptions were previously made and whether they could have been avoided. The section can also be used to register major events that have occurred over the last 12 months, for instance, investment in new equipment, introduction of a new service or the appointment of new staff. The historical review should at most be two sides of A4 and possibly only one.

4. Markets and activity

Understanding the market and fulfilling contractual obligations is fundamental to successful management, whether it be in the health service or the private sector. The separation of purchaser and provider was designed to move the NHS from a provider to a patient-driven service and in many cases this means a gradual adjustment to providing what buyers want to buy rather than what the sellers have to sell. The main purpose of this section is therefore to show that the organization understands its current contractual obligations, what its future obligations are likely to be and how it will influence them. This will involve showing an appreciation of:

- national and local purchasing priorities;
- the intentions of the purchasers themselves;
- the intentions of other service providers, DMUs, trusts or private;
- the strategic direction of the organization as a whole;
- changes in clinical practice, demography or any other matter which is expected to influence the level of activity or operation of the directorate.

It is also important to show how much emphasis or dependence is being placed on which purchasers, how much is based on existing contracts and how much is at risk. Similarly, that you have considered the alternatives that purchasers will have and what effect that could have on the organization.

Activity analysis by service and purchaser

This subsection should define who the purchasers are, both now and in the future. This involves, for example, showing which health authorities and/or GP fundholders now purchase from the directorate and which are likely to in the future.

Every attempt should be made to try and quantify the total buying capacity of each purchaser and what share the directorate might expect to get, estimating if needs be. You should also show the form of contract that already exists or may be used so that the reader can form an opinion as to the degree of risk. I suggest that most of this information is displayed in a tabular and/or graphical form, but the main 'bullet points' of data should still be included in the text. Assumptions and rationale should also be clearly expressed. In particular, you should explain why purchasers will be buying from you rather than your competitors, i.e. what is it that you offer that influences the purchasing decision, e.g. geographic convenience, reputation, specific facilities or procedures, price, waiting time? Some planners choose to approach this section after undertaking SWOT analysis, i.e. an appraisal of the organization's Strengths and

Weaknesses and how this in turn provides Opportunities and Threats.

What are the purchasers' alternatives?

It is important that you demonstrate that you understand the alternatives that purchasers have available to them, not just now but also in the future. Similarly, you need to know how they will react to your proposals. In this section, each directorate should set out a list of the units that provide a similar or competing service and it should attempt to quantify their relative size. It should also describe any known developments that these units are involved in.

Effect on support services

The directorate must consider what effect its own plans will have on other support services in the future, for example, pathology, pharmacy, anaesthetics, outpatients, theatres, radiology, hotel services and therapies, and show that it has discussed its proposals with them.

Marketing

Having made assumptions with regard to activity levels, the plan must state what efforts and disciplines will be set in place to market the directorate appropriately to purchasers. This will become increasingly important for clinical directors who will have to cope with the likely change in emphasis from a small number of large buyers to an increasing number of smaller buyers, such as GP fundholders.

5. Human resources

The purpose of this section is to explain how objectives that relate to staffing and management problems will be dealt with over the plan period and to show the knock-on effect that proposals in other areas may have on personnel. The sort of objectives are likely to cover such areas as management structure, skill mix, absenteeism, staff turnover and recruitment. The narrative should describe the problems as they are now and then set out what the objective will be for the future and over what time scale. It should then describe the proposed solution together with the ramifications. An example would be reducing junior hospital doctors' hours. What are their hours at the moment? What are the objective reductions over what time period? How is this going to be achieved? What are the financial and other ramifications? It is important to show that you have recognized the effect on human resources of other proposals. For example, increased activity levels may require additional recruitment to maintain the status quo or conversely, an existing problem may become worse. A good example would be the effect that increased activity might have on morale and staff turnover.

It is important to set out staffing plans in tabular form. This makes it much easier for others to appreciate at a glance the overall assumptions that have been made about staffing levels and also, where a plan is one of many, makes the consolidation of overall figures much easier. The table should also differentiate between the different staff grades so that again it is easier to gain an immediate understanding. Training should also be considered in this section where specific training objectives have been set. In general, though, training is likely to have already been touched upon as part of the means of attaining other personnel-related objectives.

6. Information and monitoring

The purpose of this section is to demonstrate how information systems will be used to monitor performance and help achieve objectives. Information systems in this instance relate to all forms including visual and oral and it would be wholly wrong to assume that all information systems have to revolve around computers. As part of the planning process, you should continually be considering the strengths and weaknesses of existing systems. Weaknesses should be supported by suggested remedial action plans and you should clearly state what objective is intended, how decision making will be improved and that the benefit of the information is worth the cost of collection. The narrative should summarize what data are required, how they will be collected and how often, how they will be analysed and how they will be stored. It is not necessary to describe at length how existing systems operate but where changes are proposed, or already being made, these should be discussed. Particular care should be taken to describe any likely changes that will result from changes in clinical practice, location of service and activity levels.

Quality

The purpose of this section is to set out planned procedures for achieving or maintaining quality objectives and showing that you clearly understand contractual obligations to purchasers and to patients through the Patient's Charter. Quality assurance is a process which provides for the systematic evaluation of all aspects of patient care. It includes clinical care, medical audit and all support and hotel services. The system will demonstrate improvements in quality by evaluating actual performance against agreed standards. Plans should set out the means by which it monitors all aspects of quality. Emphasis should be placed on specifying the outcomes being measured, the method of measurement, current performance levels, the targets set and the time scale for achievement.

Research

You should describe any research work being undertaken, explaining why it is relevant to the achievement of objectives. This should include reference to the purpose and benefits of the work, the parties involved, the time scale and the extent to which it is specifically funded. A similar outline should be provided for research being considered or that might be envisaged over the course of the plan period.

7. Finance

The purpose of this section is to quantify in financial terms the expected outcome of the plan and demonstrate that it satisfies overall financial objectives or constraints. More specifically, it is important to demonstrate an understanding of the importance of contracts that already exist, those that may be at risk and the financial effect of under- or overperforming against the larger ones. It is almost inconceivable that agreed objectives will not include some form of improvement in efficiency and most purchasers, in line with NHS directives, are looking for annual improvements of some 2%. Typically, this means either providing the same amount of activity for 2% less cost or an increase in activity for the same cost. For an acute provider it is generally expected that they will find these savings by, for example:

- improving bed occupancy;
- increasing the proportion of day surgery;
- moving some services into the primary care environment;
- improving the utilization of their assets.

Financial information can only realistically be shown in tabular form and the text should be used only to highlight major changes, many of which will have been touched upon already in other sections of the narrative. An explanation should then be given for significant changes in the assumed level of income and cost in the future years compared to the immediate past history and current budget. Further tables that support and clarify arguments are helpful. It is often useful to identify, by estimate if necessary, which particular cases account for the major proportion of expenditure, split between pay and non-pay costs. The purpose is to show an understanding of the impact that changes in case mix could have on costs. For example, a 10% increase in the activity related to hip replacement has a more significant effect on cost than a 10% increase in the surgical treatment of hernias.

Capital expenditure

One of the ways of satisfying the constant drive for efficiency is the use of new equipment and this section of a plan should be used to set out proposals. The major problem that most people experience with this is that they interpret it as a form of 'wish list' and are consequently frustrated and disappointed when they don't succeed in gaining the approval they want. Whilst capital expenditure that improves patient care is of course essential, this is a separate argument and one which must be put to the purchaser. What is being proposed here relates to what is 'cost effective' and this must be quantified in some form. Those with supporting detail and compelling arguments stand better chances than those without. You also need to show that you are aware of the financial significance of the major items of equipment used by your organization, particularly when replacement is due during the plan period and is likely to cost a significant amount of money. To help with this discipline, a list is prepared of the most expensive items of equipment and it would not be unusual to find that 80% of the value of all equipment is in fact accounted for by only 20% of the actual number of items.

8. Risks and sensitivity

It is fully appreciated that circumstances change and that what will ultimately happen in practice will not be exactly as planned. The planning process must therefore identify what assumptions and future events, if not as predicted, would have the most damaging effect on the organization's plans and how it would react to them. This is frequently referred to as risk and sensitivity analysis. Typically, this might include reference to one major purchaser who accounts for a particularly large proportion of income or changes in case mix which would have a significant impact on cost. Out of this process, it should become obvious that there are a few things which are absolutely fundamental to the success or failure of the organization and these are often known as the 'key success factors'. You should list them.

9. Action plan

The purpose of this final section is to provide a clear

picture of the main action points that the plan has highlighted. These are frequently referred to as 'milestones'. It is intended as a useful internal management document for the directorate itself as well as a simple way of communicating to the board. It should take the form of a table or list of actions or objectives. In the case of objectives that involve achieving a relative or specific level of performance, the measure should be stated together with the goal and the timetable for achievement. Where responsibility can be attributed to an individual or group then this should also be shown. The list should be restricted to the major objectives, all of which should have previously been discussed in other sections of the plan.

A clinician faced with preparing a business plan for the first time would be forgiven for feeling daunted by the prospect of completing all the tasks described above, especially if the amount of administrative support available is limited and the quality of existing data poor. However, the most important thing to remember is that business planning is essentially an internal process and should concentrate on only the most important objectives and management problems for your organization. You should not dogmatically consider and write endless pages against all the suggested headings above and if they are of little relevance they should be ignored. They will provide a useful checklist and act as a catalyst for thought.

A typical business plan layout

Section	Contents	Number of pages
1.	Executive summary	2
2.	Introduction	1
3.	Historical review	1
4.	Markets & activity	4
	Activity analysis by service & purchaser	
	What are purchasers' alternatives?	
	Effect on support services	
	Marketing	
5.	Human resources	2
6.	Information & monitoring	1
	Quality	
	Research	
7.	Finance	2
	Capital expenditure	
8.	Risks & sensitivity	2
9.	Action plan	1
	(Total pages	16)
10.	Appendices	

REFERENCES

Argenti J A 1968 Corporate planning: a practical guide. Allen & Unwin, London

Argenti J A 1993 Your organization. What is it for? McGraw-Hill, Maidenhead

West A 1988 A business plan. Pitman/National Westminster Bank, London

24

Marketing, marketing strategy and contracts

Rodney Gale

MARKETING

Of all the management paraphernalia that has come into healthcare in recent years, perhaps it is marketing that causes the most distress. Marketing is the essence of the market system and it has a large set of jargon terms. It is difficult at first to discern any real value or purpose in it. As professionals, doctors have never needed to indulge in overt or direct marketing. Professionals have always commanded a respect in society and have been assured of a steady stream of patients, mainly through rarity and licensing systems to control practice.

Marketing is a subject we feel we know about because of our cultural interest in amusing advertisements. Many people think of marketing as advertising, but it is much more. Marketing is also strongly associated with the marketing professional. The stereotype is a person with a rather unprofessional image, a persuader, a somewhat slick and insincere, lightweight intellectual who seems to command a large expense account and a big car and maintain a good lifestyle. An easy target for jealousy. We must not throw out the baby with the bathwater, just because of the negative image of some marketing practitioners. In fact, we should all learn a little about marketing so that we can harness the professional marketeers that bit more effectively.

Many people find the concept of market difficult to encompass. A street market has a series of stalls where honest traders set out their wares for all to see. Customers wander from stall to stall reviewing the goods on offer and deciding whether or not to buy them. Some stallholders will bargain, others have published prices. Stallholders adjust their prices, particularly of perishable goods, so that they clear their stalls just before going home time. Shopping late is a good strategy to catch the bargain. The market system balances supply of goods and demand for them through the price mechanism or more precisely, the value mechanism.

Markets for healthcare do not have a physical manifestation in one place but the processes take place at a number of distributed points. There are suppliers who set out their stalls in the form of a prospectus or offer to supply services. The customers only 'visit the stall' if they receive the prospectus. The bargaining takes place over a protracted period as the offer of services and the value of the contract are gradually brought into harmony or the customer looks at another stall. The bargain hunters are the purchasers, i.e. fundholding general practitioners and health commissioners with surplus cash who will often wait for the second half of the year before referring some patients in the hope that a trust will have lowered its prices in order to attract more work.

We must look at marketing more thoroughly and try to understand what it is and what it can do to help us survive in the emerging healthcare marketplace. We will use the example of service contracts to illustrate some of the issues and we will also go on to discuss strategy and competitive advantage.

WHAT IS MARKETING?

My early scientific indoctrination taught me to start from definitions. In marketing there is no one universally accepted definition. There are several different definitions, each of which conveys some of the aspect of marketing. I will use two.

Peter Drucker gives us: 'Marketing is the whole business seen from the point of view of its final result, that is, the customer's point of view'. The Institute of Marketing include in their definition: 'Marketing is the management process which identifies, anticipates and supplies customer requirements efficiently and profitably'.

The first point to make is that the customers are the final arbiters of the quality of the services you offer. It is their needs you must satisfy by supplying the services they want in the ways they want them. Although your perception of your organization's skills and competences will be important in projecting an image, it is the customer who will decide what to buy. It is a hard lesson to learn that the market may not have the same opinion of your unique skills as you do; it may not think your ways of organizing medicine are as good as you do. It is also very difficult in healthcare because treatment is given to patients but they are not the ultimate customers. The service is delivered to patients but is purchased by others. In principle, 'the money follows the patient' but there is still a large element of 'the patient follows the money'. In this latter case, the purchasers' needs play a large part. The standards of care that a doctor would wish to apply to an individual patient are potentially in conflict with the need to treat more patients at lower unit costs within a cash-hungry NHS.

The second issue is the responsibility for the whole enterprise that marketing assumes. This includes operational matters such as ensuring that you can actually perform the task that constitutes the service you offer efficiently and profitably. It is here that marketing and medical practice must meet. It also includes strategic tasks such as identifying which sector of the market you should approach and what type of image you wish to project through the mix of services offered and the style of service proposed. Marketing, in today's healthcare industry, is about deciding the types of customers, or purchasers or commissioners as they are variously titled, you should approach. It is also about deciding the range of services you wish to supply. To do this you need to review your skills from the standpoint of the purchaser. Marketing reaches into just about every aspect of the life and work of a hospital in today's NHS.

There is a circularity in the marketing problem in that you will not know what the market wants until you try and sell to it and you will not be able to see what the market wants unless the market knows what you are offering. Getting the balance right is an iterative process. In terms of attracting income to a trust through service contracts, it will need a number of discussions and modifications of the offer before agreement can be reached. It is relevant to say that such negotiations should always be supported by a clinician who is able to specify the level of service accurately and to understand the clinical consequences of the decisions taken. Contract negotiation is not to be handed over to professional marketing managers. This holds true for both purchasers and providers because of the complexity of the service being traded.

MARKETING THEORY

There are many ways to present aspects of marketing depending on the message to be conveyed. The standpoint of this chapter is to provide a broad introduction. Marketing, in common with other mystical religions, attracts and sustains gurus. In my jaundiced view these people have something to offer but usually neglect to describe the parts played by circumstances and sheer luck in achieving the success upon which their fame rests. So, reading their views can be illuminating but there is no substitute for getting down to basics. Marketing is an art form underpinned by a little theory and is therefore subject to an extreme range of views. One view is as below.

ALPHABETICAL MARKETING

Marketing wisdom can be summarized in the 3 Cs and 6 Ps. These stand for:

- Customers
- Competitors
- Channels
- Product
- Price
- Place
- Promotion
- People
- Process

These are not independent since a change in the product will affect price and possibly promotion. The overall choice made about each of the variables is known as the marketing mix.

We will examine each of these elements in more detail and try to add some thoughts relevant to the situation that many of you are in, wrestling with the world of purchasers and providers linked together through service contracts. The first group deal with external market conditions and the second group with internal decisions – the marketing mix. The 6 Ps are interconnected and interact one with another. A choice made about price, say, has implications for the product or service which must suit the price and the type of promotion needed and the type of people who will be able to deliver the required standard of service.

Customers

The fundamental questions are:

- Who are the potential customers for your service?
- Where are they?
- How do you get to them?
- What do they want from you?

It is not possible fully to answer these just yet, but there are some points to make. Most doctors spend their professional lives treating patients and could be forgiven for thinking that patients matter. Patients do not buy the service directly, they receive it. They are the means through which the service is provided for the purchaser and they may influence choices indirectly. Generally, the health commissioner is the customer or the fund-holding general practitioner because they have the power to spend resources on your services. Patients are referred to hospital by GPs or they refer themselves through casualty. If they are subsequently admitted and they are not local residents or covered by a contractual agreement, their health authority will be charged for their treatment.

How many districts could you reasonably approach in view of the fact that patients must travel to receive the services? What is the optimum mechanism for approaching them? what sort of services are they looking for? They may only have short-term work to reduce waiting lists or they may only be willing to purchase top-up services to complement their bulk contracts. There are costs in trawling for business: costs of preparing contracts, costs of negotiation and later, costs of administering several contracts each with a potentially different payment procedure.

Competitors

Assuming you know what it is you wish to sell and that this coincides with what a purchaser is seeking to buy, a very good place to start marketing analysis is with your competitors. What are you offering to the potential purchaser that is superior to the other trusts seeking to win the contract? Trusts must publish their service prices, but these do not reveal everything about the quality of the services on offer, nor the range of services.

It is probably not too difficult to predict who your competitors are, although you should watch out for rail links, motorways or air routes that might make far-flung competitors viable opposition. The car-owning democracy is also more willing to travel in order to receive quicker or specialized treatment. Informal medical networks and royal college contacts will probably tell you how good competitors are or what advantages they have. It is futile to take a headlong rush at a very strong competitor. It is better to try to take just a small piece of the market and to grow slowly from there, by offering something different that the customer wants.

If you are in a fortunate position of being a potentially monopolistic supplier because of some advantage of equipment or knowledge, then competitors are not your main concern, customers are.

Channels

Channels are more relevant to the marketing of consumer goods than to marketing of healthcare services because they are usually concerned with the ways the goods or services will get to the consumers. Channels might be relevant to a trust planning to franchise its cost-effective and efficient treatment patterns as, say, 'St Kidding's Medical'. Channels can be looked upon as communication links to your hospital for patients representing customers. St Thomas's Hospital in London is close to British Rail's Waterloo Station and to Waterloo International. Its customers could come from anywhere on the rail route or indeed anywhere within a couple of hours of the Channel Tunnel. We can expect French-speaking staff there soon!

Product

Product in this context is all, or part of, the range of treatments that you wish to offer. Product is a residual of the industrial marketing origins of the theory. Perhaps, 'pservice' would be better – where the 'p' is silent . . . .

The next decision to consider is the range of services you are offering to supply. Are you going to offer a full range of services or are you going to specialize or concentrate on providing core services efficiently? This may differ by speciality. It is perfectly reasonable to be a world leader in organ transplants whilst offering standard medical and surgical services to the resident population. The approach having the greatest merit depends upon the precise nature and degree of competition that you face in your chosen sectors of the market. Sector is another convenient shorthand to describe a grouping of customers. A geographical sector would be concerned with purchasers in a particular area, a speciality sector would cover all purchasers wanting to buy, say, ear, nose and throat services.

Purchasers are seeking to maximize the volume of healthcare they can purchase within a fixed money allocation. They are seeking improved quality at lower unit cost and increased volume of activity at lower overall cost. Providers are seeking long-term stability and continuity of contracts at reasonable rates of reward. There is more to this type of marketing than buying and selling. There is an aspect of building partnerships and relationships between the parties so that each understands the other's needs and desires and the two parties grow together beneficially. The alternative adversarial model of contracting where purchasers switch suppliers every year can only drive out suppliers to the detriment of healthcare provision.

Price

The price you charge is very important. Firstly, the service and the price together are the major elements that the customer or client uses to determine value for money. Secondly, the price you charge is the only means you have of generating revenue from your activities; everything else is a cost. Price is not independent of the other elements in the marketing mix so it is important to judge your position on the spectrum of perceived quality. Purchasers are under pressure to demonstrate that the unit price of treating patients, the cost per patient within a group of diseases, is constantly reducing. It is a wise provider that is able to offer a reduced cost. The market system is the hidden hand that guides your actions and the sure knowledge that some other supplier will take your contract if you do not offer the best value for money is the spur to action.

The connection between price and the nature of your offering is also important. If you are supplying a widely available service or one that is a substitute for others that are widely used, you will be forced to accept the going rate for the service. If your service is special or in demand you can adopt a 'skimming' approach whereby you price at the top end of the range and make large profits from a few customers before the opposition catch up with you. This is the prime motivation for differentiating your service from its competitors by the way you present it or deliver it so that, for a short space of time at least, it will be perceived as special by the market and will be afforded high value. Uniqueness and superiority are service attributes that correlate with success in this strategy.

Types of contract

There are currently several types of contract in use in the NHS.

Block contracts These are usually negotiated with the local health commissioners. They cover the supply of basic medical services to the resident population. The contracts contain a quality specification and a service level or agreement over the numbers of each type of disease to be treated. These are based on averages from past experience and are updated regularly. If the prescribed volume of activity is exceeded, there is no reward. There may well be praise, but there is no money. In principle, you are free to return to the purchaser and ask for more but purchasers usually commit nearly all their funds and have very little left.

Cost and volume contracts As the name implies, these contracts specify the quality and the precise volume of treatments required. If you do too few, you lose money and if you exceed the quota, by agreement, you may gain money and be financially rewarded for the extra effort. A sliding scale usually applies so that increased activity leads to a lower unit price.

Cost per case This form of contract is highly attractive to the medical profession because it is designed to remunerate the supplier fully for all services provided to an individual patient. It is not often used.

Providers have to publish their costs and have to charge the same to all purchasers, unless winning work through tendering processes. This has led to some wide variations in price for ostensibly comparable treatments, many of which have been used politically to denigrate inner city hospitals. A more sophisticated analysis of costs reveals that not everyone is using the same system.

Providers have to recover the full costs of providing services from the various contracts they have agreed in order to balance their books. The full costs contain all the fixed costs of the estate and buildings, all the overheads of administration, management and the trust board and all the support services. Costs used to be recoverable on inpatient episodes only, so they had to cover the costs of outpatient treatments and consultations. The current system identifies inpatient elective procedures, inpatient emergencies, outpatient and day case episodes, each of which has associated overheads. Accident and emergency services are contracted for as part of the block contract. If an A&E patient is admitted and is not from a district having a contract with the trust, they are treated and the bill is sent to the relevant purchaser.

Costing systems were relatively unsophisticated and are still so, but improving under Department of Health guidance. For instance, an orthopaedic department fixed a single cost for any procedure by dividing the total cost of running the department by the number of patients treated. This meant that simple procedures were overpriced and complex ones underpriced. It also meant that sophisticated purchasers chose to buy the complex procedures only and, as a result the department started to lose money. More sophisticated systems band procedures into five, six, seven or more bands which represent procedures of similar complexity. This gives more sophisticated recovery of actual costs provided the case mix does not alter significantly due to population changes or changes in referral patterns.

The differences in published price did certainly contain an element due to differential efficiency and differential sophistication of technique. They did, however, contain many more distorting factors which depended upon exactly how the costing had been arrived at and which costs had been included. As an example, the costs of running an ITU need to be recovered in some way. They could be put into the A&E budget and so reduce surgical and medical prices or they could rest with surgery and reduce A&E prices. It makes sense to operate within the legal variations so as to put a large proportion of overheads onto those items that are remunerated in full and to leave them out of block contracts or out of procedures that were in strongly competitive domains.

In the early operation of the market system, providers strove to keep flexibility over the setting of prices so that they had some fine tuning capacity to satisfy the different needs of the various contracts they held. Not surprisingly, purchasers wanted to be able to compare hospitals on price, given a sufficient quality standard. Purchasers are now trying to have providers calculate their prices in a similar fashion and on a common basis. This is another attempt to create a 'level playing field'. Markets survive having unequal suppliers and unequal purchasers. Trying to rig the market to give all suppliers an equal chance leads to unnecessary bureaucratization and stifles the creativity and drive needed to succeed. The market mechanism can deliver more efficient healthcare, initially, by forcing providers to review critically their procedures and practices.

The choice of price must take into account local competition, purchasers' needs, the case mix and the scarcity value of the service. It should signal whether your trust aims to be a standard service supplier locally or whether it seeks to take work from neighbouring units. In this case lower prices may attract more work and a busier hospital uses its facilities and support services more efficiently. It is very little use trying to charge a premium price if your services are not perceived by your purchasers as being of appropriately premium quality.

Place

The place where the service is provided has been static for a number of years. People went to the hospital. This remains largely the case, but the market mechanism has caused some specialities to offer outreach clinics. These take place in general practices and the hospital consultant travels to the patients, rather than the other way round. These schemes need to be properly evaluated, despite their popularity, because there are some potential disbenefits to patients and to the hospital. In the general practice setting, the patient is a more significant customer. Even though the FHSA remunerates the GP, there is a capitation element and a service provision element, both of which depend on patient numbers.

Patients have much more freedom to exercise choice and can change their GP, in principle.

We are also facing a shift of resources from secondary to primary care. This will mean that a larger range of services will be available locally. Services are moving closer to the patient. There are some question marks over quality of services which are yet to be resolved.

Promotion

Promotion is much more than direct advertising. A major part of it is termed passive advertising. This is the creation of an image and favourable perception in the eyes of the purchasers by providing an excellent service, being helpful to purchasers, by publishing academic articles, by avoiding litigation and scandals and so on. Passive advertising is very powerful.

Direct advertising may be necessary to establish contact with fundholders or health commissioners that you have not previously worked with. Even here, such advertising would be more akin to communication and information than an explicit attempt to persuade. You may need to promote special offers, but this too would be done in a low key manner rather than a banner headline in the daily paper announcing, 'A massive 25% off all operations at St Kidding's Surgical Super Unit. Hurry, this crazy offer cannot last, be ill now!'

The best form of business is repeat business. It takes time to get to know a new customer and to harmonize the contracting arrangements, to get to know the staff involved and to sort out payment systems. This investment provides a comfortable cushion for both sides and prevents rapid switching from customer to customer because there are costs and risks involved. It follows that keeping a customer avoids the cost of finding a new one.

People

People are an essential component of the marketing mix and have at last attracted the formal recognition they have always deserved. When marketing a service, you are implicitly marketing the people who will be providing it. You are marketing their individual skills, their collective teamwork, their reputations. It is a sound policy to attract and retain good staff because they can deliver a good and efficient service and can provide those rare and specialized skills that are needed.

People and people management policies play an important part in the marketing mix.

Process

The business or service process has lately come into

consideration as part of the marketing mix in consumer goods markets and in company-to-company marketing. It relates to the duties and responsibilities of each partner in the transaction. It concerns the internal systems of each contracting party and the tasks that each has to perform as part of the deal. It covers the paperwork and the reporting. Business advantage can be gained by paying attention to ways in which the process can be streamlined and made simpler for both parties.

CUSTOMERS AS RELATIONSHIPS

In the last decade marketing theory has addressed itself to the growth in service industries and started to identify the essential differences between physical goods and services. These are presented below as absolute contrasts to physical goods, whereas they actually represented degrees of difference.

- Services are not tangible.
- Services are not durable, they cannot be stored.
- Services are not testable in advance.
- Services are produced and consumed at the same time and involve the customer in their production.

These factors lead to the perception of customer relationships and indeed influence the ways in which services can be promoted. Because the service cannot truly be predicted in advance, then past practice and past reputation become important ways in which a customer minimizes the risk of a service-purchasing decision. This concept helps to explain why the brassy hard sell approach does not have much place in healthcare marketing.

Because of this relationship element, trusts should not view their purchasers as adversaries but as partners, even friends, with a shared interest. They should encourage visits, they should send news of successes and warn of failures very early.

SELLING

Marketing is about creating the image and potential, selling is about doing the deal, getting the contract and fixing the terms. Selling involves negotiation and entrepreneurial flair. Some people find selling suits their personality and others find it demeaning and too commercial, lacking in any professional mystique. In today's NHS selling has to be done. Good marketing only creates the platform, selling is the final performance.

Selling has elements of an attempt to obtain money from the unwary by trickery. Our legal system enshrines the concept of 'buyer beware' which only seems to deepen the suspicion. Selling is about convincing someone they need your services and that it is risk-free to buy them. We all need to sell, if only to sell ourselves in the job market.

In terms of negotiating contracts and selling the final deal, there are great dangers in allowing marketing professionals to dominate. They have undoubted expertise, but, in my experience they need to be used as technical supports to the clinicians who will ultimately deliver the service. This is because only the clinical staff can fully appreciate the consequences of any proposed deal on the care delivered to patients. They are best placed to judge. This applies to both sides of the contracting process. They both need sound clinical advice.

STRATEGY

Business strategy and marketing strategy are closely related. The former sets the target and the latter is the route to get there. It appears as the marketing plan. The topic is often distorted by mechanistic planning methods that fail to capture the simplicity that a good plan needs. As Benjamin Franklin said, 'The planning is everything, the plan is nothing'. The important part is the systematic review of what the organization is trying to achieve and how it will achieve it, not the massive paper mountain that spews forth as the plan itself. There is another very sound rationale for concentrating on the process, because the parameters and circumstances that produced the details of the plan can and always do change during the life of the plan. The plan soon becomes a historical record and not a blueprint. I am an advocate of tearing up the plan once it is finished and planning all the time. I am, however, realistic enough to accept that bureaucratic organizations need physical plans. In the new world of purchasers and providers, plans are central to contract negotiations. Plans cover volumes and levels of activity as well as quality issues.

The centralizer's view of the world of business planning is from the top down. It is also a structured and rigid view. The main tenets are largely imports from American private sector business practices where marketing is a dominant force and where the population is in greater need of icons to salute. The centralizer's view starts with a mission statement from which comes the strategy and then the plan.

Everything stems from the mission statement, those few words that capture the essence of what the organization is in existence to achieve. As an example, the London Business School's mission is: 'To be world leader in helping individuals and organizations to enhance their managerial effectiveness. To do so by pursuing a balanced excellence that links theory to practice in teaching and research that are innovative, rigorous and relevant to international, career-long learning'. That really covers everything!

The strategy flows from the mission and describes, in more detail, where the organization is trying to go, what its next goals are.

The other polar extreme of strategy formation starts from the activities of the organization. It collects together what the organization is currently doing reasonably well and decides to continue doing much the same, with a few marginal adjustments. The components are then lumped together in natural groupings and possible gaps in the service are identified and plugged.

Strategy formulation by the second method has the virtues of involving virtually all the organization in advocating its part of the empire. It is more messy and mirrors reality, unlike the clear tones of the centralist's views.

As the NHS internal market develops, business and marketing planning will become more pertinent, particularly if purchasers combine to exert greater influence over buying decisions. The hope is that quality of treatment will become a major determinant of market success; the fear is that price alone will influence the placing of contracts.

Business and marketing planning can be applied as a rationing process. Rather than deciding what it is your unit is capable of doing and then trying to find the resources to do it, the process is one of being allocated a share of resources and being asked to maximize activity within that ceiling.

SWOT

Many of you will have heard of or participated in SWOT (Strengths, Weaknesses, Opportunities, Threats) analysis. This is part of strategy formulation which examines the strengths and weaknesses of the current organization and its market position. It also looks at the strategic opportunities that are emerging and the threats to its business that are just over the horizon.

We look at strategy in two ways. The first is the competitive forces model. Fig. 24.1 illustrates this model in the context of the NHS. In the centre of the figure is the current competitive environment with individual trusts competing on price and service specification, on location and local relationships to supply services against contracts. This is the arena in which the 6 Ps operate. The marketing mix and the service specification will mark you out from the others. Each industry is characterized by positive or negative growth. Growth makes room for everyone to grow and increase their services. In healthcare, there is downward pressure on the trusts as spending, although increasing in absolute terms, is

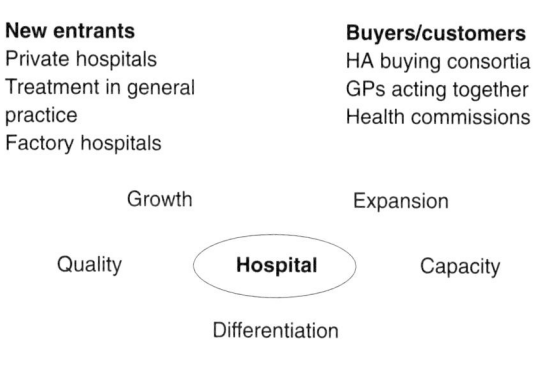

New entrants
Private hospitals
Treatment in general practice
Factory hospitals

Buyers/customers
HA buying consortia
GPs acting together
Health commissions

Growth — Expansion
Quality — Hospital — Capacity
Differentiation

Suppliers
Stores combines
GP referral patterns
Pharmaceutical companies

Substitutes
Preventative medicine
Alternative medicine
Private medicine
New consumer needs

Fig. 24.1 Competitive forces

not covering the growth in demand or the complexity of treatment. Exit barriers are also mentioned. These are the costs of switching to new modes of operation. They are more relevant to the private sector where capital seeks the maximum return and the cost of abandoning plant and machinery has to be considered.

Treatments at different hospitals are not very clearly differentiated in the public mind, although the profession may make distinctions between, say, cardiothoracic surgery at hospital A and hospital B, or between particular consultants.

The 3 Cs deal with the wider environment and the four corners of the figure cover similar territory. The axis from bottom left to top right is the one that represents opportunity in strategic terms. A merger of business interests up the axis is known as forward integration and the other direction is backward integration. General practitioners supply patients to hospitals through the referral system. Giving GPs funds to purchase elective treatments, and possibly others, amounts to them taking over part of the hospital's business. Mergers could take place in the reverse direction and trusts could set up their own general practices to ensure a steady patient flow. It is possible for hospitals to be influenced by concerted patient action, hence the growth in patient satisfaction surveys. Although patients cannot take over the hospital, they can influence its operations.

The other axis presents the threats from new market entrants possibly diluting your share of the cake and from alternative ways of meeting the underlying need: substitute services. These could include the substitution of private sector providers of healthcare or complementary medicine.

At the department level, substitutes, in the form of alternative treatments or alternative techniques, may well prove threatening. The threats from new entrants may well be more significant. These could take the form of private hospitals or specialized clinics. The current shift of powers and services to primary care is equally problematic. Purchasers are the most worthy of scrutiny. Beware the combined purchasing authority with the power, and desire, to place a limited number of contracts. Beware the combination of FHSAs and HAs into health commissioners with the power to alter the balance between primary and secondary care. There is currently no danger of them taking over provider units for the reason that such a move would recreate a unified health authority.

SWOT analysis takes place within the overall context described above. Strengths are the things you are good at doing or better at doing than your competitors. They could be accidents of geography that give you a large catchment area or provide you with newer facilities and equipment. The skills mix within your team could also be a strength. It is clear that strengths and weaknesses are the opposite poles of each continuum, so that lack of skills or inappropriate skill mixes can be disadvantageous. Quality problems in systems or staff need to be identified honestly and addressed.

Opportunities are those things you could do, either by growth to accommodate new services or by switching resources from one area to another. Opportunities may rest on new technological or procedural advances or new demands for services. Threats are those things that could thwart your ideas and plans. They might include a neighbouring hospital undercutting your contract price or a change in public attitude towards travelling further for treatment or a growth in private insurance or a sudden upswing in the value of land or a change of government (could also be an opportunity). At the department level, the potential loss of a key consultant, difficulties in recruiting nursing staff of the correct skill level or the growth in surgical treatment of a particular condition could be threats.

INFORMATION

Information about the state of the market, the purchasers and the competitors is needed in order to review your current position. The management of information is itself becoming a strategic issue. Successful organizations are able to make use of a wide range of data sources and to extract the useful information from them in a speedy and efficient manner. For these organizations, data collection is not a stylized, annual ritual, it is a continuous process of scanning the external environment and absorbing new pieces of the information jigsaw. The remaining community health councils and patient groups may represent powerful sources of information on consumer interests.

A lack of reasonably accessible sources of data is a major barrier to competitive success. Consultants will need to be alert to this issue and take steps to ensure they have the information needed to make sound decisions in a competitive environment.

DISTINCTIVE COMPETENCE

Distinctive competence is something your organization is known to be good at. Having a distinctive competence in a particular part of the service is a building brick in the search for competitive advantage. It is also wise to root out any distinctive incompetence!

SUSTAINABLE COMPETITIVE ADVANTAGE

An alternative view of the current state of the competitive environment is provided by analysing sustainable competitive advantages. Advantages can come from geographical location, control of raw materials, superior skills, better integration of services, better facilities, scale of operations or whatever. It is worth remembering, however, that some advantage is in the perception of the consumer or purchaser and can be eroded if those perceptions change.

Fig. 24.2 captures the ideas in sustainable competitive advantage. It is adapted from the work of Michael Porter (see Further Reading), one of the leaders of thought on competitive strategy. To be successful in a competitive environment, there are certain functions of the enterprise which need to be well organized and managed. The following relate to company policy issues. The enterprise needs to have an adequate organizational structure that is in harmony with the balance of products or services. It needs to secure human resources of the correct skill and at the best prices. It must look to its own technological development and have viable procurement functions; in other words, efficient ways to secure the materials and equipment it needs.

The concept of the value chain relates to the manufacturing process that takes raw materials and converts them into manufactured goods that people need. It can also relate to the production of services, where the raw materials are the customers themselves. In hospitals, there is a mixture of production/manufacturing and service provision, so both views may need consideration. The notion of after-sales service is not terribly relevant.

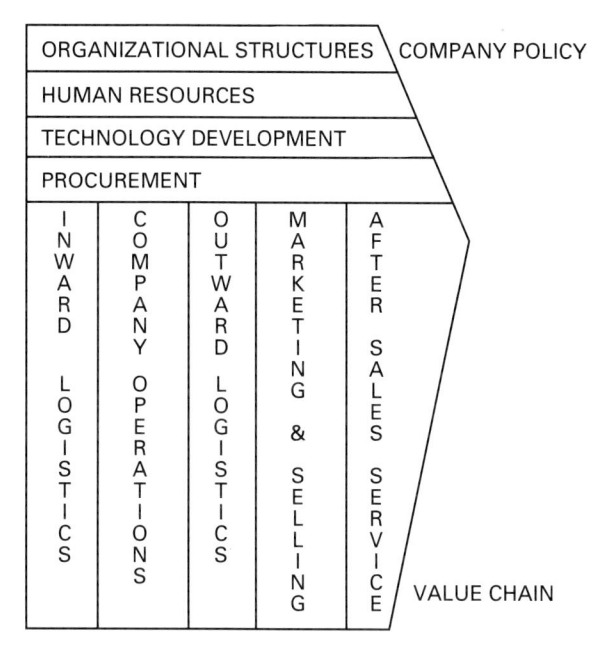

Fig. 24.2 Competitive advantage

Inward logistics relate to the sources of supply and the ways these are handled. In current NHS terms, we would be considering the quality and number of contracts, relationships with GPs and the ambulance service, the state of car parking and road access and problems with the bus services. These are all related to getting the money in or getting the patients and their visitors in.

Company operations relate to the services delivered within the hospital or even outside it, if under hospital control. It is possible to have competitive advantage by having a well-functioning clinical team, access to advanced techniques or a good physical layout of the wards. Outward logistics are concerned with distribution channels or advantages in distribution like one's own railway line. Advantage, in NHS terms, can flow from efficiency in discharge procedures, good relations with community services, proper information flows to GPs to handle follow-up treatment, good ambulance or hospital car services. At department level, the layout of the hospital, the location of beds, postoperative recovery areas and others may be sources of advantage that can be sustained until capital building programmes, elsewhere, erode them. Outward logistics can also relate to the quality of relationship a hospital enjoys with the community and Social Services. Successful relationships can aid the smooth transfer of patients from the hospital and back to the community. This can increase bed utilization by getting the healthy out of hospital.

BCG MATRIX

This was invented, if that is not too high an accolade, by the Boston Consulting Group. It has the simplicity needed to succeed in America and it is now being adopted on these shores with increasing frequency. It uses two dimensions against which to judge the products or services of a company: the size and nature of the market, especially its growth potential, and the share of the market held. Fig. 24.3 illustrates and describes this concept further. Underlying the matrix is the concept of a product life cycle or service life cycle. New ideas come along and are gradually taken up and become routine services. Demand for these services remains steady until a better procedure or treatment comes along and the original service declines. This is called a life cycle because it contains birth, youth, maturity, decline and death.

The BCG matrix has four quadrants. We don't like dogs. They are in markets of little value where we have little share, so we should get out of them fast. We tolerate cows. Cash cows make lots of money because we have high market share in what may be a mature market or even a declining one. We only need bung them a bit of grass and they go on producing. Stars are what we seek. They are products or services that are dominant in their markets and their markets are growing fast. They have the potential to make lots of money and deserve a concentration of resources and effort. Question marks are products in good markets which have not yet achieved market share, so we give them the resources and effort needed to become stars or crash down to dogland.

Where does all this take the average consultant? The answer is that it may help to balance the services you provide and enable you to determine where new services are needed. The market axis could be replaced by one

Fig. 24.3 The Boston Consulting Group matrix

representing public demand and purchaser desire, be that health commissioners or the growing number of fundholding general practitioners. The market share axis could be a blend of quality and cost of the service. A well-balanced service needs lots of cows, a few stars, no dogs and not too many question marks. Services should be clustered around those things the purchasers want to buy and that you can provide at good quality levels. You should be grooming some new services for the future, but not too many, and you should be quietly trying to get out of other lines of work or to make them more attractive.

Such thought processes lead to the strategy for your department and similar processes can lead to the strategy for the hospital. In this case the departments themselves can be looked at as cows, stars, dogs or question marks.

FURTHER READING

Berry L L, Parasuraman A 1991 Marketing services. Free Press, New York

Bourne H, Miles C 1993 Marketing: its place in organizational structure. Health Services Management Volume 89: 18–20

Courtis J 1988 Marketing services: a practical guide. Kogan Page, London

Davidson H 1987 Offensive marketing. Penguin, London

Drucker P 1973 Management: tasks, responsibilities, practices. Harper & Row, New York

Joseph D, MacBurnie T 1989 Marketing plus. Heinemann, Oxford

Kotler P 1994 Marketing management, 8th edn. Prentice-Hall, New Jersey

MacDonald M H B, Morris P 1987 The marketing plan: a pictorial guide for managers. Butterworth-Heinemann, Oxford

MacDonald M H B, Morris P 1987 Selling services and products. Butterworth-Heinemann, Oxford

Ovretveit J 1992 Health service quality. Blackwells, Oxford

Pearson B, Thomas N 1991 The shorter MBA – a practical approach to business skills. Thorsons, London

Porter M E 1985 Competitive advantage. Simon & Schuster, New York

Sheaff R 1990 Marketing for health services. Open University Press, Milton Keynes

Stapleton J 1989 How to prepare a marketing plan. Gower, Aldershot

Stewart D M 1992 Gower handbook of management skills. Gower, Aldershot, ch 24

Weitz B A, Wensley R 1984 Strategic marketing: planning, implementation and control. Kent, Boston, Mass.

25

Economics for clinicians

Karin Lowson

WHAT IS ECONOMICS?

Paul Samuelson (1970), a celebrated American economist, has written:

> Economics is the study of how men and society end up choosing, with or without the use of money, to employ scarce productive resources which would have alternative uses, to produce various commodities and distribute them for consumption, now or in the future, amongst various people and groups in society.

The underpinning assumption of economics, therefore, is that 'resources are always and everywhere scarce'. Scarcity means that choices have to be made and priorities established regarding resource allocation. Economics is therefore not about saving money, reducing costs, budgets or finance. These are inputs to economics. Economics is more than just costs and spending money. Economics is a discipline, in other words a way of thinking which is considered to be more important than a particular technique. It is also a toolkit, a set of techniques that can be applied to a problem.

Finally, since economics is about making choices, the question must be posed, 'Who makes the choices?'. In a perfect marketplace, the answer is the consumer or, on a larger scale, society. In other words, society's values must be taken into account when setting priorities and making choices.

THE MARKETPLACE

Within the widget industry, widgets are produced because consumers wish to purchase them. The consumption of widgets adds satisfaction to the consumer and the number of widgets purchased is the result of the balancing out of the price against the satisfaction gained. In other words, the consumers take their income, which is finite, and make decisions as their purchases: choices are made against priorities.

Conversely, the widget manufacturer will buy in raw materials and employ labour and capital in order to produce widgets at a price which will make the manufacturer a profit, but which also will be attractive to the consumer. Goods so produced are bought and sold in the marketplace. What are the characteristics of this market?

- Consumers have perfect information about all the products in the marketplace. They know the prices and they know what alternative products are available.
- Consumers know the satisfaction that they will gain from consuming the products. They also know how to measure the quality of the products.
- No product dominates the marketplace, so that all producers will adjust their prices and quantities accordingly.

DEMAND AND SUPPLY

A consumer's demand can be described in algebraic and graphical forms by the demand curve. This describes the relationship between the quantity demanded of a good and the factors influencing that demand, such as income, taste and the price of other goods, where:

$$Q_i = f(P_i, Y_i, P_1, P_2 \ldots P_i, T)$$

where Q_i = the amount of good i demanded in a particular time period;
P_i = the price of good i in that same time period;
Y_i = income in the same time period;
$P_1, P_2 \ldots P_i$ = prices of other goods in the same time period;
and T = tastes in the same time period.

The demand curve is also shown below in graphical form as in Fig. 25.1.

Conversely, the supply curve can be described as the relationship between the quantity supplied of a good and factors influencing that supply, such as price and technology, where:

$$Qi = f(Pi, P_1, P_2, \ldots Pi, T)$$

where Qi = the amount of good i supplied in a particular time period;
Pi = the price of good i in that same time period;
$P_1, P_2, \ldots Pi$ = prices of other goods in the same time period;
and T = technology involved in the production.

The supply curve can also be shown in graphical format as in Fig. 25.2.

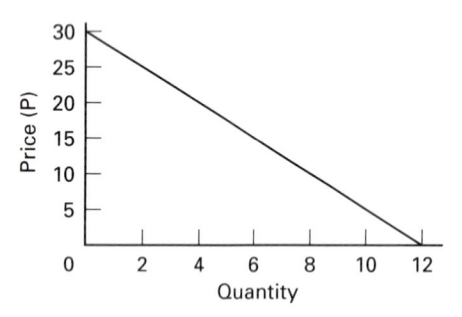

Fig. 25.1

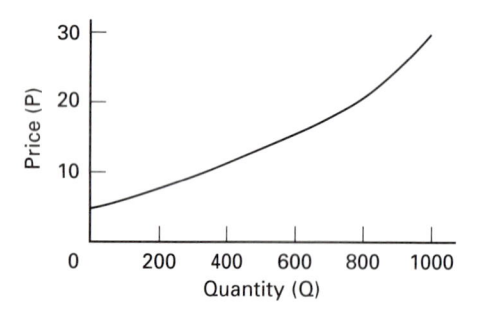

Fig. 25.2

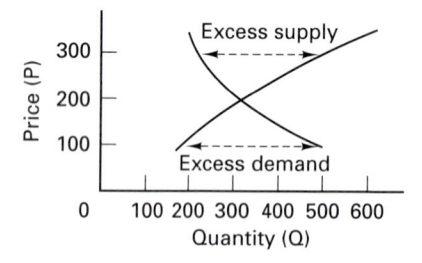

Fig. 25.3

Equilibrium of supply and demand is reached where prices and quantities demanded and supplied are equal. This is shown in graphical form in Fig. 25.3.

IS THE HEALTHCARE GOOD DIFFERENT?

The section above described the characteristics of a marketplace under the ideal conditions of perfect competition. Do these conditions pertain in the healthcare marketplace? The answer is not really, since there is a basic asymmetry in the healthcare marketplace between the professional (i.e. the supplier) and the patient (i.e. the consumer).

On the demand side the consumer's ability to make decisions is impaired; they are dependent on the suppliers to make decisions on their behalf and they also have little or no information on quality, alternatives or price. Consumers are likely to be ignorant about both their current state of (ill)health and the probable future state. They are also unlikely to know the range and effectiveness of treatments available.

In a marketplace with full consumer knowledge and participation, consumer sovereignty rules. In a marketplace with imperfect consumer information and decision making, and therefore where professionals (such as doctors) make decisions on behalf of the consumer, such as the healthcare market, the product is known as a 'merit good'. The professional makes the decision based on their judgement of the patient's 'needs'. Therefore needs-based decisions regarding demand and supply conflict with decisions based on consumer sovereignty.

The supply side of the marketplace is also restricted. This is true of any supply which is under the control of 'professions', which restrict entry to the profession, self-regulate, keep prices high and control knowledge about products and outcome.

NEED AND DEMAND

Need is a concept that is much used, but not necessarily well understood. How often do we hear the exclamation, 'We need a new accident and emergency department/hospital . . . etc.'? But what does this 'need' mean?

Many economists have written about need, most notably Culyer (1976) and Mooney (1986). Mooney has made a list of key points about need, which are replicated below:

1. There is a lot of confusion and illogical thinking surrounding the concept of need, sometimes perhaps deliberate in an attempt to stifle debate.

2. 'Need' ought not to be determined without con-

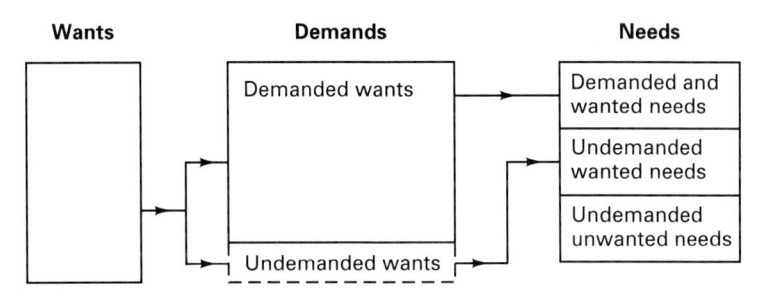

Fig. 25.4 Wants, demands and needs revised (from Mooney 1986)

sidering what end is being sought and to which the services in question are instrumental means.

3. Ignoring the possibilities for substitutability in meeting needs is likely to lead to inefficiency.
4. Almost always, no matter how need is defined, it embraces the idea of some third party party being involved in the valuing process – unlike 'demand', where it is the consumer who is sovereign.
5. Which third party is relevant and which decisions are the key issues in the need/demand debate.
6. Need is not absolute.
7. Needs have to be ranked and should be costed.
8. The particular contribution of economics to 'needology' derives from the proposition that the degree to which any given need will be met will depend upon the costs and benefits of meeting it.

The relationship between wants, demands and needs has been described by both Cooper & Culyer (1973) and Mooney (1986). Mooney's approach is shown in Fig. 25.4.

Need may be:

- demanded and wanted;
- undemanded and wanted;
- undemanded and unwanted.

If a woman has cervical cancer, there are three alternatives:

1. If she does not realize that anything is wrong, this will be undemanded and unwanted, although objectively she needs treatment;
2. She may want treatment, but not visit her GP since either she is too worried to attend or does not realize the importance of attending. This will be wanted but undemanded need;
3. She wants treatment, visits the GP and is given treatment. This is wanted and demanded need.

There is also a scenario in which treatments are demanded and wanted but not deemed as needed, such as some forms of plastic surgery. Where the professionals do not deem treatment to be needed, it may not be provided by the NHS. However, in the marketplace where consumer sovereignty rules, i.e. private healthcare markets, it will be provided.

MUST THERE ALWAYS BE SCARCITY IN THE HEALTHCARE MARKETPLACE?

There are never enough resources to satisfy all human wants and desires. This means that every time resources are committed to the production of one commodity, those resources are not available for the production of another commodity. In other words, society foregoes the opportunity to use those resources in other beneficial activities. This is known as the concept of opportunity cost; it is this concept that probably best crystallizes the economist's view of the world.

At all levels choices have to be made and priorities established. This is true despite the system of funding the production of healthcare. Individual consumers have scarce resources and will choose whether to purchase healthcare against the consumption of other commodities such as food, housing and travel. Governments have a multitude of calls on their scarce resources, such as education, housing and defence. Companies, who fund work-based insurance schemes, can only spend a limited amount of their profits on healthcare.

Within the NHS, a healthcare system funded predominantly by government taxation, decisions have to be made at a purchaser level and a provider level. Purchasers address the macro level; examples of these decisions are shown in Table 25.1.

WHAT IS HEALTH ECONOMICS?

Samuelson's definition refers to the employment of resources, the production of commodities and their distribution. What is produced and distributed in the healthcare industry?

Resources are nurses, doctors, drugs, operating theatres which, combined together, produce a commodity such as an episode of care for the treatment of a broken leg. This commodity is consumed because

Table 25.1 Resource decisions (from Lowson 1993, p 8)

- *What*: via needs assessment
- *How*: via models of care
- *Where*: which locations
- *When*: on the continuum between primary prevention and tertiary intervention
- *Who*: via priorities
- *How much*: via clinical trials for treatments or allocation methods
- With what resources

the patient (i.e. the consumer) wants an improvement in healthcare. Economists argue that the demand for healthcare is a 'derived' demand, because it is not the healthcare per se that is valued but the resulting improvement in health.

It is therefore possible to apply the principles of economics to the healthcare marketplace. Indeed, it is most important to recognize that the production of health must compete for scarce resources along with the production of other commodities that are valued.

A diagrammatic representation of health economics is shown in Fig. 25.5. What can be seen from this overview is that:

1. Elements such as 'What influences health?' (box A) and 'What is health?' (box B) are not the prerogative solely of health economists. Indeed, one could argue that the most efficient and effective ways to improve health are by improving housing, education and employment possibilities, rather than investing in healthcare. However, as we shall see later in the chapter, decisions on improving health and the relationship between preventive and curative healthcare do benefit from an economic analysis.

2. Economics is a wide-ranging subject covering many aspects of healthcare delivery, from the traditional demand and supply to planning and distribution.

3. Most empirical economics is at a micro level (box E) and it is this area on which this chapter will concentrate, although it will touch upon other areas.

4. Delivery and evaluation of healthcare is multidisciplinary; clinicians and managers have as much of a role as do economists. Indeed, it is preferable that these groups of influential people embrace the discipline and thinking of economics, rather than adopt the stance that economics is only what economists do.

ECONOMIC APPRAISAL

Drummond has written extensively on the subject of economic appraisal and its application (see, for example, Drummond et al 1990). He asserts that:

> Appraisal is concerned with the analysis of alternative courses of action with a view to assisting choice. While there is no simple single basis for making community wide choices, it is possible to identify a number of relevant criteria for choice. One such criterion is economic efficiency.

The criterion of economic efficiency means that choices in respect of healthcare should be made in order to maximize the total benefit from the resources available to society, with due regard to the costs of achieving those benefits.

Much economic appraisal hinges on the three concepts of economy, efficiency and effectiveness.

Economy

Economy is concerned with good housekeeping, with the costs of the inputs and efforts at reducing those costs.

Efficiency

Efficiency is concerned with doing things right; the relationship between the inputs and the outputs are maximized for given inputs or inputs minimized for given outputs.

Effectiveness

Effectiveness is concerned with doing the right things; the relationship between the inputs, the outputs and the outcomes.

The technique of economic appraisal needs to be performed in conjunction with three other techniques:

1. *Efficacy* Does the health treatment or procedure provide benefit?
2. *Acceptability* Is the treatment acceptable and hence useful?
3. *Availability* Does the treatment reach those who may benefit?

The first two questions may be answered by clinicians who are undertaking clinical trials; the third may equally concern health service managers.

Finally, there is the concept of ethics. Economists believe that it is unethical to invest in treatments that are not maximizing benefits for a given sum of resources. By not maximizing benefits, patients are being denied treatment or health gains that could be available to them, since resources are being wasted.

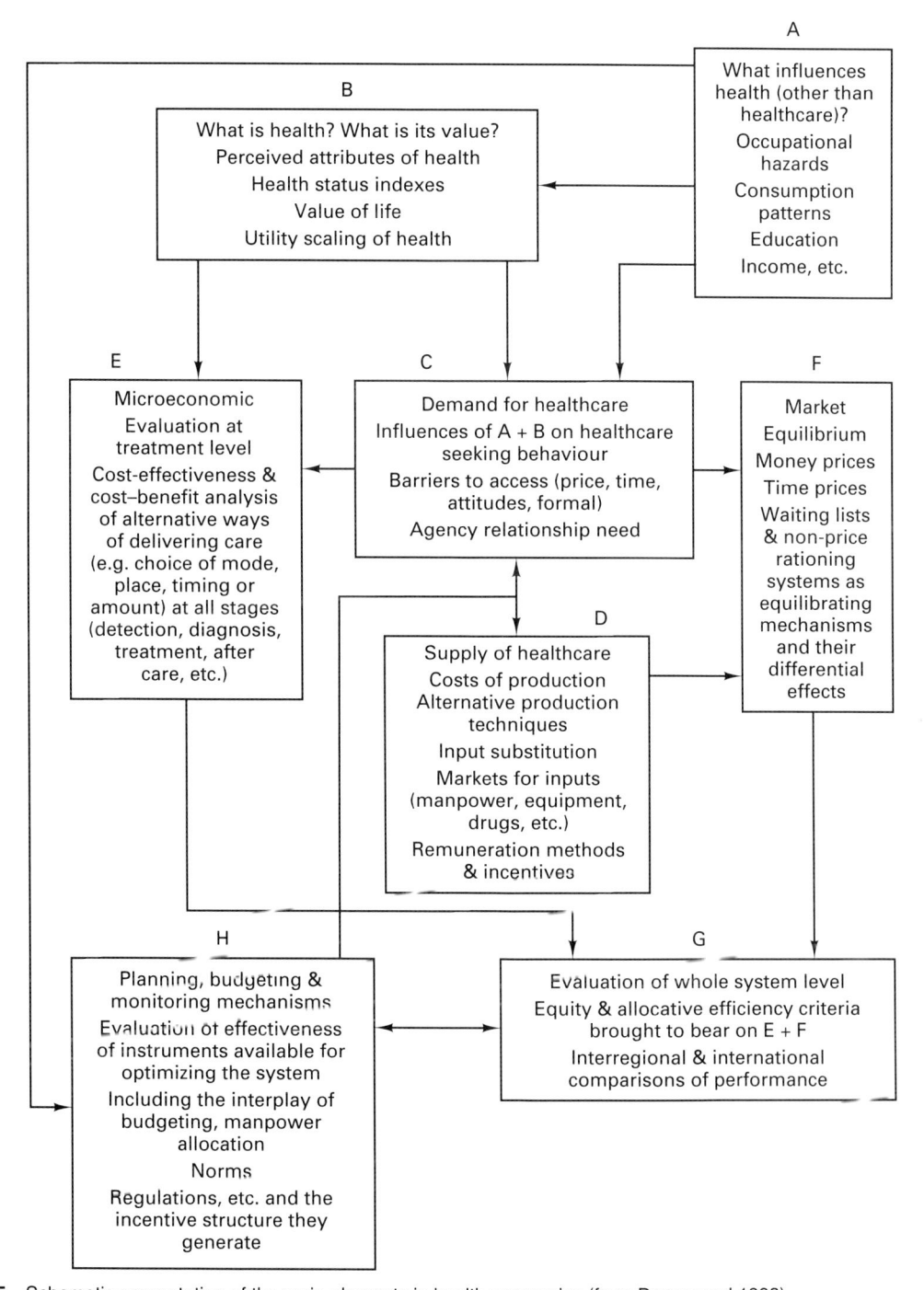

A
What influences health (other than healthcare)?
Occupational hazards
Consumption patterns
Education
Income, etc.

B
What is health? What is its value?
Perceived attributes of health
Health status indexes
Value of life
Utility scaling of health

E
Microeconomic
Evaluation at treatment level
Cost-effectiveness & cost–benefit analysis of alternative ways of delivering care (e.g. choice of mode, place, timing or amount) at all stages (detection, diagnosis, treatment, after care, etc.)

C
Demand for healthcare
Influences of A + B on healthcare seeking behaviour
Barriers to access (price, time, attitudes, formal)
Agency relationship need

F
Market Equilibrium
Money prices
Time prices
Waiting lists & non-price rationing systems as equilibrating mechanisms and their differential effects

D
Supply of healthcare
Costs of production
Alternative production techniques
Input substitution
Markets for inputs (manpower, equipment, drugs, etc.)
Remuneration methods & incentives

H
Planning, budgeting & monitoring mechanisms
Evaluation of effectiveness of instruments available for optimizing the system
Including the interplay of budgeting, manpower allocation
Norms
Regulations, etc. and the incentive structure they generate

G
Evaluation of whole system level
Equity & allocative efficiency criteria brought to bear on E + F
Interregional & international comparisons of performance

Fig. 25.5 Schematic presentation of the main elements in health economics (from Drummond 1993)

ECONOMIC EVALUATION

An overview of economic evaluation is shown in Fig. 25.6. This shows that a health programme, in order to give benefits, must consume resources. It also shows the relationships between the techniques outlined below.

There are two elements that characterize economic evaluation, regardless of which aspects of the health

```
                    ┌─────────────────────┐
                    │  Health treatment   │
                    │    or programme     │
                    └─────────────────────┘
              Consume resources │ Gives improvements
                     ↓          │    in health ↓
        ┌──────────────────┐         ┌──────────────────┐
        │      Costs       │         │     Benefits     │
        │ What is forgone? │         │ What is obtained?│
        └──────────────────┘         └──────────────────┘
                     ↓                          ↓
                    ┌─────────────────────┐
                    │ The cost–benefit    │
                    │      approach       │
                    └─────────────────────┘
       Costs and benefits │         │ Benefits not
         in money terms   ↓         ↓  in money terms
        ┌──────────────────┐        ┌──────────────────┐
        │  Cost–benefit    │        │ Cost-effectiveness│
        │    analysis      │        │     analysis     │
        └──────────────────┘        └──────────────────┘
         Treatment objective          Treatment objective
          can be questioned            not questioned
```

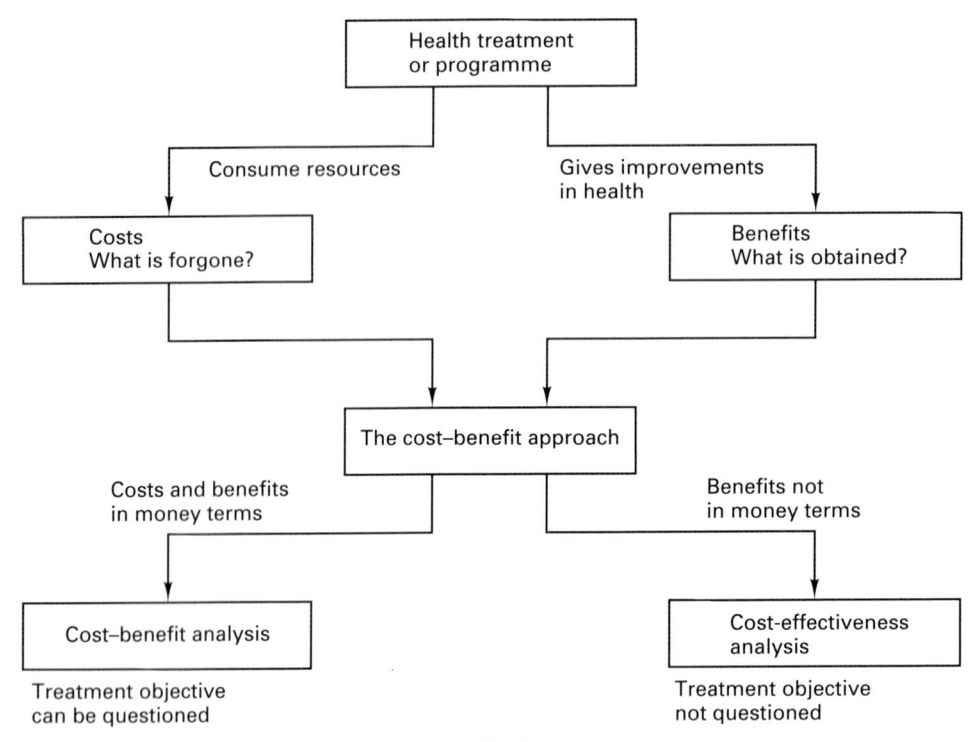

Fig. 25.6 Costs and benefits in healthcare (from Drummond 1984)

service they are applied to. The first is that economists will always argue that there are alternatives; although resources appear to be committed, changes can always be made. The second is that economic analysis looks at both inputs and outputs and, wherever possible, at outcomes.

Fig. 25.7 pulls these ideas together and shows the relationship between resources consumed (the inputs), the healthcare programme (the output) and the health improvements (the outcomes).

Assessment of inputs

In Fig. 25.7, Drummond refers to 'resources consumed'. What are these resources and how can they be measured and costed?

There are three categories of resources:

1. *Health service resources*   Resources are expended, for example, during a hospital stay or a GP visit. Inputs to these will include, for example, staff time, usage of land and buildings, and consumables.

2. *Other support services*   These include services provided by local authorities, police and the voluntary sector. Inputs are as per health services.

3. *Patients' and carers' resources*   This includes their personal time, adaptations to home and expenditure associated with the care, such as travel and drugs. In addition, there are intangible costs associated with pain and suffering.

How will the usage of these resources be measured? Those under categories (1) and (2) will attract a market value. Staff costs will be evaluated using wage rates, drugs and consumables by the price paid in the marketplace, capital usage by the application of depreciation to capital resources.

Those under category (3) pose more of a dilemma. Market rates can be applied directly, such as wage rates for patients' or carers' time, or can be imputed, for example for housewives. Methods of measuring pain and distress are discussed in more detail in the section on outcome measures.

Costing methodologies

The question 'How much does a pathology test cost?' can be answered in many ways, depending on the definition of cost adopted. Table 25.2 demonstrates some of the commonly used costing techniques and definitions.

A simple example of calculating the cost of an input is shown in Table 25.3, which illustrates the methodology for calculating the cost of a radiology test.

ECONOMICS FOR CLINICIANS

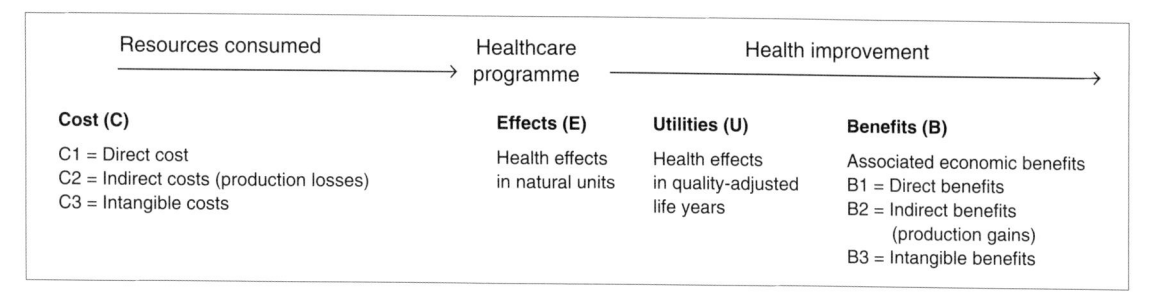

```
         Resources consumed           Healthcare              Health improvement
    ───────────────────────────►      programme      ───────────────────────────────►

    Cost (C)                          Effects (E)       Utilities (U)        Benefits (B)

    C1 = Direct cost                  Health effects    Health effects       Associated economic benefits
    C2 = Indirect costs (production losses)  in natural units  in quality-adjusted   B1 = Direct benefits
    C3 = Intangible costs                               life years           B2 = Indirect benefits
                                                                                  (production gains)
                                                                             B3 = Intangible benefits
```

Fig. 25.7 Components of economic evaluation (modified from Drummond et al 1990)

Table 25.2 Examples of costing methodologies (from Lowson 1993, p 10)

Definition	Examples of costs
Capital	A one-off large purchase, whose benefit is long term; strictly speaking anything over the cost of £5000, e.g. large item of equipment
Revenue	Day-to-day running costs, e.g. staff salaries
Direct	Resources that are directly identified with the production of the test, e.g. chemicals
Indirect	Resources that cannot be directly attributable to each test, e.g. electricity
Total	Includes both direct and indirect costs
Average	Total costs divided by the number of units of production, e.g. tests
Fixed	Costs that do not change as the number of tests change, e.g. the departmental manager or the auto-analyser
Variable	Costs that do change as the volume of tests change, e.g. chemicals
Marginal	The cost of producing one more unit
Standard	What it ought to cost

Table 25.3 Management of a radiology department (from Lowson 1993, p 11)

	Illustrative time	Illustrative cost
Direct inputs: staff time		
Time of clerk to book patient in, pull notes, ensure records are correct, etc.	10 mins	£1.25
Time of radiographer to take X-ray	15 mins	£3.75
Time of radiographer assistant to process film	5 mins	£0.90
Consumables: sheets of film	2 sheets	£2.00
		£14.15
Indirect inputs: shared throughout the department		
Staff: overhead time associated with above staff: order film, attend courses, manage staff. Overheads associated with staff not directly involved in producing radiological tests, e.g. the medical secretary	Apportion on basis of direct time	
Non-staff: miscellaneous items, e.g. paper, notes, uniforms, etc.	Apportion on basis of direct time	
Overhead costs: heating, lighting, cleaning, etc.	Apportion on size of dept & direct time	
Capital cost: radiological equipment	Apportion on basis of direct time	
Overhead costs outside the dept: finance, hospital canteen, etc.	Dept overheads may be 50% Additional overheads an extra 50%	
Total cost of radiological examination is £28.30		

Measures of output

Outputs can be measured in terms of the end product of the healthcare system as a production process. Examples of outputs are inpatient days, completed operations, radiology tests, district nurse contacts and GP visits.

A measure of output does not imply any measure of quality. In other words a completed consultant episode may be an output, but we do not know if the patient was discharged alive or dead, cured or in the same condition as when admitted.

Outputs, however, are relatively easy to measure and therefore tend to be used as the currency in contracts between purchasers and providers. Contracts may be set on the basis of, say, 50 hip replacements, 100 000 district nurse contacts or 50 000 finished consultant episodes.

Measures of outcome

Health improvement should be the natural consequence of resources employed in healthcare. The three categories of health improvement in Fig. 25.7 are described in more detail below.

Effects, as in cost-effectiveness

The outcomes are measured in 'natural units', such as years of life gained, cases correctly diagnosed, points of blood pressure reduced and disability days saved. There is no attempt to ascribe a value to these units, they are merely counted.

Effects are relatively straightforward to measure, provided that the question is posed correctly and at an early enough stage in the measurement process for the data to be collected or available. The outcomes may in fact be intermediate and hence be outputs, such as patients appropriately treated or positive cases found, but these can have value in their own right, such as reassurance.

Utilities, as in cost–utility analysis

The outcomes are measured in time units, adjusted by utility weights, such as 'quality adjusted life years'. This approach means that quality is also brought into the equation so that comparisons can be made between treatment regimes which, for example, extend life but at the expense of quality, such as with some chemotherapy treatments.

This technique is used where quality is an important aspect of the regime, for example in programmes which improve social and physical functioning but where mortality is not an issue or where the quality of survival is as important as survival itself, as in the treatment of neonates.

Appendix 1 gives more detail about the derivation and calculation of QALYs.

Benefits, as in cost–benefit analysis

The outcomes are translated into monetary terms, so that they can be commensurate with the costs. Herein lies the problem, as not all benefits can be translated easily into monetary terms. For example, there are many ways in which a human life could be valued, two of which would produce different results – lifetime earnings as against how much a court has awarded in a similar situation.

TECHNIQUES OF ECONOMIC EVALUATION

There are four basic economic techniques that can be applied to any evaluation of a healthcare programme. Each technique concerns itself with costs since, as Fig. 25.6 shows, it is not possible to produce a healthcare programme without consuming resources. The main difference between the techniques is how they deal with the benefits.

Technique 1: cost minimization analysis (CMA)

Cost minimization analysis is used when comparing programmes that are known to produce equal and proven benefits. For example, there are two programmes of minor surgery: one programme involves an overnight stay in hospital and the other is performed on a day-case basis. Providing that evidence exists to indicate that the difference in outcome from the programme will be very small, then a study of cost minimization will suffice.

Technique 2: cost-effectiveness analysis (CEA)

Cost-effectiveness analysis can be used in comparing programmes with similar therapeutic objectives. The outcomes, although common across programmes, will be different in terms of success factors. For example, the comparison of costs and outcome between different renal programmes or the provision of antenatal care can be undertaken via CEA. In the former example, the outcome may be measured in life years that are saved while in the latter, it may be in terms of birth weight of baby.

Technique 3: cost–utility analysis (CUA)

Cost–utility analysis can be used to compare differing healthcare programmes, provided that the benefits or utilities can be measured and hence compared. The utility units can be, for example, quality adjusted life years (QALYs) or healthy days.

Technique 4: cost–benefit analysis (CBA)

Cost–benefit analysis relies on being able to quantify the benefits, as well as the cost, in monetary units; for example, disability days avoided or life years gained can be ascribed a monetary value. This is not, of course, necessarily easy or without ethical questions.

ECONOMIC APPRAISAL AT A PROVIDER LEVEL

The hospital production function

Let us look at the use of economic evaluation at a provider level. A production function is described in Fig. 25.8. It shows what is produced in a hospital (it could equally apply to any provider unit), who is responsible for managing the resources at each stage of the production process and how the production process is combined to produce an outcome, for example a treated patient.

The first two stages of the process relate to economy and efficiency and are largely the concern of the departmental or functional manager, for example the clinical manager of the pathology laboratories who has to purchase chemicals, decide on the appropriate staffing levels and choose equipment. These decisions concern economy. Combining chemicals with staff and machinery time to produce a test result leads to the production of what can be referred to as an intermediate product and concerns the concept of efficiency.

The third stage concerns combining intermediate products, such as operating room procedures, days of care on the ward, drug regimes and pathology tests, to produce a treatment regime that should be effective. The management of this part of the process is certainly under the control of the clinicians.

The fourth stage concerns the combination of 'products' as measured, for example, by healthcare resource groups (HRGs), diagnosis related groups (DRGs) or procedures as given on the GPFH list. The choices at this stage may be under the control of an epidemiologist, who measures patients' needs, or GPFHs.

The cost curve

One method of describing an output is via the cost curve, which draws together the inputs and the costs. Suppose the output being described is an inpatient case such as a hip replacement; it is possible to show what the daily cost profile might be for that patient. Fig. 25.9 shows the 'intermediate products' consumed during each day of the patient's stay and the costs incurred. The care profile indicates that the most expensive days are at the beginning of the stay. The whole cost of the episode of care is the sum of the daily totals.

Suppose the length of stay is reduced. Days 1 and 2 can be removed, since the operation could be done on the day of admission. Days 8 to 10 could be removed as the patient could be discharged on day 7, with the patient convalescing at home. The result is that the total cost of the case is reduced, but the average cost per inpatient day has increased.

What effect will this reduced length of stay have on the efficiency and cost-effectiveness of the hospital?

- The case is more cost-efficient;
- Savings can be made, provided that the bed days saved are not utilized for other cases. However, these savings will be at the margin;
- The savings will be at the margin. There are fewer bed days over which to apportion the fixed costs, which by definition are incurred regardless of the volume of activity;

Hospital production function	Raw goods →	Intermediate products →	End products →	Product lines
	• Labour • Supplies • Capital	• Nursing • Lab tests • X-rays	• DRG • ICD-9-CM • Surgical procedures	• HMO/PPO • Speciality services
Type/level management	Departmental		Clinical	Finance/planning/marketing
Managerial objectives	Manage the cost of raw goods and services	Manage the unit cost of Intermediate products	Manage the utilization of intermediate products	Market existing products products to new markets Market new products to existing markets Improve bottom line
Economic evaluation	Economy	Efficiency	Efficiency Effectiveness	Market forces Competition Equity

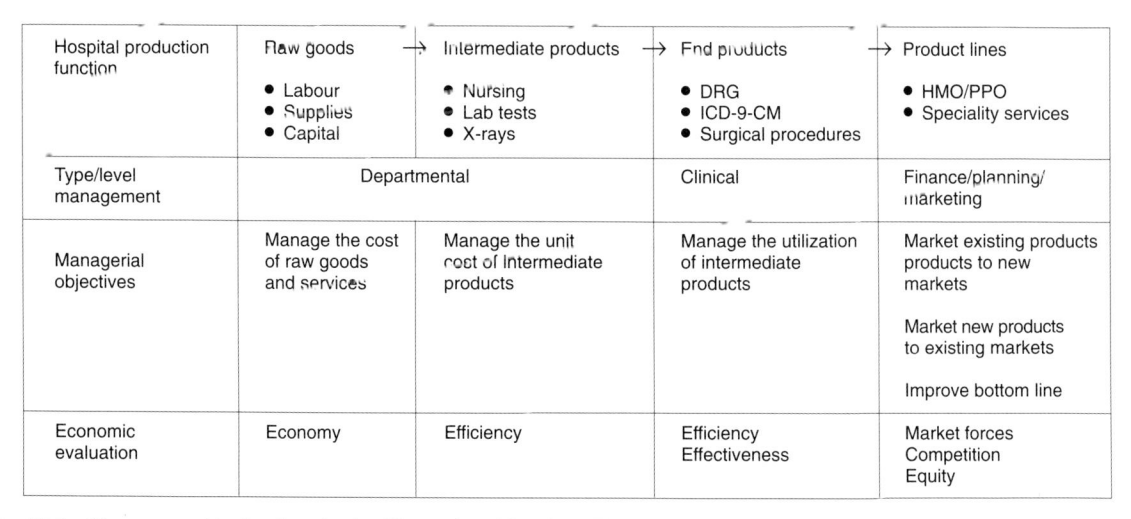

Fig. 25.8 Management technology for healthcare (modified from Transition Systems 1989)

Fig. 25.9 Hypothetical patient–cost profile (from Lowson 1993, pp 9–10)

Key:
- A: Fixed costs
- B: Hotel costs
- C: Administrative costs
- D: Treatment costs

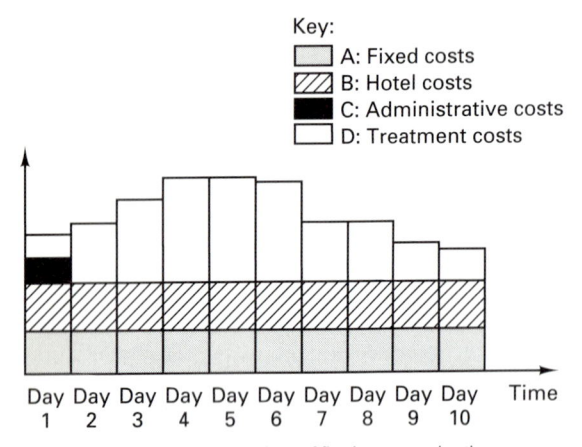

A: Indicate the patient's share of fixed costs, e.g. heating, lighting and capital charges

B: Indicate the patient's share of what are often called 'hotel costs' incurred each day the patient is in hospital, e.g. laundry, cleaning, general staffing of wards and basic nursing care

C: Indicate the administrative costs, e.g. booking in, clerical time associated with case notes, and discharge procedures

D: Indicate the treatment costs associated with that case, e.g. diagnostic procedures, drugs, operation and care in an intensive care unit immediately postoperatively

- Conversely, additional cases could be treated at marginal cost;
- Each inpatient day utilizes resources more intensively.

The management of intermediate products

The production of radiological examinations is under the control of the radiologist and radiology staff. Table 25.3 (see p 247) describes in more detail the inputs to a radiological examination, in this case erect and supine abdominal films. The manager of the radiology department can influence the costs of the radiology test in many ways:

- purchase less costly film or negotiate better prices for the same film;
- reduce film wastage, e.g. changing practices through the education of staff;
- improve management of staff time;
- changing grade or staff mix.

The manager can also influence the way colleagues use the radiology department by persuading them to:

- send patients promptly to the department;
- not to order 'unnecessary tests';
- seek advice regarding the appropriateness of tests.

Much economic evaluation of intermediate products examines issues such as:

- the location of the function, in other words whether to take the technology to the patients or the patient to the technology;
- substitution of staff, such as how to use trained and untrained staff in the best combinations;
- how to use the high cost capital investment, for example of a radiology suite, by means of a throughput, such as attracting business from GPFHs or the private sector;
- the appropriateness of the procedure, for example the value of preoperative chest X-rays or skull films following head injury.

The management of the final product

In the parlance of the hospital production function, treatment for varicose veins is an 'end product' and the surgeon undertaking the treatment is managing the utilization of intermediate products. Table 25.4 shows the combination of possible intermediate products, which are the inputs for the treatment.

Economic evaluation of the final product looks at issues such as:

- when to intervene. Is it preferable to screen and treat rather than wait for a disease to emerge and then treat?
- whether surgical intervention is justified;
- whether to administer therapeutic or surgical intervention;
- the effect of changing length of stay, such as not admitting patients for 1 or 2 days preoperatively or reducing postoperative length of stay;
- location of care, such as hospital at home schemes, with postoperative care taking place in the patient's home;
- the increased use of outpatient care, such as in the care of mental illness;
- the types of prosthesis or materials used for sutures;
- the postoperative management of wounds including dressings and drugs.

How to use economic appraisal

The application of economic appraisal in the majority of clinical situations is certainly within the scope of clinicians and clinical directors or managers who are managing a department providing intermediate products or managing the treatment regimes of the patients.

Table 25.4 Hypothetical treatment for varicose veins (from Lowson 1993, p 11)

Treatment regime 1	Treatment regime 2
3 days on inpatient ward	Treatment in 1 day on day-case unit
Minor operation under general anaesthetic	Minor operation under local anaesthetic
Wound management using dressing type 'x' and drugs type 'y'	Wound management using dressing type 'p' and drugs type 'q'
Amount of physiotherapy, excluding outpatient treatment	Amount of physiotherapy, including outpatient treatment
3 district nurse visits	1 district nurse visit
Total cost: £1200	**Total cost: £950**

However, the effect of the marketplace should also be considered, for example:

1. Supposing spare capacity is created through an appraisal of pathology services or the introduction of day-case surgery; how will this spare capacity be utilized if there is no purchaser?
2. The effect of the introduction of day-case surgery is to create space on wards, meaning that financial savings can be accrued. But how will these savings be calculated – at an average cost or marginal cost – and what will be the effect on prices?
3. Day-case surgery will create savings, but capital investment is required to equip a day-case unit. Can the purchaser be persuaded to support the business case for the extra capital?
4. All the evidence indicates that day-case surgery is cheaper and has equivalent outcome, yet organizational rigidity, such as the flexibility of staff shift patterns and relationships between hospital and community nurses, is hindering change.

The examples given above have concentrated on ways of delivering care for certain conditions or groups of patients. They have not allowed decisions to be made across different types of care groups or the relationship between preventive and curative medicine. This is because providers mostly manage raw goods, intermediate products and end products, as given on the hospital production function. Alternatively, referring to the overview of health economics, they mostly look at the micro level. It is the role of the purchasers to look at the bigger picture, to determine which client groups should be treated, which product lines should be available and issues regarding equity and distribution.

ECONOMIC APPRAISAL AT A PURCHASER LEVEL

Purchasers include such diverse organizations as:

- the National Health Service Management Executive (NHSME) who purchase healthcare direct, for example from the special hospitals and the Public Health Laboratory Service;
- district health authorities who act as local purchasers of secondary healthcare for the majority of the population and purchase from NHS trusts (both hospital and community) and occasionally from private hospitals;
- general practitioner fundholders (GPFHs), who both provide healthcare for the individuals on their practice lists and purchase a range of secondary (mostly non-acute procedures, outpatient care such as mental health and diagnostic tests and paramedical treatments) and community nursing care. Evaluations are also taking place of GPFH consortia (for example, the Worth Valley Consortium in West Yorkshire) and individual GPFH practices (for example, Castlefield Practice in Runcorn, Cheshire) who are purchasing the whole range of services for their practice;
- the Social Services departments of local authorities, who also both purchase and provide services. Under the Care in the Community legislation, local authorities may purchase a range of care from NHS trusts, who are deemed 'independent organizations' in the context of providing care following Social Services assessment.

Funding sources

The first issue that affects purchasing decisions both at governmental and local purchasing levels is the source and size of funding.

Table 25.5 shows the variation in health expenditure as a percentage of GNP. In 1990, it can be seen that the UK had one of the lowest expenditures. However, when converted to 'what can be purchased for each $', the UK can be seen to get 'value for money' and it is argued that the UK has a very cost-effective healthcare system.

There are many reasons for this:

- Wages in the UK healthcare market are not as high as those in other countries, for example France, Germany and the USA.
- A system whereby the majority of the funding comes from taxation is a very cost-effective method of collection. Compare this to the complex methods of the USA (a mixture of private, taxation and insurance) and many European countries.
- A system whereby the healthcare providers receive

Table 25.5 Healthcare expenditures per person for 18 OECD countries, converted by exchange rates and purchasing power parities ($US, 1980) (from Appleby 1992)

Country	Exchange rates (rank)	GDP purchasing power parities (rank)	Medical care purchasing power parities (rank)
Norway	964 (5)	773 (6)	1440 (1)
France	1040 (3)	839 (3)	1267 (2)
Netherlands	988 (4)	777 (5)	1168 (3)
Finland	684 (11)	564 (11)	1157 (4)
Austria	722 (10)	607 (9)	1119 (5)
Japan	569 (12)	537 (13)	1118 (6)
Germany	1065 (2)	818 (4)	1108 (7)
USA	1089 (1)	1089 (1)	1089 (8)
Luxembourg	836 (7)	707 (7)	1070 (9)
UK	548 (13)	484 (15)	907 (10)
Belgium	747 (9)	596 (10)	906 (11)
Denmark	880 (6)	668 (8)	894 (12)
Canada	788 (8)	853 (2)	890 (13)
Italy	479 (15)	541 (12)	854 (14)
Ireland	480 (14)	510 (14)	684 (15)
Spain	334 (16)	376 (16)	544 (16)
Portugal	150 (18)	237 (17)	502 (17)
Greece	175 (17)	211 (18)	388 (18)
Average per cap. spending	696	670	952

funds directly from a few purchasers, as in the UK, is also more cost-effective than the complex method of billing a variety of sources, almost on a per case basis (as in the USA, for example).

- The UK, relatively speaking, is not dramatically 'overbedded' and the UK's inpatient facilities are very intensively used, with high bed occupancies, and also waiting lists.
- Expensive, high tech medicine has historically been rationed, with services provided on a few sites only; specialities, such as cardiac surgery, neurosurgery and plastic surgery, tend to be located at regional hospitals. Thus equipment, such as CAT and NMR scanners, has also been restricted.

In addition, expenditure on healthcare has increased dramatically over the last 10 years:

- There has been an increase in the over-65 age group. The elderly consume a disproportionate amount of healthcare, not just in the traditional speciality of 'geriatrics' but also in most surgical specialities, such as orthopaedics, ophthalmology and cardiac, as well as in general medicine.
- Technology has improved and the range of equipment has increased, for example with the advent of sophisticated CAT and NMR scanners, prostheses and lithotripters.
- There has been a development in drugs and methods of treating diseases such that not only are established diseases being treated with more expensive drugs, sutures, dressing packs and anaesthetics but also new diseases are being treated with new drugs, for example AZT for AIDS.
- More people are being treated, which is due to a combination of consumerism, which increases expectations, and physician-led demand, as well as improved techniques, for example shorter lengths of stay and increased day-case and outpatient treatments.

Not all of the changes above are for the good of the patient or the NHS. Maynard (1993) argues that many technological advances 'have not been investigated thoroughly, and much of the expenditure inflation is produced by innovations of unproven cost-effectiveness'.

The role of purchasers

The role of purchasers is to ensure that the needs of their population are served by appropriate healthcare. Thus purchasers will be concerned about:

- health needs assessment
- equity
- cost-effective purchasing.

Health needs assessment as a methodology for allocating resources is relatively new, although the formula adopted to redress inequalities in the RAWP process (see next section) addressed need via the inclusion of standardized mortality ratios (SMRs).

Health needs assessment

Health needs assessment, at a district purchasing level, is the prerogative of the epidemiologists, occasionally assisted by health economists. All purchasers, via their departments of public health, are now obliged to draw up a health plan. This document addresses the needs of the population served, by reference to the illness patterns, the uptake of, for example, immunizations in children, and comparative figures on, for example, number of hip replacements per 1000 population.

In addition, GPFHs, who are now significant purchasers in some localities, are addressing the needs of their patients by, for example, more thorough screening programmes and a focus on prevention. This emphasis has been encouraged by financial incentives.

Equity

Equity has been an issue for many years. The RAWP (Revenue Allocation Working Party) process was an attempt to address the inequalities in resources and spend across regional boundaries, which still exist. The continued move to weighted capitation-based funding will tackle inequality based on need. Increased equality in funding, however, does not necessarily result in equality in provision of treatments.

Inequality has to be tackled on many fronts. It has to be acknowledged that inequality can be both a supplier problem and a demander problem. Thus inequalities may be tackled by not only changing the volume and method of delivering healthcare, but also by altering consumer perceptions.

Cost-effective purchasing

The move to cost-effective purchasing has been slow, in part because purchasers are not able to judge what is cost-effective. Purchasers themselves may not be able to judge what are desirable levels of delivery. For example, there is enormous geographical variation in the rate of surgical procedures, as shown in Table 25.6. However, what is the acceptable rate and who is to decide?

Nonetheless, there are many initiatives and methodologies that can be utilized by purchasers.

Guidelines The development of guidelines for the treatment of certain conditions, which include criteria for treatment, by the royal colleges and the Scottish Health Management Efficiency Group should ensure a more uniform and equitable approach to treatment.

Initiatives A series of initiatives, commissioned by the Department of Health, has been set in train to facilitate the spread of good practice in the treatment of patients:

Table 25.6 Geographical variations in surgical procedures in England (from Maynard 1993)

Procedure	Rate per 10 000 population (age and sex adjusted)			
	Districts		Region	
	Low	High	Low	High
Herniorrhaphy	10.0	20.0	8.5	14.5
Haemorrhoidectomy	1.0	4.6	1.3	3.0
Prostatectomy	4.5	9.5	5.8	13.2
Cholecystectomy	7.0	11.0	5.7	9.7
Hysterectomy	7.5	15.0	18.1	28.7
Appendicectomy	14.0	21.0	12.9	19.4
Tonsillectomy with and without adenoidectomy	7.5	27.5	14.0	25.0

- York University publishes bulletins on effective healthcare;
- the Nuffield Institute researches epidemiologically based needs assessments, which examine the health needs associated with common conditions such as diabetes and coronary heart disease and cost-effective ways of providing the services.

Outcomes

This work is in its infancy, since many outcomes are long term, and also much of the data for carrying out such studies are not routinely collected.

Nonetheless, many examples do exist, such as:

- deaths on discharge, taking account of case mix;
- readmission rates;
- hospital acquired infections, such as postoperative wound infections and bed sores;
- life years saved, such as measured within cancer studies or alternatively, using methods of quality for weighting life years to derive QALYs.

Purchasers may work with their providers, as determined in the contracts, in order to increase quality. Evidence from the USA and also from the private sector suggests that low quality uses more resources than high quality, since the cost of 'reworking', i.e. the infections, the iatrogenic diseases and the unplanned readmissions, as well as the cost of litigation, can be high.

Cost containment

The NHSME also undertake initiatives which are designed to contain costs rather than deliver cost-effectiveness, such as:

- monitoring the prescribing habits of GPs via the PACT (Prescribing Analysis and Cost Data). Currently, this is a crude tool to reduce variation in prescribing costs amongst GPs, but with some imagination the data could be combined with other GP-related data, such as referral patterns, or linked to the above 'best practice' guidance;
- the introduction of the 'limited list' of drugs that can be prescribed routinely by GPs; in addition GPs are encouraged to use generic rather than branded drugs;
- increasing the percentage of certain procedures that are undertaken on a day-case basis.

The delivery of much of the above, such as the use of guidelines, the adoption of best practice or the percentage of day-case activity, are within the remit of the providers. However, it is possible, through the contracting process, for purchasers to request that such approaches are used.

Priority setting

A purchaser's healthcare plan, by taking account of need, should address priorities. There are alternative methods for this but the most common and well documented are the use of QALYs and the Oregon experiment.

QALYs The principle behind the usage of QALYs is that purchasers should seek treatments that either maximize the number of QALYs per pound of expenditure or minimize the pounds spent per QALY.

North Western Regional Health Authority carried out an experiment in 1987 into using QALYs for helping in the allocation of its regional speciality fund. In the event, it did not prove possible to do so; problems included the derivation of a QALY for a diagnostic procedure (such as tissue typing), for an untried treatment (AIDS) and for treatments which may be for life against those that are a one-off, as well as the adverse political and media interest (Allen et al 1989).

Table 25.7 provides a league table of treatments the outcomes from which are relatively easy to measure, which could influence purchasers' intentions. Although the findings are tentative, the range of cost per QALY must give purchasers some guidance.

Oregon experiment This comprised a method of deciding priorities for treatment regimes, in response to cost pressures on Medicaid. The method comprised the drawing up of 709 pairs of 'conditions with treatments', from which a list of 587 had to be prioritized for funding by the state government. This represented a 15% reduction in spend.

Public meetings determined 13 basic values, which included quality of life and equity, against which the list of preferred condition/treatments could be judged.

This method has been criticized on many counts, for example, the lack of a random selection of people attending the meetings, the lack of cost data and the initial strange priorities, such as the fact that tooth capping was rated higher than acute emergency operations. In addition, economists have criticized the approach by arguing that if only cost-effective treatments were used, there would not have been a problem and that the final listing could reinforce non-cost-effective treatments.

In the event, this process was an explicit approach to involving the general public in the thankless task of prioritizing treatments and recipients.

Prioritizing in the UK Many purchasers have now stated that they are not prepared to pay for such treat-

Table 25.7 Quality adjusted life year (QALY) of competing therapies: some tentative estimates (from Kind & Gudix 1993)

	Cost/QALY (£ Aug 1990)
Cholesterol testing and diet therapy only (all adults, aged 40–69)	220
Neurosurgical intervention for head injury	240
GP advice to stop smoking	270
Neurosurgical intervention for subarachnoid haemorrhage	490
Antihypertensive therapy to prevent stroke (ages 45–64)	940
Pacemaker insertion	1100
Hip replacement	1180
Valve replacement for aortic stenosis (narrowing)	1410
Cholesterol testing and treatment	1480
CABG (left main vessel disease, severe angina)	2090
Kidney transplant	4710
Breast cancer screening	5780
Heart transplantation	7840
Cholesterol testing and treatment (incrementally) of all adults 25–39 years	14 150
Home haemodialysis	17 260
CABG (1 vessel disease, moderate angina)	18 830
CAPD	19 870
Hospital haemodialysis	21 970
Erythropoietin treatment for anaemia in dialysis patients (assuming a 10% reduction in mortality)	54 380
Neurosurgical intervention for malignant brain tumours	107 780
Erythropoietin treatment for anaemia in dialysis patients (assuming no increase in survival)	126 290

CABG, coronary artery bypass graft; CAPD, continuous ambulatory peritoneal dialysis

ments as minor plastic surgery and IVF. Therefore, patients have to receive private treatment or find a GPFH who is prepared to fund or provide this treatment inhouse.

General practice fundholders In addition, GPFHs are changing their referral patterns by searching for providers who offer cheaper treatments within a quality framework and offering inhouse care such as minor surgery and stress counselling. They also search for the shorter waiting lists. Cost-effectiveness of treatment and prioritization seem to play important roles in their purchasing decisions.

Innovative purchasing

There are alternative ways of improving health which may involve working with the housing and education departments of the local authorities. Purchasers can work with their local authorities in providing, for example, 'one-stop shops', funding community workers, looking at nutrition and the types of shops on housing estates and running mother and toddler groups. In addition, health-related initiatives, such as Health at Work, need to be run in conjunction with local industry as well as the local authority.

THE WAY FORWARD FOR HEALTH ECONOMICS

The overview of health economics, as given in Fig. 25.5, shows that it has an effect on most aspects of the delivery of health and healthcare. Clinicians have an important role to play in ensuring that resources are used such that the improvement in health is maximized. That clinicians have a role is indicated by the fact that the *BMJ*, the *New England Journal of Medicine* and speciality-orientated journals such as the *Journal of Psychiatry* regularly run articles on health economics.

Clinicians now have a greater management orientation; clinical directors take responsibility for budgets, skill mix of staff, volume and case mix of activity and quality standards within their directorate and also are increasingly involved in contract negotiations. Therefore at a micro level, as this chapter has described, it is critical that clinicians manage resources such that cost-effectiveness and efficiency are taken into account.

At a purchaser level, epidemiologists are exhorted by the NHSME to take economics into their decision making. Provided that clinicians understand the toolkit that is the economics approach, they should know when and how to apply the tools.

APPENDIX 1 THE USE OF QALYS

QALYs are quality adjusted life years and they represent a mechanism for incorporating quality and quantity into outcome measurements.

Their use is based on two tenets of health economics:

1. We want to generate *beneficial* healthcare, i.e. healthcare that does not just add years to life but life to years (i.e. positive QALYs).
2. We want to have *efficient* healthcare, i.e. where each QALY generated is low cost or as high a number of QALYs as possible is generated for each £1000 invested in healthcare.

We therefore need to look at the *measurement* of the benefits of healthcare, where the benefits are outcomes and not just outputs.

QALYs are a way of incorporating life expectancy and the quality of life such that society's values are also reflected. This is done by weighting life years gained, derived from societal weightings.

The assumptions underpinning QALYs are therefore that:

- we can define health (and ill health);
- we can elicit values from individuals so that states of (ill) health can be ranked and weighted;
- the rankings can be aggregated.

The philosophy is that:

- a year of 'healthy' life is worth 1;
- a year of 'unhealthy' life is worth less than 1;
- the more 'unhealthy' the year of life, the lower the value it has;
- death equates to zero;
- there are states worse than death, which have a measure of less than 1 (i.e. negative).

Years of life are weighted using the Rosser Index (Kind et al 1982). The problem in weighting a condition of ill health is being able to quantify and compare a state in which, say, an individual is in little pain but is immobile to a state of extreme pain but some mobility.

The Rosser Index allows the bringing together of disability and distress onto a single index. The classification has eight states of disability and four states of distress, each of which has a weighting, derived from interviews with a societal cross-section.

Table 25.8 gives the classifications. Thus a year of life in State V disability and C distress (i.e. unable to undertake paid employment or to continue education; old people are confined to home except for escorted outings and short walks and unable to do shopping, and housewives able only to perform a few simple tasks and in moderate distress) is worth 0.9 of a healthy year of life.

Figs 25.10 and 25.11, taken from Williams (1985), show how QALYs can be used in choosing treatment regimes. Patients who are treated for severe angina and left main vessel disease have two options – medical management and a coronary artery bypass grafting (CABG). The CABG is given to 70%, of whom 3% die postoperative (profile C). The remaining 67% (profile A) live for 11 years, which is approximately 6 more years gained than the 30% who have medical management (profile B). However, the profile A patients don't just live longer, they have a higher quality of life. The gain in life years *and* quality is given by the shaded area.

Table 25.8 Rosser's classification of illness states (from Kind et al 1982)

	Disability		Distress
I	No disability	A	No distress
II	Slight social disability	B	Mild
III	Severe social disability and/or slight impairment of performance of work. Able to do all housework except very heavy tasks	C	Moderate
		D	Severe
IV	Choice of work or performance at work very severely limited. Housewives and old people able to do light housework only but able to go out shopping		
V	Unable to undertake any paid employment. Unable to continue any education. Old people confined to home except for escorted outings and short walks and unable to do shopping. Housewives able only to perform a few simple tasks		
VI	Confined to chair or to wheelchair or able to move around in the house only with support from an assistant		
VII	Confined to bed		
VIII	Unconscious		

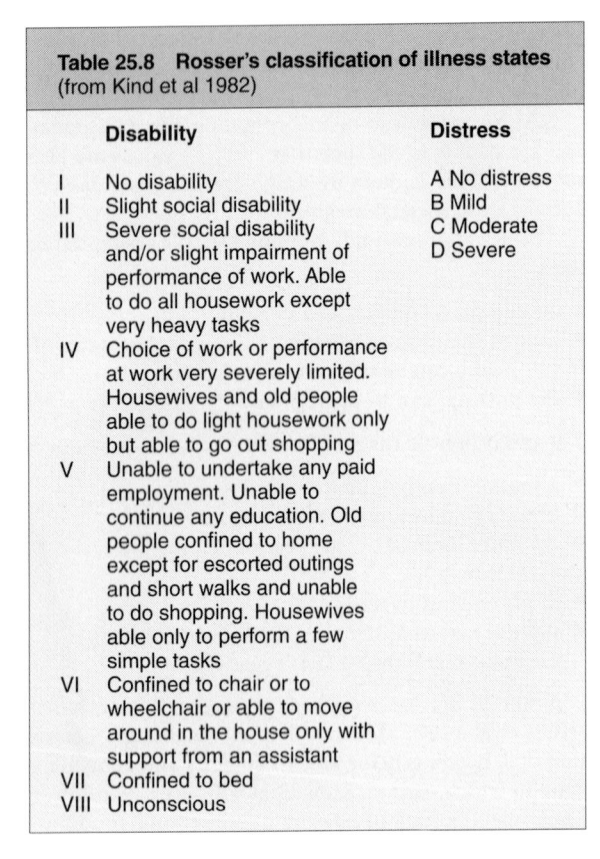

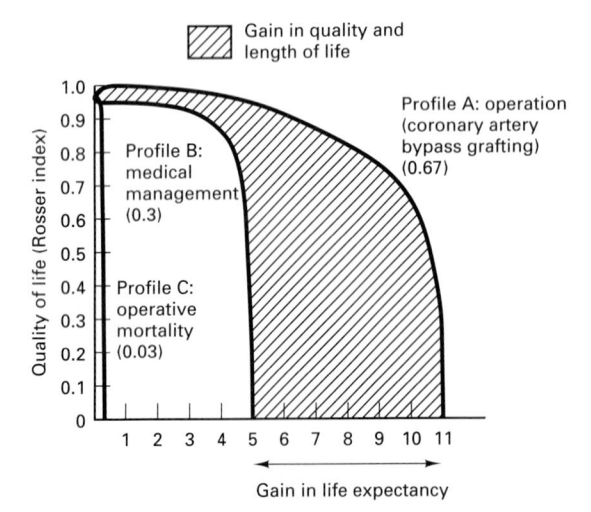

Fig. 25.10 Expected value of quality and length of life gained for patients with severe angina and left main vessel disease (from Williams 1985)

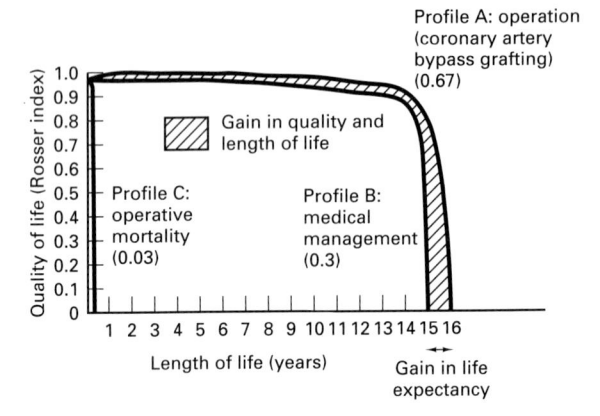

Fig. 25.11 Expected value of quality and length of life gained for patients with severe angina and one vessel disease (from Williams 1985)

REFERENCES

Allen D, Lee R, Lowson K 1989 The use of QALYs in local health service planning. International Journal of Health Planning and Management 4: 261–273

Appleby J 1992 Financing healthcare in the 1990s. Open University Press, Buckingham

Cooper M H, Culyer A J 1973 Health economics. Penguin, Harmondsworth

Culyer A J 1976 Need and the NHS. Martin Robertson, London

Drummond M 1984 Principles of economic appraisal in health care. Oxford University Press, p 2

Drummond M 1993 The contribution of health economics to cost-effective healthcare delivery. In: Drummond M, Maynard A (eds) Purchasing and providing cost-effective health care. Churchill Livingstone, Edinburgh, p 20

Drummond M F, Stoddart G L, Torrance G W 1990 Methods for the economic evaluation of health care programmes. Oxford Medical Publications, Oxford

Kind P, Gudix C 1993 In: Drummond M, Maynard A (eds) Purchasing and providing cost-effective health care. Churchill Livingstone, London

Kind P, Rosser R, Williams A 1982 Valuation of quality of life: some psychometric evidence. In: Jones-Lee M W (ed) The value of life and safety. North Holland, Amsterdam

Lowson K 1993. Health economics for clinician managers. The clinician in Management 2(3)

Maynard A 1993 The significance of cost-effective purchasing. In: Drummond M, Maynard A (eds) Purchasing and providing cost-effective health care. Churchill Livingstone, London

Mooney G 1986 Economics, medicine and health care. Wheatsheaf, Hemel Hempstead

Samuelson P 1970 Economics. McGraw-Hill, New York, p 4

Williams A 1985 The economics of coronary artery bypass grafting. British Medical Journal : 326–329

26

Personnel, performance and staff appraisal

Helen Witt

In any organization it is vital that its managers and staff are clear about key objectives that are to be attained and how these relate to the work of themselves and others. To appraise (performance review) or not? The appraisal process, or individual performance review (IPR) to use current language, is a management process, a systematic way of achieving clarity of purpose, a process used by many organizations (including hospitals and healthcare services) to:

- ensure that goals and objectives are communicated to all staff and understood;
- ensure that the opportunity for feedback on performance is provided;
- ensure that staff are sufficiently skilled to meet the requirements of the organization;
- identify any gaps and ways of meeting them;
- identify, monitor and meet if appropriate individuals' needs and training/career development plans.

In other words:

- Where am I?
- Where do I want to go?
- Where does the organization want me to go?

Performance review looks at:

- What was set out to be achieved during the year?
- Was it achieved?
- What is to be done next?
- What measurement will be used to identify if it has been achieved or not?

Historically appraisal tended to be the once a year or once every 2 years 'telling off'. Both staff and management, particularly within public bodies, used the process in a negative way, concentrating on the past, taking the formal opportunity to reprimand staff or discipline

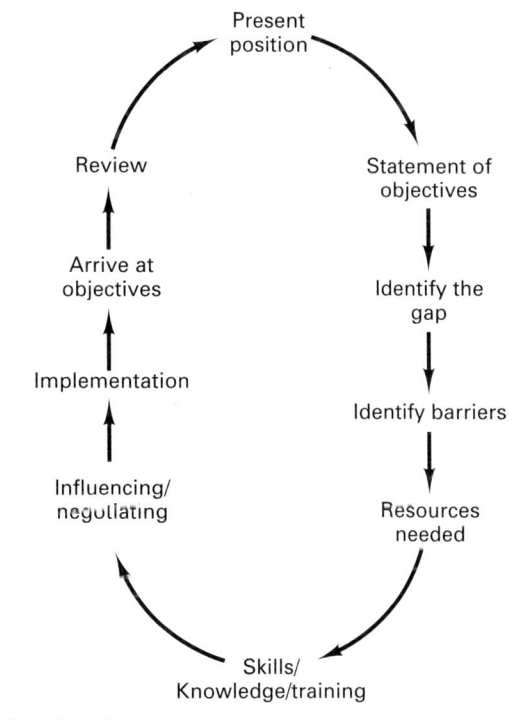

Fig. 26.1 IPR is part of the overall management process

them and to identify faults requiring correction. Very little attention was paid to all the good that had happened, skills that had been perfected and progress that had been made. In a way this made a mockery of the process. Any fault requiring attention should be dealt with at the time of occurrence via the processes available, not saved up and dealt with once a year when memories have faded and the troublesome employee has become even more troublesome or the circumstances leading to the fault have become so overwhelming that the employee leaves or is more severely disciplined than would have been appropriate at an earlier stage.

It would be reasonable to say that the appraisal process within the NHS in the past has been misused, due to lack of training and understanding by those both applying the process and those receiving appraisal. Appraisal systems should be flexible and able to take account of organizational changes, with constant monitoring to ensure that the process is up to date and live, so that staff can learn how they are doing, acquire new skills and correct mistakes. Good organizations build in long-range requirements for achievement as well as short-term objectives (usually 12 months). This practice also tends to be applied by those successfully using the process within the service, as this assists both the organization and employees in making positive growth and reducing the need for firefighting activity only.

There are many types of performance review schemes. The best are those which are flexible to meet the current need. Previously systems may have used personality factors to demonstrate success or failure but these have generally fallen into disuse, as such measures are difficult to apply, depending upon personal relationships rather than performance. Similarly some systems have devised complicated measurement and ranking scales to demonstrate success or failure, the difficulty here being that such systems may not be equally applicable to all staff nor equally applied by those administering the system. Objective setting, which is becoming the more acceptable method, allows greater freedom to both parties in determining how performance is measured.

Performance review should be a special two-way session – reviewing progress to date and identifying and agreeing future objectives, concentrating on skills rather than traits. When considering performance reviews within the health sector environment it is useful to use the following headings:

- Why have IPR?
- The process and the concept
- Interested parties and who they are
- The paperwork
- Training – identification of and meeting the needs
- Objectives
- Appraisal interview and review
- The appraisee
- Why appraisal can fail.

WHY HAVE PERFORMANCE REVIEW/ APPRAISAL?

Individual performance review (IPR) as a management process reviews the recent past (usually the last 12 months) and plans for the future to ensure that a hospital's objectives and needs are in harmony with potentially its most expensive resource, the staff. This resource needs to be sufficiently trained and skilled to meet the future needs identified via business plans and objectives and any other formalized plans of how the hospital or service wishes to move forward, as well as meeting individual development needs.

There are three parties to the process – organization, appraiser and appraisee. IPR exists to:

Motivate

Most staff, while being self-motivated, value time being set aside for a formal appraisal. They welcome the opportunity to explore privately the success (and failures) of the past, their levels of performance and value to the organization, in addition to identifying training/development needs and planning them to be of mutual benefit.

In effective organizations communication is ongoing. The appraisal process enhances this and provides for unique extra special communication. It gives time for two individuals to discuss confidentially and privately success or failure and the way forward, leaving the employee motivated as they have received feedback on their own performance plus providing them with the opportunity to have their say and be clear on the direction for the coming period.

Improve performance

Employees receiving constructive feedback on performance will use it to build on strengths and resolve weaknesses, to enable them and the organization to move forward. Negative feedback can be destructive if used in a careless, unmanaged way, leaving the employee demoralized and potentially dangerous to the employer. The employee will lose their way and the employer may resort to other formal processes (mainly discipline or counselling) to manage a situation which should not have occurred in the first instance. That is not to say that negative criticism should not be used in the appraisal process. Arguably it is as important as the use of positive criticism. The secret lies in the way the appraiser presents the criticism and how the appraisee receives it. If done in a sensitive, encouraging, supporting fashion, the appraisee's reception should be positive. Any criticism given in an unplanned way can be highly destructive.

Chance to give view of the department/ directorate

As the appraisal interview is a special session, most

employees will have spent some time preparing, giving order to their thoughts, thinking of objectives they would like to work to and other needs.

Employees have views on how the department and/or the hospital is functioning and should be encouraged to express them in a constructive positive way. Employees' comments and criticisms can be of great value. Their views must be treated seriously if an atmosphere of trust is to be developed. The appraisal interview creates the right environment for such an opportunity to occur.

Promotion and/or future prospects

It is natural for discussion relating to promotion and future prospects to occur in the interview. Future prospects are related to and are an integral part of the objective setting process.

Employees 'have a mortgage to pay' and likewise the hospital is looking for the highest possible return on its investment in human resource terms. Employees need a clear idea of their value and future prospects. Management must be able to deal with this question and give an honest answer. A high flyer with nowhere to fly can be just as disastrous as the constant poor performer who has never been told or the employee who has reached their own plateau and has never had this identified for them. All types of employees have a value to the organization. It is the way they and their progress are managed which makes for success or not.

Training needs

Identification of training needs, like future prospects is also an integral part of the process. It is the identification of the 'gap' between needs and skills (Fig. 26.2) and how the gap can be closed, thus ensuring that the employee is suitably skilled to meet the needs of the organization and their own individual needs. This is vital to the overall motivation of the employee.

Exercise control

The appraisal process and in particular the interview should be as close to 50/50 participation of appraisee and appraiser as possible. While to some such a statement may represent employee/employer utopia in reality it is an expectation to be striven for. Such a balance represents the openness and fairness of the process and can be a positive statement to an employee that they really are a respected player. Some will argue that such a balance is impossible as 'someone' has to remain in control, if only to ensure that it is the hospital or service that comes first. However, if the process is handled positively and properly both participants can succeed. In reality, acknowledging the need to have some form of recognized control, participation perhaps should be at a level of 56/44.

Identify weaknesses

Because the process is private and confidential between immediate manager and subordinate, it presents the opportunity for weaknesses to be identified and assistance given through training and development to turn weakness to strength. Employees, while enjoying hearing what they are good at, also benefit from having weakness identified and planning how, if necessary, it can be overcome or accepting it as something that both

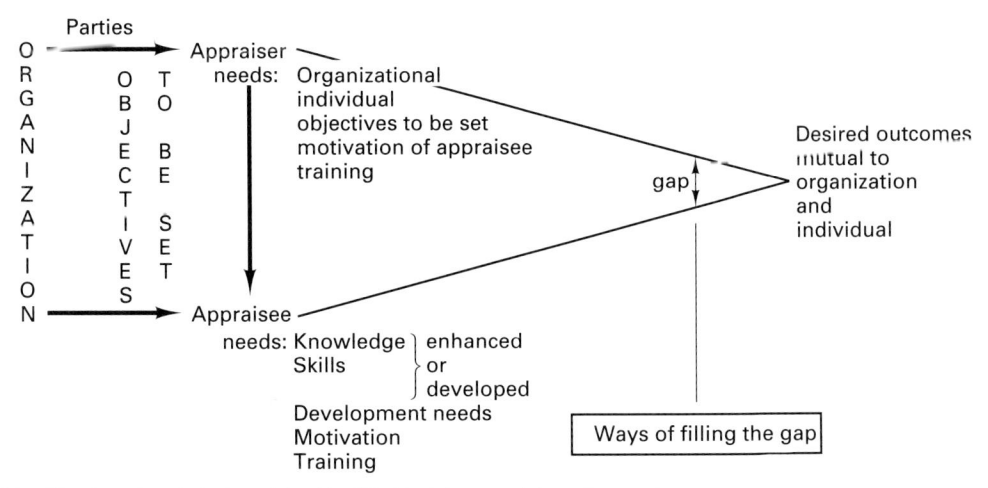

Fig. 26.2 Identification of and closing of the identified training needs/development gap

the organization and individual can live with. It is not only poor performers who have weaknesses, good performers and the high flyers can have them as well. The skill in the appraisal process is identifying the weakness and then planning and agreeing between both parties how it will be managed and improved upon. Employees find it easier to participate in this assessment process when they know what their objectives are rather than looking at personal qualities and characteristics.

Impress the boss

Employees, given the opportunity, wish to impress their boss. Receiving praise has a 'glowing effect': motivation is enhanced, their feeling of belonging is increased, appreciation of the hospital or service is added to and the relationship between manager and subordinate improved. Good management should be able to say thank you and give praise at all times when appropriate.

Subordinates do not always have opportunities to 'impress the boss' in their everyday activities. The appraisal process provides the environment, albeit formal, for management to say thank you and for the employee to make management aware of how good an employee they have.

Review salary

In some organizations salary review is linked to the appraisal process. In the main this is not something that the NHS does (except for those on senior managers pay where pay is linked with achieving objectives). Linking pay to the appraisal process can have questionable results. If the appraisee has performed throughout the year solely to achieve the objectives set and a good salary review, this can be to the detriment of the hospital or service and others (and themselves). Money is not always the main reason why a person undertakes a particular job so rewarding with money may not be that great a motivator. For the poor performer a low salary increase is not necessarily the most appropriate way of getting the best from them. Money is a motivator but it usually achieves the best results when linked to other things, e.g. recognition of ability, appreciation and value acknowledged. When linked to the appraisal process it can undermine other important factors of the interview, e.g. identification of training needs, and have a negative effect on the whole process. However, reviewing salary as part of the appraisal process can also have a very positive effect.

In the main, organizations which link salary review to the appraisal process usually do so by two different interviews, treating the issues separately.

Set goals/objectives

The setting of goals and objectives is dealt with later in this chapter. Suffice it to say here that the setting of goals or objectives is vital to the whole appraisal process. Goals or objectives provide the basis for reviewing, planning the future and meeting training needs.

WHAT IS IPR?

The process and concept. IPR is a special session which concentrates on looking ahead. There are nine components of the IPR process and six stages to the process.

The nine components are:

1. Present position
2. Future aim
3. The gap – objectives
4. Barriers and resources
5. Skills and knowledge
6. Negotiating/influencing
7. Decisions/implement
8. Reach aim
9. Review.

1. Present position

Where are the appraisee, appraiser and hospital or service currently and how did they get there? If already in the IPR cycle, progress is made by achieving the objectives set the year before. If the process is being used for the first time, all parties need to consider how they have got to their present position; this may produce some diversity of views!

If you are about to embark on the process for the first time, it should be recognized that it will take time. The skill is in ensuring that this time is used constructively and not just as a moan session from either party. When already in the process this review of the present position may still take time and should not be unnecessarily hurried. Circumstances will have changed in the year, 'goal posts' moved, objectives not reached for good (or bad) reasons. All factors need to be fully explored if previous objectives and performance are to be successfully evaluated and the coming year's requirements properly and fairly set in new objectives (Table 26.1).

2. Future aim

IPR should never be undertaken by an appraiser if they themselves have not received their own individual performance review. Most systems work on a cascade process (which within the health environment would commence with the chief executive appraising the

Table 26.1 Time taken to complete the IPR process

Preparation	Interview	Complete documents	Review	Repeat process	Time taken
1st Time Round					
Appraiser/ee undertakes research and preparation. Time spent depends on degree of research required. Time span 2–3 h 1–2 weeks before the appraisal	Appraiser/ee formal interview. Normal time span 2–3 h. If unanticipated difficulties present themselves, it may take longer	Appraiser/ee conduct 2nd meeting to check and agree paperwork from interview and areas agreed. Objectives finalized. Time span usually 30 mins–1 h	Appraiser/ee review meetings throughout the cycle, aim being to adjust objectives depending on circumstances and if required. To monitor progress. Time span no more than 15–30 mins each time	End of year. Evaluate success or failure. Commence process again, i.e. start again on year 2	Total time taken approx 7–8 h in a year (a working day)
2nd Time Round					
Appraiser/ee prepares for year 2. Time span depends on degree of updating required as much of the foundation work has been done in year 1. Time span no more than 2 h in advance of the appraisal	Appraiser/ee formal interview. As for year 1. Normal time span 2–3 h	As for year 1	As for year 1	As for year 1. Prepare and start cycle for year 3	Total time taken approx 5–7 h in a year
3rd Time Round					
As for years 1 & 2 above	As for year 2 above with increase or decrease in time and activity for certain sections, depending upon need and development issues	As for years 1 & 2 above	As for years 1 & 2 above	As for years 1 & 2 above. Move into year 4	Total time taken approx 4–6 h in a year
Note on time spans and inputs Time spans and inputs can and will vary at any time depending on any changes that may occur in the cycle, e.g. appraisee changes, new manager appointed, objectives changed, training not being readily available, other problems or barriers to be overcome and not anticipated or planned for in critical stages					

hospital or service directors, (both clinical and non-clinical).

It is important to maintain the relationship between appraiser and subordinate as closely as possible, i.e. the appraiser undertakes only their immediate subordinates, who in turn review those subordinate to them and so it goes on. For example, in a ward environment, the E grade nurse may review the nursing auxiliary if they are the closest to each other and work together in the team. This enables the process and educational and professional development to link together in a beneficial and compatible way rather than be treated as three separate components. This theory (and practice) does not sit easily with some but consideration does have to be given to time factors, particularly if you're a clinical director with 300 staff!

262 TEXTBOOK OF MANAGEMENT FOR DOCTORS

Future aims can only be identified and planned for if the appraiser has themselves been appraised as it is predominantly the linking of organizational needs with individual needs that moves the process forward. How can objectives be set locally if those participating in the process have no idea of where the hospital or service is going or what its needs are? These can be found in the trust's or unit's business plans and other strategy documents and Department of Health documents and plans. The process would therefore be similar to the chart in Fig 26.3.

As the process moves to the more junior levels of staff it may take on a 'local identity' to meet the needs at shopfloor level, e.g. junior staff who regularly rotate around different sections of a department or directorate present the question of who can most effectively undertake their appraisal.

For the more senior staff objectives and future aims will be more global than those on the shop floor. For example, a clinical director may be charged with increasing theatre usage and number of cases dealt with in a year.

For an E or D grade nurse, their part in helping to meet this wider objective would relate to their immediate sphere of care and control such as increasing their levels of skill, using new patient documentation procedures or changes in clinical practice.

Similarly a junior doctor may need to look at their clinical practices and development needs to enable them to assist in meeting such an objective, in addition to identifying their education needs.

Future aim links an employee and their individual skills and abilities to the overall aims of the hospital or service which are honed down to the particular department and management structure within which they work. This aim or aims will not stand alone and will be interrelated with what colleagues, managers and directors are doing.

3. The gap

If you examine the present position and the future, you will be able to identify what is known as the 'gap', the

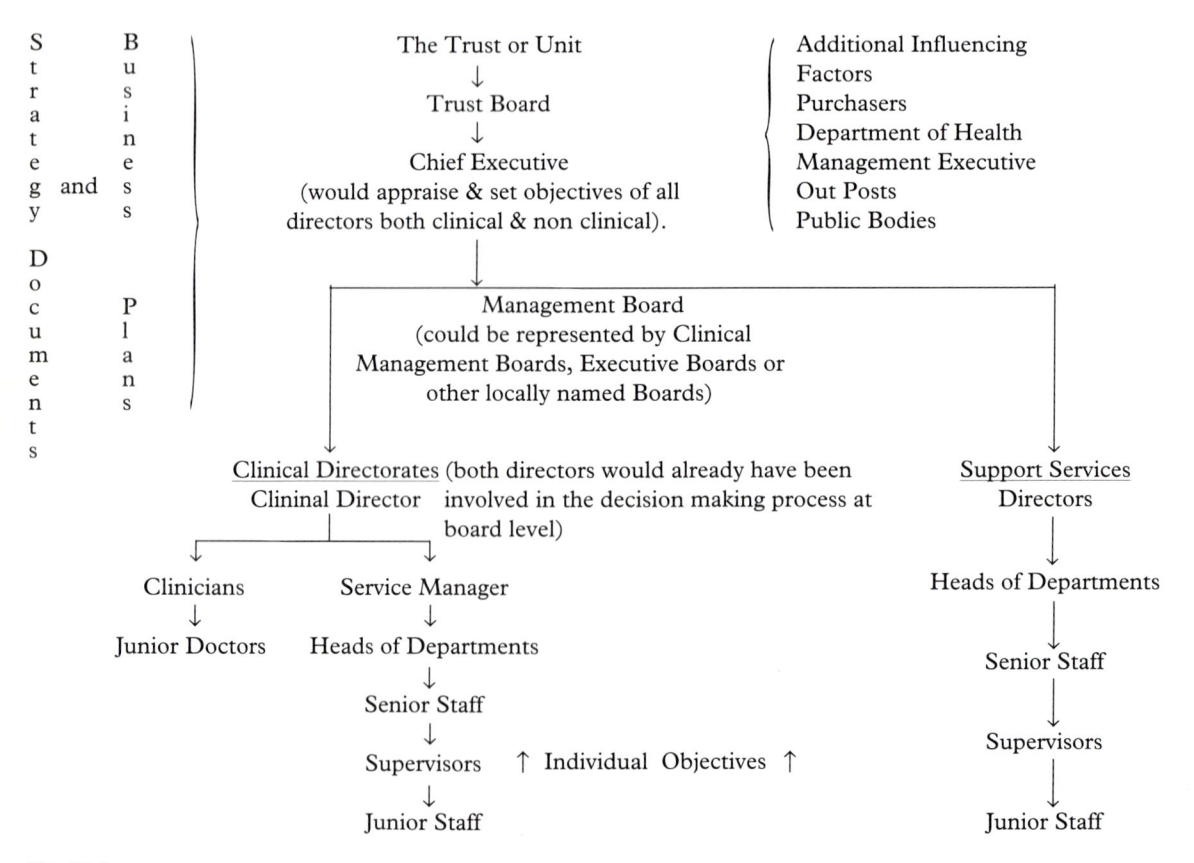

Strategy Documents / Business Plans

The Trust or Unit
↓
Trust Board
↓
Chief Executive
(would appraise & set objectives of all directors both clinical & non clinical).
↓
Management Board
(could be represented by Clinical Management Boards, Executive Boards or other locally named Boards)
↓

Additional Influencing Factors
Purchasers
Department of Health
Management Executive
Out Posts
Public Bodies

Clinical Directorates (both directors would already have been involved in the decision making process at board level)
Clininal Director

Clinicians
↓
Junior Doctors

Service Manager
↓
Heads of Departments
↓
Senior Staff
↓
Supervisors   ↑ Individual Objectives ↑
↓
Junior Staff

Support Services Directors
↓
Heads of Departments
↓
Senior Staff
↓
Supervisors
↓
Junior Staff

Fig. 26.3

void to be overcome to enable the future aim to be met or worked toward. The gap generates the objectives by which the overall aim will be achieved; it is getting from A to B via a variety of resources depending on the need.

A manager may wish to devolve budget management to the lowest manageable level. For the ward sister receiving their appraisal an objective may be to take budget responsibility for their ward. In order to implement this, the objective needs to be broken down into smaller component parts.

Objective

For ward sisters to take budget responsibility for their wards.

Actions

1. Budgets to be broken down correctly in the first instance. Liaison between finance manager and ward sister.
2. Ward sister to receive training in budget management.
3. Ward sister to shadow their manager in budget management for final quarter of the year.
4. Complete budget management to be handed over to ward sister at commencement of new financial year.

In effect, for the ward sister there are three objectives to be achieved in the current objective-setting year (1–3) with objective 4 being carried into the coming year. This would be reflected in the objective-setting process as identification of long-term goals (usually over a rolling 5-year period).

The appraisal process is not all one way and appraisees will also have their own personal set of objectives. These can range from enhancing skills, achieving promotion, going on a course, undertaking study, meeting educational needs and reducing hours to moving department or team. The skilled appraiser will recognize the value of allowing some individual objectives to be agreed. Preferably they should be related to achieving hospital or service needs as well. The request to attend a course or receive further training may be agreed if it enhances the appraisee's ability in their current area of work or as part of a planned development/educational programme. A request to undertake study not related to the area of work may be considered less favourably.

Under the old style of appraisal employees saw the process as first meeting their own training needs with little consideration of the value of this to the hospital or service. An example relating to a technical department relates how technicians would regularly request and receive the opportunity to undertake business studies. While the manager was to be commended for being farsighted enough to see that such skills would stand the department in good stead, the questions to be asked were: did the technicians need these skills? Were these skills useful back in the workplace? How many technicians left after receiving such training? Would the technicians (and the department) have benefited more from further technical training?

It is important to strike a balance between the needs of the organization and the desires of the individual.

4. Barriers and resources

No objective should be set for an appraisee that is virtually impossible to achieve. The process is not a test but the mutual development of the individual and the hospital or service. Therefore objectives must be realistic and achievable with normal activity.

Recognition of barriers and resources relates to the identification of obstacles to the achievement of an objective. There is no value in asking an employee to undertake computer work if they are not computer literate, the department does not have a computer or time scales for going live are not known. An objective that involves another department can only be achieved if management have gained acceptance from that department to have access to it and its staff. It would be wrong to set an objective knowing that those who are involved in it are going to be absent for some or all of the duration of the objective.

The appraiser must consider the difficulties objectives may present and enable the appraisee to be as well resourced as possible for their achievement. Barriers and resources may also relate to the appraisee's skills and abilities.

5. Skills and knowledge

There is no point in setting an objective for which the appraisee is not skilled unless the development of such skill or knowledge is acknowledged as part of the package. The identification of skills and knowledge – current and future – is critical, being undertaken predominantly at the objective-setting part of the process. If action is not subsequently provided on the needs identified, this will lead to disillusionment with the system and declining performance by the employee.

6. Negotiating/influencing

There can be a trade-off between hospital or service and

individual objectives. The normal number of objectives for most would range between four and eight. The appraiser is responsible for prioritizing objectives and gaining the acceptance of the appraisee to take them on board. If the appraiser has identified eight objectives which the appraisee accepts but the appraisee also has two or three of their own, a wise appraiser may be prepared (subject to criteria identified previously) to drop one or two of theirs to allow the individual one or two personal objectives. This acts as a motivator, demonstrates that the appraisee is important to the process and keeps the number of objectives manageable and achievable. Both parties will negotiate what comes out of the process; the success is in ensuring that all parties achieve a win–win situation.

7. Decisions/implement

Once objectives have been clarified, barriers and resources resolved and training needs identified and planned for, objectives can be implemented and progress monitored throughout the year. Although objectives are set for the year, some are short-term and some long-term. Some can only start once something else has happened. In terms of time scales not every objective has to start on 1 April and end on 31 March every year. The timing of all objectives should be identified and be workable, with priorities being identified at the beginning. Objectives should allow for changes, if known; the unknown should be taken into account at the mini review stages throughout the year.

8. Reach aim

Agreed and workable objectives should be achieved at the end of the year, but due to unforeseen circumstances they may be on their way to achievement or have been dropped as unrealistic. The process must be flexible to work. If the process is inflexible it will be open to abuse and distrusted and may close a line of communication throughout the organization.

9. Review

The main review of the process should occur at the end of the cycle (12 months) and the beginning of the new cycle. If the process is to remain live, periodic review should also occur throughout the cycle (usually quarterly, with a 6-month review as a minimum) taking no longer than 15–30 minutes. Such reviews provide the opportunity for support, counselling or coaching. They allow the ability to amend any objective, identify problems or barriers and agree action plans to overcome these, for communication and to keep the process flexible and timely.

A small team of junior doctors in ENT, when asked if they saw any benefit in such a process, responded with an overwhelming yes. They perceived that such a process provided a framework within which to work and periodically check direction and needs. It also provided the opportunity for structured feedback, which they felt was sometimes not as constructive as it could be, particularly on issues where it may be most needed, i.e. career direction or educational needs.

The six stages of the process are:

Stage 1

| Give IPR documents to individuals at least two weeks prior to interview. |

Stage 2 ↓

| Individual considers and completes the documents. |

Stage 3 ↓

| Individual and manager meet, discuss progress and set objectives for future performance. |

Stage 4 ↓

| Meet regularly to monitor progress. |

Stage 5 ↓

| At the end of the year have a major review meeting. |

Stage 6 ↓

| Start the process again. |

Fig. 26.4

While stages 3–6 have been adequately covered, stages 1 and 2 are considered here.

Stage 1 Preparation

If the IPR process is to work and be believed in as an open, partnership process, much can be achieved by establishing openness right from the very beginning. Most systems rely on paperwork of some kind to assist this process. If there is to be nothing secretive about the process, there is value in giving a blank document to the appraisee in advance of their appraisal (stage 1) to enable them to prepare themselves as much as the appraiser might. Such documents may contain the following headings:

- Personal preparation form (includes current job and its strengths and weaknesses, career interests and development needs)
- Performance plan (objectives)
- Aspects of performance skills
- Personal development plan
- Notes.

Most documents require the appraisee to have some thoughts on their needs. It is better to ask the appraisee to consider this in advance rather than spring it on them at interview, when even good intent can be misconstrued. Advance planning by both parties can only lead to a more constructive interview.

Reference points for the appraisee may be last year's appraisal document, evaluating a piece of work, talking to colleagues, thinking of other managers/clinicians they worked for in the course of their work and what they would say regarding their performance, analysing what needs to be done, setting some objectives to discuss or some quite personal reflective thought on where they want to go and what their skills and abilities are. The appraiser may turn to last year's appraisal document and the job description, talk to users of the service provided by the appraisee or department, use their own objectives, business plans or strategies if appropriate and any other source of information.

Stage 2 Completion of documents

Stage 2 relates to advance completion of the document where appropriate. An appraisee certainly should have stated something in most sections, including the performance plan (objectives) and skills sections, although in the main these sections will be identified and completed at interview. Most employees have concerns about forms, particularly those which are formal and confidential. It should be stressed that the appraisee's copy of any document used to undertake advance preparation remains their property. It does not have to be shown to the appraiser or used at interview. Comments from appraisees in the past have included 'I'll fill it in pencil as that doesn't photocopy' and 'I'll use invisible ink'! Neither of these precautions is necessary. The appraiser will be using exactly the same form and it is their copy which will be used at interview.

THE PAPERWORK

Different organizations use different forms of paperwork and systems for the process. There is no one standard form. The reasons for using a form are to prompt, provide a sequence and consistency and a record. Paperwork must never be used to collect information which may be perceived as being available for use against an employee at a later date. In good organizations this is not necessary anyway. In poor organizations the appraisees will soon come to suspect such a system, rebel against appraisal and the process dies.

Most documentation will include the headings previously referred to on this page plus a record sheet of the appraisee's and appraiser's names, relationship and review date and notes. A breakdown of each heading is as follows.

Personal preparation form

Usually optional for the appraisee and relates to an individual's current job and its strengths and needs, career interests and development needs. Usually it will ask questions such as:

- Have you been clear what your objectives were?
- Under what conditions do you work most effectively?
- Has your job changed significantly in the last 12 months? If so, how?
- What is your main career interest?
- What are some alternative career interests?
- What are your main development needs?
- What additional education, training or experience do you need?
- Do you feel there are any major constraining factors outside your control?

All questions will be geared to make the appraisee think about their strengths and weaknesses and what could be done to help.

For medical staff the personal preparation form may vary slightly from that used for non-medical staff, to take account of or possibly emphasize the need to link the process with professional and educational development and support needs. These in themselves may be external to the objective needs of the immediate area of work, e.g. a junior house surgeon may wish to plan their future career in surgery as well as meeting the needs of their current post. Therefore additional questions may be included on the preparation form, such as:

- Is the provision of and access to postgraduate education suitable to your needs?
- Are you clear in your educational and career plans? Are there areas which require some attention?
- Have you considered properly the alternative career opportunities within medicine that are available to you?
- Do you feel there is sufficient educational support/input in your current post and clinical firm? What development/adjustments could be made?

Table 26.2

1. Key ojectives for coming period	2. Priority order	3. Action required and by whom and when	4. Identified personal development needs	5. Any changes to objectives	6. Review of achievement
To take responsibility for management of ward budget	1	i) Identification and agreement of budget to be devolved – Appraisee – Appraiser – Finance department May 199 ii) Appraisee to receive training in budget management – Appraisee – Appraiser – Training department Sept 199 iii) Appraisee to shadow management budget for remaining 1/4 of year – Appraisee – Manager – Subordinate March 199	– Enhanced knowledge of how budgets work – Attend budget awareness training – Receive detailed training on individual budget – Raise awareness amongst subordinates of change – Undertake team management training	– Identification took longer due to illness – Budget training delayed due to oversubscription of course	Success

Performance plan (objectives)

Normally this section is in the shape of a table (see Table 26.2) and allows for the recording of objectives, their priority order and who leads, action required and who helps, development needs which have been identified for the appraisee in relation to their objectives and potential career plans, changes to objectives and review.

Alternatively, for a junior doctor objectives may be set around the following areas of activity:

1. Key objectives:
   - to take responsibility for 'x' aspects of a clinical trial;
     or
   - to undertake a new pharmaceutical activity;
     or
   - to develop/test a non-invasive procedure;
     or
   - develop team relationships as required under the Care in the Community Act;
     or
   - learn, develop, practise a new clinical skill (a) for personal development and (b) to meet the needs of the department, e.g. skills required for day surgery provision;
   - Other.
2. *Priority*   The same principles for priority setting would apply as for any other group, i.e. which objective needs to be met first or which needs to be started first or what factors influence the priorities being considered, e.g. the need for new surgical skills may take priority over the Community Care Act.
3. *Action required*   Requires the identification of all those involved in the process and why and who will do what.
4. *Identify personal development needs*   As for the nurse or other employee – what are the personal development needs of the doctor to enable them to successfully meet objective?
5. *Changes*   Are any adjustments to objectives required and if so for what reason?
6. *Review*   Success or not – why?

Aspects of performance and skills

This section will usually be completed by appraiser and appraisee at the interview stage. It is designed to help analyse the abilities and performance of the appraisee. Together with the personal preparation plan, it will provide the basis for the development plan. Again, this section will usually be in the form of a table with headings such as:

- organization and management work

- foresight and depth of thought
- oral and written communication
- overall performance

with space alongside each question for comments. The appraiser should consider the appraisee's performance in each facet.

Most documents used at this stage contain space for both appraisee's and appraiser's signature, the main purpose for this being an acknowledgement that the process has been conducted and that the review and the plans in it are a fair reflection of what was agreed. The date is useful to identify when the appraisal took place to allow for effective measurement throughout the cycle. Some appraisees are not prepared to sign the form but every encouragement should be given to them to do so, allowing them to record any additional comments they may wish to make as these can be referred to in the review process and the opportunity taken to turn any negative thoughts to positive. As this document is confidential between the two parties the normal process is for each party to keep a copy of the finally agreed form, with the appraiser keeping their copy private and confidential. It does not automatically go to the appraiser's manager, unless the appraisee requests it or is agreeable to the form being passed on.

The fact that the form is not automatically passed on to the manager above (grandparent) does cause some appraisers concern. They may feel they want a safety net or that it is difficult to implement some of the training needs without referring upwards, if only because it is the manager above who holds the purse strings! Both points are valid. However, the process is reliant on confidentiality between two parties, the two parties who work most closely together and for whom the appraiser is responsible. Dialogue can and does go on between the appraiser and their own manager, but it is better to do it with the acknowledgement of the appraisee. Also, if the appraiser has undertaken their preparation, they will know the boundaries within which they can work and be able to identify the need to refer anything on at the interview stage and get back to the appraisee with an answer, rather than promise everything and provide nothing.

Role of the grandparent

The grandparent, or manager once removed from the process, has a role in overseeing the process. Where there is disagreement between appraiser and appraisee, the appraisee may request an interview with their grandparent. Ideally grandparents will have contact with the individual and know their role. The grandparent is important in ensuring the equitableness of the system as they provide a further level of review but are removed from the immediate process, with a greater span of control. Such a function reinforces the fairness of the process.

Personal development plan

Usually in table form, this part of the documentation is used to focus:

. . . primarily on those learning/development needs identified in the performance plan (objectives) and then on development needs related to the individual's realistic career expectations in the next 2–5 years. Production of the personal development plan will be accepted as confirmation that a performance plan has been agreed. It supersedes any previous development plan. (SUH NHS Trust)

The table will usually include reference to the objectives set and their training needs, timing, jobs for which an individual could be considered, which work experience, special assignments, personal improvement, education and training information would be helpful to the employee and which party will do what to help meet those needs. A copy of this form, once completed and accepted, is usually sent to the training department for use in building the organization's training and development programme.

Notes

Primarily notes for the appraiser but useful for the appraisee as well. Normally notes will give advice on the value of the IPR process, what will make IPR work well, objective setting, who is involved in the process and how to use the paperwork.

IDENTIFICATION OF TRAINING NEEDS

As the process includes the identification of training needs, it is worth considering these and how they can be met before moving on to the objective setting part of the process.

A definition of training is: 'To bring to desired standard of efficiency by instruction and practice; teach and accustom to' (*Oxford Dictionary*).

There are many ways of identifying training needs, of which the IPR process is just one. Other ways include questioning, sampling, job analysis and critical incidents. Just as there are many ways of identifying needs, there are many ways of meeting needs. Some are more cost-effective than others and some require no cash outlay at all; going on a course is not necessarily the best way of meeting a need.

Training falls into three categories:

On the job

- Training manuals
- Job/work rotation
- Projects/assignments
- Coaching
- Delegation
- 'Sitting next to Nellie'
- Structured work experience.

Off the job

- Films/videos
- Role play
- Business games
- Lectures
- Simulations.

On or off the job

- Computer assisted learning
- Demonstrations and guided practice
- Self-directed learning
- Distance learning
- Discovery/experimental learning
- Action learning
- Seminars/workshops
- Briefing groups.

Some of the above may also be found in the provision of professional training and/or can supplement professional training, as well as being used to meet the needs identified through the objective-setting process.

Just as there are many ways of identifying and providing for needs, there are many different times when training may be needed, for example:

- job changes
- new systems introduced
- new technology
- job expansion
- transfer
- promotion
- professional development.

All types of learning have their use. It is the job of the appraiser to identify the most appropriate method to be used that will make training useful and valuable and not just another awayday for the appraisee!

Provision of effective training relates to:

- skills needed in present job;
- skills needed in the future;
- skills needed for promotion/new post/professional development.

OBJECTIVE SETTING IN THE IPR PROCESS

Examples of objective setting are given earlier in the chapter.

To improve the performance of the organization everyone has to be clear about what is important and what should be achieved. Reaching agreement about key objectives and their definition is critical. If not done well, the whole of the rest of the process will contribute little to the success of the organization.

(SUH NHS Trust)

Objectives come from work experience, business plans and strategy documents, which have to be translated into personal responsibilities and reflected in individual performance plans (objectives).

The purpose of objectives setting is to ensure progress and performance on those issues which are agreed as key to the success of the organization.

(SUH NHS Trust)

If too many are agreed, little significant progress will be made on any of them. Objectives should not include tasks that need to be done as a matter of routine.

They should be challenging to ensure progress, but achievable, to avoid frustration because of failure. If the number of objectives reaches double figures there are possibly too many.

(SUH NHS Trust)

Objectives should be defined, clear about what should be achieved and written so that they:

- are capable of being tested (constraints within which they are to be achieved being defined);
- are quantifiable (objective and measurable);
- are precise (well defined in as few a words as possible);
- are within a definite time scale;
- address the right problem;
- are achievable and realistic;
- identify costs (what resources are required);
- allow for changes to be made if agreed upon.

Overall, objectives must be kept simple.

Objectives can be categorized as follows:

1. *Innovative* New initiatives, identifying areas for improved efficiency.
2. *Maintenance* Keeping up or improving existing standards of performance.
3. *Human resources* To further develop the human resource, e.g. ensuring that staff have performance and development plans. To ensure that investment in training is realistic and linked to organizational

objectives and that talent spotting and succession planning exist.

Objectives usually deal with short-term aims (12 months) but should also include longer term goals (say, 5-year rolling period) and include action required to begin to move towards them. You should recognize that some will be conceptual in nature and may be expressed in general terms, which should still remain 'measurable'.

Once the IPR process is in use, long term will roll into short term as the cycles progress. Objectives need to be as precise as possible using few words. You shoud try to avoid the following words when setting objectives:

Desirable	As soon as possible	Minimum
Increased	Approximate	Adequate
Maximum	Optimize	Reasonable
Reconcile	Decreased	etc.

In the appraisal process what do they mean? Many others can be added to this list.

In addition to identifying how to make objective setting successful, it is also important to identify why some objectives are not achieved and some are bettered.

Objectives not achieved

Why	Action to take
Objective too high	Amend to realistic level
Failed to meet requirements of job	Consider use or benefit of training, counselling, reduce size of job, commitment
Lack of support from others	Examine and consider procedures, communication, relationships, authority, delegation, coordination
Other causes	Consider resources, suitability. Will it happen again?

Objectives achieved or bettered

Why	Action to take
Objective too easy	Amend objective
Unforeseen favourable circumstances	Will they recur?
Highly effective efforts	Can they be rewarded?
Other	Tighten up objective so they have time to do other things

THE IPR INTERVIEW

The IPR interview, like all other formal employment interviews, is a planned discussion between appraiser (manager) and appraisee (subordinate). Its purpose is to review how the appraisee has carried out their job since the last appraisal and to plan how to move forward for the next 12 months.

Most interviews contain a mix of telling and selling, listening and problem solving. The most successful interviews are likely to be those which tell and listen and problem solve. The structure of the interview should be planned in advance to be constructive:

- Review of appraisee's performance in advance (collect information and refer to previous appraisals including reference to specialist advice if appraising a person with specialist skills other than appraiser's own).
- Agree at interview with the appraisee what problems exist and what action to take.
- Record the interview; copies of documentation given to both parties.
- Afford the same etiquette as for other interviews, including sufficient time set aside, confidentiality, privacy and peace with no interruptions.

Throughout the interview process the appraiser in particular should demonstrate:

- listening skills
- feedback skills
- paraphrasing skills
- ability to reflect feelings
- use of open and closed questions appropriately
- focusing skills.

Such skills can also be of benefit to the appraisee.

A large proportion of the interview relates to giving feedback on performance. Feedback should be supported with examples. It is not uncommon for appraisees to blame poor performance on the situation and circumstances rather than themselves, while appraisers can view performance as being due to the appraisee's characteristics rather than the situation itself. In order for an appraisee to improve their performance they must have feedback on:

- the performance that was expected (using the objectives set for the past year);
- what their performance was (whether or not the objectives were achieved and why?);
- the nature of their strengths and weaknesses (exploring the reasons for good and bad work);
- how they can improve their performance (what help or training is required to improve weaknesses and help with future objectives?);

- what help is available, e.g. training (what can be done to help improve, what is available, how will it be carried out?).

For the appraiser to enable feedback to be as constructive as possible, the following factors will aid the process.

- Focus on the job not the person. The appraisal interview is not the place to correct character traits. Other processes are available to deal with these.
- Concentrate on the good things at least as much as the bad. Keep the interview balanced and focused. Do not concentrate on a positive or negative to the detriment of the other.
- Go into detail about good and bad points. If staff are to improve or are excellent they need to know and understand why.
- Explore reasons for good and bad points. Validate and correct reasons given, as reasons for poor performance may be out of the appraisee's control.
- Ensure feedback is regular/create opportunities for giving feedback. In the formal interview this includes allowing the appraisee time to have their say. External to the interview, it is to do with keeping lines of communication open.
- Go beyond feedback. Identify and provide additional help and assistance as necessary. The successful employee will also mean a successful manager.

Above all, for the interview to succeed it should leave the appraisee feeling encouraged and with a sense of purpose.

THE APPRAISEE'S ROLE IN IPR

So far predominance has been given to a management or appraiser's perspective of IPR. It is worth giving consideration to the appraisee's perspective.

Appraisees may be cautious about participating in the process particularly if it has not been fully explained to them. So it is advisable not to appraise staff who have not had the process explained to them. Staff need to understand that it is not a process to be feared, but that the hospital or service chooses to use it to help progress.

Appraisal happens at a basic level to everyone in their everyday lives and is carried out by family, friends and colleagues. The formal IPR process used at work is designed to be more constructive, allowing time for discussion on points raised and to cover all the issues raised in this chapter.

It is beneficial for the appraisee to prepare for their interview, as the appraiser will be prepared, as this helps with the flow of information. The appraisee should recognize that some frank discussion will be taking place so to avoid feeling defensive, the appraisee should try and identify what the appraiser is likely to say about their skills, ability and past performance. It is also a good idea to have same suggestions for improvement or training that they could take to the interview.

WHY APPRAISAL CAN FAIL

Appraisal can fail because there are too many objectives, it is disjointed with no real structure of any sort, it concentrates on personal qualities and is of no real help to the appraisee and service in diagnosing potential.

WHY IPR SUCCEEDS

IPR succeeds when it concentrates on performance, considers strengths and weaknesses and is concerned with future career and progression. It is a complex interpersonal process. Individual competence can be enhanced through skills training but a great deal can be achieved by ensuring that:

- there are regular and frequent informal review discussions about progress using the documentation associated with the process. IPR is not and should not become a 'once a year' event;
- review between appraiser and appraisee is truly open, within clear understandings about confidentiality;
- dialogue between the two is positive, supportive and forward looking, providing the opportunity for exploring new ideas and improving performance rather than seeking alibis or excuses;
- there is recognition that no performance review process is easy. It requires working at by all involved and will improve with practice and feedback. The hardest part is getting started.

It is worth remembering that IPR:

- is a process;
- is not an end in itself;
- is results orientated;
- is not wholly to do with personal qualities;
- is developmental;
- is not disciplinary;
- is individual to each employee.

As an integral part of the management process, it is continuous but with a formal focus annually. The management process is about maintaining and developing services. IPR is about maintaining and developing individuals. Managed effectively, the two can be totally compatible.

REFERENCES

Southampton University Hospital NHS Trust IPR documentation
Southampton University Hospital NHS Trust IPR documentation
Southampton University Hospital NHS Trust IPR documentation
Southampton University Hospital NHS Trust IPR documentation
Southampton University Hospital NHS Trust IPR documentation

FURTHER READING

Andrew Stewart Performance appraisal
Gower Handbook of training and development.
NHSTD IPR publications.

27

Quality in health care

Richard Thomson

INTRODUCTION

This chapter covers the reasons for the present emphasis on quality, the history of quality assessment and improvement in the National Health Service (NHS), definitions and concepts of quality, the main approaches to quality improvement and what the future may hold.

An important contribution to NHS quality activity has been the recent promotion of medical and latterly clinical audit (DoH 1989a, 1990, 1991a,b, 1993a,b). This is likely to remain a focus for some time to come and has already been covered in detail. Therefore, I will say less about audit and more about other methods and approaches. However, I will consider professional audit in the context of other methods and how it may be integrated into wider quality strategies.

WHY QUALITY TODAY?

The NHS is having to address quality as never before. There are a number of reasons for this, including:

- increasing demonstration of unexplained variation in clinical practice and health outcomes, as well as variation in access to and availability of services or interventions (Charlton et al 1983, Ham 1988);
- increasing public knowledge and expectations (Joule 1993);
- a drive for greater accountability of public services (Pollitt 1990);
- the burgeoning costs of health care (OECD 1987, 1992);
- the volume and pace of change of clinical knowledge (Lowry 1993);
- the recent NHS reforms, including clinical audit and the purchaser–provider split (NHS and Community Care Act 1990).

This focus on quality has not been limited to health care. There has been a similar emphasis in industry, stimulated primarily by the success of Japanese companies whose approach to quality has put them to the fore in such areas as motor and electronics manufacturing. An emphasis on quality before productivity, informed by theoretical and applied statistical and behavioural knowledge, has been stated as the reason for their success (Deming 1986, Juran 1964,1988, Crosby 1979, Neave 1990).

QUALITY IS NOT NEW

If a doctor has treated a gentleman with a bronze lancet for a severe wound and has caused him to die, or if he has opened with a bronze lancet an abscess of the eye of a gentleman and has caused the loss of the eye, the doctor's hands shall be cut off.

The code of King Hammurabi of Babylon (1728–1688 BC)
(Pritchard 1969)

A focus on quality in health care is not a new phenomenon. Fortunately, however, our methods have become much more refined since the time of the ancient Babylonians. As long ago as the Crimean war, Florence Nightingale undertook a classic audit study with dramatic effect (Strachey 1948). After noting the high mortality at the Scutari Military Hospital, she enforced higher standards of care and hygiene, reducing mortality rates from 40% to 2% within 6 months. Furthermore, professional, educational and regulatory bodies, such as the royal colleges, medical and nursing schools and the General Medical Council, have long been concerned with assuring the quality of professional practice.

Whilst a more extensive approach to quality has been in place in North American health care for many years, there have been a number of initiatives in the United Kingdom concerned with quality assessment and improvement. These include national confidential enquiries such as the Confidential Enquiry into Maternal Deaths (CMD) (Ministry of Health 1957), the Confidential Enquiry into Perioperative Deaths (NCEPOD) (Buck et al 1987, Campling et al 1990, 1992, 1993) and the Confidential Enquiry into Stillbirths and Deaths in Infancy (CESDI) (National Advisory Body 1994).

Examples of external quality monitoring in the United Kingdom include the Hospital (latterly Health) Advisory Service (HAS) (Department of Health and Social Security 1984), the nursing homes inspection requirements (Registered Homes Act 1984) and the National External Quality Assurance Scheme (NEQAS) for pathology laboratories (UK NEQAS 1993). Recently, more sophisticated accreditation programmes for hospitals, community units (Shaw & Brooks 1991, Shaw & Collins 1995) and pathology departments (College Accreditation Steering Committee 1991) have developed, although experience of accreditation of GP training practices has evolved since the late 1970s (Joint Committee on Postgraduate Training for General Practice 1976, Gray 1984, 1992).

In the area of patient and public representation, community health councils were created and given powers in 1974 to act as a voice for their local population (Hogg & Winkler 1989).

The Royal College of General Practitioners (1985) has been a prominent proponent of quality for many years, producing the 1983 Quality Initiative which included the aims that every general practice should be able to describe their work and services and should incorporate audit into their routine practice. In addition to support for audit from the medical colleges, the Royal College of Nursing implemented a major standard-setting initiative in its dynamic standard-setting system (DYSSY) (RCN 1990) and there are a number of examples of nursing quality assessment instruments (Redfern et al 1993).

Recent years have seen several important initiatives, many of them stimulated or implemented as a result of the NHS reforms, including the Department of Health quality and total quality management initiatives (NHSME 1993), the Patient's Charter (DoH 1991c), enhanced roles for the Audit Commission (Davies 1992) and the National Audit Office (1990), the creation of the Clinical Standards Advisory Group (CSAG) (Higginson 1992) and the purchaser–provider interaction, including the requirement for quality clauses in service contracts (DoH 1989b,c).

Although there is a long history of NHS quality initiatives, until recently many of these have been the province of enthusiasts or have had limited powers or effect. We now have an opportunity to introduce systematic means of quality improvement, thus beginning to meet the WHO target that: 'By 1990, all member states should have built effective mechanisms for ensuring the quality of patient care'.

Before describing the mechanisms for quality improvement in health care, the definitions, concepts and models that inform such approaches will be discussed.

WHAT IS QUALITY? CONCEPTS AND DEFINITIONS

A commodity that is damaged if any changes whatsoever are made in the structure or financing of the current system of medical practice.

(Caper 1988)

There are a multitude of definitions of quality in addition to Caper's ironic example, many of which are no more than attempts at succinct statements of particular philosophies (Table 27.1). There are, however, common components within the different approaches and models. Indeed, attempts to define quality may deflect us from an understanding of the general attributes of quality which might better support mechanisms of quality improvement.

The key features of quality that are fundamental to effective means of assessment and improvement are that quality is:

- *comparative* some things are better than others. For instance, a surgeon with a wound infection rate of 1% is providing higher quality care than one with an infection rate of 8%, other things such as case mix being equal.
- *dynamic* today's high quality is tomorrow's acceptable quality. For example, prior to the implementation of effective treatments for childhood leukaemia, high quality care was concerned with palliation, appropriate terminal care and family support.
- *consumer defined* in many other settings the ultimate arbiters of quality are the customers or users of the product or service. Customers of health care can be identified: in addition to the obvious patients and their families, there are also 'internal customers'. For example, general practitioners are internal customers

Table 27.1 Definitions of quality

- Meeting the customers' needs.
- Doing the right things well.
- The totality of features and characteristics of a product or service that bear on its ability to satisfy stated or implied needs.
- Fitness for purpose.
- Right first time, every time.

of the radiologist reporting a chest X-ray result and rely on the quality and timeliness of the report to make appropriate decisions.

These features of quality are as important in health care as in service or production industries, although some of the terminology (for instance, customers) may still seem somewhat alien to the NHS.

A corollary of the dynamic and changing nature of quality is the necessity to utilize some form of cyclical approach to ensure that data on quality are used to create change. In the absence of methods of change and review there is a risk that efforts at collecting and displaying data on quality of care will remain an incomplete exercise. This is the underlying rationale behind the audit or quality assurance cycle (Fowkes 1982).

Definitions and models of quality in health care encompass such features, but have to recognize the complexity of health care. This is reflected in the American Institute of Medicine's definition of quality of care constructed as part of its remit in reviewing the Medicare quality assurance program (Lohr 1990):

Quality of care is the degree to which health services for individuals and populations increase the likelihood of desired health outcomes and are consistent with current professional knowledge.

Whilst this is commendable in its comprehensive elegance, simpler concepts have been more helpful in practice. The two classifications of health care quality attributes that have most clearly influenced approaches in the UK are those of Avedis Donabedian (1966, 1980) and Robert Maxwell (1984).

Donabedian conceived quality as having three interlinked attributes:

1. structure
2. process
3. outcome.

Structural attributes include the building blocks of health care such as premises, equipment, staff and funding. *Processes* include those activities which impact upon patient care including diagnosis, treatment and intervention, explanation and communication, as well as more mechanistic elements such as record keeping, test ordering and selection, and delivery or handling of results or specimens. Both structural and process variables contribute to the *outcomes* of care, which broadly speaking encompass change in health status and other effects of care, including patient knowledge and satisfaction. Outcomes are also affected by factors outside the immediate influence of health care including patient age and social circumstances, as well as other patient characteristics which may be amenable to change, such as comorbidity (coexistent ill health), patient compliance and lifestyle factors such as smoking.

The importance of this Donabedian triad lies in the interrelationships of structure, process and outcome (Donabedian 1988). Taken alone, measurement of health care outcome is of limited value without a clear understanding of the factors that influence outcome, including, most importantly for the purpose of healthcare quality improvement, those that are amenable to change within health care itself.

The major contribution of Robert Maxwell is his six dimensions of quality, recently revisited by the author (Maxwell 1984, 1992). These are:

1. *access* factors such as geographical siting, on-site accessibilty and waiting times;
2. *relevance to need* appropriate to the health profile of the population and groups within it;
3. *effectiveness* the ability of the treatment or service to produce the desired results;
4. *equity* fair distribution of health care resources within a publicly funded system;
5. *social acceptability* including environmental conditions, communication and privacy;
6. *efficiency and economy* the best possible service for the best possible price.

These dimensions go beyond the individual clinician–patient focus of the Donabedian approach to take cognizance of features of the publicly funded NHS, including the quality of care provided to communities. They have been used to inform health policy, for example in the East Anglian Regional Health Authority's strategic role in health care development and evaluation (Maxwell 1992).

Before leaving these concepts, it is worth describing a second Donabedian classification of quality into the technical, interpersonal and amenity elements of care. *Technical* elements include structural features such as the presence of diagnostic or investigative equipment, as well as the complex processes of clinical practice concerned with patient treatment. *Interpersonal* elements of care include communication with patients and other important components of clinician–patient interaction such as treating people with dignity and respect. *Amenity* elements would include the quality of the environment within which health care operates, as well as hotel services such as laundry and catering. To this triad could be added a fourth element, that of the quality of care provided *to the community*. Thus, the best technical, interpersonal and amenity elements may be in place, for example in the treatment of patients within a regional cardiothoracic unit, leading to excellent outcomes, but care to the local community would be less than ideal if those with potential to benefit were denied access to such services.

The above conceptualizations of healthcare quality offer frameworks within which quality of care can be assessed or measured, but they do not include within them the means of improvement. For improvement in healthcare quality, application of these concepts to the assessment of healthcare quality needs to be appropriately incorporated alongside effective methods of quality improvement. The next section addresses the main methods of quality assessment and improvement at present applied within the NHS (see also Chapter 33 on multiprofessional audit).

METHODS AND MODELS OF QUALITY IMPROVEMENT

The approaches available for quality improvement depend upon the perspective of assessment (for example external monitoring or internal audit), the means of data collation and evaluation (for example confidential enquiry, use of quality indicators) and the focus of interest (for example predominantly on outcome or on process). These are not mutually exclusive. For instance, guidelines can be developed and evaluated within a provider unit or hospital speciality for the purpose of clinical audit or they may be implemented through the contracting function of the purchasing authority. Quality indicators, or performance measures, may be utilized to identify problem areas for a speciality's audit programme or published in the form of league tables for public consumption. External assessment or monitoring may be entered into voluntarily by an organization seeking to enhance its quality, for instance in pursuing BS5750 (ISO9000) accreditation (Smith & Hart 1992) or may be a statutory requirement such as that of nursing home registration (Registered Homes Act 1984). For reasons of presentation, I have divided this section into: confidential enquiries and national audits; standards, protocols and guidelines; the outcomes movement; the patient and public perspective on quality; indicators and performance measures; and external monitoring and accreditation. Finally, I have considered the still developing purchaser–provider interaction.

Confidential enquiries and national audits

The value of confidential enquiries depends upon:

- an external unbiased professional review of cases;
- confidentiality/anonymity, thus stimulating reporting of cases free from threat of censure;
- the collection of populations of often rare events enabling identification of common features or themes.

Confidential enquiries can support and encourage local investigation, whilst allowing data collation on larger populations for epidemiological, audit and research study.

We now have three nationally managed confidential enquiries. The first of these is the triennial Confidential Enquiry into Maternal Deaths (CMD) established in 1952 to identify reasons for avoidable maternal mortality (MoH 1957).

An enquiry is initiated by the director of public health and enquiry forms sent to relevant clinical staff for completion, before both regional and national confidential expert assessment. Cases are categorized as direct causes (resulting from obstetric complications of the pregnant state, from interventions, omissions, incorrect treatment or from a chain of events resulting from any of the above), indirect deaths (resulting from pre-existing disease or disease developing during pregnancy not due to direct obstetric causes) and fortuitous deaths (other causes happening to occur in pregnancy). The central assessment mechanism also seeks evidence of substandard care.

Despite considerable improvements in care since the introduction of this enquiry, the most recent report still identifies opportunity for improvement (DoH 1994a). The main avoidable causes are hypertensive disorders (18.6% of direct maternal deaths), pulmonary embolism (16.6%), deaths in early pregnancy including abortion and ectopic pregnancy (10.3%) and obstetric haemorrhage (15.2%). Evidence of substandard care was present in half of the 238 maternal deaths between 1988 and 1990. For hypertensive disease, 88% of cases were felt to involve substandard care.

In 1987 the Royal College of Surgeons and the Royal College of Anaesthetists published the results of a pilot Confidential Enquiry into Perioperative Deaths (CEPOD) occurring in hospital within 30 days of surgery (Buck et al 1987). CEPOD was subsequently extended nationally (Campling et al 1990, 1992, 1993). National CEPOD (NCEPOD) depends on local reporters providing data voluntarily.

Each year a sample of cases are reviewed in more depth by central advisory groups. The first NCEPOD report concentrated on care of children (Campling et al 1990). The second reviewed a random sample of one in five deaths (Campling et al 1992), whilst the most recent report explored a selection of specific surgical procedures in greater detail (Campling et al 1993). A number of important quality issues have been identified within these reports. In the most recent these include:

- the continuing problem of thromboembolism leading to death after surgery;
- the critical importance of fluid balance in elderly patients;
- access to 24-hour emergency services;
- appropriate supervision of trainees by consultant staff;
- a need to increase the post-mortem rate;
- the need for better information on perioperative deaths;
- problems with the storage and retrieval of medical notes;
- appropriate selection of cases, particularly those whose death is inevitable and imminent.

Most recently, a national Confidential Enquiry into Still Births and Deaths in Infancy (CESDI) has been implemented (Chalmers 1989, National Advisory Body 1994). A model preceding this within the Northern Region involves the central notification of still births and deaths in infancy, with local audit meetings and regional analysis and feedback, including reports, publications and an annual conference (Northern Regional Health Authority 1993). This has stimulated further research and audit studies (Northern Regional Health Authority 1984).

The national programme requires central reporting of a minimum data set on all deaths. Regions have formed multidisciplinary confidential assessment panels to review a proportion of cases (in 1993 these were normally formed intrapartum and early neonatal deaths and (in selected regions) sudden unexpected deaths in infancy).

The confidential enquiries described above are extensions of a particular audit approach – the critical incident technique – where a significant event is reviewed to identify opportunity to improve practice (Flanagan 1954, Buckley 1990). It is likely that confidential enquiries act partly through requiring contributors to consider such cases in greater detail than might otherwise have happened, in addition to shining a general spotlight on areas where improvement is possible.

A number of other national audits have been initiated through, by or with the support of the royal colleges and have been summarized in a recent national report, also available on computer disk, which it is intended to update annually (Department of Health 1994b).

A difficulty with national audits and confidential enquiries is in assessing how effective they are in changing practice. They may provide valuable comparative and case study data, but do not in themselves include the means for implementing change. Whilst maternal mortality has fallen following the introduction of CMD, it was already falling as a result of a multiplicity of factors including improvements in social conditions as well as in health care. Whilst anecdotal examples of change in practice abound, improvement in the quality of care depends upon the results of such enquiries stimulating review and change in practice at all levels of the service, a situation that will be heavily dependent upon both local and national responses to their findings.

However, there are examples of improvements following passive feedback of comparative data, for instance in the case of the multicentre St Mark's large bowel audit study (Fielding et al 1980). This collated and fed back data showing wide variation in anastomotic integrity and infection following large bowel resection. Following feedback there was a reduction in the overall rate and in the variation between centres. A recent review of the effectiveness of different methods of feedback on changing practice has addressed this area in greater detail (Mugford et al 1991).

Standards, protocols and guidelines

There are a number of overlapping concepts encompassed within the terms standards, protocols and guidelines. Multiple synonyms are somewhat liberally applied. Some clarity is provided by the following definitions (Clinical Resource and Audit Group 1993):

- *criterion* a carefully selected element to measure and assess a clearly defined aspect of care. For example, a criterion of quality of surgical care would be the wound infection rate;
- *standard* a specific statement relevant to a particular criterion of care against which practice can be assessed. For example, a standard could be that wound infection following hip replacement should not exceed x %;
- *guideline(s)* systematically developed statements which assist in decision making about appropriate healthcare for specific clinical conditions;
- *protocol* a fixed set of instructions to follow in the management of conditions designed to reduce treatment variation and improve outcome.

Guidelines and protocols may include or comprise a set of standards. Alternatively, they can support the explicit local development of standards. Guidelines have been developed at all levels of the service, including national or regional development. National examples would include guidelines on investigation and management of stable angina (Royal College of Physicians 1993) and on asthma management (British Thoracic Society 1993). Local protocols on the treatment of patients with stable angina or asthma can be developed, drawing upon these national guidelines, taking account of local organization and facilities.

Table 27.2 A taxonomy for clinical guidelines

Probability of effectiveness	Development strategy	Dissemination strategy	Implementation strategy
High	Internal	Specific educational intervention	Patient-specific reminder at time of consultation
Above average	Intermediate	Continuing medical education	Patient-specific feedback
Below average	External local	Mailing targeted groups	General feedback
Low	External national	Publication in professional journals	General reminder

Adapted from Russell IT & Grimshaw J 1992

Standards may be expressed as ideal, optimal or minimal. Minimum standards have their place, particularly in areas where precise quality control is critical, for instance in aspects of the blood transfusion service where minimum standards for blood product collection and distribution minimize the risks to patients. However, a reliance on minimum standards alone will offer no incentive for improvement in the majority of service provision.

In contrast, a statement of ideal standards may offer something to aim for, but in many cases may be effectively unachievable. Aiming for such standards may be counterproductive, acting to demotivate and diminish morale. Perhaps the appropriate approach from the point of quality improvement is to set (optimal) standards which are kept under regular review. This should not be equated with complacency; such standards should be set as a challenge to improvement and should be equivalent to those that conscientious staff can best achieve within the constraints under which they work.

Guidelines and protocols are receiving increasing emphasis in the NHS today, including a central NHSME initiative to promote guidelines which inform the purchaser–provider interaction and contracting (DoH 1993c). There have been several recent extensive and detailed reviews of the effectiveness and potential impact of guidelines, as well as suggested frameworks for their development (Lomas & Haynes 1987, Institute of Medicine 1992, Eddy 1992, Russell & Grimshaw 1992, Grimshaw & Russell 1993a,b, 1994, Grol 1992, Thomson et al 1995). These recognize that the effectiveness of guidelines depends upon several inter-linked phases: development, dissemination, implementation, evaluation and review. Each of these is critical to ensure that guidelines promote the desired health outcomes.

The factors that are likely to promote effective development, dissemination and implementation are summarized in Table 27.2. However, there are inevitably inherent tensions and trade-offs. Thus, whilst guidelines developed by those who are going to apply them are more likely to be followed, rigorous development using extensive literature review and effective consensus methods in multiple sites would appear to be an inefficient and probably unachievable means of guidelines development. Nationally or regionally developed guidelines may more readily be able to draw upon the skills, expertise and time necessary for such rigorous development, but at the cost of requiring enhanced dissemination and implementation strategies to overcome the potential barrier of lack of ownership.

Perhaps the most efficient compromise lies in nationally or regionally produced guidelines which can be seen to involve appropriate multidisciplinary professional input and expertise and which can then be adapted or adopted to meet the requirements of varying local circumstances into more detailed local protocols. This may well be further supported by explicit inclusion within contracts or by negotiation between purchaser and provider to ensure that key guidelines and protocols are utilized and assessed within audit programmes.

Whilst structured development is necessary to ensure that guidelines actually reflect research evidence, dissemination and implementation methods require equally careful consideration. The best developed guidelines are set to fail if they do not reach those responsible for implementing them (Madhok et al 1993). Dissemination linked to educational initiatives appears most effective, whilst publication in professional journals is much less so (Russell & Grimshaw 1992, Grimshaw & Russell 1994). Even if the guidelines reach their target audience, implementation of their recommendations requires further effort. Implementation strategies based upon patient-specific reminders at the time of consultation would appear to be most effective (Russell & Grimshaw

1992, Grimshaw & Russell 1994). In primary care, the development of computerized guidelines on the GP's desktop computer may offer considerable potential, although such an approach may be less practicable in the hospital setting.

The introduction of systematic audit offers potential to support and evaluate the implementation of guidelines and protocols, both through assessing the process of their implementation and measuring outcomes to see if they are leading to the desired or predicted effects.

Furthermore, as clinical knowledge develops at an increasingly rapid pace, there is a need to build in systems for regular review and refinement of guidelines to take cognizance of emerging knowledge. Moreover, the development and implementation of guidelines should increasingly be informed by a health economics perspective, taking account of the cost and benefits implications, as well as increasingly being informed by and informing the patient perspective (Eddy 1992).

The introduction of the NHS Research and Development strategy offers a real opportunity to support and integrate guidelines into the reformed NHS (Peckham 1991). R & D provides the information upon which evidence-based guidelines can be constructed; the audit programme offers the means of supporting their implementation and assessment and also helps identify further research needs. R & D can further enhance this triangle by funding studies into the factors that influence the use and impact of guidelines and their effect on clinical decision making. To this can be added the potential of the purchaser–provider interaction to stimulate the use and audit of guidelines.

Outcome measurement

Whilst outcome measurement is but one approach to support quality assessment and assurance, the recent emphasis in this area, aligned with the rapid development of outcome-based measures, merits separate consideration (Frater & Sheldon 1993, Long et al 1993, Frater & Costain 1992, Hopkins & Costain 1990, Ellwood 1988). I will concentrate on the relevance of outcome measurement to quality assessment and assurance of health care provision and interventions. This enhanced emphasis on outcomes is to be welcomed, although the necessary measures and their interpretation are still in their development phase.

Historically, health outcomes have often tended to be negative – disease, death, disability, discomfort and dissatisfaction. Recently research in this area has concentrated upon the development of more positive and patient-centred measures of outcomes (Ware 1993, Hopkins & Costain 1990, Hopkins 1992). These range from patient satisfaction (see below) to generic and disease-specific health status or quality of life measures (McDowell & Newell 1987, Spilker et al 1990, Fallowfield 1990, Bowling 1991, Bowling 1994, Wilkin et al 1992, Guyatt et al 1993, Morris & Watt 1993).

Generic measures are not developed for a specific patient group but aim to be suitable for use across a range of patient groups, often summarizing the state of health as a single score or brief profile. Their advantages lie in evaluating the effects of disease and treatment on several life domains and allowing comparison across different disease and patient groups. Their disadvantages lie in the fact that they may be insufficiently focused on the particular impact of different disease states.

Generic health status measures tend to encompass several domains reflecting a wide concept of health – for instance, the SF36 health status measure, developed and validated in the United States but increasingly used in the United Kingdom, includes measures within the domains of physical functioning, social functioning, role functioning, mental health, vitality, pain and general health perceptions (Stewart et al 1988, 1989, Wells et al 1989, Tarlov et al 1989, Jenkinson et al 1993, Garratt et al 1993, Brazier et al 1992, Stewart & Ware 1992, Ware & Sherbourne 1992, McHorney et al 1993). Other widely used instruments include the Nottingham Health Profile (Hunt et al 1986) and the Sickness Impact Profile (Bergner et al 1981).

Disease-specific measures are available in a range of areas, including rheumatic diseases (Meenen et al 1982, Roland & Morris 1983), stroke and cardiovascular disease (de Haan et al 1993) and cancer (Maguire & Selby 1989). They may be more sensitive to the quality of life factors directly relevant to particular patient groups, but are unable to allow comparison between different patient groups.

Quality of life measures can be applied in several ways in health care including:

- screening and monitoring for psychosocial problems in individual patient care;
- population surveys of perceived health problems;
- professional audit;
- outcome measures in health services or evaluation research;
- clinical trials;
- cost-utility analysis.

Use in a quality assurance setting depends largely upon their validity and reliability in the patient group under evaluation and upon their sensitivity to change following intervention or treatment. Instruments must be carefully selected dependent upon their intended use. Several good sources of advice are available on development, selection and use of such instruments (McDowell & Newell 1987, Fallowfield 1990, Bowling 1991, Bowling 1994, Wilkin et al 1992, Streiner & Norman 1989).

The legitimate interests in health care outcomes should not deflect us from recognizing the limitations of the approach. For a health care provider these are:

- the need to understand the links between structure, process and outcome if appropriate changes are to be instituted to improve patient care (Donabedian 1988);
- the effects of patient case mix on outcome – particularly critical if comparative analysis is to be undertaken;
- the importance of *appropriate* outcome measures, preferably informed by patient views as well as clinical knowledge;
- an understanding of the issues of validity, reliability and sensitivity to change of available measures and of the development and assessment of future measures;
- the effects of factors beyond health care on outcome, such as patients' social and economic circumstances;
- the often long time interval between intervention and outcome, for instance in assessing survival in treatment of cancer patients;
- the additional difficulty of assessing outcome in chronic conditions.

Undoubtedly there is a need to develop the outcome emphasis further through well-conceived and extensive research. In summary, greater emphasis on outcomes is to be welcomed, but not to be rushed. Application and interpretation of outcome measures must be developed with a clear understanding of both the benefits and limitations and increasingly supported by necessary outcomes research. Arnold Epstein (1990), in commenting on the outcomes movement in the United States, has stated that:

Our expectations must be moderate if we are to avoid disappointment. The danger we face is that we will undermine a healthy evolution and allow revolutionary zeal to lead us to carry a good thing too fast and too far.

The patient and public perspective on quality

The NHS has been insufficiently responsive to the views and wishes of its users – one of the main conclusions of the Griffiths Report on health service management (DHSS 1983). The opportunity for patients to comment upon health care quality has relied over-heavily on complex, ponderous and adversarial complaints procedures, without the means of obtaining wider user or community views on quality of services and care. Even when the views of patients have been actively sought, the methods used and the areas addressed have tended to be extremely limited, largely relying upon self-completion patient satisfaction questionnaires, usually concentrating upon the amenity and, to a lesser extent, interpersonal areas of care. Moreover, it is commonly felt that patients are not in a position to comment validly upon the technical elements of care. Another concern has been that despite consistent feedback from patients on characteristics of the service that could be improved and despite the increasing number of patient satisfaction surveys, the messages received are not seen to lead to corrective actions. Furthermore, patients have appeared to have a very limited choice or involvement in their own care.

Fortunately for the purpose of quality assessment and improvement, attitudes and policy within the NHS are changing, but there is still some way to go before the 'customer's' views become a fully articulated and appropriately influential voice.

Donabedian (1992) has reviewed the role of the patient or public in the quality of health care and has identified several key elements in this role. He sees consumers (his term) as having three ways of *contributing* to quality assurance: by defining quality, by evaluating it and by providing information for others to evaluate it. In addition to this he sees them as having more subtle (but no less important) roles as 'targets' for quality assurance, for instance as sharing in the governance of their own care through education by, and discussion with, their doctors and as reformers of health care, including expressing choice and taking part in political action.

This recognizes that responsiveness to user views can and should occur at an individual level, in the contact between the service and the patient and their family and carers, as well as in response to the views of groups of patients or the public as a whole. For such responsiveness to lead to appropriate action requires, amongst other things, a better communication and information exchange between the service and its users or potential users.

Patient assessment of health care

One of the central tenets of modern quality theory and practice in other settings is the primacy of the customer (Davidow & Uttal 1989). Within the NHS, this is an attitude still in its infancy. Whilst doctors have become less paternalistic and more skilled in communication, the means for patient or public views to influence the quality of health care are still limited in both their methods and application.

Skills are required to obtain and respond to user attitudes and opinions (Jones et al 1987). The cursory question about whether a patient is satisfied or not is likely to elicit an equally perfunctory response. Moreover, if that response is one of dissatisfaction, the provider may be none the wiser when it comes to implementing change. Hence, the design of instruments and selection of methods to elicit views require considerable care.

The most widely used method for obtaining patient views has been the self-completion patient satisfaction questionnaire. Unfortunately, patient questionnaires are too often rapidly constructed without reference to already available and validated instruments and are neither piloted nor validated, thus providing information of dubious value. Increasingly, there are sources of advice and support in the design, use, interpretation and response to patient-centred assessment of care (Stone 1993, Carr-Hill 1992, Cleary & McNeil 1988, Fitzpatrick 1990, 1991a,b, 1993, McIver 1991a,b, Caplan & Ware 1989), as well as access to the skills of epidemiologists, psychometricians, social scientists and health service researchers. Given this, there should be no excuse for poorly designed and inadequate studies and instruments.

Whilst self-completion questionnaires have the advantage of collating information from a large population at relatively low cost, they have the disadvantage of lack of depth. Moreover, information obtained by questionnaire is limited by the structure and content of the questionnaire itself.

Greater depth of information can be obtained by more detailed techniques, including face-to-face, telephone or group interviews (Smith 1972, Beed 1985, Abramson 1990, Mishler 1991). These may be more costly but may provide richer information. The choice of method depends upon the objectives of the study, the data needed to meet those objectives and the target group. Different methods are complementary. For instance, the problem of appropriate content of self-completion questionnaires can be partly addressed by careful development and design, including effort to ensure content validity by obtaining views from a range of expert and other opinion on the content of the instrument. Appropriate content can be determined in part by an initial qualitative approach with the specific purpose of identifying areas of concern or patient interest to be subsequently explored in a structured questionnaire (Streiner & Norman 1989). On the other hand, a questionnaire may identify an area of concern where more focused qualitative study is required to explore the expressed concerns.

Obtaining views from certain groups, such as children, the visually handicapped and those with learning difficulties, can present particular challenges.

As with other sources of information on quality of care, patient assessments may be collected locally or externally to support monitoring, patient information and choice. At present there are no established UK examples of external monitoring of patient views, although it is likely that this will occur. However, there are examples where an external organization is responsible for managing the collation, analysis and feedback of patient-elicited opinion using validated instruments in order to inform local services, with the added advantage of allowing comparative data analysis and feedback (Gritzner 1993, Black et al 1993, Eccles et al 1992).

In the United States several examples of short validated self-completion questionnaires have been developed, some of which are being adapted for the NHS (Hays et al 1991). In the United States, at the time of writing, the Clinton reforms are proposing the use of a standardized 'report form' to obtain comparative quality information which will be made available to corporate purchasers and the public to inform choice and contracting (Caplan 1993, The Health Security Act 1993).

Validated patient satisfaction questionnaires and other methods are available in many areas including generic inpatient and outpatient questionnaires (McIver 1991a,b, 1992, Gritzner 1993), day-case surgery (Black & Sanderson 1993, Black et al 1993), accident and emergency care (McIver 1992), primary care (Baker & Whitfield 1992, Baker 1993, Bamford & Jacoby 1992, Eccles et al 1992, McIver 1993), mental health services (McIver 1991c) and maternity services (Mason 1989).

Patient choice

The introduction of the internal market was partly concerned with making the service more consumer responsive, in line with the primacy of the consumer being recognized as a key component of quality approaches in manufacturing and service industry (Deming 1986, Davidow & Uttal 1989). However, the internal market within health care is a quasi-market (Le Grand & Bartlett 1993); it differs from true markets in a number of fundamental ways, one of which is that the direct user (in the NHS, the patient) rarely exercises choice. This is delegated to a third party, the district health authority or the GP fundholder.

However, there is considerable potential to empower patient choice in terms of their greater involvement in decision making on their own care. This would appear to be particularly pertinent when considering the considerable elements of uncertainty that remain in clinical decision making and which have contributed to variation in practice. Furthermore, the era of the paternalistic clinician making choices on behalf of patients is fading fast. It could also be argued that greater involvement of patients in shared decision making, based upon clear advice and information on likely prognosis, risks and outcomes, is desirable at a time of rising litigation.

Of course, there are challenges to supporting greater patient choice – what should be done if patients express preferences that appear to be contrary to their best interests or the best interests of others? How can the necessary information be conveyed to ensure that informed choices are made? Nevertheless, there are already good examples of innovative approaches to empowering patients in choosing between treatment options, for instance between operative intervention and watchful waiting for prostatic hypertrophy (Kasper et al 1992).

If the service is to develop effectively into a more patient and public-focused entity, and if patients and public are to stimulate appropriate change, several features will need to evolve in parallel. These include:

- applying a wider range of methods other than self-completion questionnaires to obtain opinion including, for instance, focus groups, interviews, patient participation groups;
- demonstrably acting upon and responding to elicited views;
- communicating with and educating the patient and public, such that their expressed views are well informed and based upon realistic expectations;
- offering opportunity for people to express opinion in a non-threatening environment;
- changing long held attitudes and beliefs within the service itself about the validity of such views;
- greater participation of patients and the public – for instance, with health care decisions made cooperatively between patient and clinician;
- increasing use of patient-focused measures of health and health status (see above).

The Patient's Charter

One part of the government's quality initiative has been the introduction of the Patient's Charter (DoH 1991c). This articulated a series of rights and standards for health care, many of which were already encompassed within the statutory frameworks of the NHS. These were built into the contracting and review mechanisms within the reformed NHS and districts are required to produce annual reports for the public on their Patient's Charter status. Health authorities were required to develop and publish their own local standards and charters.

As part of the Patient's Charter initiative, regions were required to institute accessible telephone information lines covering NHS services, waiting lists, Patient's Charter standards, self-help and voluntary groups, complaints procedures and other local or national information. This health information line is now available on a national free call number with calls routed to the regional offices.

Another effect of the Patient's Charter has been an increased emphasis on information leaflets and other media for better communication with patients and the public. There has been a considerable increase in patient information, but this has often been developed inappropriately, producing leaflets which communicate poorly with their intended readers (Smith 1992, Albert & Chadwick 1992).

In 1992, a Patient's Charter for family doctor services was produced to meet recognized criticism of the hospital and secondary care emphasis of the earlier charter, again encompassing basic rights and development of service standards (DoH 1992).

Most recently indicators of Patient's Charter performance, including accident and emergency and outpatient assessment times, ambulance response times, cancelled operation rates, day surgery rates and waiting time indicators, are being centrally collated and published as league tables, although concerns have been expressed about both the likely data quality and the value of league tabling as a means of stimulating quality improvement.

Whilst the Patient's Charter addresses some of the areas necessary to make the service more responsive to its users, it is unclear as to whether the emphasis on certain measures and indicators is really getting to the heart of the problem. Is the considerable effort being expended justified? For instance, do waiting time targets risk distorting decisions on clinical priority? Has the implementation of the charter led to changes in quality that are obvious to users of the service? Could the time spent on collecting data on Patient's Charter standards be better spent in applying patient assessment methods?

Complaints

One means of service users expressing their views is through complaints. Indeed, some industries and service organizations have used complaints as a means of identifying and rectifying problems. It has been suggested that the NHS could similarly utilize complaints.

The NHS has long-standing statutorily defined complaints procedures (DHSS 1981, 1988, Association of Community Health Councils 1990). These differ between primary and secondary care and are dependent upon whether the complaint concerns clinical or administrative procedures.

The hospital clinical complaints procedure is a three-stage process. If the complainant is not satisfied by stage one, which normally involves discussion with the consultant in charge, the complaint can proceed to the second stage which will involve the regional medical officer (RMO), who may then institute stage three. This involves an external independent review by consultants chosen by the joint consultants committee of the British Medical Association, who will review the case records and interview appropriate staff, as well as the complainant. They convey their findings verbally to the complainant and in a report to the RMO, who writes to the local staff involved. The complainant will receive a final letter from the district health authority outlining the findings of the review. This represents the final stage. If unsatisfied the complainant can refer the matter to the health service commissioner, but his powers extend only to an investigation of the administration of the procedure: he cannot investigate further the cause of the complaint (Health Service Commissioner 1990).

The design and process of the complaints procedures have been criticized for being cumbersome, slow, poorly responsive to complainants' needs and wishes, opaque, adversarial, lacking in impartiality, poorly communicating findings and not leading to appropriate change (Association of Community Health Councils 1990, Geffen 1990, Scott 1985). One of the fundamental problems has been the lack of a systematic overview of complaints as a means of identifying common themes and priorities for action, as well as a tendency to see a complaint as a negative event rather than an opportunity for improvement.

Nonetheless, persistent themes occur in the analysis of, and research into, complaints. A recurrent problem is communication, including failing to treat people with appropriate respect and dignity. Even when a clinical problem has occurred, it is often compounded by an initially defensive or insensitive response (Simanowitz 1985). In many cases early recognition and apology for a mistake would have prevented subsequent detailed, expensive and extensive procedures.

The Patient's Charter addresses some of these concerns (see above) but much more could be done. There have been calls for fundamental reviews of the systems (Donaldson & Cavanagh 1992), including suggestions for enhanced arbitration functions. The Wilson Committee (1994) has reviewed complaints procedures in the NHS and recommended the development of a unified system, with an initial immediate response by front-line staff, followed by investigation, conciliation and action, if necessary. Only if not adequately dealt with at this stage would a second stage be invoked, in difficult cases employing an independent panel with a majority of lay members. It is intended that such an approach would be less adversarial. A new procedure, taking account of many of the Wilson Committee recommendations, was implemented on 1st April 1996 (DoH 1995).

Community health councils and patient representative groups

Community health councils were established in statute in the 1974 NHS reorganization with the role of representing communities' interests in the NHS, usually one CHC per district (DHSS 1974). They have certain rights including: access to information from NHS authorities; access to certain NHS premises; consultation on substantial changes or variations in services; and meetings with district health authorities and family health service authorities (Dunham & Smith 1993). However, they have few formal powers and their relationships with authorities have been fraught with difficulty and tensions. A major part of their work has been in supporting complainants through the complex procedures.

The recent NHS reforms have provided a further challenge to the CHC role, including some lack of clarity as to whether they relate more to the purchasers' or providers' perspective (Dunham & Smith 1993, Hogg & Winkler 1990). Formal mergers of authorities and commissioning alliances further threaten their role and status. Their effectiveness is highly dependent on local circumstances and relationships. Whilst in some areas the emphasis on patient and public views has led to additional opportunities, the role and future of CHCs are unclear.

In addition to the statutory CHCs, there are a wide range of patient and public representative groups or associations, again with very variable purpose and impact. The British Diabetic Association is an example of an active and well-integrated body, largely through its capacity to work with and alongside both patients and clinicians (Williams 1992). The College of Health has achieved prominence in its work on waiting lists as well as other areas, the Patient's Association has stimulated debate and action at a national level and organizations such as MIND and Age Concern are regularly consulted by government. Other patient representative organizations offer valued support, advice and guidance to sufferers from particular diseases or problems. Information on such groups may be obtained from the Patient's Charter health information lines or the National Council for Voluntary Organizations.

Indicators and performance measures

The concept of indicators in the NHS is not new, but has attracted criticism and scepticism following the publication of performance indicators as a result of the Griffiths reforms in the 1980s (Pollitt 1985, Skinner et al 1988). These were largely structure and activity indicators and were often based upon data of questionable quality. Moreover, whilst the standard of presentation of indicators using computerized graphs and charts was of increasing quality and sophistication, the underlying data could be up to 2 years out of date (DHSS 1987).

If health services indicators are to be of real value in supporting quality improvement, they should meet the majority, if not all, of the following attributes. They should be:

- valid
- reliable
- timely
- appropriate
- comparative
- relevant to the quality of care
- interpretable
- capable of change.

Even if they meet these attributes, the way that indicators are utilized may well influence their effectiveness. Indicators are not *absolute* measures of quality. They should be seen as a barometer rather than as a thermometer of quality, as flags or screens capable of identifying opportunities for further study or as measures to support the evaluation of temporal change (Kazandjian 1991, Quality Review Bulletin 1989). Given this assertion, one can see the potential pitfalls of using indicators to externally monitor and evaluate performance, if their nature is poorly understood or the measures given undue prominence. This was driven home by the publication in the US of comparative hospital mortality rates in the mid 1980s (US DHHS 1987). The prominent media response was matched by the responses from the hospitals themselves – often concerned with questioning the quality of the data or explaining the mortality rate in terms of case mix or comorbidity, rather than using the data as a launching pad for quality improvement (Dubois et al 1987, Greenfield 1988, Dubois 1989).

In the UK, the Department of Health performance indicators introduced avoidable mortality indicators in 1986, including deaths from tuberculosis, chronic rheumatic heart disease, hypertensive and cerebrovascular disease, asthma, common surgical conditions (appendicitis, abdominal hernia, cholecystitis and cholelithiasis), Hodgkin's disease and cervical cancer. Unfortunately, at a district level, these indicators were largely constructed from small numbers of deaths, thus limiting their usefulness. They were also presented by population of residence, such that the small number of deaths following hernia operation may have occurred in more than one hospital, thus limiting their value as a way of assessing provider quality of care.

It is likely that the uses and interpretation of indicators will differ dependent upon whether they are developed at a population or provider level. Increasingly, purchasers and government will wish to utilize population-based indicators of health to monitor and assess progress of the *Health of the Nation* initiative (DoH 1991d). The Department of Health Central Health Outcomes Unit has published a consultation document on such population-based indicators drawn from routinely available health service statistics (DoH 1993d). This encompassed previously published avoidable deaths indicators, but extended the potential range of indicators to a much wider body.

However, in order to support provider-based quality improvement, there is a need for development of and access to indicators focused upon providers rather than populations. At a provider level, experience with clinical or outcome indicators (in contrast to structural or activity indicators which formed the core of the Health Service Indicators package) is at an early stage in the United Kingdom, although models exist and are developing elsewhere, particularly in the United States (Joint Commission on Accreditation of Health Care Organizations 1990, O'Leary 1987, Quality Review Bulletin 1989, Buckland 1989, Maryland Hospital Association 1990, Kazandjian et al 1995).

Indicators may be utilized by providers in a number of ways including professional audit (for instance, using wound infection rate as an indicator of the quality of surgical practice (Hancock 1990)). Within a single hospital, the value of such indicators may be limited by their lack of comparability with other services or hospitals – the concept of benchmarking applied widely in non-health settings (Camp 1993). However, systems for the production and publication of provider-based comparative indicators have potential pitfalls and problems, including concerns about the value of 'league tabling'. A move towards externally published clinical process or outcome-based indicators is likely to create tensions and considerable debate, although mechanisms that would allow providers to assess their status comparatively and anonymously could support provider quality strategies and audit.

A pilot study in the Northern Region has been assessing the potential of including acute hospitals in the Maryland Hospital Association quality indicator project which provides comparative assessment of performance utilizing a small number of acute hospital inpatient, A & E and day-case indicators with an outcome focus (Maryland Hospital Association 1993, Kazandjian et al 1995). These are collated by the participant units and forwarded electronically to the central office of the quality indicator project on a quarterly basis. They are then analysed and fed back to participant units to enable them to assess their position relative to aggregated data from all hospitals involved in the project (currently more than 800 in the United States). In addition to providing a rapid analysis and turnaround service (with quarterly data fed back within 45 days), the project provides supportive documentation to enable managers and clinicians within the participant units to appropriately interpret and utilize such indicator data in a continuous quality improvement model, recognizing the limitations of such measures.

In summary, there is likely to be an increasing push for use of comparative indicators of quality of care. The effectiveness of indicators in driving improvements in patient care is likely to depend markedly on the methods of data collection, the quality of the data, the perspective of those interpreting and using the data and whether they are applied as a stimulus for quality improvement or in a judgemental or sanctional way.

External monitoring and assessment

One form of quality assessment relies upon external inspection with or without accreditation. Such an approach is widespread in the United States, although it has been widely criticized (Roberts et al 1987, Wareham 1994a,b, Thomson 1994). In the UK there are examples of external inspection or visiting enshrined in law, as well as developing models of voluntary organizational audit which assess organizations against explicit standards.

Health Advisory Service (HAS)

The Health (formerly Hospital) Advisory Service was introduced in response to the Ely Hospital scandal of 1967 (Ely Report 1969) to report on the management, organization and standards of patient care predominantly in long-stay hospitals for the elderly and mentally ill. Its remit has been extended from hospital to community services, and the links between them, and has subsequently incorporated the Drug Advisory Service (NHS Health Advisory Service 1993). Until the end of 1991, the HAS carried out about 40 visiting team reviews of health and social services annually, reporting to ministers and the health and local authorities concerned. These routine visits have now ceased. A ministerial review concluded that the HAS should retain its remit for the same services, but that the role should change to take account of the NHS reforms. It was charged with developing its work in two main areas: in undertaking an inspectorial and advisory role under commission from ministers and in providing advisory services to the intermediate tier of the NHS. It has also been given responsibilities to monitor the performance of purchasers.

Their method relies on the appointment of review teams and on their expertise and upon implicit standards applied by these expert teams. This approach may suffer from a lack of objectivity; the findings and interpretation of such visits will depend upon the particular views of the visiting team and the individuals within it. Furthermore, there is no system of subsequent follow-up and review. The director recognized in his annual report of 1992–3 that the HAS should move towards adopting more explicit standards, but in an evolutionary way, aligned with development of the selection and training of seconded staff (NHS Health Advisory Service 1993).

An evaluation of the HAS (Henkel et al 1989) concluded that it had something of a hybrid role, being neither truly inspectorial nor having the resources necessary for a true consultancy and advisory service. Hence its effects were felt to be marginal. It remains to be seen whether the revised HAS, which has still not apparently resolved this conflict, will be considered of value to those responsible for commissioning its services and on whom its future may depend.

Nursing home registration

District health authorities are required to regularly inspect and register nursing and mental nursing homes under the terms of the Registered Homes Act 1984. However, the guidance included within the act has been criticized for being vague and ill defined and subsequently has not been significantly revised (Arai 1993). As a result, the guidelines developed by DHAs vary widely in their content and detail and may be limited to covering the environment and physical standards, with no element requiring or supporting quality assessment or audit within the home itself. Registration decisions rely on the integrity, skills and knowledge of the individual inspector, without the requirement for either national qualifications or training. The National Association of Health Authorities has published widely used guidance, recently supplemented by guidance on independent acute hospitals (National Association of Health Authorities 1988, National Association of Health Authorities and Trusts 1993).

The effectiveness of the approach is likely to depend

upon the relationships between inspectors and the homes; for instance, inspectors can disseminate good practice and advice. However, concerns about the variability of the approach have raised the question as to whether a more formal accreditation scheme should exist. Subsequently, the 1990 Community Care Act has introduced contracting requirements between DHAs and nursing homes which have offered a means of more explicit statements of standards of care and their monitoring.

The King's Fund organizational audit and similar programmes

The King's Fund has piloted and now offers an external organizational audit programme for acute hospitals (Shaw & Brooks 1991, King's Fund 1990), modelled upon the Australian and, to a lesser extent, the North American experience (Sketris 1988, King's Fund 1989). It involves a detailed 3-day visit from a trained audit team consisting of a manager, a nurse and a doctor. Prior to the visit, the participating hospital prepares for a year before undertaking its own self-audit using a large volume of explicit standards ranging across all functions and departments within the hospital. In addition to this, the audit team reviews key documentation, including for instance the minutes of quality and audit committees. The visit is prearranged, drawing upon the team's prior review of the self-reported standards. At the end of the visit, a draft report is shared with the senior management team in an immediate debriefing. Subsequently, a final report is sent to the participating hospital. Unlike its counterparts in other countries, there was initially no award of accreditation status, although such as system has now been implemented.

Following a 2-year pilot, the King's Fund have developed a similar primary care programme which is now available to interested general practices (Blakeway-Phillips 1993). Furthermore, there are pilot projects in community hospitals, nursing homes, mental health services and services for learning disabilities. In addition, there is a pilot of organizational audit for purchasers, beginning with six authorities (Bradbury B 1994, personal communication).

Other accreditation programmes exist or are in development. The South Western Regional Health Authority has an accreditation programme for community units (Shaw & Brooks 1991, Shaw & Collins 1995) and there is a similar voluntary scheme available for pathology departments (College Accreditation Steering Committee 1991).

As with similar programmes elsewhere, these assessments largely concentrate on structures and processes: they ask the question 'Can this organization provide good quality care?' rather than 'Does this organization provide good quality care?'. Thus, their effectiveness will rely, at least in part, on the appropriateness of the derived standards and their likely association with (unmeasured) positive health outcomes.

Accreditation of training posts by the Joint Commission on Higher Medical Training and royal colleges is an important professional method of assuring quality of care.

BS5750/ISO9000

The BSI has provided external accreditation standards for industrial and manufacturing organizations since 1979 – BS5750 (ISO9000) (British Standards Institute 1987, 1991). This tells purchasers and providers of goods what standards are required of a quality system by identifying the basic disciplines and specifying the criteria and procedures to ensure that customers' requirements are met. This is a voluntary scheme, although it is increasingly common for private sector purchasers to contractually require their suppliers to be accredited.

The enhanced focus on quality within the NHS has stimulated an interest in BS5750 (ISO9000) (Dickens & Horne 1991, Hoare 1991, Smith & Hart 1992, Davies 1993, Sloan 1993). Initially, technical and support services were attracted to this approach. More recently there have been examples of clinical functions or whole services attaining BS5750 (ISO9000) including a general practice, an occupational health department, an obstetric service, mental health services, an ambulance service, a regional medical physics organization and a regional blood transfusion service.

BS5750 (ISO9000) depends heavily upon documentation and policies, as well as on evidence of quality assessment and assurance activity. An accrediting team assesses the applicant and, if accredited, further assessment visits occur at intervals and the BS5750 (ISO9000) registration and kite mark can be withdrawn. If close to attaining registration, an organization can be offered an early re-audit after opportunity to rectify identified problems.

Recently the BSI has developed standards specifically for the service sector (British Standards Institute 1991), which may be particularly applicable to some elements of health care.

The value of BS5750 (ISO9000) lies in its enforcement of a systematic and organization-wide approach. However, there are problems with the burden of documentation and systems development. Furthermore, BS5750 (ISO9000) may not change the attitudes or style of managers and staff. In addition, whilst its value is clear if an organization seeks accreditation as part of its commitment to quality, the value may be less when contractually required. Nevertheless, being encouraged to take a systematic view of policies can have considerable benefits and be a valuable launching pad for later, more extensive, total quality management approaches.

The Audit Commission and the National Audit Office

Both of these organizations have statutory roles to audit the accounts of the NHS. With the increasing emphasis on the quality dimensions of economy, efficiency and effectiveness (Maxwell 1984, 1992) within a cash-limited public service and the more explicit consideration of rationing and prioritization decisions (Drummond & Maynard 1993), their profile in quality is growing.

The Audit Commission's statutory role in local authorities, including its value for money studies, was extended in 1990 to health authorities (Davies 1992). It selects three to five topics each year for in-depth study. A discussion paper on the NHS approach to quality improvement concluded that there were still weaknesses, including insufficient attention to patient views, lack of coordination across professional and geographical boundaries, a concentration on the measurable rather than the important and limited evaluation of quality improvement activities (Audit Commission 1992a).

It has already published influential reports on day-case surgery (Audit Commission 1990); the use of medical beds in acute hospitals (Audit Commission 1992b); and the use of laboratory services (Audit Commission 1991).

The day-case surgery study has influenced national and local policy including the setting of targets to increase the appropriate utilization of day-case treatment. This study also illustrates the Commission's desire to develop practical tools to enhance quality in the NHS, in this case a patient satisfaction questionnaire (Black & Sanderson 1993, Black et al 1993). It is now developing its role in quality, in particular in the public/patient perspective, improving local audit and in assisting with change (Audit Commission 1992a). The developing emphasis on quality assurance and outcome work with the NHS also includes an expressed wish to develop a voluntary good practice network, including the potential for publishing comparative information and the possible production of league tables and performance measures.

The National Audit Office (NAO) is an independent organization with powers to report to Parliament through the public accounts committee on the economy, efficiency and effectiveness with which resources are used (National Audit Office 1990). Recently, the NAO has increased its role within the NHS, including studies into use of operating theatres (National Audit Office 1987, 1991a), outpatient services (National Audit Office 1991b), services for the young physically disabled (National Audit Office 1992) and for HIV and AIDS (National Audit Office 1991c). A report into arrangements within the NHS for monitoring the effectiveness of clinical care provided in hospitals identified need for more coordinated audit activity, facilitated nationally and undertaken locally, as well as making recommendations for further development of the NHS advisory bodies such as the Health Advisory Service (National Audit Office 1988). Recently, the NAO have undertaken a study of the implementation of the national clinical audit programme in Scotland and selected regions in England: their conclusions are awaited.

The study into the use of operating theatres identified need for more efficient use of facilities and influenced the development of the national waiting list initiative (National Audit Office 1987). The follow-up report (National Audit Office 1991a) identified good progress, partly due to this initiative, although not without some criticism. Further recommendations included more dedicated day-case units, better information, greater validation of waiting lists and better understanding of the factors influencing the management of lists, factors that have subsequently been investigated and resourced.

The Clinical Standards Advisory Group

The multidisciplinary Clinical Standards Advisory Group (CSAG) was established in 1991 as part of the NHS and Community Care Act, to advise government and the NHS on standards of care and on access to and availability of services (Higginson 1992). Its establishment occurred in response to concerns expressed by the medical profession about the potential impact of the NHS reforms. The first series of reports covered childhood leukaemia, cystic fibrosis, neonatal intensive care, and coronary artery bypass grafting and percutaneous transluminal coronary angioplasty (Clinical Standards Advisory Group 1993a,b,c,d,e).

Whilst not strictly an external monitoring body their work, commissioned from research units, has included: analysis of routine data; surveys of and interviews with clinicians, managers and patients; and visits to facilities. Common findings relate to variations in access and activity, the need for improved information and for supra-district planning and purchasing for specialist services. Much of the initial data were from before or at an early stage of implementation of the NHS reforms. There is a recognized need to revisit these areas in 2 to 3 years to identify any effects of the reforms. The government's lacklustre response to the Group's recommendations leaves some doubt as to the impact of their work as a catalyst for change (DoH 1993e).

Summary

A variety of external monitoring and inspection models are in place or developing in the UK, but at present their impact is difficult to assess as there has been very little evaluation of their activities. Furthermore, the purchaser–provider split has led to further development of monitoring and inspection role for purchasers, although concerns have been expressed about both the capacity and the desirability of purchasers undertaking such a role (Boufford 1993, Thomson 1994). Whilst there is undoubtedly a place for such approaches, it is unlikely that we will develop external systems to the extent seen in North America. In particular, the government have shown reluctance to develop national accreditation schemes, although it is possible that purchasers will see benefits in requesting or subcontracting some form of third party assessment of their providers (see below).

Purchaser–provider systems and quality improvement

The purchaser–provider separation and interaction offers new means of quality of care enhancement, including the negotiation of contracts focusing upon quality standards and the stimulation of provider-based audit (Hopkins & Maxwell 1990, DoH 1989b,c). However, this interaction is still at an early stage of maturation, particularly in the development of the purchaser role (Gill 1993). The role of the purchaser in terms of population health and health care needs assessment is clarified by the new role of DHAs and FHSAs and clearly encompasses important issues of quality of care for populations, including equity, access and relevance to need. Thus, purchasers will wish to influence, and invest in, services to better align provision with population needs. However, the role of the purchaser in provider-based quality of care improvement is less clear.

Considerable emphasis has been placed on the role of contracts for services. Initial government guidance on contracting emphasized the importance of building quality specifications into contracts and gave early examples of good practice (DoH 1989b,c). Contracting offered an opportunity to make explicit statements about standards of service provision against which services could be monitored. However, contracting was introduced at a time when there was little explicit standard setting within clinical practice, hence the need for a parallel emphasis on the wider development of professional audit. Moreover, information systems are still extremely limited in their capacity to provide data on quality of care. For these reasons, many early contract quality clauses concentrated upon already measurable, albeit important, factors such as waiting times. In addition, many quality specifications made admirable statements regarding, for example, treatment of patients with respect and dignity, but the value of such statements relies upon providers' responses, as the means or measures for purchasers to evaluate or assess such clauses were largely unavailable. Furthermore, purchasers had insufficient resource to adequately monitor such quality clauses themselves, at the same time as developing the wider purchasing role of needs assessment and health strategy (Gill 1993, Boufford 1993).

There has been surprisingly little assessment of contracts and quality clauses content, let alone their monitoring, since the implementation of the NHS reforms, although concerns have been expressed about the present potential for quality issues to survive in competition with cost and volume emphasis, particularly in the light of limited information availability (Gill 1993).

There has always been a risk that quality clauses in contracts might become a bureaucratic exercise exceeding the capacity of the purchaser to monitor and the provider to respond. It is clearly of limited value to include clauses that are impossible to monitor or evaluate or that providers will wilfully or by default ignore.

To an extent, the effectiveness of contracting relies on the fact that the purchaser–provider interaction should be a continuous process of negotiation and discussion and not an intermittent event of contracting. However, real concerns have been expressed about the appropriate involvement of clinicians in contracting for services as well as concerns about the expertise and seniority of purchasing contracts managers.

This raises the important issue of the appropriate involvement of the purchaser in provider quality. Purchasers undoubtedly feel some responsibility to ensure that the care purchased is of good technical and interpersonal quality and delivered in an appropriate and safe environment. In broad terms, several different approaches can be envisaged on a spectrum ranging from requiring providers to have appropriate quality systems (such as clinical audit) in place and being assured of their effectiveness, through to detailed inspection and monitoring of provider quality, requiring extensive data exchange and analysis. Moreover, the purchaser–provider relationship could be cooperative or to a greater or lesser extent adversarial (Gourlay 1992).

Purchasers will need to consider how they can most effectively and cost-effectively influence and be assured of the quality of the clinical care purchased. Where does the balance lie between extensive purchaser involvement in provider quality and a hands-off approach that some might consider an abrogation of purchaser responsibility? In a quasi-market, such as that implemented in the NHS internal market, an important consideration is balancing the benefits of contracting, and the associated costs of information needed, with the transaction costs of implementing such systems (Le Grand & Bartlett 1993).

The American experience may provide important pointers here. Firstly, external monitoring systems are expensive, heavily reliant on extensive data collection and widely criticized by providers (Wareham 1994a, 1994b). For example, the mandatory external peer review organizations (PROs) have consumed considerable resources, but have largely developed into bodies whose function appears to be cost containment and the identification of bad care (Lohr 1990). This approach, not surprisingly, has generated defensiveness and antagonism from clinicians (Berwick 1989).

Secondly, multiple purchasers producing differing demands are both inefficient and a costly burden on providers – a feature recognized within the proposed Clinton reforms (Caplan 1993). Thirdly, external comparative monitoring, such as publication of hospital mortality data, is problematic. The publication of such data in the US produced an immense media response (Brinkley 1986) but also led to an explosion of approaches to risk adjustment of such data, much of which appears to have been focused on explaining variation, rather than on stimulating quality improvement activity (Blumberg 1986, Iezzoni 1989). Fourthly, whilst external accreditation models are widely applied, they are costly, both to organize and for providers to subscribe.

If purchasers are to develop means of effectively assuring themselves of the quality of care they are purchasing, they may best focus their efforts upon insisting that providers have well-developed and demonstrably effective quality systems in place, rather than trying to develop external assessment or make judgements on provider quality based upon inadequate data or understanding.

That is not to say that providers should be insulated from appropriate and legitimate external interest in the quality of their care: they should increasingly be able to demonstrate that their systems lead to quality improvement and they will equally have a responsibility to ensure that their priorities for quality assessment and audit are driven by much more than their own interests and aspirations. Mechanisms are needed to ensure that purchaser, patient and public views, amongst others, inform priorities for quality improvement.

The American experience suggests that we should actively explore co-operative relationships between purchasers and providers in pursuing their joint aspirations for high quality care. The primary purchaser emphasis should be on the population dimensions of quality and on purchasing the 'right things', whilst providers should be required to demonstrate effective quality improvement systems, albeit increasingly responsive to the expressed priorities of purchasers and founded in open dialogue between purchaser and provider (Thomson et al 1993a). Perhaps the final word here should rest with Avedis Donabedian who, in emphasizing the value of the organization-wide approach to quality, wrote:

> The challenge is to introduce quality monitoring and its associated controls so that they become an organically functioning part of an organization, rather than a foreign irritant to be neutralized or repudiated.
>
> (Donabedian 1988)

QUALITY IN HEALTHCARE: THE FUTURE

The methods and mechanisms for assessing and improving health care quality described above are multiple and varied, as perhaps befits the complexity of health care. Whilst recent NHS reforms, particularly the introduction of professional audit, have opened up opportunities for more systematic approaches, there is still concern that approaches remain to an extent fragmented. In particular, one wonders whether a synthesizing philosophy of quality improvement could enhance and inform present methods and allow for their greater consistency and coordination.

It is perhaps worth briefly caricaturing the development of quality systems in the industrial setting. Once industrial approaches had succeeded the primacy of the individual craftsman, systems for quality control became necessary. Initially, these relied on systems of inspection. Quality control inspectors were employed to identify poorly manufactured widgets at the end of the production process and discard them. At best they would be returned to the beginning of the production process and refashioned. Such an approach had the potential to prevent substandard products reaching the market. However, it is a wasteful system leading to rework and relying upon the accuracy and quality of the inspection process.

As a result, quality theorists began to develop the concepts of statistical process control (Feigenbaum 1991, Ishikawa 1985, Juran et al 1979). In effect these shifted the emphasis from inspection to prevention. Examination of the product was used only as a mechanism for feeding back into refinement of the processes of production. These were then continuously improved, using and applying statistical measurement techniques, in order to increasingly ensure that the production process led to predictable manufacture of high quality widgets by continuously reducing variation and improving the processes of production.

However, whilst this approach led to considerable forward progress in quality improvement within industry, particularly in post-war Japan, it was still insufficient. Increasingly it was recognized that much of the resource available to organizations lies in the skills and abilities of the workforce. Furthermore, they are often best placed to identify opportunities for improvement in work processes. In addition, there is more to developing a quality organization than introducing statistical processes. The recognition of the human aspects of organizational success, aligned with an increasing emphasis on the desires and wishes of the customer of the service or product, added to the further development into the area of total quality management (Deming 1986).

In the United States, Berwick (1989, 1992) has championed the introduction of such a philosophy into health care, coining the phrase 'continuous quality improvement' and contrasting this with the 'bad apple' approach which he perceives as being more prevalent in present quality initiatives in the United States. The continuous quality improvement or total quality management (TQM) approach relies on a number of fundamental components. These include:

- commitment from the top;
- an organization-wide approach;
- use of quality improvement tools;
- concentration on the customer;
- staff development and training;
- process improvement;
- a participative environment;
- investment in quality.

Much of the present debate on health care quality in the United States focuses on how present systems can encompass this continuous quality improvement approach (O'Leary 1991). It has not only a clear theoretical and practical basis in other settings, but also has considerable face validity in terms of the potential to create lasting and effective improvement when contrasted with the 'bad apple' approach, in which concentrating on the outliers runs the risk of game playing and efforts focused on explaining away or defending a position, whilst potentially having little effect on the great majority who exceed the implicit or explicit threshold standards (Berwick 1989). In contrast, approaches that offer the means of improvement across the board and reduction in variation can be expected to lead to a shift to the right of the quality distribution, thus leading to considerably greater quality enhancement for patients and populations.

It is also suggested that such an approach would succeed the standards-based model at present supported by clinical audit, with measures being used more as indicators to track and assess change rather than as the basis for statement of standards.

The other major feature of a continuous quality improvement approach lies in its preventive nature. At present much audit and quality assurance is retrospective. The TQM approach is more concerned with building in lasting solutions through the systematic organization-wide application of effective processes.

Of course, such an approach presupposes and requires the necessary cultural milieu, depending upon sound and supportive personnel policy, with co-operative and open relationships based upon trust and honesty. Whether the NHS reforms are conducive to such an approach remains to be seen. The NHSME invested funds into pilot schemes of TQM in healthcare and across a range of healthcare organizations, with the effectiveness of such approaches being evaluated by an independent research team from Brunel University (CEPPP 1991). Their interim conclusions suggest that the generalizable lessons from other settings are equally applicable and pertinent in organization-wide approaches to quality in healthcare. However, these studies also suggest that the range of approaches developing under the TQM banner in health care are wide – indeed many may not be recognized as such by those responsible for implementing or developing TQM in other service or production industries.

Nonetheless, both in the UK and in the United States, there are an increasing number of examples of the applicability of tools and methods of quality management in the health care setting (Berwick et al 1991, Batelden & Buchanan 1989, Thomson et al 1993b). I very strongly believe that the NHS must develop organization-wide approaches to quality improvement encompassing such issues as professional audit and guidelines, but within the wider context of a considered strategic approach to quality improvement centred upon the fact that the NHS is an employee-focused organization. Its strengths have traditionally lain in the commitment and motivation of its staff. For any approach to work in the NHS, it must recognize, support and develop its crucial human resources, within an empowering culture. Without such future development there is a risk that quality initiatives, albeit much enhanced compared to 10–15 years ago, remain peripheral rather than central to the strategic role of the NHS and health care.

Acknowledgements

I would like to thank the following for their helpful comments on drafts of this chapter: Pat Blain, Barbara Bradbury, Bruce Charlton, Brian Coapes, Norma

Doherty, Bill Ennis, Marie Johnson, Elaine Tait. Thanks are also due to Astrid McIntyre for highly valued secretarial help and to Vanessa Burgess and Catherine Smith for library support.

REFERENCES

Abramson J H 1990 Survey methods in community medicine. Churchill Livingstone, Edinburgh

Albert T, Chadwick S 1992 How readable are practice leaflets? British Medical Journal 305: 1266–1268

Anderson C A, Cassidy B, Rivenburgh P 1991 Implementing continuous quality improvement in hospitals: lessons learned from the international quality study. Quality Assurance in Health Care 3: 141–146

Arai Y 1993 Quality of care in private nursing homes: improving inspection. International Journal of Health Care Quality Assurance 6: 13–16

Association of Community Health Councils for England and Wales 1990 National health service complaints procedures. ASCHCEW, London

Audit Commission 1990 A short cut to better services: day surgery in England and Wales. HMSO, London

Audit Commission 1991 The pathology services: a management review. HMSO, London

Audit Commission 1992a Minding the quality: a consultation document on the role of the Audit Commission in quality assurance in health care. Audit Commission, London

Audit Commission 1992b Lying in wait – the use of medical beds in acute hositals. HMSO, London

Baker R 1993 Use of pyschometrics to develop a measure of patient satisfaction for general practice. In: Fitzpatrick R, Hopkins A Measurement of patient satisfaction with their care. Royal College of Physicians, London, pp 57–86

Baker R, Whitfield M 1992 Measuring patient satisfaction: a test of construct validity. Quality in Health Care 1: 104–109

Bamford C, Jacoby A 1992 Development of patient satisfaction questionnaires. I methodological issues. Quality in Health Care 1: 153–157

Batalden B P, Buchanan E D 1989 Industrial models of quality improvement. In: Goldfield N, Nash D B Providing quality care: the challenge to clinicians. American College of Physicians, Philadelphia, pp 133–155

Beed T W 1985 Survey interviewing: theory and techniques. Allen & Unwin, London

Bergner M, Bobbitt R, Carter W, Gilson B 1981 The sickness impact profile: development and final revision of a health status measure. Medical Care 19: 787–805

Berwick D M 1989 Continuous improvement as an ideal in health care. New England Journal of Medicine 320: 53–56

Berwick D M 1992 Heal thyself or heal thy system: can doctors help to improve medical care? Quality in Health Care 1 Suppl: S2–S8

Berwick D M, Blanton Godfrey A, Roessner J 1991 Curing health care: new strategies for quality improvement. Jossey-Bass, San Francisco

Black N, Sanderson C 1993 Day surgery: development of a questionnaire for eliciting patients' experiences. Quality in Health Care 2: 157–161

Black N, Petticrew M, Hunter D, Sanderson C 1993 Day surgery: development of a national comparative audit service. Quality in Health Care 2: 162–166

Blakeway-Phillips C 1993 What has organisational audit got to offer primary health care? Primary Care Management 3: 7–8

Blumberg M S 1986 Risk adjusting health care outcome: a methodologic review. Medical Care Review 43: 351–393

Boufford J I 1993 US and UK health care reforms: reflections on quality. Quality in Health Care 2: 249–252

Bowling A 1991 Measuring health: a review of quality of life measurement scales. Open University Press, Milton Keynes

Bowling A 1994 Measuring disease: a review of disease specific quality of life measurement scales. Open University Press, Buckingham

Brazier J E, Harper R, Jones N M B et al 1992 Validating the SF36 health survey questionnaire: a new outcome measure for primary care. British Medical Journal 305: 160–164

Brinkley J 1986 US releasing lists of hospitals with abnormal mortality rates. New York Times March 12th: 1

British Standards Institute 1987 BS5750 (ISO9000): quality systems part I: specification for design/development, production, installation. BSI, London

British Standards Institute 1991 BS5750 (ISO9000): quality systems part 8: guide to quality management and quality systems elements for services. BSI, London

British Thoracic Society 1993 Guidelines for the management of asthma: a summary. British Medical Journal 306: 776–782

Buck N, Devlin H P, Lunn J N 1987 The report of a confidential enquiry into perioperative deaths. Nuffield Provincial Hospitals Trust, London

Buckland A E 1989 In search of quality, Part IV. The Maryland Hospital Association Quality Indicator Project. Journal of the American Medical Association 60: 34–38

Buckley G 1990 Clinically significant events. In: Marinker M Medical audit in general practice. MSD Foundation, London, pp 144–167

Camp R 1993 Benchmarking: the search for best practices that lead to superior performance. ISF International, Bedford

Campling E A, Devlin H B, Lunn J N 1990 The report of the national confidential enquiry into perioperative deaths 1989. NCEPOD, London

Campling E A, Devlin H B, Hoile R W, Lunn J N 1992 The report of the national confidential enquiry into perioperative deaths 1990. NCEPOD, London

Campling E A, Devlin H B, Hoile R W, Lunn J N 1993 The report of the national confidential enquiry into perioperative deaths 1991/2. NCEPOD, London

Caper P 1988 Defining quality in medical care. Health Affairs 7: 49–61

Caplan A 1993 Clinton's health care reforms: an unstoppable momentum for change. British Medical Journal 307: 813–814

Caplan S H, Ware J E 1989 The patient's role in health care and quality assessment. In: Goldfield N, Nash D B Providing quality care: the challenge to clinicians. American College of Physicians, Philadelphia, pp 25–68

Carr-Hill R A 1992 The measurement of patient satisfaction. Journal of Public Health Medicine 14: 236–249

CEPPP 1991 Evaluation of TQM in the NHS: first interim report. CEPPP, Brunel University

Chalmers I 1989 Inquiry into stillbirths and infant deaths. British Medical Journal 299: 339–340

Charlton J R H, Hartley R M, Silver R, Holland W W 1983 Geographical variation in mortality from conditions amenable to medical intervention in England and Wales. Lancet 1: 691–696

Capar P 1988 Defining quality in medical care. Health Affairs 7: 49–61

Cleary P, McNeil B 1988 Patient satisfaction as an indicator of quality care. Inquiry 25: 25–36
Clinical Resource and Audit Group 1993 Clinical guidelines: report of the working group. Scottish Office, Edinburgh
Clinical Standards Advisory Group 1993a Access to and availability of specialist services: childhood leukemia. HMSO, London
Clinical Standards Advisory Group 1993b Access to and availability of specialist services: cystic fibrosis. HMSO, London
Clinical Standards Advisory Group 1993c Access to and availability of specialist services: neonatal intensive care. HMSO, London
Clinical Standards Advisory Group 1993d Access to and availability of coronary artery bypass grafting and coronary angioplasty. HMSO, London
Clinical Standards Advisory Group 1993e Access to and availability of specialist services. HMSO, London
College Accreditation Steering Committee 1991 Pathology department accreditation in the United Kingdom: a synopsis. Journal of Clinical Pathology 44: 798–802
Crosby P 1979 Quality is free. Mentor, New York
Davidow W A, Uttal B 1989 Total customer service. Harper & Row, London
Davies H 1992 Role of the audit commission. Quality in Health Care 1 Suppl: S36–S39
Davies L 1993 What is BS5750 (ISO9000)? British Dental Journal 174: 298–299
De Haan R, Aaronson N, Limburg M, Langton Hewer R, Van Crevel H 1993 Measuring quality of life in stroke. Stroke 24: 320–327
Deming W E 1986 Out of the crisis. Cambridge University Press, Cambridge
Department of Health and Social Security 1974 HC(74)4. HMSO, London
Department of Health 1989a Working for patients. Working paper 6: medical audit. HMSO, London
Department of Health 1989b Funding and contracts for hospital services: working paper II. HMSO, London
Department of Health 1989c Contracts for health services: operational principles. HMSO, London
Department of Health 1990 Health service developments – working for patients. Medical audit in the family practitioner services. HC(FP)(90)8.HC(90)15. HMSO, London
Department of Health 1991a Framework of audit for nursing services: guidance document. EL(91)72. HMSO, London
Department of Health 1991b Medical audit in the hospital and community health services: assuring the quality of medical care: implementation of medical and dental audit in the hospital and community health services. HC(91)2. HMSO, London
Department of Health 1991c The patient's charter: raising the standard. HMSO, London
Department of Health 1991d The health of the nation. HMSO, London
Department of Health 1992 The patient's charter and primary health care. EL(92)88. HMSO, London
Department of Health 1993a Clinical audit in HCHS: allocation of funds 1993/4. EL(93)34. HMSO, London
Department of Health 1993b Clinical audit: meeting and improving standards in health care. HMSO, London
Department of Health 1993c Improving clinical effectiveness. EL(93)115. HMSO, London
Department of Health 1993d Population health outcome indicators for the NHS: a consultation document. HMSO, London
Department of Health 1993e Government response to the report by the clinical standards advisory group on access to and availability of specialist services. HMSO, London
Department of Health 1994a Report on confidential enquiries into maternal deaths in the United Kingdom 1988–90. HMSO, London
Department of Health 1994b Medical audit of the royal colleges and their faculties in the UK. HMSO, London
Department of Health 1995 Government response to the review of NHS complaints procedures. EL(95)37. HMSO, London
Department of Health and Social Security 1981 Health service management: health service complaints procedure. HC(81)5. DHSS, London
Department of Health and Social Security 1983 NHS management inquiry (Griffiths report). HMSO, London
Department of Health and Social Security 1984 Health advisory service. HC(84)116. DHSS, London
Department of Health and Social Security 1987 Performance indicators in the NHS: guidance for users. HMSO, London
Department of Health and Social Security 1988 Health service management: hospital complaints procedure act 1985. HC(88)37. HMSO, London
Dickens P, Horne T 1991 A quality status symbol. Health Service Journal 12th Sept 101:25
Donabedian A 1966 Evaluating the quality of medical care. Milbank Memorial Fund Quarterly 4: 166–206
Donabedian A 1980 Exploration in quality assessment and monitoring, vols 1–3. Health Administration Press, Ann Arbor
Donabedian A 1988 Quality assessment and assurance: unity of purpose, diversity of means. Inquiry 25: 173–192
Donabedian A 1992 The Lichfield lecture. Quality assurance in health care: the consumers' role. Quality in Health Care 1: 247–251
Donaldson L J, Cavanagh J 1992 Clinical complaints and their handling: a time for change. Quality in Health Care 1: 21–25
Drummond M F, Maynard A (eds) 1993 Purchasing and providing cost effective health care. Churchill Livingstone, Edinburgh
Dubois R W 1989 Hospital mortality as an indicator of quality. In: Goldfield N, Nash D B Providing quality care: the challenge to clinicians. American College of Physicians, Philadelphia
Dubois R W, Rogers W H, Moxley J H, Draper D, Brook R H 1987 Hospital inpatient mortality. Is it a predictor of quality? New England Journal of Medicine 317: 1674–1680
Dunham P, Smith S 1993 The changing role of CHCs. Health Services Management 89: 14–17
Eccles M, Jacoby A, Bamford C 1992 Development of patient satisfaction questionnaires: II collaboration in practice. Quality in Health Care 1: 158–160
Eddy D M 1992 Assessing health practices and designing practice policies: an explicit approach. American College of Physicians, Philadelphia
Ellwood P M 1988 Shattuck lecture – outcomes management: a technology of patient experience. New England Journal of Medicine 318: 1549–1556
Ely Report 1969 Report of the committee of enquiry into allegations of ill treatment of patients at Ely Hospital, Cardiff. HMSO, London

Epstein A M 1990 The outcomes movement – will it get us where we want to go? New England Journal of Medicine 323: 266–270

Fallowfield L 1990 The quality of life. Souvenir, London

Feigenbaum A V 1991 Total quality control. McGraw-Hill, New York

Fielding L P, Stewart-Brown S, Plesovsky L, Kearney G 1980 Anastomotic integrity after operations for large bowel cancer: a multi-centre study. British Medical Journal 281: 411–414

Fitzpatrick R 1990 Measurement of patient satisfaction. In: Hopkins A, Costain D (eds) Measuring the outcomes of medical care. Royal College of Physicians, London, pp 19–26

Fitzpatrick R 1991a Surveys of patient satisfaction I: important general considerations. British Medical Journal 302: 887–889

Fitzpatrick R 1991b Surveys of patient satisfaction II: designing a questionnaire and conducting a survey. British Medical Journal 302: 1129–1132

Fitzpatrick R 1993 Scope and measurement of patient satisfaction. In: Fitzpatrick R, Hopkins A Measurement of patients' satisfaction with their care. Royal College of Physicians, London, pp 1–17

Flanagan J C 1954 The critical incident technique. Psychological Bulletin 51: 327–358

Fowkes F G R 1982 Medical audit cycle. Medical Education 16: 228–238

Frater A, Costain D 1992 Any better? Outcome measures in medical audit. British Medical Journal 304: 519–520

Frater A, Sheldon T A 1993 The outcomes movement in the USA and the UK. In: Drummond M F, Maynard A (eds) Purchasing and providing cost effective health care. Churchill Livingstone, Edinburgh, pp 49–65

Garratt A M, Ruta D A, Abdalla N I, Buckingham J K, Russell I T 1993 The SF36 health survey questionnaire: an outcome measure suitable for routine use within the NHS? British Medical Journal 306: 1440–1444

Geffen T 1990 The complaints procedure. Health Trends 22: 87–99

Gill M 1993 Purchasing for quality: still in the starting blocks? Quality in Health Care 2: 179–182

Gourlay R 1992 Negotiating health contracts: harmony or hostility? International Journal of Health Care Quality Assurance 5: 35–36

Gray D J P 1984 Selecting general practitioner trainers. British Medical Journal 288: 195–198

Gray D P 1992 Accreditation in general practice. Quality in Health Care 1: 61–64

Greenfield S F 1988 Flaws in mortality data: the hazards of ignoring comorbid disease. Journal of the American Medical Association 260: 2253–2255

Grimshaw J, Russell I T 1993a Effect of clinical guidelines on medical practice: a systematic review of rigorous evaluations. Lancet 342: 1317–1322

Grimshaw J, Russell I T 1993b Achieving health gain through clinical guidelines I: developing scientifically valid guidelines. Quality in Health Care 2: 243–248

Grimshaw J N, Russell I T 1994 Achieving health gain through clinical guidelines II: ensuring that guidelines change medical practice. Quality in Health Care 3: 45–52

Gritzner C 1993 The CASPE patient satisfaction system. In: Fitzpatrick R, Hopkins A Measurement of patients' satisfaction with their care. Royal College of Physicians, London, pp 33–41

Grol R 1992 Implementing guidelines in general practice care. Quality in Health Care 1: 184–191

Guyatt G H, Feeny D H, Pattrick D L 1993 Measuring health related quality of life. Annals of Internal Medicine 118: 622–629

Ham C (ed) 1988 Health care variations: assessing the evidence. King's Fund Institute, London

Hancock E D 1990 Audit of major colorectal and biliary surgery to reduce rates of wound infection. British Medical Journal 301: 911–912

Hays R D, Larson C, Nelson E C, Batelden P B 1991 Hospital quality trends: a short form patient based measure. Medical Care 29: 661–668

Health Security Act 1993 US Government Printing Office, Washington DC

Health Service Commissioner 1990 Annual report for 1989–90. HMSO, London

Henkel M, Kogan M, Packwood T, Whitaker T, Youll P 1989 The health advisory service: an evaluation. King's Fund, London

Higginson G 1992 Role of the Clinical Standards Advisory Group. Quality in Health Care 1 Suppl: S34–S35

Hoare T 1991 Quality management. BS5750 (ISO9000). Occupational Health 43: 25–26

Hogg C, Winkler F 1989 Community/consumer representation in the NHS with specific reference to community health councils. Greater London Association of Community Health Councils, London

Hogg C, Winkler F 1990 Community health councils: their role after the NHS white paper. Health Services Management 86: 171–173

Hopkins A (ed) 1992 Measures of the quality of life and the uses to which such measures may be put. Royal College of Physicians, London

Hopkins A, Costain D (eds) 1990 Measuring the outcomes of medical care. Royal College of Physicians, London

Hopkins A, Maxwell R 1990 Contracts and quality of care. British Medical Journal 300: 919–922

Hunt S, McEwan J, McKenna S 1986 Measuring health status. Croom Helm, London

Iezzoni L I 1989 Measuring the severity of illness and case mix. In: Goldfield N, Nash D B Providing quality care: the challenge to clinicians. American College of Physicians, Philadelphia, pp 70–106

Institute of Medicine 1992 Guidelines for clinical practice: from development to use. National Academic Press, Washington

Ishikawa K 1985 What is total quality control? The Japanese way. Prentice-Hall, Englewood Cliffs, NJ

Jenkinson C, Coulter A, Wright L 1993 Short form 36 (SF36) health survey questionnaire: normative data for adults of working age. British Medical Journal 306: 1437–1440

Joint Commission on Accreditation of Health Care Organizations 1990 Primer on indicator development and application. JCAHO, Chicago

Joint Committee on Postgraduate Training for General Practice 1976. Criteria for the selection of trainers in general practice. JCPTGP, London

Jones L, Leneman L, MacLean U 1987 Consumer feedback for the NHS: a literature review. King's Fund, London

Joule N 1993 Involving users of health care services: moving beyond lip service. Quality in Health Care 2: 211–212

Juran J M 1964 Managerial breakthrough. McGraw-Hill, New York

Juran J M 1988 Juran on planning for quality. Free Press, New York

Juran J M, Gryna F M, Bingham R S (eds) 1979 The quality control handbook. McGraw-Hill, New York

Kasper J F, Mulley A G, Wennberg J E 1992 Developing shared decision making programmes to improve the quality of health care. Quality Review Bulletin 18: 183–190

Kazandjian V A 1991 Performance indicators: pointer dogs in disguise – a commentary. Journal of the American Medical Records Association 62: 34–36

Kazandjian V A, Wood P, Lawthers J 1995 Balancing science and practice in indicator development: the Maryland hospital association quality indicator (QI) project. International Journal for Quality in Health Care 7: 39–46

King's Fund 1989 Health services accreditation: a national overview. King's Fund, London

King's Fund 1990 Organisational audit (accreditation UK): standards for an acute hospital. King's Fund, London

Le Grand J, Bartlett W (eds) 1993 Quasi-markets and social policy. Macmillan, Basingstoke

Lohr K N (ed) 1990 Medicare: a strategy for quality assurance. National Academic Press, Washington

Lomas J, Haynes R B 1987 A taxonomy and critical review of tested strategies for the application of clinical practice recommendations: from 'official' to 'individual' clinical policy. American Journal of Preventive Medicine 4: 77–94

Long A F, Dixon P, Hall R, Carr-Hill R A, Sheldon T A 1993 The outcomes agenda: contribution of the UK clearing house on health outcomes. Quality in Health Care 2: 49–52

Lowry S 1993 Trends in health care and their effects on medical education. British Medical Journal 306: 255–258

Madhok R, Thomson R G, Mordue A, Mendelow A D, Barker J 1993 An audit of distribution and use of guidelines for the management of head injury. Quality in Health Care 2: 27–30

Maguire P, Selby P 1989 Assessing quality of life in cancer patients. British Journal of Cancer 60: 437–440

Maryland Hospital Association 1990 Guidebook for quality indicator data: a continuous improvement model. Maryland Hospital Association, Lutherville

Maryland Hospital Association 1993 Quality indicator project implementation manual. Maryland Hospital Association, Baltimore

Mason V 1989 Women's experience of maternity care: a survey manual. HMSO, London

Maxwell R 1984 Quality assessment in health. British Medical Journal 288: 1470–1472

Maxwell R 1992 Dimensions of quality revisited: from thought to action. Quality in Health Care 1: 171–175

McDowell I, Newell C 1987 Measuring health: a guide to rating scales and questionnaires. Oxford University Press, Oxford

McHorney C A, Ware J E, Raczek A E 1993 The MOS 36 item shortform health survey (SF36) II: psychometric and clinical tests of validity in measuring physical and mental health constructs. Medical Care 31: 247–263

McIver S 1991a An introduction to obtaining the views of users of health services. King's Fund, London

McIver S 1991b Obtaining the views of patients. King's Fund, London

McIver S 1991c Obtaining the views of users of mental health services. King's Fund, London

McIver S 1992 Obtaining the views of inpatients and users of casualty departments. King's Fund, London

McIver S 1993 Obtaining the views of users of primary and community health care services. King's Fund, London

Meenen R, Gertwin P, Mayson J, Dunaif R 1982 The arthritis impact measurement scales: further investigation of a health status instrument. Arthritis and Rheumatism 25: 1048–1053

Ministry of Health 1957 Report on confidential enquiries into maternal deaths in England and Wales 1952–54. HMSO, London

Mishler E G 1991 Research interviewing: context and narrative. Harvard University Press, Cambridge, MA

Morris J, Watt A 1993 Assessing quality of life. In: Drummond M F, Maynard A Purchasing cost effective health care. Churchill Livingstone, Edinburgh

Mugford M, Banfield P, O'Hanlon M 1991 Effects of feedback of information on clinical practice: a review. British Medical Journal 303: 398–402

National Advisory Body 1994 The confidential enquiry into stillbirths and deaths in infancy 1992–93. HMSO, London

National Association of Health Authorities 1988 The registration and inspection of nursing homes: a handbook for health authorities. NAHA, Birmingham

National Association of Health Authorities and Trusts 1993 Independent acute hospitals: supplement to the handbook on the registration and inspection of nursing homes. NAHAT, Birmingham

National Audit Office 1987 Use of operating theatres in the National Health Service. HMSO, London

National Audit Office 1988 Quality of clinical care in National Health Service hospitals. HMSO, London

National Audit Office 1990 The role of the National Audit Office. National Audit Office, London

National Audit Office 1991a Use of National Health Service operating theatres in England: a progress report. HMSO, London

National Audit Office 1991b NHS out-patient services. HMSO, London

National Audit Office 1991c HIV and AIDS related health services. HMSO, London

National Audit Office 1992 Health services for physically disabled people aged 16–64. National Audit Office, London

National Health Service and Community Care Act 1990. HMSO, London

Neave H R 1990 The Deming dimension. SPC Press, Knoxville

NHS Health Advisory Service 1993 A unique window on change: the annual report of the director for 1992–93. HMSO, London

NHS Management Executive 1993 The quality journey: a guide to total quality management in the NHS. NHSME, London

Northern Regional Health Authority 1984 Perinatal mortality. British Medical Journal 288: 1717–1720

Northern Regional Health Authority 1993 Collaborative survey of perinatal, late neonatal and infant death in the Northern Region. NRHA, Newcastle upon Tyne

O'Leary D S 1987 The Joint Commission's agenda for change. JCAHO, Chicago

O'Leary D S 1991 Accreditation in the quality improvement mold: a vision for tomorrow. Quality Review Bulletin 17: 72–77

Organization for Economic Co-operation and Development 1987 Financing and delivering health care: a comparative analysis of OECD countries. OECD, Paris

Organization for Economic Co-operation and Development

1992 The reform of health care: a comparative analysis of 7 OECD countries. OECD, Paris

Peckham M 1991 Research and development for the National Health Service. Lancet 338: 367–371

Pollitt C 1985 Measuring performance: a new system for the National Health Service. Policy and Politics 13: 1–15

Pollitt C 1990 Doing business in the temple? Managers and quality assurance in the public services. Public Administration 68: 435–452

Pritchard J B (ed) 1969 Ancient near-Eastern texts: relating to the Old Testament. Princeton University Press, Princeton

Quality Review Bulletin 1989 Editorial: characteristics of clinical indicators. Quality Review Bulletin 15: 330–339

Redfern S J, Norman I J, Tomlin D A, Oliver S 1993 Assessing quality of nursing care. Quality in Health Care 2: 124–128

Registered Homes Act 1984 HMSO, London

Roberts J S, Cole J G, Redman R R 1987 A history of the Joint Commission on Accreditation of Hospitals. Journal of the American Medical Association 258: 936–940

Roland M, Morris R 1983 A study of the natural history of backpain. I. Development of a reliable and sensitive measure of disability in low back pain. Spine 8: 141–144

Royal College of General Practitioners 1985 Quality in general practice: policy statement. RCGP, London

Royal College of Nursing 1990 Quality patient care: the dynamic standard setting system. RCN, London

Royal College of Physicians 1993 Guidelines: investigation and management of stable angina. Royal College of Physicians, London

Russell I T, Grimshaw J 1992 Effectiveness of referral guidelines: a review of the methods and findings of published evaluations. In: Roland M, Coutter A Hospital Referrals. Oxford University Press, Oxford, pp 179–211

Scott J A 1985 Complaints arising from the exercise of clinical judgement: a report by the English regional medical officers. Health Trends 17: 70–72

Shaw C D, Brooks T 1991 Health service accreditation in the United Kingdom. Quality Assurance in Health Care 3: 133–140

Shaw C D, Collins C D 1995 Health service accreditation: report of a pilot programme for community hospitals. BMJ 310: 781–784

Sheldon T A, Barrowitz M 1993 Changing the measure of quality in the NHS: from purchasing activity to purchasing protocols. Quality in Health Care 2: 149–150

Sherwood T 1992 Exitus auditus – no fun. Lancet 340: 37–38

Simanowitz A 1985 Standards, attitudes and accountability in the medical profession. Lancet 2: 546–547

Sketris I 1988 Health service accreditation: an international review. King's Fund, London

Skinner P W, Riley D, Maelor-Thomas E 1988 Use and abuse of performance indicators. British Medical Journal 297: 1256–1259

Sloan A 1993 Keeping up standards: BS5750 (ISO9000). Occupational Health 45: 244–245

Smith J M 1972 Interviewing in market and social research. Routledge & Kegan Paul, London

Smith J M, Hart S 1992 Health authorities and BS5750 (ISO9000): a standard of purchasing. International Journal of Health Care Quality Assurance 5: 23–25

Smith T 1992 Information for patients: writing simple English is difficult, even for doctors. British Medical Journal 305: 1242

Spilker B, Molirek F R, Johnston K A, Simpson R L, Tolson H 1990 Quality of life: bibliography and indexes. Medical Care 28 Suppl: 1–77

Stewart A L, Ware J E 1992 Measuring functioning and well being: The Medical Outcomes Study approach. Duke University Press, Durham

Stewart A L, Hays R D, Ware J E 1988 The MOS short form general health survey. Reliability and validity in a patient population. Medical Care 26: 724–735

Stewart A L, Greenfield S, Hays R et al 1989 Functional status and well being of patients with chronic conditions. Journal of the American Medical Association 262: 907–913

Stone D H 1993 How to design a questionnaire. British Medical Journal 307: 1264–1266

Strachey L 1948 Eminent Victorians: Cardinal Manning, Florence Nightingale, Dr Arnold, General Gordon. Chatto & Windus, Harmondsworth

Streiner D L, Norman G R 1989 Health measurement scales: a practical guide to their development and use. Oxford University Press, Oxford

Tarlov A R, Ware J E, Greenfield S 1989 The medical outcomes study: an application of methods for monitoring the results of medical care. Journal of the American Medical Association 262: 925–930

Thomson R G 1994 The purchaser role in provider quality: lessons from the United States. Quality in Health Care 3: 65–66

Thomson R G, Cook G, Lelliot P, Baker I, Godwin R 1993a Audit and the purchaser–provider interaction. EL(93)34. Annex B. Department of Health, London

Thomson R G, Lavender M, Madhok R 1995 Fortnightly review: How to ensure that guidelines are effective. BMJ 311: 237–242

Thomson R G, Tait E, O'Brien S, Regnard C, Candlish J P, Cattan M R 1993b Introducing industrial quality management into health services: a case study. In: Chan J F L Quality and its applications. University of Newcastle upon Tyne, Newcastle upon Tyne, pp 377–384

UK NEQAS 1993 Report and directory. UK NEQAS, Sheffield

US Department of Health and Human Services Health Care Financing Administration 1987 Medicare hospital mortality information, 1986. US Government Printing Office, Washington DC

Ware J E 1993 Measuring patients' views: the optimum outcome measure. British Medical Journal 306: 1429–1430

Ware J E, Sherbourne C D 1992 The MOS 36 item shortform health survey (SF36) I: Conceptual framework and item selection. Medical Care 30: 473–483

Wareham N J 1994a External monitoring of quality health care in the United States. Quality in Health Care 3: 97–101

Wareham N J 1994b Changing systems of external monitoring of quality of health care in the United States. Quality in Health Care 3: 102–106

Wells K B, Stewart A, Hays R D 1989 The functioning and well being of depressed patients: results from the medical outcomes study. Journal of the American Association 262: 914–919

Wilkin D, Hallow L, Doggett M A 1992 Measures of need and outcome for primary health care. Oxford Medical Press, Oxford

Williams D R 1992 A proposal for continuing audit of diabetes services. Diabetic Medicine 9: 759–764

Wilson Committee 1994 Being heard. HMSO, London

28

Managing some legal issues

Gill Strawford

COMPUTER RECORDS – LEGAL STANDING

The legal standing of computer records was explained in two articles in the *Journal of the Medical Defence Union* in 1992. The courts will, following established practice, operate a 'best evidence' rule. If that 'best evidence' is a computer record, it will be admissible. Generally the admissibility of computer records in civil proceedings is provided for in the Civil Evidence Act 1968. This states that a statement contained in a document produced by a computer is admissible as evidence if:

- the document containing the statement was produced by the computer during a period over which the computer was used regularly to store or process information for the purposes of any activities regularly carried on over that period;
- over that period there was regularly supplied to the computer in the ordinary course of those activities information of the kind contained in the statement;
- throughout the material part of that period, the computer was operating properly;
- the information contained in the statement reproduces or is derived from information supplied to the computer in the ordinary course of those activities.

In addition a judge will want to be assured that the records have not been tampered with and the author of the record is identifiable. That a judge would require this assurance is not surprising given the weight attached to medical records in legal proceedings.

Lawyers frequently enquire into not only the exact meaning of the words and abbreviations contained within the written notes, but also the handwriting and layout of these notes. The reason for such detailed scrutiny of written notes, and that such weight is attached to them, is that these notes are written contemporaneously and once written, the notes become a dead record. Any attempt to add to, alter, substitute or delete an entry is usually blatantly obvious on the face of the records.

In contrast, by their very nature, computer records remain 'live' and can be substantially altered or even replaced with new data replacing old data, without any necessary indication appearing on the face of the records.

This situation can be modified if an 'audit trail' is incorporated into the programme. This will allow all previous entries and their alterations to remain on the record and to be retrieved if required. The author of each record (original or alteration) could be identified if each author is allotted a unique code and a record of the codes kept to identify all users years later.

Without an audit trail enabling the courts to confirm the validity of each entry, or to establish the derivation of the relevant entry from the original, it is unlikely that computerized records will be afforded the same status as written records. However, if regular hard copy printouts are stored in the patient's medical record envelope, these become part of the 'written' record.

CLINICAL RECORDS – DISCLOSURE AND PATIENT ACCESS

Clinical directors and consultants need to be familiar with the legislation governing the disclosure of patient records in order to advise their hospital/trust board properly following a request for disclosure.

Much of the legislation governing access to and disclosure of records is relatively recent. The relevant acts include the Data Protection Act 1984, the Access to Medical Reports Act 1988, the Access to Health Records Act 1990 and the Access to Personal Files Act 1987.

The Data Protection Act 1984

An individual's rights of access to personal data held on

computer are governed by the Data Protection Act 1984 (the Data Protection Act (Isle of Man) 1986) and in the case of medical treatment by the subsequent Order of 1987 on Modified Access to Personal Health Information.

Under the Act itself 'data subjects' (patients) have the right to be told by a 'registered data user' (a practitioner in general or private practice or a health authority or trust) whether there is information about them held on computer. If they request it, they must be supplied with a copy of that information. The initial application must be in writing and accompanied by the appropriate fee. Some data users choose to respond to oral requests or to waive fees at their discretion.

Disclosure must take place within 40 days of receipt of the request, a period which cannot be used for editing or 'doctoring' the records to the data user's advantage. The information supplied must be what was in the records at the time the request was received. During that 40-day period, routine updating is of course permitted to continue.

The Data Protection (Subject Access Modification) (Health) Order 1987 provides for 'modified access', in that the data user is permitted to withhold information:

... which is likely to cause serious harm to the physical or mental health of the data subject or any other person, or which could lead to the identification of another individual (other than a health professional) who has been involved in the care of the subject.

It is for the individual practitioner to consider the likelihood of harm to a patient's health and whether such harm may be serious; this is necessarily a somewhat subjective test. The practitioner is not obliged to tell the patient that sensitive material has been withheld.

In a health authority or trust, the data user's representative dealing directly with the patient is likely to be a lay administrator; however, the lead health professional must be consulted and allowed to decide whether access to computerized data should be modified or not.

The patient is entitled to challenge the validity of computerized data and to have errors corrected. The courts may order compensation to be paid for damage and any associated distress suffered by patients as the result of lost, incorrect, inaccurate or misleading data.

Access to Medical Reports Act 1988

The Access to Medical Reports Act 1988, the Access to Personal Files and Medical Reports (Northern Ireland) Order 1991 and the Access to Health Records and Reports Act 1993 (Isle of Man) give individual patients a right of access to reports provided by (medical) practitioners for employment or insurance purposes, in order to ensure accuracy and prevent the perpetuation of serious errors which may be prejudicial to an individual's interests.

Only reports prepared by the doctor who is or has been responsible for the patient's medical treatment are covered by the Act. Independent medical examiners and occupational physicians who do not provide any clinical care are excluded from its provisions. Clinical care is defined as 'examination, investigation or diagnosis for the purposes of, or in connection with, any form of medical treatment'.

At the time a report is requested, the patient must give their consent and must be notified – by the insurance company or the (prospective) employer – of their rights under the Act. They will be asked to decide whether or not they require to see a report prepared by their 'own' doctor (usually the GP but occasionally a hospital specialist) and the applicant will notify the doctor accordingly.

If the patient does not wish to see the report, it may be passed on to the applicant. The doctor must retain a copy of the report for 6 months after its despatch and within that period must allow the patient to see it if they ask.

If the patient asks to see the report, the onus is on them to make arrangements to see it. They are entitled to a copy of the report, for which 'a reasonable charge' may be made. If the patient fails to make arrangements, the practitioner should not send in the report until 21 days have elapsed.

If the patient considers the report incorrect or misleading, they may make a request in writing to have it amended. The doctor may refuse, but must in that event attach the patient's own comments to the report. If the doctor agrees to modification, the insurance company or employer is not entitled to know that the original report has been changed. A copy must be retained for 6 months (see above).

Access to the report may be withheld by the doctor if disclosure would be likely to cause serious harm to the patient's physical or mental health or if disclosure might reveal information about another person or give away the identity of someone (other than a healthcare professional) who has supplied information to the reporting doctor. The doctor must tell the patient in writing if access is denied in this way and must not pass the report on to the applicant if consent is withdrawn – at this or at the amendment stage.

An aggrieved patient may apply to the courts if they feel that an applicant or doctor has failed to comply with the Act's requirements. Penalties cannot be imposed, but if the court finds the patient's complaint to be justified, it may order the practitioner to show the report to the patient.

Access to Health Records Act 1990

The Access to Health Records Act 1990 gives patients the right to see and/or have copies of any records made after 1 November 1991 and to have the records explained if they are illegible or unintelligible. The Access to Health Records (Northern Ireland) Order 1993 and the Access to Health Records and Reports Act 1993 (Isle of Man), which confer the same rights upon patients, came into operation on 30 May 1994 and 1 July 1994 respectively. There is no obligation to disclose records made before 1 November 1991 (or 30 May 1994/1 July 1994, see above) unless it is necessary to see them to understand what follows. The application should be in writing, though some practitioners may allow an oral application. Access must then be given within 21 days – unless the records were made more than 40 days previously, in which case the limit is 40 days.

Application for access may be made by:

- the patient;
- a person whom the patient has authorized in writing to apply;
- a person responsible for a child (under 16), provided the child consents or cannot understand the meaning of the application;
- a child, if he or she is old enough to understand the nature of the application;
- a person appointed by a court to manage a patient's affairs, if the patient is mentally incapable;
- the personal representative (executor or administrator of the estate) of a deceased patient (though access should not be given if the patient while alive had given specific instructions against it);
- any person who may have a claim arising out of the patient's death.

Once again, the practitioner may deny access if serious harm to the patient's physical or mental health might result (*R v Mid Glamorgan FHSA and Another Ex Parte Martin*) or if the confidentiality of another person might be breached. The patient does not have to be told that information has been withheld, but is not prevented from asking the practitioner informally whether the full record has been made available and may apply to the courts if dissatisfied with the answer.

The patient may ask for inaccurate, misleading or incomplete information to be corrected. If the practitioner agrees, they should comply but if they do not, a note about the conflict of views must be added to the relevant part of the record and a copy supplied to the patient.

As with the other legislation described above, the patient may apply to the courts if they feel that the doctor has not complied with the requirements of the Act. Penalties cannot be imposed, but the court may order that the patient is given access to the records if it finds their complaint to be justified.

The Access to Health Records (Control of Access) Regulations 1993 and the Access to Health Records (Control of Access) Regulations (Northern Ireland) 1994 restrict the right of access such that access should not be given:

to any part of a health record which would disclose information showing that an identifiable individual was, or may have been, born in consequence of treatment services within the meaning of the Human Fertilization and Embryology Act 1990.

Access to Personal Files Act 1987

Practitioners are often asked to provide reports for Social Services departments. These reports will become part of an individual's 'personal file' held by Social Services and thus subject to the provisions of the Access to Personal Files (Social Services) Regulations 1989. If the patient seeks access, the requirements are exactly the same as those for the Access to Health Records Act 1990. Social Services staff are obliged to consult the practitioner concerned about exemptions from disclosure for medical reasons and about the correction of inaccuracies.

Disclosure to solicitors

If a person wishes to embark upon civil litigation in order to obtain compensation for personal injury, they and their advisers will wish to obtain the medical records, which are likely to be highly relevant, whether or not the action is for medical negligence.

Before 1971 parties to an action for damages experienced difficulties in obtaining such information before the trial because there was no provision for compelling disclosure of records prior to the trial. A solicitor could, with the plaintiff's consent, ask for voluntary disclosure from the holder of the records (e.g. a hospital or GP) by providing a guarantee not to take proceedings against the holder, who would be asked to disclose the notes to a nominated medical expert. If the holder of the records refused, a subpoena could be issued, but this only compelled the holder of the record to disclose it at the trial itself.

The two major problems arising out of this situation were firstly, that lack of medical evidence made it difficult to arrive at out of court settlements, and secondly that trials frequently would be adjourned so that the medical records could be examined. Consequently, this led to unnecessary waste of public funds.

Under the Administration of Justice Act 1970 (which came into force in 1971), a person who is likely to be a party to a subsequent action for personal injuries or death can apply to the court for an order compelling disclosure of records held by other persons who are likely to become a party to proceedings, e.g. a potential defendant health authority.

This right to preaction discovery is currently set out in Section 33 of the Supreme Court Act 1981. This section also sets out the information which the applicant (usually the plaintiff) must provide in the summons for disclosure which will be served upon the respondent, who is the custodian of the documents (e.g. medical records) and the potential defendant to any subsequent action.

The applicant must explain why they believe that the respondent is likely to be a party to subsequent proceedings, setting out the allegations (of negligence) directed against the respondent and the circumstances which gave rise to these. They must also describe the documents concerned stating why they believe them to be relevant to the proposed action and that they believe they are in the respondent's possession. An order for disclosure of medical records will usually be in favour of the plaintiff.

Solicitors frequently make a written request for the records to be disclosed voluntarily in a letter which usually contains the same information which would have to be included in a summons for disclosure as explained above. The Department of Health has, in the past (HM(59)88), advised health authorities to disclose the records voluntarily, after consultation with the practitioners concerned. Failure to disclose the records without good cause, e.g. a failure on the applicant's part to give sufficient grounds for disclosure, will usually be a pointless exercise as it may well provoke the applicant into seeking a court order for disclosure, the cost of which may be awarded against the health authority.

The Supreme Court Act 1981 also makes provision (Section 34) for disclosure of records by a person who is not a party to proceedings. The plaintiff can make an application for disclosure, after proceedings have commenced, and only needs to identify the documents concerned, the reasons why they are thought to be relevant and that they are in the respondent's custody. Again, solicitors usually seek to avoid the costs of obtaining a court order by asking for voluntary disclosure, e.g. from a health authority, after proceedings have been served against a GP or the plaintiff's employer.

Failure to disclose the records without good cause would be unwise.

For all the foregoing, only relevant records need be disclosed but it can be difficult to decide what is or is not relevant in any given case. For example, a patient's solicitor may be investigating their client's claim for back injuries sustained at work. It is just as important for the solicitor to know what their client's back was like in the years prior to the injury as it is to know what it was like in the months afterwards. Many solicitors would argue that it is for them to decide what is relevant to their client's action and not for the health authority. In practice, it is usual to disclose the entire records rather than to engage in debates about relevance.

It is relevant to note that as time passes, more and more records will fall within the provisions of the Access to Health Records Act 1990, making it unnecessary for solicitors to set out their reasons for requesting disclosure for records made on or after 1 November 1991.

The statutory provisions set out above do confer a number of rights upon a patient (or their legal advisers) to see clinical notes. Apart from exercising these rights, a patient cannot require disclosure of medical records upon demand, particularly if expert medical advice indicates that their disclosure would be detrimental to the patient, though an offer of disclosure to a medical expert nominated by the patient would be a proper step to take (*R v Mid Glamorgan FHSA and Another Ex Parte Martin*). An employee, a plaintiff in a personal injury action against their employer, may be ordered to permit disclosure of the whole of their medical history to their employers' medical advisers (*Dunn v British Coal Corporation*). In addition, disclosure of clinical notes of a deceased patient may be ordered in advance of an inquest hearing (*Stobart v Nottingham Health Authority*).

Disclosure of children's records

Children over 16 and those under 16 who are capable of understanding the significance of record disclosure should be consulted prior to disclosure and may give their own consent. Otherwise consent must be given by whoever has parental responsibility for the child under the provisions of the Children Act 1989.

The concept of parental responsibility is defined under the Act as being 'all the rights, duties, powers, responsibility and authority which by law a parent of a child has in relation to the child and his property' (Section 3(1)).

A child's natural parents both have parental responsibility if they were married at the time of the child's birth and that responsibility continues to be vested in both parents after separation or divorce unless the court acts to limit it. If the parents were unmarried at the time of the child's birth only the mother has parental responsibility unless the father acquires it under the provisions of the Act (either by court order or by a formal 'parental responsibility agreement' with the mother).

Other people, e.g. grandparents or a guardian, may be given parental responsibility by court order. Where more than one person has parental responsibility for a child, each of them may act alone and without the other(s) in meeting that responsibility unless there has been a court order to the contrary.

RETENTION OF MEDICAL RECORDS

The current health circular dealing with the retention of records is HC(89)20 Preservation, Retention, and Destruction of Records – Responsibilities of Health Authorities under the Public Records Act. This circular gives guidance on the main periods of retention of records for the purposes of the Public Records Acts 1958 and 1967 and refers to documents and records which may be worthy of permanent preservation, as well as personal health records. The guidance concerning preservation, retention and destruction of maternity (obstetric and midwifery) records was updated in the Health Service Guidelines HSG(94)11.

The recommended retention periods are:

- maternity records (including those records of episodes of maternity care that end in still birth or where the child later dies) – 25 years;
- records relating to children and young people – until the patient's 25th birthday or 26th if entry made when young person was 17; or 8 years after death of patient if sooner;
- records relating to mentally disordered people within the meaning of the Mental Health Act – 20 years from the date at which, in the opinion of the doctor concerned, the disorder has ceased or diminished to the point where no further care or treatment is considered necessary; or 8 years after the patient's death if sooner;
- all other personal health records – 8 years after the end of treatment.

Ideally, for medicolegal purposes, medical records should be preserved until there is no possibility of a civil action and the length of time involved may vary according to the type of patient and their date of knowledge. In general an action for medical negligence must be commenced 3 years from the date of the event complained of. However, this time limit may be extended if the person's date of knowledge did not fall within that 3-year period. A person's date of knowledge is defined as the date on which they had knowledge of the following three facts: the identity of the defendant; that the injury in question was significant; and that the injury was attributable in whole or in part to an act or omission. Thus there is always a possibility that a claim for medical negligence may be brought many years, occasionally decades, after the date of the alleged injury.

Lastly, for the purposes of the Consumer Protection Act 1987, records relating to product liability should be kept for 10 years 8 months.

NHS INDEMNITY

In March 1989 the Department of Health announced a scheme for NHS indemnity to cover all NHS hospital and community health service staff, both medical and dental, but not including general practitioners. The scheme became effective from 1 January 1990.

In response to an increased number of claims and higher awards by the courts, defence organizations' subscriptions had to rise in the 1980s. From 1988 these had been partly reimbursed by health authorities with a consequent, new and heavy financial outlay by them. The problem was compounded in 1989 by the decision of one defence society to institute differential subscriptions, which were related to speciality and which would have had to be paid by individuals who did not enjoy differential salaries or have the ability to charge patients more. The Doctors and Dentists Review Body 1989 concluded that to take this into account would distort both pay and pensions. In addition, this particular proposal led to concern that young doctors might decide not to take up a career in those specialities which attracted a higher defence subscription. As a result of this situation, NHS indemnity was introduced.

Under the terms of Health Circular HC(89)34, which still apply, district health authorities were instructed to 'assume responsibility for new and existing claims of medical negligence' and medical staff were relieved of their contractual requirement to belong to a defence organization. This assumption of responsibility meant that the essential decisions about handling claims and about defence or settlement devolved onto district general managers or their nominated representatives, with or without help from the defence organizations which now provide a claims handling and advisory service in the capacity of paid agents. The legal position for the medical and dental staff then became the same as it had been for other NHS employees, for whom the health authority, as employer, had always been vicariously liable.

The introduction of this scheme led to some concern that health authorities would settle claims for the sake of financial expediency without paying due regard to points of principle or the reputation of the doctor concerned. The Department held the view that since it was the health authority which was vicariously liable for its medical staff and therefore for the financial cost of defending/settling medical negligence claims, then it must have the ultimate right to decide how the defence of a case was to be handled, although claims should not be settled without good cause.

The Department's instructions about potential settlements as set out in HC(89)34 are of particular importance to the doctors themselves. They read as follows:

In deciding whether to resist a claim or to seek an out of court settlement, health authorities and those advising them should pay particular attention to any view expressed by the practitioner concerned and to any potentially damaging effect upon the professional reputation of the practitioner concerned. They should also have clear regard to any point of principle or of wider application raised by the case; and to the costs involved.

In HC(89)34 practitioners were reminded that health authority indemnity would cover only health authority responsibilities. The health departments advised practitioners to maintain their defence organization memberships in order to ensure they could apply for assistance and indemnity for any work which did not fall within the scope of the indemnity scheme. Such work would include: private practice; locums in general practice; medicolegal work; disciplinary enquiries, e.g. a GMC investigation; good samaritan acts; criminal prosecutions carried out (e.g. manslaughter) in connection with the practitioner's private or NHS practice.

In 1990 the Department of Health stated (EL(90)191) that the general provisions of the indemnity arrangements set out in HC(89)34 would apply equally to NHS trusts, who would be liable for the negligent acts and omissions of their staff from the time they were in operation. A working group was then established to consider a scheme to assist DMUs and trusts with the costs of future clinical negligence claims. In February 1991 the Department of Health circulated the detailed arrangements of this scheme (EL(91)19) and confirmed that NHS trusts would be legally and financially liable for all *new* claims of clinical negligence, i.e. those arising out of events occurring on or after 1 April 1991. Clinical negligence committed prior to that date would remain the responsibility of health authorities.

Medical negligence claims are plaintiff-led and usually begin with a letter from the patient's solicitors seeking disclosure to them of the patient's medical records. Apart from computerized records (to which the Data Protection Act 1984 applies) and manuscript notes made after 1 November 1991 (to which the Access to Health Records Act 1990 applies), a patient's solicitor must 'show cause' to the body or individual from whom disclosure of the records is sought. Experienced patients' solicitors will set out the fullest details of the prospective claim because if they do, and the body or individual fails to make disclosure, a court order can be made in the patient's favour which can involve payment of the plaintiff's solicitors' costs of the application. This letter, containing the application for disclosure of medical notes, means that medical notes, nursing notes, investigation reports, drug charts, relevant X-ray films, etc. are required. The consultant in charge of the patient's case and the relevant practitioners should be consulted about the content of this letter and the requirement for disclosure in a proper case. In some instances allegations supporting an application for disclosure are put in such detail as to amount to a letter before action (one in which court proceedings can be expected to follow if the patient's demands for compensation are not met).

The following is an account of the way in which the MDU would expect to respond to and handle a claim. Whilst the general conduct of a claim usually follows a similar pattern, there may be variations in the handling of the claim between different defendants and their legal advisers. The term defendant, when used in the following account, would apply to any corporate body affected by Crown indemnity including health authorities, health boards (Scotland and Northern Ireland), trust hospitals and special hospitals service authorities.

The letter and the relevant case notes would then be passed to the hospital's legal advisers or to the defence organization which has been contracted to handle the claim. The person appointed to handle the claim (hereafter referred to as the claims handler), having obtained the relevant clinical records, will then go through them carefully to identify those members of staff involved if the information in the letter seeking disclosure is sufficiently full. They will usually seek reports from all the doctors concerned, and also from other involved health professionals. Those members of staff who have been asked to provide reports would be sent a copy of the letter setting out the allegations and the relevant medical records. The report is privileged and intended only for disclosure to the defendant and its legal advisers.

The report would commence with an identifying section setting out the full name, qualifications, position (e.g. consultant) and speciality of the author, together with a statement giving the dates of their employment by the (named) defendant. The author would then state whether the report is compiled from an actual recollection of events, reconstructed from the notes or based upon usual practice. Any documents referred to in the report (e.g. medical records/X-rays) should be clearly identified.

The author would then set out a detailed chronological account of their personal involvement in the case. Comments upon each contact with the patient would include the history taken; the extent of any examination findings; the investigations ordered (and subsequently their results); the management decisions taken, etc. The account would also include comments upon any discussion held with the patient, particularly where consent for an operation was obtained or where a major treatment plan, e.g. radiotherapy, was discussed. That the patient gave informed consent to a particular operation/treatment can be of crucial importance in the defence of a claim. It is therefore essential to comment upon the explanation given to the patient regarding the procedure, its likely success, acknowledged risks, side-effects, complications, etc. When commenting upon the procedure itself it is helpful to give a detailed account rather than saying, 'I performed a right knee replacement' or 'This patient had a course of radiotherapy'. The expert, who will base their opinion upon the reports and notes, will need to know the technical details of the procedure, e.g. what prosthesis/suture material was used; how the operation was performed; what dose of radiation was given; whether the procedure was routine; if not, what complications arose and their management thereafter, etc.

The author would then comment upon the allegations set out in the solicitor's letter before action. Whilst it is possible that some medical staff, particularly those who are inexperienced, may not be able to give a definitive comment upon the allegations, it would be expected that a consultant would be able to provide an overview of the management of the case and to comment authoritatively upon the allegations.

Once all the relevant reports have been received by the claims handler, they will then be in a position to examine the reports, together with the clinical records, in order to identify points of strength and weakness and to clarify any gaps in the information received. Further reports can be obtained from the appropriate member of staff if required. Once all the necessary information has been gathered the claims handler will then be in a position to instruct a medical expert to provide an opinion upon the strength of the health authority's position.

The expert has to consider, when providing this opinion, firstly, whether the defendant owed a duty of care to the plaintiff; secondly, whether that duty of care had been breached (liability); and thirdly, whether that breach of the duty of care had led to the harm which the plaintiff claims to have suffered (causation).

In order to have breached their duty of care, the doctor must be shown, by the plaintiff, to have failed to apply the necessary standard of care, i.e. they have been negligent. The standard that the doctor is expected to achieve was set out by McNair J in *Bolam v Friern Hospital Management Committee* (1957) as being that of 'the ordinary skilled man exercising and professing to have that special skill'. This does not mean that the doctor has to have the highest expert skill, merely that they must exercise the skill of an ordinary competent individual in that field. In addition to this, a doctor is not guilty of negligence if they have acted in accordance with a practice accepted as proper by a reasonable body of persons, merely because there is a body of opinion that takes a contrary view (Childs 1991b). These are the standards which the expert must apply in giving their opinion.

If the expert concludes that the relevant practitioners have been negligent and that their negligence is responsible for the harm that the patient has suffered, then a decision to settle the claim may be made. However, the expert may recommend that further opinions should be obtained before this decision can be taken. In addition to this, the views of the relevant practitioners would be sought in accordance with the Department of Health guidelines.

If a decision to settle the claim is made, at an early or any subsequent stage, the claims handler will need to take steps to quantify the claim. These may include referring to previous cases which have set a precedent, arranging for the plaintiff to be examined so that a report on their current condition and prognosis can be obtained, seeking the advice of a barrister (known as counsel), particularly where the value of the claim is likely to be high. In high value claims, e.g. where the plaintiff is disabled, further opinions may need to be sought upon issues such as nursing care, earnings/pension rights, etc. It is desirable for both sides to come to a negotiated agreement on quantum, but if they fail to achieve this they will have to proceed to a trial on quantum so that a judge can determine the level of damages to be paid.

Before the introduction of NHS indemnity the decision to defend or settle a claim would have been made by a cases committee of the appropriate medical defence organization, in conjunction with the practitioners concerned. This committee, comprising experts drawn from a wide variety of specialities, would discuss the written expert opinions and the medical and legal aspects of the case in detail before reaching a decision on the future management of the claim. Under the provisions of NHS indemnity the responsibility for taking this decision falls to the chief executive of the trust, the general manager (health authority) or their nominated representative, who will be guided by the expert and legal advisers appointed by the defendant. It is to be expected that the practitioners concerned will be consulted.

The plaintiff's solicitors will be undertaking a similar exercise and if their expert concludes that the plaintiff has no case, then the claim will be discontinued. If, however, their expert concludes that the plaintiff does have a valid claim then the plaintiff's solicitors will at some point issue proceedings, which should be served within 4 months of the date of issue. A plaintiff may issue proceedings at any time but, in order to avoid a defendant raising a defence of limitation, they must be issued within 3 years of either the event giving rise to the cause of action or the date upon which the plaintiff acquired the knowledge that they might have a cause of action. The limitation period does not start to run in the case of a child plaintiff until they reach the age of majority and it does not run at all in the case of a plaintiff who is suffering a mental disability, e.g. one who is mentally handicapped.

Proceedings are in the high court if the value of the claim exceeds £50 000 and are begun by the issue of a writ and statement of claim, which is required to be accompanied by a medical report on the patient's current condition and prognosis, and a schedule of special damages. For claims valued at less than £50 000 the appropriate jurisdiction is the county court where proceedings commence with the issue of a summons which is served together with the particulars of claim, a medical report on present condition and the schedule of damages. The last document will quantify those items such as loss of earnings, cost of nursing care, special equipment, taxi hire to hospital, etc. which the plaintiff's legal advisers believe have been lost/incurred as a result of the defendant's negligence and for which the plaintiff is entitled to receive compensation. The statement or particulars of claim (hereafter known as the pleadings) will set out, in more precise terms, details of the plaintiff's allegations (the particulars of negligence) and should contain all the assertions which the plaintiff must subsequently prove in court, if their claim is to succeed. Once this document has been received, the claims handler will again seek statements from the medical (and other) staff involved, who will usually be asked to meet with the claims handler, at this stage, in order that the statement can be prepared. This statement will necessarily be more detailed than that previously submitted by the practitioner as all the plaintiff's allegations are now known in detail. The claims handler will review all aspects of the practitioner's involvement in the case and will accordingly draft the statement which will also include the practitioner's comments upon the particulars of negligence.

Although this statement may be set out in a format which is suitable for disclosure, it will not be disclosed to the plaintiff's solicitors at this stage.

A defendant has a limited time in which to respond to the pleadings by the service of his defence. The time limits are 21 days from the date of issue of proceedings in county court cases and 14 days after service of the statement of claim in the high court, although the defendant can obtain an extension of the time in which to service their defence either by agreement with the plaintiff's solicitor or by order of the court. The courts are now intolerant of 'holding' defences, i.e. the sort of defence in which the defendant simply denies or does not admit most of the pleadings. It is essential nowadays to plead a detailed defence and to set out in outline what the defendant's case will be. It is essential that the taking of witness statements precedes instructing counsel to draft a defence, in order that they are properly informed as to the defendant's case.

Thus although the statement prepared by the claims handler is not to be disclosed at this stage, it is nevertheless an important document. Doctors should, therefore, be entirely happy with the contents of the statement before they sign it. Claims handlers are used to being asked to make amendments to these statements and practitioners should be quick to point out errors and omissions which need to be amended. However, as the time for service of the defence is limited, it is essential that the doctor concerned gives this matter their prompt attention.

As one might expect, as the claim progresses and as more details of the case emerge, independent medical and other expert(s) will be asked to review and, if they consider it to be necessary, to revise their opinions. Commonly, the experts will be asked to do this once the witness statements have been obtained and the pleadings served. If the expert(s) now conclude that the claim should be settled then steps should be taken to quantify the claim as described above. If the expert(s) are still of the opinion that the claim should be defended, then a formal decision to defend will be sought from the health authority.

The progression of the claim, from service of the defence to trial, follows a timetable which sets out the time limits for exchange of lists of documents and the inspection of the documents by the other party; witness statements; expert reports. The timetable is restrictive, more so for the defendant than the plaintiff, for the plaintiff's solicitors will often have prepared their client's case, including witness statements and expert reports, before proceedings are even issued.

However, either party can apply to the court in order to vary the timetable. The court is not likely to be sympathetic to a defendant who has had the opportunity to investigate the claim prior to service of proceedings which underlines the need to give prompt assistance to the claims handler at an early stage. Where the defendant has not had prior opportunity to investigate the claim, e.g. where they were first notified of the action by service of proceedings, the court is more likely to grant an extension of the time limits upon request. The latter scenario is likely to become more common as more records fall under the provisions of the Access to Health Records Act 1990, thus enabling plaintiffs to have access to their records without having to apply formally through their solicitors, who would normally send a letter requesting disclosure to the defendant, thus alerting it to the intention to bring a claim.

Witnesses may expect to receive further correspondence from the defendant's solicitors at this stage, to advise them that the matter is progressing and that their witness statements are due to be exchanged. The solicitor now needs to review the statement to ensure that it is set out in the correct format for disclosure. It must include the witness's full name; address; occupation; a statement that the witness is either a party to the proceedings or an employee of that party; and a declaration that the contents are true to the best of the witness's knowledge and belief. The statement should be set out in chronological order in numbered paragraphs, each paragraph confined to a distinct portion of the evidence. Any documents referred to in the statement must be clearly identified and the statement must be dated and signed.

When reviewing their own statement prior to disclosure, the witness needs to bear in mind the purpose of this document. It is designed to provide, in written form, the evidence which the witness will give either in support of or in response to the allegations contained within the pleadings. A witness can expect to be cross-examined minutely on the contents of their witness statement by a well-prepared barrister, who will be able to refer to it and to identify any discrepancies between it and the oral evidence given by that witness. If the witness changes their account from that given in the witness statement, their credibility is likely to be damaged. It is therefore essential that the contents of this statement are entirely accurate. The contents should also be relevant to the issues, factual and complete. The last point is particularly important because a party may not, without consent of the other parties or the court, adduce evidence from a witness if the substance of that evidence has not been included in the statement.

Evidence which a witness may give can be an actual recollection of events, a reconstruction from the notes or be based upon usual practice. Witnesses must be careful about including hearsay in their statements as this may not be admissible. The claims handler will advise the witness about hearsay when drafting the statement.

The other event in the progression of the claim which may involve a witness is the conference with counsel, who is instructed to advise upon the merits of the defendant's case, quantum and to represent the defendant at trial. The conference is usually attended by the instructing solicitor, the experts and the witness. Although counsel should be familiar with all the relevant documents, the conference will provide them with an opportunity to address what they consider to be the relevant issues. It also provides the witness with an opportunity to discuss the case with counsel and the experts. Witnesses may not, however, expect to receive guidance as to what they should say when giving evidence. 'Coaching' of witnesses is not permitted by the Law Society or Bar Council.

The health authority or trust has to meet the cost of defence at trial, settlement and legal costs out of its budget from which it must also continue to provide necessary services to patients. It is not surprising, therefore, that health authorities and trusts are concerned that a continued increase in claims will have a deleterious effect on the resources available to provide services for patients.

CONSENT TO TREATMENT

To grant or withhold consent prior to examination or treatment is a patient's fundamental right. Treatment or investigations carried out without the informed consent of the person concerned (or, in the case of a child, a person with parental responsibility) can amount to an assault and may result in an action for damages or a criminal prosecution against the medical practitioner concerned.

The medical practitioner has a medical duty to explain to the patient in non-technical language the nature, purpose and material risks of the proposed procedure. The patient must be capable of understanding the explanation given and if necessary an interpreter should be present to ensure that the explanation is given in a language which the patient comprehends. If they are incapable, whether from unsound mind or any other cause, informed consent cannot be obtained. However, if the patient is unconscious or if there is a genuine emergency, a clinician may undertake whatever treatment is immediately necessary to attempt to sustain the patient's life or health without waiting to obtain formal consent.

The full explanation given to the patient is of paramount importance. The signing of the consent form is of secondary significance; however, it will afford documentary evidence that consent has been obtained. Where the patient has been given insufficient information the clinician may be found to be in breach of their duty of care to the patient and if harm results the patient may be entitled to compensation. The obtaining of consent is a task which should not be delegated routinely to a junior doctor, especially if a complicated or specialized procedure is contemplated. It is important that the person who discusses the procedure with the patient should, whenever possible, be the person who will carry out the procedure. If this is not possible then consent should be obtained by someone who is appropriately qualified and familiar with all the details and risks of the proposed procedure and any alternatives.

The nature and extent to which a doctor must warn their patients of the risks inherent in any proposed form of treatment was considered by the House of Lords in the case of *Sidaway v Bethlem Royal Hospital Governors and Others (1985)*.

Mrs Sidaway had undergone surgery in 1974 to relieve pressure on a cervical nerve root which had been diagnosed as the cause of long-standing pain in her neck, right shoulder and arms. During the course of the operation Mrs Sidaway's spinal cord was damaged and she was rendered severely disabled.

Mrs Sidaway did not allege that the neurosurgeon had been negligent in carrying out the operation, but rather that he had been negligent because he had failed to warn her of the risks involved. The two specific risks inherent to this operation were: a) damage to a nerve root in the area of the operation; b) damage to the spinal cord either by direct contact or by some interference with the radicular artery. The risk of either sort of damage occurring was estimated by expert witnesses as being between 1% and 2% and the severity of the ill effects could range from mild to catastrophic. Mrs Sidaway alleged that the neurosurgeon had been 'in breach' of a duty to warn her of all possible risks and that had she been given a proper warning she would not have agreed to surgery.

The trial judge, Skinner J, did not accept that the neurosurgeon had failed to provide Mrs Sidaway with any warnings at all. He found that the neurosurgeon would have explained the nature of the operation in simple terms, mentioned the possibility of disturbing a nerve root, but did not refer to the danger of cord damage or the fact that the operation was one of choice rather than of necessity.

Skinner J determined that the neurosurgeon was not negligent for failing to tell Mrs Sidaway of the risk to the nerve root or that the operation was one of choice, because the neurosurgeon was acting in accordance with a practice accepted as proper, in 1974, by a responsible and skilled body of opinion. Thus, Skinner J applied the test adopted in the case of *Bolam v Friern Hospital Management Committee (1957)* which set the standard of care as being that of the ordinary skilled person exercising and professing to have that special skill. A doctor is not guilty of negligence if they have acted in accordance with a practice accepted as proper by a responsible body of medical persons, merely because there is a body of opinion that takes a contrary view. The Court of Appeal agreed with his view and dismissed Mrs Sidaway's appeal. Mrs Sidaway then appealed to the House of Lords.

Mrs Sidaway's appeal was unanimously dismissed by the five members of the House of Lords who considered it; however, they did not reach a uniform agreement on the test to be applied. The majority view held that the test, as to whether a doctor has been negligent in failing to mention a risk to a patient, was the same test to be followed in deciding whether or not a doctor has been negligent in any other aspect of their work, i.e. they applied the standard of accepted professional practice as set out in Bolam.

Lord Bridge added an important qualification asserting the right of the law to intervene, as summarized by Childs (1991a). He said that even in a case where no expert witness in the relevant field condemned the non-disclosure as being in conflict with accepted and responsible medical practice, the judge might conclude that disclosure of a particular risk was so obviously necessary to an informed choice on the part of the patient that no reasonably prudent medical person would fail to make it. The kind of case he had in mind would be an operation involving substantial risk of grave adverse consequences, such as a 10% risk of a stroke. A doctor who respected the patient's right of decision could not fail to appreciate the need to warn of such a risk.

Although the example given by Lord Bridge carried a specific percentage risk, i.e. 10%, there are difficulties, for the law's development, in describing a substantial risk in purely percentage terms. Kennedy & Grubb (1994) discussed the two drawbacks as follows:

The first is that it represents what is really a normative exercise (of what *ought* to be disclosed) as if it were an empirical matter. The danger is that this will suggest that the law's approach is a simplistic and arithmetical one, merely concerned with expert evidence on percentages.

The second objection lies in the danger that reference to percentage risks will merely provoke disagreements among experts as to what is the precise percentage in any particular case. Furthermore, it leaves undecided what percentage is the percentage beyond which a risk is regarded as substantial. Would the law not run the risk of having experts give evidence (hand on heart) that a particular risk has only a 3½% chance of occurring if 4% had become the magic legal limit? A court would have no criteria by which to choose amongst conflicting expert views. The consequence could be that in effect the law would be handed back to the medical profession through experts.

In any event, discussion of the size of risk in isolation overlooks the fact that in matters of risk calculation it is not only whether a risk exists but of what happens if the risk eventuates which are relevant in determining whether a patient is prepared to run that risk. For example, if an operation may bring benefits but carries a high risk of causing a long-term irritating rash, the patient may decide to run that risk whereas he may not decide to run what is represented as a low risk of having a permanent limp as a consequence of the same operation. It is all well and good to refer to 'grave adverse consequences'. The above example tends to suggest that the only judge of what is 'grave' or 'adverse' can be the patient.

One example of an operation which carries a low risk of a complication which may be viewed by the plaintiff as being highly significant is a sterilization operation. Failure to warn of the risk of failure of this procedure could be negligent.

It is of interest to note that Lord Scarman took a dissenting view which was sympathetic to that set out in the American case *Canterbury v Spence (1972)* which has been adopted in a minority of US states. In that case the court adopted a reasonable and prudent patient test, requiring doctors to disclose any information which would be deemed material by a reasonable person in the position of the patient. The standard of professional practice was criticized as difficult to identify and likely to permit too much information to be withheld.

Lord Scarman asserted the patient's right to know and held that the doctor's duty was to inform the patient of the material risks inherent in the treatment. The test of whether a risk was material was whether, in the circumstances of the case, the court was satisfied that a reasonable person in the patient's position would be likely to attach significance to the risk. The materiality of the risk was a question for the court to decide on all the evidence; many factors called for consideration. The two critically important medical factors were the degree of probability of the risk materializing and the seriousness of possible injury if it did.

However, Lord Scarman also dismissed Mrs Sidaway's appeal as he concluded that she had not established that the risk was so great that the neurosurgeon should have appreciated that it would be considered a significant factor by a prudent patient in her situation, who had to decide whether or not to have the operation.

In the Sidaway case, the law therefore retained the right to overrule medical opinion if disclosure was obviously necessary for an informed choice by the patient. However, even if the risks were material, the doctor would not be liable if, upon a reasonable assessment of the patient's condition, he considered that a warning would be detrimental to the patient's health and that a respectable school of thought would have the same view.

WHOSE RESPONSIBILITY IS IT ANYWAY?

Since the advent of the healthcare reforms clinicians may have met with situations where the boundaries of clinical responsibility appear less clearly demarcated than previously experienced.

In order to reduce waiting list times, a health authority or trust (hereafter known as the health authority) may make arrangements for a number of operations upon their patients to be performed at another hospital under the care of a second consultant surgeon, who will either be employed by another health authority/trust (hereafter referred to as the trust) or who will have undertaken to perform the operations as an independent contractor in the private sector. It is conceivable that the second consultant may disagree with the decision of the original consultant (or their junior staff) to place the patient on the waiting list for that particular operation, which the second consultant is now being asked to perform. The second consultant may consider that a different operation, or even a non-operative line of management, would better serve that patient's interests.

The question now arises as to who is responsible for decision making with regard to that patient. Is the second consultant reduced to the status of a technician, obliged to perform the previously chosen operation, simply because their employers have contracted to carry out a set number of operations on behalf of another health authority?

There can be no doubt that consultants owe a legal duty of care to any patient whom they treat or upon whom they operate. In addition to this they have a professional duty to exercise their clinical judgement and to apply their skills in a way which best serves the interests of their patients. Given that this twofold duty exists, it would be wholly inappropriate to reduce the status of the surgeon to that of a technician by restricting their ability to exercise their clinical judgement. Thus, although their employers (the trust) may have contracted to perform a number of operations upon patients originally under the care of another health authority, this does not absolve the consultant from the responsibility for properly assessing the patient's condition and for advising upon the type of operation (if one is required) which, in their clinical judgement, is most beneficial and appropriate for that patient's condition and personal needs.

If a surgeon were to be placed in a position where their ability to exercise their clinical judgement was restricted, this would not only compromise them in a professional sense, but it would also have the potential of compromising the trust's position should the patient choose to pursue a claim against that trust at some point in the future. By contracting to perform operations upon the patients originally under the care of another health authority, the trust will become involved in responsibility for any claims arising out of the care/operations which it has contracted to provide. This may have considerable financial implications for the trust.

Another situation in which the consultant surgeon (or a member of their team) may be asked to perform an operation chosen by another practitioner occurs when the patient's general practitioner decides upon the operation to be performed and places the patient upon the waiting list personally. Warry (1994) reported upon a pilot scheme in Staffordshire which involved general practitioners placing patients with surgical conditions upon a consultant's waiting list, in accordance with protocols previously agreed with the consultant surgeon. The general practitioner advises the patient upon the operation and postoperative course.

The GP also performs a social and anaesthetic assessment, both of which are forwarded to the hospital with the patient's clinical diagnosis. Although the general practitioner will have thus provided the surgeon and anaesthetist with surgical and anaesthetic assessments, this does not absolve these two hospital doctors of their professional responsibility to ensure that the patient requires an operation, is having the appropriate operation and is fit for the anaesthetic.

Should the patient choose to pursue a claim arising out of this procedure or the anaesthetic, it is most likely that their solicitor will direct the claim against the trust. Claims for negligence are plaintiff-led and it is their prerogative to determine the person against whom the claim is directed. The plaintiff is therefore at liberty to direct the claim against the general practitioner as well, if that course of action is considered to be appropriate.

If the claim is only directed against the trust, it is a matter for that body and its legal advisers to determine whether it would be justified in involving the general practitioner in the proceedings.

PRODUCT LIABILITY

Doctors (and their employers) may knowingly or unwittingly assume liability for products under the Consumer Protection Act 1987 which defines a producer, for medical purposes, as being the person who manufactures the product. In many cases doctors will either be the producer or have overall responsibility for the department which manufactures the product. These include dressing packs, limb prostheses, hearing aids, blood and blood products.

A doctor can also become a producer by altering products, for example, if they mix drugs prior to injection, as is commonly done with local anaesthetic and steroid, or alters a piece of equipment for personal preference such as bending a needle prior to use or cutting or bending an orthopaedic insert to suit an individual patient.

The Consumer Protection Act 1987 requires a producer to ensure that a product is up to standard and fit for the intended purpose. Part 1 of the Act came into force on 1 March 1988 and deals with the issue of product liability which has a bearing on the practice of medicine.

The product is considered to be defective when it does not provide the safety which a person is entitled to expect taking all circumstances into account. Liability for defective products rests with the producer of the product or any person who, by putting their name on the product, holds themselves out to be the producer. If the product is manufactured outside the EEC, then the person importing the product is the producer. The ways in which doctors can become producers have already been described above. The Act enforces a strict liability, so that if the product is defective and the consumer's health is damaged (this includes personal injury or death) then the producer is liable. It is not necessary to prove negligence. However, the law of negligence as it relates to medical practice remains unchanged.

It is important to remember that liability under the Act can devolve upon the supplier of a product if that supplier is unable to identify the producer, when requested to do so by a person who has suffered damage caused wholly or partly by a defect in the product. Doctors may themselves become suppliers under the Act when they dispense any product to a patient or when they directly administer drugs to patients, both in the NHS and in private practice. Under these circumstances it is essential for the doctor to be able to identify the producer of that product, whether that producer is still in existence or not. A supplier does not automatically become liable for damages under the Act just because the producer goes bankrupt or into liquidation. Where doctors are not themselves suppliers, they should be able to identify the supplier and/or the producer of the product in question.

It is therefore advisable for doctors (and their employers) to ensure that adequate records are kept. These records should include the name of the drug (or product); the dose required; the frequency of administration; the length of treatment; the occasions when the drug (or product) was administered; the expiry date or batch number (since this confirms that in this respect the producer's recommendations were followed); and the name of the supplier and/or producer. Such records must be kept for 10 years 8 months.

Records are also important when considering equipment as the definition 'product' not only extends to pharmaceutical preparations, but also to any equipment used in treatment. If a patient suffers damage from the use of a piece of equipment in the course of treatment, the liability rests with the producer or supplier. However, the producer may escape liability if it can be shown that the equipment was not maintained or calibrated or used in accordance with their instructions. It is essential that such equipment is properly maintained and calibrated in accordance with the manufacturer's instructions and that records are kept to show this has been done. Failure to do this could result in liability devolving to the supplier who may well be the doctor.

Apart from showing that a product was not maintained in accordance with their instructions, a producer may also have a defence if the product was used for a purpose for which it had not been marketed. Doctors who become producers by altering a product may have a defence if the alterations which they made accord with the original producer's instructions and guidelines.

Lastly, a producer may have a 'state of the art' defence. That is, if all appropriate tests had been made, bearing in mind the state of medical knowledge at the time, the adverse effect could not have been predicted.

PROFESSIONAL CONDUCT – RESPONSIBILITY FOR COLLEAGUES

The position of clinical director, or chairman of a division, places many duties and responsibilities upon the incumbent. One such duty is the responsibility to investigate concerns that a professional colleague's conduct or competence is contrary to the interests of patients or endangering their safety.

The General Medical Council (1993b) places a responsibility upon all doctors to 'inform an appropriate person or authority about a colleague whose professional conduct or fitness to practise may be called into question or whose professional performance appears to be in some way deficient'.

A clinical director/chairman of division is appropriately placed to receive such information which must be acted upon to ensure that patient safety and high standards of medical practice are maintained. Failure to act upon information of this nature may result in an appearance before the professional conduct committee (PCC) of the GMC.

In July 1993 the PCC considered the case of a locum anaesthetist who faced several charges in connection with the standard of care and monitoring which he had provided for a patient during the course of an anaesthetic. As a result of that anaesthetic the patient sustained severe hypoxic brain damage. The facts in the charges against the anaesthetist were admitted by him and found proved. He was found guilty of serious professional misconduct which resulted in his name being erased from the Register.

In 1994 the PCC considered charges which had been made against the consultant who was chairman of the anaesthetic division at the relevant time, i.e. during the period that the locum was working in the anaesthetic department. The PCC found that this consultant had been advised, on a number of occasions (prior to the date of the incident described above) by a number of persons, that the locum's professional performance and conduct were giving cause for concern and that he had failed to take appropriate steps to investigate the concerns which had been expressed to him. By virtue of these findings the PCC concluded that the consultant was guilty of serious professional misconduct.

In considering the latter case the PCC took account of all the circumstances of the case including the problems concerning anaesthetic manpower and indicated that it was aware of the problems arising from procedures for the appointment of locums.

The committee decided that the public interest did not require the restriction or removal of the consultant's registration and concluded the case. The president, Sir Robert Kilpatrick, told the consultant that it was the committee's wish to remind him and all registered medical practitioners of the medical profession's duty to protect patients.

Doctors who have reason to believe that a colleague's conduct or professional performance poses a danger to patients must act to ensure patient safety. Before taking action in such a situation, doctors should do their best to establish the facts. Where there is doubt, it is unethical for any doctor to give reference about a colleague, particularly if it may result in the employment of that doctor elsewhere. References about colleagues must be carefully considered; comments made in them must be justifiable, offered in good faith, and intended to promote the best interests of patients.

Sir Robert then went on to say that doctors have a duty to activate appropriate procedures for response to reports of evident, and dangerous, incompetence, where such cases arise. His final words, which doctors would be wise to remember, were: 'At all times patient safety must take precedence over all other concerns including understandable reticence to bring a colleague's career into question'.

ADVERTISING BY DOCTORS

The guidance on advertising by doctors in the UK is laid down by the General Medical Council (1993a). The General Medical Council makes a distinction between general practitioners and specialists in this guidance, that which concerns specialists being more restrictive than that which concerns general practitioners. The GMC bases this distinction on the stated belief that:

Most individuals, when choosing a general practitioner, are in good health and able to make a rational choice on the basis of factual information. People requiring the attention of a specialist may, by contrast, be ill or in a vulnerable state and need the advice of a general practitioner before being referred for further investigation or treatment.

Specialists are permitted to disseminate information concerning the services they offer and the fees which they charge to their professional colleagues and to management. They may also include their name, professional qualifications, address and telephone number in national and local directories and in other publications of a similar nature. However, the GMC makes it clear that any information disseminated by a specialist should not be seen to 'disparage, directly or by implication, the services provided by other doctors, nor should it claim superiority for the specialist's personal qualities, qualifications, experience or skills'.

Individual specialists may not release information of this nature directly to the public in any other way, although the membership lists of associations of doctors may be released on request to a member of the public. In keeping with the nature of the guidance, any such list may not imply that doctors on the list are specifically recommended or that they are the only practitioners appropriately qualified to practise in that speciality.

Practitioners are reminded that any doctor who has a financial or professional relationship with an organization such as a hospital, nursing home, screening centre, etc. must bear some responsibility for the advertising of that organization. Doctors are therefore reminded that they 'must therefore make it their business to acquaint themselves with the nature and content of the organization's advertising' and that they should make every effort to ensure that the organization's advertising conforms with the GMC's guidance. If a doctor is reported to the GMC in connection with an alleged breach of the advertising guidance, the GMC has stated that it will not accept as satisfactory any explanation which states that the doctor was not aware of the nature or content of the advertisement or that they were unable to exercise any influence over it.

Doctors are also advised that they should not become involved in promoting the organization by 'public speaking, broadcasting, writing articles or signing circulars'.

If a specialist wishes to offer their services in providing medicolegal advice or medical examinations to a company or firm, they may supply factual information about their qualifications and services and in addition may place a factual advertisement in a relevant trade journal, providing that the advertisement does not include any statement which makes a claim of superiority, disparages another doctor or which is misleading.

Lastly, doctors who are involved in broadcasting or writing must be careful to ensure that the published material does not especially recommend that patients consult that particular doctor.

EVENT RECORDING AND ANALYSIS

A recordable event is any occurrence which affects a patient, member of staff or visitor while they are undergoing treatment or are on hospital, clinic or surgery premises, which could have or actually has caused harm or could lead to a complaint or claim. Recording of other specific events will also be important for quality assurance in a particular department. For example, event recording will also pick up that a consent form has not been correctly completed, that a patient has fallen out of bed, whether or not they were injured, that a fault has been detected in a piece of equipment or that a throat pack was inadvertently left in situ at the end of an operation, even if the patient subsequently suffered no harm.

Event recording has three main purposes:

1. to record events which have caused injuries so that they can be investigated and fully documented;
2. to record 'near misses' so that steps can be taken to prevent recurrence of 'near misses' which could cause possible harm to others;
3. to record events of particular interest to the department for quality assurance.

Event recording reports are an important part of any risk management and quality assurance programme and are intended to improve patient care and staff safety. By identifying specific criteria which are known to be a cause of medicolegal problems, event recording will help to prevent accidents and to minimize harm that has already occurred. This will have the effect of freeing trusts' and health authorities' funds which would be better spent on patient care.

It is accepted that some problems, errors or mishaps are inevitable, but by drawing attention to them it will be possible to identify trends and eliminate many of the risk factors that may have remained undetected. To ensure that the system works it is essential to have the cooperation of all staff. An undertaking from the chief executive that event recording forms will not be used for disciplinary purposes is essential for staff to participate, as is confidentiality of the data.

It is as important to record 'near misses' that have not caused harm as it is to report more serious events. For example, an incorrectly dispensed drug may be noticed before it is given to a patient, but the circumstances that led to the incorrect dispensing can still exist and next time a patient may be harmed. If such an event is recorded and a report is made, the system can be corrected immediately.

It can be difficult sometimes to decide what is or is not an event to record and report. The MDU has developed a list of specific criteria for high-risk specialities and other hospital departments. Lists of these criteria are included with each pad of reporting forms. If one or more of the criteria occurs, the facts *must* be reported on the event recording form.

The list of specific criteria is not intended to be exhaustive. If a harmful event of any kind occurs, it should be reported. When collecting data for analysis all information is important in trying to improve patient care and eliminate avoidable risks.

Any member of staff may complete an event recording form. Ideally a person who was directly involved in the incident should complete the form as soon as possible after the event, but otherwise a witness or anyone who knows what has happened is suitable. It is preferable for two forms to be filled in for the same incident rather than none at all.

The facts should be stated in as much detail as necessary to give an objective, clear account of what happened. The names of all members of staff who were involved in the patient's care at the relevant time should be included.

When the form has been completed it should be passed immediately to the consultant in charge or head of department who may wish to clarify particular details.

The consultant in charge or head of department should check that all relevant details on the form have been correctly filled in and that all staff involved have been identified (this is not for possible disciplinary reasons but is a medicolegal precaution in case a claim is made). If possible the consultant or department head should speak to whoever is involved in the incident/event to ensure that the information recorded is both accurate and complete.

Should urgent remedial treatment be required it is the responsibility of the consultant in charge or department head to take whatever action is necessary and, when indicated, to seek advice from an appropriate consultant.

One copy of the form should be retained by the consultant in charge or department head and the other should be sent to the appointed officer within 24 hours. Usually that officer is a member of the hospital's risk management committee.

Acknowledgement

Dr G. Strawford would like to thank her colleagues, particularly Dr Patrick Hoyte, and Mr James Watt of Hempsons who have kindly provided help and advice in the preparation of this chapter.

REFERENCES

Bolam v Friern Hospital Management Committee. 1957, 2 All ER 118, (1957) 1 WLR 582

Canterbury v Spence. 1972, 464 F 2d 772

Childs M 1991a Duty to warn of treatment risks. Sidaway v Bethlem Royal Hospital Governors and others (1985). Journal of the Medical Defence Union 7(3): 57–59

Childs M 1991b Professional negligence. Bolam v Friern Hospital Management Committee (1957). Journal of the Medical Defence Union 7(1): 21–22

Dunn v British Coal Corporation. 1993, 1 RLR No. 396

EL (91) 19. Clinical negligence funding scheme

General Medical Council 1993a Professional conduct and discipline: fitness to practise. GMC, London, pp 31–36

General Medical Council 1993b Professional conduct and discipline: fitness to practise. GMC, London, p 22

HC(89)34. Claims of medical negligence against NHS hospital and community doctors and dentists.

HC(89)20. Preservation, retention and destruction of records: responsibilities of health authorities under the public records act

HM(59)88. Supply of information about hospital patients engaged in legal proceedings

HSG(94)11. Preservation, retention and destruction of maternity (obstetric and midwifery) records

Kennedy I, Grubb A 1994 Medical law: text and materials, 2nd edn. Butterworths, London

R v Mid Glamorgan FHSA and Another Ex Parte Martin. The Times, Court of Appeal, 16 August 1994

Stobart v Nottingham Health Authority. 1992, 3, MED LR No. 284

Warry R (19th August 1994) Charge fee for anaesthetic test. General Practitioner: p 13

FURTHER READING

Access to Health Records Act 1990
Access to Health Records and Reports Act 1993 (Isle of Man)
Access to Health Records (Control of Access) Regulations 1993
Access to Health Records (Control of Access) Regulations (Northern Ireland) 1994
Access to Health Records (Northern Ireland) Order 1993
Access to Medical Reports Act 1988

Access to Personal Files Act 1987
Access to Personal Files and Medical Reports (Northern Ireland) Order 1991
Access to Personal Files (Social Services) Regulations 1989
Administration of Justice Act 1970
Children Act 1989
Civil Evidence Act 1968
Consumer Protection Act 1987
Data Protection Act 1984
Data Protection Act (Isle of Man) 1986
Data Protection (Subject Access Modification) (Health) Order 1987
EL (90) 191. Handling claims of medical negligence
Norwell N. 1992 GP computer records – questions answered. Journal of the Medical Defence Union 8(2): 43–44
Sidaway v Bethlem Royal Hospital Governors and others 1985 1 A11 ER: 643
Supreme Court Act 1981
Taylor J, Yates P 1992 Medical records on computer. Journal of the Medical Defence Union 8(1): 19

29

Risk management

David Bowden

INTRODUCTION

By its very nature, healthcare is a risk activity. Indeed, doctors and other health professionals should not be discouraged from taking some risks in developing more effective methods of treatment and care for patients. But, it is important that such risks are taken as a result of a positive decision to do so, on the basis of good information and a sound understanding of the possible consequences and the likely outcome of treatment. Of course, whenever possible, this should be done with the knowledge and consent of the patient concerned.

Similarly, the most effective managers are those who are prepared to take calculated risks, deliberately choosing to make such judgements from a range of fully detailed options.

What is of concern is the wide range of risks which occur by accident rather than design and through mischance, mishap or mistake. Even more worrying are those untoward incidents which result from the lack of clear policies; deficient working practices; poorly defined responsibilities; inadequate communications and staff working beyond their competence. After all, most clinical negligence is not caused by individual clinical error, but as a result of that type of systems failure or a combination of several small mistakes occurring at the same time.

The challenge for managers and clinicians alike is to eliminate, or at least reduce, the potential for such misfortunes by being proactive in the future management of risk.

Why proactive? Because being reactive is simply not good enough. Whether considering a brain-damaged baby, the administration of the wrong drug, the absence of firefighting equipment, the lack of training in lifting techniques or inadequacy of the emergency generators, it is morally indefensible to say 'It was just one of those things', if it was possible to foresee and prevent the incident from happening – even once.

WHAT IS RISK MANAGEMENT?
The nature of risk

Risks are present throughout any organization. The buildings which an organization occupies and uses may be unsafe and unsound; the equipment, chemicals and other substances used in the operation of the business may be hazardous and dangerous; and the people employed by or visiting the organization may give rise to risk through their errors or omissions.

Risk management addresses itself to every one of the various activities of an organization. It identifies the risks which exist, assesses those risks for potential frequency and severity, eliminates the risks that can be eliminated, reduces the effect of those which cannot be avoided and puts into place financial mechanisms to absorb the financial consequence of the risks which remain.

This leads to safer practices, safer systems of work, safer premises and greater staff awareness of danger and liability.

A quality system

Reducing your risks gives you a competitive, quality edge.
NHS trust director of quality

Risk management is, in fact, an essential quality system which can have a very significant beneficial effect on the quality of patient care (Fig. 29.1).

In the clinical context, risk management embraces the whole range of medical and clinical audit programmes, moving the emphasis from professional peer reviews to a more patient-centred focus (Figs 29.2 and

Risk management is a process for:

- the identification of all risks which have potentially adverse affects on the *quality of care* and the safety of patients, staff and visitors;
- the assessment and evaluation of those risks; and
- the taking of positive action to eliminate or reduce them.

Fig. 29.1

Medical audit	A professional, peer review process enabling doctors to systematically and critically analyse the quality and outcome of their treatment
Clinical audit	A patient-focused audit process involving doctors, nurses and other clinicians who comprise the clinical care team
Quality assurance	Working throughout the organization towards improving and maintaining the quality of care to patients

Fig. 29.2 Related issues

A TOTAL QUALITY APPROACH

QUALITY ASSURANCE
RISK MANAGEMENT
CLINICAL AUDIT
MEDICAL AUDIT

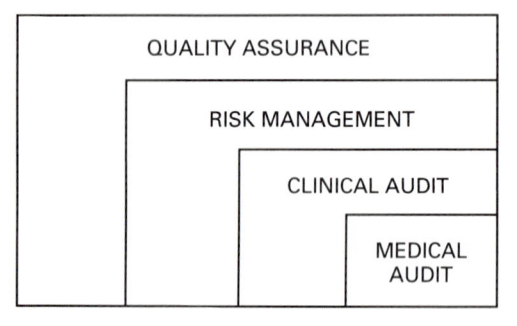

Fig. 29.3 A total quality approach

29.3). Risk management programmes do, of course, bring quality benefits, not just to acute general hospitals, but to the whole range of community/primary care services and in those services for people with mental illness and learning disabilities.

Risk management therefore provides an effective way of breaking into every healthcare provider's quality agenda.

A financial system

> This risk management programme will provide the trust with a major investment for the future.
>
> NHS trust finance director

Additionally, and very importantly, risk management is a financial system which protects the assets and earnings of the organization. It reduces unnecessary costs and minimizes the losses from material damage, professional negligence, injuries to staff and visitors, defective products, and ensures that income is not reduced through lost facilities.

A CURRENT ISSUE

A new concept

Risk management is a relatively new concept in the NHS, though it is, of course, a tried and tested management practice in commerce and industry, as it is in the United States healthcare business. There are three main reasons why it has risen in prominence in UK healthcare.

Crown indemnity

Firstly, on 1 January 1990, the government introduced the concept of Crown indemnity. This meant that district health authorities became responsible for damages and costs arising out of negligence claims. Thus, the authority became vicariously liable for the acts and omissions of all those medical and dental staff working within its organization. Prior to that time, the awards made to people as a result of a proven case of negligence by a doctor had been met by the doctor's own indemnity arrangements, provided through one of the medical defence organizations. Health authorities had hitherto, therefore, been protected from the worst financial effects of clinical negligence. Suddenly, district health authorities became fully and directly liable for these costs, and it began to concentrate their minds! It continues to do so for NHS trusts.

Loss of Crown immunity

Secondly, with effect from 1 April 1991, health authorities lost the last vestiges of their Crown immunity from criminal prosecution. Previously, as public bodies, health authorities were protected from large sections of health and safety and other legislation. As a result, there was no legal imperative for them to correct safety and hygiene deficiencies. The removal of Crown immunity has meant that authorities and trusts are now subject to severe fines and other penalties and important facilities and services can be closed down by the Health & Safety

Executive inspectors. Continued defiance of the executive's requirements can even lead to managers being imprisoned. This too has concentrated the minds of chief executives and others!

Internal market

Thirdly, the 'internal market' created by the National Health Service and Community Care Act 1990 has led the commissioning district health authorities to demand higher quality standards of service and care, at increasingly competitive prices. This has meant that trusts and other provider units are increasingly required to eliminate, or at least reduce, their whole range of risks which would otherwise compromise those standards. The 'market' environment also forces healthcare providers to reduce wasteful expenditure to maintain their competitive edge. The cost of poor quality in the NHS is thought to be over 20% of its total budget. Consequentially, the cost of not managing risks effectively contributes significantly to such avoidable costs. Too many risk situations occur time after time without action being taken. District health authorities and general practitioner fundholders will not be prepared to tolerate this and will insist on more explicit and specific references in contract specifications, unless the providers take their own steps to prove they have a more positive and proactive approach to risk management. Should they not do so, they may lose contracts and that will concentrate their minds.

Increasing litigation

These three changes are not working in isolation. Successful patient and staff litigation is increasing in both frequency and cost. Individual awards continue to rise and the indirect expenses are contributing increasingly to the cost of settling claims. The upward spiral will continue to drain resources away from an already hard-pressed service, unless something serious is done to stop it. The more effective management of risks provides a practical way to do so. It is as well that the three changes highlighted above have brought the necessary pressure to bear to ensure that its concepts are now considered. They must be embraced wholeheartedly by everyone in every healthcare organization.

THE COST OF RISK
Clinical risk

The amount and potential cost of risk is very high. This is not surprising, as hospitals and other healthcare premises are inherently full of dangerous and hazardous substances and circumstances.

So far as NHS clinical negligence is concerned, the NHS now pays out over £150M every year. In fact, actuaries have established a liability triangulation which highlights dramatically how this will increase, year on year, unless action is taken. The triangulation has been calculated with a 7 year tail, as many claims take this unacceptably long time to be settled.

The research indicates that a typical 1000 bed acute general hospital trust in the NHS, with a bed occupancy rate of 89%, can expect 5800 patient incidents per annum. A patient incident can range from the avoidable death of a patient to someone simply falling out of bed or being given the wrong drug inconsequentially.

Of this total, on average, only 116 will be potentially compensatable events, of which 38 will become claims.

The cost of settling only 50% of those claims can be up to £2.6M (93/94 costs), excluding legal/claims handling expenses. These are already too high for any such trust to maintain its financial viability. What is more worrying is the way in which the figures will evolve if the trust does not take preventative action.

It should be borne in mind that many negligence claims take several years to settle, so that, based on the 93/94 exposure of £2.6M:

- total payments will actually be £3.77M by 2000/01 (based on 10% per annum inflation);
- the base figure for 2000/01 will become £5.76M without any change in the nature of the risks, but due simply to the increased frequency and cost of claims;
- that base figure of £5.76M will give rise to total payments for the 2000/01 year of exposure of £16.29M (by 2007/08);
- In 2000/01 payments made in that year will be £7.81M, and the outstanding liability will be £48.37M.

Staff injuries

These figures are huge, but they only deal with clinical negligence claims costs. Staff injuries are also a major factor. Too many staff are injured during the course of their employment. Quite apart from the distress and discomfort to the employee concerned, major losses occur as a consequence. Much of this can be avoided with a more focused and systematic approach. Steps must surely be taken to reduce the millions of days staff are unable to contribute to the work of their respective departments. Surely, efforts must be made to reduce the annual sickness payments to staff, let alone the high cost of using locums to replace injured staff. Too little attention is paid to this issue. More thorough investigation of the trends in injuries can pay dividends, if subsequent necessary action is taken. This is likely to include more focused training in lifting, manual handling and the use and disposal of sharps/needles, as well as raising risk awareness throughout the trust.

COST CONTAINMENT
Increased costs

It is helpful to identify what costs it might be possible to contain in this context.

Firstly, there are the increased costs which occur as a result of claims, fines, damage and losses. With regard to claims, as stated above, these can be from patients and staff, but they can also come from visitors and contract workers, who sustain injury or property damage due to defects in the estate. A big issue of cost containment with claims concerns the need to manage these properly. Too often, a claim has not been anticipated, because the untoward occurrence had not been reported at the time and therefore not investigated fully when facts were still fresh in people's minds. Not only does that mean the claim is often not defendable, but also that it has not been possible to reserve funds prospectively in the budget, as would be desirable. Fines may arise from the Health & Safety Executive and they are likely to increase in number and to get bigger. There will also be occasional significant costs arising from avoidable damage to buildings and equipment and, of course, their reinstatement and replacement. Additionally, there is the extra cost resulting from the loss of equipment and personal belongings which either have to be replaced or compensated for.

It is also necessary to distinguish between those costs which are direct and those which are indirect. The direct costs are usually fairly obvious, but there are a number of hidden costs, including legal fees, locum costs and lost management and clinical time being absorbed by the investigation of serious incidents, court appearances, statement preparation, evidence gathering, etc.

Another way of considering increased costs is to make a distinction between the longer term costs which should be contained as a result of the implementation of a risk management programme and the short-term costs. As indicated earlier, the potential for an ever rising cost of negligence claims is great – that is unless we can break into the spiral. With healthcare monies being, naturally, limited, it is vital that we take steps to do so; risk management points a very clear way.

As far as the shorter term is concerned, in undertaking surveys, it is also possible to identify areas where savings can be made (e.g. the improvements of the disposal of clinical waste which actually cost less money at the same time).

Reduced income

One needs also to look at the whole issue of the income which is lost as a result of the inadequate management of risk. The internal market makes it essential that realistic contract prices are quoted and that inpatient days do not generally exceed the budgeted norm. Therefore, it is necessary to ensure that 'productivity' is not adversely affected as a result of a patient having to stay in hospital longer than they would otherwise have had to because of an unfortunate fall from their bed or wrong procedure having been undertaken.

Similarly, the loss of use of premises and equipment, unavailable due to fire, theft or other loss, is a very obvious cost to the organization because of the resultant loss of income.

Finally, there is the issue of the reputation of the hospital or community services concerned. As patients become more aware, they will express unwillingness to attend certain hospitals because of their poor reputation in risk and safety terms. This will in turn have an effect on the district health authorities and GP fundholders who will be less prepared to buy services from a hospital which is both unsafe and is more costly to maintain.

Benefits

So, we should manage risks and claims more positively because:

- prevention is cheaper than cure;
- marketability prospects will be improved;
- quality of patient care will be enhanced; and
- the public will have more confidence in the providing trust.

A COMMISSIONER ISSUE

I am not prepared to commission services from providers without having a clear idea of the risks they carry.

DHA chief executive

Risk management is no longer just a provider issue. It is of increasing importance to the commissioners of healthcare. District health authorities are striving to ensure a high quality of service delivery and to achieve greater health gains for the population they serve. Neither they nor the GP fundholders will be prepared to pay the higher prices their providers will be forced to charge to meet the whole range of costs incurred from not managing their risks more effectively. They will not be prepared to have less money to meet the health needs of the population. Neither will they accept the quality deficits arising from an unsafe environment and unsafe clinical practices. Indeed, surely it cannot be long before the Patient's Charter recognizes that patients should have the right to expect to be treated and cared for in a safe and risk-free environment.

It is therefore inevitable that the contract specifications will increasingly require providers to demonstrate they have some form of risk management programme in place.

THE RISK MANAGEMENT PROCESS

There are four stages of risk management:

1. identification – what can go wrong?
2. analysis – how severely, frequently and likely is it to go wrong?
3. control – what changes can and should be made to prevent it, or reduce the effect of it, going wrong?
4. funding – how is any loss incurred paid for if it does go wrong?

Identification and analysis

The pain of knowing the risks you face is far better than unplanned and unexpected consequences of claims, fines and unnecessary expenditure.

NHS trust director of business services

Before risks can be managed, they firstly have to be identified and then analysed as to their nature, frequency, severity and probability, in order that they can be prioritized. It is vital to approach this process holistically and in a more thorough and coordinated way than at present. An initial identification survey is the key.

This should involve a detailed audit of the entire organization, embracing all of the following services:

Detailed survey

- The estate
- Clinical activity
- Health and safety of employees
- Computer and telecommunications
- Security
- Fire
- Waste
- Environmental issues
- Infection control
- Commercial and business risks.

It is also important that each of the above elements should be reviewed from every one of the following perspectives:

- Premises and equipment
- Circumstances and activity
- Practices and protocols
- Policies, procedures and plans
- Organizational issues.

This simple matrix provides the holistic review so necessary in an organization as complex as a NHS trust. It is vital that the interdependencies of the various departments are examined and assessed for risk.

It is also important that such an all-embracing survey is undertaken by skilled practitioners who have the wide range of expertise, experience and detective skills to ensure that all risks are spotted and analysed. It is feasible that some very large trusts may be able to afford to employ some of their own staff to do this but for most, such action will be far less cost-effective than commissioning an outside agency to do so. That will also ensure a much more independent and unbiased account of the organization's risk profile.

Obtaining views from staff

Staff often have a clearer view of the risks in their work situation than they feel able to express. They also have valuable contributions to make as to how those risks should be tackled. A Merrett Health Risk Management identification and analysis survey always includes asking staff for their confidential views. The responses are collated and reflected in the detailed risk profile report, having been audited during the site visits. This process has obvious benefits, not least because it signals to the staff as a whole that management is serious about enhancing safety and resolving some often long-standing problem situations.

Assessment and analysis

Once the risks have been identified, they need to be analysed and assessed, as it will be valuable for the chief executive and trust board to be given a clear indication of the priorities for action.

To make such judgements needs a mechanism which minimizes subjective views. Merrett Health Risk Management Limited has found it valuable to use the following six factors to assess each individual risk situation:

1. Frequency

2. Severity
3. Timeframe
4. Cost
5. Ease of implementation
6. Type of action.

Each of these carries a weighting which allows overall priority rating to be given, so that it is possible to compare the urgency of corrective action of a clinical risk situation with one demanding action in, say, waste disposal. Similarly, one is able to compare infection control with fire or security control and between health and safety legislative requirements and commercial risks.

A risk profile

The value of such a holistic, prioritized risk profile of the organization cannot be overstated, particularly if it has been based on the following four modules of investigation:

1. risks which have a direct impact on patient care;
2. risks which have an indirect impact on patient care;
3. risks to the health and safety of staff and others;
4. organizational and commercial risks.

The extensive detailed report, which follows the indepth, across-the-board review, will contain many recommendations, which will be a valuable agenda for action to tackle the risks identified. It is certain to provide some real challenges for the decision makers, as many problems will be exposed. On the other hand, it is equally certain that the chief executives who commission such a report are those who are not prepared to go on sticking their heads in the sand or who manage by the 'finger-crossing' technique. They are those who want to know which risks exist so they can begin to manage them more proactively in future.

An interesting general trend of such independent reports shows that about 85% of all the recommendations made do *not* need significant expenditure to correct the deficiencies. They are, in fact, management issues. Issues about which managers need to do things differently; issues about which managers need to *do something*; and issues about which managers should stop something being done.

So there is a crucial need for a data collection system which gives the chief executive – the ultimate risk manager – good, processed and clear information upon which they can make informed judgements about whether to spend money to reduce or eliminate a risk.

Risk control and prevention

The risk management programme has been a catalyst for wide ranging change and has laid a solid foundation for the future.
NHS trust chief executive

The agenda for immediate action provided by the detailed risk profile report is a vital first step. However, the real key to managing risks on a continuous basis is the creation of some far-reaching risk control and prevention measures throughout the trust.

More focused approach

Risks which have arisen in the past need to be avoided in future and, when they do occur, they must be managed more effectively to minimize their impact. This can only be achieved by implementing a risk management process *throughout* the trust.

It is worth reflecting that all staff in any organization manage risks every day. However, the effect of such action is diluted by the ad hoc nature of the action. What is so vitally needed is a framework whereby those risks are identified very quickly and managed with a more coordinated and systematic, organization-wide focus.

Line management responsibility

At the same time, it is a golden rule that risk management is most definitely a line management responsibility, which is one of the clinical director's prime concerns. Such devolution of responsibility and authority does not make the more coordinated approach easy, as a result of which it may be appropriate for the chief executive to appoint a risk management team both to provide the vital across-the-trust oversight, and to give whatever support is required and demanded by the line managers.

Change in attitude

One thing is certain in all this; there are likely to be some major changes to the organization's value systems. The management of risks must become everyone's business. There must be an inbuilt discipline within the organization which ensures that, inevitably and without fail, an untoward incident of whatever nature is reported immediately. This can only happen if there are changes in staff's attitudes and behaviour, leading to greater openness within the organization, and a genuine willingness by all to admit to mistakes and to report their 'near misses'. Only by adopting such a philosophy can the managers in the organization spot early enough the service elements which need improvement. No longer is it acceptable for the clinical director or chief executive to first know about an untoward incident 2 years after it occurred, through the receipt of a solicitor's letter making a claim for medical negligence!

More openness and honesty

This, in turn, leads to a more open and honest approach in dealing with those untoward clinical events and complaints from patients.

Giving patients and their relatives speedy, willing and comprehensive explanations of any adverse occurrence or outcome will lead to fewer complaints and claims for negligence, not more.

Control and funding

As Fig. 29.4 indicates, in terms of controlling the risk, it can either be avoided, accepted or prevented.

Avoidance

Risks can be avoided altogether by ceasing to provide the service or function which creates the risk. This is not usually a practical solution in such a publicly run service such as the NHS.

Acceptance

So far as acceptance is concerned, one can either assume the risk by making an explicit, positive judgement that is unlikely to warrant any management action or expenditure, or one can transfer some of it.

In assuming the risk, it would be quite legitimate for the trust board to assess a situation to be a 'one million to one' risk and therefore decide to assume that chance. In such circumstances, it would be potentially very valuable to record, albeit briefly, the factors and criteria used in making the judgement. This may be valuable,

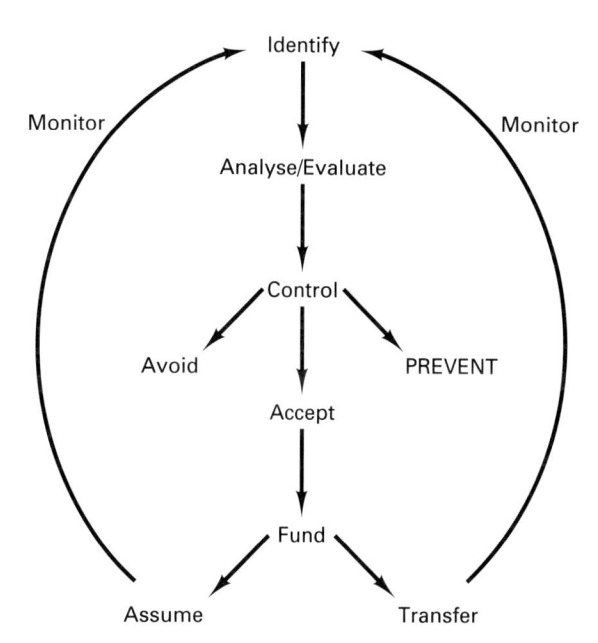

Fig. 29.4 How to manage the risk

supportive information to present in defence, if the one chance in a million did emerge and resulted in loss of lives or facilities.

Transferring costs

The most likely method of cost transference is through insurance. From 1 April 1991, NHS trusts have been free to buy insurance cover for most risks. This is expected to be a combination of self-insurance and commercial insurance. The permitted insurance arrangements can cover property, motor, employer's liability, public and products liability and directors and officer liability.

Insurance cover does, of course, have many benefits, but it is only one element of the risk management process and is no panacea. What is of concern is its tremendous potential to encourage complacency, and the fact that, of itself, it does little positively to improve patient care.

In April 1995, the Government established the Clinical Negligence Scheme for Trusts (CNST) which allows Trusts to indemnify themselves against the costs of large claims of clinical negligence. The Scheme will be the responsibility of the NHS Litigation Authority.

A key ingredient of the Scheme is the emphasis it places on 10 or 11 risk management standards being met to save significant reductions in the annual financial contributions.

Prevention

The emphasis, therefore, should be on prevention,

through the implementation of positive risk management programmes, which bring about continuous improvements.

Prevention results in better practice, better outcomes, less defensive medicine and a less expensive service. Prevention is definitely better and cheaper than cure.

HOW TO PREVENT RISKS

By addressing the quality v cost equation, we have reduced our exposure to risk.

NHS trust chairman

Address the quality v quantity issue

Many risks occur in the NHS setting because clinicians, managers and others are having to make urgent decisions under pressure or at least in the genuine belief they are under pressure. Often, the nature of the decision is guided by intuition rather than an analysis of all the facts. Indeed, such a detailed assessment is often not possible in an emergency situation. Similarly, these daily decisions can be affected by an overstretched operating theatre, an overcrowded accident and emergency department and an understaffed community nursing service. In such circumstances, individual professionals are forced to make immediate, individual judgements about who to treat first and who not to. Such situations increase the risks to the patients concerned, well in excess of the inherent risk involved.

To reduce the potential for increased risk in these ad hoc situations, the trust concerned needs to address the whole quality v quantity issue. This needs to be done positively, involving a wide range of clinical views, and with an open-minded attitude. It is necessary to ask the question 'Are there any circumstances in which the trust would knowingly compromise the quality of patient care?'. In reaching its conclusion, the trust will want to determine if the quality of care is not up to its defined standards. If the answer to the question is 'No', but the reality is that standards are not being met, then the trust must decide whether or not it needs to reduce the quantity of activity. However, if the answer is 'Yes', then the trust board should recognize quite explicitly the quality deficiencies it accepts. Once having reached its conclusion, the trust will no doubt wish to debate the issue with its main purchasers of service.

This is not a simple or straightforward matter. Healthcare is, of course, a complex service industry. It is concerned with quality of life and life and death issues. As such, it has emotional and emotive aspects with which British risk managers have not had to contend before. Only those who specialize in this arena recognize fully the delicate interdependence of the wide and multifaceted range of departments and functions. Nevertheless, unless this crucial issue is addressed, fundamentally, a vast range of risk situations will continue to occur on an ad hoc basis, and without any sense of control. This cannot be acceptable any longer. Clinicians and managers must be given clear guidance and support in this highly vulnerable arena.

Recognize systems failures

Most adverse events and untoward incidents, which have resulted from uncontrolled risks, do not occur because a single person has made a single mistake. They happen because a number of small mistakes, insignificant in themselves, occur together to form a large untoward incident. The answer is to try to spot the potential for these small errors and 'near misses', by more proactive surveillance systems. However, more importantly even than that is that critical adverse events occur because of a systems failure. Clinical directors can prevent such events and eliminate or reduce risks by identifying these failures and taking action to make them less likely to happen.

In outlining some important examples of systems failures, it is helpful to distinguish between:

- risks which have a direct impact on patient care;
- risks which have an indirect impact on patient care;
- risks to the health, safety and well-being of staff and others; and
- organizational and commercial risks.

Avoiding direct patient care risks

I have selected the following patient risk situations for brief attention here. These apply across the range of service provision, from acute general hospital care to services for people with mental illness or learning disabilities, and to both primary and community care.

Avoid breakdown in communications

A great deal of clinical risks occur because of poor communications between doctors and nurses/midwives in the same clinical team; senior staff and their juniors; professionals in one department and those in another; and between clinicians and their patients. The maxim is 'You haven't told them unless they've heard it'. Risks occur because of misguided communication; wrong information being given; indecipherable or inaudible information or simply because there has been *no* communication.

Good communication need not take more time and not all good communicators are born with the talent. Clinical directors can do much to identify those in need of improvement, to help them perform better through training and support and, of course, to develop systems where communications become easy. Clinical team management and team briefing are just two ways to help.

Duty to exercise reasonable skill and care

Negligence is a tort, and for a claim to be successful it must be established that a duty of care exists, that the defendant was in breach of that duty and that there was a causal link between the negligent act or omission and the injury sustained by the injured claimant. The effect of the double action is such that if the defendant can be shown to be in breach of a statutory duty, it only remains for the claimant to prove the causal link.

As long ago as 1822 (Pippin v Sterrad), it was established that a medical practitioner owes a duty to exercise reasonable skill and care in their treatment of a patient. However, a doctor is not negligent if 'he acts in accordance with the practice accepted at the time as proper, by a reasonable body of medical opinion, even though some doctors adopt a different practice. In short, the law imposes the duty of care, but the standard is a matter for medical judgement'. The Bolam Test, as it is called, is applied to both diagnosis and treatment. It has, however, been confirmed more recently (Sidaway v Bethlem Royal Hospital Governors and others (1985)) that the court is the final arbiter of a professional standard – this being defined as acting in accordance with a practice *rightly* accepted as proper by a body of skilled and experienced medical people.

The NHS Management Executive has also expressed a view about this. As Figs 29.5 and 29.6 show, central guidance does exist with regard to a breach of a duty of care.

Managers and clinicians alike should ensure that well-considered clinical practices and protocols are developed and agreed through the clinical audit process. Managers also have a responsibility in this context to ensure adequate staffing levels, suitable skill mix for service provision, and proper facilities and equipment.

Ascertaining the facts

The 'reasonable standard of care' argument can also be applied where a failure to provide case notes or test results affects the activities of clinicians.

Clinical negligence is a breach of duty of care by members of the healthcare professions (including medical and dental practitioners, nurses and midwives, professions allied to medicine, ambulance personnel, laboratory staff and relevant technicians) or by others consequent on decisions or judgements made by members of those professions acting in their professional capacity on relevant work, and which are admitted as negligent by the employer or are determined as such through the legal process.

(NHS Circular EL (91)19)

Fig. 29.5 Clinical negligence

The following must all apply before liability for negligence exists:

a) There must have been a duty of care owed to the patient by the relevant professional(s).
b) The standard of care appropriate to such duty must not have been attained and therefore the duty breached, whether by action or inaction, advice or failure to advise.
c) Such a breach must be demonstrated to have caused the injury and therefore the resulting loss complained about by the patient.
d) Any loss sustained as a result of the injury and complained about by the patient must be of a kind that the courts recognize and allow compensation for.
e) The injury and resulting loss complained about by the patient must have been reasonably foreseeable.

(NHS Circular EL(91)19)

Fig. 29.6 Breach of a duty of care

It is of vital importance that all medical and other patients records are complete, legible and securely held, so that:

- correct treatment and medication is given;
- confidentiality is maintained; and
- a defence can be clearly proven in instances where the trust has not been negligent, and in cases where negligence is obvious, a speedy settlement can be reached without incurring unnecessary legal costs.

The obligation to keep records confidential rests on the trust board. A breach by an employee could lay the trust open to legal action.

With regard to these important issues, managers will need to ensure that medical records, X-ray and pathology departments are properly organized and realize the importance of their function. This means adequate storage of written and computerized records, early filing systems and the need for strict rules of confidentiality.

A more important and challenging job for clinical directors is to persuade, if necessary through incentives or sanctions, all their clinical colleagues to record *whenever necessary and very clearly*, any contact with a patient. This is a very high priority for improvement, not least because present gross inadequacies in this respect lead to enormous areas of risk.

Informed consent

There are hundreds of cases each year in the NHS whereby patients have not realized the risk in a particular operation or treatment or have not been provided with the range of options open to them, from which they can give informed consent to proceed. This can lead both to unnecessary risks, because instructions have not been followed, and to disgruntlement because something has happened to them which they did not expect.

Managers must ensure that all patients undergoing a treatment carrying risk sign a written consent. Furthermore, the practitioner receiving the consent should record and sign briefly that he or she has explained the risk. Not to ensure this could well bring claims of clinical negligence, if not serious deficiencies in overall care.

Undertaking work beyond one's competence

It can be said that, in general, inexperience is no defence to an allegation of negligence and that, in essence, the standard of skill expected of a doctor would be that expected of practitioners with whom they claim to have similar skills. However, if an inexperienced doctor does not seek the advice of a senior or specialist when a prudent junior would do so, they may be considered negligent. Similarly, if novices undertake procedures in which they are not experienced, other than in an emergency, they are effectively claiming the skills of a suitably trained practitioner and will be judged on that standard.

In Wilsher v Essex Health Authority, the court of appeal held that a practitioner must attain the standard of skill to be expected from a person holding his post in the hospital. It was irrelevant that he was new to the post and still in training. However, junior doctors may discharge their duty to a patient by consulting their senior colleagues, who then take over or endorse their treatment.

Likewise, the United Kingdom Central Council Code of Professional Conduct for Nurses, Midwives and Health Visitors states that in the exercise of their professional accountability, they should 'acknowledge any limitations of competence and refuse in such cases to accept delegated functions without having first received training in those functions and having been assessed as competent'.

The Code also states that they should:

have regard to the environment of care and its physical, psychological and social effects on patients/clients and also to the adequacy of resources, and make known to appropriate persons or authorities any circumstance which could place patients/clients in jeopardy or which militates against safe standards of practice.

Key areas here for clinical directors are the employment of locums and the proper induction of staff. Locum clinical staff can create a highly risky set of circumstances, with the locum being unfamiliar with agreed local practices and protocols, not knowing how to obtain support services and being generally unsure of the geography of the hospital, clinic or locality. Like every other member of staff, locums need some form of proper induction upon commencement of duty. Directors also need to be sure that secure procedures are in place to check references and up-to-date professional registrations, etc.

Clearly defined responsibilities

Many clinical risks occur as a result of junior members of the clinical team being unsure of their levels of responsibility and authority, particularly in an emergency situation. A classic example concerns a senior house officer in the obstetric team not being absolutely certain what action to take with a difficult birth at a weekend, with the consultant 'on call' but miles away from the hospital. These circumstances need to be predicted in advance and talked through with all members of the team. Staff need to be clear exactly what is expected of them in a range of potentially difficult situations.

Timeliness of treatment

Patients are able to sue NHS trusts for failure to provide correct diagnosis/treatment. It is possible that a claim could succeed if a delay in treatment caused additional pain and suffering, death or bodily injury to a patient, including a delay in treatment caused by an administrative problem.

A delay in treatment can also occur if equipment is out of action or breaks down. It is also worthy of note that care should be taken when drawing up contracts for the provision of services that any time scales incorporated are realistic and that these can be met. Failure to meet the terms of these service contracts will have a detrimental effect on the trust's reputation and lead to patients asking to be referred elsewhere.

The above issues are just a few of the many risk areas affecting clinical services. The summary message is that the action to prevent such risks is well worth the effort in terms of maintaining and improving quality and safety standards, let alone the considerable potential for reducing unnecessary and wasteful expenditure. Such action can be taken through a more proactive and focused approach which leads to greater cooperation between professions and between departments.

Some clinical departments and services are more vulnerable to risks than others. Maternity care is the highest clinical risk speciality, with far too many babies being born with brain damage as a result of inadequate care and attention during birth. General and orthopaedic surgery also carry big risks, as do accident and emergency departments and mental health services. Traditionally, anaesthetic, imaging and pathology departments have installed satisfactory risk control processes, but these need to be checked vigorously and regularly.

Avoiding risks in the support services

There is also a whole range of risks arising from the estate and support services, including security, fire precautions and building and plant maintenance. These are concerned largely with physical loss or unavailability of buildings or equipment and the control and disposal of clinical and other waste. However, they also include consideration of liability risks, where appropriate and, of course, potential loss of life in the fire and security areas.

Security

Most NHS trusts will have some form of security focus, but this is more than likely to be inadequate to meet the wide range of issues, from theft and fraud to violence, assault and vandalism, and it is helpful to distinguish between patients and staff in these respects.

From the surveys undertaken by Merrett Health Risk Management Limited, it emerges that, on average:

- one in five staff do not feel safe in their place of work during daylight hours;
- two thirds do not feel safe on duty at night;
- three quarters do not feel their property is safe from pilfering; and
- two thirds do not consider the trust's property is safe from pilfering.

In practical terms, the following simple actions by *everyone* in the trust can save so much money:

- remove targets from sight;
- place targets behind barriers;
- make potential thieves, etc. highly detectable (e.g. install security alarms, identification badges, stock control, access control, etc.).

Fire

In society at large, the threat posed by uncontrolled fire is generally recognized. In those activities where the risk of fire is greater than the average, special precautions need to be taken. However, the incidence of large fires in hospitals and community care buildings is not particularly great (though they rank third as the target for arsonists) and the level of fire precautions often reflects this.

The aims of a fire precautions programme should be:

- to minimize the probability of a fire starting;
- to avoid, so far as is possible, the likelihood of a fire causing death or injury to patients, staff or visitors;
- to minimize the likely damage to the buildings and equipment;
- to minimize the effect of the fire on the provision of healthcare.

So far as the second point is concerned, the avoidance of death or injury can only be assured by the most stringent forethought and planning, followed by regular training and practical experience. This should include practical training in evacuation procedures, the correct use of firefighting equipment and the clear identification of alarm points and exit routes. Clinical directors should ensure that all their staff are included in this.

Buildings, plant and equipment

Hospitals and other healthcare premises are totally dependent on reliable equipment and continuous services, so it is important that they are safe and free from defects, are adequately maintained, and that maintenance records are kept. If these are not available or in place, huge financial, safety and quality risks will be present.

This means the need for planned preventative maintenance programmes, quick responses to requests for emergency repairs, etc. and satisfactory emergency equipment.

Whilst not a specific responsibility of clinical directors, they do have a role to play in monitoring the effectiveness of the service they receive and notifying the chief executive of any deficiencies.

Waste and environmental issues

NHS trusts have a legal responsibility to dispose of all waste so that no harm is caused to either people or the environment. The particular issues for attention are:

- the segregation, collection and storage of waste;
- the disposal of drugs and chemical waste;
- the disposal of clinical waste;
- general waste.

Significant in this complex issue is the great potential for staff to be injured by the incorrect initial disposal, by wards and departments, of sharps and used needles, etc. The hepatitis and HIV scares have highlighted this high risk situation and yet, time and time again, porters, domestic staff and nurses are seriously damaged. Similarly, in community clinics, it is not uncommon to find small children inquisitively putting their hands into the sharps disposal container awaiting collection on the floor of the clinic.

Typically, these serious risks do not require money to be spent in eliminating them. They require appropriate management attention, and clinical directors should ensure there is a greater risk awareness on the part of all their staff.

Control of infection

The importance of effective infection control cannot be overstressed. The temporary closure of wards and community clinics is not unknown, and as the public become more litigious, the financial cost of such an incident could become a serious consideration. More importantly, the high incidence/low severity effects of inadequate control of infection will create a drain on resources. These 'hidden' costs arise from extended hospital stays, readmissions and unavailability of staff, etc.

Control of infection needs to be examined thoroughly under four headings as follows:

- responsibility for control of infection;
- information and awareness;
- staff uniforms, protective clothing and changing facilities;
- other infection control issues (e.g. refrigerators, microwave ovens, food handling, etc.).

In most organizations, some attention is paid to all of these issues. However, this is usually undertaken in an uncoordinated and reactive way. The important message to come through here is that a less ad hoc and more proactive approach can pay huge benefits in cost, safety and quality.

Health and safety legislative liabilities

Most line managers underestimate significantly the risks to which their staff are subjected and consider the legislative requirements of, for example, the Health & Safety at Work etc. Act 1974 as someone else's responsibility. This is flawed thinking, not least because of the large number of 'man' days lost to the NHS every week as a result of injuries sustained at work. Clinical directors have a real role to play in this respect.

The focus is concerned primarily with the health, safety and well-being of employees, although there are areas in which the same concerns apply to patients, residents and visitors. A useful way of examining these issues is to base the survey on the headings used in the Health & Safety at Work etc. Act 1974.

In 1987, the Single European Act added a new Article 118a to the Treaty of Rome, specially relating to health and safety at work. As a result, several new directives have been adopted. The framework directive sets out general duties and principles which apply to all sectors of work activity and includes a requirement to assess workplace risks. Other, more specific directives relate to the workplace, use of work equipment, use of personal protective equipment, display screen equipment and manual handling of loads.

It is vital that the trust has copies of all the directives and regulations which incorporate them into UK law, and key officers become familiar with their requirements. Early planning and foresight can often cut the cost of implementation, simply by the phased replacement of out of date equipment with items which comply with future requirements.

The legal framework

Most legal liability claims by employees against their employer are double action, claiming breach of statutory duty coupled with a claim for negligence.

The breach of statutory duty is normally a breach in the duty of the employer, as defined in the Health & Safety at Work etc. Act 1974. This act is framed in general terms, with the result that it is becoming increasingly difficult for employers to prove that there has not been a breach of the act if there has actually been an accident at work.

The Health & Safety at Work etc. Act also imposes a duty on individual employees to take care of their own health and safety and that of their fellow employees.

Nevertheless, experience demonstrates that there is a much heavier onus upon the employer to ensure compliance with the act, so the best that can be hoped for is that the amount of any compensation will be reduced by virtue of the contributory negligence of the injured party.

For example, taken to its logical conclusion, this would mean that any employee who feels at risk of injury through not having been adequately trained or not having adequate assistance in lifting ought to refuse to carry out any task which involves a risk of injury. This would bring almost any hospital to a standstill. If the trust was to insist on perpetuating the existing situation, there would be virtually no defence against claims brought by injured employees arising out of injuries caused by lifting. Similar comments would apply to other breaches of the Health & Safety at Work etc. Act referred to in the following sections.

Safe systems of work

It is a particular duty of employers under Section 2(2)(a) of the Health & Safety at Work etc. Act 1974 to ensure 'the provision and maintenance of plant and systems of work that are, so far as is reasonably practicable, safe and without risks to health'. A breach of this duty would support an action in negligence against the trust.

The Manual Handling Operations Regulation 1992 (90/269/EEC) requires employees to take steps to avoid the need for manual handling and, where this is not possible, to take appropriate measures and use appropriate means to avoid or reduce the risk to workers.

Where manual handling cannot be avoided, employers must organize work situations so as to make manual handling as safe as possible. Employers must also assess, where possible in advance, the health and safety conditions of the type of work involved and take appropriate measures to avoid or reduce the risk, taking account of the various factors in Annex 1 (of the directive) relating to the characteristics of the load, the physical effort required, the work environment and the requirements of the task.

As stated previously, unless adequate training, aids and assistance are available to employees when required to lift or handle, it would be considered that the Health and Safety at Work etc. Act 1974 and the relevant EC directive have been breached. In order to create a defence that training is provided, it is necessary to keep full records of the nature of training provided, together with the date of delivery.

The cost of back injury cases is escalating. In February 1991, damages of £184 603 were awarded to a nurse who sustained a back injury whilst helping three porters to lift a 16 stone patient (McGowan v Harrow Health Authority (1991)). Reports of such awards are frequently well publicized and could well influence others to make similar claims.

Control of substances

It is a particular duty of employers under Section 2(2)(b) of the Health & Safety at Work etc. Act 1974 to make 'arrangements for ensuring, so far as is reasonably practicable, safety and absence of risks to health in connection with the use, handling, storage and transport of articles and substances'. A breach of this duty would support an action in negligence against the trust.

Control of Substances Hazardous to Health Regulations (COSHH) apply to substances that have already been classified as being very toxic, toxic, harmful, corrosive or irritant under the Classification, Packaging & Labelling of Dangerous Substances Regulations 1984, and to those substances which have maximum exposure limits or occupational exposure standards. COSHH also covers substances that have chronic or delayed effects (e.g. carcinogenic, mutagenic or teratogenic).

A substance hazardous to health is not just a single chemical or compound, but also includes mixtures of compounds, microorganisms, allergens, etc.

The COSHH regulations place specific duties on employers as follows:

- assessments (Regulation 6);
- prevention or control of exposure (Regulation 7);
- use of control measures and maintenance, examination and test of control measures (Regulations 8 and 9);
- information, training etc. (Regulation 12).

Protective clothing must be provided for staff involved with handling contaminated substances or linen. Masks and gloves should be provided and staff should be given instruction in the correct use thereof.

The COSHH Regulations 1988 came into force on 1 October 1989. It is therefore not only a matter of risk, but also of legislative compliance that the trust ensures that COSHH Regulations are implemented.

NHS trusts should by now have carried out an assessment of the health risks associated with the substances used within their organization and put in place any resultant changes, information, training and health surveillance, as required under the regulations.

Information, instruction, training and supervision

It is a particular duty of employers under Section 2(2)(c) of the Health & Safety at Work etc. Act 1974, to provide 'such information, instruction, training and supervision as is necessary to ensure, so far as is practicable, the health and safety at work of his employees'. A breach of this duty would support an action in negligence against the trust.

The importance of adequate instruction and training for *all* staff, especially in lifting and handling of either patients or objects, cannot be overemphasized.

To provide an adequate defence to a breach of statutory duty, not only should training be provided, but there should be documentation showing the date of the course, the content and signed verification of the employees having received training. This should include a statement from the trainee confirming that he or she feels competent and confident to perform as trained, and the opportunity to state additional training required.

Safe place of work

It is a particular duty of employers, under Section 2(2)(d) of the Health & Safety at Work etc. Act 1974, to ensure:

so far as is reasonably practicable as regards any place of work under the employers control, the maintenance of it in a condition that is safe and without risks to health and the provision and maintenance of means of access to and egress from it that are safe and without such risks.

A breach of this duty would support an action in negligence against the trust.

Without risks to health

The Health & Safety at Work etc. Act 1974, Section 2(2) (e), states that the employer is responsible for:

The provision and maintenance of a working environment for his employees that is, as far as is reasonably practicable, safe, without risks to health, and adequate as regards facilities and arrangements for their welfare at work.

Competent and suitable fellow servants

The common law responsibility of an employer includes the provision of competent and suitable fellow servants. The responsibility for employing suitable staff for each post rests with the trust concerned.

As can be seen from the foregoing, the legislative and statutory requirements resting with the trust cannot be ignored. To do so would incur the wrath of the Health & Safety Executive and lead to closure of facilities, the imposition of fines and, in extreme cases, senior managers imprisoned.

Organizational liabilities and commercial risks

Many risks occur within the trust because it has not been sufficiently specific or explicit about the liabilities of shared accommodation or the sale of income generation products or services. It is also important to reduce the risks of fraud and stock losses, etc. through a more formalized approach to internal audit. Regular checking of the usage of up-to-date standing financial instruction, for example, will reduce the organizational risks.

In the new 'market' environment, trusts are more than ever vulnerable to the commercial uncertainties of lost contracts. Therefore, it is important that the management of such risks is developed as a fundamental part of the regular business planning reviews.

THE MEDICAL ROLE IN RISK MANAGEMENT

As the function of clinical directors and clinical directorates continues to develop, the opportunities for medical staff to become directly involved with management decision making should increase.

Consultants who are appointed as clinical directors will be able to ensure two-way communication between management and clinicians on issues key to risk management. Those adopting a proactive and positive attitude to the subject may wish to take the following steps to facilitate this communication:

- designate a group of a few interested and key people within the directorate to draw up a risk management policy and plan for the directorate;
- ensure the group identifies a more focused and systematic approach to managing risk within the directorate;
- make it very clear what is expected of each member of staff within the directorate;
- regard the creation of departmental protocols and procedures as a vital, team activity;
- develop early warning, untoward occurrence systems;
- have a holistic risk identification and assessment survey undertaken;
- make sure the recommendations for risk control and prevention are prioritized across the various modules of focus;
- involve all the clinicians at an early stage, as an extension of their medical and clinical audit activities;
- gain the commitment of the trust chief executive;
- acknowledge risk management as an essential quality system.

It is essential that an approach to managing risk is adopted which allows clinicians to:

- identify the key risks to clinical care within their area;
- explore the relationships between audit activities and other risk analysis, prevention and control methods;
- identify the priorities for preventing and controlling risk in their area.

Establishing a risk management process

The following pointers give some indication of what needs to be done to get started with a risk management process, following the creation of a risk profile for the directorate or department.

There are eight elements which require attention if a risk management programme is to be successful.

1. Risk management structure;
2. Reporting and communication;
3. Tracking, trending, monitoring and projection;
4. Investigation and administration of adverse events;
5. Education programme;
6. Standards, policies and procedures;
7. Risk control objectives;
8. Contingency/disaster plans.

Risk management structure

Commitment of senior staff

The overall responsibility for the management of risk within a clinical directorate rests firmly with the clinical director. To be effective, risk management requires the commitment of that director and this must be communicated throughout the entire directorate by a structured approach. In departments where the risk management programme is not structured, the departmental head receives information and advice which is individually related, which can lead to good risk management practices being conducted in some areas of the department whilst, in similar parts elsewhere, poor risk management practices are allowed to continue.

A line management responsibility

As has been referred to earlier, risk issues are present throughout any organization, and the management of risk must become the concern of every member of staff. The need, therefore, is for a focused approach and attitude to the management of risk. This requires the central pool of trust expertise to supplement and support the risk management activity of individual departments and to encourage a holistic and systematic approach to the management of risk.

Reporting and communication

One of the most important foundations for an effective risk management programme is the communication of timely and accurate information relating to adverse incidents. It is important for the clinical director to track the untoward incidents which occur, in order that they may be studied and analysed effectively, so that preventative measures may be put in place to avoid similar future events. This applies equally both to incidents which have given, or may give, rise to property damage and to actual or possible personal injury.

Unfortunately, efforts directed at the identification of medical loss prevention problems have been historically the least effective. The first notification of a potentially compensatable occurrence received by a health authority or trust has often been in the form of a solicitor's letter. At times, this notification occurs a year or more after the date of the occurrence and, occasionally, as much as 20 years later. Prior notice of the potentially compensatable occurrence was usually not provided by a 'traditional' incident reporting system. As a result of this system deficiency, the healthcare provider is at a great disadvantage. It is extremely difficult to reconstruct details of the occurrence several years after the fact; medical records may be unavailable, witnesses or staff move on or expire, individuals relocate and memories fade. These factors make the development of a successful defence much more difficult.

Early identification of potential liabilities will not only affect the likely outcome and final cost of liability claims, but will also lead to early identification of systems, practices or equipment which are not contributing to the highest standard of patient care. As risk management is an essential quality system, this should, in turn, facilitate the introduction of preventative measures and quality assurance objectives.

Tracking, trending, monitoring and projections

The importance of gathering data and the manner in which it should be gathered have been addressed above. However, that data must be analysed and categorized in some meaningful manner, in order to provide the clinical directors or departmental heads with good, clear information upon which they can make sound judgements. It is for the director to ensure that a critical incident reporting system is in place and supported by a computer software package to allow such analysis to be undertaken.

Investigation and administration of adverse events

A more proactive approach to the investigation and administration of adverse events is required for several reasons. Firstly, corrective action can be taken; the speedy reporting of incidents and identification of liability should lead to physical hazards being improved and practices which are hazardous being amended soon after the time of incident. In the past, it has been possible for a whole series of similar incidents to arise from one proximate cause in the same department, before being identified and amended.

Secondly, investigation of clinical incidents will enable clinicians to address matters through their clinical audit arrangements, enabling them to develop increasingly sophisticated standards of practice and outcome, etc.

Thirdly, early investigation of an adverse event allows the clinical director to fully document the matter and ensure that, should a claim arise, sufficient information exists upon which to base a decision regarding liability.

Finally, early reporting allows a more honest and open approach with the patient(s) affected. All members of the team advise patients, or relatives, very shortly after an adverse event has occurred.

Establish education programme

It is feasible that risk situations develop in isolation, but experience tells us that they normally arise because of human involvement. People contribute to risk by being unaware of the nature of risk and of their contribution to that risk. An employee who is unaware of risk might, for example, leave valuable personal possessions in clear view on a desk whilst leaving a room, whereas a risk aware employee would secrete the valuables in a locked drawer. An employee unaware of their contribution to risk would be the one who leaves a bag of clinical waste outside the locked container into which such waste should be placed, thus enabling anyone who comes into contact with it to be exposed to infection, should the bag burst. A nurse who leaves an elderly patient unattended on the commode could be contributing to the risk of that patient sustaining a fall and a longer inpatient stay.

The control of the human element in risk is primarily one of information and education. The trust should therefore undertake a systematic and ongoing education programme for its entire workforce regarding the human factor in risk. This education can be incorporated into existing training schemes, but should also include the development of new education modules. It is recommended, particularly when training staff in matters relating to health and safety at work, that courses should be well documented on the personnel files of individual staff.

Develop standards, policies and procedures

Written standards, policies and procedures have many benefits in respect of comparing the quality of services of various providers and letting staff know what is expected of them. However, they do also have disadvantages. It is good to be seen to have an ultimate goal of perfection, but it is inadvisable to have a written standard which is breached. In some circumstances, particularly in the area of health and safety at work, the standard is set by statute and, in these cases, every effort must be made to comply with the required standard, as a breach may lead to an adverse decision regarding liability in the event of a claim for compensation. Standards, policies and procedures should therefore be written on the basis that they should be attainable. It may be preferable to have a written standard which requires an improvement of a percentage on existing performance, rather than to have one which sets out the perfect but unattainable goal.

Standards, procedures and protocols should be prepared within each department or clinical directorate, although it is important to coordinate them centrally to ensure that they do not give conflicting instructions and are readily available for consultation by the claims manager within the risk management team. It is important that an incident can be checked against the appropriate standard, as this will provide the first indication of whether or not liability exists.

In this context, it is also recommended that a trust risk management strategy be prepared. This should be simple and achievable. The objective of the strategy should be clearly stated, as should the method of implementation and it should make clear what are the clinicians' responsibilities for its achievement.

Risk control objectives

When looking at eliminating or reducing risk, much can be done with very little expenditure. However, some risk management decisions incur considerable expenditure, for example, the replacement of x-ray equipment. In order, therefore, that a risk management programme fulfils one of its key objectives to reduce the cost of risk, it is necessary for both clinicians and managers to understand the quality/cost equation and to have available sufficient information to make valid risk management decisions.

Contingency/disaster plans

Contingency and disaster planning is particularly important in order to avoid possible and unexpected events which could seriously hamper the functioning of the trust and its directorates and departments. Some activity has been undertaken in this area in the past, but often it has not been coordinated or continuous.

It is recommended that each area should develop its own set of contingency plans and ensure that it develops and is updated appropriately.

THE BENEFITS OF A HOLISTIC RISK MANAGEMENT PROGRAMME

Should the trust decide to implement a genuine, holistic risk management programme, it will:

Know its risks

The risk management programme will enable the trust to identify the whole range of risks it faces and to analyse them in order that they may be quantified in terms of frequency, severity and probability.

Choose its priorities for action

Having identified the risks, the information can be used to make sound business decisions regarding preventative action. In some cases, preventative action can be taken without spending further money, but simply by undertaking some organizational or procedural change.

Monitor adverse events

The risk management programme will encourage an increase in gathering information regarding adverse events occurring, by clinical directorates, including those incidents which did not give rise to claims. This will enable the directorates to reduce the number of repeat pattern incidents and eliminate or reduce potential claims.

Manage untoward incidents and claims

When loss or injury does occur, the risk management programme will ensure that an untoward incident is identified immediately. This will mean that the witness statements and other information required to defend the claim are gathered at the time when the incident is fresh in the memory of the parties involved. This will enable the trust to anticipate future financial outlays for claims.

Educate trust staff

The human element in risk is most important. When individuals are aware of the consequences of a certain course of action, that awareness alone will cause them to modify their behaviour. As an education programme progresses, there will be fewer 'repeat pattern' incidents and claims. The emphasis will be on getting things right the first time and every time. The education process will also concentrate on postoccurrence activity, which will lead to reductions in the cost of those losses which are not avoided.

Plan for disasters

The risk management programme will enable any shortcomings to be identified in the range of internal and external contingency plans.

Save money

A key objective of risk management is to prevent, wherever possible, adverse events and therefore avoid the significant financial consequences of claims, fines and losses.

SOME NEW DIRECTIONS

Just as advances in medical research and technology are constantly changing the clinical perspective on healthcare, there are developments in the management of risk which will affect the provision of care.

Perinatal outcomes analyst

A concept developed in the United States, the perinatal outcomes analyst is now being introduced into the NHS. POAs provide a vital focus in the investigation of maternity mishaps. They are usually trained nurses with several years' experience in obstetrics and neonatology. They investigate all untoward incidents immediately, whether or not the mother or baby has been injured, so that changes in practice can be put in hand straightaway to avoid a recurrence. The POA also provides a link between the professionals and the mother in explaining exactly what went wrong, what is being done and what are the implications for the parents and the child.

Experience in the States suggests that the POA will

become a key mover in the reduction of patient distress, the enhancement of the patient/clinician relationship at a potentially damaging time and the reduction in the cost of clinical negligence claims.

Risk management standards

While there are several audit programmes currently used for hospitals and other healthcare organizations to assess the quality of their service provision, as yet there is no approved accreditation scheme for risk management.

With the creation of the CNST (see section above), however, there will be a need for a recognized set of criteria against which to assess a trust's approach to managing risk.

Risk management consultancies will therefore work with clinicians and NHS managers to identify how to meet these key criteria.

Proactive claims management – an end to the adversarial approach?

As has already been stated in this chapter, prompt incident reporting and accurate record keeping are crucial to the effective management of claims.

The clinician has the key role in handling clinical negligence claims proactively. Developing a positive attitude to untoward incidents and to communicating with an injured patient is the first and most important step in this process.

Clinicians must be prepared to acknowledge that something has gone wrong without the fear that they may incriminate themselves. Experience shows that sympathy and openness at the outset between the doctor and patient improve the outcome for everyone involved:

- litigation may be avoided altogether;
- where negligence is clear, settlements can be made more quickly and thus more cheaply;
- the aftercare of the patient can be conducted more effectively for the patient;

- staff are supported through the process by management.

While the move to openness and honesty in clinical negligence cases may be more of a cultural change for some organizations and/or individuals than others, the effort is sure to be worthwhile.

CONCLUSION

The consequences of not taking risk management seriously are that trusts will continue to have quality deficiencies, and to pay claims, fines, additional staff costs, additional replacement costs and extended stay costs. There will also be unexpected litigation and unplanned losses of facilities and services, resulting in the need for managers to realign their priorities constantly – a difficult enough task at the best of times.

On the other hand, the benefits of a risk management programme are:

- improvements in the quality of patient care;
- reduction in damage and injury to patients;
- enhanced security and safety of buildings and equipment;
- better environment for staff;
- reduction in wasteful expenditure;
- increases in patient activity.

All of us do, and should, take risks. The point is that managers must identify, analyse and control the risk appropriately, to manage through informed choice and judgement. By being positive and proactive in the management of this future uncertainty, clinicians can play a crucial part in securing a continuous improvement in the quality of patient care.

REFERENCES

McGowan v Harrow H A 1991 *Kemp & Kemp* volume 2: E3–005/2
UKCC Code of Professional Conduct 1992 *UKCC*, London
Wilsher v Essex H A 1986 *3 ALL ER 801 Court of Appeal*

30

Information and information technology in healthcare

Tim Scott

*I have five honest serving men,
I call them, Who, What, Why, Where, When.*
(Kipling)

INTRODUCTION

Management is not, or shouldn't be, about maintaining the status quo. It is about constantly striving to improve what the organization does and indeed to modify what it does in response to its customers' requirements. This proactive style of management has as its prime approach a constant questioning and Kipling's honest serving men provide a very comprehensive set of tools.

When management teams start to ask these probing questions about the basics of what the organization does, it is easy to fall back on anecdote, soft information, opinion and hearsay. Often the most effective orator or indeed the loudest, will ensure that their view becomes the group view and their choice becomes the group decision. The only safeguard against such behaviour is an insistence on information; timely, accurate and properly presented. But such information can itself be a minefield. How many of us have participated in endless arguments about the validity of the information, rather than applying that energy to trying to understand the data themselves?

Clinicians involved in management need to gain a broad understanding of the information systems in the organization and the information technology (IT) that supports those information systems, in order to be able to use information in management. They need to know how it is constructed, its limitations and its degree of accuracy to decide the extent of reliance they should place on it. Additionally they need to gain a broad understanding of the 'cost' of information, that is, the cost of the resources involved in collecting and collating it.

INFORMATION TECHNOLOGY

We live in a society where the computer, or more generally information technology, is driving change at a pace which we find hard to comprehend. It has been called the IT revolution and parallels have been drawn to the Industrial Revolution, but the Industrial Revolution took place over some 50 to 100 years, not the two or three decades that we have experienced. There is no doubt that information technology is transforming not only the organization of hospitals and their business processes but the fundamentals of medicine itself. The enhancement of images possible through computerization makes radiology and other diagnostic approaches far more powerful than they were previously. The ability to store and compare information and add to the global clinical database means that huge trials on alternative therapies can be conducted in a way that was not previously possible.

However, an information system doesn't necessarily mean a computer system. One of the best information systems in most hospitals is the theatre book. This manual record of what goes on in operating theatres is usually well maintained and highly specific and provides a valuable source for a variety of tasks. In most cases the need to computerize an information system is a result of a high volume of transactions. For example, a small company of perhaps 20 employees will happily use a manual payroll system. Each week the clerk can write into a multipart stationery booklet the hours worked, calculate the earnings, calculate the tax to be deducted and National Insurance and complete the pay slip. By adding up the page the total amount the company has to

331

pay to the Inland Revenue can be calculated. It's only when the number of employees increases and the task of addition becomes significant that the potential for computerization is there. When operational computer systems are installed, the benefits are usually to be found in relieving people of tedious and routine calculation or other tasks. In fact, if those benefits aren't there, then there should be questions about the need to computerize. Of course, in looking at the costs of computerization benefits, the dramatic decrease in costs of computers means that many simple applications which 10 or 15 years ago might have been best performed manually are now most cost-effectively performed on computer.

ACTIVITY

The key area of information for most clinical managers will relate to the activity of the directorate. This is the measure of what the directorate actually does and at its heart, of course, is the treatment of patients. A basic element of data recording in all healthcare systems is the patient record.

Why is there a patient record? What purpose does the big binder of case notes really serve? Setting to one side legal requirements, what other purpose does the record hold? Some might answer that clinical medicine is almost invariably delivered by a team of people and that the record helps any one member of the team to understand the totality of what's going on. Others might argue that it covers for the gaps in human memory and that it reminds us what we've already done, what provisional diagnosis we may already have reached. The clinical record is the basic information system in the treatment of an individual patient. It provides the hard facts, the data if you will, resulting from pathology tests, X-ray, interview, examination or some other approach to gaining an understanding of the patient as well as documenting the therapies applied and their perceived results. For hospital patients, it is a detailed document of the visible aspects of their ill health episode and, like the tip of the iceberg, may indicate a much greater wealth of data about periods prior to hospital admission and subsequent to discharge which have not been captured.

If we talk to any consultant or consultant team and ask them what they do, they could easily point to a pile of patient records and say 'That's the patients we treated last year'. In itself this wouldn't tell us much. We might want to count the number of files and gain a quick assessment of how many cases were treated. If the files were colour-coded, we could count how many were male and how many were female. Then we would want to gather some more detail. We would try to form some broad classification of the cases treated, either by outcome – 'how many died and how many were discharged alive?' – or more likely by diagnosis – 'how many were hernia repairs?'.

CLASSIFICATION

This immediately points up the need for some type of classification, preferably a standard one. Yet any classification brings us up against the uniqueness of the patient.

Clinicians rightly insist on the uniqueness of the individual patient. Each patient presents a unique set of symptoms reflecting their background, environment, genetic make-up and so on. No two patients react in the same way to a virus and no two patients will react in the same way to medication. However, the very basis of medical teaching and knowledge and of treatment is to seek to categorize and classify individuals. If we can determine the diagnosis, then we can select appropriate therapies and by monitoring the patient's reactions and categorizing them further (for example, penicillin allergic), we seek to tailor the generic therapies to the individual patient. The tension in the practice of medicine between the general principles and their unique application is reflected equally in clinical information systems.

The most perfect information system would capture everything that we can write down about the patient as well as investigations, such as X-rays and lab test results, in a completely free format, which would then be available for analysis. Even the electronic medical record, a long-term strategy both in the US and the UK, will find it difficult to capture the true richness of data about individual patients held by the clinical team.

Clinical hunches and intuition can often be traced to subconscious and highly specific observation and recall from experience. Given that not all the richness can be captured in an electronic data record, any attempt to capture facts about individual patients inevitably involves some form of classification. If we can at least put the patient in to some kind of pigeon hole, then we will be able to analyse and think about the different groups of patients, the different types of patients and the different treatments.

Most doctors will be familiar with the basic coding and classification systems in use in hospitals: International Classification of Diseases (ICD) (NHSME 1991, WHO 1977), the Office of Population Censuses and Surveys classification of surgical operations (OPCS 1987) and the detailed and extended Read codes, named after Dr James Read who developed them (Chisholm 1990). A hospital inpatient must, after discharge, be assigned a primary diagnostic code which indicates the reason, subsequent to investigation, for their stay in hospital. This primary diagnostic code, the underlying reason, can be amplified by secondary diagnostic codes indicating associated or multipathological conditions. Any procedures carried out in an operating theatre must also be coded according to the OPCS classification and identified in the basic data set which is passed to purchasers under the contract. The important point to consider in looking at issues of classification within the information system is the full path from the medical record through to the coded data. Understanding the way in which individual hospitals go about this task, the people involved and their responsibility and management structure is an important step in beginning to ensure quality control. If the basic data held in information system are incomplete or inaccurate then it will be difficult to use them to support sophisticated decision making, and indeed this may lead to poor quality decisions.

CODING

Until 10 years ago, most hospitals had a small, dedicated group of clinical coding staff, usually part of the medical records team, who coded all diagnostic codes from the medical record itself. They had little opportunity to refer back to clinical staff, were seen as part of 'administration' and were in no way linked into the clinical structure. Nowadays, many hospitals have either devolved coding (and coders) to directorates or made much stronger links between individual coders and the directorates they support. Only clinicians can decide which is the correct diagnosis to code, but they will need to work with coders to understand how the particular classification system in use locally is applied and the ambiguities that can arise (Read and Benson 1986). Most directorates will want to receive regular reports on the percentage of records being coded within 1 month and review the flow of records to prevent any bottlenecks.

GROUPING

Given the number of cases being treated, say 2000 per annum for a typical clinical directorate, and the wide range of diagnostic codes that they can carry, we need some broader clustering of similar patients in order to review activity. The NHSME, having done development work with diagnosis related groups (DRGs), an American developed analytic tool (Fetter et al 1980), have settled on a UK variant, known as healthcare resource groups (HRGs) (Sanderson 1992). Standard computer programmes are available from the Department of Health for hospitals to use in assigning patient records to HRGs. These HRGs provide a clinically sensible group of patients who are likely to use the same basic pattern of hospital resources within a statistical range.

CASE MIX

Provided the basic patient activity data are available and coded, they can be brought together with financial data and pathology, X-ray and other therapy data in a case mix system.

Introduced as a consequence of the original resource management programme (DHSS 1986), many acute hospitals have now developed or purchased the necessary software to provide case mix reports. Such reports, if the data are available from the other operational systems, allow directorates to review their spend against budget and determine whether any variation is due to a change in volume of activity, a change in the mix of patients or a change in patient treatment patterns.

STRATEGIC OVERVIEW

Most hospitals seem to have a wide variety of information systems, hungry beasts that need feeding with data by armies of clerks and which yet seem to provide little useful information. These disparate systems are often described as vital to some third party: the purchaser, the region or the Department of Health. Trying to understand what is in place and how these apparently disparate systems fit together, either now or at some point in the future, is often difficult. To gain this kind of overview you need to understand the organization's strategy.

Information and information technology are a basic support for the organization. In that sense they must never drive the organization, but must rather be responsive to the business and clinical needs. In other words, once the organization has formulated a clear view on its overall strategy, on what it is trying to achieve, then a necessary component is information to support that and the information technology to support the information requirement. Drawing up an information strategy is something that should be undertaken at least every 3 years and more frequently if major aspects of the organization change. Most information strategies are based on a simple three or four-step process:

1. Where are we now?
2. Where do we want to be? (Where will momentum take us?)
3. How do we get there?

The element in brackets is sometimes omitted but it is always important to acknowledge that there is an existing momentum to the organization and that some changes will take place in any event. Many health service strategies of the 1960s failed to acknowledge the continuing rise in referral rates and assumed hospital activity was essentially static. Not surprisingly, they grossly underestimated the costs of hospital care in the 1980s. All strategies need to acknowledge changes in external environmental factors.

NATIONAL IM & T STRATEGY

It will be important to consider national developments as one of the major external influences.

There is a national information management and technology strategy now for the NHS as a whole (NHSME 1992a,b). Some important elements of the national strategy which will need to be considered in developing local strategies are:

- the establishment of a national network;
- the clinical terms project;
- new format NHS number;
- integrated clinical work stations;
- electronic clinical records.

National network

The national network which is currently under discussion and development will enable data to be passed from one part of the NHS to another with suitable controls to ensure confidentiality. The possibility of transferring data from hospitals to general practitioners will be of interest to clinical staff. As more and more general practitioners become computerized, the potential for rapid electronic transfer, for example of discharge letters and even of information during a patient's stay, becomes a possibility. Whilst the national strategy will endeavour to put the infrastructure in place to enable such communication to take place, it will still leave individual hospitals with choices as to the extent to which they might take advantage of such interchange possibilities. Any local strategy would have to address such questions and involve hospital staff in consideration of the issues.

Clinical terms

The clinical terms project is developing a controlled vocabulary for clinical medicine to enable computerization of a far greater range of clinical information. It should enable local synonyms for particular conditions to be used confidently in discharge letters and other such documents, with agreed mapping back to nationally understood terms. The project looks to create a halfway house between numerical classification systems, such as ICD, and full text.

NHS number

Whilst all adults have, in theory, an NHS number, the wide number of different formats and a number of other problems mean that it is not possible to use NHS numbers as a unique identifier within computer systems. The potential to retrieve records from other hospitals, for example, is severely limited by the establishment of local patient numbers and an element of the national strategy is to establish and implement a national NHS number in a single format. As and when this is achieved hospitals will need to consider their own strategies, the way in which they take advantage of this possibility and the extent to which they move to a new NHS number as the core patient identifier in their systems.

Integrated clinical workstation

Hospital doctors are increasingly confronted with a variety of terminals which they need to access as part of their work in the hospital. They may wish to log on to a management information system, they may want to order drugs or request pathology tests through a ward-based terminal, they may want to access a bibliographic database or they may want to review a set of patients audit details. As the physical possibilities of integrating these systems together on to the same network are seized, then potential for them all to be presented at one terminal becomes apparent. The information management group of the NHSME are currently undertaking some project work on the way in which such systems might best be brought together for the benefit of clinicians and in particular, ways of presenting and working with this variety of information.

Electronic clinical record

The last element within the Department's strategic framework is the potential for electronic clinical records. It is important to emphasize that both in this country and in America, it has been recognized that the electronic clinical record is some way from being reality. The major problems involved in, for example, incorporating X-ray data into computer records mean that interim solutions and systems will develop and it is unlikely that significant and useful electronic clinical records will appear in less than a decade. Nevertheless it is important to be aware of their potential and the

Department hopes that by maintaining a development project in this area, it will be possible to keep the NHS at large advised on potential and progress.

OPERATIONAL SYSTEM OVERVIEW

Strictly speaking it is possible to write an information strategy without an information technology strategy and an information technology strategy can be seen as a logical consequence of, and associated with, an information strategy. Nevertheless, most organizations prepare a single strategy covering both aspects, but it is useful in reading them to endeavour to separate out the two strands. If you can get hold of your own hospital's information technology strategy you will find a considerable amount of information about the current basic information systems set up. You might want to match this against the basic systems diagram in Fig. 30.1.

In general most hospitals have a range of operational systems serving specific departments. Typically, we will find at least one or more pathology systems in each of the various pathology disciplines and an X-ray system. In general these areas have been computerized at some point in the past, because of the very high volume of individual transactions taking place. The number of requests which need to be managed by the laboratory in order to ensure that the correct test result is linked to the correct specimen and reported back to the original enquirer is a major administrative task. Similarly, radiology departments quite often have a system to manage the administration of X-ray requests. In addition, both departments are likely to have computer-supported equipment. X-ray machines increasingly have built-in 'intelligence' as do auto-analysers and other tools of the laboratory. Because staff are often computer-literate and interested in developing information systems, they have often been heavily involved in system choice, if not in system design.

Whilst most pharmacy departments have some form of computerization, particularly to produce labels, it is often not linked to a full information system. In particular, a considerable quantity of drugs are dispensed as top-up to ward stocks and cannot be tracked to individual patients. Whilst the existing system helps the pharmacy with its operational business, it does not provide the information which will be useful in a wider management context.

Many hospitals have now installed a theatre information system. Frequently this does not replace the theatre book but adds a further data collection load to the work of theatre staff. Information is collected about the operation, coded appropriately, the time it took and often some data about the prostheses and consumables used.

FROM APPLICATIONS TO FUNCTIONS

Thinking about and designing hospital computing is currently undergoing a massive conceptual shift. In the past, computer systems were usually application systems, that is, designed to do a particular set of jobs. In particular, most hospitals have what was called a patient administration system (PAS). This was essentially designed to help with the administrative task

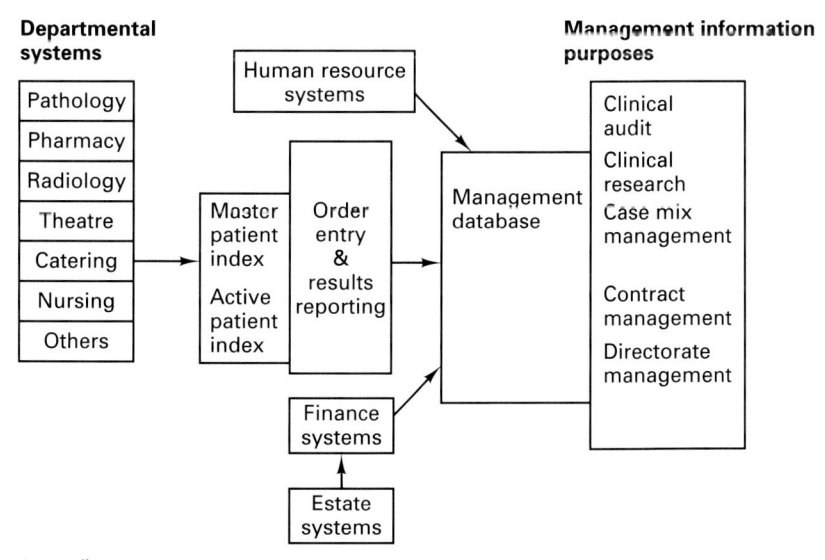

Fig. 30.1 Basic systems diagram

involved in patients attending either as inpatients or outpatients, providing them with an appointment and generating letters for admission, discharge letters and so on. They were precisely what they were called, administrative systems to deal with all the administrative tasks associated with a patient's hospital episode. What they didn't do, or did poorly, was provide any kind of analysis of the data on hospital activity. The PAS system was usually a large mainframe, had probably been bought by the region and was a very major and massive piece of computer technology. It was often seen as the core of the hospital's information technology and subsequent systems would attempt to link with it or in some way grow out of it. In fact PAS suppliers often went on to develop systems for radiology and other departmental usage.

As hospitals began to consider the wealth of data locked up in operational systems and the need to link data about, for example, use of X-ray with other patient data, they increasingly began to look to link the operational systems. The key to this was the realization that a core element of the traditional PAS systems was a patient index. The conceptual shift was to understand that this is the central database around which cluster a variety of functions. The principle of capturing data as few times as possible, preferably once and as close to the patient as possible, suggests that each of the departmental systems will want to draw down basic patient data, such as name, date of birth, address and so on, from the master patient index and, provided a unique hospital-wide identifier can be unambiguously assigned to the patient, will be able to use the central master patient index for this purpose. This is of course the key to being able to assemble any kind of patient activity database, reflecting all patients' use of the hospital resource.

The major step facing most hospitals in taking further advantage of technology for operational systems is to move from the variety of individual systems towards a full electronic environment with the functionality of order entry and results reporting. These two elements, which can be separated, are capable of transforming a hospital and the way in which staff go about their work with significant advantage if properly done. By order entry, we mean that the appropriate member of a clinical team can order or request a diagnostic test or therapeutic intervention from a support department electronically. For example, following the ward round, the ward sister on behalf of the clinical team can tap a password into the computer and put in a request for a particular test for a particular patient. The second element, results reporting, clearly has further complexities. For example, a pathology laboratory may receive a request for a battery of tests, perform some of those, get results that indicate to them that further different tests are required and also fail to perform other parts of the overall request. This partial completion and extension of requests requires sophistication of the reporting system.

One clear and significant consequence of the move to order entry and/or results reporting is a full communications network, linking all the systems together. This requires detailed consideration as part of an overall technology strategy. Not only the communication standards of the various systems need to be considered, but also the possible links to clinical communication systems and future communication requirements, for example audit systems or management information systems. Laying cabling around hospitals is an expensive operation and therefore requires a great deal of planning.

MANAGEMENT INFORMATION

Clinicians in clinical teams treat individuals and their record systems and note keeping are oriented around the individual. To think of groups of individuals, as we do in medical audit when we review care of a particular clinical group, is something done as part of the overall clinical management of the practice. In essence this is the difference between operational information systems and managerial information systems. Operational information systems are designed to provide immediate benefit to the task being undertaken, whilst managerial information systems, the data of which should always be derived from operational information systems, are intended to review the totality of work undertaken in a specific area and allow planning of future work.

The difference between operational and managerial information systems is a critical and important distinction when looking at information systems and information technology. Looking at Fig. 30.1, we see a variety of departmental systems, including those of the finance department and human resource (or personnel) department, all feeding data into a management database. This means that the wide variety of management information requirements shown as purposes can be supported by this database. In IT terms it is important to keep operational systems distinct from management information systems; after all, you don't want to cause a delay in the pathology system reporting a result because of some management report on all pathology tests for the last 3 years!

MANAGEMENT STRUCTURE AND REPORTS

A management information service needs to be structured around the organization's management structure.

If, for example, the organization includes a tertiary hospital (for hip replacement, say) and a DGH, managed as separate units, then an organizationwide report on drug costs will not be useful, cutting as it does across two different management domains. The basic reporting structure must be set up to reflect the management structure, providing data on those things that are within an individual manager's control.

An important task facing many clinical directors is to begin to organize the wide variety of reports already being provided into a routine package. Information specialists can usually help to determine the significant reports, and in particular to help construct high level reports which can indicate the need, or not, for more detailed analysis.

HUMAN RESOURCES

Few hospitals have a comprehensive human resource information system which can provide a range of management information. Those hospitals with no system usually rely on data generated as a byproduct of payroll processing, which can sometimes be ingeniously adapted. Clinical managers will want to monitor routinely data about recruitment and retention difficulties: unfilled vacancies and turnover rates, for example. Recent Audit Commission reports have highlighted the high costs associated with current levels of sickness absence and provide a useful set of comparative data. Other current issues may require ad hoc data analysis – any attempt to come to grips with the full potential implications of the Calman Report and the reduction of junior doctors' hours will need a very full analysis of current staffing, with probably a need to construct a model incorporating retirement and other variables.

ESTATE

Consideration of effective use of the estate was until recently the lone (and lonely) province of the works officer. The advent of capital charging and the inevitable devolution to clinical directorates of 'their share' of the estate costs means that clinical managers will want to review information on their use of land and buildings. Most trusts will have an estate information system capable of providing a range of management reports.

EXTERNAL COMPARISON

Internally generated information is the first concern in managing services but, given a detailed understanding of the activity of the directorate and its resource use and costs, managers will want to know how well they perform comparatively. There are a variety of sources of external comparative data (Lowry 1988). The Department of Health issue a performance indicator package (DoH 1990) allowing comparisons to be made across some 400 key ratios. A number of commercial concerns will provide anonymized comparison with a range of similar providers. The unit labour costs projects, initially sponsored by the Department of Health, allow review of productivity comparisons. Even clinical trials can provide a useful source of comparative data. Such comparisons pinpoint areas for more detailed local analysis.

OUTCOME

The principal focus of discussion has been on activity and use of resources. Clinical managers can review and improve both the structure and process of healthcare delivery. Ultimately, however, they will want to target such review, and measure its impact, by considering outcome.

A few clinical specialities, such as renal medicine, have a well-developed outcome measurement framework. Data supplied by units to the European Dialysis and Transplantation Association (EDTA) enable rates of 5-year survival post-transplant (for example) to be reviewed and compared. Most specialities, however, lack any such standardized data collection or even any agreement on what data to collect. Increasingly, however, clinicians will need to take a lead in suggesting local data to measure outcome.

The multidimensional nature of healthcare quality is now well understood and as well as clinical outcome, clinical managers will increasingly want to measure patients' own perceptions, perhaps using instruments like the Short Form 36 (Brazier et al 1992).

CONFIDENTIALITY

All personal data held on computer systems are subject to the Data Protection Act. The hospital has to register such systems and the uses to which they are put and individuals can request data about themselves from such systems for their own interest and review. Controls need to be in place to ensure that only those authorized to look at individual patient data can do so and that any unauthorized access is where possible prevented but at worst noted for subsequent investigation. As soon as you link computers together into a network you make the possibility of 'hacking' much more feasible and when any such network is linked to the outside world through telephone access, then sophisticated controls must be put in place. Apart from problems of unauthorized access there are the problems of a virus striking the system. Any users of a network system have responsibilities for only using disks which have been checked for viruses and avoiding otherwise infecting their system.

TRAINING

The NHS has increasingly recognized the needs for training for information management and information technology. Special initiatives in the past mean that most hospitals should have reasonably well-organized training centres teaching the basics of information technology and the use of a number of standard packages in the areas of word processing, spreadsheets and databases. Any new application which the hospital implements should, as a matter of routine, have a linked training programme for users. So if your hospital is installing a case mix management system or an executive information system then, if you are likely to be a user, expect to be consulted and offered training.

Additionally doctors may still wish to develop some basic understanding and knowledge of the standard computer tools of word processing, spreadsheets and databases. Enquiries of a local training specialist should indicate a variety of options including some classroom tuition and self-teach packages. It is often easiest to learn such tools around a real problem. For example, a budget proposal for service development may be most easily developed using a spreadsheet and would be a good simple application with which to gain understanding of technology. The ability to vary some of the basic numbers and recalculate the proposal quickly and accurately provides the 'pay-off'. Similarly a small-scale research project in a particular clinical area might be an appropriate guinea pig for learning to use databases. The ability to calculate statistical coefficients on a number of parameters and link that to graphical output might make it easier to write a research paper.

PROJECT CONTROL AND MANAGEMENT

The recent history of the NHS, and indeed of many other large organizations, is not a happy one in the area of information technology. Organizations do make mistakes and they are sometimes costly and in a public environment like the NHS, there are now a variety of procedures and controls designed as far as possible to ensure that sensible decisions are made in an appropriate and legal fashion. Increasing legislation in this area, particularly from the European Community, means that any system costing above about £90 000 needs to be advertised and tenders received in a structured way. Increasingly most NHS trusts are going out to tender for even smaller purchases.

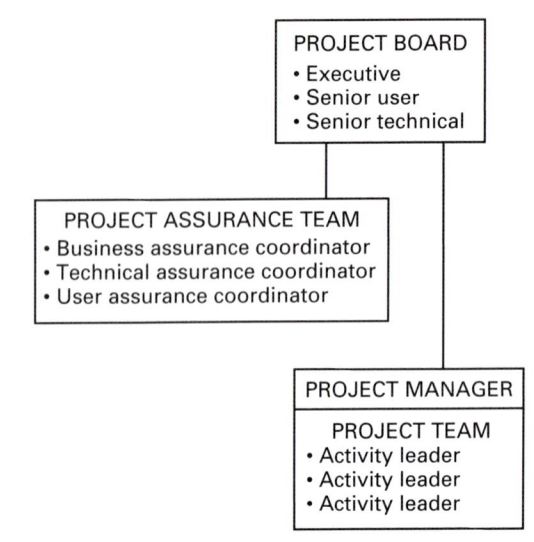

```
PROJECT BOARD
• Executive
• Senior user
• Senior technical

PROJECT ASSURANCE TEAM
• Business assurance coordinator
• Technical assurance coordinator
• User assurance coordinator

PROJECT MANAGER
PROJECT TEAM
• Activity leader
• Activity leader
• Activity leader
```

- The project board takes overall control of the project on behalf of the CEO
- The project assurance team monitor the progress of the project and assure the quality of product
- The project manager takes day-to-day responsibility for the project and manages individuals taking responsibility for specific elements of the project

Fig. 30.2 Typical PRINCE project structure

The procurement and implementation of new information technology systems should in most cases be managed as a project. In fact, the NHSME has recommended use of a standard known as PRINCE for project management within the NHS. Although this sounds like another area of jargon and bureaucracy, in fact the principles set out in any project management methodology are basic common sense and, interpreted sensibly for local use, should considerably reduce potential problems. A typical PRINCE project structure is shown in Fig. 30.2. Clinicians are increasingly likely to find themselves asked to join one of the teams set out. A notable feature is the existence of an identified individual, the project manager, working on a full or part-time basis, taking lead management responsibility for the project. This individual provides a point of focus for all those working in or affected by an information technology project and should be the key person trying to ensure the project is brought home on time, within budget and to a successful conclusion.

SUMMARY

Information is a critical resource for clinical managers.

An appreciation of data available in local information systems and the way in which such systems are structured is a necessary knowledge base. Clinical managers need to ensure that wherever possible relevant information is considered in management decision making and that the organization has a robust strategy to develop and deliver such information.

REFERENCES

Brazier J E, Harper R, Jones NMB et al 1992 Validating the SF36 health survey question. British Medical Journal 305: 160–164

Chisholm J (1990) The Read Classification. British Medical Journal 300: 1092

Department of Health 1990 Health service indicators guidance dictionary. HMSO, London

Department of Health and Social Security 1983 NHS management inquiry. HMSO, London

Department of Health and Social Security 1986 Health service management – resource management (management budgeting) in health authorities. Health notice HN (86)34. HMSO, London

Fetter R B, Shin Y, Freeman J L, Avverill R F, Thompson J D 1980 Case mix definition by diagnosis related groups. Medical Care 18: 1–53

Israel R A 1990 The history of the international classification of diseases. Health Trends 22: 43–44

Jenkins L, McKee M, Sanderson H 1990 DRGs: a guide to grouping and interpretation. CASPE, London

Lowry S 1988 Focus on performance indicators. British Medical Journal 296: 992–994

NHS Management Executive (a) 1991 International classification of diseases, 9th revision, with UK amendments and extensions. St Anthony, Alexandria, VA.

NHS Management Executive (b) 1992 IM & T infrastructure overview. HMSO, London

NHS Management Executive (c) 1992 IM & T study overview. HMSO, London

NHS Management Executive 1992 A view for hospital doctors. HMSO, London

Office of Population Censuses and Surveys 1987 Classification of surgical operations and procedures, 4th edn. OPCS, London

Read J D, Benson T J R 1986 Comprehensive coding. British Journal of Healthcare Computing 3: 22–25

Sanderson H 1992 Measuring case mix. British Medical Journal 304: 1067–1068

United States National Committee on Vital and Health Statistics 1980 International classification of diseases, 9th revision. Clinical Modification, 2nd edn. US Government Publishing Office, Washington DC

World Health Organization 1977 International classification of diseases: manual of the international statistical classification of diseases, injuries and causes of death, 9th revision 1975. WHO, Geneva

31

Management of learning and professional development through clinical audit

Gifford Batstone, Mary Edwards

INTRODUCTION

Effective clinical practice requires not just healthcare professionals who have up-to-date knowledge and skills and appropriate attitudes. It also needs these professionals to combine in collaborative and cohesive clinical teams, supported by organizations which are responsive to a changing environment of both patient and strategic needs. More importantly, professionals, teams and organizations need to learn from the experience of current practice in order to be proactive in determining the future direction of clinical developments rather than merely reacting to pressures from purchasers and professions. This chapter indicates the importance of clinical audit in this learning process at the level of the individual professional, the clinical team within which they work and the organization (unit, trust or primary healthcare team) in which that team functions. Clinical audit demonstrates the quality and effectiveness of clinical care and helps determine future learning needs. This relies on a fundamental principle that practice is based as far as possible on research evidence, using clinical guidelines where appropriate but remaining responsive to clinical needs together with the values, preferences and choices of the individual patient.

This chapter reviews the nature of learning and professional development in the current climate of change before describing clinical audit and how this may enhance learning. The role of the organization in promoting learning and improved practice is described as well as the need for proper education in audit techniques if the audit process is to enhance clinical effectiveness. Further information on multiprofessional clinical audit is given in Chapter 33.

NATURE OF LEARNING AND CONTINUING PROFESSIONAL DEVELOPMENT

One of the key discriminating features of a professional is the maintenance of standards. This may be organized through a professional body or more usually is achieved by the individual in a self-directed fashion, often in combination with professional bodies. The essential role of professional bodies such as the medical Royal Colleges is to set standards for membership and maintain public safety by promoting continuing education. However despite discussions concerning reaccreditation with professional bodies and the requirement to demonstrate continuing participation in educational activities, the maintenance of professional standards is still regarded by the majority of healthcare professionals as being a matter to be determined by the individual practitioner. In this sense the key factor of self-motivation in enhancing professional roles and activities is in accord with Brookfield (1986) when he describes the principles of motivation to participate in such self-directed learning as:

- voluntary participation;
- mutual respect of other professionals and their roles;
- collaborative spirit in seeking a common goal;
- praxis – a set of examples for practice to promote and implement change;
- critical reflection on current practice;
- self-direction.

The concept of continuing professional development as compared with traditional views of continuing education is important because it expands the curriculum outside the areas of diagnostic and therapeutic advances to include effects of healthcare delivery on individuals and society through personal, team or organizational activity. Continuing professional development as a broader phenomenon includes (Batstone & Edwards 1994):

- acquisition/application of new knowledge;
- better application of existing knowledge;
- enhanced management of healthcare
  — working in clinical teams
  — working within the organization;
- enhanced communication
  — with patients
  — within and between clinical teams
  — with managers;
- improved teaching skills;
- attention to social, cultural, ethical and psychological influences;
- effective use of information technology;
- maturation as a person.

Perhaps there is a need to differentiate between education and learning. Education is an activity which combines three essential elements:

1. a specified set of tasks to be achieved or knowledge to be acquired – basically some form of curriculum;
2. a person or group of persons who are present in order to come to terms with that curriculum – in short, a pupil;
3. another person or group of persons whose task it is to promote an effective and fruitful coming together of pupils and curriculum – a teacher.

To the individual however the process of learning may not require either a teacher or even a curriculum. In this sense learning, in the view of the person undertaking that learning, comes through a staged process of:

- reception of new material;
- engagement with it;
- development of new perceptions;
- undertaking new forms of activity.

Learning is often unrecognized and certainly underreported as it is often incidental or an implicit part of, say, clinical audit rather than a purposeful process. Learning may be:

- incidental – an automatic response to a finding, circumstance or information;
- purposeful – a structured change aimed at mastery which may involve the uptake of a curriculum and use of a facilitator.

Further, learning may lead to a variety of outcomes:

- confirmation of current practice, views or knowledge;
- reinforcement of certain aspects of a process of care leading to a greater determination to achieve specific ways of working;
- change in practice which may involve just the individual but more likely the range of professionals with whom that individual works.

It is in this sense that the word learning is used in this chapter and is not necessarily synonymous with education.

Learning in a changing environment

Motivation to participate in continuing professional development is difficult in an environment where reforms in the organization of healthcare delivery, increasing patient empowerment and thus expectation, purchaser demands and so on are often interpreted as perturbing the traditional role of staff delivering healthcare. Such changes are commonly considered to diminish professional learning through generation of frustration. Perhaps the truth is found in Winston Churchill's comment that 'the most important thing about education is appetite'. In such a changing and perturbed environment, learning and the educational aspects of audit need to be promoted not just as another duty or chore to add to the burden of the day but as a positive strategy for dealing with the changing environment.

Learning enables people:

- to overcome threats of a changing environment by anticipating change and promoting those areas which will lead to improved patient care;
- to gain power to meet the load of daily tasks through finding novel approaches to care;
- to maintain professional independence and direct interdependence.

This approach to learning may be enhanced through:

- critical review of current practice;
- seeking opportunities for improvement;
- considering alternative perspectives;
- experimenting with options.

In this environment, which needs to be stimulated from the top of the organization, learning is seen as proactive response anticipating change to meet:

- factors identified through the care of individuals;
- local needs of the unit/trust/primary healthcare team;
- patient needs as assessed by satisfaction surveys, comments/complaints, community health councils, consumer organizations, etc.;

- purchaser requirements based on needs assessment of the population served;
- *Health of the Nation* and other strategic targets.

Later in this chapter we will address the role of the organization in which a healthcare professional works in helping to maintain and even promote that appetite for learning that Churchill described. In addition the nature of learning organizations will be described.

Role of education in changing practice

The impact of continuing education on clinical practice has been reviewed by a number of authors. Davis et al (1992), in their review of 50 randomized controlled trials of continuing medical education interventions in various fields of clinical practice, concluded that changes in physician behaviour were achievable. Of more interest was the style of intervention or combination of interventions used and the effect on the performance of doctors and the benefits achieved in patient healthcare. Simple dissemination of information generally led to negative or inconclusive results. When dissemination was combined with practice visits, provision of printed materials, workshops, clinical flowcharts or computer-generated prompts there was a greater change in doctors' performance but little change in patient care. Dissemination when combined with feedback and reminders in addition to printed materials and other predisposing techniques had a greater effect on improving patient outcomes. More complex approaches combining all the above with the use of opinion leaders and clinical audit gave the greatest change in both doctors' performance and patient healthcare, although the number of trials for the last category was rather small. Similar results have been found with the uptake of clinical audits as summarized below.

Studies by Fox et al (1989) have highlighted the role of education when doctors decide to make change(s) in their practice. The research they report asks the question about the effectiveness of continuing education in a different fashion. By interviewing doctors who had made changes in practice, they were able to assess the reasons/stimuli for that change, the interventions that were used to achieve it and the effectiveness of the change process.

The reasons for change in practice cited by the interviewees were:

- desire for enhanced competence (24%);
- perception that their clinical environment pressed for change (14%);
- to improve personal financial status (9%);
- to further career development (8%);
- promotion of personal well-being (8%);
- pure curiosity (4%);
- relationship with colleagues at work (11%);
- professional pressures (9%);
- response to regulations (10%).

The doctors studied linked their changes to episodes of evaluation or the effects of transitions in their lives. Over two thirds of the changes involved some kind of learning and the greater the change undertaken the larger the educational input was evident.

Continuing medical education/ continuing professional development as a provider function

As part of the White Papers introducing the NHS reforms, an unnumbered working paper on postgraduate training and continuing medical education (DoH 1990) was produced which indicated that the responsibility for continuing professional development of doctors is a provider function and not that of purchaser or regional health authority. As part of the same process Working Paper 10 set down the arrangements for the

Table 31.1 Factors influencing the uptake of guidelines (after Grimshaw and Russell 1993)

Relative probability	Development strategy	Dissemination strategy	Implementation strategy
High	Internal	Specific educational intervention	Patient-specific reminders at consultation
Above average	Intermediate	Continuing medical education	Patient-specific feedback
Below average	External local	Posting target groups	General feedback
Low	External national	Publication (prof. journal)	General reminders

purchase of non-medical preregistration/undergraduate training. Working Paper 10 does not cover continuing professional development of non-medical staff, which therefore is also, presumably, a provider function. In general practice the Postgraduate Education Allowance (PGEA) scheme rewards general practitioners for participation in educational programmes which are approved by the regional adviser in general practice or the GP tutor on behalf of the adviser. Here CPD is a provider role but with a professional oversight of its content.

This approach is consistent with the contractual arrangements for healthcare professionals working in trusts or in general practice. As CPD is part of the mechanism by which organizations should pursue their objectives, they should have some responsibility for promoting its uptake and should influence its content. For professional staff this creates concerns especially where they perceive CPD not as part of a mechanism for organizational development, but as an isolated professional issue leading to continual squabbling between professionals and managers. Purchasers also have a responsibility in ensuring that sufficient funding is available within contracts to meet educational needs. For the purchaser this may of course be linked to achieving specific targets as part of their own or national strategic goals. For instance purchasers may agree funding for education of appropriate professionals in the use of limited access surgery, improved care of head injury or reduction in pressure sores. Unfortunately most provider organizations do not have a multiprofessional approach to education. Whilst medicine has a system of clinical tutors responsible to the postgraduate dean and college tutors responsible to specific medical Royal Colleges, the structures for other professions are varied and there is little integration at local level between professional groups and those interested in educational matters for individual professions. Such integration will be essential if organizations are to effect improvements in clinical practice especially through the implementation of multiprofessional clinical guidelines.

Role of professional bodies in continuing education

Increasingly professional bodies are taking a lead by increasing their area of influence from the setting of standards for membership into continuing education. Few, however, have widened their area of interest to include the agenda of continuing professional development.

An example of this is the United Kingdom Central Council's proposals for the re-registration of nurses based on professional updating known as Postregistration Education and Practice (PREP). This enables nurses to demonstrate their learning by highlighting areas for study, ways in which learning was achieved and most importantly how this learning modifies their clinical practice. Clinical audit is an aspect of learning which is encouraged in the PREP scheme (UKCC 1994) and fits well in the portfolio learning approach (see below). The Institute of Biomedical Sciences have for the past 4 years organized a scheme leading to a diploma based on the acquisition of credits over a 5-year period (Allison & Loaring 1992). Credits are linked both to formal educational activities and professional activities such as task force membership or learning new skills. Recognized activities are recorded in an activity record card. Most medical Royal Colleges are promoting continuing medical education by requiring members to obtain a given number of cognate points earned by attendance at approved courses or activities. These approaches parallel methods of re-registration and recertification of professional clinical staff in the USA based on points accumulation from courses/conferences.

The Postgraduate Educational Allowance (PGEA) scheme in general practice links attendance at educational activities in the areas of practice management, disease management and disease prevention to financial reward.

Such approaches give healthcare professionals an approved set of educational activities from which to choose but do not help individuals target any objectively defined educational/learning needs. Often the choice relates to special areas of interest and areas of established expertise. The Royal College of Pathologists is promoting a project in Wessex region by which this cognate point approach is linked to needs assessment through a paired peers approach. It is anticipated that pathologists will meet at least twice a year with a colleague from another trust to discuss areas of development within their speciality, areas of personal strength and weakness, possible ways of meeting educational needs and monitoring progress in achieving learning targets. The RCGP fellowship scheme goes further in setting specific targets of performance for general practitioners which are formally reviewed by a team of peers to obtain fellowship status.

Some professional bodies have incorporated participation in national clinical audit activities within their cognate point system, e.g. the Royal College of Pathologists, whilst the UKCC accept local audit activity as part of PREP. The reason why medical Royal Colleges have not included local audit activity within their points systems for continuing education is not that they do not recognize its educational value but because of the contractual obligation of medical staff to participate in audit.

The Dynamic Standard Setting System (DySSSy) project (Kitson et al 1994) which focused on helping nurses agree standards demonstrated the importance of group dynamics in achieving change in clinical practice through the standard-setting process. The approach is based on professional interaction, which was found to require expert facilitation to be effective. The Royal College of Physicians and Surgeons of Canada has introduced a maintenance of competence programme (MOCOMP 1993). This involves a diary approach to self-directed continuing medical education which indicates a topic and methods of learning both formal and informal used to address that topic. Further the doctor indicates whether as a result of the activity clinical practice will be modified. Educational activities are collected into an annual profile of self-directed projects, uptake of formal educational events and use of self-assessment and practice evaluation schemes – very similar to portfolio learning. This annual profile is compared with that of specialists in the same field and the range of CME topics offered by the college as a form of review to help determine further educational needs.

Critical thinking, reflection and learning

The concept of thinking critically about clinical activity is a positive force in the development of clinical services and appears to be the cornerstone of self-directed and team-directed learning. There are a number of phases of critical thinking as described by Brookfield (1987):

- trigger event which raises the potential for change;
- appraisal of the current situation;
- exploration of options for change;
- developing alternative perspectives;
- integration with current philosophy, knowledge and practice.

Those who understand clinical audit will recognize the close similarity of this series of steps to those of the audit cycle (see Chapter 33 for more detail) shown in Fig. 31.1.

Both critical thinking and audit start with a stimulus event which leads to some consideration of current practice and its purpose. Audit uses the discipline of standard setting and practice monitoring followed by peer review as the process of 'appraisal of the current situation' and as a basis for considering options for change. (Often when considering an audit topic, options for change may follow the stage of 'reflection on service' and the audit process used to review the effectiveness of the improved aspect of care.) Both critical thinking and audit require some development of new perspectives and integration of these into practice.

Clinical expertise – personal mastery

Donald Schon (1991) has described interesting insights into the nature of the expert practitioner. He indicates the need for clinical practitioners to learn from experience; a process which has five stages:

Fig. 31.1 The audit cycle

1. The first stage, termed 'knowing in action', assumes that practitioners cannot practise effectively unless their knowledge is action-orientated as opposed to theoretical. This knowing in action includes those practices which are so ingrained that they are almost automatic such as the recognition of common symptoms and signs of a clinical diagnosis.

2. The second stage deals with the occasions when patient findings do not fit with the current stream of knowledge in action – the element of surprise such as an inconsistent clinical findings, laboratory test or response to therapy.

3. This leads to the third stage of 'reflection in action' when in response to this surprise knowledge, skills and events are reconstructed to meet the challenge of the surprise to resolve any ambiguity or conflict. This process occurs not after the event but during the interaction between practitioner and patient to develop a response appropriate for that encounter.

4. Schon's fourth stage is termed 'experiment' in the sense of trying to find further information by rephrasing a question, listening to the patient view, repeating part of the physical examination, changing a procedure, etc. This indicates the ability of the practitioner to seek data and reconstruct existing information to meet the unusual features of a particular clinical case.

5. The final stage of integration takes place after the interaction and seeks to make sense of the surprise and the way in which it was resolved. This enables the recent experience to modify established personal practice and gives a new frame of reference for future cases.

Another way of perceiving the way in which practitioners learn from their daily clinical experience has been described by Argyris (1993) as the difference between what he calls single and double loop learning. This difference is demonstrated in the simile of a radiator. The single loop learning radiator knows to warm a room when the temperature falls to a certain level and allow it to cool when a given upper temperature is achieved. The double loop learning radiator has this knowledge but asks pertinent questions about the span of the day for which this temperature is required, other ways of achieving the temperature balance, etc.

The role of reflection on clinical practice is important in the approaches to learning of both Schon and Argyris. Another author, David Boud (Boud et al 1985), describes the role of reflection as a series of events:

- returning to the experience in a factual and objective fashion;
- attending to feelings surrounding the experience;
- reevaluating the experience in the light of further thought;
- association of the experience with new information;
- integration with other ideas;
- validation by testing against other models;
- appropriation as part of a new way of thinking;
- outcomes and action based on implementation of appropriated thought.

This approach emphasizes that both the objective data and the individual or group response to that data need to be resolved for learning to occur from an experience. As will be shown later in this chapter these stages are close to those of the clinical audit cycle.

Learning diaries and portfolio learning

Keeping leaning diaries or journals of professional development is recognized as an important method of promoting learning whilst monitoring its effect on professional practice and reflecting on practice (Holly 1987). Portfolio learning is a learning cycle that enables self-development and group development through the achievement of personal or team goals. Warren Redman (1990) described the process of portfolio building as a five-stage process:

1. The starting point is the person's existing experience, commencing with the breadth of experience.
2. The next step is to reflect on specific aspects of that experience and describe what has been learnt from it.
3. The following stage is that of demonstration of learning from experience.
4. From this, learning needs are assessed building on known strengths and weaknesses with respect to the area of activity.
5. The final stage is the identification of learning opportunities and development of a personal or group programme of educational activities.

He regards the process as being cyclical in that the identification of learning opportunities leads back to considering the breadth of experience and reflecting on the depth of prior learning.

In practical terms the portfolio is a way of recording the results of 'critical reflection' concerning an area of professional activity. Normally the learner has a learning file in which to jot down ideas, thoughts, insights, challenges, etc. which have arisen from everyday work and also a portfolio in which a more considered record of thoughts are kept together with key photocopies, photographs, diagrams, etc. which are pivotal to the thinking described.

To the learner the portfolio, as a record of learning, provides a means of assessment of professional development, of evaluation of possibilities for future change and a means of demonstrating this learning for accreditation and similar purposes, e.g. receipt of educational funding (PGEA) or education credits (PREP). Use for accreditation purposes involves an assessment of the portfolio by a senior professional or group of professionals. Recently the Royal College of General Practitioners (1993) has described an approach to portfolio learning for primary care.

NATURE OF CLINICAL AUDIT

Clinical audit has been described as being 'essentially educational' in a variety of Department of Health and NHSME documents including Working Paper 6 (DoH 1989), speeches by Secretaries of State for Health (Clark 1990) and the NHSME publication *Clinical audit: meeting and improving standards in health care* (DoH 1993). This concept has been supported by professional bodies such as the Royal College of Physicians 1989 who consider education to be the most important outcome from participation in audit. A more recent publication *The evolution of clinical audit* (DoH 1994a) links audit to both educational systems and professional development. It describes audit as systematically looking at the procedures used for diagnosis, care and treatment, examining how associated resources are used and investigating the effect care has on the outcome and quality of life for the patient. Clinical audit has also been defined by Batstone & Edwards (1994) as 'multidisciplinary, professional, patient-focused audit, leading to cost-effective, high quality care delivery in clinical teams'. As such it is a professional process leading to enhanced quality of care for patients achieved through the continuing professional development of health professionals as individuals and in teams.

A more detailed discussion of clinical audit is given in Chapter 33.

Learning from clinical audit

Learning opportunities occur in three areas of the audit cycle as shown in Fig. 31.2.

These three areas for learning are:

1. The first (A) linking the stages of reflection and negotiation of standards including recognizing the importance of the roles of other professionals and views of patients/carers whilst ensuring that clinical care and audit standards are based on sound research evidence.

Receiving a stimulus This may arise from published guidelines, research evidence, observing others' practice, untoward events, complaints, purchaser input or proposed clinical service development.

Reflecting on current service/practice This stage may include reflecting on the purpose and nature of the service required to achieve care needs through a critical review, redefinition of the service, reflection on the style of the service, reading research findings, guidelines, etc. The aim is to ensure that standards set for the service

Fig. 31.2 Learning opportunities in the audit cycle

are both relevant to patient need and are evidence based.

Negotiating standards At this point the team negotiate objective indicators of good practice together with the frequency with which they should be achieved. Specific exceptions are defined and sources for data concerning these indicators identified. It is vital that these indicators are agreed with all the professional groups having a legitimate interest and role in the area of patient care under consideration.

2. The second (B) relating to the process of peer review and considering options for change.

Monitoring practice At this stage data are collected and analysed and then a report is prepared for presentation to the peer review meeting.

Peer reviewing of findings At the review meeting, peers note compliance and non-compliance with standards, reviewing facts initially but allowing time for attitudes and concerns to be expressed. It is vital that known, surmised and other possible reasons for the cause of problems are considered. It is necessary to be aware of the natural tendency of all those who are keen to perform in a professionally correct fashion to rationalize their behaviour and generate defensive attitudes which may on occasion perturb the open review of the data. As the Alment Report (1976) stated 'The purpose of both peer review and self-assessment for practising doctors should be educational'.

Considering options for change This is based on the diagnosis of any problems found. The aim is to consider all possible options, even those which may have been considered initially as 'unthinkable'. Involvement of general managers in appraising options, especially if their help will be needed in implementation of change, is essential. Before selecting the best option it is necessary to consult widely about change whilst being aware of defensive comments and their negative effects and influences. The process of considering all the options openly and without bias is another part of the learning from audit.

3. The third area (C), of more directed and purposeful learning, is often one of the key methods in an implementation plan for effecting a change in clinical service. In this respect the audit activity is recognized as a method of needs assessment for education and learning.

Planing and implementing change Changes in clinical practice may involve operational or educational elements or, more frequently, both:

- Operational changes deal with structure, e.g. equipment and/or process, e.g. clinical procedure, skill mix, local protocols, etc.
- Educational input to change may involve feedback on performance, further review of guidelines, training about guidelines, specific educational programmes for groups, clinical teams or individuals. This educational approach may involve self-directed learning, tutor-initiated education, a wide variety of learning styles and comparison of local audit findings with those of other professionals and clinical teams.

A fourth aspect of learning is the demonstration that learning has not only happened but has also changed clinical practice to meet the standards of care agreed by the clinical team – a process called closing the loop. This stage involves moving through the cycle again to ensure that practice has changed. This is part of attempts to constantly improve the quality of service involving reflection on the new service, renegotiation of the standards of care and reaudit at a specified time. Further, this stage may be used to demonstrate the learning and development achieved as a summative rather than a formative assessment.

If learning needs have been discovered in an audit cycle and addressed through an appropriate learning programme, then subsequent cycles will demonstrate the effectiveness of that learning process in behavioural terms. As a way of evaluating learning this is the most important, as demonstrated by Kirkpatrick's (1975) hierarchy of learning:

1. Reaction – satisfaction with educational programme
2. Learning – demonstration of knowledge/skills
3. Behaviour – transferring learning to everyday practice
4. Results – changes in outcome: patient and organization.

Clinical audit of process will indicate whether learning has changed behaviour and audit of outcomes will show the results of that changed behaviour.

As the process of clinical audit involves reviewing current practice against standards of care developed by team consensus it is essentially a reflective process based on clinical experience of the style described by David Boud (Boud et al 1985).

Linking clinical audit findings to formal educational processes

As indicated above, clinical audit will indicate learning needs of individuals, professional groups, clinical teams and even organizations. These learning needs at individual, professional and clinical team level may be of knowledge, skills or attitudes, which may appear as inappropriate application of existing knowledge or skills. Where knowledge, skills or attitudes are limiting factors to performance (Batstone 1992) the following approaches may be used:

- literature review
- programmed reading
- self-assessment exercises
- tutorials
- demonstrations
- shadowing
- secondment
- feedback or even counselling
- courses
- (re-)writing guidelines.

The Industrial Society in an internal memo lists 48 ways of developing an individual of which lectures and attending conferences are but two. Perhaps this indicates the excessive interest placed by most healthcare professionals and managers on educational processes outside the normal place of work, whereas the Industrial Society, like many interested in professional development, emphasizes importance of work-based and workplace learning. This is not only because workplace learning may be less expensive with less loss of staff time but primarily because it is a more effective way of improving professional practice, promoting team development and helping to meet the needs of patients.

Here clinical audit becomes a method of assessment of educational needs by comparison of actual practice with the style and values of practice declared in the negotiation of standards or criteria. As indicated these educational needs may be individual or relate to a specific profession, clinical team or even the entire organization.

Clinical audit as a process of experiential learning

The audit cycle may be considered and redrawn from the viewpoint of experiential learning. This style of learning concentrates on the process of reflection on the experience of clinical practice, as described by Boud et al and discussed above. The cycle may be considered as a process of reconsidering the assumptions and values by which clinical practice is undertaken, interpreting stimuli received during current clinical experience – as in the early stages of the audit cycle – and linking these to specific learning activities such as those listed in the section above. This leads to a new style of practice, whether technological, organizational, etc., which becomes the subject of further refinement through reflection.

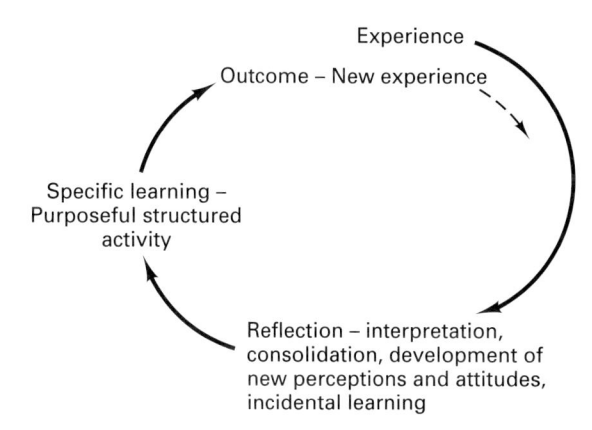

Fig. 31.3 The experiential audit cycle

To the learner, the personal aspects of clinical audit seem paramount, but to improve clinical practice, organizational change needs to parallel this experiential cycle. The balancing of these two routes is a key factor in the success of clinical audit. The response of most acute trusts to the CEPOD findings is an example of where professional learning appears to have outstripped organizational change to the great frustration of clinical staff. For example, the need to provide additional operating time during daylight hours was immediately appreciated by professionals when they reviewed the evidence but for this to change, the pattern of operating required a considerable rethink of resource deployment by the trust managers which inevitably took much longer. On the other hand many managers recognized that improvements in resuscitation and avoidance of fluid overload were also important and within the remit of clinical staff who often appeared to show less interest in this than additional operating time.

The role of group learning in clinical audit

Learning associated with the standard-setting process involves review not of current practice but of research evidence, clinical guidelines from professional bodies, patient/carer views and information on clinical effectiveness. It is critical to success that standards used in clinical audit are evidence driven and not simply a statement of current custom and practice and to ensure that guidelines are implemented successfully requires a change management and education process that includes (Batstone & Edwards 1994):

- dissemination to all relevant healthcare professionals;
- adaptation to meet local needs/skill mix;

- adoption by all healthcare professionals involved;
- implementation of modified practice;
- monitoring of this process;
- evaluation of outcomes.

The first two stages and the third in part are educational processes, with the third and fourth being part of change management and the last two clinical audit of process and outcome.

However, the educational strengths of audit spread more widely and include (Batstone 1990):

- small group work, which is effective in modifying attitudes and management of clinical conditions;
- critical review of current practice, which encourages learning about new techniques and treatments and when to use them;
- review of current practice, leading to reinforcement of agreed procedures and thus making the teaching of trainees more explicit and practice based;
- observation of practice, which may indicate gaps in knowledge, skills and attitudes for which appropriate educational programmes may be developed.

With the evolution to clinical audit further educational strengths may be added:

- learning from other professionals about roles, approaches to care, objectives, ways of working, etc.;
- greater consideration of the appropriateness and timeliness of interventions.

Overcoming barriers to learning from clinical audit

Learning associated with enhancing the quality of care is a wider agenda involving not only individuals and the clinical team but the structure, processes and priorities of the organization. Specific educational activities may also arise from audit findings for individuals, professional groups or the clinical team as a whole. For this learning to be effective it is important that the team has a leader capable of promoting learning from the audit process. Within this context the factors for effective learning are:

- arousal of interest in those involved;
- gaining acceptance of potential benefit, that it is worth the effort;
- learner goals are determined as the project develops;
- goal colineraity – that everyone shares a common purpose;
- listening/contributing in small groups;
- acceptance of equality of views of participants;
- environment for learning – critical thinking, hospitality to novel ideas;
- presentation of material for discussion – objective data accepted by the team;
- other learners' experience – prior knowledge and experience;
- own experience;
- creating desire to reach a solution.

For the leader of clinical audit it is necessary to develop strategies to overcoming barriers to learning from clinical audit:

- *'Unsafe' environment* Creation of an environment for effective learning from clinical audit depends on creation of such an atmosphere by both senior clinicians and general managers. Within the context of specific audit meetings the way in which the room is arranged, data presented and many other environmental features are important (Batstone 1992).
- *Educational versus service pressures* For learning to occur there needs to be a margin of power over load, where load represents the quality and complexity of tasks to be achieved in the working day and power the ability to achieve these tasks (McClusky 1970). Education can increase the power of both the team and the individual.
- *Limited view of professional education* The need to recognize the wider agenda of continuing professional development.
- *Failure to promote reflection* As indicated above, Boud (Boud et al 1985) has indicated the steps in the reflective process leading to change in clinical practice which need to be promoted.
- *Lack of critical thinking* In this context critical thinking is seen as a positive force for improving patient care.
- *Lack of openness* This covers openness in accepting professional roles as well as weaknesses in oneself and others.
- *Poor understanding of adult learning* The principles of adult learning based on Malcolm Knowles (1990) are given below and act as a guide to promoting learning from audit as well as indicating why the audit process is a valuable learning mechanism.
- *Failure to develop educational plans* Development of individual, team and organizational learning plans from clinical audit activity is essential if the maximum benefit is to be achieved from audit.
- *Unwillingness to accept learning needs* Acceptance of learning needs comes with openness and a sense of common purpose with respect to the audit topic.

Another approach to considering the value of clinical audit as a learning process is to consider audit with respect to the principles of adult learning described by Knowles (1990):

- individuals know what they might gain from the effort of learning;
- they determine the course and pace of their learning;
- learning is related to their own experience;
- topics are those which help them deal more effectively with everyday problems;
- topics relate to actual tasks and problems;
- learning is seen to enhance job satisfaction and self-esteem.

Certainly audit concentrates on learning based on personal experience, relates to actual tasks and problems, helps individuals deal more effectively with such problems and has the potential to enhance job satisfaction. However, it also involves elements of challenge, confrontation and critical analysis of oneself, the team of which one is a member and the role of that team in patient care which Brookfield (1986) describes as being important stimuli to learning.

Learning from audit is very different to the more traditional education received at school, college or university (Batstone & Edwards 1994) as follows:

Traditional	Audit
Curriculum based	Needs based
Authoritarian	Rational
Teacher centred	Learner centred
Individual	Group
Competitive	Open
Accepting	Critical
Theoretical	Experiential

The value of audit comes from its learning format which meets individual and team needs in a style which is more likely to generate changes in behaviour leading to enhanced clinical care rather than simply involve the uptake of knowledge and skills – see Kirkpatrick (1975).

The process of change, even to enhance clinical care, involves a variety of emotional responses and associated attitudes which the leader of clinical audit will need to recognize to help individuals take a positive attitude to changes arising from audit activity. These changes have been described by Lewin (1975) as shown in Fig. 31.4.

In response to a challenge on personal performance or the assumptions concerning care delivery there is a natural tendency for individuals and groups of individuals to follow the curve shown in Fig. 31.4. Initially there is a phase of denial of the force for change (the challenge) which is followed by active resistance to the

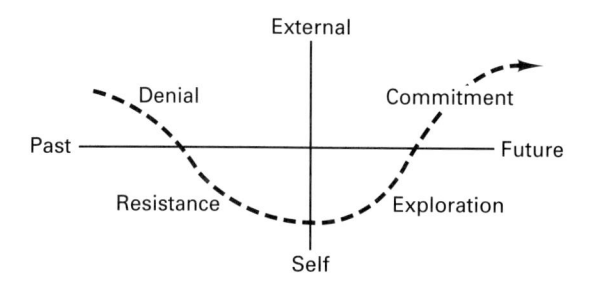

Fig. 31.4 Emotional responses to change

change and those trying to implement that change. With time there develops an exploration of the new proposals, especially to find points that may be of personal advantage. When areas within the change that are considered valuable are recognized, these are then incorporated into practice as commitment to the change happens. Full participation in clinical audit requires the challenging of assumptions concerning clinical care, a phenomenon which is uncomfortable and which, if not handled carefully, will lead to denial of the need for change, resistance to change and entrenchment in current practice. Leaders of clinical audit will need to help colleagues through these processes especially at the stages of resistance and the tendency to waste effort 'chasing hares' at the stage of exploration.

Examples of the learning aspects of audit

Patrick Jeffrey (personal communication, 1994) has allowed us to use his experience of being involved in an audit of breast cancer services. We have attempted to tell the story with annotations indicating the learning activities being undertaken whether conceptual or problem specific, experiential or deliberate, formal or informal (Fox et al 1989). Problem-specific learning deals with a specific issue whereas conceptual learning is more about the assumptions on which care is based or the linking of ideas. Deliberate learning refers to use of library facilities, courses, etc., whereas experiential learning is that achieved through reflection on audit findings. Informal learning occurs at an individual or group level when the purpose of meeting is not to achieve that learning as opposed to formal learning opportunities where attendance is to gain specific education. Key learning aspects of this audit are shown in Table 31.2.

This audit has led to considerable change in the delivery of service but more importantly has modified clinical practice with an emphasis on assessing and meeting patient needs and feelings. The story also indicates the learning that comes from patient input to the clinical audit process.

Table 31.2 Learning aspects of audit

The audit as it unfolded	Learning aspects of the audit
Patrick, a surgeon who has a special interest in the surgery for and treatment of breast cancer, began to consider whether his joint follow-up clinics with a radiotherapist were appreciated by both patients and general practitioners and indeed whether they were worthwhile. The concept of an audit of the care of patients with breast cancer was conceived and consideration of standards commenced.	Curiossity – conceptual, informal, experiential Literature review – deliberate, problem solving
Whilst attending a national meeting to hear a discussion of risk management, he listened to a lecture about the role of consumers in healthcare given by Marianne Rigge, director of the College of Health. This confirmed his curiosity and extended the area of interest to a much more patient-orientated view of the audit.	Information association – conceptual, informal. Elaboration – deliberate, conceptual
Contact was made with the College of Health in order to learn of their experience in assessing patient perceptions of clinical care. This involved the staff of the audit department and the nurse responsible for promoting the quality of care. At this point a list of all interested parties was made and Patrick undertook to contact them concerning the audit project.	Communication – deliberate, conceptual, informal Disseminating awareness – deliberate, informal
A previous audit of fine needle aspiration had involved histopathologists, who were readily recruited to the new project. Discussions with radiologists and radiographers concentrated thoughts on areas of their work which were relevant and standard setting began. Standards from the National Breast Screening Programme were adapted to suit patients presenting with disease by surgical and nursing staff. The radiotherapist concentrated on standards for access to the service whilst pharmacy considered the delivery of chemotherapy.	Literature review – deliberate, problem solving Revision of guidelines – deliberate, problem solving Consensus standards – deliberate, informal
The College of Health undertook semistructured interviews with patients based on findings from their previous studies. Ethical committee approval had been sought for these interviews, criteria agreed and a patient selection procedure for a retrospective audit undertaken.	Seeking patient views – deliberate, conceptual
The findings of the audit were discussed at a number of peer review meetings. The College of Health findings were initially reported to Patrick and the lead audit assistant before being discussed by a wider group including medical, nursing, OPD and quality staff. Other peer groups discussed data relevant to their particular input and proposals discussed within the wider group. From this an action plan with dates for completion was agreed.	Peer review meetings – experiential and deliberate Agreeing change – deliberate, formal, problem solving
Some actions were undertaken immediately in response to patients' views, e.g. suggesting patients brought someone to drive them home because they might find breast aspiration uncomfortable, whilst others required planning, e.g. making pyjamas rather than openback gowns available for mammograms. Some senior staff have attended courses in counselling techniques. Over the next 6 months an agreed programme of improvements was implemented. Further, it was agreed to repeat the audit including the consumer element in 18 months to confirm that learning and change had taken place to find out what new lessons need to be learnt.	Implementing change through explanation – conceptual, deliberate, informal Further learning – formal, deliberate, problem solving Planned review – openness to further possibilities for learning and problem solving

ROLE OF ORGANIZATIONS

The development of the healthcare team regarded as critical for successful clinical audit may be based upon the model identified by Adair (1988) which sees the need for a successful organization to:

- develop the individual
- build the team
- achieve the task.

Healthcare organizations will only achieve their aims through creating a style which promotes learning and critical review at both individual and clinical team levels.

In the study by Batstone (1994) the development of clinical audit within organizations was seen as a process which had five stages of maturation each with its own style of audit and each having prerequisites to meet that stage – see Table 31.3. The five stages are:

1. personal
2. professional
3. clinical team
4. own organization
5. multiorganization or interagency.

For audit to move into the last three stages required a certain type of organization in which clinical team development was promoted, there was close alignment of views of the direction of the unit/trust from both managerial and professional staff, and an open approach to problem solving was evident. Overall the key factors for success were:

- General managers' understanding of and involvement in audit;
- shared aims of senior clinical and managerial staff;
- confidence in discussing problems and potential solutions;
- quality and number of audit support staff;
- quality of leadership of audit;
- shared vision and collaboration of medical and nursing/PAMs directors.

The nature of organizations in which audit was most successful was characterized as being:

- high trust as opposed to command and control;
- common purpose of clinical staff, managers, purchasers and patient advocacy groups, together with a hunger for optimum performance;
- anticipating impacts of change rather than simply reacting and certainly not reacting in a negative or obstructive fashion;
- involving clinical staff in the contract processes.

Organizations which use audit effectively and learn to develop improved clinical care recognize a set of links necessary to facilitate improvements in healthcare and which help define direction, roles and functions in improving healthcare as shown in the box below (Batstone & Edwards 1994).

- Informed by health strategies
- Based on research findings
- Implemented through education
- Evaluated by audit

The model highlights the key role of education in the development of improvements in healthcare and the role of clinical audit in demonstrating the effectiveness of the improved care.

Organizations demonstrating the value of learning

There is a strong tradition of independent professional determination of the need for continuing education coupled with an anticipation that the organization within which the professional works will supply the necessary funding or that funding will come from the pharmaceutical or instrument industries. The discussion on continuing education revolves around perceptions of a right to study leave and the shortfall in revenue to meet costs. For consultant medical staff the average uptake of study leave is about 60% of the 'allowance' of 10 days per annum, with less than two thirds funded by the employing authority. The funding for other professional groups is less generous with no allowance of time. With the introduction of PREP, this may need to be reviewed as the UKCC recommends 5 days study in 3 years. To professional staff lack of funding and allocation of time is interpreted as lack of interest and even low esteem of professional staff by managers.

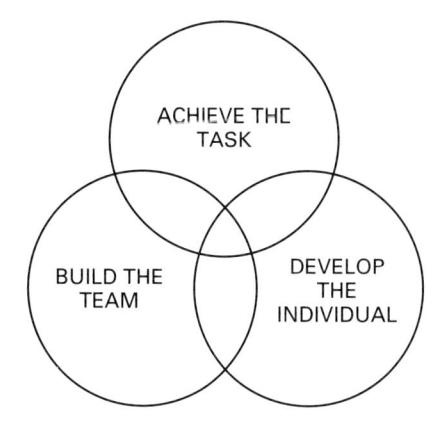

Fig. 31.5

Table 31.3 Maturation of clinical audit

Level	Style	Prerequisites
Personal	Case review/care plan review Condition series review Clinicopathological conference	Tradition Personal learning Pursuing specialist interest
Professional	Criterion-based method National/regional speciality audit Interspeciality/profession audit	Training in audit techniques Perception of benefit High quality audit staff
Clinical team	Multiprofessional care plan/profile Critical incident review Variance assessment Patient focus Interprofessional	Team spirit 'No blame' culture/openness Team development Group learning Recognition of professionals' roles Alignment of professional frames
Organization (own)	Linking to business objectives Seeking purchaser input Supporting *Health of the Nation* targets Linking to other quality initiatives	Confidence in general managers Input to the contract process Organizational development Involvement of business managers Inclusion in business planning process Collaborative approach between medical & nursing director
Interagency	Linking with other agencies Considering purchaser objectives Focusing on care management approach	Recognition of health needs Confidence in purchasers More holistic view of healthcare Active sharing of information between agencies

Further, any educational activities associated with management of healthcare delivery are seen by clinical staff as being outside the remit of study leave and requiring additional funding and time. Very few clinical directorates build study requirements into their business plans and fewer link study requirements to the strategic direction of the directorate.

To most professionals study is about conferences and attending meetings/lectures, etc. outside the organization. There is less interest in workplace learning such as that which comes from clinical audit activity although it is more likely to meet strategic aims and local plans for service development. Educational needs demonstrated through audit activity will in future be more likely to gain funding than those determined solely by personal interest because they will be seen as promoting the future of the organization.

Professional staff will need to link educational plans for individuals and groups of individuals to clinical audit findings and areas of service development to meet the needs of the organization in which they work. Educational plans need to take account of three influences:

1. the professional body to which an individual belongs and the approach to CME/CPD taken by that body and the review of the educational activity which it undertakes;
2. the review of services undertaken by general managers, both purchaser and provider, and the need for those services to meet strategic aims both locally and nationally determined, e.g. *Health of the Nation*;
3. clinical audit as a team review of current practice compared with desired practice gives an input from a variety of healthcare professionals within the clinical team.

One way of approaching the development of a personal learning plan which incorporates these three elements is shown below as an example:

1. Stimuli to learning plan

   - Discussions with professional colleagues on the way clinical practice is developing.
   - Findings of service review by general managers.
   - Educational requirements of professional body, e.g. medical college and courses offered.
   - Educational programmes offered by clinical societies and associations.

Fig. 31.6 Input to educational plans

- Findings of clinical audit projects.
- Findings of patient satisfaction surveys, complaints, etc.
- Views of primary care/secondary care/tertiary care.
- Need to continue producing papers for publication.
- Need to review ways of service management.
- Need to review ways of organizing clinics, use of new assays, etc.

2. Learning objectives derived from stimuli

- Develop communication skills and how to use them more effectively.
- Develop IT skills using 'in house' training sessions.
- Review guidelines, select one or two and develop them locally.
- Determine in discussions with colleagues which clinical areas need updating by reading programmes, visiting experts, attending meetings.
- Write up papers for publication.
- Updating on clinic organization and range/style of service.

3. Proposed ways of meeting objectives

- Attend course on communication skills and undertake audit of this.
- Attend 'in house' training course on IT.
- Select suitable area for guidelines development and work through a process to do this.
- Consider planing a regional workshop on a key area of practice.
- Agree with colleagues which conference to attend.
- Write papers.
- Undertake portfolio learning approach for clinic management changes.

4. Markers that objectives have been achieved

- Audit of communication skills and possibly video interviews.
- Use IT skills in guidelines development.
- Effective uptake of guidelines as shown by clinical audit.
- Use CHC to help in satisfaction survey of clinics.
- Obtain college CME credits.
- Review papers presented for publication.
- Present portfolio for peer review by colleague with whom educational needs have been discussed.

Organizations which learn

As indicated earlier in this chapter, clinical effectiveness requires not just professionals with mastery of their science and art, and not only such professionals working well in clinical teams, but also organizations which are responsive to change. This involves both external stimuli to change, as for example meeting purchaser needs, but also internal stimuli such as the findings of clinical audit activity and service reviews.

Peter Senge (1990) describes how successful organizations are also learning organizations. He identifies five 'competent technologies' which provide the essential dimensions for building organizations which can learn:

1. *Systems thinking* a conceptual framework of all the interrelated factors in a changing environment rather than just a snapshot.
2. *Personal mastery* continually clarifying personal vision and proficiency in an objective fashion. This is regarded as the cornerstone of a learning organization.
3. *Mental models* these are ingrained assumptions about people and groups that may need to be modified for an organization to be successful.
4. *Building shared vision* an ability to create and hold a shared view of developments and generate genuine commitment to them.
5. *Team learning* this occurs when team members learn more rapidly than could have occurred by individual effort in the production of outstanding results.

The concept of team learning begs the questions 'What are teams about and what makes them effective?'. The 'wisdom of teams' has been described by Katzenbach & Smith (1993) as a series of features which they divide into commonsense (readily anticipated characteristics) and uncommonsense (those which may be surprising) findings.

Their commonsense findings are:

- a demanding performance challenge tends to create a team;
- attention to size, purpose, goals, skills, approach and accountability promotes team development;
- team performance opportunities exist throughout the organization;
- teams at the top are more difficult to achieve;
- team accountability rather than individual accountability builds teams.

Their uncommonsense findings are:

- organizations with strong performance standards spawn more effective teams;
- high degrees of personal commitment help create high performance teams;
- teams integrate and enhance formal structures and processes;
- teams naturally integrate performance and learning;
- teams are the only size of unit that can help organizations respond to performance challenges.

For the findings of clinical audit to effect appropriate change in improving clinical performance, the role of clinicians within teams needs to be recognized. Organizations will help performance by the way in which they utilize teams, recognize team rather than individual performance and respond to the learning of teams as ways of promoting team development.

Role of purchaser/provider interaction

With the devolution of funding for clinical audit in England to purchasers from April 1994, resources for clinical audit become a part of the interaction between purchasers and providers. EL(94)20 (DoH 1994b) recommends that simple contracts for clinical audit are organized by a lead purchaser ensuring sufficient funds to meet the needs of crossboundary flows and tertiary referrals. Part of the annex to this EL is a code of practice to promote good quality audit and interaction between purchasers, providers and professionals.

Clinical teams would be wise to state in their business plans the educational requirements to meet development objectives and their intended use of clinical audit to demonstrate the effectiveness of these developments, both process and outcome aspects. Clinical directorates will compile learning and audit intentions into the directorate plan and hence into the trust plan, which will inform the contracting process. Similar approaches may be undertaken by general practice.

This approach to planning audit will enhance the purchaser/provider interaction in funding and promoting audit activity. Certainly purchasers are increasingly unlikely to sign a cheque for whatever audit activity an organization wishes to undertake. Provider organizations would be wise therefore to link audit activity to areas of clinical development and national strategies such as *Health of the Nation* as well as any local strategies negotiated with purchasers. However both purchaser and provider organizations must recognize the educational input to change in clinical practice, such as the implementation of guidelines, and the learning needs demonstrated through clinical audit and the educational resources necessary to meet them.

Purchasers will recognize a need to collaborate in major initiatives to gain an effective mass of educational, professional and change management expertise. Take head injury, for example, with its implications for a variety of clinical staff and organizations including ambulance, specialist neurosurgery, A&E, rehabilitation, therapists of many types, primary care, Social Services, etc. Programmes to improve head injury cannot be undertaken by a local provider or purchaser in isolation. Instead purchasers should coordinate a collaborative approach to ensure a full range of effective services are available and promote clinical audit of the whole care process.

Demonstrating clinical effectiveness and learning through clinical audit

Clinical effectiveness may be just the latest buzz word as this chapter is written – but let's hope this one stays with us. To professionals this phrase has implications of leading edge proven clinical practice based on research evidence. To the patient it gives assurance that procedures are not experiments where n = 1. To the provider manager it gives assurance that unnecessary procedures are not being undertaken. In the purchaser–provider relationship it gives opportunity for disinvestment in poor and outdated practice and reinvestment in up-to-date techniques arising from research findings.

In this environment trusts and primary healthcare teams will be asked by fellow professionals, provider managers, purchasers and the public to demonstrate their clinical effectiveness. This will also mean that clinical effectiveness can be demonstrated in a much more meaningful fashion than finished consultant episodes, length of stay and cost per case.

TRAINING HEALTHCARE STAFF IN CLINICAL AUDIT

Until clinical audit is part of the curriculum of the basic training of all healthcare professionals, both clinical and non-clinical, there is a major task in training existing staff to undertake audit projects.

For medical staff there has been the stimulus of colleges requiring evidence of clinical audit in their review of posts for doctors in training. Clinical pathology accreditation has similarly required evidence of participation in clinical audit. King's Fund organizational audit takes a similar approach to audit.

Much audit training is undertaken in single profession, speciality groups in order to learn the basic elements. Our experience, like that of many others, is that courses in audit techniques are best organized as two sessions separated by a period of 4–6 weeks during which the participants undertake a simple audit. This bases the training in the experience of audit practice and gives an opportunity to demonstrate the role of audit in continuing professional development.

When audit training is organized for multiprofessional groups working in clinical teams it is our experience that there needs to be incorporated in the programme a substantial section on teams and team building in order that individuals recognize and value the various roles individuals play in the dynamics of the team.

Different courses are required for those who intend to lead clinical audit for speciality groups or clinical directorates. These need to emphasize ways of helping individuals and groups to deal with change and learn from their audit findings. For audit support staff a wide variety of training courses may be needed including use of information technology, presentation skills, statistical analysis, etc. as well as clinical audit techniques.

CONCLUDING COMMENTS

In order to achieve clinically effective healthcare, there is a need for clinical directorates and primary healthcare teams to establish real and effective links between their clinical work, clinical standard-setting processes and clinical audit to monitor their clinical performance in order that these teams identify the necessary knowledge and skills they require to achieve the aim of clinical effectiveness. General managers should help promote this process by recognizing clinical staff as their greatest asset and supporting their continuing education and professional development, promoting clinical audit as part of the process of determining these needs.

Development of personal and clinical team learning plans informed by service needs, professional needs and personal desires coupled with the findings of clinical audit is critical in this process. Business plans should include clinical audit activity and learning plans in order that these costs are incorporated.

The role of general managers in promoting this style of approach to learning is key to success. Clinical staff with managerial roles should help promote the concept of the learning organization and the role of clinical audit as part of the process of achieving this.

As the aim of adult learning is to reveal, describe and interpret the past experience of individuals in order to illuminate the present and make manifest the potentialities of the future, then clinical audit is an attractive mechanism to promote this whilst at the same time meeting both patient and strategic needs.

REFERENCES

Adair J 1988 The action-centred leaders. The Industrial Society Press, London

Allison R, Loaring L 1992 Continuing professional development. IMLS Gazette 652–653

Alment Report 1976 Competence to practice. Committee of Enquiry into Competence to Practice, London

Argyris C 1993 Teaching smart people how to learn. In: Howard R (ed) The learning imperative: managing people for continuous innovation. Harvard Business School Press, Boston

Batstone G F 1990 Educational aspects of medical audit. British Medical Journal 301: 326–328

Batstone G F 1992 Using audit for education. In: Making medical audit effective. Joint Centre for Education in Medicine, London

Batstone G F 1994 A model for the development and maturation of medical/clinical audit derived from a review process: implications for medical/clinical education. Dissertation University of Wales College of Medicine

Batstone G F, Edwards M 1994 Clinical audit – how do we proceed? Southampton Medical Journal 10(1): 13–19

Boud D, Keogh R, Walker D 1985 Promoting reflection in learning. In: Boud D, Keogh R, Walker D (eds) Reflection: turning experience into learning. Kogan Page, London

Brookfield S D 1986 Understanding and facilitating adult learning. Open University Press, Milton Keynes

Brookfield S D 1987 Developing critical thinkers. Open University Press, Milton Keynes

Clark K 1990 Speech to the joint meeting of the National Association of Clinical Tutors, the Conference of Postgraduate Deans and the National Association of Postgraduate Centre Administrators, York, 6 July

Davis D A 1994 The dissemination of information: optimizing the effectiveness of continuing medical education. In: Dunn E V et al (eds) Disseminating research/changing practice. Sage, Thousand Oaks

Davis D A, Thomson M A, Oxman A D, Haynes R B 1992 Evidence of effectiveness of CME: a review of 50 randomized controlled trials. Journal of the American Medical Association 268: 1111–1117

Department of Health 1989 Medical Audit Working for Patients, Working Paper 6, command 555. HMSO, London

Department of Health 1989 Working for Patients, Working Paper 10, command 555. HMSO, London

Department of Health 1990 Postgraduate training and continuing medical education. HMSO, London

Department of Health 1993 Clinical audit: meeting and improving standards in healthcare. HMSO, London

Department of Health 1994a The evolution of clinical audit. NHS Executive, Leeds

Department of Health 1994b EL(94)20. Future funding of clinical audit: 94/95 and onwards. HMSO, London

Fox R D, Putnam P E, Masmanian R W 1989 Changing and learning in the lives of physicians. Praeger, New York

Grimshaw J M, Russell I T 1993 Effect of clinical guidelines on medical practice: a systematic review of rigorous evaluation. Lancet 342: 1317–1322

Holly M L 1987 Keeping a personal professional diary. Deakin University, Victoria

Katzenbach J R, Smith D K 1993 The wisdom of teams. Harvard Business School Press, Boston

Kirkpatrick D L 1975 Evaluating training programs. American Society for Training and Development, Washington

Kitson A et al 1994 The impact of a nursing Quality Assurance Approach, The Dynamic Standard Setting System on Nursing Practice and Patient Outcome. National Institute for Nursing: Report No. 4, Oxford

Knowles M 1990 The adult learner: a neglected species. Gulf, Houston

Lewin K 1975 Behaviour and development as a function of the total situation. In: Cartwright D (ed) Field theory in social science. Greenwood Press, Westport

McClusky 1970 An approach to a differential psychology of the adult potential. In: Grabowski SM (ed) Adult learning and instruction. ERIC, Syracuse

MOCOMP 1993 The maintenance of competence program. Annals of the Royal College of Surgeons and Physicians of Canada 26(5) Suppl: S12–S17

Redman W 1990 The portfolio approach to learning. Counselling, p 56, British Association for Counselling, Rugby.

Royal College of General Practitioners 1993 Occasional Paper 63. Portfolio-based learning in general practice. RCGP, London

Royal College of Physicians 1989 Medical audit: a first report. What, why and how? RCP, London

Schon D 1991 The reflective practitioner: how professionals think in action. Avebury, Aldershot

Senge P M 1990 The fifth discipline: the art and practice of the learning organization. Century Press, London

United Kingdom Central Council for Nursing, Midwifery and Health Visiting 1994 PREP – Government supports UKCC proposals. Register 14: 4–5

32

Further principles for clinical directors

Tony White

Equo ne credite, Teucri. Quidquid id est, timeo Dantos et dona ferentis.
(Virgil 70–19 BC)

INTRODUCTION

It requires considerable management skills to manage and maintain a balance in a large and dynamic structure such as a hospital department with such diverse medical and paramedical professionals, managers and others, facing increasing demands on services, the need to complete more FCEs, achieve greater and measurable quality standards while at the same time constantly saving money.

MANAGEMENT SKILLS

Just as there are different levels of commitment (see Chapter 21) so there are different levels of commitment by consultants to management.

1. *The leaders* Those who understand and are committed to the contribution of management to patient care.
2. *The helpers* Those who see it as in their interest to get involved in management.
3. *The followers* Those who can detect a shift in the balance of power and realize that it is in their interest to get involved in management 'to be on the winning side'.
4. *The opposers* Oblivious to management and are here 'to treat patients'.

People can of course vary according to mood and circumstance but on the whole it is an evolutionary process to proceed up the scale. There are some who will always stick at the bottom. Some of those who seem to be helpers may also be dangerous as they are there for the wrong reasons and see no reason or value in becoming leaders.

THE EXPECTATIONS OF OTHERS

There are pressures and demands from the management board, the medical director, other clinical directors and maybe other executive directors (finance, nursing, human resource, etc.). It might be helpful at this stage to consider what it is that management generally expects from doctors involved in management. This has been summarized as demanding integrity, hoping for the best and expecting considerable variation in performance.

What usually happens is that there are varying levels of competence at the job. Some doctors have a natural ability even though they may doubt this. There are those who have trainability and who can do a reasonable job when trained. Unfortunately there are a few who exhibit what might be called 'unbelievability'. They are the ones who think they can do it but somehow never learn how.

CLINICAL DIRECTOR'S SELF-EXPECTATIONS

How will you survive? You will need support from colleagues and the organization. You will need to decide in consultation with your colleagues what you are going to give up in order to make time for the role. If you do not consider this you will stop doing your own things and encroach on home and family time. Always remember there is nothing wrong in doing what you enjoy and making sure you have time to do so.

You need to prioritize your time for different activities in your life. You have to face the fact that you cannot do everything but once your time allocation is decided try not to feel guilty about it. Nor is it helpful to waste time chasing elusive goals. Expectations can be, may even need to be challenging but should always be realistic.

If a task falls outside your range of duties or desires, cultivate the ability to refuse assertively and with a clear conscience. Learn to delegate tasks or areas of duty to others. This can be a powerful way of helping others to feel part of the team, creating ownership of problems and solutions and concentrating your time on more important issues. You will need to select those to whom you delegate with care or you may waste time sorting out their mistakes.

You need to work to make yourself not indispensable but dispensable. A vital colleague is your business manager; your relationship with this person and the importance of making the right selection when appointing them cannot be overemphasized.

You will need to consider what meetings and committees you must attend but, more importantly, what you can safely miss. Many meetings are held unnecessarily, for the wrong reasons, are badly chaired or achieve very little. Meetings and committees should be time limited and every committee should ruthlessly review its role annually.

Your most vital job is not to stint on communication; if you are poor in other respects at least you can gain support and credibility by maintaining superb communication, not only with your peers but downwards to all members of the directorate, laterally to other clinical directors and upwards. Time sorting out organizational issues and ensuring that people know their duties, roles and tasks is an investment that repays the effort. Try to be available at predictable times; this enables other people to find you and solve minor problems before they become an urgent crisis.

DELEGATION

Delegation of responsibilities should not be regarded as their abdication. Some important aspect is usually left under your control. For a clinical director this usually means working within some financial control, usually a budget, and with limited authorization on expenditure. So you must equally give freedom to others but within reasonable constraints. If the fine details of the achievement of the delegated task are important to you, it should probably not be delegated although you may get someone to carry it out under your control. Delegation is not just giving someone instructions, it is about giving responsibility and as such it should enhance the esteem of those on whom it is bestowed.

The problem with delegation is that it does carry risks, so you must not delegate if you cannot afford to get it wrong. You may occasionally want to take that risk. People need to develop their managerial skills so you must present opportunities which stretch and develop staff but do not overwhelm them.

Thus delegation can enhance what you can achieve within time constraints but you need to decide who can be trusted with tasks, who can maintain harmony and who may be seeking to distort matters with their own agenda. Also who has potential to accept greater responsibility and who has reached their current maximum potential. It is thus an attractive option but not always easy and requires effort and often considerable interpersonal skills to achieve success. (See also section on delegation in Chapter 13.)

LEADERSHIP AND POWER

Leadership style also has close similarities to managing the change process. What needs changing may be considered under the headings of structure, technology and people (Leavitt 1964). How changes are produced is very closely related to approach and therefore leadership style. The work of Greiner (1967) identifies seven frequently used managerial approaches.

There are three forms of unilateral power:

1. *The decree approach* A one-way instruction from a person in higher authority to someone in lower authority. The manager makes the decision and tells everyone else what to do.
2. *The replacement approach* A key individual in an organization is replaced in order to bring about a change. It might be a business manager, chief executive or even the consultant.
3. *The structural approach* The organizational structure and relationships are changed in order to bring about required change.

Two forms of shared power:

4. *The group decision approach* where group members choose from several alternative solutions specified in advance by their manager. There is no problem identification or problem solving, only obtaining agreement to a particular course of action.
5. *The group problem solving approach* where problem identification is shared and problem solving is through group discussion.

Finally there are two forms of delegated power:

6. *The data discussion approach* where members of a group are encouraged to develop their own analyses of the original data.
7. *The sensitivity training approach* where managers are trained to be sensitive to the underlying processes of individual and group behaviour. Changes in work patterns are assumed to follow changes in interpersonal relationships and by working on these interpersonal relationships, improvements in work performance are encouraged.

It is rare for only one of these strategies to be used. A balanced approach using several methods is usually necessary. The least successful approaches are those which use exclusively one or other of the extremes. Kolb (1983) analysed the decision-making processes in organizations and identified similar categories of leadership:

- *Telling* Dictatorial, where the manager makes the decision and tells everyone what has been decided. Very similar to the decree approach discussed above.
- *Selling* Where the manager may make the decision but have some consultation after the decision has been made. The ideas are thus being sold rather than imposed. Rather similar to the group decision approach.
- *Consulting* This time the manager consults before the decision is made but still makes the decision personally, although based on the views expressed.
- *Delegating* The manager remains in control of the process but may delegate the decision making to the group. Rather similar to the group problem solving approach.
- *Democracy* The manager may not lead the process and has no greater input than any other group member.

While these analyses are useful and we all have a natural style, it is important to know and recognize what that approach is and if necessary to suppress it when that style is inappropriate. Change and its management is a complex process and you may find it helpful if you are introducing any change to think of it as a series of evolving stages. Lewin (1951) identified three phases:

1. *Unfreezing*, when people recognize the need for change or the status quo is jolted.
2. *Changing*, involving the introduction and implementation of change.
3. *Refreeezing*, which reinforces the new patterns of behaviour.

Unfortunately change is not always easy to achieve, when a whole department has to undergo change and especially if other departments outside your control are involved. How change is managed, how you ensure that everyone is willing to get involved in the change and give it their full support is helped by studying the change process and the various factors involved and this is considered in detail in Chapter 21.

INFLUENCE AND DEVELOPING A POWER BASE

Influencing is a skill that you need if you try to alter the actions of fellow consultants. It has already been discussed elsewhere (Chapters 4, 5, 6 and 10) as one limb of the triad of responsibility, accountability and authority. In more pragmatic terms there are many forms of influencing style which might be used.

- *Positional power* is the power conferred by office or role. Consultants are familiar with this in relation to their own position as head of a firm or team.
- *Authority power* is conferred by being given responsibility for a particular task or set of tasks. This may be independent of your normal position in the organization. Authority power can sometimes be borrowed; for example, if you do not have the power it can be delegated or borrowed from someone who has, although it is vital to make sure the person you borrow power from knows and agrees beforehand. A similar type of power is connectedness power from your relationship with someone else in the organization; for example, you might be married to someone influential.
- *Information power* is determined by the control you have over access to information, your influence as a filter of information to others or, better still, if you have better sources of more reliable information.
- *Resource power* is held by those who control access to human, material or financial resources and who have the potential to influence their use. Often the person with ultimate control may not be high in the organization. For clinical directors this resource power is exercised through control of the budget.
- *Expert power* is the ability to perform certain tasks or to control certain systems that others are less able or unable to do. Being an expert in some matters may encourage others to listen to your advice on other, unconnected matters.
- *Charismatic power* is the power of your personality. This may be related to your charm, your smile, your willingness to listen or just your presence. Closely related to this is example power which relates to what you do, setting an example, sometimes known as leadership by example.

The two final forms of power are indebtedness where you may have influence over someone who owes you a favour in return for past efforts you have put in on their behalf, and self-disclosure power. Openness and honesty about your views and feelings can be surprisingly effective in causing others to reveal their thoughts and be more open to influence.

MOTIVATION

There is considerably more written than understood about motivation. Managers are often required to 'motivate' staff. It is probably much more important to avoid 'demotivating' them. It is also important to distinguish lack of ability and lack of suitable training from lack of motivation. Lack of motivation can be a dustbin into which staff with whom the manager has difficult interpersonal relationships, does not respect or does not like can be conveniently dumped.

Nor is motivation an essential part of job satisfaction. You can achieve high job satisfaction without being motivated in the managerial sense. To genuinely motivate staff as a manager you need to understand and identify the motivational needs of staff and adjust the structure and reward system accordingly. But there are pitfalls; others may not share your outlook on the world.

There are various theories to explain motivation at work. The classic work of Maslow (1987) suggests that all humans have needs in an ascending hierarchy (see also Chapter 13). As the lower needs are met so higher ones become more relevant. At the bottom are the basic survival needs of food, drink and warmth, followed by security from danger. From there one progresses to a need to belong whether it be to the group or society. Next there is the need for recognition and self-esteem, and finally the top level, described as self-actualization, where the person can assert their full potential. In practical terms, this means that if the person feels insecure or psychologically unsafe they are unlikely to be able to operate in a group and equally a self-actualizer would not welcome an overspecified task.

Herzberg (1968) recognized a similar approach with factors whose presence signified positive motivation and feelings of satisfaction and others whose effects tended to be negative. The motivating factors relating to the content of the job were achievement, recognition, responsibility, advancement, work interest and growth potential. The negative or hygiene factors are those which tend to be ignored as long as they are satisfactory and relate to organization (be that hospital, unit, department or practice) policy, quality of administration, status issues, salary levels, work conditions and reporting relationships. Thus while you need to have reasonable levels of hygiene factors effort needs to be put into job content. Increasing salaries will only prevent further loss of morale, whereas an increase in recognition, status or positive feedback could increase motivation. The clinical director has only limited control over the hygiene factors but much greater control over the content. Set goals that are hard to achieve but not impossible and make sure that goals are detailed and specific rather than general. Ensure that there is adequate feedback and above all ensure that the goals are developed and owned by the staff within the directorate.

COMMON PROBLEMS ENCOUNTERED

These include the following:

- that managers do not believe in and covertly do not support the concept;
- information and information systems are often poor and access to financial expertise is often lacking;
- the alarmingly common tendency to revert to or increase centralization thus stifling innovation and initiative, presumably as a result of the constant squeeze on resources;
- the continuing tendency to monitor performance and standards centrally with consequent delay in timely data being available to control performance;
- the delay in asking clinical directors to input clinical advice to the business planning process, but particularly the contracting negotiations.

At directorate level the role of the members of the clinical management team is fixed rather than influenced by expertise, experience and enthusiasm and although this is desirable it does need to be explicit so that everyone in the team knows their role and responsibility. Teamwork and the value of each team member needs to be respected. The members need to identify with the team first rather than their professional or discipline background.

THE CRITICAL SUCCESS FACTORS

Management research has increasingly focused on observing what managers do rather than on what they should do. Boyatzis (1982) tried to identify the characteristics of excellent performance. He concluded that a job is performed most effectively when three elements are congruent: the job demands, the organizational environment and the competence of the job holder. Competence for the task involves personality, values, motives, attitudes and behaviour, as well as skills and knowledge.

There are technical skills associated with the particular profession or speciality. These are basic skills and knowledge possessed to achieve success in a professional role. There are basic managerial skills appropriate to any managerial situation, for example leadership, people management, social skills, supervision and working with others. And there are special skills which distinguish the excellent manager. Some are personality features which cannot easily be learned. Others are more amenable to change or can be taught and learned. Making these distinguishing skills explicit can be an agent for change.

Making things happen involves identifying goals and carrying them through, determining the direction of the directorate, providing a clear focus and setting standards for the work of other members of the directorate, delegating tasks to get the work done and develop others and generally organizing resources to achieve the objectives.

You need to show enterprise and initiative, be decisive, get things done and try to improve the service. Improving the service means doing things better either faster with less resources or to a higher level of quality. However, never forget the Chinese Laundry (Bailey 1990) which advertised a Fast Service, Quality Service, Cheap Service, but also pointed out that customers could only pick two out of three. Look for improvements in both effectiveness of the service and the efficient use of available resources, recognize inefficiencies in current practice and generally search for ways of improving how things are done.

To undertake these tasks you need to be able to think conceptually, analytically and strategically, breaking issues into component parts or smaller manageable pieces, then connecting the parts into a coherent whole to think about the totality of the problem. You need to be able to identify the key factors in a complex situation and question the basic premises and assumptions. Analytical thinking should feature highly amongst doctors because of their scientific training. You need to be able to relate issues to the broader picture and make connections between different parts, develop and use clear criteria for evaluating options, expect problems and develop contingency plans.

You should develop a long-term vision of the future of your speciality and directorate based on an analysis of its purpose and the future environment it will be working in and formulate strategic goals in line with that analysis. You then need to influence strategy by persuading, trading and negotiating and planning interventions. Remember that only one method of influencing is likely to be inadequate. You should also identify the key people who need convincing and tailor your influencing strategy to the concerns of those key individuals/groups. You may need to use networks to gain support, use personal relationships to shortcut bureaucracy and lobby influential people in advance of formal meetings and always remember to keep key people informed. You will need to organize and present data and use logical arguments to influence and appeal to the greater good of the hospital or community.

Turrill et al (1991), in a study of the characteristics of excellent doctors in management, referred to three types of characteristics as competencies and found that:

These occur with sufficient frequency to suggest that they are too important to the role to be ignored. They may be termed the threshold variables in that they suggest the minimum conditions for fully acceptable performance.

1. *Achieving* Demonstrating enterprise and initiative.
2. *Thinking* Thinking analytically.
3. *Influencing* Influencing strategically and persuading rationally.

Technical and managerial competencies are eminently teachable whereas these more primary behaviours may be improved but only within the limits of the individual's innate potential. They result from the underlying characteristics of the individual's personality and are the building blocks for managerial process competencies such as team leadership, negotiation, etc.

Possession of these attributes alone is insufficient. Success is unlikely unless the clinical management teams possess the full range of managerial process skills and the unit has management systems in place which are appropriate to the new arrangements. This is unfortunately not always the case. Some doctors display a somewhat restricted range of managerial process skills. Unless the managerial systems are in place and the clinicians have the managerial process skills to use them, the clinical directorate initiative will be frustrated.

The overall climate set by the chief executive and the managerial systems provide the arena in which successful clinical directors can display their primary behaviours using their managerial process skills. Some outstanding managerially aware doctors have a very clear view of their own role and the part they have to play within the overall process. Their common view is that management is about trying to do more with less, pursuing excellence with limited resources. For many reasons, not least of which is the time they have available, it may be that they are better placed to do this if they act as transforming leaders rather than transactional managers. Their choice of role will have a significant effect upon the process competencies required by them and their immediate team.

The operation of a successful directorate rests heavily

upon a team approach and the nurse manager and business manager must play a significant part, so their capabilities are critical. A senior nurse or technician who has been successful in different situations will not necessarily have the correct distinguishing competencies for this new one. Perhaps the key role for the lead clinician is just leadership. If so, it is important that the business manager and nurse manager develop their managerial skills to complement and support the leader.

Stewart (1982) describes the manager's job as made up of constraints, choices and demands, although 'the individual has some discretion in shifting the balance (by pushing back constraints, for example)'.

- *Demands* include minimum criteria of performance and procedures that cannot be ignored.
- *Constraints* include resource limitations, physical location, attitudes and expectations of others.
- *Choices* include how work is done and what work is done.

The dilemmas which need to be taken into account as directors develop their role are the professional and organizational tensions. No longer are you just a clinician and equal member of a peer group, but leading a management team while at the same time still engaged in clinical activity. You may be a respected clinician but you are also now possibly a complete beginner in management skills. As director you are fully responsible for performance but at the same time your involvement with day-to-day decision making is part-time, maybe peripheral and delegated. With perhaps a passion for one's own speciality, clinical work and maybe research, the problem is how to make room for understanding and concern about others. Having learned to represent corporate directorate interests, you now have to learn to put these aside for hospital corporacy.

Try not to give in to the pressure of being all things to all people, attempting to be informed of all directorate business and being party to all decisions, as this is not only unrealistic but intrusive upon others and obstructive to their proper functioning and personal development. As clinical director you have to do your fair share of devolving authority and decision making. All staff need to have confidence in their director's common interest in all of them and holistic approach to the directorate. As a key player you must be trusted to sacrifice your self-interest for corporate well-being and development. Staff motivation and goodwill will be lost if they see any sign of their director seeking personal or professional power from the position.

Another dilemma is how to cope with a chief executive who appears to lack the ability or confidence to devolve. Poor organizations do not think through what they need or ought to do and when they do they do it poorly. They do not ask the 'what ifs' and the 'how woulds', they do not plan the implications of change for the staff, do not train the staff for the change and lack the right sort of communication. A bureaucracy is very difficult to dismantle, although it is possible to rehabilitate a chief executive in difficulties with the changes. When did your chief executive last come and see you operate or spend time with reception in outpatients or stay in the ward during one of the more busy periods, so as to be involved in and understand the organization?

Some poor managers are supported and maintained by the medical staff with neither the manager or the medical staff even being aware of this collusion, such is the loose management structure that some hospitals have. It is sometimes necessary to understand the chief executive's perspectives. They have a career too. You need to understand where they come from and if possible where before that. You need to understand the influence of their mentors, referees and background. Even if they come from outside the health service there are likely to be role models within the service. There is usually a supporting network. You need to understand the whole person, then you will understand how to cope with them as an individual.

Hospitals will look radically different in 20 years' time and an increasing ageing population will not alter that basic concept. Primary care is taking on more and more of the functions, day surgery is increasing but is at present only a fraction of what it will be in the future. Yet in spite of these signs many US and UK trust hospitals say in their plans that they envisage continuous expansion over the next few years. Have you considered the effects of these and other changes on your directorate over the next 10 years? Doctors are able to provide long-term continuity to balance the constant change of managers every few years which leads to the managers thinking much more short term than is realized.

It is essential that the skills of the clinical management team members are fully used and developed. This requires central managers to 'let go' and also invest in the continuing education, training and professional development of all clinicians and professionals and members of the healthcare teams. This involves investment of resources and time and also a major cultural change on the part of many organizations. The culture also needs to be changed to create an environment where innovation and risk taking are encouraged and individuals are empowered to improve all aspects of patient care.

The decisions at organization level on the use of available resources need to be explicit and within previously defined goals, which need to be shared both at directorate and organization level. These goals also need to move towards improvement in quality, efficiency and effectiveness of healthcare.

CONCLUSIONS

Do not neglect the importance of being aware of the formal and informal workings of the whole organization. Develop an attitude of strategic and corporate thinking. Learn to read selectively and quickly all the documentation that comes your way, no matter how long and tedious. They may contain some vital piece of information about your directorate's future or give you the spark of an idea for development. Write concisely. Keep a database of useful information together with references to sources.

Allow papers to pass through your hands only once. Review your post with your secretary, making immediate decisions on actions where possible. Review with your business manager information and notices for meetings of the directorate. Make actions lists at meetings and have these identified on the minutes in the right-hand column so that everyone is clear later whose responsibility it was to do things. Do not put items on directorate meetings agendas for information when the original document can be circulated.

Work with your support staff. Medicine tends by nature to be a rather solitary activity, breeding self-reliance and encouraging autonomy. You are now involved in team working. Always be punctual and encourage it in others. Do not delay the start of meetings. Try to negotiate the 'win–win' situation where everyone gains something and therefore everyone is happy. Always try to identify key figures. Remember the importance of developing networks. Be positive and at the end of the day reflect on what has been achieved and what you have done well.

THE FUTURE OF CLINICAL MANAGEMENT

It seems helpful to end this chapter by restating that successful clinical management results in improved patient care, professional development is enhanced, there is more effective use of resources, relations between clinicians and managers improve, the various disciplines in the healthcare team work closer together, there is more influence on the management of the organization. But also a word of caution from Watson (1994, personal communication):

It is clear that the activity of hospitals will in future be driven by increasingly sophisticated contracts and there can be no meaningful role for clinical directorates unless they are an integral part of the negotiating process. This is now the most important issue facing clinicians in management.

REFERENCES

Bailey B J 1990 Somehow we have to stop the train wreck. Archives of Otolaryngology and Head and Neck Surgery 116: 669–700

Boyatzis R E 1982 The competent manager: a model for effective performance. Wiley, New York

Greiner L C 1967 Patterns of organizational change. Harvard Business Review

Herzberg F 1968 Work and the nature of man. Staples Press, London

Kolb D A 1983 Problem management: learning from experience. In: Staivastva S et al (eds) The executive mind. Jossey-Bass, San Francisco

Leavitt H J 1964 Applied organization change in industry: structural, technological and human approaches In: Cooper W W, Leavitt H J, Shelly M W III (eds) New perspectives in organization research. Wiley, New York

Lewin K 1951 Field theory in social science. Harper & Row, New York

Maslow A M 1987 Motivation and personality, 3rd edn. Harper & Row, New York

Stewart R 1982 Choices for the manager. McGraw-Hill, Maidenhead

Turrill T, Wilson D, Young K 1991 The characteristics of excellent doctors in management. A report produced for NHS Management Executive, Resource Management Unit. Turrill Ltd, Thirsk

33

Multiprofessional audit

Mary Edwards, Gifford Batstone

INTRODUCTION

All health professionals are being encouraged to move towards collaborative multiprofessional clinical audit as part of the growing realization that healthcare is a team-based function. This development is supported by the Department of Health and the professional organizations such as the royal colleges. It has been recognized, however, that the evolution of clinical audit is not a simple process because the various professions have had different approaches to audit to date which need to be recognized and strategies developed to support healthcare teams as they move into more collaborative approaches.

The key themes developed in this chapter emphasize the need to develop clinical audit which is multiprofessional in nature and focused on the patient. The clinical team will be auditing the overall plan of care but within that, individual professions' care may still be appropriately considered using uniprofessional audit.

BACKGROUND

Audit was formally introduced into the NHS in 1989 when the White Paper *Working for Patients* (DoH 1989) proposed that all doctors should be actively involved in formal audit of their work. This was endorsed by the royal colleges and faculties and was further supported by specific funding from the Department of Health. The last year of this protected funding, 1993–94, saw a total budget of £41.9 m for medical audit in England. Medical audit was defined in the White Paper (DoH 1989) as 'the systematic, critical analysis of the quality of medical care, including the procedures used for diagnosis and treatment, the use of resources and the resulting outcome and quality of life for the patient'. Government encouragement for audit in general practice occurred in 1990 (DoH 1990) with funding being made available to FHSAs to support medical audit advisory groups (MAAGs), £12.2 m in 1993–94. The nursing and therapy professions were then encouraged to develop audit by the Department of Health in 1991 (DoH 1991b). Again specific funding was provided to pump-prime this activity and for 1993–94 the total budget for England was £8.2 m.

Following these quite separate developments and programmes to introduce audit into the health professions, there was a growing realization of and desire to support the move towards multiprofessional clinical audit. This was encouraged by the Department of Health in England in 1993 with the announcement of the cessation of ringfenced separate funding for the various uniprofessional audit programmes and demand for moves to be made to integrate these approaches (DoH 1993a). Extra funds were provided as a one-off allocation in 1993–94 to support the emergence of clinical audit and this was further emphasized by the publication of a policy statement which set out the fundamental principles of clinical audit (DoH 1993c). These state that audit should:

- be professionally led;
- be seen as an educational process;
- form part of routine clinical practice;
- be based on the setting of standards;
- generate results that can be used to improve outcome of quality care;
- involve general managers in both the process and outcome of audit;
- be confidential at the individual patient/clinician level;
- be informed by the views of patients/clients.

There are differences in the way in which audit has developed which have been influenced partly by the level of funding made available by the Department of

Health and how this funding has been used; medical audit funding was mostly allocated to units/trusts on the basis of the number of consultants employed whilst the nursing/therapy money was distributed to regions on a population basis and mainly allocated to units/trusts on a project bidding system. Further, the White Paper introducing medical audit resulted in a contractual requirement for doctors in hospital and community services to undertake audit. This requirement does not apply to GPs or other health professionals, however, although there is an expectation that all health professionals will participate in audit.

The recommendations within Working Paper 6 (DoH 1989) have also led to a greater emphasis on professional development through audit undertaken by doctors compared with other professions. There are also variations related to audit structures with most units/trusts having established medical audit committees and employing audit assistants/analysts to support doctors undertaking audit. The other health professions do not have such structures and are often unaware of the help to be gained from audit support staff. Other variations relate to the level of training in audit provided and the culture within which audit was developed; audit was generally seen as a monitoring process by non-medical health professionals rather than having a professional development role, highlighted for medical staff, as mentioned earlier.

The key issue, however, when moving towards multiprofessional audit is the need to recognize that different professional groups are progressing at different speeds along a continuum of audit technique. Recognition of these different approaches and respect for individual sensitivities is required in order to encourage rather than delay the move to clinical audit. This is particularly true when planning training programmes and establishing an infrastructure to support clinical audit locally.

The key principles that need to be built upon in developing this multiprofessional approach include:

- maintaining and enhancing the continuing education/professional development aspects of audit;
- the potential to enhance integration across professions by achieving collaborative audit programmes;
- making audit mainstream business by integrating it within the corporate quality programme and involving general managers at all levels in audit;
- developing an audit plan that looks at the totality of healthcare from disease prevention and health promotion to treatment and rehabilitation;
- working across the primary/secondary care interface involving the whole healthcare team;
- emphasizing the patient focus and input to the audit process.

CHARACTERISTICS OF CLINICAL AUDIT

Clinical audit has been described in the following way in a policy statement issued by the Department of Health's Clinical Outcomes Group (DoH 1993c):

Clinical audit involves systematically looking at the procedures used for diagnosis, care and treatment, examining how associated resources are used and investigating the effect care has on the outcome and quality of life for the patient.

An alternative description has been developed to emphasize the collaborative nature of clinical audit as: 'multiprofessional, patient-focused audit leading to high quality, cost-effective care delivery through clinical teams' (Batstone & Edwards 1994).

Clinical audit is often described as a cycle whereby teams are encouraged to move through a process of setting standards, collecting and analysing data, comparing these data to the standards in a peer review process and then finally taking some action to improve the quality of care. This traditional view of audit excludes a vital part of the process, that is indicated in Fig. 33.1, in which teams are required to reflect on the service they are providing and reach agreement on the purpose and value of that service. This reflection has a two-fold role: firstly it helps the team learn about each other's roles (often a novel experience for multiprofessional teams) and secondly, it ensures that they have jointly agreed what they are trying to achieve with their particular group of patients.

The key elements for assessing that clinical audit is developing successfully are that (DoH 1994a):

- it is undertaken by multiprofessional healthcare teams;
- it is focused on the patient;
- there is development of a culture of continuing evaluation and improvement of clinical effectiveness focusing on patient outcomes.

This clearly emphasizes that the patient should be the central focus of the audit process which will also enable teams to identify which professions need to be involved for any given audit project. This approach does not mean, however, that uniprofessional audit cannot or should not be undertaken where professions can identify clearly their own singular contribution to patient care. There will therefore need to be a mixture of uni- and multiprofessional audit depending upon the clinical intervention being evaluated.

It may be worth considering at this stage what would

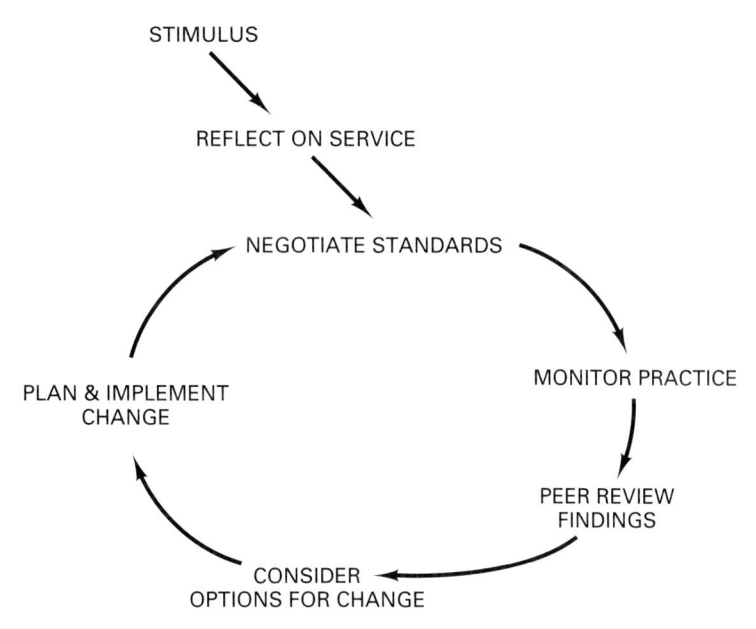

Fig. 33.1 The audit cycle

happen if health professionals do nothing to support the evolution of clinical audit. Firstly, purchasers will ensure that no funding is forthcoming for audit. Secondly, if consequently no audit is undertaken and clinical effectiveness is not demonstrated, contracts will be moved to other service providers. There is already some evidence of these steps being taken in England. It would therefore seem rational for health professionals to be proactive in moving towards patient-focused clinical audit.

The individual contributions within the healthcare team can be shown by the 'fishbone' in Fig. 33.2. This approach can be used to ensure that all the relevant professions are involved in planning care, developing guidelines and care profiles as well as auditing these processes. The composition of healthcare teams will obviously vary depending upon local need and patient groupings and will include primary healthcare teams in general practice. The diagram can also be used to show the linkages between uniprofessional audit and the overall multiprofessional audit of the patient's total care package. Healthcare team is used as a generic term to encompass all types of clinical team because clinical team is often seen as a hospital-based phenomenon, not suiting all community and primary care settings.

The other key element outlined above is the need to constantly evaluate clinical effectiveness in order to achieve health gain for patients (again, patient is used as a generic term to cover all recipients of healthcare). The factors to consider when evaluating effectiveness have been suggested by Batstone & Edwards (1994) as:

T	Timeliness	Multiprofessional standard setting
A	Appropriateness	Multiprofessional standard setting
P	Process	Uniprofessional standard setting
E	Effectiveness	Multiprofessional standard setting

Timeliness, appropriateness and effectiveness refer to the assessment of whether an intervention was the correct one, undertaken at the correct time and performed correctly. These are seen as requiring multiprofessional agreement both in terms of standard setting and the formulation of desired outcomes. On the other hand, the process used by each individual professional as their contribution to the patient outcome is seen to need individual professional determination and judgement. It is clearly not logical nor appropriate, for example, for a nurse or physiotherapist to judge whether a surgeon's technique is correct; they do not have the background knowledge for this. In the same way it is not appropriate for a doctor to judge an occupational therapist's training skills. The team, however, do need to reach

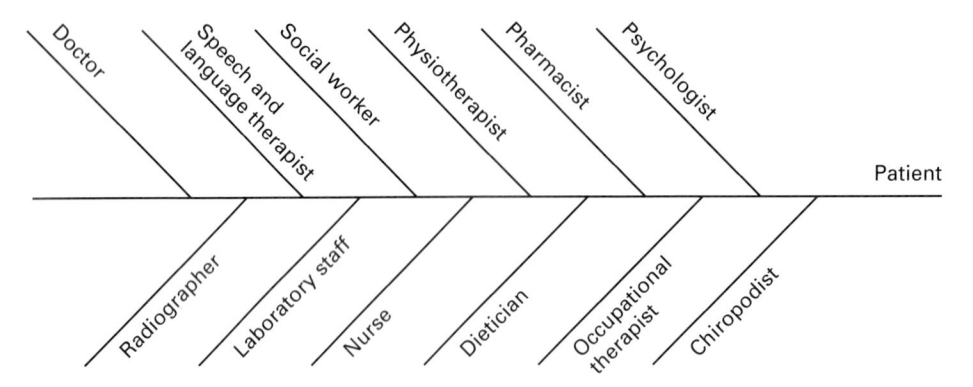

Fig. 33.2 Contributions within the healthcare team

agreement on their aims and objectives for the total package of care in order to achieve desired patient outcomes because it is conceivable that, without this agreement, they may all be travelling in different directions and pursuing contradictory care processes. This also indicates again where uniprofessional audit fits into multiprofessional clinical audit. It may be appropriate, however, in the early stages of the development of collaborative clinical audit, to undertake uniprofessional review of multiprofessionally agreed standards of timeliness, appropriateness and effectiveness until the team is confident in working together in an open and honest way. This avoids professionals being forced into exposing themselves too early in this evolutionary process as they will become defensive and reticent which does not best serve the purpose of clinical audit or the patient.

For clinical audit to be successful it is important to focus all this activity at the healthcare team level, whether that be the primary healthcare team, community mental health team or surgical department within an acute hospital. The development of the healthcare team could be based upon the model identified by Adair (1988) which sees the need for a successful organization to:

- achieve the task;
- build the team;
- develop the individual.

All three components are inextricably linked for a successful outcome (i.e. improving patient care) and thus audit as a professional development activity can be used to link education to evolving professional roles within healthcare teams; in other words, team learning.

The evaluation of patient care undertaken through the audit process must not be seen as an isolated activity and so clinical audit must be integrated with the organization's quality management programme, whilst main-

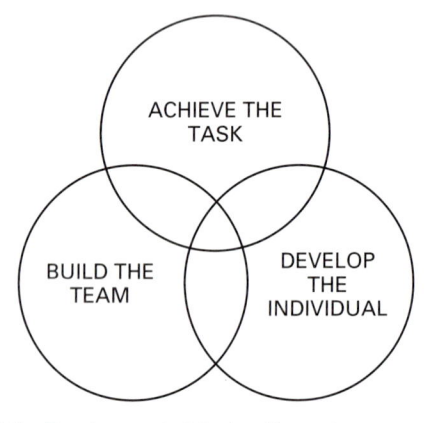

Fig. 33.3 Development of the healthcare team

taining its fundamental professional development role. This must be associated with open critical review of current practice and implementation of changes as indicated. This will ensure that audit becomes mainstream business and is used appropriately within the healthcare commissioning process. Both health professionals and general managers should therefore seek ways of harnessing, with clinical audit, other quality improvement programmes, some of which are listed below:

- infection control structures;
- health and safety activities;
- prescribing monitoring;
- continuous quality improvement programmes (CQI);
- total quality management (TQM);
- professional standard setting;
- drug and therapeutic committees;
- immunization rate monitoring;
- radiation protection systems;
- laboratory external quality assurance;
- patient satisfaction/user involvement activities.

Some of these activities may be found in all

healthcare provider organizations, but many of them are orphan structures which had definite functions before the internal market was introduced to the NHS but are no longer linked to the mainstream business of their organizations. This is particularly true where they were formerly districtwide activities (e.g. drug and therapeutics committees). The topics they deal with, however, are very relevant to audit, either in terms of producing standards or raising potential problems.

It is also important that audit addresses questions of cost-effectiveness and value for money at the healthcare team level; these issues are becoming increasingly important in the market-based NHS. Value for money must be seen in this context as the attempt to achieve the highest possible quality of service within the given resources; in other words making the best use of a finite resource, not, as many health professionals perceive it, merely cost-cutting. Links must also be developed between audit and research and development programmes as well as ensuring that the full potential for education and professional development is enhanced through clinical audit. These themes will be further developed later in this chapter. In addition links should be made to other activities undertaken within healthcare organizations such as resource management, risk management and the work being undertaken to tackle specific health strategies such as *Health of the Nation* (DoH 1992).

PATIENT BENEFIT THROUGH CLINICAL AUDIT

Multiprofessional audit must be seen to have patient issues, rather than professional issues, as its focus. It incorporates technical and therapeutic advances together with organizational developments and professionally generated guidelines. The key therefore is to promote the adoption and monitoring of uptake of these advances in order to demonstrate patient benefit; clinical audit can be used to monitor uptake and assure patients and professionals alike that the best possible care is being provided based upon the best scientific knowledge to date. In addition the audit process may develop realistic goals by increasing the use of patient perceptions of care as source material for peer review.

With the growth of consumerism and patient involvement in healthcare, there is a growing emphasis on lay input to the audit process, but this still needs to be further encouraged and supported. Patients and their advocates are able to influence all stages of the audit process from topic selection and standard setting through audit design to drawing up recommendations for change following analysis. It is quite feasible, for example, for individuals or groups of patients to be asked to help in topic selection and standard setting prior to an audit; this does not mean that the professionals' views will be disregarded, rather that both sides will learn from each other and reach agreement on the key elements to be audited. Patients can then be involved where appropriate in drawing up audit tools, particularly if questionnaires are to be used to test their opinions on certain service aspects. Finally, patients can be consulted about proposed changes before implementation to ensure that these are feasible and desirable from their viewpoint; many changes, supposedly for patient benefit, have been introduced without this consultation and ended in failure.

The mechanisms for involving patients are not well developed, but several organizations have piloted the use of patient focus groups, particularly where these already exist. Focus groups have been used, particularly by mental health units, to draw together real users to share their views and opinions on the quality of the service. Another potential mechanism is to seek out users of the service by, for example, advertisements in local newspapers and to train them to participate in the audit process. Patients clearly do not need indepth knowledge of the audit process, but they do need to understand what their role is in the process and what audit's role is in the organization. It is also important not to pick one or two 'professional' patients who may have their own agenda or pressure groups for the same reason. An early start may be made by using the CHC if there are already good relationships, although they may not be a good substitute for real service users.

Lay input is also important when considering membership of clinical audit committees at whatever level of the service, including directorate/care group/primary healthcare team level. These committees tend to have a key role in setting the audit agenda and allocating funding for specific audit projects and so a patient view here is clearly vital. Many organizations are now inviting a lay member onto their committees; however, it is advisable to have more than one individual so that peer support can be given. It is quite daunting for a member of the public to contribute to a debate lead by highly skilled, knowledgeable health professionals.

SKILLS REQUIRED FOR CLINICAL AUDIT

In order to achieve integrated clinical audit, organizations will need to promote interprofessional development and education. As training courses are developed to meet these needs, the following issues will need to be considered.

Focus on the healthcare team

Training provision should wherever possible be focused on the healthcare team to utilize fully the benefits of multiprofessional collaboration as highlighted above. This will enhance the prospects of achieving the key elements of clinical audit in that it is multiprofessional and patient focused. A target for organizations would be to have a trained audit leader within each healthcare team as a minimum. The professional background of this individual is not relevant; they should be selected by the team on the basis of their commitment to audit and ability to motivate and lead the team through a change process. In particular, attention should be paid to the culture required for learning through small groups to be effective (Jaques 1984).

Assessment of training needs

Organizations will need to assess training requirements at three levels to support the clinical audit programme. It is clearly not feasible nor desirable to equip all team members with the necessary methodological skills to undertake audit.

Firstly, therefore, a leader should be identified within each healthcare team to motivate and cascade change within the team. This individual, chosen for their interest in audit and leadership skills, will need training in change management as well as enhanced understanding of the audit process. Secondly, individual team members from all professions will require training on the benefit of audit and their contribution to it. Finally, the clinical audit programme will need to be supported by well-trained audit support staff who are able to provide advice on audit design and methodology, carrying out data collection and analysis as appropriate. The audit support staff should work in partnership with the audit leaders. Training will be required for all participants within the audit process to enable them to utilize fully patient input to the audit programme. General managers will also need to understand their roles at all stages of the audit process and may need training for this.

Access

Use of resources for training must ensure equity of access for all relevant health professionals. This will ensure that all team members have the opportunity of obtaining appropriate skills. Account should be taken of the various start points of the professions as indicated earlier to give those with less opportunity previously the chance to catch up. This should ensure that no specific professional group is seen as the natural leader of clinical audit.

This emphasis on training to bring about change must be recognized and supported by senior managers and will enable them to achieve the integration of clinical audit within the mainstream business of the organization. Senior managers must perceive the benefits to be gained from establishing an organizational culture of constant evaluation as well as having the ability and desire to respond to the findings from audit.

AUDIT AND PROFESSIONAL DEVELOPMENT

One of the fundamental principles of clinical audit is that it is seen as an educational process as well as being related to the moral and professional accountability for practice. It would also be appropriate to link audit with the wider concept of professional development as proposed in Chapter 31. This requires that healthcare organizations see the benefit of the longer term development aspects of audit. This in turn will add further value to quality improvement resulting from audit and avoid it being seen merely as a contract monitoring process. As developed elsewhere in this book, learning can take place at a number of stages within the audit process and participation in audit can help to identify learning needs from which educational plans may be developed (Batstone 1990). This learning may take place at a number of levels within the organization:

- personal
- healthcare team
- organization.

Clinical audit can be seen as a means to enhance the team by developing reflective practitioners (Schon 1991). This development is achieved through the solution of everyday problems of healthcare delivery and learning through the provision of better care.

Audit may also be linked to portfolio learning whereby an individual indicates their particular development needs and develops plans to meet these educational objectives. Experiences, thoughts, notes and other sources of learning are collected as a portfolio to demonstrate that learning has taken place. This concept is being increasingly used in professional and non-professional education and the Royal College of General Practitioners is showing great interest in this approach (RCGP 1993). The system of accreditation of prior learning (APL) which has recently been introduced is based upon individuals building portfolios of their prior learning, both formal and experiential. This portfolio may then be used to gain credits towards certain types of qualifications. The system has not been used extensively by health professionals but may be expanded in the future.

Portfolio learning may also become a key component for assessing professionals' learning and development as moves towards professional accreditation increase. The UKCC, which governs nurses' registration and professional conduct, is introducing this system as part of its reaccreditation recommendations. The therapy professions are also involved in credit accumulation based upon experiential learning. Most of the medical royal colleges are developing a system of cognate points for accreditation; these mainly relate to lectures and study days rather than experiential learning, although some incorporate points for participation in national audit projects.

There is clearly great potential for the learning that takes place through participation in the audit process to be recognized and accredited as part of any individual's continuing professional development, but to date the professional organizations have been slow to capitalize on this potential. These approaches are also in accord with the principles of adult learning and generate effective learning as proposed by Knowles (1990) which is expanded upon within Chapter 31.

INFRASTRUCTURE TO SUPPORT CLINICAL AUDIT

The concept of multiprofessional, patient-focused audit that is being proposed in this chapter requires an infrastructure to support it. There are a number of key elements which need to be identified as part of this, including:

- coordination;
- audit support staff;
- resources, including time and money;
- links to education providers and professional organizations.

The first issue to be emphasized here is the need to ensure that this infrastructure is provided in an equitable way for all professional groups. This should be developed from existing structures in such a way that it does not send negative messages to non-medical professionals and thus result in raising interprofessional barriers rather than having the desired effect which is the opposite of this. Each organization will need to assess and plan its own strategy for evolving this infrastructure. As part of this process it will be necessary to test with key opinion formers locally whether existing structures (e.g. medical audit committees) can include sufficient other professionals to achieve a multiprofessional forum or whether they will need dismantling before new ones are set up. Early successful attempts at this have included building an audit committee to reflect the management structure of the organization; for example, selecting a nurse, therapist and doctor from each directorate/care group, one of whom attends the audit committee. There is implicit encouragement with this system to ensure that a good mix of professionals actually attend the committee. This model emphasizes a multiprofessional view of audit, shares the load of leading audit locally and enhances the links to the management structure of the organization. In primary care, successful models are evolving which include practice nurses and managers and, where possible, other members of the team, e.g. health visitors, district nurses, community therapists, etc. It is an important objective to avoid the potential for tokenism as the move towards collaborative audit evolves. Equally, multiprofessional cohesion will not be embedded by establishing several parallel structures for each profession which report to a central coordinating mechanism. This will merely delay the move towards genuine collaboration.

Whatever structures are put in place must be closely integrated within the rest of the corporate business of the organization including areas such as quality management, resource management and risk management. As mentioned earlier, clinical audit must also link to other quality-enhancing activities such as infection control, organizational audit, patient satisfaction and complaints systems. This will speed up the process of making audit mainstream and less of an 'add-on' and therefore be more successful in achieving change. The principle to follow is evolution from existing good practice.

To support the totality of patient care clinical audit must be integrated across the primary/secondary care interface and the infrastructure should support that. Examples of good practice in this area show that it is possible to share audit resources between secondary care services and primary healthcare teams. This collaboration may ultimately be taken into the broader view of community care to involve other agencies such as Social Services and education services.

The key elements to be identified to support clinical audit include:

Coordination

A focus for the coordination of audit by all professionals will be required and may be achieved by the establishment of a clinical audit coordinating group/committee. The chairperson of this committee should be an individual who commands the respect and support of clinical colleagues and managers. Existing models of good practice include inviting a non-executive trust director to chair the committee as a powerful way of reducing the problems of professional sensitivities. Another possibility is to rotate the chair between senior professionals; this mirrors the practice of the Department of Health's clinical outcomes group in England which is jointly chaired by the chief medical officer and the chief nursing officer. A further strength is realized by asking the audit committee to report directly through the chairperson to the full trust board. This will ensure that audit is seen as mainstream business. These suggestions are obviously more appropriate to hospital and community provider organizations, but the principles are equally applicable to coordinating committees such as medical audit advisory groups (MAAGs) in primary care. These uniprofessional groups are rapidly evolving into multiprofessional groups and will need to consider the same issues as their hospital/community counterparts. It is also vital, as argued earlier, that any committee avoids tokenism by simply adding one or two non-medical professionals to an existing medical audit committee.

Organizations should also include lay representation to any audit committee and should support these individuals to enable them to make a meaningful contribution to the audit programme, including training for the role. There should be more than one lay member to counteract isolation and to enable the individuals to receive peer support in a potentially daunting situation (see earlier section on patient input to audit).

Audit support staff

Audit support staff must be trained to support the multiprofessional team and should be seen as a significant source of expertise in terms of planning and implementing the audit process. They will need to understand the previous experience of all the professions in improving the quality of care in order to extract the best from all approaches as they move towards clinical audit. Health professionals will also need to receive information on the role of the audit department because many staff may not realize the expertise available to them; this is particularly true of non-medical professionals who do not have a history of using this source of support.

The work of the audit department will need to be developed to coordinate and support the full audit programme. This should be linked to the coordination provided for quality programmes to enhance integration of related work programmes, whilst ensuring that audit maintains its fundamental professional and educational principles.

Resources

Organizations must recognize the time required by health professionals to undertake clinical audit and offer equitable arrangements to permit staff to participate. This is more likely to occur where organizations recognize the benefit to be gained from individual and team development by participating in audit.

The funding to support individual audit projects will need to be made available where necessary. The majority of this funding may be invested in employing well-trained audit support staff, but there are other cost implications for audit such as retrieving notes, accessing data and the provision of computer analysis where necessary. Organizations will need to decide what mechanisms should be put in place for allocating funding. Currently this is mainly coordinated through audit committees but some hospital services are devolving the funding down directorate/divisional structures. This is wholly appropriate where it is linked to the whole organization's priorities and ensures value for money through the audit programme. Several organizations are ensuring that this devolved system is successful by including audit programmes in directorate/divisional business plans, thus enabling linkage to the organization-wide business plan. Whatever system is implemented must permit some flexibility to meet additional audit requirements mid-year, for example to meet specific problems or purchaser requests.

LINKS TO EDUCATION PROVIDERS AND PROFESSIONAL ORGANIZATIONS

As indicated earlier, clinical audit is an important professional development activity and it is therefore important that clear links are developed with postgraduate education providers, particularly at local level. These links should also take account of the benefit of using audit as part of portfolio learning in professional accreditation. It should be recognized that links may be easier to forge with postgraduate medical structures such as clinical tutors and college tutors. The difficult development will be linking to education structures for non-medical professions which are less easily defined and may be geographically distant.

In order to support audits organized through professional bodies such as the medical royal colleges, the Royal College of Nursing, Chartered Society of Physiotherapy, etc., provider organizations, both primary and secondary care, will need to make clear links to relevant organizations. Staff should be enabled and encouraged to participate in nationally and regionally organized audits for the benefit of professional development and to enhance clinical effectiveness within the team. The professional organizations will also need to develop collaborative links with each other to ensure that audits take account of the totality of care across both primary and secondary care sectors.

CLINICAL EFFECTIVENESS

Clinical audit must be placed in context with other activities that enhance the quality of patient care such as research, development and evaluation. The 1993 Advisory Committee on Science and Technology Report (ACOST 1993) supports this approach in recommendation 4.6: '... ensure that validated procedures are effectively implemented and outdated techniques supplanted. Any implementation programme must be underpinned by monitoring of adoption and uptake'.

Fig. 33.4 illustrates how these activities link to enhance clinical effectiveness by showing how research, evaluation and audit all influence standards of care. Research is used to achieve solutions to questions where there is no existing evidence to support a particular pattern of care. The impact of that proposed solution must then be evaluated to determine its impact in clinical practice and then, once the particular research evidence has been implemented, audit may be used to assess the degree of compliance with agreed best practice. This model can therefore be used to demonstrate how a culture of constant evaluation of clinical effectiveness can be developed by linking research, evaluation and audit together. This must, as always, be focused at the healthcare team level in order to gain maximum effectiveness.

There is a growing realization that health professionals need assistance in achieving the objective set out in the ACOST Report, partly stimulated by the introduction of a national research and development strategy (DoH 1991a). Many professional organizations, particularly the medical royal colleges, have gradually been producing clinical guidelines on specific issues such as asthma (British Thoracic Society 1993) and diabetes (British Diabetic Association 1993). In an attempt to coordinate this work on guidelines and clinical effectiveness and to encourage professionals to make use of this work the Department of Health in England published an executive letter in December 1993 (DoH 1993b) asking purchasers to include in contracts at least one of a list of seven clinical guidelines which were commended to the service. This was followed by a further executive letter in September 1994 (DoH 1994b). These guidelines were assessed to see if they met the relevant criteria in that they were:

- developed and endorsed by the relevant professional bodies;
- based on good research evidence of clinical effectiveness;
- practical and affordable;
- where appropriate, multidisciplinary;
- aware of patient choices and values.

Guidelines are not meant to restrict individuals' clinical freedom, but they should be useful for informing discussions between purchasers and providers on clinical aspects of the service. They also clearly have a role in informing clinical audit programmes both in terms of agenda setting and agreeing standards for individual projects. This will only be possible, however, if an emphasis is placed on their effective dissemination to relevant professionals. Systems for ensuring that they reach their target audience will need to be developed using the full range of professional networks, publication in journals and education structures as well as more imaginative methods. This dissemination process will also need to consider who are the target audiences and what type of messages they require. It is clear, for example, that the diabetologist will need detailed clinical information whereas the provider general manager will need information on resource implications and potential risks. The purchaser, on the other hand, will wish to know about outcomes and key issues for quality monitoring.

The second issue to consider under this heading is how to ensure that health professionals actually implement this guidance. The mere production of a piece of paper will clearly not achieve this. The process required to introduce guidelines is a lengthy one and will need to incorporate all relevant health professionals. It has been

Fig. 33.4 Cycles enhancing effectiveness

suggested (Batstone & Edwards 1994) that the following stages need to take place at local level:

- informing all relevant healthcare professionals;
- adaptation to meet local needs/skill mix;
- adoption by professionals and general managers;
- implementation of modified practice;
- monitoring of this process;
- evaluation of the anticipated outcomes of implementing the guidelines.

The earlier elements involve essentially an education process; all require a multiprofessional approach. Clinical audit will cover the last two areas listed and will be reported through professional networks and findings conveyed to purchasers, including planned and implemented change.

As more multiprofessional guidelines are introduced and taken up by health professionals, it will be easier to develop multiprofessional care plans or profiles. These may include anticipated pathways and times for recovery (where appropriate) that reflect the planned nature of interventions to respond to individual patients' healthcare needs. These can then be used as part of standard setting and variance identified through an audit project. It is important, however, that care plans/profiles are not seen as recipes for patient care, thus inhibiting clinical decision making. As guidelines, they are merely indicators of best practice and should not

Table 33.1 Criteria for the assessment of clinical audit

Professionally led	a) Infrastructure for CA is professionally led with sufficient audit support staff b) Equity of professional involvement including selection of change agents in clinical teams c) Participation in college/regional audits d) Link audit to other professional functions, e.g. infection control, antibiotic policy

Essentially educational	a) Identifying and meeting learning needs demonstrated through audits
	    – individual
	    – healthcare team
	    – organization

Addressing timeliness, appropriateness and effectiveness of interventions	a) Topic & criteria selection based upon these requirements
Using criterion-referenced approach	a) Use of 'audit of audit' to assess audit projects b) Use of criteria developed from guidelines & consensus statements
Focus on patient/carer	a) Lay input to appropriate stages of the audit process
Undertaken by clinical teams	a) All relevant professionals have an input to standard setting and peer review of findings b) Audit programme included within business plans c) Demonstration of clinical benefit from audit activity
Involving general management	a) Managers informed of topics selected for audit b) Audit programme included in business plans c) Managers' participation in proposed service changes arising from audit d) Managers facilitate linkages to other quality improvement programmes e) Demonstration of the value of audit in enhancing the quality of care
Maintaining confidentiality of individual patient and healthcare professional	a) Reporting mechanisms maintain confidentiality in accordance with the Wessex policy statement
Informing purchaser and provider strategies	a) Evidence of audit informing the development of purchasing strategies and priorities b) Evidence of audit informing provider development c) Audit programme contains some negotiated topics
Linking to HOTN, R&D, DEC	a) Evidence of topics based on HOTN targets b) Using audit standards which have a scientific basis where available c) Negotiated topics to include relevant DEC recommendations

aim to produce standardized care ignoring patient individuality.

Guidelines, care plans and audit generally should not stifle innovation. Change requires outliers to indicate that improvement may be possible and where this is identified through audit, it should be fed into the research planning process to enable rigorous testing of this potential innovation. This will then feed through the cycle identified earlier, returning to the audit process following the production of valid and reliable research findings.

MAKING AUDIT WORK FOR THE ORGANIZATION

As part of the monitoring mechanism for audit in the Wessex Region, a series of review meetings were held with all trusts in the region (24 in total). As a result of this review process a number of themes emerged as potential success criteria for the trust's audit programme. With the changing responsibilities for the funding of audit, we needed to take into account the enhanced role of the purchaser in steering the audit programme and supporting the evolution of a truly multiprofessional approach by providers and themselves. Criteria were therefore developed which assess purchasers' success in promoting audit within trusts and their achievement in meeting the fundamental principles of audit set out in the Department of Health's policy statement (DoH 1993c). These criteria are set out in Table 33.1.

CONCLUSION

It is worth emphasizing in conclusion that there are three vital elements to be tackled as we develop truly multiprofessional clinical audit:

1. Audit activity must be focused at the clinical team level. This will include building audit plans, undertaking actual audits, reviewing findings and planning and implementing change as a result of the peer review. All this must take place within a team that is honest and open with one another and where the traditional status issues are not considered relevant.
2. Clinical audit will be more successful if it is patient focused at all stages of the audit process. This is clearly a difficult target to achieve but vital if audit is to be meaningful and thus valued by all concerned, professionals and managers, purchasers and providers.
3. Audit should be developed in conjunction with other activities to improve clinical effectiveness. Audit is one of the tools capable of demonstrating effectiveness both in terms of process and outcomes and, as a vehicle for professional development, will assist professionals wishing to improve the care they provide.

REFERENCES

Advisory Council on Science and Technology 1993 Medical research and health committee. A report on research and health. HMSO, London

Adair J 1988 The action centred leaders. The Industrial Society Press, London

Batstone G F 1990 Educational aspects of medical audit. British Medical Journal 301: 326–328

Batstone G F, Edwards M 1994 Clinical audit: how should we proceed? Southampton Medical Journal 10(1): 13–19

British Diabetic Association 1993 Recommendations for the management of diabetes in primary care.

British Thoracic Society 1993 Guidelines on the management of asthma. BMJ Publishing Group

Department of Health 1989 Working for patients. Working Paper 6, Command 555. HMSO, London

Department of Health 1990 Medical audit in the family practitioner services. HC(90)15, NHS Management Executive, London

Department of Health 1991a Research for health: a research and development strategy for the NHS. London

Department of Health 1991b Framework of audit for nursing services: guidance document. EL(91)72. NHS Management Executive, London

Department of Health 1992 Health of the nation: a strategy for health in England. HMSO, London

Department of Health 1993a Clinical audit in HCHS: funding for 1994/95 and beyond. EL(93)104. NHS Management Executive, London

Department of Health 1993b Improving clinical effectiveness. EL(93)115. NHS Management Executive, London

Department of Health 1993c Clinical audit: meeting and improving standards in healthcare. London

Department of Health 1994a The evolution of clinical audit. NHS Management Executive, Leeds

Department of Health 1994b Improving the effectiveness of the NHS. EL(94)74. NHS Management Executive, Leeds

Jaques D 1984 Learning in groups. Croom Helm, London

Knowles M 1990 The adult learner: a neglected species. Gulf, Houston

RCGP 1993 Occasional Paper 63. Portfolio-based learning in general practice. RCGP, London

Schon D 1991 The reflective practitioner: how professionals think in action. Avebury, Aldershot

34

Doctors and management in the reformed NHS

Alan Maynard

INTRODUCTION

The NHS reforms have altered the balance of power between clinicians and managers. Hospital consultants are challenged increasingly not only by their institutional managers but also by their professional colleagues, especially general practice fundholders. The pressure on consultants within hospitals is the culmination of changes begun over 10 years ago by the Griffiths Report which identified not only 'where the buck stopped' but also made the chief executive more sensitive to the needs of government to produce 'efficiency savings' (currently mandated at 3% per annum) and reduced waiting times. The health reforms, with their creation of an NHS market, reinforced these managerial pressures.

Many clinicians within the NHS feel that change has been too rapid and destabilizing. They should console themselves with the knowledge that compared to the United States, they are having a quiet time! In the USA aggressive managed care (i.e. purchasing) may make 167 000 doctors redundant by the year 2000 (Weiner 1994), fees are being reduced and all elective treatment decisions are subject to rigorous managerial review. Also compared to Canada, the British doctor is having a quiet life; the Alberta government has reduced physicians' fees by 10% at a stroke and the Nova Scotia government has cut these fees by 5%.

The medical profession is entering a period of rapid change and its members, instead of denying the existence of the need to improve efficiency, have to face this challenge, understand its causes and facilitate the production of efficiency gains. If this does not happen the status and power of the profession will be eroded and its decision-making role will be taken over by a management structure which, if it follows the US model, will be expensive (costing 15% than 5% of NHS expenditure) and of uncertain quality in terms of producing demonstrable health gains for the public.

HEALTHCARE DECISION MAKING

Convincing the Treasury that it is efficient to increase NHS funding

The British have been remarkably successful in terms of producing a healthcare system which is both relatively cheap and universal in its coverage. Each year the Cabinet agrees a new expenditure figure for the NHS. It does this after an elaborate ritual 'dance' in which the Secretary of State for Health and his or her advisers seek to convince the Treasury that they have a strong case for increased NHS expenditure. The Health Department's arguments typically include the 'guestimated' effects on expenditure of the ageing of the population (which is declining in the 1990s due to demographic trends), technological advance and public expectations (e.g with regard to reduced waiting times).

Conventional wisdom in the 1980s was that productivity gains in the labour-intensive public sector were small. Thus, as a result of this relative price effect (whereby productivity in the NHS rises more slowly than the manufacturing sector), the Department of Health argued that the NHS needed additional funding. This 'wisdom' has been shown to be erroneous. During the late 1980s and early 1990s 'efficiency gains' (i.e. increases in activity) have been produced at significant levels. This has convinced the Treasury to press for continuing and growing increases in productivity (as measured in completed consultant episodes) and has removed an argument for increased funding which was used intensively by the Department of Health in the 1980s.

However, the task of the departmental advocates of increased funding for the NHS is facing even greater challenges: if the Treasury is to agree to additional NHS funding it has to be convinced that existing NHS resources are spent efficiently. Clinicians have to facilitate this process rather than oppose it. The Treasury mandarins are getting increasingly effective at opposing NHS expenditure increases because of the absence of evidence of efficiency and the profession's opposition to openness and accountability.

The need for cost-effectiveness data

Over 20 years ago Cochrane (1972), himself a doctor, argued that most interventions had not been evaluated systematically and were of unknown effectiveness and unknown cost-effectiveness. He argued that these defects could be remedied by 'better science', in particular the use of randomized controlled trials (RCTs).

The use of RCTs is expensive and complex but unavoidable if efficacy and effectiveness are to be evaluated systematically. However, such information is only half of the decision-making equation and cost data are also needed. If intervention A for condition X produces 5 years of good quality life (i.e. 5 quality adjusted life years or QALYs) and intervention B for the same condition produces 10 QALYs, a doctor may choose the latter intervention. This may be an inefficient choice if intervention A costs £500 (i.e. £100 per QALY) and intervention B costs £5000 (i.e. £500 per QALY). Thus, as Cochrane agreed, treatment and diagnostic choices have to be informed by cost-effectiveness data if efficient choices are to be made.

Choices based on effectiveness data alone may be inefficient. Thus treatment B above is not cost-effective and if used, results in unnecessary consumption of scarce resources which could be used elsewhere in the NHS. Such inefficiency is thus unethical: it deprives potential patients of care from which they could benefit.

Cochrane's discussion of the failure to evaluate medical practices concluded optimistically with a statement of his belief that things were set to improve:

> Allocations of funds and facilities are nearly always based on the opinions of senior consultants, but, more and more, requests for additional facilities will have to be based on detailed argument with 'hard evidence' as to the gain to be expected from the patients' angle and the cost. Few can possibly object to this.
>
> (Cochrane 1972, p 82)

Efficiency and incentives

Why, after all this time, do consultants' opinions still determine resource allocation in the NHS and all other healthcare systems? Education, information and incentives are three elements in the answer to this question.

Medical education, both in medical schools and in the training grades of the NHS, is seriously inadequate. In the education system there is an emphasis on the acquisition of 'facts' rather than the creation of an ability to synthesize and critically evaluate evidence about effectiveness and cost-effectiveness. This is as unfortunate as it is deeply embedded. The failure to train junior doctors in research methods ensures that they and their consultant supervisors add to the pool of published and biased papers in medical journals. All too often such inadequate clinical data are used as the basis of models by economists: the sum of rubbish and nonsense is often of little utility to a decision maker in a cash-limited NHS (Freemantle & Maynard 1994). Altman (1994) has argued that this research process is aimed more at the development of the curriculum vitae to facilitate career advancement than at the enhancement of the size and quality of the knowledge base. Further elaboration of the deficiencies in the training of junior doctors has been provided by the Audit Commission (1995).

With technological change the skills and knowledge acquired in university and in training as a junior, limited though they may be, also age. In some areas of medicine where the evidence base is changing rapidly, the expertise of some practitioners may be out of date in 5 years. The NHS is a frenetic place with intense managerial pressure to increase activity. This pressure, together with the audit and managerial roles that have become an essential part of the clinician's life, means that the scope for keeping up to date is limited. As a consequence the role of continuing medical education over the life cycle is of great importance but not well developed. One consequence of the defects in medical education is that effectiveness data, let alone cost-effectiveness data, from good clinical trials take time to be disseminated, appraised and translated into practice. Much of the effort to keep doctors up to date is poorly targeted and of unevaluated cost-effectiveness, e.g. the use of written material about 'best practice' appears to have minimal effect on doctors' behaviours (e.g. Lomas & Haynes 1987, Lomas 1991).

Efficiency: deficits in the knowledge base

Even if better training and well-evaluated dissemination practices were established, the stock of information available about demonstrably cost-effective interventions is limited. The Cochrane database on pregnancy and childbirth (1993) provides a systematic review of trials in a wide range of areas. It shows that some interventions (e.g. the prophylactic use of antibiotics for caesarian sections) are demonstrably effective but have not been adopted by all specialists. It has been shown that D+C rates are about six times higher in England than the United States and that much of this excess is not useful (Coulter et al 1993). The insertion of grommets in many children with glue ear is unnecessary (Freemantle et al 1992). For these and other interventions where there are systematic data, clinical practice can improve considerably as can the efficiency with which resources are deployed.

However, in many diagnostic and therapeutic areas the cost-effectiveness of interventions is unproven (Cochrane 1972, Fuchs 1984). Furthermore, the routine data which are collected about activity and outcome are not used to inform clinical or managerial behaviour. There are variations in activity levels between consultants: some appear to be very 'active' and some appear to be 'lazy'. Are 'lazy' consultants with low activity rates dangerous, i.e. more likely to damage the health status of their patients? Is their low activity due to 'on the job leisure' or inappropriate levels of private practice (Audit Commission 1995)? Do higher volume consultants, for instance those carrying out coronary artery bypass grafts, get better results, in terms of mortality and morbidity, than low volume surgeons? There appears to be a consensus that low volume surgeons can damage your health but this may be due to the incomplete analysis of available data (Sowden et al 1995). Perhaps low volume surgeons working to strict protocols and with good audit can achieve outcomes similar to high volume surgeons?

Data about such questions can be augmented by comparison of readmission rates, post-operative infection rates and other information. All of these data are contentious and incomplete. Their great virtue is that they facilitate the creation of managerial activity, both clinical and non-clinical, which is more focused and may facilitate the improvement of patient care.

In 1841 the editor of *The Lancet* argued for the systematic collection and publication of activity data:

> All public institutions must be compelled to keep case-books and registers, on a uniform plan. Annual abstracts of the results must be published. The annual medical report of cases must embrace hospitals, lying-in hospitals, dispensaries, lunatic asylums and prisons.
> (Lancet 1841)

Florence Nightingale advocated the measurement of hospital outcomes in terms of whether patients were dead, relieved or unrelieved and argued, like a management consultant today:

> I am fain to sum up with an urgent appeal for adopting this or some uniform system of publishing the statistical records of hospitals. There is a growing conviction that in all hospitals, even in those which are best conducted, there is a great and unnecessary waste of life ...
> In attempting to arrive at the truth, I have applied everywhere for information, but in scarcely an instance have I been able to obtain hospital records fit for any purpose of comparison. If they could be obtained, they would enable us to decide many other questions besides the ones alluded to. They would show subscribers how their money was being spent, what amount of good was really being done with it, or whether the money was doing mischief rather than good.
> (Florence Nightingale 1863)

Over 130 years after this advocacy and over 20 years after Cochrane's comments, data about activity, process and outcome, where collected, tend to be underutilized both by the profession itself and by managers. Such behaviour is unacceptable and dangerous: in particular it ensures Treasury parsimony in the funding of the NHS.

Overview: professional duty in the NHS market

Traditionally the focus of medicine in the NHS has been on the individual practitioner who has acted with great autonomy. The essence of this professional behaviour has been that the practitioner is motivated by the public interest and their duty to care for the patient to the best of their ability. In most markets the motive of duty is the principal way in which exchange between buyers and sellers is governed, as Adam Smith, the 18th century political economist, emphasized:

> Those general rules of conduct when they have been fixed in our mind by habitual reflection, are of great use in correcting the misrepresentations of self-love concerning what is fit and proper to be done in our particular situation.... The regard of those general rules of conduct, is what is properly called a sense of duty, a principle of greatest consequence in human life, and the only principle by which the bulk of mankind are capable of directing their actions.
> (Smith 1976)

However, if professions fail to exercise their duties vigorously and explicitly, they will inevitably be challenged by those concerned with 'value for money'. So it was in the 1980s when Margaret Thatcher and her government, anxious to challenge vested interests which impeded change and increased efficiency in the use of public expenditure, began to focus on the apparent inadequacies of medical practice. The proposed solution for the problems of inefficiency was the creation of the internal market.

THE NHS REFORMS
Market regulation

The 'market' solution to the poorly articulated problems of the NHS was conceived rapidly and implemented with a vigour and short-sightedness that ensured that systematic evaluation of its costs and benefits was practically impossible.

A 'market' is a network of buyers and sellers who exchange goods and services. No market is ever free: always and everywhere public and private decision makers regulate the ways in which prices, volume and quality are determined. This is very evident in the recently privatized public utilities. In telecommunications, water, electricity and gas the government, prior to selling this 'family silver', recognized the inevitability of regulation, setting up independent regulators such as Offgas and Offwat.

It is perplexing that in the NHS reforms the need for regulatory rules about the price, quality and volume of care and an independent regulator was ignored. Not only is there no independent NHS regulator (presumably it would have been called Offsick!), it was not until December 1994 that the government made any attempt to articulate market rules (DoH 1994) and when it did, it set itself up as the market regulator! The architects of these rules are seeking to create competition amongst NHS providers. They tend to ignore the costs of implementing such a policy and seem ignorant of the fact that NHS trusts and purchasers can be referred under the Monopolies and Mergers Act (1980) for non-competitive behaviour (Dawson 1995).

How should such regulation be articulated? The purpose of the NHS is to meet patient 'needs' within a cash-limited (global) budget. What is need? Let us assume that the definition of need which governs NHS behaviour is the delivery of care to those patients who benefit most at least cost. If this benefit principle is adopted it is essential to identify both the cost (i.e. the value of the alternatives foregone) and the benefit (i.e. the enhancement of the length and quality of life, e.g. QALYs) of competing therapies so that they can be ranked or prioritized to inform clinical choices.

It is important to recognize that the results of economic evaluation are used to inform, not determine, clinical choices. If clinicians, for personal or public reasons, decide to ignore the results of economic evaluation they can be held to account and asked to explain why they are being inefficient. If such behaviour is the product of Whitehall attempts to buy votes, this will become apparent and pressure exerted hopefully to prevent such inefficiency.

Market regulation and efficiency

Have the NHS market reforms facilitated the achievement of greater efficiency in NHS resource allocation? The purchaser–provider mechanism is very uneven and its behaviour is constrained tightly by centrally determined guidelines and advice. Most of the medical expertise and, in many cases, the better management capacity is in the provider units. The purchaser units generally have little expertise in clinical medicine and their managers do not possess the skills necessary to synthesize data, to interrogate its strengths and weaknesses and to apply the results of such work to formulate more efficiency-inducing contracts.

Management in provider units have been under much pressure from the NHS Executive to carry out tasks of uncertain efficiency. Increased resources for waiting list initiatives, pressure to develop rapidly day-case surgery and the Patient's Charter have been demanding immediate attention from local managers, especially as their effectiveness was judged in relation to their responses to these centrally determined imperatives.

The efficiency of such goals is unclear. Is it more cost-effective to expand day-case surgery in activity X rather than allocate the resources to the creation of assessment wards in which the false-positive myocardial infarctions are discharged rapidly? The Patient's Charter targets of waiting times in outpatients and A & E are related neither to cost nor effectiveness. Allocating scarce resources to reduce waiting times for minor illnesses may, at significant cost, produce relatively little health benefit.

This failure to set performance targets in relation to evidence of cost-effectiveness uses considerable amounts of scarce managerial and clinical time. The opportunity cost of this is a lack of time for many decision makers to use routine activity data intelligently and develop more helpful targets which begin to switch managerial attention away from 'doing more' (i.e. activity) and towards 'doing better' (i.e. producing health gains at least cost or demonstrating cost-effectiveness).

The routine use of activity data reveals large variations in clinical activity. Why do some ophthalmologists do far more procedures than others even after adjustment for case mix? Why do some surgeons specialize (e.g. in lumpectomy and mastectomy) and others 'do a little bit of this and a little bit of that'? Do those who specialize get better results, in terms of the quality and length of survival of patients? Do ophthalmologists who do few NHS operations spend an unacceptable amount of their time in the local private hospital? Without the thorough and intelligent use of activity data by trust managers and purchasers such questions cannot be asked. When they are asked they facilitate a debate about success (outcomes) and obligations to the NHS.

It is unfortunate that routine data of this nature have been collected for decades and largely ignored. Often the excuse for such behaviour is that the data are inaccurate. Little effort will be made to collect accurate data until it is used for managerial purposes. Once used in this way there is a strong incentive for those collecting and using the information to ensure the basic data are accurate and interpretations of the data are presented with care.

Kind (1988) showed that, after adjusting for age and sex, there were considerable variations in mortality rates between NHS districts. Possibly these variations can be explained by case severity and the socioeconomic background of patients rather than the quality of the care provided by doctors, nurses and other staff in hospitals. Yet 7 years have elapsed since Kind's work began and still the majority of purchasers and providers do not use these data to identify variations, to explain their causes and to demonstrate their cost-effectiveness.

In part this is due to the sometimes strong opposition of the medical profession to such data analysis. However, such opposition is a product of their professional failure both to do this routinely and incorporate such practices into clinical audit. The architects of the NHS reforms set much store by the creation of medical audit, invested over £200 million in it in the early 1990s, permitted the medical profession to capture it and produced little of real merit for patients and taxpayers.

Such failures are a product of the inadequate regulation of the new NHS market. There is an acute need for purchasers to be obliged to incorporate into their contracts service standards where they exist (e.g. material from the Cochrane database on childbirth and pregnancy and the advice in the Effective Health Care bulletins). Additionally, the Executive should be requiring purchasers to monitor such data as readmission rates, pressure sore rates and postoperative infections both to identify and minimize their resource implications to hospitals and primary care and to cut their levels. It is well known that a considerable proportion of postoperative infections are avoidable with minimal practice changes (in particular, more careful personal hygiene of those in theatre) and at low cost (Maynard 1992).

Such measures have many limitations but they are a good start in the process of focusing attention on the cost-effective production of healthcare. Unfortunately the reforms have added only limited impetus to these trends. Indeed, the government was so obsessed with the radical 'redisorganization' of the structure of the NHS that only latterly is it beginning to focus on the nature of exchange, the rules for such trading and how these market rules might be designed to facilitate the achievement of greater efficiency in the NHS.

Incentives for efficiency

Why is this? In part there was a belief in government that the 'competitive market' would translate the incentives inherent in the new NHS into better devices for inducing efficient behaviour. In fact, of course, many of the incentive structures have remained unaltered. The system of payment of hospital doctors remains much as it was at the inception of the NHS: basic salary, plus private practice (where available), plus distinction awards. Distinction awards remain expensive (costing over £100 million per year) and are allocated largely in secret (Bloor & Maynard 1992). Chief executives of trusts participate in the determination only of the lowest award (the 'C') but their organizations have to finance the awards even if they are not consistent with the board's strategy.

The reform of the consultant contract is inherently risky for trust management. The present contracts for consultants are for the working life and thus the risks associated with declining income and underutilization of staff lie with the trust. If contracts were short term, the risks associated with income fluctuations and underutilization would fall on the consultants: their contracts would not be renewed if service contracts were lost. This risk would have to be compensated with higher salaries for doctors. Perhaps it is more efficient for trusts to shoulder contract fluctuation risks, be able, as a consequence, to pay lower salaries and also seek to induce collaboration in the context of corporate responsibility of management, clinical and non-clinical, to maintain contract income.

The reform of the GP contract has been a mixed blessing. Much of the content of this contract is of uncertain cost-effectiveness (Scott & Maynard 1991). Although the effect of this contract has been to reinforce nurse substitution trends (Maynard & Walker 1995), work pressure on GPs has been increased and entry into general practice has declined sharply. Thus the new contract may have led to the provision of possibly inefficient services which cannot be withdrawn (e.g. screening of the over-75 year old population) and may be inducing changes in skill mix of uncertain cost-effectiveness. Such dilution of the skill mix is a central part of US managed care policy but the knowledge base, reviewers of which assert that 70% of what a doctor does can be done by a nurse, is limited both in quality and quantity and is a perilous basis for such radical policy changes (Richardson & Maynard 1995).

The structural reforms of the NHS have changed incentive mechanisms extensively. However, the effects of these changes have been evaluated quite poorly. For instance, GP fundholding has grown rapidly in the past, perhaps due to quite generous funding (National Audit Office 1994). Whilst this new form of primary care has been studied extensively with qualitative methods (i.e. descriptive techniques) the number of studies with comparators is quite limited and give ambiguous results (Gosden & Torgerson 1995). This incomplete evaluative basis has encouraged the government to extend the GPFH expenditure into total fundholding from April 1996, whereby the whole of the budget will be controlled by primary care/general practice cooperatives. As ever, reform of the structure of the NHS is all too rarely informed by careful evaluation and review of the knowledge base.

Conclusions

The reforms altered the structure of the NHS radically but the government has largely failed to articulate a comprehensive and coherent set of rules to govern trading between purchasers and providers. The failure to develop this framework has been accompanied by central determination of a set of ambiguous activity targets (e.g. waiting times in outpatients and for elective procedures) which have diverted managerial attention away from the imaginative use of existing data sets and the process of creating routine measures of patient outcome and cost-effectiveness. The management of the NHS, encouraged by the Executive and the Department of Health, continues to be reluctant to identify 'what works' in healthcare, let alone facilitate the translation of this knowledge into changed, and improved, professional behaviour.

OVERVIEW

If the efficiency of resource allocation in the NHS is to be improved, unevaluated reform of the structure of purchasing and providing is unhelpful. Cochrane (1972) articulated clearly both the need to measure the cost-effectiveness of alternative diagnostic and therapeutic healthcare interventions and the need to use this information to determine which patients will be prioritized and treated. Whatever the structure of the NHS, be it a regulated internal market or not, these data are central as is the need to identify how to translate such knowledge into changed provider behaviour.

Reform designed to enhance the cost-effectiveness of patient care is difficult to design and implement. Changes in healthcare expenditure create changes in the distribution and level of providers' incomes. Increased efficiency means that the amount of labour used to generate a given healthcare benefit is reduced. If incomes and employment are reduced and/or redistributed, political pressures to limit change and protect provider interests are created even though such opposition reduces the quantity and quality of patient care. However, disturbing the status quo may make structural reform potentially attractive to politicians if it gives the pretence of advance and is marketed 'imaginatively' to a gullible electorate by, for instance, claiming that reduced waiting times are a product of reform rather than the increased funding with which it is associated (Maynard 1994).

The role of clinicians in the management of NHS is central if efficiency is to be increased. If the profession opposes change and increased accountability it will induce increased bureaucracy, as in the US managed care systems, and reduced status and power. Such changes would not be in the patients' interests but may be unavoidable if the medical profession fails to heal itself by becoming knowledge based in its practices and accountable through collaboration with the managers of trusts, purchasers and GP fundholders.

REFERENCES

Altman D G 1994 The scandal for poor medical research. British Medical Journal 308: 283–284

Audit Commission 1995 The doctors' tale. The work of hospital doctors in England and Wales. HMSO, London

Bloor K, Maynard A 1992 Rewarding excellence? Consultants' distinction awards and the need for reform. Discussion Paper 100. Centre for Health Economics, University of York

Cochrane A L 1972 Effectiveness and efficiency. Nuffield Provincial Hospitals Trust, London

Cochrane Pregnancy and Childbirth Database 1993 Derived from the Cochrane Database of Systematic Reviews. Published through Cochrane Updates on Disk, Oxford. Update Software, Disk Issue 2

Coulter A, Klassen A, MacKenzie I Z, McPherson K 1993 Diagnostic dilation and curettage: is it used appropriately? British Medical Journal 306: 236–239

Dawson D 1995 Regulating competition in the NHS. Discussion paper 131, Centre for Health Economics, University of York

Department of Health 1994 A Guide to the Operation of the NHS Internal Market: local freedoms, national responsibilities

Freemantle N, Maynard A 1994 Something rotten in the state of clinical and economic evaluation. Health Economics 3: 63–67

Freemantle N, Long A, Mason J, Sheldon T, Song F, Watson P, Wilson C 1992 The treatment of persistent glue ear. Effective Health Care 4. School of Public Health, Leeds University

Fuchs V 1984 Rationing health care. New England Journal of Medicine 311(24): 1572–1573

Gosden T, Torgerson D 1995 Prescribing and referral patterns: does fundholding make a difference? National Primary Care Research and Development Centre at the Centre for Health Economics, University of York

Kind P 1988 Hospital deaths – the missing link: measuring outcome in hospital activity data. Discussion Paper 44. Centre for Health Economics, University of York

Lancet 1840–41 (editorial) pp 650–651

Lomas J 1991 Words without action? The production, dissemination and impact of consensus recommendation. Annual Review of Public Health 12: 41–65

Lomas J, Haynes R B 1987 A taxonomy and critical review of tested strategies for the application of clinical practice recommendations: from 'official' to 'individual' clinical policies. American Journal of Preventive Medicine 4: 77–94

Maynard A 1992 Is it worthwhile reducing hospital infection rates? In: Taylor E W (ed) Infection in surgical practice. Oxford University Press, Oxford, pp 119–122

Maynard A 1994 Can competition enhance efficiency in health care? Lessons from the reform of the UK National Health Service. Social Science Medicine 39(10): 1433–1445

Maynard A, Walker A 1995 Managing the medical workforce: time for improvements? Health Policy 31: 1–16

National Audit Office 1994 General practitioner fundholding in England. Report by the Comptroller and Auditor General. HMSO, London

Nightingale F 1863 Some Notes on Hospitals. Longman, London

Richardson G, Maynard A 1995 Doctor–nurse substitution: a review of the literature. Centre for Health Economics, University of York

Scott T, Maynard A 1991 Will the new GP contract lead to cost effective medical practice? Discussion Paper 82. Centre for Health Economics, University of York

Smith A 1976 A theory of moral sentiments. Oxford University Press, Oxford, ch IV, para 12, ch V, para 1

Sowden A J, Deeks J, Sheldon T A 1995 Volume and outcome in coronary artery bypass graft surgery: true relationships or artefact? British Medical Journal 311 (6998): 151–155

Weiner J 1994 Forecasting the effect of health reforms in US physician workforce requirement – evidence from HMO staffing patterns. Journal of the American Medical Association 272(3): 222–230

35

The culture of a health commission: management or medicine?

Barbara Longley, Madeleine Gantley

INTRODUCTION

Two people have contributed to this chapter. Barbara Longley is a medical doctor and provided the second section and the interview data for the third section; Madeleine Gantley is a medical anthropologist and undertook the analysis that forms the third section. The chapter therefore arises from, and addresses, the meeting of rather different perspectives and a shared interest in making use of anthropological insights.

The chapter focuses on health commissions. These are, at the time of writing in early 1995, a relatively new addition to the organizational infrastructure of the NHS and are the result of the merging of district health authorities and family health service authorities. The second section offers a description of health commissions, their origins, structure and functions. The third section introduces some of the analytical perspectives of social anthropology into the discussion of health commissions. It draws on informal interview data that make explicit some of the tensions for both doctors and managers working within health commissions. The analysis introduces the concept of 'cultural borderlands' (Rosaldo 1993) as a way of 'reframing' interactions between the contrasting agendas of doctors and managers. It uses an anthropological concept of culture as constantly under negotiation within specific sets of circumstances. The analysis centres on the constant change that is a feature of working within the NHS and on issues such as language and identity that are focal points of difference; it discusses too the exercise of power at different levels within the NHS and within commissions.

How is such an approach relevant in terms of this book? In conceptualizing the health commission as a cultural borderland, a place where differences in language and identity become explicit, this chapter offers those involved within NHS organization a chance for reflection. It may well be that by the time this book appears, new political debates will be aired; nonetheless, we hope that the essentially reflective nature of anthropological analysis will continue to offer useful insights.

HEALTH COMMISSIONS
The evolution of health commissions

The following references were used in compiling this section: Flynn 1992, Ham & Heginbotham 1991a,b, Kerr et al 1993, King's Fund 1993, Lawton & Rose 1991, NHSME 1991, Nichol 1994, Shapiro 1994.

Health commissions are basically the result of bringing together the functions of the family health services authority (FHSA) and the district health authority (DHA) for any given geographical area. As yet they are not statutory bodies and have no legal powers, a state of affairs that will change on 1 April 1996, assuming things continue in the direction currently planned. (At the time of writing, the Health Authorities Bill, which is the statutory representation of proposed changes, is due to be presented before Parliament.) To understand the nature of a health commission, it will probably be helpful to look more closely at DHAs and FHSAs.

Prior to 1 April 1991, a district health authority was responsible for the running of the hospitals and community services that provided care for the population of the relevant geographical area. It also held the budget and controlled expenditure of the funds allocated by the regional health authority to pay for those services. FHSAs managed the services provided by GPs, dentists, retail pharmacists and opticians, for their population. Their area geographically conformed to the boundaries of the major local authority and were not therefore necessarily coterminous with the DHA (Ham 1991).

The government White Paper *Working for Patients*

(DoH 1989) provided the framework for changes in the management and funding of the NHS, which were implemented in April 1991. These basically involved the creation of what is now recognized as an internal market within the NHS. This necessitated the separation of the job of buying services to care for a given population from the job of delivering them. Thus, whereas a DHA had previously done both, it now became the prime purchaser, only being involved in the running of those services which had not adopted trust status as independent providers. The focus became identifying health needs and buying services to meet those needs. Since 1991, many DHAs have merged to reduce management and running costs and now serve much larger populations, with concomitantly larger budgets with which to apply leverage on provider units.

The FHSA has the task of assessing the need for, and ensuring provision of, primary health care services according to that need. The FHSA should also monitor the quality, efficiency, and cost-effectiveness of these services, being partly enabled to do this through management of funds for GP practice development and thereby theoretically being able to target resources according to need. All this places considerable demands on the infrastructure required to provide and assimilate the requisite information.

The rationale behind creating health commissions is that bringing together DHA and FHSA will allow:

- a cohesive approach to assessing the health needs of the local population;
- the development of a comprehensive strategy;
- the integration of funding and purchasing of primary, secondary and community services.

In addition, the thinking is that it will:

- facilitate the development of local links, thereby enhancing sensitivity and responsiveness to local issues;
- give better, i.e. reduced, management costs;
- facilitate the development of the involvement of GP fundholders.

A recent publication (NAHAT 1994) expressed this latter point as 'the development of a shared and devolved commissioning environment within which all GPs are fully involved'.

The internal market

It seems prudent at this point to discuss some aspects of the creation of the internal market within the NHS. The impetus for this came from the perceived need not just to contain but to drive down costs. Enthoven's recommendations in 1985 suggested that applying the principles of a market economy would provide the incentives and the competitive environment necessary to do that. The Griffiths Report in 1983 had previously stated that the transfer of private sector principles to public sector organizations was possible and the so-called New Right which had emerged in British politics was anxious to apply economic thinking to the public sector. Signs of this prior to 1991 were the encouragement of contracting out, competitive tendering, quality monitoring and consumer power.

Thus, the thinking was that the internal market would:

- reduce costs, promote efficiency of service provision, increase service quality;
- allow for the purchasing of services most likely to maximize health outcomes for resources available, i.e. best value for money, and targeting of service purchasing according to health needs;
- promote working in liaison with other public, private and voluntary sector bodies, i.e. the development of 'healthy alliances';
- increase consumer choice and involvement;
- decentralize management responsibility and reduce central regulation.

Purchasing authorities were seen as pivotal in maintaining market mechanisms and tensions.

They were able to ask a new question, 'Who should we buy from?' as well as the question, 'What should we buy?'.

The work of a health commission

This has conveniently been described as consisting of two main strands (Prowle 1992):

1. The setting of a *health strategy* which acts as the basis for decisions regarding what the optimum pattern of services for the local population would be. Answering this question 'what do we buy?' requires:

- identifying existing service norms, levels of and gaps in provision;
- health needs assessment requiring data on morbidity, mortality, demography, socioeconomic and environmental factors;
- setting objectives, establishing priorities and allocating resources accordingly;
- consulting with 'consumers' and GPs on the above;
- an awareness of the evidence of effectiveness of different treatments, technologies, etc. in terms of clinical outcome and cost.

2. Having a *contracting strategy* to get the best provision of service required, aiming to promote efficiency in provider units, introduce greater specification into contracts, change patterns of service as appropriate and encourage alternative treatment patterns, e.g. day surgery. It requires:

- analysing the market, assessing alternative providers;
- deciding who to purchase from and overcoming any inertia due to the 'steady state' of provision existing prior to 1991, if it is seen as necessary to alter existing patterns of service provision;
- negotiating and agreeing contracts, budgeting and planning expenditure according to developed purchasing intentions, contracts for action, health investment plans, etc.;
- evaluating performance in terms of quantity, quality, timing, pricing, e.g. monitoring waiting times and lists, complaints, consumer views, producing audit and financial reports;
- developing integration of primary and secondary care purchasing by working more closely with GPs and other local authorities.

The workings of a health commission

Formal organization

Since the full merging of DHA and FHSA functions is not yet achieved, most health commissions resemble the FHSA/DHAs of origin in structure, with a chief executive, a director of finance and usually three or four other directors. These usually cover purchasing and contracting, public health, corporate business, acute, community and primary care, in differing constellations. The chairperson, who is appointed by the Secretary of State, and up to five non-executive members make up the board, together with the chief executive and the directors.

Using the terminology of management theory, which is explained elsewhere, the structure of the organization can usually be described as vertical. However, the rapidity of change and reorganization has necessitated the evolution of more of a matrix style (Mintzberg 1983), with the need for diverse and transferable skills to break down traditional divisions of labour. During turbulent and uncertain times, an organic structure works better than a more rigid or mechanistic (Burns & Stalker 1961) set-up. Paradoxically, however, a more hierarchical style of leadership with clear lines of authority up a vertical system is often what is required to provide direction and focus in uncertainty. Most health commissions seem to be still finding their feet in these respects, which means that old modes of operating tend to persist. The features of a bureaucracy which have tended to characterize public sector organizations, e.g. hierarchy, continuity, expertise, clear internal systems of promotion, career development and remuneration, are no longer appropriate within an organization supposed to be operating according to market economy principles. Whilst the formal structure may appear to be changing, the informal structures as manifest by the way people relate to each other and actually behave often belie the preexisting system of power and authority, with the chief executive as head of a hybrid body. (The informal structure is dealt with more fully in the third section of this chapter.)

Values, motivation and morale

Traditionally, public sector organizations have certain core values to which their employees are supposed to aspire. These include equity, trustworthiness, professional honour, neutrality, permanence, confidentiality and accountability.

Purchasing bodies still technically belong to the public sector, but are being required increasingly to operate according to private sector principles. Since ultimately the political dimension determines present and future directions, it can be difficult to get the right balance between central direction and local discretion.

In addition, short-term political considerations make long-term planning and stability difficult. A change of organizational culture is being demanded and this can produce conflict for the individuals working within the organization. When change is too rapid and produces a perceived state of continuous upheaval, motivation and morale suffer, especially if change is imposed externally or from above, which is most often the case in purchasing authorities. Employees may be reluctant to speak the new market economy language or feel that they are not involved in the formulation of mission statements and other official authority documents and therefore cannot 'own' them. At the same time the current trend to merge and 'down-size' or, as the Americans now call it, 'right-size', within NHS organizations can leave people feeling trapped by the need to express their discontent and fear for the security of their jobs. These and other issues of informal organization are elaborated in the third section.

Working together

The recent alterations in the fundamental structure of the NHS have generated a fair degree of diversity and discontinuity, in which change is one of the few things that people consider they can be sure of. Some people feel that too much and too rapid change reduces effectiveness and productivity and has an overall disruptive effect at a personal and organizational level. This climate of change requires new ways of working, which are based on influence and networks rather than on command and control, which are more flexible and interactive, and collaborative rather than competitive.

The merging of DHAs and FHSAs is another time of upheaval when differing organizational cultures, with their own rules and objectives, must 'harmonize' as well as adapt to these new ways of playing the game. Having clearly demarcated the separation of purchaser and provider, two things are now being required. One is greater involvement of professionals in commissioning, partly because of the increasing focus on clinical effectiveness and the need to base decisions on sound evidence about outcomes. The other is a shift in focal point of purchasing towards primary care.

Looking at the first of these points, the early days of the purchase–provider 'split' (as it was somewhat ineptly called) were often characterized by rather 'macho' behaviour on both sides, with mutual accusations of incompetence, as people struggled to find new ways of working and relating to each other in what was often referred to as the 'Brave New World'. As with any separation, this was not always easy or without hostility. The 'arms length' stance sometimes taken by DHAs, who were trying to disentangle themselves from management responsibility for provider units, was often too great to allow understanding of the provider point of view. As the dust begins to settle, it is apparent that the one cannot work effectively without the cooperation of the other. This requires clear ground rules for contracting on both sides, open strategy statements, an explicitness and involvement in risk taking and the implicit dangers of altering service patterns and, idealistically perhaps, openness and trust. It is not always apparent how these characteristics are to be generated within the competitive environment purposely generated by the internal market.

Regarding the shift towards integrated purchasing, this requires that commissions work in close collaboration with GPs. From 1991, fundholding practices were able to purchase a limited range of non-urgent services for their patients. The first wave of GP fundholders was seen by DHAs as something of a threat, although they were too small and too few really to be so. A major problem arises, however, when the size of GP purchasing power is so large that it inhibits a commission from initiating major strategic change in service provision or it curtails their budget. The GPs' freedom of referral is inconsistent with the principles of the internal market but, as with the wider issue of professional autonomy versus managerialism, it is a freedom which many doctors may not find easy to relinquish.

Somehow, commissioning authorities will need to persuade GPs of the advantages of integrated purchasing, without appearing to stage a takeover. From reading that part of the ongoing dialogue that surfaces in the medical press, it would seem that some GPs have been pleasantly surprised by the emerging interest, some confused, whilst others have taken a more cynical stance. Most would recognize that they lack purchasing skills, together with the requisite knowledge and expertise. Thus they can maybe see some advantage in working together with commissions. Some may be excited by the opportunity of developing this themselves or indeed of buying in this expertise from, for example, specialists in public health medicine. There are a small number of experimental projects underway, in which GPs will be able to purchase the full range of hospital and community health services for their patients. Much of the future of commissioning will hinge on the evaluation of the results of such initiatives.

Health commissions also have to reappraise their thinking in the area of 'consumer participation'. The shift of the power base from professional to patient encouraged by the internal market means that the debate on healthcare is being opened up to the views, priorities and preferences of the general public. The structural mechanisms and the expertise necessary to allow this are not commonplace in health commissions, who are now trying to find ways to be more 'user friendly'. However, many of the issues of concern for local people are matters over which health professionals have no direct control. The new *zeitgeist* of collaborative working must embrace not only local people but also local authorities, non-statutory and voluntary bodies. DHAs and local authorities have been struggling to develop this for many years already and the Community Care Act in 1993 added impetus to the need to find the right level of relationship to allow joint targeting and commissioning. The question of leadership is crucial here. Public health specialists, to whom the concepts of networking, healthy alliances and multisectorial collaboration to secure health gain are not new, have a key role to play.

Getting purchasing to work

This section aims to give a non-polemic overview of what health commissions are and what their job is. Purchasing authorities are at different stages in their development and are having to mature rapidly to keep up with the pace of centrally determined change. One of the problems which most seem to have encountered is the need to develop a better information technology infrastructure. Another is the lack of adequate mechanisms to provide the knowledge and expertise to support evidence-based purchasing. The contracting process itself requires clear game rules and good information which should be available to all parties. To date, experience has shown that accurate costing is actually very difficult to achieve. Another key feature of a market mechanism is the presence of competitors, but in reality it can be difficult to help new providers break through into the market. Also, there is no competition on the purchasing side, which can lead to imbalance. Markets do not of themselves guarantee lower prices and have running costs themselves.

The next section picks up and develops another of the central problems, one that is not easily addressed, understood or solved. This is the meeting, sometimes clashing, of values implicit in the establishing of internal market mechanisms within the public sector domain of healthcare, which is seen here as representing the meeting of different cultures. This problem exists at a more abstract, less tangible and measurable level, but has profound and concrete effects. For example, many doctors and other healthcare professionals do not find the competitive logic of the internal market acceptable. They fear a substantive shift in the value base of decision making from health gain to financial gain, do not welcome management involvement in clinical matters and are concerned about the potential of the profit motive to distort behaviour (Bourn & Higgins 1988). Some of these conflicts are discussed in the third section of this chapter.

AN ANTHROPOLOGICAL PERSPECTIVE

Anthropologists in the past have worked in unfamiliar distant societies; in modern industrialized countries, however, some anthropologists are starting to use historical insights in working within more familiar Western contexts. This entails adopting a crosscultural perspective and recognizing and working in those areas which may be regarded as 'cultural borderlands'. The doctor-patient consultation, for instance, could be regarded as a cultural borderland, a time and place in which a member of the culture of biomedicine comes into contact with a non-member of this culture. The doctor's view of smoking, for example, may well be very different from that of the smoker; within this encounter, recognizing how each person views smoking – as a serious risk to health or as an important coping strategy – is a vital step towards developing useful communication. It is within intermediate situations that potentially conflicting perceptions may emerge. Often they remain unstated; the deliberate adoption of an outsider's perspective, that of the anthropologist, allows the observer to identify situations in which interactions may conceal implicit knowledge and values. Such situations, or cultural borderlands, allow the informed observer to reflect on potential disjunctures in meaning and understanding.

We hope to offer a way of reflecting on personal experience by creating an analytical distance, by adopting in some measure the 'participant observer' stance of anthropologists. This analytical distance is achieved through the approach of 'making the familiar strange' (Clifford & Marcus 1986) in order to adopt the perspective of the outsider observing and analysing specific interactions. There may be some parallels between the English speaker visiting a foreign but English-speaking country, such as the USA: there is an expectation that both participants in any exchange will understand the language being used, yet we know that speakers of American English use specific terms in very different ways to speakers of British English. One anthropologist (Rosaldo 1993) cites the example of his Mexican-born father's surprise at a veterinary surgeon describing a pet dog as a 'patient': for Rosaldo's father, 'patient' was a term that was attributed only to humans and was inappropriate when applied to domestic animals. Rosaldo cites this as an example of a cultural borderland, in which two different perspectives meet and a disjuncture in meaning is identified.

It is the shared implicit understandings that contribute to the culture of an organization or a profession: within medicine, for instance, the relatively low status of the general practitioner in relation to that of the surgeon is 'inside knowledge'. The acquisition of this informal or implicit knowledge is part of the process of what social scientists term 'professional socialization'. In one early but frequently cited definition, this means the 'collection of processes by which people acquire values and attitudes, interest, skills and knowledge – in short the culture of a profession' (Merton et al 1957).

Becoming a member of a particular profession has implications for identity: individuals become members of a group with well-defined boundaries. One of the ways in which they make this distinction explicit is through learning a new language: they are quick to define themselves as 'medics' and other students as non-medics; they learn to distinguish between doctors and patients. They acquire the specific language of medicine and the values attached to medical knowledge.

One of the ways in which a profession has been characterized, and in which organizations are sometimes described, is through their particular 'culture'. This term, however, needs some further discussion. A recent anthropological discussion of organizations

(Wright 1994) suggests that within organizational studies the 'culture concept' is used in four ways. These include multinational companies characterizing outlets in different countries in terms of their national 'cultures' or companies attempting to integrate workers of varying ethnic origins into one working environment or 'culture'. Similarly, 'culture' may be the term used to describe either the informal values of an organization or the more formal values imposed on an organization by managers. For anthropologists, however, 'culture' is an analytical concept that is constantly refined through research. In one definition, 'Culture is an active process of meaning-making and contestation over definition, including of itself' (Street 1993).

In discussing the introduction of health commissions, this chapter concentrates on the process of defining culture. Health commissions are the result of combining the district health authorities and family health services authorities. They are therefore organizations in which the very different agendas of doctors and managers may become visible. In a discussion of the contrasting ways in which the term 'community' is used, Cohen (1985) comments that: 'People become most sensitive to their own culture when they encounter others'.

The new 'culture' of the commission is a constant negotiation between the doctor and manager perspective. This chapter results from a period of observation and participation in a commission and introducing both the theoretical perspective of anthropology and qualitative research methods.

Qualitative research

Qualitative methods are most frequently used by anthropologists, sociologists and educationists, all of whom have an interest in recognizing and explaining the contrasting perceptions of particular situations, for instance, sickness or the schoolroom. For an example of their use in organizational studies, see Turner (1983). The term 'qualitative' refers to the research method used, as well as the nature of the data collected. Qualitative methods are frequently contrasted to quantitative research methods; the two approaches offer different but complementary ways of conducting research, the quantitative being appropriate for the collection of large data sets using techniques such as questionnaires and the qualitative being more appropriate for indepth observation or semistructured interviews in naturalistic settings.

Grounded theory and data analysis

'Grounded theory' refers to a process of developing theory from data rather than collecting data in order to either prove or disprove a particular hypothesis (Glaser & Strauss 1967). Analysis involves identifying specific issues within the data, grouping these issues into broader categories and linking these categories around one or more shared themes. The process entails first coding the data (usually transcripts of interviews or fieldnotes) line by line, marking issues as they are discussed, then grouping issues into categories and broader themes in order to form an outline analytical framework. Once the broad framework of themes and issues has been prepared, data analysis entails using this framework in order to code the complete data set. This process may reveal points at which the analytical framework needs adjustment or extension in order to reflect the nature of the data themselves. Data collection and analysis takes place as an iterative cycle, so that identification of issues and development of the categories for the analytical framework starts relatively early and continues throughout the research process.

Sampling and data collection

It is the close relationship between the data and the analysis that allows qualitative research to deal with data that are rich in context and give new insights into little-understood situations. This chapter is an example of qualitative research, used specifically to explore a little-understood set of circumstances. There is no intention to use a representative sample of a larger population. Instead, informants are recruited in order to clarify a specific situation: here a small number of people working within the commission were recruited as a 'maximum variety sample' (Patten 1990), that is, a sample that allows the researcher to explore the views of as wide a range of informants as possible.

Data collection took the form of confidential tape-recorded interviews, which were analysed as described above, in order to identify the range of ways in which working within a health commission could be experienced and described. Semistructured interviews explicitly encourage the interviewee to shape the priorities and topics to be covered. Interviewers undertake initial research in order to sensitize themselves to the issues that are likely to emerge or to identify specific topics that they wish to explore with an interviewee. This preliminary research may combine literature reviews, observational and experiential work and initial interviews. Interviewers use open rather than closed questions or may ask the respondent to comment on a given situation. Once the interviewee has had the opportunity to respond to open questions, the interviewer is in a position both to ask the interviewee to extend comments on a particular area or to request a comment on an issue that has not been raised. The cycle of data collection and analysis offers the unique opportunity for the interviewer to incorporate new topics, or perspectives on particular situations, into future interviews. In this way, new ideas or insights may be described as 'grounded' in the data and may be verified or explained further through later interviews. In this way the data have 'field validity', through the process of being reflected back to later interviewees. This chapter does not address the question of the reliability of qualitative research: in brief, the criterion of transferability has been proposed as more appropriate (Kirk & Miller 1986). Transferability entails the researcher making explicit the circumstances under which the validity of the data holds, in order to allow an assessment of the extent to which findings would be transferable.

Writing up qualitative data is necessarily a wordy process. The data themselves take the form of quotations from interviews, rather than numbers. However, it is the analytical framework developed from the data that provides the outline of the analysis, with quotations from interviews acting as data to illustrate and support arguments. Analysis seeks to show the diversity of ways in which particular situations are experienced or understood; for this reason the number and frequency of the appearance of particular issues are of less importance than the nature of such variety.

Reflexivity

Just as we are suggesting that people working within health commissions may find it useful to be offered a reflexive distance on their own experience, so we open our discussion of the data section by reflecting on our own roles in this process. It is an integral part of anthropological work to consider the relationship between the observer and the observed and to reflect on the perspectives that observers bring to their fieldwork and the impact their presence has had on those taking part in the research. In this instance, there were two researchers, a social anthropologist (MG) working in a primary care group and a medical doctor (BL) based in an institute of public health medicine. Both contributed to the collection and analysis of the data. BL capitalized on her own experience of the impact of the internal market in order both to gain confidential interviews and to develop extended discussions with respondents. Her role enabled her to form relationships that fostered confidentiality and informality for extensive, semistructured interviews. In analysing the data MG drew on theoretical perspectives within the social sciences, in particular the negotiation of power within organizations. It is an essential part of qualitative research of this kind to reflect on the influence of the interviewer. This is an example of the use of adopting a specifically distancing perspective such as that of 'making the familiar strange'.

At the time the interviews were conducted, in late 1994 and early 1995, they were considered extremely sensitive. During the data collection period the BMJ initiated a debate on 'The rise of Stalinism in the NHS' (Smith 1994), drawing attention to the restrictions being placed on staff who wished to voice in public their dissatisfaction about the reforms. These concerns were echoed by our informants. Such was the measure of concern that one interviewee reserved a private room, rather than a shared office, in order to ensure confidentiality. They were assured that every effort would be made to ensure confidentiality. Their views are therefore cited indirectly for the most part and any direct quotations are deliberately short. It would be good practice in presenting a piece of research of this kind to include a brief biographical description of each respondent; here, however, only outline general data are provided. Informants were a mixture of managers, public health doctors, doctors in other specialities and people working with but not employed by one health commission. They were informed that the data were being collected for inclusion in a chapter of a book about management for doctors. They are identified in the text by letters, to allow readers to attribute quotations to particular individuals. The informants' serious concerns about their own futures were not only a practical and ethical issue within the research. They provided the first of our research findings, identifying the important but often unspoken dimension of power.

Power and change

Life is not very clear or certain for anyone at the moment. [C1]

In presenting the interview data, our broad aim is to reflect on how individual experiences differ from the rhetoric of the many documents that have been published during the establishment of the health commissions and in particular, the climate of fear in which many people find themselves working. In this way we hope to counterpoise the documentation that is summarized in the second section of this chapter and the experience that provides the basis of the present section. One respondent commented on the dilemmas he faced in trying to maintain his employment but at the same time recognizing the contrast between his own priorities and the values implicit in the new organization:

I think if you really cared we would actually be challenging a lot of the policies we are asked to formulate and put into practice. I don't do it, because I need a job. [A4]

This informant did not mention power explicitly but it is implicit in his comments, which relate to responding to policy change made at a higher level either by government departments or by more senior NHS managers. These comments identify, too, the personal tensions of dissatisfaction with policy, accompanied by the need for employment and income. Similar sentiments were expressed by another manager:

Any senior manager, who is going to be a good one, must say what they do and don't like, but at the end of the day you must agree a particular direction.

For this person, there could come a point at which you would have to 'bale out', but:

At the end of the day you need a salary. [C7]

One informant commented directly on the exercise of power. In the context of a discussion of perceptions of the NHS Executive, the interviewee described the organization as distant and having little direct knowledge of patient care; the people who worked for the NHSE were described as trying to achieve an agenda that was different from that of an NHS which was established to provide healthcare. They were seen instead as:

a bunch of people posturing for positions of power. [B8]

with little interest in patients or their care or the NHS as many longer-standing employees saw it.

In the face of the continuous change, both doctors and managers faced the problem of maintaining continuity. Informants identified this as an issue that concerned them all and the strategies they adopted are discussed below.

Maintaining continuity in the face of change

In the face of an environment of constant change and uncertainty about roles and responsibilities interviewees spoke of the importance of maintaining existing networks, built up over several years. This was essential in order to maintain personal credibility with professional medical colleagues and to achieve collaboration on specific objectives, such as drafting strategy documents. [B2]

One public health doctor, having attended a management course, commented on the 'enormously useful' aspect of building new relationships and developing others, which laid the groundwork for approaching people informally – outside the formal strategies and plans – in order to achieve urgent objectives:

The job gets done by informal relationships. [B5]

This applied too to dealings with general practitioners, which were maintained on an individual basis rather than through the organizationally decreed – but, in his experience, inefficient – route of health commission and family health services authority.[B6] It was also through personal friendships, rather than official channels, that it had been possible to deal effectively with the Department of Health.

The importance attached to informal relationships, and to goodwill, was also perceived to be of only limited duration. It was described by one manager as:

keeping things going, but it won't last for ever.

He spoke of the long-term damage to relationships brought about by imposing changes and disregarding expertise and long service. [D4]

The central theme of these data, the core of the interview material, was that of change. Interviewers spoke of their reactions to responding to change and having to introduce changes with which they did not agree. 'The changes' to the organization of the health service, described in the second section, were a constant feature of the discussions. They were also the subject of extensive national debate, focusing particularly on the possibility of the change of national government and the implications of any change in governing party for maintaining or reversing NHS reorganization.

Life in the health commission: the 'change agenda'

The second section of this chapter has described the process of the introduction of health commissions and some of the rationale on which it was based. The present section shows how the commission was viewed from a range of perspectives and the extent to which interviewees did or did not identify with it.

Within the commission, there was a view that senior managers were expected to 'toe the party line', to develop policy that was in line with national politically defined targets. In practice, however, it was at middle management level that unresolved tensions had to be worked out. It was precisely at this level of introducing change through the contracting process that it was 'less easy to do business' because of the different priorities and perspectives of those with backgrounds in management or in public health. [D3]

The personal and organizational experience of change was identified in a number of ways. A term that was used widely was the 'change agenda'. In this way the process of change became reified: that is to say that it shifted from a process to a constant state, to which organizations and individuals adapted to a greater or lesser degree.

Interviewees spoke of the impact of change in a variety of ways. These included the creation of new organizations, for instance health commissions; insecurity about individual roles, identities and futures; and finally the importance of using informal networks to maintain personal and organizational continuity during these periods of change.

One of the ways in which people had been affected immediately by change was in the use of the names of newly constituted organizations. One employee of a newly formed health commission was wary of using the old title: 'It was always called the health authority. You have to be careful what context you use the word authority in'. Staff involved in consultation exercises found public perceptions of the structure of the health service were vague both before and after current changes; their problem was essentially that of using appropriate language with colleagues within the NHS, rather than in their dealings with the public. Respondents dealing with GPs found them similarly unaware of the shift from DHA and FHSA to HC incorporating FHSA, as it had had little impact on their practice.

Within the commission, there was a lack of clarity about its role. This centred on the introduction of change, with some people conceptualizing change as being achieved through the powerful contracting process and others describing a process of developing partnerships of mutual benefit to purchaser and provider. In practice, the contracting process had been an unrealistic 'fairyland' – in one manager's words – of negotiating contracts where there was in fact no choice of provider.

The inclusion of the FHSA in new commissions was spoken of as drawing GPs into a more managed framework, rather than in terms of the administrative function of the FHSA. [D1] Integrating primary and secondary care, and bringing primary care within the commission, was seen as the key element of the changes to the NHS: 'It really does bring it together, it lays the foundation to apply management to primary care'. [C3] From this perspective, fundholding GPs, or GPs involved in purchasing consortia, were seen as being offered more control and influence over secondary services. [C3] One of the interesting paradoxes here, however, was in how GPs perceived these changes: while some were becoming actively involved in fundholding or purchasing consortia (and these were the ones with whom the commission came into contact), others were distrustful and resentful of the changes. [A16]

People talked about change in a variety of ways. For some, the changes in the NHS were part of a broader climate of economic change. One manager saw NHS change as only one feature of broader societal change, commenting that 'Life is not very clear or certain for anyone at the moment'. For others, the changes were specific to the political climate that was introducing the 'internal market' into the health service. Some respondents distanced themselves from the actual changes they were called on to make by prefacing their remarks with comments such as 'In a situation where . . .'. Others saw positive elements in their role as implementing the 'change agenda':

I think I personally get a lot of reward out of not maintaining the routine, but thinking how to cope with change. [C5]

At the same time, however, this respondent commented again on the prevailing climate of uncertainty about employment:

With each change, security and job are on the line. [C6]

The way in which the changes were being introduced also had the effect of isolating people within specific commissions: one manager, in commenting on the national situation, drew attention to the limited opportunities for collaborating with colleagues in similar roles:

The changes are all happening at different rates across the country. [A2]

The process of introducing change was described by one manager as part consultation and part persuasion. Managers had observed many different reactions, but 'all had to learn their new role': DHA staff, for instance, had to relinquish operational control and shift to their new identity as staff of a purchasing commission. [C5] In the early days of the purchaser–provider split, those involved had been 'fumbling'. The impact of the health commission was characterized in terms of giving power to providers who themselves wanted to change either the quality or quantity of their services, a process that could be initiated by providers as well as purchasers. [D4] On the other hand, health commissions were seen by some trusts as holding the power through the control of budgets and through dictating what provider services trusts should offer.

Interviewees who found themselves, reluctantly, working for the commission spoke of being charged humorously with being a 'poacher turned gamekeeper' or 'going over to the enemy'. 'People jokingly refer to it [the commission] as "the enemy".' Previously flexible arrangements allowing posts to be split between hospital and district health authority had become untenable due to organizational change which had led to a loss of flexibility in colleagues' attitudes. Indeed, the loss of flexibility, which had resulted from the DHA's direct involvement in the running of hospitals, had on some occasions become a polarization of attitudes. The separation of the DHA's functions into provider and purchaser had had the effect of reducing flexible working opportunities, with implications for both the individuals involved and the functioning of the services.

The view of the commission as alien emphasized the difference in informants' role perceptions as public health doctor or community care manager and their expectations of what it was to work for the National Health Service.

If people go into health in any aspect, they go into it because they care, because it is a sort of vocation . . . but [now] I wouldn't see it like that, you are an agent of government, a civil servant, we are doing what we are told basically. [A4]

The climate of the health commission as an organization had many unfamiliar features for respondents. They spoke of constant 'rushing around', a tense working environment, lack of secretarial support, pending knowledge of redundancies, absence of routine social courtesies, the insecurity of being employed on short-term contracts, having to reapply for a currently held post following a change in job title, a 'paper-heavy organization', communication among physically proximate colleagues via electronic mail and crowded offices. One manager focused on 'the ethos of the work world', which involved longer working hours, an increased workload and the need to be seen to be working hard. Entailed in this was the constant feature of change and with that, job security: 'With each change, security and job are on the line'. [C6]

The commission was observed to be different from working in a hospital in that it worked office hours and staff wore 'grey suits', an unfamiliar form of dress to those from a hospital background. It was seen as remote from patient care, staffed by people with little experience of healthcare and dominated by a language of management. The issue of language recurred throughout: at the same time as staff communicated by electronic mail, a vast amount of documentation was circulated – 'strategies for everything' written in dense, unfamiliar language that often led to documents simply not being read.

While this documentation was a source of frustration for some people, for others it offered clear purpose and identity: when asked to explain the role of a commission, one manager commented that:

paper could get you a very definite answer. [C1]

Another produced a copy of the health commission's 'Strategic Goals' when asked to describe the role of the commission. [E1] For people working from this management-dominated perspective, the role of the commission was clear and its advantages evident. It was seen as offering the potential of bringing together community care, Social Services and voluntary groups in particular areas. For the participant observer in these circumstances, the existence of such documentation, and the particular language in which it was couched, suggests the importance of introducing the idea of 'strategic thinking' into the health service through health commissions. As one participant put it:

The new thing is we are thinking strategically. [B6]

Such thinking emphasized the need to adopt both a longer term and broader view and to consider developing strategies – such as bringing together the purchasing of services from different places – that would demonstrate improved management function, such as cost-effectiveness.

The lack of knowledge and experience of patient care among some managers resulted on some occasions in a lack of understanding of medical priorities; similarly, those with a health service background found the language of the internal market, of contracting, purchasing and providing, equally unfamiliar. The distance from patient care recurred in discussions of the NHSE:

The higher you get in the power political echelons the more removed you are from what matters in terms of delivering a service. [B7]

This tension between the role of the doctor and manager became particularly clear in the case of public health doctors, whose functions bridged the medical and the managerial. The next section focuses on the meeting of these two perspectives.

Medicine and/or management: 'This is not what I became a doctor for'

Within the commission, the environment was clearly easier for those able and willing to use the language of management. However, some managers used this within a broader ethos of public service, of attempting to achieve the best for the community as a whole with the resources available. This perspective placed the budgeting function as a significant contribution to the NHS – 'It needs my sort of person'[C7] – and viewed doctors who failed to consider financial implications, or saw management as irrelevant to them, as 'defaulting' in their responsibilities.

Surviving in what was for some a hostile environment was achieved more or less successfully. For one it was 'clearly a game' that could be played quite cynically up to a certain point. For others, it was a question of surviving because they needed that job. This highlighted dilemmas about individual roles and expectations of working within the health service. The change in ethos associated with the commission led to reflections such as 'This is not what I became a doctor for' and 'This is not why I joined the health service'.

It was in their views of the NHS that some informants made explicit their reservations about the new organization. If the old NHS had been perceived as based on an ethos of equality of access, the new structure was summed up as 'command and control', with:

power running straight down from the chief executive. [A1, B9]

In this particular informant's understanding, the chief executive was responsible to the NHSE and neither the individual nor the commission was perceived to have any significant or realistic opportunity to step beyond their specific instructions.

The place and role of public health doctors were described as an example of a disjuncture between the ethos of the health commission and the responsive, immediate nature of some public health work. In particular, the working of albeit long office hours meant that no switchboard services were available after 5.00 pm and access to some information sources was similarly restricted. Attitudes to information varied from the 'open-handed' approach of public health to the more restrictive ethos of the commission which maintained an interest in the commercial value of certain data sets.[B5]

The responsive nature of public health work on the control of communicable diseases seemed to be ill-suited to description in detailed planning documents. For one person this:

forces you into an unnatural way of working. [B4]

In particular, devoting time to developing potentially restrictive plans, for instance in 'outbreak control', had resulted in the loss of flexibility and effectiveness. It was the informal networks that 'made things work in reality' [B4], a point developed further below.

For the less urgent aspects of public health work, the speciality was seen as particularly vulnerable. It was unclear why tasks such as organizational review or strategy development should be done by a doctor; similarly, contracting for specific numbers of particular operations, done to agreed standards, could perhaps be better achieved by a manager. [B4–5] One manager spoke of the development of a 'ready reckoner' that would summarize the health needs of the local population, the cost-effectiveness of particular treatments and issue contracts accordingly. His enthusiasm for this possibility did not take into account the debates being aired in a variety of health service journals about the feasibility of providing information that would be up to date, sufficiently flexible to respond to change and able to respond to the requirements of special needs groups.

If the managers saw public health as a maverick, not controllable, having sympathy with providers, the public health doctors themselves saw the management agenda as simplistic and unable to respond to the critical thinking of public health. One doctor commented, for instance, on the limitations of the use of measures such as 'finished consultant episodes' or 'efficiency indices' as indicators of good care.

For some participants in the research, public health doctors were seen by provider units as the 'good guys' within the commission, as opposed to managers acting as purchasers or contractors. On the other hand doctors were seen to be using a 'professional cloak as a disguise' and using their own professional identity as a way of demonstrating their status and expertise and at the same time questioning the status of managers:

They're not even professionals. [D1]

This was echoed in the view expressed by some managers that doctors need 'reining in'; managers may understand some of the issues, but underestimate the professional solidarity and cohesiveness of doctors as a group.

Cultural borderlands

This chapter has introduced the notion of an anthropological perspective through a strategy of introducing reflective distance or 'making the familiar strange'. It has drawn on the experience of the discipline of anthropology in observing and reflecting on the process of defining culture within the 'cultural borderland' of a newly formed health commission.

We have introduced a set of data showing how the relationships within a health commission, particularly those between doctors and managers, may be seen as a cultural borderland and the individuals concerned involved in the negotiation of culture. There is, however, a further dimension that has emerged, that of power. On the one hand there is the power of the medical profession that is being challenged in certain aspects (for instance the expertise of public health in defining health needs) or being increased in others (fundholding in general practice); on the other hand, there is the increasing power of managers within the health service.

The chapter has shown how, during a period of constant change, the life of a health commission was very distant from that of the official documentation describing organizational change. For doctors and managers involved in such organizational change, or for doctors as managers involved in change, we offer this rather different perspective in the hope that it will offer insights into the roles of doctor and manager and into ways of introducing or questioning change.

CONCLUSION

In this chapter we have provided a new way of looking at working within a changing health service. In order to do this, we have drawn on some of the concepts used by social anthropologists. Much of this book is devoted to the different approaches, understandings and languages of managers and doctors and the problems that arise at the interfaces between them. By regarding these interfaces as 'cultural borderlands', we have attempted to tease out some of the differing perspectives that have emerged within a health commission and in health commissions' relationships to other organizations. We have used culture as a dynamic and continuously negotiated category, rather than as a fixed attribute of a particular organization.

The adoption of a reflective distance is key to an anthropological analysis, allowing the researcher both to participate in and observe interactions. The capacity to stand back and reflect constitutes the 'participant observer' role: we suggest that this is a useful intellectual strategy for those involved in situations such as those we have described. We have taken from contemporary anthropologists, working in cultures within which they themselves are 'natives', the idea of 'making the familiar strange'. We believe that this approach is useful and constructive.

REFERENCES

Bourn A, Higgins J 1988 Internal markets in the National Health Service. Institute for Health Policy Studies, University of Southampton

Burns T, Stalker G M 1961 The management of innovation. Tavistock, London

Clifford J, Marcus G E 1986 Writing culture: the poetics and politics of ethnography. UCal Press, Berkeley

Cohen A P 1985 The symbolic construction of community. Tavistock, London

DoH 1989 Working for patients. HMSO, London

Enthoven A C 1985 Reflections on the management of the National Health Service. Nuffield Provincial Hospitals Trust, London

Flynn R 1992 Structures of control in health management. Routledge, London

Glaser B, Strauss A 1967 The discovery of grounded theory. Aldine, Chicago

Griffiths R 1983 NHS management inquiry. Department of Health and Social Security, London

Ham C 1991 The new National Health Service – organization and management. Radcliffe Medical Press, Oxford

Ham C, Heginbotham C 1991a Purchasing with authority: the new role of the DHAs. King's Fund, London

Ham C, Heginbotham C 1991b Purchasing together. King's Fund, London

Kerr R, Liddell A, Spry C 1993 Towards an effective NHS – a personal contribution to the debate. Office for Public Management, London

King's Fund 1993 The commissioning experience: learning the art of purchasing. King's Fund, London

Kirk J, Miller M L 1986 Reliability and validity in qualitative research. Sage, California

Lawton A, Rose A 1991 Organization and management in the public sector. Pitman, London

Merton R K, Reader G G, Kendall P L 1957 The Student Physician Harvard University Press, USA cited in Hafferty E W 1991 Into the Valley: Death and the Socialisation of Medical Students New Haven: Yale University Press, USA

Mintzberg H 1983 Structure in fives: designing effective organizations. Prentice-Hall, New Jersey

National Association of Health Authorities and Trusts 1994 Managing the new NHS: unified commissioning of health care. NAHAT, Birmingham

NHSME 1991 Purchasing for health. Conference Report May 16 1991, NHS Management Executive, London

Nichol D 1994 Changing the machinery: a perspective of market reforms in government. European Policy Forum, London

Patten M 1990 Qualitative evaluation and research methods. Sage, California

Prowle M 1992 Purchasing in the NHS: a managerial perspective. Studies in decentralization and quasi-markets. School for Advanced Urban Studies, University of Bristol

Rosaldo R 1993 Culture and truth: the remaking of social analysis. Routledge, London

Shapiro J 1994 Shared purchasing and collaborative commissioning within the NHS. NAHAT, Birmingham

Smith R 1994 The rise of Stalinism in the NHS. British Medical Journal 309: 1640–1645

Street B V 1993 Culture is a verb: Anthropological aspects of language and cultural process pp 23–43. In: Graddol D, Thompson L Language and Culture Clevedon, UK

Turner B A 1983 The use of grounded theory for the qualitative analysis of organizational behaviour. Journal of Management Studies 20(3): 333–348

Wright S 1994 Anthropology of organizations. Routledge, London

36

Clinical and professional freedom

Tony White

Quidquid agas, prudenter agas, et respice finem.
(*Gesta Romanorum*)

INTRODUCTION

Clinical freedom is of major significance to a doctor's participation in management. It has a pivotal role in the relationship between doctors and managers. The management of professions is a key issue in the running of a healthcare organization and it is important to consider in detail the concept of clinical freedom which is often misunderstood. Clinical freedom has grown since the formation of the NHS as the doctor no longer had to worry about the patient's ability to pay before deciding on treatment. This freedom is now seen by doctors to be under threat from government, who want them to be more accountable for their work, whilst believing it is trying to strike a balance between organization and freedom. As Griffiths (1983) put it: 'Involve the clinicians more closely in the management process, consistent with clinical freedom'. However Ham (1994), referring to consultants' professional independence, feels that: 'It's a fantasy to believe that doctors can ever reclaim the clinical freedom they once enjoyed'.

CLINICAL FREEDOM

But what is clinical freedom? Alternative words are autonomy, liberty, autocracy, sovereignty or independence, of which the latter is perhaps the most suitable. Limitless freedom is an unworkable concept as there are limits to freedom even in a doctor's independent practice. If limits are exceeded penalties or sanctions may be used including the controls of criminal and common law. The limits of acceptable professional practice include:

- those set by the medical profession themselves as being the 'responsible body of opinion' which sets the standards of good or acceptable medical practice;
- the guidelines set by the General Medical Council;
- the constraints of the NHS, local health authority or trust;
- in the case of employees, the limits, explicit or implicit, within an employment contract;
- case law, i.e. the courts.

So freedom is not the most appropriate word, although common usage makes it difficult to change. Study suggests that clinical freedom is not a single, but a group of concepts. Such a possibility would go some way to explaining not only certain people's instinctive sense that some consultants in the NHS have always enjoyed more clinical freedom than others but also the confusion about what is meant by the term.

Tolliday (1978) has written in some detail on clinical autonomy in the NHS. She feels that there are two views on the constitution of clinical freedom:

1. that doctors have it by the very nature of medical work and that the medical culture is inconsistent with making a doctor subordinate to a manager;
2. doctors and only doctors legitimately command clinical freedom.

Indeed the Merrison Committee (1975) stated that the argument was widely accepted in the NHS that doctors cannot be managed because of the damage such an arrangement would cause to medical self-respect and dignity and there was a need to maintain the self-respect of the profession.

Another view is that doctors have clinical freedom,

firstly because of the nature of illness itself and secondly because of the determination in the NHS to provide healthcare through confidential relationships between doctors and patients, creating a personalized service as opposed to an agency service, an issue to be addressed later. It is this, and the need for clinical freedom which follows from it, that makes it impossible for consultants to be subordinated to a manager. Not having a manager does not mean, however, that doctors in the NHS are free to do just as they please. Control mechanisms have been set in place which set limits upon the work which consultants undertake within the NHS.

Consideration of these two ideas suggests that the concept of clinical freedom embraces not one or two but many distinct and separable elements which might be unravelled for individual consideration. It is helpful to group them under the headings of those which embrace the idea of clinical freedom and those which, although part of the concept, are in reality arguments for retaining clinical freedom.

The first group includes:

- independent practice with unmanaged status;
- patient choice;
- practitioner choice;
- primacy;
- prime responsibility.

The second group comprises:

- personalized service;
- the nature of illness;
- medical dignity.

THE ELEMENTS OF CLINICAL FREEDOM

Independent practice with unmanaged status

A doctor forms opinions and makes decisions without these being subject to inspection or modification by anyone else. This independent practice rules out management of the practitioner by a manager whose approval is necessary for work carried out. Cang (1978) argues that this independent practitioner status precludes consultants from having a managerial superior. They are managerially freestanding, working within the very broad terms of reference established by their contracts with a health authority or trust. The quality of their clinical work and decisions is not subject to managerial scrutiny or review, unlike junior doctors who are in a manager/subordinate relationship with a consultant, although this may not be overt. These ideas may make managerial control of consultants problematic, but whether they make it impossible is open to debate.

Independent status is sometimes alleged, to amount to doctors being endowed with enhanced or special status in society. However, independent status can be justified if it provides the patient with a personal and confidential doctor–patient relationship thought to be essential for the management of the anxiety associated with illness. There is also the question of whether doctors in general (although not exclusively, as access to dental care, for instance, is an exception) act as gatekeepers to the NHS. A medical qualification may be thought to provide the holder with a better understanding of the needs of patients in totality than any non-medical professional qualification. But such an assumption is increasingly being challenged in healthcare, that it is not a single field of care but separate fields of care and this may complicate the allocation of the elements of clinical freedom to professional roles.

Patient choice

Clinical freedom entails the right of the patient to choose a doctor. This patient choice is personal, freely entered into and based on confidence and trust. In general practice patient choice is more explicit than in hospital practice. For some specialities there may be little opportunity or relevance, e.g. pathology in general, radiology and possibly anaesthesia. Choice is often limited to the patient's general practitioner choosing a particular consultant to undertake prime responsibility (see below), on the patient's behalf; allowing the patient to state a preference for a particular consultant; or granting the patient's right to ask for a second specialist opinion. This preservation of freedom of the choice of doctor within the resources available can ensure for the patient the same degree of personal quality and confidentiality of care under a national service as under other types of service.

Practitioner choice

In addition, the doctor has a right to refuse an individual as a patient. According to Enthoven (1985):

In the name of clinical freedom consultants can choose the kinds of cases they want to see, accept or refuse referrals, arrange their operating schedules, pursue their intellectual interests independently of patient needs, and keep patients waiting for months,

although in the NHS this right is to some degree limited by the terms of service of most medical practitioners. Klein (1985), discussing the decision-making autonomy of clinicians, says: '.. clinicians are free to determine whom they select for treatment and how they treat them'. And Light (1991), in his observations of the NHS, and the work of Pope (1991), on waiting lists, reinforce the idea that consultants may use considerable choice in whom they treat:

> They are not a first come, first served queue but more like a singles dance, where (simply) the gals whom the guys pick are determined by what the guys are looking for, how much time they have, and how skilfully or persistently the chosen put themselves in the minds of the choosers.

While such researchers identify examples of this, White (1992), primarily referring to surgical waiting lists, suggests that usually patients were before the 1989–90 reforms admitted in chronological order according to strict clinical priority and need, with an additional case mix adjustment according to the needs of training for junior doctors. The introduction of the internal market largely changed that to one of selection according to the priority or ability of the purchaser to pay (i.e. the health authority, health commission or general practitioner fundholder). The consultant remains in the position, however, of assessing priority of an individual case within a group contract.

Prime responsibility

Healthcare is rarely now within the competence of a single profession and whilst ensuring that other necessary professionals are not only available but coordinated effectively, prime responsibility for the care of each patient is normally allocated to a specified doctor and may be transferred from one doctor to another.

Treatment in hospital, whether as an inpatient or outpatient, may involve members of a variety of professions for investigations, diagnosis and treatment, but the consultant who has prime responsibility is ultimately in charge of the case. The consultant coordinates all doctors brought in and ensures that the needs of the patient are met. Jaques (1978) sets this out neatly under two headings: firstly that it will be necessary to make an assessment of the general needs of the patient at the time of assumption of prime responsibility, to undertake any action needed or to initiate such action through junior medical or ancillary staff and to refer when necessary to colleagues and other professionals for collaboration in further assessment or action or for action in parallel, while remaining continuously aware of the progress of the case and taking further initiatives as necessary. In other words this is a coordinating rather than a managerial role. And secondly the doctor with prime responsibility has a right and duty to decide when to relinquish extended collaboration with colleagues or when to terminate all further action on the case. However, as Jaques points out this is probably only true for personalized medicine.

In this context it is worth noting that difficulties do arise in linking clinical freedom to particular roles. For example, consultant radiologists and pathologists do not fit the criteria agreed for clinical freedom. Many of them (although there are exceptions, e.g. chemical pathologists with lipid clinics and haematologists) do not have their own patients but work on problems presented by doctors carrying prime responsibility for the patient, usually a clinical consultant. They only perform tests upon receipt of a written request; if they feel that further investigations or tests are required they only advise on this. It is then for the doctor with primary responsibility to decide whether to write a further request for additional investigations. Nonetheless all groups of doctors are afforded clinical freedom although as a group they fail many of the criteria associated with the concept. They do not have primacy or prime responsibility, nor do they provide a personalized service or have a personal relationship on a named basis with patients.

There are therefore certain doctors who regularly carry prime responsibility as defined above and others who do not. In general, it includes all who can talk about 'their' patients: general practitioners, surgeons, physicians, psychiatrists, etc. Anaesthetists, radiologists and pathologists generally do not carry prime responsibility. There are, however, exceptions such as haematologists investigating and treating patients with blood disorders, anaesthetists treating patients in intensive care units and pain clinics, etc. There appears to be a very well-developed etiquette in medicine itself as to who carries prime responsibility in any case and at what point it transfers, but there are significant pockets of doubt, such as consultants and general practitioners regarding, for example, patients in cottage hospitals (Rowbottom et al 1973).

It seems, therefore, that the automatic allocation of prime responsibility as so far defined must always be limited to some particular field of work. Jaques (1978) summarizes prime responsibility:

> In a situation where many members of a variety of professions are involved in the consideration of a particular case, the practitioner who has prime responsibility is ultimately in charge of the case. He coordinates the actions and discussions of all those practitioners brought into the case and ensures that all underlying needs are met. More specifically he has coordinating but not managerial authority to: a. make a personal assessment of the general needs of the case at the time of assumption of prime responsibility; b. undertake personally any action needed or to initiate such action, through subordinate or ancillary staff; c. refer, when and as necessary to colleagues and other independent agencies for

collaboration in further assessment or action or for action in parallel; d. keep continuous awareness of the progress of the case and take further initiative as necessary . . . Further, although it may not be true for agency service, where the practitioner with prime responsibility is in independent practice he has the right and duty to decide when to relinquish extended collaboration with colleagues or when to terminate all further action on the case.

Primacy

The idea of primacy springs from prime responsibility. Cang (1978) defines it as the automatic allocation of prime responsibility. According to Tolliday (1978):

> Where one profession is held to have a more encompassing and comprehensive knowledge of all the fields of care available in the National Health Service than any other discipline or profession, such that prime responsibility automatically falls in the first instance to a member of that profession. Thus that profession may be said to have primacy.

Except in dental care, where a dentist may carry out all his own work, it is only doctors who have primacy in the NHS. The identification of independent practice, primacy and prime responsibility as separate components of clinical freedom, however, makes it possible to recognize that the apparent influence and power of doctors and consultants arose not so much from their status as from their primacy. Tolliday states (1978): 'They make the National Health Service what it is'. They are the group authorized to determine who shall be patients and receive the services of the NHS and are further empowered to determine what other skills are appropriate to the care of patients. Primacy always remains with the doctor, even though prime responsibility for care may be transferred to other professions.

THE REASONS FOR MAINTAINING CLINICAL FREEDOM

Personalized medicine

A fundamental reason for the retention of clinical freedom was that patients have a continuing right to a confidential, personal relationship with their own named doctor. A personal, private and confidential relationship between doctor and patient is built on the clinical freedom of the doctor. Full clinical freedom contains a number of constituents, all of importance to the patient, namely independent practitioner status and the carrying of prime responsibility by the doctor and mutual patient–doctor choice. Clinical freedom ensures doctors work as independent practitioners who are then free to diagnose and treat in accord with their own best clinical judgement and in the best interests of the patient. White (1992) discusses how the individual clinician is responsible by name for service to the patient and the consequences that flow from that for the doctor–patient relationship. Society has placed confidence in the individual clinical judgement of a highly trained and selected group of people, relied upon as professionals, given genuine freedom but not absolute licence, freedom within the five limits previously listed.

Although care is state provided, doctors have clinical freedom in the NHS because current policy is for personalized care. Patients have their own doctors in whom they can place their trust and confide the most intimate of their desires, fears and secrets without anxiety that such information will become public property for use other than in the management of their illness. It is this policy of providing personal care that predominantly, if not completely, provides doctors with their right to unmanaged status. In other words, clinical freedom is directly linked with the work of, not membership of, the medical profession. More importantly, far from being a matter of concern only to doctors, clinical freedom is crucial for patients if they are to continue to have personalized care.

The nature of illness

Traditional thinking has justified the unmanaged status of doctors on the grounds of possession of specialized knowledge and skills. In discussions concerned with management arrangements for the NHS, some doctors have argued that they should retain their clinical freedom because of their professional status. Tolliday (1978) feels that:

> Exploration of some of the practical problems arising from general and sociological explanations of doctors' clinical autonomy had led us to the realization that the real reason for the NHS's retention of clinical autonomy for doctors, despite the attacks on it, was far more important than anything related to doctors' self-interest or self-esteem: that reason lay in the nature of illness and arising from that, the form of healthcare most likely to benefit the patient.

Medical dignity

One argument is that doctors cannot be managed because of the damage such an arrangement would cause to medical self-respect and dignity. Reference has already been made to the Merrison Report (1975) which spelt out the need for the medical profession to maintain its self-respect.

MANAGERIAL IMPLICATIONS OF CLINICAL FREEDOM

Providing healthcare on the basis of a personal doctor–patient relationship has profound consequences for the organization and structure of the NHS. Because of the emphasis on accountability in the service, many have been in favour of establishing chief executives and general managers carrying responsibility for health services within a hospital or unit, in the same way as managing directors in industry. However, because of the nature of healthcare as established in the 1946 Act and based on the personal doctor service, consultants could not be subordinated to a hospital or district chief executive or general manager.

This did not mean that consultants cannot be made accountable. Confusion seemed to exist in the minds of many people about this, some using the arguments previously discussed that consultants could not have managers because of the work they perform but following from that, they could not be involved in management or even made accountable. Clinically autonomous practice, whether in the private sector or within the NHS, is not entirely free practice. As we have already shown, all doctors are accountable for staying within certain limits, the limits established by the medical profession representing acceptable medical practice, as well as the limits binding on the behaviour of all citizens and of course financial limits, etc.

The NHS, together with doctors, is held liable for negligence. It uses a monitoring authority to keep informed of work carried out, advising doctors where work is contravening limits and, if necessary, suspending or terminating the contracts of individual doctors. There are of course difficulties with such monitoring and these are well known. The binding standards of any profession change with changing social attitudes and technology and the boundaries of acceptable practice are shifting constantly. Speller (1971), in quoting Lord Justice Denning's judgement, shows this:

> It would, I think, be putting too high a burden on a medical man to say that he has to read every article appearing in the medical press; and it would be quite wrong to suggest that a medical man is negligent because he does not at once put into operation the suggestions which some contributor or other might make in a medical journal. The time may come in a particular case where a new recommendation may be so well accepted that it should be adopted.

Until recently, employment in the NHS curtailed medical professional practice no more than it is curtailed when undertaken privately. What has occurred recently is that cost control has become more explicit and the limitations of budgets have dictated amounts of healthcare in a hospital or district. The devolution of budgetary control to the individual faculty or firm has now set financial considerations higher on the agenda for individual consultants when considering individual patient care.

To provide for this monitoring of clinically autonomous doctors and ensuring that their practice keeps within the policy and resource limits determined for the NHS as a whole and locally, the policies and resource limits have to recognize consultants' need to accept responsibility for treatment prescribed for their patients. If these policies and resource limits mean that consultants feel that what they do for their patients is unacceptable, then who carries responsibility? In the words of Tolliday (1978): 'If prevailing policies leave doctors feeling that what they are able to do for their patients is personally unacceptable, no one carries responsibility'. Ways have to be found to ensure that policies are acceptable. The practical way is for consultants to gather together to establish a medical view acceptable to all, i.e. what they think of proposed policies or what they themselves wish to propose. This may use the representative principle developed in the past with local hospital medical committees where the consensus views are negotiated through elected representatives, although this role has been subject to change (White 1992).

Much of the writing on the creation of the NHS assumes that doctors' clinical freedom was built into the service because the medical profession wanted it so and the government of the day was not strong enough to refuse it. Foot (1962), in an account of Aneurin Bevan's negotiations with the medical profession in the 1940s, suggests that doctors' clinical freedom and unmanaged status in the NHS was the price the government had to pay to get doctors to enter into the health service in the first place. In such accounts, clinically autonomous practice was seen as consistent with a contract for service between doctor and patient where the patient pays, but inappropriate to practice where the state, and not the patient, employs and pays the doctor. In other words, doctors have clinical freedom in the NHS because they insisted on practising in a state-provided health service in an identical fashion to the way they practise privately. Clinical freedom in the NHS is thus argued to be an anachronism and anomaly, only preserved because of the preference and power of doctors.

In the radical reorganization embarked upon in the 1989 reforms it was the doctors who were ardent defenders of a nationalized structure because clinical freedom had been increased by the formation of the NHS. Honigsbaum (1990) states:

Clinical freedom had been enlarged as well, as the doctor no longer had to worry about the patient's ability to pay before deciding on treatment. The profession was enjoying greater freedom than at any time since club practice began in the 1820s.

According to Tolliday (1978): 'Thus far then employment in the NHS has curtailed medical practice no more than it is curtailed when undertaken privately', although that probably is no longer the case as cost controls have become ever more explicit. Even in the 1974 reorganization Klein (1989) felt that:

In the case of the medical profession, the new managerialism presented a potential threat to their clinical autonomy as traditionally conceived, their immunity from scrutiny appeared to be at risk. In short the basis of the implicit concordat on which the NHS was founded – that ministers would decide on resource levels while consultants would have complete autonomy within any given budget – seemed to be in the process of being eroded . . . No wonder too, that the medical profession's sense of insecurity translated itself into low morale and a tendency to see the chronic shortcomings of the NHS as an acute crisis. If rationing by consultants had always been a fact of life in the NHS, it was perhaps becoming less attractive to accept responsibility for it during the second half of the 1980s and more tempting to blame the government.

A sense that doctors' clinical freedom is vulnerable in the NHS has been increased with the expansion in the number of separately established professions in healthcare during the last 10 years or so. The assumption in the service that clinical freedom is in the gift of the medical profession, and is awarded to all its members, means that if other professions reach maturity and full professional status, they too will expect their members to have full clinical freedom. Such an eventuality would appear to present the NHS with an impossible management problem. One way to avoid this would be to deny everyone clinical freedom. It is this scenario, perhaps, which many doctors most fear.

CLINICAL FREEDOM AND OTHER HEALTHCARE PROFESSIONS

Not only has clinical freedom of consultants been preserved in the NHS, but professional independence in the form of independent practitioner status is being granted to an expanding number of professions within the service. The issue of liberty thus reappears not only in the retention of clinical freedom for doctors but also in the possible extension of prime responsibility to professions other than medicine. Some members of established non-medical health professions have began to question the clinical freedom of consultants' monopoly in hospital.

To see this in context one needs to consider the definition and the aspirations of a profession. There have been many attempts to define a profession. There is a considerable body of sociological literature on professions, all filled with attempts to find an adequate definition. Possession of a body of particular and specialized knowledge, adoption of a service ethic, existence of a professional association, control of training and testing of competence, public registration, length of training and many other factors have been given due weight by various commentators (Wilensky 1964, Goode 1969, Hickson & Thomas 1969).

Others claim that the whole attempt to find a rational definition is misguided, that professions are simply those occupational groups who have been lucky or clever enough to negotiate themselves into a situation of high status and power (Johnson 1972). The word profession is significant and must be defined accurately. Clearly the word has everyday use and conveys more than the general term of an occupation. There is an implication that a professional brings specific theoretical knowledge and insight to bear which non-professionals do not have, or have in a lower degree, in assessing real needs and appropriate responses. There is also an expectation that the professional will exercise judgement in particular cases as impartially and objectively as possible. In other words there is the implication of some kind of ethic. The one question in the demands of various groups to gain clinical freedom is, are these based on a wish to enjoy a confidential one-to-one relationship or merely the desire for unmanaged status? The increasing demands for clinical freedom by other professional groups are a problem for the NHS, for if they are successful and if they are based on demands for unmanaged status rather than the other reasons, then the difficulties of managing the organization will increase.

THE CONSEQUENCES OF CLINICAL FREEDOM

The NHS is a very large organization and much of its complexity arises from the provision of personalized rather than agency healthcare and from the multiprofessional nature of modern health services. The association of clinical freedom with the nature of the work done, rather than with the status of the medical profession, allows some recognition of the nature of illness and the response of the NHS. Further analysis leads to the identification of elements of clinical freedom and the possibility that this might lead other professions within healthcare to achieve unmanaged status, even for non-medically qualified professionals to assume the right to practise independently and to assume prime responsibility. This analysis also raises questions about the boundaries of the various professions, their relationships to NHS activity and policies bearing on that activity. Clinical freedom is not just about how much freedom doctors should have, it is also about freedom for patients to make choices about the nature of healthcare.

Elliott (1978) talks about criticisms of a grey mediocre uniformity under a national governmental monopoly service, the serious issues raised and problems not easily avoided. He lists a number of conditions which must be established if these criticisms are to be answered.

1. Patient choice of doctor.
2. Reciprocal right of doctor not to treat a particular patient.
3. Private and confidential relationship between doctor and patient.
4. Doctors' right to independent practitioner status.
5. Avoidance of records on patients, unknown or unavailable to patient.

He feels these criteria should apply to any health service, governmentally provided or otherwise, which perhaps reinforces the view that clinical freedom is not just about the interest of doctors. Hayek (1960) states that:

There are so many serious problems raised by the nationalization of medicine that we cannot mention even all the important ones. But there is one the gravity of which the public has scarcely perceived and which is likely to be of the greatest importance. This is the inevitable transformation of doctors, who have been members of a free profession primarily responsible to their patients, into paid servants of the state, officials who are necessarily subject to instruction by authority and who must be released from the duty of secrecy so far as authority is concerned. The most dangerous aspect of the new development may well prove to be that, at a time when the increase in medical knowledge tends to confer more and more power over the minds of men upon those who possess it, they should be made dependent on a unified organization under single direction and guided by the same reasons of state that generally govern policy. A system that gives the indispensable helper of the individual, who is, at the same time an agent of the state, an insight into the other's most intimate concerns and creates conditions in which he must reveal this knowledge to a superior and use it for purposes determined by authority opens frightening prospects.

However, the growing independence for other professional groups may make it possible for the NHS to move in exactly the opposite direction to that predicted by Hayek. In the words of Jaques (1978):

Not only has the clinical autonomy of both consultants and general practitioners been preserved in the NHS, but professional independence in the form of independent practitioner status is being steadily granted to a wider and wider range of professions in the service. The issue of liberty thus reappears not only in the retention of clinical autonomy for doctors but also in the possible extension of prime responsibility to professions other than medicine.

MANAGEMENT AND CLINICAL FREEDOM

Concern has been expressed by consultants that if they were organized into managerial hierarchies they would lose their clinical freedom. Given the nature of clinical freedom according to Rowbottom (1978) some of the issues that are encountered are to do with how far external management or direction of professional work is appropriate or possible in medicine. Can doctors be managed by their employers and if so in what sense of the word? Can they appropriately be placed under the control of senior general managers or lay administrators? How far can employing authorities themselves properly guide or direct the work of their professional employees? Secondly, could doctors appropriately manage other doctors without improper interference with the exercise of professional judgement? And thirdly if doctors have authority over nurses or other paramedical staff, for example, how far should it extend and what justifies that authority? For this there is no one set of answers which apply equally to all the various occupational groups under consideration but Rowbottom (1978) identifies four characteristics:

1. *Degree of professional development* – whether the group possesses its own specific body of theory and practice which has moved beyond the stage where non-members can be expected to appreciate emerging possibilities for extension and further development.

2. *The practice assumption* – whether the assumptions, explicit or otherwise, of the nature of the practice in any given situation are consistent with what may be called agency service or whether they demand what might be called independent practice for the individual practitioner.

3. *Existence of an 'encompassing' profession* – whether or not another profession or occupation exists which is regarded as having a deeper or more encompassing view of practice in the field concerned.

4. *Primacy* – whether members are recognized as automatically carrying prime responsibility where members of other occupational groups regularly work together with them on the same cases or projects.

In considering these characteristics it is useful to develop the ideas about the relationship between the management of the doctor and clinical freedom. I shall develop further only the arguments about the first two, because the last two have been covered earlier in some detail as well as clarifying the issues of primacy and prime responsibility, which the above classification confuses.

Degree of professional development

The key question is just how far it is possible or appropriate for a senior manager, general manager or chief executive to exercise control over doctors. The issue here is not whether they could physically do, with equal proficiency, all the work of those of various specific professions or crafts of whom they are in charge, nor even whether they could give detailed technical instructions to the doctors. The real issue is whether they actually understand enough about the work and the needs which it has to meet to manage the performers of that work, the doctors. One is now obliged to define what is meant by the word 'manage' (and manager). I can find no universally accepted definition of a manager, management or the management process. Nor, it seems, am I alone in this. Heirs & Farrell (1989), discussing management and managers, say: 'It seems so often to mean different things to people in different professions, or even to different organizations within the same profession. Unfortunately, there are no satisfactory substitutes'. For them, however, a manager is: 'an individual who has responsibility for making major decisions and for determining policy and plans within any organization'. According to Drucker (1968): 'The first definition of management is therefore that it is an economic organ, indeed the specifically economic organ of an industrial society. Every act, every decision, every deliberation of management has as its first dimension an economic dimension'. Boyatzis (1982) seems more helpful: 'A person in a management job contributes to the achievement of organisational goals through planning, coordination, supervision, and decision making regarding the investment and use of corporate human resources'. Appley (1969) agrees that a manager is someone who 'gets things done through other people'.

Handy (1985), in discussing the problem, suggests that if it is a problem it is one of roles. Almost any manager has an array of roles to choose from. This can result in a feeling of role overload and stress or it can be a licence to play all the parts in an ever-changing drama. All this is a reference to Mintzberg (1973) who describes 10 roles for a manager although this work was based on the observations of five chief executives. Other managerial jobs may not be so wide or so complicated and Stewart (1983) has based work on a much wider field at lower and middle levels, the latter being probably more comparable to the operational role of the clinical director. Interestingly Handy (1985) draws a medical analogy with the manager as a general practitioner:

The analogy of general practitioner has been hauled in from the medical world to characterize one role that is not emphasized by Mintzberg but underlies all the other 10 roles. The manager, like the GP, is the first recipient of problems. However he may deal with them, whatever role he may choose to assume, he must first (like the doctor) decide whether it is a problem and, if so, what sort of problem it is, before he proceeds to act. He must in other words: identify the symptoms in any situation; diagnose the disease or cause of the trouble; decide how it might be dealt with – a strategy for health; start the treatment.

It is therefore not an exact science and for that reason often does not appeal to a doctor's basic instincts and scientific training. The search for universal principles is frustrating. Management is an art with a science base. (In the same way that Russell (1958) describes history as both a science and an art.) It has generally to be learnt by experience and being complex, it is interpreted differently by different people. The manager is concerned with setting goals and achieving objectives. The effective manager is many things, a historian learning from past success and failures, a psychologist who must understand the way people act in, and react to, group situations and an innovator who can develop new ways to achieve desired objectives and apply them in an appropriate manner.

Health service organizations are frequently said to be unique in a number of ways, so management study and practice have to take account of that uniqueness. These unique features include: the absolute necessity for high quality of work, the involvement of high technology, the use of a wide range of human resources, the coexistence of automated and manual work methods, many separate professional groups, etc. Some of these features may be found in other organizations, but the most unique feature is doctors' professional clinical freedom. For this discussion I shall first use the definition of Rowbottom (1978): 'A manager is someone who is accountable for his subordinates' work in all its aspects, who is not only able to assess the quantity and quality but the effectiveness of the work of his subordinates'. This definition is to some extent supported by Jaques (1976) who talks of: 'the accountability of a manager for the work of a subordinate to his own superior'.

Clearly with this definition the more developed a professional group becomes the more difficult it is for a non-member, however generally capable, to perform this managerial function adequately. When a manager cannot help their subordinates with technical problems encountered, where they cannot really judge their all-round competence in any precise degree and where they lack any perception for emerging possibilities of practice or ability to guide the practitioner in important new developments, it is necessary to question in what sense the word manager is being used. Some hospital managers were willing to assert, privately if not publicly (White 1993), their collective competence to manage doctors or any other profession in hospitals, however specialized or advanced the nature of their work. However, further exploration would demonstrate that these same managers did not mean by this that they would feel able, for example, to assign priority to clinical cases, allot particular clinical cases to doctors or to make effective assessments of their clinical as well as general abilities. Nor would they feel able to carry full accountability for all aspects of the work of doctors or indeed of any other professionals, in the same way that they would naturally do for the work of their own immediate assistants. Nor would they feel competent to guide doctors in important developments in medical practice. But this is normal for many managers; lack of competence to undertake the task of a subordinate does not prevent a person managing. The difficulty in identifying a universally agreed definition of managing has already been discussed. As Boyatzis (1982) states: 'Having the word manager in one's job title does not necessarily mean that person is a manager'. Boyatzis, synthesizing the work of Appley (1969) and Drucker (1977), describes management as five basic functions: planning, organizing, controlling, motivating and coordinating. Clearly the managers referred to above were carrying some relationship of control or guidance in respect of the doctors and other professionals.

Problems arise where a manager is fully accountable for the work of another or a manager is expected to help in the selection and instruction of an individual in the role expected and to assign work and allocate resources. A manager usually expects to be informed about an individual's work and help deal with problems. It is normal for a manager to appraise general performance and ability and in turn keep the individual informed of assessments, arrange or provide training, change roles or arrange transfers or dismissals.

A monitoring role arises where it is felt necessary to ensure that the activities of an individual conform to satisfactory standards in some particular respect and where a managerial supervisory or staff relationship is impossible or requires supplementing. The aspect of activity to be monitored might, for example, be adherence to contract of employment, i.e. attendance and hours, etc., safety, financial propriety and security, levels of expenditure, technical standards of work or adherence to personnel policies. The monitor would be expected to obtain adequate information on the effects of the activities of a particular individual and to discuss possible improvements with them or their superior, to report to a manager or superior body any sustained or significant deficiencies and to recommend new policies or standards where required. The monitor needs authority to obtain first-hand knowledge of the individual's activities and problems, to persuade the individual to change performance but not to instruct, but does not need the authority to make or recommend official appraisals of the individual's work nor to set new policies or new standards. According to Rowbottom (1978):

> What neither relationship includes is either the right to issue final or binding prescriptions in the face of strongly conflicting views, or the right to make or act upon fine assessments of performance of personal competence, as is expected in the managerial relationship.

One might question why the roles of certain doctors do not fit the aforementioned facts. Why is it, for instance, that doctors employed as civil servants and junior medical staff are organized into managerial hierarchies, which it is claimed are absolutely incompatible with the type of work performed by a qualified doctor? The answer to these apparent inconsistencies lies in the nature of the work of doctors in these examples. In the first case the civil servant doctors are not primarily employed as doctors but as civil servants and they have no direct doctor–patient relationship and no prime responsibility as a named doctor to a patient; they are not engaged in personalized medical practice. In the second case the junior doctor is only an agent of the consultant, carrying no prime responsibility; the consultant remains the named doctor responsible for the personal medical care of the patients.

It is thus possible to see from these exceptions the importance of the provision of personalized medicine in the concept of clinical freedom. This leads to the second of the four characteristics outlined by Rowbottom (1978), the establishment of a strong one-to-one therapeutic relationship, which argues for independent practice in medicine. For doctors who are employed outside clinical work without an involvement with individual patients, for instance epidemiological work, medical administration, screening or immunization programmes, then the same arguments do not apply.

The practice assumption

The possibilities for managerial organization caused by the characteristics of medical practice described so far have significant implications. They affect management, but they do not prohibit some form of managerial control. Either the profession is incorporated into pre-existing managerial hierarchies, which is now being pursued by many hospitals in the UK implementing the new reforms from the White Paper (DHSS 1989), or an independent professional managerial hierarchy may be created on its own under the employing authority along the lines that used to exist before the 1974 reorganization. Bureaucratically, management organization is therefore still possible.

A patient arriving in a hospital has their medical care supervised by a particular, identified and named consultant, an independent practitioner exercising clinical autonomy and employed to pursue a professional practice as they think most appropriate within the broad terms of a contract. The patients have confidence that their doctor has complete freedom within certain broad limits to diagnose, investigate and treat as they personally judge best. Under these circumstances mutual trust is likely to be the outcome. Thus independent practice is linked in this particular case to the requirement to establish a strong clinical relationship. This in turn implies the possibility of choice and I have discussed the importance of freedom of the patient to choose or change their doctor and indeed the ability of the doctor to transfer their patient where a minimal necessary level of trust and cooperation cannot be established.

However, there are circumstances, for instance when one psychiatrist or one geriatrician automatically deals with all cases arising from one predetermined geographical area, in which there is no effective choice for the patient. Pathologists, radiologists or anaesthetists in independent practice rarely have patients of their own and patient choice is again usually non-existent. The question therefore arises whether pathologists and radiologists, etc. are in independent practice. There seems to be only one firm ground rule, that of a voluntary relationship of trust and cooperation between a specifically identified professional and a specifically identified patient. Independent practice is therefore the basis of personalized medicine.

Clinical freedom and resource constraints

What of the effect or possible effect that limited resources might have on clinical freedom? A consultant has discretion to make decisions about patients now under treatment without review or the possibility of anyone else, even someone from the same discipline, reversing that decision. What is done can be shared in a peer review context, where it can be discussed, but this is voluntary; no one can insist on knowing why something was done nor can they change it. Clinical freedom has to do with treatment of patients, it does not affect management work. It is also concerned with current patients being treated; there is no clinical freedom to make decisions about future patients. Those are planning decisions. It is the issue of resources through contracts which seems to be the major fear for clinical freedom.

IMPLICATIONS OF INDEPENDENT PRACTICE

The question of the management of professionals by non-professionals often leads to the comparison of doctors with airline pilots. It is widely accepted that planes need well-trained independent professionals to cope with whatever situation develops. But it is also accepted that the autonomy can be exercised within limits of financial and organizational efficiency set by the airlines (West 1988). The pilot does not, however, have a personal, confidential or individual relationship with the passenger. The passengers do not have a right to personal choice of pilot. Although the pilot is not able to choose passengers the pilot probably does have a right as captain to put off the plane anyone considered a danger to other passengers. The pilot does not have primacy and although there is prime responsibility while in the air, the pilot's position could be seen as that of an agency service as opposed to a personalized service. It has to be recognized that many patients may not realize that they have this choice of consultant.

Managerial control may be inconsistent with independent practice and therefore with personalized medicine. Where independent practitioners work together there can be a monitoring and coordinating relationship. Although doctors may be difficult to manage there is a need to see that they are coordinated and integrated with other work and developments. Thus as clinical directors emerge, this title implies not so much a managerial role but rather a monitoring and coordinating one carrying within it a limited authority and only applicable within the general terms of any policies or practices adopted by the unit, department or hospital as a whole.

The personal attitudes and styles adopted in the interaction are, of course, another matter. Having authority does not necessarily mean behaving in an authoritarian way. Equally, encouraging participation in decision making does not necessarily mean relinquishing authority. According to Rowbottom et al (1973): '.. no prescriptive rights exist between doctor and doctor, other than where the second doctor is in training or specifically employed as an assistant'. This applies even between surgeons and anaesthetists or physicians and pathologists.

Even for professionals attracted by independent practice, there are advantages to working in a larger organization and a number of ways of arranging this.

The professional may work alongside fellow professionals some of whom may be more senior or eminent, but if independent practice is required, this is counter to the establishment of a managerial relationship. At present even an employing authority has no right to impose particular rules or policies or to demand that specific tasks be accomplished or that specific methods be followed, unless these have been the subject of specific contract negotiation.

The NHS recognizes no right on the part of a sponsoring body such as a FHSA, health board, HA or trust to tell the professional how to diagnose or treat or what priorities to give to patients or how to organize their work. Although hospital consultants are actually in the salaried employment of HAs or trusts who provide their premises, supporting staff, equipment and materials, they too recognize no constraints on work that are not the subject of specific agreement.

Doctors are usually grouped with fellows into divisions or departments and firms and it is usual for a senior member chosen by the group to act as spokesperson and coordinator. However, the role of elected representatives has limits and they cannot be held accountable by the employing authority. In addition, certain designated senior staff, not necessarily of the same professional group, act as agents or officers of the employing authority with the job of carrying out additional and broader focused coordination, as well as monitoring adherence to contract conditions.

Where a number of specialities exist, questions on how many should have separate representation to speak and negotiate on their behalf may arise. How many specialities should be banded together? It is difficult for non-members of any distinct professional group or subgroup to be able to command adequate understanding of the specific needs and emerging possibilities for new developments and so to act as effective spokespersons and this is an issue discussed in Chapter 4 and returned to in Chapter 6.

As any profession develops, members exchange ideas with one another through professional associations and develop common practice and extend knowledge. This is additional to a motive to protect their collective interests, a desire they may share with less well-developed occupational groups. They will take an interest in training and the setting of qualifications. They will wish to control practice development in specific organizations where they are employed in large numbers and they will look to establish management posts filled by their own members with direct access to policy forming bodies. In recent years the gathering together of social workers in Social Services departments, headed by directors who are often chosen from the ranks of qualified social workers, suggests a recognition that social workers have now reached a stage of professional development which prohibits effective management by non-members.

One issue that seems appropriate to raise is that a professional manager has to work within a professional code of conduct whereas a non-professional manager or administrator has no such code (Heys 1991): 'Managers have a unique position within the NHS. In contrast to almost every other discipline in the service there is no code of conduct to judge their actions against'. Although Dixon (1991), former director of the Institute of Health Service Management, said: '. . that although the conduct issue had been discussed frequently it was dismissed as "inappropriate"'. An all-party select committee of MPs, however, felt that managers should also be held accountable for their mistakes (HMSO 1990). The issue has been revisited recently in a discussion on the case for a code of ethics for managers (Bayliss 1994, IHSM 1994).

SUMMARY AND CONCLUSIONS

The question is how much independence doctors should have, when in theory and practice they are employed within an organization. From the discussion there is almost no general answer. It appears, however, that where the work assumptions of the professional group in certain situations demand independent practice, as appears to be the case with doctors involved in clinical work, this is inconsistent with managerial hierarchy or technical direction, although coordinating and monitoring relationships are feasible. But in the words of Rowbottom (1978):

Over and above this they offer definite statements about the conditions under which any professional may be assimilated into bureaucratic organization, and the specific circumstances in which radically different organizational arrangements become necessary.

One difficult issue in the NHS is that of the development of an adequate managerial structure. There is a desire to establish a unified managerial structure, neatly and tidily organized under a single manager or chief executive, but for reasons outlined this has not proved easy. It has been rejected because consultants, it is claimed, cannot be managed and it is not organizationally possible to place a chief executive in a position of managerial accountability to consultants and retain clinical freedom as the foundation of personalized services for patients. It is not possible to do so even if the chief executive is also a doctor. Another possibility, according to Jaques (1978), was to separate doctors from the rest of the services:

A role might then be established which would carry coordinative authority only in relation to the doctors, but managerial authority with respect to the other services. This concept, however, also proved unacceptable since it was found to run counter to the professional independence required in a wide range of medical services including, for example, nursing, community medicine, medical administration, many paramedical services, and the administrative services.

The questions arise as to who should be the leader of the teams and who in the final analysis should be responsible if anything goes seriously wrong. It is these questions which reflect the lack of provision for explicit allocation of primacy or of prime responsibility to professions other than medicine. For if primacy or prime responsibility could be specifically allocated to one member of a team, then the uncertainty concerning leadership and final responsibility would not arise. When things go wrong individual accountability can all too easily be lost or hidden in a group. Finally, and the most difficult question of all, what is the future of clinical freedom? What effect does the introduction of guidelines and treatment protocols based on outcome studies have on clinical freedom? Watson (1994) feels that the governmental outcome initiative is a threat and claims that the creation of the internal market has introduced the notion that purchasers are imposing treatment protocols on providers, although this is denied by the CMO (Calman 1994), a view supported by the Health Secretary who tried to allay concern that there might be a threat to clinical freedom and independence from clinical guidelines (Bottomley 1994). She felt that these should be advisory rather than prescriptive and preserve doctors' freedom to treat each patient as an individual. This is an area where ethical considerations need to be introduced and is discussed further in Chapter 37.

REFERENCES

Appley L A 1969 A management concept. American Management Associations/Arrow Books, New York
Bayliss P 1994 A case for a code of ethics. Health Services Management
Bottomley V 1994 Opening address, Conference of the British Association of Medical Managers, Brighton
Boyatzis R E 1982 The competent manager. A model for effective performance. Wiley, New York
Calman K 1994 Report. Hospital Doctor 16 June: 8
Cang S 1978 Professionals in health and social service organizations. In: Jaques E (ed) Health Services. Heinemann, London, Ch 5
Dixon M 1991 Cited in: Heys R Code of conduct needed to keep managers in line. Hospital Doctor C11(45): 28
DHSS 1989 Working for patients. HMSO, London
Drucker P F 1968 The practice of management. Pan Books, London
Drucker P F 1977 Management. Tasks, responsibilties, practices. Pan Business Management, London, pp 137–147
Elliott J 1978 Health services. Heinemann, London
Enthoven A C 1985 Reflections on the management of the National Health Service. Nuffield Provincial Hospitals Trust, London
Foot M 1962 Aneurin Bevan: a biography. MacGibbon & Kee, London
Goode W J 1969 The theoretical limits of professionisation. in Etzioni.
Griffiths R 1983 NHS management inquiry. DHSS, London
Ham C 1994 Cited in: Agnew T (ed) Should doctors practise from chambers? Medicom (UK), Kingston on Thames, pp 16–18
Handy C B 1985 Understanding organizations, 3rd edn. Penguin, London
Hayek F A 1960 The constitution of liberty. Routledge & Kegan Paul, London, p 300
Heirs B, Farrell P 1989 The professional decision thinker. Our new management priority. Grafton, London
Heys R 1991 Code of conduct needed to keep managers in line. Hospital Doctor C11(45): 28
Hickson D J, Thomas M W 1969 Professionalisation in Britain, a preliminary measurement. Sociology 3(1): 37–53
HMSO 1990 Select committee on the parliamentary commissioner for administration. Third report. HMSO, London
Honigsbaum F 1990 The evolution of the NHS. British Medical Journal 301: 694–699
IHSM 1994 Regional consultation on ethics for health service managers. Institute of Health Service Managers, London
Jaques E 1976 A General theory of bureaucracy. Heinemann, London
Jaques E 1978 Health services. Heinemann, London
Johnson T J 1972 Professions and power. Macmillan, London
Klein R 1985 Who makes the decisions in the NHS? In: NHS management perspectives for doctors. King's Fund, London
Klein R 1989 The politics of the NHS, 2nd edn. Longman, Harlow
Light D W 1991 Observations on the NHS reforms: an American perspective. British Medical Journal 303: 568–570
Merrison A W 1975 Report of committee of inquiry into the regulation of the medical profession. HMSO, London
Mintzberg H 1973 The nature of managerial work. Harper & Row, New York
Pope C 1991 Trouble in store: some thoughts on the management of waiting lists. Sociology of Health and Illness 13: 193–212
Rowbottom R W 1978 Professionals in health and social service organizations. In: Jaques E (ed) Health services. Heinemann, London
Rowbottom R W et al 1973 Hospital organization. Heinemann, London, Ch 9
Russell B 1958 Portraits from memory. Allen & Unwin, London
Speller S R 1971 Law relating to hospitals and kindred institutions, 5th edn. H.K. Lewis, London, pp 150–151
Stewart R 1983 Choices for the manager. McGraw-Hill, Maidenhead

Tolliday H. 1978 Clinical autonomy. In: Jaques E (ed) Health services. Heinemann, London

Watson J 1994 Report. Hospital Doctor 6 June: 8

West P A 1988 Understanding the NHS: a question of incentives. King's Fund, London, p 99

White A 1992 Management for clinicians. Edward Arnold, London, Ch 5

White A 1993 The role of hospital consultants in management, decision making and change. PhD thesis, University of Bath

Wilensky H L 1964 The professionalisation of everyone? American Journal of Sociology 70: 137–158

37

Ethics

Roger Higgs

If major change has recently been afoot in medicine and management, then the same can be said for ethics, both as an academic subject and in its applied form related to healthcare or business studies. Twenty years ago talking about medical ethics in a professional context was not easy. In the hospital where I was a medical registrar I invited fellow doctors to an ethical debate. 'No thanks, I've got antibodies to those sorts of things,' said one colleague over her shoulder. 'When I hear the word ethics, I reach for my golf clubs,' joked a consultant (I don't think he realized the original quote came from Nazi Germany!).

But now medical ethics is an established and growing area of interest on both sides of the Atlantic (as is business ethics) and an accepted part of the undergraduate curriculum and of continuing professional development. Starting as it has done from the realities of medical problem solving, particularly in relation to new technology, research and consumerism, medical ethics is now a legitimate area for public debate in the media and has even created a reaction in philosophy itself, kickstarting a new approach to applied ethics in many academic centres.

But because of its relative youth, we can say that the contribution of ethical thinking to the actual practice of healthcare remains unclear. How often and how much does it help in day-to-day work? Will it help in management? I hope to show that in spite of the many different ways in which people think about moral problems, there are a number of different contributions that ethics can make. There are accepted frameworks we can use which will be constructive and coherent and may help managers in healthcare in real ways when faced with a problem or difficult choice. For instance, there may be confusion in an organization, or part of organization, where a conflict, say between cost saving and providing a comprehensive service, may be difficult to resolve. There may be the need to address the values or aims of the service or to help new entrants or learners to understand what these are in order to distinguish a professional from a purely personal response.

WHAT IS BEST?

How does this differ from the sort of thinking that clinicians and managers are used to doing anyway? There is certainly a school of thought which suggests (and has suggested since Plato) that we could find out what to do if only we knew more. 'No one does wrong knowingly' was the gist of the words put into Socrates' mouth well over 2000 years ago and, like a modern parody, there is a tendency for some people when presented with a difficult decision simply to demand or go in search of more medical data. This may well be helpful but equally may not get us off the hook. Medical ethics is asking questions which are much broader. What is right here? What is best, all things being considered? What is the better or the least bad decision amongst those presented to us? As such the details of the service, clinical, administrative, political and so on, may be of relevance but the moral decision demands more. I should say here that I don't see an important distinction between morality and ethics or the words 'moral' and 'ethical'. The important distinction is between a judgement about facts, what is so, and about values, what should be so. Even if some thinkers maintain that this line is hard to draw – and I agree with them – the implications are clear. We need to be able to decide about right and wrong, ourselves, in context. No amount of research, questionnaires or statistics will finally answer the questions of right or wrong in medicine and management. We need an understanding of how to ask and answer these questions in their own right and this may entail a new understanding of the insights of medical ethics.

WHY A NEW SUBJECT AREA?

But why do we need new understanding? Isn't the working of our own conscience or a knowledge of the values we hold as people quite enough? Quite possibly, yes, and certainly nothing that is proposed here is being suggested as separate or different from the moral standards we have been used to since a child. Quite the reverse: a lie is a lie whenever it is told and promises should be no more broken in the board room than they were in the playground. But we need to know something of our own ways of thinking and reasoning before we can expect others to be ruled by them, even if we don't change our conclusions as a result. The issues are not, largely, to do with what will just impinge on us.

There are likely to be greater complexities and conflicts, potential and real, in modern healthcare than simple moral rules have prepared us for. We have probably been used in our clinical work to some of the dilemmas that doctors face, in particular through the understanding that it is not only our own moral standards and structures but also those of the patients and staff which have to be taken into account. In addition, providing healthcare for a pluralistic society, with a developing set of aims and against an altering political and financial background, may mean that decisions may have to be taken about problems which we have not faced before. Perhaps we personally would not have made those choices had things been different but if they become policy they have to be adhered to. So if we are to remain in post, they'd better be good. As the Hippocratic tradition has it, 'If treatment is good, treatment after thought will be better'. Given the pressure of work, in clinical and management arenas, it just may be that some of the thinking has to be done before we meet the problem.

WHEN DO WE NEED IT?

There are several ways in which the need for this type of thinking may present itself. As we have suggested, many of the decisions made in clinical care already are based on judgements or moral values rather than pure medical fact, for instance: Is this man an alcoholic? Is this properly a health problem? What resources should come from the public coffer? And so on. (In almost all cases, ethical 'evidence' is only one part of the total picture, to be weighed with other concerns.) But changes in the structure and funding of healthcare may well mean that an organization will need to examine the values it works to at the earliest possible opportunity. Also, anyone changing their role within such an organization is well advised to work with colleagues to do something similar on a personal basis.

Moving from proactive to reactive mode, moral problems may appear in several guises. Some may come ready labelled, so we can say 'Ah, this looks like an issue of confidentiality' or whatever and know where at least to start. Others may be new: for instance, if a member of staff complains that she is taking part in a procedure which she feels is experimental. But many issues will appear in disguise and take us by surprise whatever we do. Here the marker is a feeling of unease about a decision or an emotion we had not expected, perhaps sudden anxiety or distrust. It is important not to dispose of these feelings immediately without noting them (even if we have to be equable on the instant), as they will indicate in all probability that there is a moral issue which should be examined. And finally, it is likely that we should use ethical thinking in general in any assessment of the organization or its work. Are we responding as we should to real need and if so, whose and how well?

LEVELS

In order to look at these issues we shall need some frameworks. These in turn will often have been shaped by thinkers, authorities and processes which are quite beyond the scope of this article. But we can now see that there is a possible series of levels and we may wish to be aware where we are and at which level we wish to work (Fig. 37.1).

I shall largely be working at the fourth level, for several reasons. One is that to take several particular issues and do them all justice will not be easy, although we shall use examples. The second is that this is an area where answers do not come by rote and although routines and procedures may be of help, they will be of process and not of content and require us to be skilled.

Appropriate range and depth

This chapter aims to move and focus mainly on the fourth level, in order to offer a way of thinking about a broad range of areas rather than attempt a spuriously

---

1. Sensation of something not being right.
2. The stated need, in a concrete situation, that something needs to be examined.
3. The moral issues, stated in ways we can recognize – such as the abortion debate, clinical freedom, confidentiality, employees' health.
4. Possible ethical frameworks.
5. Philosophy, law or religious belief underpinning these.

Fig. 37.1

confident answer to a narrow range. Equally, to go beyond and look at the fifth level, the background to moral thinking, takes us not just into volumes but into libraries. A framework should enable us to check that we have considered an issue from different angles, in sufficient depth. This already outlines two approaches. The first has been implied already: that a simple statement, one which could be called a rule or guideline (if looked at positively) or a 'knee jerk response' (if you don't like it!), is unlikely to be enough. Even if we are looking at principles (and we shall be), the grounding of any principle in its practical context is vital for the judgement to make sense and an examination of the principle, its words and its meanings and the way in which it may with benefit be used in thinking about a particular policy or problem, is a prerequisite of nuanced moral behaviour. The manager who says to themselves 'tell no lies' and then divulges to the visiting journalist the details of a particular situation without any consideration may be a saint, but they may also be simply thoughtless and dangerous. There may often not be time to think through things in great depth but not thinking through them at all is a particular form of moral ineptitude. In the situation we have quoted, for instance, many other ethical issues would come to mind: for instance, the right of the enquirer to know, the question of public safety, confidentiality for individual patients, the responsibilities of employees, the prejudicing of a possible legal case, and so on. It may be that, having considered the options, a manager would simply tell what they considered to be the facts – what we might want to call 'the truth'. It would certainly be refreshing in comparison with the usual style of 'official statements'. But before the choosing of a simple and clear road through there is other rough but fertile ground to be checked.

How much checking out is enough? No one can answer this. Healthcare, like politics, has its own particular time scale and rhythm, and time is seldom on our side. A manager needs to make competent decisions quickly or may begin to seem incompetent. Sometimes the best may be enemy of the good. What we are suggesting here is that being able to identify speedily a moral issue or component in a problem and to think it through adequately is a skill like many others, capable of being learned and developed or not as desired. Once that skill is deployed, good decision making may be speeded, not impeded. This implies, like all skills, that they should be internal, creative and available to individuals, not external, restrictive and necessarily conforming. Hence our second requirement, that a moral position is one examined from more than one angle and is thus a rounded or three-dimensional assessment.

Three-dimensional thinking

There has already been enough from Marcuse and others to make this sort of language perhaps a little confusing. All I wish to imply is that where there is a moral question to be considered, there is already likely to be more than one viewpoint and for a proper moral evaluation, these viewpoints should be visited. I shall propose two different ways of doing this here. One is by using *four principles*, a reasonably common currency within Anglo-American healthcare now, to analyse and challenge a particular view. For instance, in the confrontation between manager and press quoted above, we could see one potential conflict if a member of staff were rumoured to be HIV positive. The conflict might be between the public interest – in the sense of promoting health benefit and minimizing harm, rather than prurience – and the manifest needs of an individual patient (for, though a professional, such the infected person undoubtedly is) for confidentiality and control of information about their own person, which we might designate as within the realm for respect of personal autonomy. The second way is by examining the *perspectives, roles or relationships* of those involved in the decision or on whom it impinges. If we continue the same example, these undoubtedly include the professional, their partner(s), the staff they work with, former and future patients or children of patients, but also might include the views of groups or services – a ward, a health authority, a government department, a defence association, a family. Some of these views might be quite clearly articulated, some not.

But surely, someone may ask, something is either right or wrong irrespective of to whom it happens? Otherwise the spectre of special pleading or privilege may arise: we may be engulfed (to change the metaphor) by the shifting sands of moral cynicism. There is always this danger, to which we should be alert. But I am not implying that we alter rules to fit cases as we wish: I am arguing that ethical thinking in this area must deal with the concrete and the particular and that part of that has to be the views and thinking of those actually or potentially involved. The context matters: it will be quite different if the professional involved (in the case above) is a consultant gynaecologist or a laboratory technician. But equally, whatever decision is made, the 'other views' – views of a differently conducted response or a different potential outcome – will not go away. They have to be taken into account as part of the analysis, respected as valid and heard; and they have to be dealt with afterwards, just as a surgeon would follow up a patient who had been operated on. If, for instance, the decision is taken that information has to be divulged against a person's wishes (and this is deliberately extreme as there may be many ways in which this could be negotiated differently), there are issues about that person's future, the broken trust, employer–employee relationships, responsibility and so on to be considered.

Consequences and duties

This points us down towards the fifth level, to consider briefly two ways of looking at moral decision making which are often in conflict. One is to take decisions by weighing the *consequences* which might be judged to stem from any of a series of different actions or stances. The clearest form of this in philosophical thinking is utilitarianism, which suggests that decisions can be made by weighing between choices which would confer the greatest benefit to the greatest number (adding that each person be counted as one and no one as more than one). However difficult this is in practice, utilitarian thinking is part of modern healthcare and most of us respond to consequentialist styles of thinking – indeed, the whole concept of 'outcome' could be seen to revolve round it.

The other way of thinking, associated again in its purest form with the philosopher Immanuel Kant, is *deontology* (Beauchamp & Childress 1989), responding to moral rules, commitments or duties seen as powerful and immutable in themselves and not altered by consequences. (The origin of the word is not, as some think, from the Latin *deus* = god but from the Greek *dei* = it must (be done, etc.).) Again, we can all recognize duties which we should initially agree upon as universal rules – not to kill someone, to tell the truth and so on. In pure form, Kant saw these duties as absolute, and many, particularly those who follow a directive religious faith, may find this certainty comforting. Such duties are also the reciprocal of rights: a right implies that someone has a duty to respond to it (and it is worth noting in passing that if a right does not confer a duty on someone, the language may not be helpful). But we should not take too long to realize that binding ourselves to an inalienable duty may be very different from expecting the same of others, who may have a different set of absolutes or feel that there are no absolutes at all. We should expect not to kill and not to be killed, for instance, but are brought up a little by discovering that polls show that a sizable minority of the British people do not share that view in certain circumstances: for instance when it comes to assisting the death on request of the irredeemably suffering terminally ill, while others think that the British abortion law could be construed as flaunting that key duty.

Thus ethics in management is likely to suggest that, whatever our own personal moral stance, it is going to be very difficult to take a rigid or absolute stance on any of the major issues in terms of moral duties but equally that we cannot afford (morally) only to be guided by contingent consequences. There has to be a 'bottom line'. Via media anglicana? Another mixed economy? Or another of the spurious sayings of Confucius: 'He who sits on fence sees further'? So be it.

Detecting the moral issue

Let us for a moment revisit the five levels which were formerly proposed. It is suggested that some issues present themselves immediately at level 3, having been identified as 'issues', that is, areas which we know as being contentious, fraught with conflict or simply ones where people already have expressed moral disagreements. Any clinician or manager who shrugged their shoulders at this point could reasonably be considered to have failed at the very least on an educational level. It isn't good enough for a manager (or clinician) to know nothing at all about different people's views of, say, abortion, blood transfusion or care for the dying. There are texts available and if there are not, then it is always right to ask the people themselves.

Levels 1 and 2 may seem more problematic. There are certain situations which should suggest to a manager the need for moral as well as other forms of evaluation. These are where conflict emerges, either in the form of a complaint or where there is unresolved disagreement between different groups of workers. It suggests that values and aims need to be examined. In practical terms, it also suggests that strong emotions have been aroused or at least a feeling of discomfort or confusion. 'This doesn't seem quite right, but I'm not sure why not' – the sort of sensation one has when something done by rule, perhaps correctly according to the book, doesn't quite fit in this instance. Perhaps, between people, it may be a feeling of anger or disappointment.

FEELINGS

This may seem a surprising idea for a book on management, but at this point I should declare that my account is somewhat at odds with the impression of conventional wisdom amongst philosophers as I read them. There has been a suggestion – stronger in the last 300 years in the West, since the Enlightenment – that emotional issues, feelings, only serve to muddy the clear waters of ethical thinking and they should be disregarded or minimized. Just be cool, stay calculating, some texts or teachers seem to say, and the debate can be resolved in nice, quiet, intellectual terms. I have no desire to question the intellectual abilities of the thinkers who might be accused of taking this view, but what is clear to a practising clinician/manager is that moral conflicts or issues are certainly *detected* by our emotions: and if so detected, we also need probably to involve emotions in the analysis. Without our feelings we may be able to argue ourselves to a certain conclusion, only to find that it just doesn't seem to fit. Philosophers tend to say that something turns out to be 'counterintuitive'. (On the streets of South London, the language is briefer but more robust.)

We need our emotional understanding to be *part* of our cognitive apparatus. To use an extreme example, we can be pretty sure that at least some of the people who planned and carried out the gassing of Jews or the bombing of Dresden in the last war were good, ordinary folk who somehow put their emotional responses in neutral. I certainly remember carrying out as a houseman a treatment for my consultant which I knew then was no longer treatment but torture to the patient, even though it was 'good clinical medicine': I am ashamed now that I didn't respond to my repugnance by challenging the decision of a good but very blinkered senior clinician. Emotional discomfort is the sign either that there may be a problem to be examined or that the solution remains unsatisfactory. In management, as we are at one remove from the clinic or the bedside, we may choose to use this distance either to give us the false peace of 'out of sight, out of mind', being remote and keeping well out of the heat, or to give us the benefit of committed objectivity which will allow us to make a good assessment and to support and if necessary guide those who may be too close to the issue to see the best way forward.

FRAMEWORKS

Thus we can construct a process of increasing skill which leads from *detecting* that there may be a moral problem to be considered in our work (or life) to beginning perhaps to name it or *describe* it – all processes of perception or recognition. However, there remains the most difficult skill, an analysis: thinking it through and having the courage to make a decision and to cope both with enacting it and with its 'shadow', the arguments or viewpoints not chosen or responded to. In all this, I have tried to keep the concepts as concrete as possible, both because I believe that doctors are mostly better decision makers in this mode and because management involves the use of skill and 'practical wisdom' (Aristotle's phrase) which makes it (or should make it even in the extremes of refined policy making) a human activity steeped in the realities of everyday life for ordinary people. So with this proviso, I suggest a framework, choosing two of the many suggested ways of looking at issues. These are based on the Four Principles and Scope approach, outlined in this country particularly by Raanon Gillon (1985) and in USA by Beauchamp & Childress (1989), and the perspectives/roles/relationships approach, which can be gathered from my own work with Alastair Campbell (Campbell & Higgs 1982) and links with the approaches of some recent feminist thinkers. I suggest that these two are both necessary and neither by itself is sufficient.

FOUR PRINCIPLES AND SCOPE

The suggestion is that, whatever background in belief or philosophy a person may have, four important principles underpin moral decision making in medicine. These may be in conflict or in balance: indeed, in anything which may seem a 'dilemma' they usually are. So, a final judgement may have to be made by 'weighing' principles against each other as it were. But at the very least, they can be vital in clarifying a situation and at best may lead us to a good conclusion. The principles have been expressed as *respecting autonomy, promoting good, minimizing harm and being just or fair*. It is worth looking into these in more depth.

Respecting autonomy

That an individual has the right to make choices about things which properly concern them (and others must respect that) is so much part of Western culture now that it is hard sometimes to see the challenge of this principle. However, it is not so clear in many societies and was not so in our own until recently. It has become an important principle in modern medicine for several reasons.

The first is in reaction to the 'doctor knows best' or paternalistic approach which ruled the wards and clinics until recently. Medical power enabled and encouraged doctors and nurses to get on and do what they knew to be good medicine and nursing without needing to ask. The increasing understanding that there might be choices, other ways of doing things, was a triumph of consumerism. But more basic was a realization that doing things to people without permission could be an assault and that recovery could be delayed or prevented by not involving people in their own care whenever possible. When a person is 'ill', they probably mean by that word that there is some process at work in the mind or body which is not in control and in this sense that person's ability to make choices is under threat ('self-rule' is an approximate translation of the Greek origin of 'autonomy'). Thus, illness specifically puts autonomy at risk. There may be no question that in some medical circumstances (when the patient is unconscious, for instance) others have to take over. But the key additional word is *respect*. Nurses, doctors and managers must act in a way which respects that person's choices or respects what they take to be those choices. If those choices are not respected, we have suggested that an apparently healthy person may still not be returned to full health. Thus, medicine can pose a triple jeopardy: the illness or disease in itself, the loss of control (or income, etc.) that may go with it and the risk that in the process of care or cure others may take over who do not have the patient's way of looking at things. This is particularly so when society gathers together to agree that those choices are themselves not healthy. In severe mental illness, for instance, the judgement may be that such people are not competent to make their own choices. To repeat, if they are not, they are in some views not entirely healthy. But in some circumstances, their return to healthy status may necessitate a shift in other people's views, rather than their own. The reasons for making or not making that shift need to be examined carefully.

Beneficence or promoting good

Medical care aims to make people better. Even if it hurts or feels bad in the meantime, its ultimate aim is recovery or perhaps something more: some have suggested that achieving health is best understood as realizing one's full potential. The first statement would appear to offer no problems – it is almost otiose, but not quite. It would be possible for a therapeutic enthusiast to impose treatment where none was necessary. Who is to decide what is best for a patient? If someone can only cope with life in a particular family or on a certain urban estate by smoking and thereby poses risks to their health, who is to decry this? We can define what *should* be best: what *is* best in the circumstance depends, it seems, more on the person than the professional and it is the professional's role to follow that lead wherever possible. The professional may find themselves acting as an advocate of that benefit, as well as providing it.

We can see some problems here. We may wish to do good to everyone, in a sudden rush to the head, but that is not only impossible or impractical but probably, in this sense, not good moral thinking. The patient has to be in a relationship with a professional and vice versa; thus there are limits to the principle. They must wish to have good done to them and we must be able to do it: 'ought implies can'. So the thyroid lump in the bus queue next to you is free to ride another day. But the more general or basic issue may become blurred with that of preventing harm. What of the person who risks harming themselves or others?

Minimizing or preventing harm : non-maleficence

Medicine puts not only autonomy at risk: it also risks real physical or other harm to the patient. 'The operation was successful, but the patient died', and so on. It is for this very reason that there are regulated professions in medical work. People who risk harming others in the course of a therapeutic relationship should relate to certain standards and act within certain frameworks, so that people can trust that they are in good hands. The risk of harm is intrinsic to medical activities: hence my 'minimizing' where others use 'avoiding'. It is just not possible to avoid harm in medical work. A patient comes in for a check-up with no problems and goes out with a problem, say, hypertension. A well-run ward is visited as part of a routine inspection procedure, the handover process is found to be defective and conflict arises. And so on. This is a general principle, unlike the specific relationship of beneficence. But it will also be strong in individual relationships, where (in serious mental illness, say) a patient's condition is definitely harmful and is beginning to harm others: so we are justified in stepping in to override their autonomy.

Justice or fairness

The above may in some senses hold few problems for the thoughtful, although making it operational usually brings surprises. But much more difficult is the process of fair distribution of healthcare. This is a problem whatever your political stance, because it is impossible to shrug and say 'It is up to the individual'. Self-care is not an option for much of medical work and so by definition, problems of distributive justice creep in. And creep in now they have with a vengeance. The early hope of nationalized healthcare, that as people become healthier, their needs, as expressed to and perceived by the relevant health services, would diminish has been shown to be misplaced beyond all doubt. 'Needs' can be made to seem endless but resources to respond to them are finite. Whether this is true or not, it is true to say, as above, that an individual professional's own time, energy and skill are finite. A budget certainly is also and paymasters for health expenditure the world over have reacted by trying to clamp down on rapidly rising expenditure. So how will distribution be made fairly and justly?

Such is the interest in this area that this section could

have been expanded to the whole chapter and still not have due space. This has to be avoided because there is so much more to ethics and management than equitable use of budgets, but a few headlines are vital.

The first is that the essence of justice here has to be equity, that is, fair and consistent use of resources. We like judgements to be based on open arguments, so that people can judge for themselves if the system is fair. This also presupposes that there is a system for people to engage with and a system for that process of engagement. It feels more than cumbersome, for instance, that a complaint about not getting treatment should have to go to law or a decision need to be challenged through the upper echelons of the executive. A consequence of most forms of thinking here is that there will be an equalizing process in addition – equality within equity. Thus, we shall also need impartiality. Health economics has stepped in to provide vital data and different ways of looking at distribution problems. But however hard one tries, there often remain comparisons between different entities. So the discomfort of choice remains.

John Rawls, in his major work (1976), suggested the image of distributive judgements being made 'behind a veil of ignorance' by people who did not know in what role in society they were going to end up. This idealistic concept, nevertheless, reminds us of the different perils of mixing clinical and distributive judgements and of allowing these different types of decision to be made by the same person. The clinician has to be an advocate for the patient, while the manager or public health professional has to make judgements for the system or the group. This is one of the many features which makes the present writer very uneasy about general practice fundholding. Experiments, like that at Oregon, by making an explicit hierarchy of different healthcare expenditures, provide a prior statement, separate from individual cases, that can be debated and determined. Individual advocacy then has to make its special case. Our pragmatic style in Britain makes us anxious about where this might lead, but there is no getting away from the debate unless it is by a method of complete randomization. Gillon (1985) suggests that the competing claims of different approaches should be clarified – between those of welfare maximization, medical need, merit or contribution to society, for instance – but that it will be difficult to give these values consistent ranking. He quotes Calabresi & Bobbitt (1978) who make the suggestion that on the whole, a society will make efforts to 'limit the destructive impact of tragic choices between fundamental values by choosing to mix approaches over time'.

This may seem to be abandoning the argument, but it provides us with exactly the focus we need in deciding medical need also, because there is no doubt that both the public's and professions' views of what constitutes medical need change slowly but definitely and constantly require analysis. The corrosive and crippling effects of unacknowledged stress, for instance, can no longer be left out of the picture and the potential progress to be made by altering genetic make-up pulls resources in another direction. Neither would have been part of a British health system's expenditure list 20 years ago, for quite different reasons. Each requires further analysis, scientific and ethical, but both are perceived currently as legitimate claims on the healthcare system in certain circumstances.

Scope or limits

Thus we return medical judgements to centre stage, as part of a new dialogue with society based on the above four principles. But since these principles will often be pointing in different ways, we have to acknowledge that each will have its limits – endless assessment of priorities, for instance, may itself take resources from urgent clinical tasks, or the desire to help everyone may mean that no one gets proper attention – and that these principles, by keeping watch on each other, as it were, will help to provide the checks and balances that a thoughtful system needs.

There is another sense in which the scope of this thinking is important and that is about the actual concepts within our debate. Much of the concern about abortion or persistent vegetative state, for instance, may hinge on whether the fetus or the body on the ventilator is a *person* and if so, what claims this person has on the rest of us in comparison with other claims. The manager's judgement also contains a view of the scope of their own work and an understanding of the point when an issue becomes of too great importance to be contained within the policy or implementation system in which that manager acts and wider debate is needed. Limits are key to individual action too. It is vital for us, in whatever role we may be acting, to be able to say no when a particular line is crossed. This is the essence of judgement at all levels.

JUDGEMENTS AND PROFESSIONALISM

Thus, returning to the vexed question of clinical autonomy (discussed in a previous chapter), we can see within this a series of points where judgements have to be made. A health service commits itself to a certain range of work: we can campaign to change that range of work, but not behave in an arbitrary way. If we are managers within that system, we bring to it our own personal and professional judgement, but if we have been part of a group which has had to make a difficult decision we should stick to it, unless there has been a substantive change in the facts presented or the scale or type of need. However, we remain individuals with our own principles and if we find that the collective decision causes us personal discomfort we should, at the least, recognize and analyse and, at best, declare this. A decision not to accept certain sorts of patients, for instance, may create suffering which we suddenly perceive, or an employee may be dealt with in an expedient but unjust way and we have no choice but to speak out.

The way a professional person can act autonomously here brings in another approach, more acute and difficult perhaps for doctors and nurses, but existing for any professional. A profession has a certain range of skills and knowledge which marks it off and which defines it. But in the helping professions these skills are gained, and used, as society requests in defined ways and circumstances. Elsewhere it is different. A painter is free to paint, in some senses, as they wish: reward results if artists communicate their perceptions effectively. The service or helping professions are given a different set of freedoms on the understanding that they do serve or help, which is a prior assumption. Society becomes uneasy when it is the individual professional's path that is followed or the individual professional appears to act without due regard to society's proper needs. These needs are both for committed attention to individuals – respecting the autonomous choices of those patients, avoiding harming them and looking to their best interest in a fair way – but also for an understanding and response to people with medical problems as a group, however expressed. This second need will necessitate a different 'distance' for people and problems and there may be conflicting arguments for different processes and outcomes. A clinician may, for instance, think that a certain expensive treatment should be provided for the patient, but professional autonomy in this regard has limits, as we have suggested. Assuming the doctor is right, there still may be arguments which suggest that such massive expenditure is not justified for particular reasons: perhaps that this patient is not different from others with similar problems treated in the usual way. The expenditure may harm other patients by depriving them of care. It may not be justifiable in relation to the benefit it confirms, and so on.

Working within a system, a professional must accept the limits of it or seek to change that system; or may have to find another one in which to work if the restrictions are too great. Clinical autonomy is hugely to be defended, if only because of the personal benefit it confers on individual patients who are part of that professional–patient relationship, but it cannot be an absolute principle: it has its limits like personal autonomy. The manager should respect it, which means that there is still remedial action to be taken when it is trumped by other arguments. But it is also a freedom to use in the service of others and so others may challenge it.

RELATIONSHIPS AGAIN

How is this resolved? The impression is gained that the power struggles between different groups within healthcare can easily become issues in themselves and yet again the whole purpose of the system, the care of the patient, can become sidelined. Just as the notice 'road works' actually indicates that it doesn't, the new sign 'trust' has raised suspicion that this, of all values, is most honoured in the breach. A modern clinician 'manages' the patient with regard to the broadest remit possible, in terms of their social, psychological and physical health. The narrow focus is only helpful for specific moments, for particular purposes. The power here is within the doctor–patient or nurse–patient relationship. Similarly, with administrative management, the broad view remains of paramount importance. It is the system managed which has to be healthy, which requires sometimes detailed attention but always an understanding of the overall aims and values of the system and its potential.

PERSPECTIVES

This brings us back to a recurring theme for medicine and management, that policy can and should be made but that it must be based on real life and its judgements and that, unless the policy is so broad as to be useless, there will come times when it is challenged by context. One of the criticisms it is possible to make of the above approach of principalism is that it is mechanical: two similar situations are likely to produce the same answer. The problem in management, as in medicine, remains, however, when this just doesn't seem to fit: the perception, however reached, that this case is somehow different. We have looked elsewhere (Campbell & Higgs 1982) at ways in which this can be examined logically: the argument for the situation being a 'borderline case' where the main proposal is challenged by an 'unless' or a 'provided that'. The complexity of such discussions suggests that before that last point is reached, as we have noted, the different points of view of stakeholders in the decision have to be visited. Within the realm of management, however, a further complexity may arise because the roles of particular individuals or groups and their particular responsibility may be confused or may not have been identified clearly enough.

ROLES AND RESPONSIBILITY

We tend to feel that modern life has made everything more complex but there is some suggestion that in small societies or groups, the wearing of many different and potentially conflicting 'hats' may be common and potentially uncomfortable. In a large organization, or higher up the executive tree, roles may be single or more 'pure'. However, the nurse or doctor manager needs to be aware of their own mixture of roles and be prepared to help others define whether there is a conflict here and if so, which role takes precedence. A proper ethical stance suggests that we have, by entering a particular post, taken on a special responsibility to the system and must abide by its decisions, if we have a proper relationship to those decisions. However, we also have responsibility to ourselves, as professionals, and through this to our patients, perhaps in a different way from our clients when we are managers, and to ourselves as individuals.

Systems theory has suggested that defects may be mirrored up and down the structure. As an example, a British physician who responded to the requests of a desperately crippled patient in great pain by assisting her death was recently found guilty of attempted murder, running counter to broader clinical judgement of most who know the details of the case. Few commented on the fact that the ward had been set up to deal both with quick turnround cases requiring intervention on one side (urological) and with patients with long-term conditions for which there was no cure (rheumatology) on the other. This dysfunctional combination suggests that management may have made a decision which created, at best, an environment which needed a lot of attention. How much responsibility did management have for the suffering which ensued?

Luckily, medical ethics holds no brief for providing the final answer to this type of question. But what it can do is suggest that at all points of healthcare (ward rearrangement no less than others), there are questions of value and aim to be addressed and that by using a framework of principles set against the necessarily different perspectives and roles of people or groups involved, we may create a healthy manager–system relationship within which professionals and patients can flourish.

REFERENCES

Beauchamp T L, Childress J F 1989 Principles of biomedical ethics. Oxford University Press, New York
Calabresi G, Bobbitt D 1978 Tragic choices. Norton, New York
Campbell A V, Higgs R 1982 In that case: medical ethics in everyday practice. Darton, Longman & Todd, London
Gillon R 1985 Philosophical medical ethics. Wiley, Chichester
Rawls J 1976 A theory of justice. Oxford University Press, Oxford

Index

Page numbers in *italics* refer to tables, and those in **bold** type to figures.

Access to Health Records Act (1990) 297, 299
Access to Medical Reports Act (1988) 297, 298–9
Access to Personal Files Act (1987) 297, 299
accessibility
 of healthcare services
  and marketing strategy 233, 235, 239
  and quality assessment 275
 to training for audit 372
accountability
 and business planning 223
 of clinical directors 91
 and discipline, problems of 194–5
 and team building 195–6
accountants, and budgets 211, 216–7, 219
accreditation schemes
 accreditation of prior learning 372–3
 for quality in healthcare 274, 286–7
achievement, and motivation 131–2
action plan, in business planning 229–30
activity levels *see* work load
Addison, Dr Christopher, first Minister of Health 5–6
Administration of Justice Act (1970), and disclosure of medical records 300
administrators, in management of hospitals 27–8
adult learning 350–1
adverse events
 control of 84
 investigation of, in risk management 328, 329–30
advertising
 by doctors 165, 310
 in marketing of services 235
 and staff recruitment 136–8
 as unethical behaviour 165
agendas, for meetings 158–9, 164
aims
 for meetings 157, 159
 and staff appraisal 260–2
aims *see also* objectives
amenity, in healthcare 275–6
Annual Review Process, and NHS reorganization 14
anthropological perspective, in development of health commissions 391–8
appointment procedure
 for clinical and medical directors 99–102
 in staff recruitment 143
appraisal
 economic, in healthcare 243–4, 249–55
 of staff 146–7, 257–70
  clinical directors 101
appropriateness, in healthcare 369–70
assertive behaviour, and personal effectiveness 185–7, 360
audio-visual aids, use of 106, 107, 110–11, 180
audit *see also* clinical audit; medical audit
Audit Commission
 on quality in the NHS 274, 287
 on the role of clinical director 92
audit cycle, in clinical audit 345, 347, 349, 368, **369**
audit programme, by the King's Fund 286
audit trail, and computer records 297
auditing education 176–8
audits, national, and quality improvement 276–7
authority

and chairmanship of meetings 158, 161
of clinical directors 91–2
concept of 130
and NHS organization 19
autonomy, respect for 417–8

BAMM (British Association of Medical Managers) 21, 23–4
BCG (Boston Consulting Group) matrix 239–40
bed holding, and status 35
Bevan, Aneurin, and foundation of the NHS 7, 9
Beveridge, Sir William, report on social policy 7
BMA *see* British Medical Association
Bolam v Friern Hospital Management Committee (1957) 303, 306, 321
Boston Consulting Group (BCG) matrix 239–40
bottom line, in accounts 216, 218
brainstorming meetings 157, 158
breach of a duty of care 321
British Association of Medical Managers (BAMM) 21, 23–4
British Medical Association (BMA)
 on the clinical director 63, 100–1
 on consultants' responsibilities 91
 and foundation of the NHS 7
 in hospital complaints procedures 283
 on NHS management teams 15
 on staff selection 135
 on stress amongst doctors 76
British Standards Institute (BSI), accreditation schemes 286–7
budgetary authority, and role of clinical director 91, 93–4, 100
budgets
 and business planning 222
 flexibility of 215–6
 management of 211–20
 monitoring of 215–6

423

424 INDEX

budgets (contd)
  setting of 214
  types of 213
  use of 212–3
business managers
  and business planning 223
  in clinical directorates 63, 64, 92–5, 101, 360, 365
  in management of human resources 97
  role of in contracting 83
business planning 221–30
  and role of clinical director 94
business strategy, in marketing of services 236–7
buzz groups, in active learning 112

Calman Report
  and junior doctors' conditions of work 82, 83
  and management development needs 70
  on specialist training 85, 175
capital expenditure, and role of clinical director 94
career path
  and doctors' management learning 75–6, 77
  and job finding 149, 151
  problems of doctors in management 39, 64
  problems of hospital managers 43
  and staff appraisal 259, 265, 270
CEPOD (Confidential Enquiry into Perioperative Deaths) 274, 276
Certificate of Completion of Specialist Training 175
Certificate of Service-Based Learning 180
CESDI (Confidential Enquiry into Stillbirths and Deaths in Infancy) 274, 276
chairmanship
  of clinical audit teams 374
  in the clinical directorate 61–2
  of meetings 158, 161–3
  and role of medical director 87
change
  coping with the threat of 51, 52
  cultural impact of 387–98
  in development of health commissions 393–7
  emotional responses to 351
  process of 205–8
change grid, in personal construct psychology 51–2
change management 201–10
  and clinical audit 350
  in the clinical directorate 97
charitable funding, and budgets 213
CHCs (community health councils) 283
chief executive
  and distinction awards 383
  and role of clinical director 91, 92, **93**

  and role of medical director 82, 84, 87
children, disclosure of medical records 300–1
Christian Church, in the history of hospitals 2
Civil Evidence Act (1968), and computer records 297
claims handlers, and medical negligence 303–5
classification systems, in healthcare 332–3
clinical advisor, in organizational structure of hospitals 40, 61–2
clinical audit 368–71
  assessment of, criteria for *376*, 377
  and the audit cycle 345, 347, 349, 368, **369**
  and clinical director, role of 91
  in hospital trusts 17, 83
  and learning 341–57, 372–3
  maturation of 353–5
  multiprofessional 367–77
  in a quality system 96, 313, **314**
  and standardization 26
  training in 356–7, 371–2
clinical audit committees
  membership of 371
  support for 373–4
clinical autonomy, and patient care 417–21
clinical budgeting 37
clinical director
  appointment of 90, 99–102
  assertive behaviour by 360
  and business planning 221–2, 223
  and clinical freedom 408
  and health and safety legislation 324
  and information technology 337
  management skills of 359–65
  and medical directors 84–5
  power of 205
  problems of 22–3, 24
  responsibility for professional conduct of colleagues 309
  risk management by 318, 326–8
  roles of 62–3, 89–98
  as teacher-managers 173
clinical directorate
  and decentralized management systems 59–60
  evolution of 41–3, 57–60
  information in 332
  models of 41, 60–3
  in organizational structure of hospitals 38–9
  and study requirements of staff 354, 356
  teams in hospital management 24
  working of 63–6
clinical freedom 399–410
  consequences of 404–5
clinical management teams 22, 62, 64–5
clinical manager, in organizational

  structure of hospitals 40
clinical practice, of clinical and medical directors 85, 89, 100–1, 102
clinical responsibility 307–8
clinical services, responsibility for 84–5
Clinical Standards Advisory Group (CSAG) 287–8
clinical terms, controlled vocabulary for 334
CMD (Confidential Enquiry into Maternal Deaths) 273–4, 276, 277
coding systems, in healthcare 332, 332
Cogwheel Reports, on hospital services 12–13
commercial risks 316–17, 318
communication
  by the medical director 81–2, 83, 87
  and change management 206
  in clinical directorates 65, 92, 360
  and corporate management 19, 23–4, 96–7
  lack of, and complaints 283, 320–1
  and the media 166, 168
  and meetings 161
  and personal effectiveness 185, 186
  in risk management 320–1, 327–8
communication *see also* presentations and talks; writing
community health care
  accreditation programme for 286
  management in 60, 71
  in the NHS 10, 12–14, 17
  staff appointments in 140
community health councils (CHCs) 283
community physician
  representation on management boards 40
  role of 15
competition, in marketing of healthcare services 233, 238–9
complaints
  against the media 172
  procedures for patients 280, 282–3
  role of medical director in dealing with 84
computers
  in budget monitoring 216
  and guidelines, use of by general practitioners 279
  and medical records, legal standing of 297
  in writing for business planning 226
computers *see also* information technology
conceptual learning 351, *352*
conditions of employment, and job finding 151–2
Confidential Enquiry into Maternal Deaths (CMD) 273–4, 276, 277
Confidential Enquiry into Perioperative Deaths (CEPOD) 274, 276
Confidential Enquiry into Stillbirths and Deaths in Infancy (CESDI)

274, 276
confidentiality
　and ethics 414–15
　and information technology 334,
　　337–8
conflicts
　in ethical thinking 415–16
　and management of human resources
　　98
consent to treatment 303, 305–7, 322
consequences, and moral decision
　　making 416
consultants
　appointment of 138, 139, 144
　as clinical director 91–2, 99, 100
　clinical and managerial roles
　　combined 61, 62
　and clinical responsibility 307–8
　continuing medical education of 83
　in disciplinary hearings 86
　and distinction awards 383
　freedom of choice of patient 400–1
　and hospital trusts, creation of 12,
　　16–17, 379
　independant practitioner status of
　　34–5, 400–10, 417–21
　in management, incentives for 24,
　　63–4, 100–1
　as medical director 82, 85, 99, 100
　in medical staff committee 86
　positional power of 361
　and power shift to managers 44
　and primacy of patient care 407–8
　and risk management 326–7
　status of, and bed holding 35
　as teacher-manager 173, 176
　on unit management teams 14–15,
　　39–40
consumer demand, and economics
　　241–2
Consumer Protection Act (1987), and
　　product liability 308
contextual learning 106–11
continuing professional development
　　(CPD) 341–57
continuing professional development
　　see also professional
　　development
contract
　of employment
　　of the clinical director 24, 100–1
　　and job description 136
　　of the medical director 87, 100–1
　　specimen, and job finding 149
contracts
　and budgets 212
　in the business plan 227, 229
　and clinical freedom 399, 409
　management of, and role of clinical
　　director 94–5
　negotiation of, and marketing 232,
　　234, 236, 274
　and NHS hospital trusts 16–17, 82,
　　83–4

for postgraduate medical education
　175, 177
and quality 274, 288–9
risks of fluctuation in 383
role of chief executive 62
and role of medical director 87
strategy in, and health commissions
　388–9
types of 234
control and prevention, of risk 318–20
Control of Substances Hazardous to
　Health Regulations (COSHH)
　(1994) 325
coordination, in management of human
　resources 97
core services, and NHS hospital trusts
　17
core values
　in health commissions 389
　individual, identification of 49–52,
　　54–5
corporate management, and the clinical
　directorate 96–7
COSHH (Control of Substances
　Hazardous to Health
　Regulations) (1994) 325
cost control
　implications in patient care 403, 404
　need for, and management 58
cost-benefit analysis, in economics of
　healthcare 249–50
cost-cutting
　in healthcare, worldwide 379
　and internal market 388
cost-effectiveness
　data needed for 380–1, 382–3
　in healthcare 249, 371
　in healthcare purchasing 253–6
cost-minimization analysis, in
　economics of healthcare 249
cost-utility analysis, in economics of
　healthcare 249
costs
　dilemmas of 18
　of healthcare 246, 247
　of the National Health Service 9, 165
　of risk
　　and insurance 319
　　and medical negligence litigation
　　　301–5
　　in poor risk management 316
counselling interviews 147
CPD (continuing professional
　development) 341–57
critical thinking, in learning 345
criticism, handling of 187
Crown indemnity, in healthcare 314–15
CSAG (Clinical Standards Advisory
　Group) 287–8
cultural borderlands 391, 397
culture
　change in 201–2, 204
　in development of health
　　commissions 391–2

in the management process 25, 29–30
and organizational changes 387–98
curriculum vitae 149–51, 152
customers, in marketing of healthcare
　232–3, 236
customers see also purchasers

Data Protection Act (1984) 297–8
day-case treatment
　and cost control 58
　and efficiency 84
　and pressures of NHS reforms 382
decentralized management
　and clinical directorates 63, 64–6
　development of 58–9
decision making
　by managers 127
　by meetings 162–3
　conflicts in 415–16
　staff roles in 98
　in staff selection 143
defensive medicine, and overusage of
　resources 36
delegation
　by clinical directors 360, 361, 363
　and managing people 129–30, 133
　and personal effectiveness 185, 188
deliberate learning 351, 352
deontology, concept of 416
Department of Health
　criteria for assessment of clinical
　　audit 376, 377
　and external comparative data 337
　and funding for audit 367–8
　and NHS reorganization 13–14
　as a source of news 168
desirable outcomes, and motivation, in
　management 49–50
development, concept of 67–70
DHAs see district health authorities
diagnostic codes 332, 333
disability and distress, Rosser Index of
　255, 256
disability legislation, and staff selection
　145
disaster, plans for 329
discipline
　and accountability, problems of
　　194–5
　and professional conduct 309
　role of medical director in 86
　and staff appraisal 257
discrimination, in staff selection 139,
　141, 144–5
disease-specific measures, of outcome
　279
district health authorities (DHAs)
　and development of health
　　commissions 387–8
　and hospital trusts, creation of 16–17
　and indemnity 301–2, 314–15
　membership of 40
　and nursing home registration 285–6
　as purchasers of healthcare 251

district management teams (DMTs)
  membership of 40
  and NHS reorganization 14–15
districts, and NHS reorganization
    12–14
doctors
  advertising posts for 136–8
  appointment of, in management of
      human resources 97
  discipline of 86
  in the evolution of clinical directorate
      41–3
  freedom of choice of patient 400–1
  history of profession of 2–7
  in hospital management 21–30, 33–4,
      47–55, 379–84
    development for 67–78
    and the Griffiths Report 15–16
    problems of 39
  and incentives in the NHS 12, 39
  lack of interest in management 15,
      39, 57
  in media employment 170
  and product liability 308–9
  in resource management 37–8
  system of payment of 383
doctors see also consultants; junior
    doctors; registrars; senior house
    officers; senior registrars; staff
    grade doctors
documents see paperwork
Donabedian, Avedis, on quality in
    healthcare 275, 280, 289
duties, in decision making 416
Dynamic Standard Setting Systems
    (DySSSy) 345

economics, in healthcare 241–55
education
  and changes in healthcare 343
  continuing, role of professional
      bodies in 344–5
  meaning of 342
  needs for, and clinical audit 348–9
  providers of, and clinical audit 374–5
  in risk awareness 328
education see also learning; medical
    education; postgraduate medical
    education; training
educational management 173–81
effectiveness
  in healthcare 369–70
    and clinical audit 375–7
    and employee morale 34
    and quality 275
efficiency
  and audit 287
  dilemmas of 18
  improvements in 84, 85, 379, 380
  incentives for 383–4
  and market regulation 382–4
electronic medical record 334–6
Elizabethan Poor Law (1601), and care
    of the sick 1, 2

emergency care
  costing of 234, 235
  risks in 320
emergency services
  and contracts 92
  and NHS hospital trusts 17
equal opportunities, monitoring of 146
equal opportunities see also racial
    discrimination; sexual
    discrimination
equal opportunities guidelines, and
    staff recruitment 135, 136
equal opportunities legislation 139,
    144–5
equipment maintenance, records of,
    and product liability 308
equipment and plant, risks in 323–4
equity, in healthcare 253, 275
ethics
  in economics of healthcare 244
  in healthcare 413–21
evaluation, in business planning 225
event recording, and analysis 310–11
"expectancy theory", and motivation
    132–3
expenditure
  and budget setting 215, 217, 219–20
  and business planning 94, 222, 229
  containment of 253–4
  on healthcare, national statistics
      251–4
experiential learning 72–3, 77, 78, 351,
    352
  stages in 345–7, 348, 349
experimental treatments, and ethics 414
external comparative data, and use of
    IT 337
external monitoring and assessment, in
    healthcare 285–8

family doctors see general practitioners
family health services authorities, and
    development of health
    commissions 387–8
family practitioners see general
    practitioners
feedback
  in learning 107, 108, 113
  and motivation 362
  on performance, and team
      membership 197
  in staff appraisal 258, 260, 269–70
feelings, in ethical thinking 414, 416–7
finance, and business planning 229
finance departments, and support for
    clinical and medical directors
    101
financial constraints, and management
    development needs 70
financial control
  by clinical directors 360
  by the consultant manager 62
financial director
  and the clinical director 94

representation on management
    boards 39
financial independence, and
    decentralized management
    systems 58
fire, risks of 323
Fog index, of language complexity 110,
    117, 121, 123
force field analysis, and change
    management 209
formal learning 351, 352
four principles and scope, in analysis of
    moral issues 417–19
funding
  for audit 356, 367–8, 374
  and budgets 213–4
  and business planning 223
  of health authorities, and NHS
      reorganization 16–17
  lack of, and doctors' responsibilities
      57–8
  of the NHS 10, 379–80
  and purchasing decisions 251
  and study leave 353–4

gap, in staff appraisal 262–3
General Medical Council
  on advertising by doctors 310
  and constraints on clinical freedom
      399
  and postgraduate medical education
      174, 175
general practice
  and health commissions 388, 390
  and King's Fund organizational audit
      286
  outreach clinics in 235
  postgraduate training in 344
  and recruitment of doctors for 136–8
general practitioners
  and clinical responsibility 308, 401
  cost-containment by 254
  and information on hospital services
      83
  power shift to 44
  as purchasers of healthcare 233, 237,
      251
  reform of contracts of 383–4
  representation on management
      boards 40
  and role of medical director 87
  role of, in the NHS 10, 13, 395
  selection of 146
  on unit management teams 14–15
  use of computerized guidelines by
      279
  work of 5, 7, 136, 383–4
general practitioners see also Royal
    College of General Practitioners
General Whitley Council, on equal
    opportunities 145
generic health status measures 279
goal setting
  and motivation 133

and personal effectiveness 183–4
and team membership 197
grammatical construction, in effective writing 119–20, 122
Griffiths Report (1983)
 on clinical freedom 399
 on clinicians to be involved in management 15–16, 25, 37, 48, 58
 and internal market 388
 and performance indicators 284
group learning, in clinical audit 349–50
guidelines
 and clinical effectiveness 375
 and quality improvement 277–9
Guy's Hospital, clinical directorates in 63

handouts, in talks and presentations 109
HAS (Hospital/Health Advisory Service), on quality monitoring 274, 285
Health Advisory Service (HAS) 285
health commissions
 culture of 387–98
 development of 387–9
 working of 389–91
health economics 243–4, **245**
health improvements, measurement of 247, 248–9
Health of the Nation initiative
 and clinical audit 354, 356
 and performance indicators 284
health needs assessment, by purchasers of healthcare 252
Health and Safety at Work etc. Act (1974) 324–6
Health and Safety Executive, powers of 314–15, 316
health and safety legislative liabilities 324–6
Health Service Guidelines, and retention of medical records 301
health strategy, and health commissions 388–9
healthcare
 assessment of, by patients 280–1
 changes in, and education 343
 decision making in 379–81
 economics of 247–8
 legal issues in 297–311
 quality in 273–91
healthcare professions, and clinical freedom 404–5
healthcare resource groups, and healthcare information systems 333
healthcare team, and clinical audit 369, 372
Henry VIII, King, dissolution of monastic infirmaries by 2
Hospital Advisory Service (HAS), on quality monitoring 274

hospital committees, and role of medical director 84
hospital committees *see also* hospital trust boards
hospital estate
 management of, and IT 337
 risks in 323–4
hospital management *see* management
hospital services, economic appraisal of 249–51
hospital trust board
 and medical director appointments 99–100
 and organizational structure of hospitals 41
 and role of medical director 81–4, 85, 87
hospital trusts
 and business planning 221–30
 clinical audit in 368
 and clinical freedom 409
 creation of 16–18
 doctors' payment in 383
 organizational liabilities in risk 326
 as purchasers of medical education 176
hospitals
 aims and purposes of 25, **26**, 33
 doctors in management of 21–30
 historical development of 1–7
 organizational structure of 33–44
human needs, concept of 131
human resources
 and budgets 214, 219–20
 and business planning 228
 and change 202
 in the clinical directorate 97–8
 in healthcare 243
 and information technology 337
 and management of costs 250
 in marketing of services 235
 and staff appraisal 257–70
human resources *see also* personnel; staff

income
 and budget setting 213–4, 215, 217, 219
 and business planning 222
 in the clinical directorate 94
 income generating activities 213–4
 loss of in poor risk management 316
indemnity, of the National Health Service 301–5
independant practitioners
 consultants 400–10
 doctors in the NHS 408–9
 other professions in the NHS 404, 409
individual performance review (IPR) 257–70
industry, lessons for NHS from 18–19
inexperience, and risk 36, 322

infection, control of, risks in 324
influence competance, of managers 127–8
informal learning 351, *352*
information
 and budget setting 216, 217–8
 and business planning 225, 228–9
 and clinical effectiveness 278–9, 375–6
 in contextual learning 109–10
 dissemination of, and role of managers 92, 127
 importance of 331–9
 and marketing of services 238
 the media as a source of 165–6
 need for
  in management 23–4
  in purchasing 390–1
 and work of clinical directorates 65
 power of 28–9, 205–6, 361
 provision of by hospital trusts 83
information processing, in learning 106
information strategy 335
information systems
 in decentralized management systems 58, 61
 patient-based 29
 and problems of management 362
 and quality management 96, 97
 in resource management 38
 and support for clinical and medical directors 101
information technology (IT), in healthcare 331–9
information technology (IT) *see also* computers
informed consent, and risk 322
injuries
 cost of 315–16
 recording of 310–11
 risk of 315–6, 318
inner and outer worlds model, in management 67, **68**, 70–1, 73–5
Institute of Health Service Managers, on NHS management changes 43
Institute of Health Services Management, on clinical management structures 62
insurance, and costs of risk 319
integrated clinical workstation and IT 334
intellectual or cognitive competances, of managers 127–8
internal market
 and health commissions 388
 and hospital efficiency 36
 and NHS changes 390–1
 and NHS hospital trusts 17
interview panels, size and membership of 139–40
interviewing skills 141–3

interviews
  being interviewed 153–4
  core process interviews, in personal construct psychology 52
  and the media 168–72
  and staff appraisal 146–7, 258–62, 269–70
  and staff development 146–7
  and staff selection 139–44
IPR (individual performance review) 257–70
IT *see* information technology

job, and training needs 267–8
job description
  for clinical and medical director appointments 100–1
  and individual role 196
  and job finding 149, 152
  and staff recruitment 135–6
job satisfaction
  and management style 129, 131
  and motivation 362
John Hopkins Hospital, Baltimore, and cost control 58, 63
junior doctors
  changes in conditions of work of 70, 82, 83
  deficiencies in training of 380
  and medical directors 86
  and overusage of resources 36
  and performance appraisal 146–7, 262, 265–6
  and primacy of patient care 407

King's Fund organizational audit 286

laddering, in personal construct psychology 50–1
language, in effective writing 110, **117**, 121–2, 123
lay representatives, in clinical audit 371, 374
leadership
  by clinical directors 359, 360–1
  of clinical audit teams 372
  in health commissions 389
  and managing people 128–9, 133
  and team building 193–5, 197–8
learning
  by adults 350–1
  and clinical audit 341–57, 372–3
  effectiveness of 105–6, 350–1
  and management development 68–70, 72–8
  materials for 105–6, 179–80
  meaning of 342–3
  in organizations 353–6
  systems
    managed 180–1
    service-based 178–81
  theories for 105–13
  types of 351, *352*
learning *see also* education; training

learning credits 179–80, 372–3
learning diaries 345, 346–7
legal issues
  in healthcare 84, 297–311
    and constraints on clinical freedom 399
  of negligence 321
legal responsibility, of the appointments committee 144–6
legislation, on health and safety 324–6
litigation
  avoidance of, and risk management 330
  and disclosure of medical records 299–303
  increasing costs of 315
litigation *see also* medical negligence; negligence
locums, competance of, responsibility of colleagues 309
lump sum, in budgets 93, 213

management
  and business planning 223
  decentralized, and clinical directorates 63, 64–6
  and doctors
    and clinical freedom, implications of 403–10
    relationship in the NHS 379–84
  of doctors, untenable concept 399–410
  doctors' lack of interest in 15
  doctors' role in 21–30, 47–55
  and the Griffiths Report 15–16
  ethics in 416
  and information needs 331
  and medicine, changes in roles 396–7
  models of 39–41
  in the NHS, and reorganization 12–14
  process of 25–30
  of risk 313–30
  roles in 89
  staff appraisal in 257–70
  success factors in 362–5
management *see also* change management
management attributes, and learning 72–3
management board
  and clinical directorates 64, 89
  and decentralized management systems 59
  and medical director 86–7
  need for 24
management budgeting 37–8, 211–20
management contracts, and consultants 63–4
management of costs, of hospital services 250
management development, for doctors 47, 48, 53, 67–78
management information systems

336–9
management reports, and writing style 123
management skills
  acquisition of 72–7
  of clinical directors 359–65
management structure
  in health commissions 389
  and NHS reorganization 12–19
  in resource management 38
management training
  and clinical and medical director appointments 99, 102
  needs of junior doctors 86
managerial competances 127–8
managerial relationships 128
managerial skills, success factors in 362–5
managerial style, of clinical directors 359–62
managers
  and business planning 221
  in the clinical directorate 41–3, 61
  effective writing 115–25
  power shift to 44
  roles of 127, 406–7
  status of 57
  and success of audit 353
managing people 127–33
managing for personal effectiveness 183–9
Manual Handling Operations Regulations (1992) 325
market regulation, in NHS reforms 381–3
market systems, and budget setting 214
marketing 231–40
  and business planning 227–8
  and role of clinical director 95
marketplace, in healthcare 241, 242, 243
media, dealing with 165–72
media doctors 170
medical defence organizations 301–2, 314
medical director
  appointment of 99–102
  and the clinical director 91, 92, **93**
  deputies for 84
  role of 81–7
Medical Directory, The, and job finding 149
medical education
  change in 203–4
  historical development of 3
  and job finding 151
  management of 173–81
  needs of junior doctors 83, 86
  and performance appraisal 146–7
medical education *see also* postgraduate medical education
medical ethics 413–21
medical insurance, and friendly

societies 5
medical negligence
  identification of 321
  liability for 403
medical negligence claims
  and clinical responsibility 307–8
  cost of 315
  and Crown indemnity 314
  and records 299–305
  and standards 330
medical negligence claims *see also* litigation
medical officer of health, role of 15
medical records
  access to 297–301
  and information technology 334–6
  and medical negligence litigation 321–2
  and patient care teams 198
  retention of 301
  systems for 332, 334–5
medical reports, access to 298–9
medical royal colleges
  and postgraduate medical education 174, 177, 344–5, 347
  and professional standards 341, 367, 374
medical staff committee (MSC) 86
medical training, and pre-NHS 17–18
medicine
  historical introduction 1–7
  and management, cultural changes in 396–7
medicolegal matters, control of 84
meditation and relaxation, and stress handling 188
meetings
  management of 157–64
  in postgraduate medical education 174, 180
  and role of medical director 82, 86–7
  and time management, of clinical directors 360, 365
  and work of clinical directorates 66
memos and letters, effective writing of 124
mental health care, in the community 60
mentally disordered patients, records of 301
Merrison Committee, on unmanaged status of doctors 399, 402
Minister for Health, and NHS reorganization 14
Ministry of Health, creation of 4, 5
mission statements 33–4, 236–7
monitoring
  of clinical standards of doctors 403
  in management 407
moral issues, detection of 416–19
moral values, and ethics 414–15

morale
  and change, in health commissions 389
  and effectiveness, in NHS hospitals 34
motivation
  assessment of 49–52, 55
  and change, in health commissions 389
  in management 19, 49, 362
  and management development for doctors 71, 72
  in managing people 97, 130–3
  and staff appraisal 258, 260, 270
MSC (medical staff committee) 86
multiprofessional clinical audit 367–77

National Audit Office (NAO), and quality in the NHS 287
national audits, and quality improvement 276–7
national confidential enquiries, on quality in healthcare 273, 276–7
National Council for Voluntary Organizations 283
National Health Service Act (1946) 9
National Health Service Management Executive, as purchasers of healthcare 251
National Health Service (NHS)
  and business planning 221–30
  changes in
    and clinical directors 364
    and learning 342
    and management development needs 70–1
    and market regulation 381–4
    and resource constraints 202
  clinical freedom in 399, 403–5
  costs of 9
  doctors and management in 379–84
  evolution of 6–7, 9–19
  guidelines and protocols in 276
  and history of medicine 1–7
  indemnity of 301–5
  and market systems of budget setting 214–5
  national strategies in 334–5
  and politics 165
  project control and management in 338
  quality initiatives in 274, 290–1
  reorganizations of 11, 12–18
national information management and technology strategy 334–5
national initiatives, and management development needs 70, 71
National Insurance Act (1911) 5–6, 9, 10
national strategies, and clinical audit 354, 356
"near misses", and event recording 310–11, 320
negligence claims, by employees 324

negligence claims *see also* medical negligence
New Deal, for junior doctors, and management development needs 70
news agencies, and the medical profession 167
newsletters 83, 124–5
newspapers, and the medical profession 165, 166–8, 169
NHS *see* National Health Service
Nightingale, Florence (1820–1910)
  on measurement of hospital outcomes 381
  on need for accurate information 23–4
  and nurse training 4
  on purpose of hospitals 33n
  on quality in healthcare 273
notes *see* medical records
nurse managers
  in the clinical directorate 63, 64, 92, 93, 94, 101
  and support for the medical director 101
nurses
  appraisal of 98
  continuing education of, and professional bodies 344–5
  history of profession of 2, 4
  and incentives in the NHS 12
  management accountability of 61, 62–3
  in management of human resources 97, 98
  management roles of 14–15, 39–40
  and NHS reorganization 13
nurses *see also* Royal College of Nursing
nursing directors, and cost control 58
nursing home registration 285–6
nursing sisters, as managers 44, 63

objectives
  in business planning 223–4, 227, 230
  in clinical audit 347–8
  and meetings 157, 158
  need for 19
  for risk management 328–9
  in staff appraisal 258, 266, 268–9
objectives *see also* aims
operating theatre information system 331, 335
operating theatres, use of 35–6
organizational psychology, and power 28
organizational strategy, use of information in 333–4
organizational structure of hospitals 33–44
outcome measurement
  and IT 337
  and quality assessment 279–280

outcomes
  in healthcare
    economics of *247*, 248–9
    efficient use of data from 380–1, 383
    and internal market 388
    and quality 275
    role of education 343
  and motivation, in management 49–50
outreach clinics, and marketing of healthcare 235
overspend, in the clinical directorate 94

paperwork
  management of, and personal effectiveness 185
  and meetings 158–9, 164
  in staff appraisal *261*, 264–7
  and work of the clinical directors 365
paperwork *see also* documents
Pathologists, Royal College of, in continuing education 344
pathology laboratory departments, IT in 335
patient administration system (PAS) 335–6
patient care
  autonomy in 417–18
  and business planning 224, 228, 229
  and clinical audit 83, 347, 367–71, 375–7
  and clinical responsibility 307–8
  improvement of 65, 347
    and work of clinical directorates 65
  and medical records 332
  and quality management 96, 313–14
  risks in 314, 315, 318, 320–3
  teamwork in 198–9, 239
patient choice
  of doctor 400, 405, 408
  in healthcare 281–2, 417–18
  and internal market 388
patient demand, and expenditure on healthcare 252
patient groups
  representative function of 283
  and resource allocation 11
  sharing of views of 371
patient identification numbers, and IT 334
patient needs
  and demand, in economics in healthcare 242–3
  and fairness of distribution 418–20
  in the NHS 382
patient satisfaction questionnaires 280, 281
patient treatment
  economics of 247–8, 250
  as a product, in marketing of healthcare 233
patients
  and customer relations 35

  and disclosure of personal data 297–301, 337
  expectations of, and overusage of resources 36
  in marketing of healthcare 233
  role of in quality of healthcare 280–3
  welfare of, and the media 165–6
Patients' Association 283
Patients' Charter 282, 283
  and business planning 228
  and management development needs 70
  and pressures of NHS reforms 382
  and quality 274
Patients First (1980) 14
PEAKit (Postgraduate Education Audit Kit) 177–8, 181
People Chart, and change management 208
performance appraisal 146–7, 257–70, 266–7
performance managers, and team building 191–9
performance measures, and indicators 284–5
performance monitoring, and business planning 228–9, 230
performance plan, and objectives 266
performance review, individual (IPR) 257–70
perinatal outcomes analyst 329–30
person specification, and staff recruitment 135–6, **137**
person-oriented culture, and management 30
personal construct psychology, in engaging doctors in management 49–51, 53–5
personal development plan 76, 265, 267
personal effectiveness, managing for 183–4
personal learning plans 354–5
personality
  and being interviewed 154
  and change management 205–6
  and power 92, 361
  and stress handling 187–9
personalized medicine, and doctor-patient relationship 402, 403, 407–8
personnel management
  job descriptions 136
  and meetings 161
  and staff appraisal 257–70
personnel management *see also* human resources; staff
perspectives, in analysis of moral issues 417, 420
PGEA (Postgraduate Education Allowance), in general practice 344, 347
pharmaceutical companies, and income-generating activities 213–4

physical conditions
  in interview rooms 141
  of meeting rooms 158, 350
planning
  in budget management 211–12
  and change management 207, 208–9
  in hospital trusts 221–30
  in marketing of services 236–7
  for meetings 157–9, 164
  and personal effectiveness 183–4
  for writing 116, 118
policies, written, for risk management 328
political correctness, in effective writing 122–3
politics
  and NHS reforms 388
  and NHS reforms and management 379–84
Poor Law (1837), influence of on healthcare 1, 3–4, 6
portfolio learning 344, 346–7
  and clinical audit 372–3, 374
postgraduate deans, as purchasers of medical education 173, 174, 175–6
Postgraduate Education Allowance (PGEA), in general practice 344, 347
Postgraduate Education Audit Kit (PEAKit) 177–8, 181
postgraduate medical education
  assessments of 175
  and clinical audit 374
  management of 83, 173–81
  responsibility for 343–4
  service pressures in 174, 350
  shortcomings of 146
postgraduate medical education *see also* continuing professional development; medical education
postgraduate medical tutor, role of 82–3, 86
Postregistration Education and Practice (PREP) 344, 347
  and study leave 353
"pot-filling" educational model 105–6
power
  of clinical directors 91–2, 360–2
  in the management process 25, 28–9, 30, 205, 208
  shift of, in NHS changes 44, 390, 393–4, 397
practice assumption, and clinical freedom 405, 407–8
preinterview visits
  and job finding 151–2
  and staff selection 138–9
PREP *see* Postregistration Education and Practice
preparation, for media interviews 168, 171
presentations, and being interviewed 154

presentations and talks 105–13
press, and role of medical director 87
press releases, and effective writing 124
press statements 169–70
price, in marketing of healthcare 234–5
primary healthcare, under the NHS 10, 60, 71
prime responsibility, in patient care 401–2, 404, 405, 407–8, 410
PRINCE project structure 338
priorities
 of clinical directors 360
 in healthcare purchasing 253–4
 identification of, and personal effectiveness 184
 in patient care 320
 for risk prevention 318, 329
problem solving learning 351, *352*
problem-solving meetings 157, 158
procedures, written, for risk management 328
product liability, and medical treatment 301, 308–9
professional bureaucracy, and NHS organization 19, 26–8
professional competence
 accepted standard of 321
 legal aspects of 303, 306–7
 and risk 322
professional conduct, responsibility for colleagues 309
professional development
 clinical audit in 368, 372–4
 and clinical freedom 405, 406–7
 continuing (CPD) 341–57
 role of medical director 82–3
professional freedom 399–410
professional judgement, and clinical autonomy 419–20
professional organizations
 and clinical audit 374–5
 in continuing education 344–5
professional socialization, in the culture of a profession 391
professional standards
 and the medical royal colleges 341, 367, 374
 and professional organizations 26
promotion, in marketing of services 235, 236
protected time, for postgraduate medical education 174
protective clothing, provision of 325
protocols, and quality improvement 277–9
providers
 and postgraduate training 343–4
 and resources for clinical audit 356
public health work, ethos in 396–7
publications
 and curriculum vitae 150

and effective writing 123–4
purchasers
 and audit 356, 377
 economic appraisal by 251–5
 and postgraduate training 343–4
purchasers *see also* customers
purchasing, effects of development of 390–1

QALYs (quality adjusted life years), and cost-effectiveness 254, 255–6, 380, 382
qualitative research, and culture in health commissions 392–3
quality
 in healthcare 273–91, 274–6
 and audit 375–7
 and contracts 83–4
 improvement of 276–89
quality adjusted life years (QALYs), and cost-effectiveness 254, 255–6, 380, 382
quality assurance
 and business planning 228
 in healthcare 279–80
 in total quality 314
quality of life measures 279
quality management, in the clinical directorate 91, 96
quality system, risk management in 313–14
questions
 and being interviewed 153–4
 and interviewing skills 141–2

racial discrimination, and staff recruitment 136–8, 144–5
radio and television, and the medical profession 166, 167–8, 170–2
radiology departments, information technology in 335
RAWP (Resource/Revenue Allocation Working Party) 11, 16, 253
RCGP (Royal College of General Practitioners), and portfolio learning 372
records
 of drug administration, and product liability 308–9
 of equipment maintenance 308, 323
 of learning activities 344
 manual systems 331
 medical *see* medical records
 of postgraduate medical education 175, 176, 179–80, 181
 in staff selection 138, 143
 of training in health and safety 325, 328
 of untoward events 310–11
records *see also* learning diaries; portfolio learning
recruitment and selection of staff 135–47

reentry problems, of clinical and medical director appointments 101–2
references
 and job finding 149, 152–3
 and staff recruitment 138
reflection, in clinical audit 346, 347–8, 350
reflexivity, and cultural research 393
regions, and NHS reorganization 12–14
registrars, appointment of 139
relationships
 in analysis of moral issues 417, 420
 in the clinical directorate 65, 91, 92–3, 95–6
 consultants and managers, development of 48–9, 53, 55
 doctor-patient 35
 and personalized medicine 402, 403, 407–8
 doctors and managers 21–4
 managerial 128
 of the medical director 84–7
 and organizational changes 394–6
 and team membership 197–8
research
 and business planning 229
 efficient use of data from 380–1
 funds for, role of medical director in allocation of 83
 and job finding 151
 for writing 116–18
Research and Development strategy, in the NHS 279
Resource Allocation Working Party (RAWP) 11, 16
resource management 38
Resource Management Initiative (RMI) (1986) 29, 48, 62
resources
 allocation of
  and economics 241, 243, *244*
  and fairness 418–19
  in the NHS 11–12, 384
 and work of clinical directorates 65
 and budgets 212
 for clinical audit 367–8, 374
 constraints on
  and clinical freedom 408
  present dilemmas 18
 and hospital planning 33, 34
 management of 35–7, 37–8
 and power 28, 361
 service controlled 36
 and training for audit 372
 use of 35, 246, *247*
responsibility
 of clinical directors 91
 concept of 130
 and risk 322
Revenue Allocation Working Party (RAWP) 253
review, in staff appraisal *261*, 264

reward
    for clinical directors 24, 64, 100–1
    lack of
        for doctors in management 39
        in the NHS 12
        for medical directors 100–1
    and power 28
risk
    acceptance of 319
    assessment of, and informed consent 305–7
    cost of 315–16
    identification of 317–18
    in inexperience 322
    in infection, control of 324
    prevention of 319–26
risk management 313–30
    medical role in 326–9
    process of 317–20
    programme for 329
    and role of medical director 84
    standards in 328, 330
    structure of 327–8
RMI see Resource Management Initiative
role culture, and management 30
roles and responsibility, in analysis of moral issues 417, 421
Rosser Index, of disability and distress 255, 256
Royal College of General Practitioners (RCGP)
    and portfolio learning 372
    on quality 274
Royal College of Nursing, on quality 274
Royal College of Pathologists, in continuing education 344
royal colleges see medical royal colleges

salary review, and staff appraisal 260
secondary health care, in the NHS 10, 18
Secretary of State for Health, and NHS reorganization 14
security, and risk avoidance 323
self-assessment
    in service-based learning systems 179, 180
    and team membership 197
self-awareness
    and management development 71–5
    in personal construct psychology 52
self-disclosure
    and confidentiality 29
    and power 362
senior house officers
    appointment of 139
    training for 173–81
senior registrars, and management development 75, 76, 77
service departments, and decentralized management systems 59
service-based learning systems 178–81

sexual discrimination, and staff recruitment 136–8, 144–5
Sidaway v Bethlem Royal Hospital Governors and Others (1985) 306–7, 321
situated learning, and postgraduate medical education 174–5
skills, for clinical audit 371–2
skills training, and clinical directorates 65
social bonding, and team building 193
social class
    and medical care before the NHS 3, 5
    and resource allocation 11
social services departments
    and NHS reorganization 13
    personal files in 299
    as purchasers of healthcare 251
solicitors, disclosure of medical records to 299–300, 302–3
speaking, at meetings 158
specific learning 351, 352
staff
    appraisal of 98, 146–7, 257–70
    in the clinical directorate 97–8
    needs of, in NHS hospitals 34
    selection procedures 135, 138, 139
    training, and business planning 228
    view of risks 317
staff see also human resources; personel
staff grade doctors, appointment of 139–40
standards
    and clinical audit 348
    and quality improvement 277–9
    and quality management 96
    and team membership 196–7
    written, for risk management 328, 330
steady state budgets 93, 213
strategic direction documents 221–3
strategic overview, use of information in 333–4
strategy formulation, in marketing of services 236–7
Strengths
    Weaknesses
        Opportunities & Threats (SWOT) analysis
            in business planning 227–8
            in marketing of services 237–8
stress, handling of 187–9
structure and systems, in the management process 25–8
study leave
    allowance for 180, 353–4
    and job selection 151
succession planning, for clinical directors 101–2
support services
    and budget setting 214–15
    and business planning 228

and management of hospitals 27, 28
    risks from 323–4
support staff
    for clinical audit 353, 368, 372, 373–4
    for clinical directors 24, 61, 101, 365
    for medical directors 101
    secretarial
        of clinical directors 365
        and personal effectiveness 184, 185
Supreme Court Act (1981), and disclosure of medical records 300
SWOT see Strengths, Weaknesses, Opportunities & Threats

talks and presentations 105–13
task culture, and management 30
teacher-manager, in postgraduate medical education 173
team building
    aspects of change in 201
    and clinical directorates 65
    in organizations, and clinical audit 353, 357
    and performance managers 191–9
teams, learning in 345, 346, 355–6
teamwork
    and decision-making roles 98
    and meetings 157, 159–60
    need for in the new NHS 85
    in patient care 239
    and success in management 364
technical changes, management of 96, 97
Thatcher, Mrs. Margaret, and NHS reorganization 16, 17
"three wise men" system, in disciplinary hearings 86
time management
    by clinical directors 359–60
    and personal effectiveness 183, 184, 185, 188
time-wasting
    in meetings 86, 157, 160–1, 163
    and personal effectiveness 185
timeliness
    in healthcare 369–70
    and risk of litigation 322–3
total quality management (TQM) 290–1
training
    by clinical audit 356–7, 372
    concept of 68, 69
    in health and safety 325–6
    in information technology 338
    and problems of talks and presentations 105–6
    in risk awareness 328
    staff, role of medical director 82–3
training see also education; learning
training needs
    for clinical audit 372
    and staff appraisal 259, 263, 265–6, 267–7

treatment
  accessibility of, and contracts 84
  as a product, in marketing of healthcare 233
trusts *see* hospital trusts

untoward events *see* adverse events

values *see* core values; moral values
variance analysis, and budget monitoring 217–8
viruses, in IT systems 337–8
voluntary hospital movement 3–4, 5, 6

waiting lists
  and contracts 84
  and practitioner choice 400–1
  and pressures of NHS reforms 382
ward sisters *see* nursing sisters
waste disposal, risks in 324
women, value of assertive behaviour by 186
work environment, and risk 316–18, 323–6
work groups, and team building 191, 193
work load
  anticipated, and business planning 94, 222
  and budgets 93, 212, 213, 214, 215, 216
work patterns, in the clinical directorate 94
workhouse infirmaries 4
Working for Patients (1989)
  White Paper 11, 16
  and audit 367, 368
  on consultants to be involved in management 58
  and development of health commissions 387–8
writing
  for business planning 225–6
  for managers 115–25
  for the media 165–6
writing style 119–23

zero-based budgeting 93, 213